3 FREE Minutes
of weather information and save up to 60% on long distance calls!

Let **The Weather Channel®** help you pack! Get all the information you need before you leave.

- Current conditions & forecasts for over 900 cities worldwide

- Severe weather information including winter and tropical storm updates

- Wake-up call complete with your local forecast

- Special interest forecasts featuring ski resort, boating and other outdoor conditions

Remove card and see instructions on back.

Plus:

After selecting any additional payment optio,   ill receive
5 FREE MINUTES of long distance service!

Easy. Convenient. Fast.

It's The Only Phone Card You Will Ever Need!

During your free call, an automated operator will offer you an option to add $10, $20 or $30 to your phone card using any major credit card.

Use your card to:

- Save 20% on comprehensive weather information!
- Save up to 60% on long distance calls to **anywhere** in the U.S., **anytime**!
- Save 20% on other helpful information including lottery, sports, and more!

Domestic long distance service costs $0.25 per minute and all other options cost $0.75 per minute when using your TWC phone card.

Take the worry out of wondering! Carry the power to access all of these essential services with you in your wallet, wherever **Frommer's** may take you!

THE WEATHER CHANNEL®

No place on Earth has better weather.™

Travel Discount Coupon

This coupon entitles you to special discounts
when you book your trip through the

 TRAVEL NETWORK®
RESERVATION SERVICE

Hotels ◆ Airlines ◆ Car Rentals ◆ Cruises
All Your Travel Needs

Here's what you get: *

◆ A discount of $50 USD on a booking of $1,000** or
more for two or more people!

◆ A discount of $25 USD on a booking of $500** or more
for one person!

◆ Free membership for three years, and 1,000 free miles
on enrollment in the unique Miles-to-Go™ frequent-
traveler program. Earn one mile for every dollar spent
through the program. Earn free hotel stays starting at
5,000 miles. Earn free roundtrip airline tickets starting
at 25,000 miles.

◆ Personal help in planning your own, customized trip.

◆ Fast, confirmed reservations at any property
recommended in this guide, subject to availability.***

◆ Special discounts on bookings in the U.S. and around
the world.

◆ Low-cost visa and passport service.

◆ Reduced-rate cruise packages.

Visit our website at http://www.travnet.com/Frommer or
call us globally at 201-567-8500, ext. 55. In the U.S., call
toll-free at 1-888-940-5000, or fax 201-567-1838. In
Canada, call toll-free at 1-800-883-9959, or fax 416-922-
6053. In Asia, call 60-3-7191044, or fax 60-3-7185415.

---

* To qualify for these travel discounts, at least a portion of your trip must
  include destinations covered in this guide. No more than one coupon discount
  may be used in any 12-month period, for destinations covered in this guide.
  Cannot be combined with any other discount or program.
**These are U.S. dollars spent on commissionable bookings.
***A $10 USD fee, plus fax and/or phone charges, will be added to the cost of
   bookings at each hotel not linked to the reservation service. Customers
   must approve these fees in advance.

Valid until December 31, 1998. Terms and conditions of the Miles-to-
Go™ program are available on request by calling 201-567-8500, ext 55.

COL123

Frommer's®

4th Edition

Colorado

by Don & Barbara Laine

Macmillan • USA

ABOUT THE AUTHORS

Don and Barbara Laine have traveled extensively throughout the Rocky Mountains and the Southwest. In addition to *Frommer's Colorado,* they are the authors of *Frommer's Utah,* and the co-authors of *Frommer's New Mexico,* as well as the regional editors of *Frommer's America on Wheels: Arizona and New Mexico.* The Laines reside in northern New Mexico.

MACMILLAN TRAVEL

A Simon & Schuster Company
1633 Broadway
New York, NY 10019

Find us online at **http://www.mgr.com/travel**
or on America Online at Keyword: **Frommer's.**

ISBN 0-02-860920-4
ISSN 1053-2463

Editor: Erica Spaberg
Production Editor: Whitney K. Ward
Map Editor: Douglas Stallings
Design by Michele Laseau
Digital Cartography by Ortelius Design
All maps copyright © by Simon & Schuster, Inc.

SPECIAL SALES

Contents

Appendix 384

Index 390

List of Maps

AN INVITATION TO THE READER

In researching this book, we discovered many wonderful places—hotels, restaurants, shops, and more. We're sure you'll find others. Please tell us about them, so we can share the information with your fellow travelers in upcoming editions. If you were disappointed with a recommendation, we'd love to know that, too. Please write to:

Don and Barbara Laine
Frommer's Colorado, 4th Edition
Macmillan Travel
1633 Broadway
New York, NY 10019

AN ADDITIONAL NOTE

Please be advised that travel information is subject to change at any time—and this is especially true of prices. We therefore suggest that you write or call ahead for confirmation when making your travel plans. The authors, editors, and publisher cannot be held responsible for the experiences of readers while traveling. Your safety is important to us, however, so we encourage you to stay alert and be aware of your surroundings. Keep a close eye on cameras, purses, and wallets—all favorite targets of thieves and pickpockets.

WHAT THE SYMBOLS MEAN

✪ Frommer's Favorites

Hotels, restaurants, attractions, and entertainment you should not miss.

⑤ Super-Special Values

Hotels and restaurants that offer great value for your money.

The following abbreviations are used for credit cards:

AE	American Express	ER	enRoute
CB	Carte Blanche	JCB	Japan Credit Bank
DC	Diners Club	MC	MasterCard
DISC	Discover	V	Visa

The Best of Colorado

The old and the new, the rustic and the sophisticated, the wild and the refined—all of these experiences exist practically side by side in Colorado, amid what is arguably the most breathtaking mountain scenery in America.

Colorado's booming cities—Boulder, Colorado Springs, and Denver—and its admittedly somewhat glitzy resort towns—especially Aspen and Vail—offer excellent dining and some of the finest jazz, rock, blues, and film festivals around. Throughout the state, you'll also find testaments to another time, when life was simpler but rougher, and only the strong survived—historic Victorian mansions, working turn-of-the-century steam trains, old gold mines, thousand-year-old adobe-and-stone Anasazi villages, and authentic Old West towns complete with false-fronted saloons, dusty streets, and boardwalks.

Colorado truly comes alive for the visitor outdoors—among the towering peaks of the Rocky Mountains, the mesas of the western plateaus, and the broad plains in the east. You'll discover what inspired Katharine Lee Bates to pen the lyrics to "America the Beautiful" here in 1893 after you too have experienced the view from the top of Pikes Peak. Go horseback riding, hiking, mountain biking, skiing, snowboarding, jeeping, rafting, or rock climbing; or simply sit in the sun and gaze at the mountains. Whatever you do, though, don't stay indoors. Enos Mills, an early 20th-century environmentalist, and the driving force behind the creation of Rocky Mountain National Park, said that a knowledge of nature is the basis of wisdom. In other words, get out and get smart. That's the essence of Colorado.

Planning a trip can be a time-consuming experience, and all of us have less free time on our hands than we'd like. If it's a vacation you're arranging, the task can be doubly frustrating since the purpose—to kick back and relax—can easily get lost in the logistics of making it happen. Mindful of this, we've designed this chapter to make your trip-planning less stressful and, we hope, easier. We've done the legwork, so you don't have to spend hours searching for the restaurant that prepares the best Rocky Mountain game or plotting the most scenic drive through the Rockies. Instead, you can do what you're supposed to do—enjoy your visit to Colorado in the most relaxed way possible.

1   The Best Ski Resorts

- **Aspen:** Not only do Aspen and its affiliated mountains have predictably superior ski terrain that ranges from some of the most fantastic expert skiing in Colorado to what *Ski* magazine has called the best mountain in America for those just learning to ski (Buttermilk), but it is also one of the most fun, genuinely historic ski towns in Colorado. Although one's first impression is that the town is somewhat glitzy and certainly expensive, Aspen is a real town, with longtime, year-round residents and a history that goes beyond the slopes. All of these reasons make it among our top picks to spend a week. See chapter 11.
- **Breckenridge:** The lure of Breckenridge, somewhat like Aspen, lies in its fabulous skiing for skiers of all abilities, its location in an old gold-prospecting settlement, and its abundance of ski-in, ski-out lodging. Breckenridge is also a bit less expensive than Aspen and more down-home in feel. It's especially attractive to families because of its welcoming attitude toward snowboarders and variety of après-ski activities. One can easily keep oneself fully occupied here for a week. See chapter 11.
- **Vail:** This is it, the big one, America's most popular ski resort as well as its largest, with more than 4,000 acres of skiable terrain, 120 trails, and eight high-speed quad lifts. Every serious skier needs to ski Vail at least once, and it would be very easy to spend a week here and hardly ever cross the same path twice. Vail is probably the easiest major resort to get around; everything's convenient via the resort's very efficient—and free—bus system. But be prepared for steep prices and don't come to Vail looking for Victorian charm—all you'll find are rows of condominiums. See chapter 11.
- **Purgatory:** One of Colorado's best-kept skiing secrets, this resort in the state's southwest corner is known for its beautiful sunny days, heavy annual snowfall, and exceptionally friendly and easy-going atmosphere. More than $4 million in trail and facilities improvements recently helped bring Purgatory into the major leagues of Colorado skiing. See chapter 13.

2   The Best Active Vacations

- **Cowpunching on a Cattle Drive:** To really step back into the West of the 1800s, join working cowboys on a genuine cattle drive. **Broken Skull Cattle Company** near Steamboat Springs (☎ 970/879-0090) offers a 9-day drive with a herd of longhorns; you'll ride horseback, help with the wrangling chores, eat chuck wagon meals, and sleep in tents. See chapter 11.
- **Bicycling the San Juan Mountains: Backroads** (☎ 800/GO-ACTIV or 510/527-1555) offers a fabulous 5-day biking trip through the San Juan mountains. Atop 21-speed road bikes, participants whizz through the historic mining town of Telluride, passing the remains of buildings constructed by the ancient Anasazi more than 1,000 years ago. A few off-bike activities are included, such as a ride on the Durango & Silverton narrow-gauge steam train, and nights are spent at charming Victorian inns. It's expensive (approximately $1,200 per person), but an unforgettable experience. See chapter 13.
- **Skiing the San Juan Hut System:** Ambitious cross-country skiers who want to put a few miles behind them and ski among 14,000-foot alpine peaks love the San Juan Hut System's trail and series of shelters between Telluride and Moab, Utah. Designed for those of intermediate ability, skiers can tackle small sections or the

entire trail, staying overnight at the huts, which are equipped with bunks, a pro-pane cook stove, a wood stove, and kitchen equipment. See chapter 13.

- **Rafting with a String Quartet:** Lots of companies offer rafting trips, but how many take along an ensemble of professional musicians? **Dvorak's Kayak and Rafting Expeditions** (☎ **800/824-3795** or 719/539-6851) does just that. You won't get a lot of white-water excitement on this trip, but your full week on the Dolores or Green rivers won't be boring either, as plenty of time is set aside for listening to the musicians perform in the riverside sandstone canyons. You can explore the canyons and forests, or just loaf in the sun. See chapter 14.

- **Rock Climbing Penitente Canyon:** Technical rock climbers from around the world flock to this canyon near the tiny village of La Garita, some 43 miles north-west of Alamosa. The sheer cliffs produced by this wall of giant boulders look to most of us like an insurmountable obstacle, but experienced rock climbers love it. See chapter 14.

3 The Best Hiking Trails

- **The Buttes Trail at Pawnee Buttes:** This easy day-hike lets you see some of the "other" Colorado—the prairie on the state's eastern plains. A 1 1/2-mile trail leads to Pawnee Buttes, the Rattlesnake Buttes made famous in James Michener's *Centennial.* It's also a good trail for spotting coyotes, a variety of birds, and other wildlife, and has colorful wildflowers in the spring. See chapter 10.

- **The Colorado Trail at Kenosha Pass:** This easy section of the Colorado Trail near Breckenridge is a fun day's walk or can be the starting point for a serious back-packing trip. Off U.S. 285 (some 60 miles southwest of Denver), pick up the trail where the highway crosses 10,001-foot Kenosha Pass. This access point provides opportunities for short or long hikes through the aspen and bristlecone forest. See chapter 11.

- **The Bear Creek Trail:** Just south of Ouray, this national forest trail is particu-larly noted for its lush open meadows loaded with wildflowers in spring, and its old mine shafts, buildings, and equipment. Allow a full day. See chapter 13.

- **The Four-Wheel–Drive Track in Great Sand Dunes National Monument:** This moderately difficult hike along the eastern edge of the dunes provides great views of the 700-foot-tall sand dunes and surrounding mountains. The trail follows a sandy four-wheel–drive track that becomes a rough and rocky trail as it heads from the national monument into the Rio Grande National Forest. See chapter 14.

4 The Best Mountain Biking

- **Colorado State Forest:** Located in the mountains some 75 miles west of Fort Collins, this beautifully rugged country offers miles and miles of trails, as well as strategically located shelters for those on multiday treks. You may find that you're not alone on the trails, though; the resident moose sometimes use them, too. See chapter 10.

- **Tipperary Creek Trail:** Considered by many to be Colorado's very best moun-tain biking trail, this 30-mile ride from Fraser to Winter Park runs through dense forest and wildflower-covered meadows, offering views of rugged snowcapped peaks. It is strenuous, rising from an 8,600-foot elevation to more than 10,000 feet. See chapter 11.

- **Zephyr Express (Winter Park):** A chair lift for skiers in winter, the Zephyr Express hauls mountain bikers to several exciting trails from early June through

Labor Day. Ambitious bikers can tackle the Roof of the Rockies Trail, which takes them to 11,200-foot Lunch Rock, or the easier Long Trail, which meanders some 6 miles down and around the mountain. See chapter 11.

- **Crested Butte:** Crested Butte vies with Winter Park for the title of mountain biking capital of Colorado. The highly skilled will want to try Trail 401, a strenuous single-track loop that combines scenic beauty with steep grades and rough terrain. The less ambitious will be more interested in the Cement Creek Trail, a dirt road that follows Cement Creek, with many side trails to explore higher terrain. See chapter 14.

5 The Best Wilderness Experiences

- **Hiking the Colorado Trail:** For some 500 miles, this trail winds from Denver to Durango, through some of the state's most spectacular—and rugged—terrain, crossing the Continental Divide, eight mountain ranges, and six wilderness areas. Just to the west of Leadville, the trail passes through the Collegiate Peaks Wilderness with a view of some of Colorado's most prominent fourteeners (mountains more than 14,000 ft. in elevation) and fields of wildflowers. The more hardy might take a side trip to the top of Mount Elbert, the state's tallest peak at 14,433 feet. See chapters 5 and 11.
- **Hiking the Mills Lake Trail in Rocky Mountain National Park:** Though it's packed at first, it usually becomes much less crowded after you've logged a few miles. At trail's end (elevation 10,000 ft.), there's a gorgeous mountain lake ringed by towering peaks. The trail head is easily accessible from Estes Park. See chapter 11.
- **Rafting Glenwood Canyon:** Running the rapids of the Colorado River is one of the best and surely most exciting ways to see one of the West's most beautiful canyons. Though a bit too popular to provide a genuine wilderness experience, this stretch of river has sections rated for experts during the high spring runoff as well as quieter areas appropriate for everyone. See chapter 12.

6 The Best Places to Discover Native American Culture

- **The Manitou Cliff Dwellings:** These easily accessible cliff dwellings, moved by preservationists at the turn of the century to protect them from marauding treasure seekers, accurately depict how the people of the Southwest lived some 900 years ago. See chapter 8.
- **Ute Indian Museum:** One of Colorado's few museums dedicated to an existing Indian tribe, this excellent collection, run by the Colorado Historical Society, shows how Utes lived in the 19th century, as they were being forced to reconcile their way of life with that of the invading white pioneers. There's a particularly good exhibit of Ute ceremonial items. See chapter 12.
- **Mesa Verde National Park:** Home to by far the most impressive prehistoric cliff dwellings in the Southwest, Mesa Verde (Spanish for "green table") overwhelms you with its size and complexity. The first national park set aside to preserve works created by humans, it is located just outside Cortez and is spread over some 52,000 acres. Among the most compelling sites are Spruce Tree House and Square Tower House. Be sure to take the short guided hike to the Cliff Palace, the park's most famous attraction, a perfectly preserved four-story apartment-style dwelling. See chapter 13.

- **Ute Mountain Tribal Park:** What makes this group of ruins different from others in southwest Colorado is its location on the Ute Mountain Indian Reservation. The only way to see it is on a guided tour conducted by members of the Ute tribe. You'll see ruins and petroglyphs similar to those in Mesa Verde, but with an informed personal guide and without the crowds. See chapter 13.

7 The Best Places to Recapture the Old West

- **Old Town (Burlington):** On Colorado's eastern plains, right next door to Kansas, is this living-history museum, containing 2 dozen buildings (many from the 1880s). You can see a can-can show, a melodrama, or a gunfight, all in a setting that's much more reminiscent of Dodge City than Colorado's Victorian mountain towns. See chapter 10.
- **Creede, Lake City, Leadville, and Other Genuine Old Mining Towns:** With their extensive historic districts, stone jails, and false-fronted buildings, these mountain towns transport you back 100 years to the time when Butch Cassidy, Doc Holliday, Wyatt Earp, and other infamous characters stalked the saloons in search of the next card game. See chapter 11 for Leadville and chapter 14 for Creede and Lake City.
- **Bent's Old Fort National Historic Site (La Junta):** Reconstructed to the way it was in the 1830s and 1840s, this adobe fort shows life as it really was, when pioneers spent their time either trading peaceably with or fighting off plains warriors. Keep in mind that this is a reconstruction—not an original—but it's a faithfully rendered one at that. See chapter 15.
- **Buckskin Joe Park & Railway (near Cañon City):** This movie set and western theme park not only looks like the Old West, but it lets you hear, smell, and feel it, with staged smoky gunfights and bouncing stagecoach rides. A bit commercial, but still a lot of fun and fairly authentic. See chapter 15.

8 The Most Scenic Views

- **Garden of the Gods:** There's nothing like sunrise at Garden of the Gods in Colorado Springs, with its fantastic and sometimes fanciful red sandstone formations sculpted by wind and water over hundreds of thousands of years. Although you can see a great deal from the marked view points, it's worth spending some time and foot-power to get away from the crowds on one of the park's many trails, to listen to the wind and imagine the gods cavorting among the formations. See chapter 8.
- **The Black Canyon of the Gunnison:** Among the steepest and most narrow canyons in North America, the Black Canyon of the Gunnison, near Montrose, offers breathtaking and sometimes eerie views into the darkness below or, for ambitious hikers, from the canyon depths to the daylight above. The sheerness of its 2,500-foot-high walls, the narrowness of its 40-foot-wide base, and the resulting darkness at its core evoke a somber, almost religious mood. See chapter 12.
- **Colorado National Monument:** Located just west of Grand Junction, this national monument provides stunning distant views across its red-rock canyons and sandstone monoliths. The 23-mile Rim Rock Drive offers incredible views, and a series of short walks and back country trails provide additional vistas and a lot more solitude. The best light is either early in the morning or late in the afternoon, when the rocks are deep red and shadows dance among the stone sculptures. See chapter 12.

- **The San Juan Skyway:** This 238-mile circle drive that passes through the towns of Durango, Telluride, and Ouray is among the most beautiful scenic drives in America, crossing five mountain passes, past historic mining camps, fields of wildflowers, stately forests, snowcapped peaks, and cascading waterfalls. It's a thrilling drive but not necessarily for those who don't do well at high elevation (Red Mountain Pass is 11,008 ft. above sea level) or on steep, winding roads. Except in summer, it's wise to check first to see if the passes are closed due to snow. See chapter 13.

9   The Best Family Vacations

- **Panning for Gold and Other Adventures in Idaho Springs:** This excursion from Denver offers kids and adults alike the chance to pan for gold, explore a gold mine, take home an ore sample, and visit a mill and museum. The Argo Express is a one-half scale replica of an old-time steam train, providing rides at the Argo Mill. While in the area, you can take a drive to the summit of 14,260-foot Mount Evans, or go horseback or pony riding. See chapter 7.
- **Ropin' Dogies at Sylvan Dale Guest Ranch:** Nestled in the mountains outside Loveland, this is a real cattle-and-horse ranch where guests are encouraged to pitch in with chores when they're not horseback riding, swimming, fishing, or busy loafing. There's an outdoor swimming pool, tennis and volleyball courts, an indoor recreation room, and a kids' play area. Guided nature hikes, square dancing, and hayrides are popular. See chapter 10.
- **Riding the Durango & Silverton Narrow Gauge Railroad:** Based in Durango, this 1880s steam-train excursion is a trip into the past, complete with smoke in your eyes and cinders in your hair. In addition, it's an exciting way to see the beautiful San Juan mountains, just as travelers here saw them 100 years ago. See chapter 13.
- **Exploring Great Sand Dunes National Monument:** There's no ocean, but this gigantic beach, about 40 miles northeast of Alamosa, is a great place to explore, camp, hike, or just play in the 700-foot-tall dunes. Rangers provide guided nature walks and campfire programs during summer, and a hiking/off-road vehicle trail leads out the back of the monument into the national forest. See chapter 14.

10   The Most Unusual Travel Experiences

- **United States Mint (Denver):** This is where all that money comes from—at least the coins. If you've ever wondered just how those heavy chunks of metal actually become legal tender, this is your opportunity to find out as you watch the stamping of some of the five billion coins produced here each year. But let's be honest—the real reason to visit the mint is simply to be surrounded by all that cold hard cash. See chapter 7.
- **Hakushika Sake USA:** Located in Golden, just outside Denver, this brewery produces the unofficial national drink of Japan. Sake is created much like beer, and the brewery has been designed to give visitors an excellent view of the process. There's also an exhibit of brewing techniques from past centuries. A bonus is the exquisite display of Japanese art. See chapter 7.
- **The San Luis Valley Alligator Farm:** Alamosa, one of the coldest spots in America, is not where you'd expect to find alligators, but geothermal wells apparently make conditions just right for breeding the not-so-friendly beasts, who share the site with a fish hatchery. See chapter 14.

- **The Colorado Territorial Prison Museum and Park (Cañon City):** Located in a former women's prison, this museum may be a bit too macabre for some. It contains an actual gas chamber, the last hangman's noose used legally in Colorado, and other reminders of what became of some of those Old West outlaws we've heard so much about. See chapter 15.

11 The Finest Luxury Hotels

- **The Brown Palace** (Denver; ☎ 800/321-2599 or 303/297-3111 in North America; 800/228-2917 in Colorado): Denver's finest hotel, the Brown Palace has been open continuously since 1892, serving high society and celebrities—from President Dwight Eisenhower to the Beatles—with elegance and charm. Although most of the rooms are Victorian in decor, with Tiffany lamps and other accoutrements, our favorites are the art deco rooms, with an undeniable feel of the 1920s and 1930s. See chapter 6.
- **The Broadmoor** (Colorado Springs; ☎ 800/634-7711 or 719/634-7711): Colorado's top-rated resort hotel has it all—excellent dining, golf courses, pools, tennis courts, exercise facilities, and shopping, plus extraordinary service—in a fascinating historic building with extensive and well-kept grounds. Although some might consider the Broadmoor a bit pretentious, it certainly knows how to pamper its guests. See chapter 8.
- **Hyatt Regency Beaver Creek** (Avon; ☎ 800/233-1234 or 970/949-4164): This plush ski-in, ski-out resort at the foot of the Beaver Creek lifts combines a casual, comfortable atmosphere with superb service in a handsome, elegant building. The rooms' decor is a quirky combination of Old West and French countryside that works. See chapter 11.
- **The Ritz-Carlton** (Aspen; ☎ 970/920-3300): At the base of Aspen Mountain, the Ritz-Carlton offers great views of the mountains or town, impeccable service, splendid rooms, and all the services and amenities you'd expect in a fine hotel. Although a bit pricey, especially over the Christmas holidays, the hotel is supremely elegant in a comfortable, cozy way. See chapter 11.

12 The Best Moderately Priced Lodgings

- **Hearthstone Inn** (Colorado Springs; ☎ 800/521-1885 or 719/473-4413): This Colorado Springs gem, situated in two adjoining historic Victorian homes, is perfect for those who like the charm and amenities of a bed-and-breakfast but the privacy of a hotel. All rooms are different, but each has antiques, collectibles, and brass beds. A definite plus here is the breakfast, which is included. See chapter 8.
- **Days Inn Boulder** (Boulder; ☎ 303/499-4422): Perhaps the best managed chain motel we've ever seen, this four-story Days Inn is quiet, handsomely appointed, and the upper floors offer great views of the mountains. What's surprising is the better-than-average continental breakfast, included in the room rate. See chapter 9.
- **Baldpate Inn** (Estes Park; ☎ 970/586-6151): This small inn near Rocky Mountain National Park is open only in summer, and most rooms share baths, but it has personality galore. There are handmade quilts, early 20th-century furnishings, and a large stone fireplace in the living room. Named for the novel *Seven Keys to Baldpate,* the inn takes its theme seriously, inviting guests to add their own keys to a collection that now exceeds 20,000. It also offers an excellent soup-and-salad buffet dinner. See chapter 11.

- **Mid-Town Motel** (La Junta; ☎ 719/384-7741): Those looking for a clean, quiet mom-and-pop motel at extremely good rates will do no better than the Mid-Town in La Junta. Solo travelers get rooms with recliners, and pets are welcome. See chapter 15.

13 The Best Bed-and-Breakfasts

- **Holden House 1902 Bed & Breakfast Inn** (Colorado Springs; (☎ 719/471-3980): When you picture a storybook Victorian home, filled with family heirlooms and antiques, this Colorado Springs bed-and-breakfast is it. Of course, there are so many objects around, it's sometimes hard to find a place to put down your suitcase—but you gladly will. Homey touches include the two resident cats, who will happily curl up on your bed if you leave the door open. See chapter 8.
- **The Alps** (Boulder; ☎ 800/414-2577 or 303/444-5445): This historic log lodge on a mountainside west of Boulder is a perfect country bed-and-breakfast inn. It has spacious rooms, all with lots of wood, working Victorian fireplaces, British antiques, and views of the mountains and forests. Although only a few minutes from downtown Boulder, the inn is secluded and very quiet—a great getaway spot. See chapter 9.
- **Echo Manor Inn** (Pagosa Springs; ☎ 800/628-5004 or 970/264-5646): Pagosa Springs is not where one would expect to find this magnificent, four-story, Dutch Tudor-style inn, complete with turrets and towers, but here it is, all handsomely decorated with country-style furnishings. Climbing the narrow, circular stairs to the fourth floor can be dizzying, but there's a splendid view; and the little nooks and crannies throughout the house make it perfect for a kids' game of hide-and-seek. See chapter 13.
- **Cottonwood Inn** (Alamosa; ☎ 719/589-3882): Decorated with regional art, this 1908 bungalow in Alamosa has a variety of rooms, each unique, including one that is great for small families, with stuffed animals and children's books. Another room contains a fascinating combination of southwestern and art deco furnishings. See chapter 14.

Getting to Know Colorado

The heart of the Rocky Mountains, the backbone of North America, Colorado has more than 50 peaks that soar above 14,000 feet. The Rockies—with their evergreen and aspen forests, racing streams and rivers, and wealth of wildlife—are perfect for recreation throughout the year, from summer hiking and rafting to winter skiing through deep powder snow.

But Colorado is not *only* mountains. It is also the wheat and corn fields of the vast eastern prairies, the high plateau country of the west, and the modern, sophisticated cities of the Front Range.

Take the time to see the sights of cosmopolitan Denver, the "Mile High City"; Colorado Springs, home of the U.S. Air Force Academy and U.S. Olympic Training Center; and the university towns of Boulder and Fort Collins. Indulge in luxury hotels, gourmet cuisine, and year-round recreation at thriving resort communities such as Aspen, Vail, Beaver Creek, and Steamboat Springs. Ride the narrow-gauge steam trains and relive the mining-boom days in rejuvenated towns such as Durango, Georgetown, and Creede, straight out of the Old West but alive with 20th-century verve. Immerse yourself in the natural and human-made wonders of national parks and monuments such as Mesa Verde, Rocky Mountain, Great Sand Dunes, Dinosaur, Black Canyon of the Gunnison, and Bent's Old Fort, each with its own unique fascination.

1 The Natural Environment

First-time visitors to Colorado are often awed by the looming wall of the Rocky Mountains, which come into sight a good 100 miles away, soon after drivers cross the line from Kansas. East of the Rockies, a 5,000-foot peak is considered high; yet Colorado has 1,143 mountains above 10,000 feet, including 53 over 14,000 feet! Highest of all is Mount Elbert at 14,433 feet, southwest of Leadville.

The Rockies were formed some 65 million years ago by pressures that forced hard Precambrian rock to the earth's surface, breaking through and pushing layers of earlier rock up on end. Then millions of years of erosion eliminated the soft surface material, producing the magnificent Rockies of calendar fame.

An almost-perfect rectangle, Colorado measures some 385 miles east to west, and 275 miles north to south. The ridge of the Continental Divide zigzags more or less through the center of the 104,247-square-mile state, eighth largest in the nation.

2 The Regions in Brief

Colorado's basic topography can be visualized by dividing the state into vertical thirds: The eastern part is plains; the midsection high mountains; and the western third is mesa land.

That's a broad simplification, of course. The central Rockies, though they cover six times the mountain area of Switzerland, are not a single vast highland but a series of high ranges running roughly north-to-south. East of the Continental Divide, the primary river systems are the South Platte, Arkansas, and Rio Grande, all flowing toward the Gulf of Mexico. The westward-flowing Colorado River system dominates the western part of the state, with tributary networks including the Gunnison, Dolores, and Yampa-Green rivers. In most cases, these rivers are not broad bodies of water like the Ohio or Columbia, but streams heavy with spring and summer snowmelt, which are reduced to mere trickles during much of the year by the demands of farm and ranch irrigation. Besides agricultural use, they provide life-giving water to wildlife and offer wonderful opportunities for rafting, fishing, swimming, waterskiing, and boardsailing.

The forested mountains are essential to retaining precious water for the lowlands. Eleven national forests comprise 15 million acres of land, and there are eight million acres controlled by the Bureau of Land Management also open for public recreation. Another half million acres are within national parks, monuments, and recreation areas under the administration of the National Park Service. In addition to all this, the state operates more than 40 state parks.

Colorado's name, Spanish for "red," derives from the state's red soil and rocks. Some of the sandstone agglomerates have become attractions in their own right, such as Red Rocks Amphitheater west of Denver and the startling Garden of the Gods in Colorado Springs.

Of Colorado's 3.3 million people, some 80% live along the Front Range, the I-25 corridor, where the plains meet the mountains. Denver, the state capital, has a population close to 500,000, with another million in the metropolitan area. Colorado Springs has the second largest population, with about 280,000 residents, followed by Pueblo (99,000) and Boulder (83,000).

3 Colorado Today

Ask any seasoned Coloradan what makes the state unique, and his response is most likely to be: mountains. It's almost impossible to overemphasize the spectacular beauty here, or the influence it has had on the development and present-day character of the state. Colorado has been a prime tourist destination practically since the day the first settlers arrived, and many of these visitors liked the place so much they stayed. Particularly in the 19th century, but also in the first half of the 20th century, those attracted to this rugged land tended to be independent types—sometimes downright ornery and antisocial—who sought wide-open spaces, untamed wilderness, and plenty of elbow room. Of course, the dream of riches from gold and silver mines helped, too.

These early transplants established the state's image as the domain of rugged individualists—solitary cowboys, prospectors, and others—who just wanted to be left alone. Much of that feeling still survives, and today's Coloradans have a deserved reputation as a feisty, independent lot. Colorado has the distinct honor, if you can call it that, of being home to some of the most politically active liberals and conservatives in the country. They don't follow trends: they make them. It's where some

Colorado

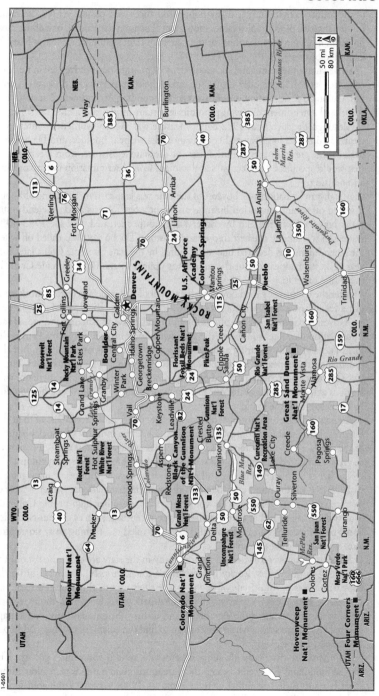

0-0501

11

of the country's first municipal gay-rights ordinances were passed; yet it's also home to the vanguard of the family values movement (Focus on the Family, one of the most powerful lobbying organizations for the Christian right's political agenda, is based in Colorado Springs).

Somewhat understandably, such a diversity of political perspectives doesn't exactly engender accord. In the early 1990s, the rest of the country got a quick lesson in politics, Colorado-style, during the controversy surrounding Amendment 2, a state constitutional amendment aimed at prohibiting certain antidiscrimination laws.

Although the successful 1992 ballot measure was vaguely worded, its intent was clear: to eliminate local gay-rights ordinances that Aspen, Boulder, and Denver had passed, and prevent other communities, or the state legislature, from creating laws that would specifically protect gays and lesbians from discrimination in employment and housing.

A high-profile nationwide boycott of the state was launched in 1993, and although it scared off some convention business and kept a few tourists away, the end result was a bit of a wash: tourism by conservative groups increased, and the 1992–1993 ski season was among the best in the state's history. The boycott was called off when the amendment was declared unconstitutional by the state Supreme Court later that year. The state appealed, but the ruling was upheld by the U.S. Supreme Court in the spring of 1996.

After the controversy died down, further proof of Colorado's maverick streak came just a few months later, when former three-term governor Richard Lamm—known as "Governor Gloom" for his philosophy of fiscal conservatism and individual sacrifice—announced he would seek the presidential nomination from Ross Perot's Reform Party, virtually ensuring a showdown with the megalomaniacal Perot, but also broadening the appeal of Perot's creation. Not surprisingly, he lost to Perot, but in true Colorado spirit, he went down fighting, describing the toe-to-toe experience with Perot as akin to drinking water out of a fire hydrant, but also admitting he wouldn't have missed it for the world.

An issue on which almost all Coloradans agree, pretty much regardless of their differences, is the need for controlling tourism. While the industry's financial benefits to the state are well-understood, it's generally acknowledged that, if tourism is allowed to grow unchecked, the cost to the state's natural resources will be tremendous.

To that end, town officials in Vail reached an agreement with resort management in 1995 to limit the number of skiers on the mountain and alleviate other aspects of overcrowding in the village. The word from Vail and other high-profile Colorado tourist destinations is that visitors will be given incentives, such as discounts, to visit at off-peak times. Ski area officials also have not ruled out turning away skiers after a set number of passes are sold.

In addition to overcrowded ski resorts, many in the state are concerned about the increasing popularity of Rocky Mountain National Park. In autumn, during the elk-rutting season, hundreds of people make their way to the Moraine Park and Horseshoe Park areas every evening. National park officials say that motor vehicle noise is starting to affect the experience and disturb the animals' routines. Disappointed visitors are asking where they can go to find the quiet serenity they had hoped to experience there.

Another issue that has wide support across the state is controlling growth. The rugged mountains and scenic beauty that lure tourists and outdoor recreation enthusiasts has also fueled an influx of transplants—a 1990s version of the gold-seekers and pioneers who settled Colorado. Colorado has gained new residents at the staggering rate of three times the national average, just since 1990. According to recently released figures from the Census Bureau, 11 of the nation's 30 fastest-growing counties in the first half of the 1990s were in Colorado. Six are within 75 miles of Denver, including the two fastest growing, the wealthy southern suburbs of Douglas and Elbert.

Many of these new residents are active, outdoorsy types who relish the idea of riding their bikes to work, and came to the state to escape the pollution, crime, and overcrowding of the East and West coasts. But perhaps inevitably, many native and long-term Coloradans have begun to complain that these newcomers are changing the character of the state, and bringing with them the very problems from which they sought to escape.

The challenge for Coloradans as they approach the next century is to solve the twin riddles of tourism and growth that are plaguing much of the American West: How do we achieve a balance between preserving a state's unique character and spectacular natural resources for future generations, while still enjoying all it has to offer today?

4 History 101

To explore Colorado today is to step back into its history, from its dinosaur graveyards, impressive stone and clay cities of the ancient Anasazi, reminders of the Wild West of Bat Masterson and Doc Holliday, and elegant Victorian mansions, to today's science and technology. The history of Colorado is a testimony to the human ability to adapt and flourish in a difficult environment. And this land of high mountains and limited water continues to challenge its inhabitants in the 1990s.

The earliest people in Colorado are believed to have been nomadic hunters, who arrived some 12,000 to 20,000 years ago via the Bering Straight, following the tracks of the now-extinct woolly mammoth and bison. Then, about 2,000 years ago the people we call the Anasazi arrived, living in shallow caves in the Four Corners area, where the borders of Colorado, Utah, Arizona, and New Mexico meet.

At first hunters, they gradually learned farming and basket making; then came pottery making, the construction of pit houses, and eventually complex villages, such as can be seen at Mesa Verde National Park. For some reason, possibly drought, they deserted the area about the end of the 13th century, probably moving southward into present-day New Mexico and Arizona.

Although the Anasazi were gone by the time Spanish conquistadors arrived in the mid-16th century, in their place were two major nomadic cultures: The mountain dwellers of the west, primarily Ute; and the plains tribes of the east, principally Arapahoe, Cheyenne, and Comanche.

Dateline

- **12,000 B.C.** First inhabitants of Colorado include Folsom Man.
- **3000 B.C.** Prehistoric farming communities.
- **A.D. 1000** Anasazi cliff-dweller culture peaks in Four Corners region.
- **Late 1500s** Spanish explore upper Rio Grande Valley, colonize Santa Fe and Taos, New Mexico.
- **1776** U.S. declares independence from England.
- **1803** The Louisiana Purchase includes most of modern Colorado.
- **1806–07** Captain Zebulon Pike leads first U.S. expedition into Colorado Rockies.
- **1822** William Becknell establishes Santa Fe Trail.
- **1842–44** Lieutenant John C. Frémont and Kit Carson explore Colorado and American West.
- **1848** Treaty of Guadeloupe Hidalgo ends Mexican War, adds American Southwest to the United States.
- **1858** Gold discovered in modern Denver.

continues

- **1859** General William Larimer founds Denver. Major gold strikes in nearby Rockies.
- **1861** Colorado Territory proclaimed.
- **1863–68** Ute tribe obtains treaties guaranteeing 16 million acres of western Colorado land.
- **1864** Hundreds of Cheyenne killed in Sand Creek Massacre. University of Denver becomes Colorado's first institution of higher education.
- **1870** Kansas City–Denver rail line completed. Agricultural commune of Greeley established by newspaperman Nathan Meeker.
- **1871** General William Palmer founds Colorado Springs.
- **1876** Colorado becomes 38th state.
- **1877** University of Colorado opens in Boulder.
- **1878** Little Pittsburg silver strike launches Leadville mining boom, Colorado's greatest.
- **1879** Milk Creek Massacre by Ute warriors leads to tribe's removal to reservations.
- **1890** Sherman Silver Purchase Act boosts price of silver. Gold discovered at Cripple Creek, leading to state's biggest gold rush.
- **1893** Women win right to vote. Silver industry collapses following repeal of Sherman Silver Purchase Act.
- **1901–07** President Theodore Roosevelt sets aside 16 million acres of national forest land in Colorado.
- **1906** U.S. Mint built in Denver.

continues

Spanish colonists, having established settlements at Santa Fe, Taos, and other upper Rio Grande locations in the 16th and 17th centuries, didn't immediately find southern Colorado attractive for colonization. Not only was there a lack of financial and military support from the Spanish crown, but the freedom-loving, sometimes-fierce Comanche and Ute made it clear that they would rather be left alone.

Nevertheless, Spain still held title to southern and western Colorado in 1803 when U.S. President Thomas Jefferson paid $15 million for the vast Louisiana Territory, which included the lion's share of modern Colorado. To explore the area, Jefferson sent Captain Zebulon Pike, for whom Pikes Peak, Colorado's landmark mountain and a top tourist attraction near Colorado Springs, was named.

As the West began to open up in the 1820s, the Santa Fe Trail was established, cutting through Colorado's southeast corner. Bent's Fort was built on the Arkansas River between 1828 and 1832, and you can visit the reconstructed fort, a national historic site, today near La Junta.

Much of eastern Colorado, including what would become Denver, Boulder, and Colorado Springs, was then part of the Kansas Territory. It was populated almost exclusively by plains tribes until 1858, when gold seekers discovered flakes of the precious metal near the junction of Cherry Creek and the South Platte, and the city of Denver was established, named for Kansas governor James Denver.

The Cherry Creek strike was literally a flash in the gold-seeker's pan, but two strikes in the mountains just west of Denver in early 1859 were more significant: Clear Creek, near what would become Idaho Springs; and in a quartz vein at Gregory Gulch, which led to the founding of Central City. The race to Colorado's gold fields had begun.

Abraham Lincoln was elected president of the United States in November 1860, and Congress created the Colorado Territory 3 months later. The new territory absorbed neighboring sections of Utah, Nebraska, and New Mexico to fill out the boundaries that the state retains today. Lincoln's Homestead Act of 1862 brought much of the public domain into private ownership, and led to the platting of Front Range townships, starting with Denver in 1861.

Controlling the Native American peoples was a priority of the territorial government. A treaty negotiated in 1851 had guaranteed the entire Pikes Peak region to the nomadic plains tribes, but that had been made moot by the rush of settlers in the late 1850s.

The Fort Wise Treaty of 1861 exchanged the Pikes Peak territory for five million fertile acres of Arkansas Valley land, north of modern La Junta. But when the Arapahoe and Cheyenne continued to roam their old hunting grounds, conflict was inevitable. Frequent rumors and rare instances of hostility against settlers led the Colorado cavalry to attack a peaceful settlement of Cheyenne—flying Old Glory and a white flag—in November 1864. About 200 Cheyenne, two-thirds of them women and children, were killed in what has become known as the Sand Creek Massacre.

The Cheyenne and Arapahoe vowed revenge and launched a campaign to drive whites from their ancient hunting grounds. Their biggest triumph was the destruction of the northeast Colorado town of Julesburg in 1865, but the cavalry, bolstered by returning Civil War veterans, managed to force the two tribes onto reservations in Indian Territory, what is now Oklahoma.

Also in 1865, a smelter was built in Black Hawk, just west of Denver, setting the stage for the large-scale spread of mining throughout Colorado in years to come. When the first transcontinental railroad was completed in 1869, the Union Pacific went through Cheyenne, Wyoming, 100 miles north of Denver, but 4 years later the line was linked to Denver by the Kansas City–Denver Railroad.

Colorado politicians had begun pressing for statehood during the Civil War, but it wasn't until August 1, 1876, that Colorado became the 38th state. Coming less than a month after the United States' 100th birthday, it was natural that Colorado would become known as "the Centennial State."

The state's new constitution gave the vote to blacks, but not women, despite the strong efforts of the Colorado Women's Suffrage Association. Women finally succeeded in winning the vote in 1893, 3 years after Wyoming became the first state to offer universal suffrage.

At the time of statehood, most of Colorado's vast western region was still occupied by some 3,500 mountain and plateau dwellers of a half-dozen Ute tribes. Unlike the plains tribes, their early relations with white explorers and settlers had been peaceful. Chief Ouray, leader of the Uncompahgre Utes, had negotiated treaties in 1863 and 1868 that guaranteed them 16 million acres—most of western Colorado. In 1873, Ouray agreed to sell to the United States one-fourth of

- **1913** Wolf Creek Pass highway is first to cross Continental Divide in Colorado.
- **1915** Rocky Mountain National Park established.
- **1934** Direct Denver–San Francisco rail travel begins. Taylor Grazing Act ends homesteading.
- **1941–45** World War II establishes Colorado as military center.
- **1947** Aspen's first chair lift begins operation.
- **1948–58** Uranium rush sweeps western slope.
- **1955** Environmentalists prevent construction of Echo Park Dam in Dinosaur National Monument.
- **1972** Colorado voters reject a chance to host the 1976 Winter Olympics.
- **1988** Colorado Senator Gary Hart, a front-runner for the Democratic presidential nomination, withdraws from race after a scandal.
- **1992** Colorado voters approve Amendment 2, a controversial constitutional amendment banning laws that protect gays and lesbians from discrimination.
- **1993** Denver becomes 15th U.S. city with three major professional sports teams with the acquisition of the Rockies, a new major-league baseball franchise.
- **1995** The $4.2-billion state-of-the-art Denver International Airport and $2.16-million Coors Field baseball stadium open. Denver goes sports-crazy when it obtains its fourth major professional sports team, the Avalanche, a member of the National Hockey League; and there's rejoicing statewide when the Avalanche wins the Stanley Cup a year later.

continues

■ **1996** The U.S. Supreme
Court strikes down Amend-
ment 2, saying it denies gays
and lesbians constitutional
rights afforded all Americans.

that acreage in the mineral-rich San Juan Mountains in exchange for hunting rights and $25,000
in annuities.

But a mining boom that began in 1878 led to a
flurry of intrusions into Ute territory and stirred up
a "Utes Must Go!" sentiment. The Utes were
moved in 1880 to small reserves in southwestern Colorado and Utah, and their lands
opened to settlement in 1882.

Colorado's real mining boom began on April 28, 1878, when August Rische and
George Hook hit a vein of silver carbonate 27 feet deep on Fryer Hill in Leadville.
Perhaps the stir over the strike wouldn't have been so great had not Rische and Hook
8 days earlier traded one-third interest in whatever they found for a basket of groceries from storekeeper Horace Tabor, the mayor of Leadville and a sharp business-
man. Tabor was well acquainted with the Colorado "law of apex," which said that
if an ore-bearing vein surfaced on a man's claim, he could follow it wherever it led,
even out of his claim and through the claims of others.

Tabor, a legend in Colorado, typifies the "rags-to-riches" success story of a common working-class man. A native of Vermont, he had mortgaged his Kansas homestead in 1859 and moved west to the mountains, where he had been a postmaster
and storekeeper in several towns before Leadville. He was 46 when the silver strike
was made. By 50, he was the state's richest man and its Republican lieutenant governor. His love affair and marriage to Elizabeth "Baby Doe" McCourt, a young
divorcée for whom he left his wife, Augusta, became both a national scandal and the
subject of numerous books, even an opera. Today the town of Leadville is among the
best places to relive the West's mining days.

Although the silver market collapsed in 1893, gold was there to take its place. In
the fall of 1890, a cowboy named Bob Womack found gold in Cripple Creek, on the
southwestern slope of Pikes Peak, west of Colorado Springs. He sold his claim to
Winfield Scott Stratton, a carpenter and amateur geologist, and Stratton's mine
earned a tidy profit of $6 million by 1899, when he sold it to an English company
for another $11 million. Cripple Creek turned out to be the richest gold field ever
discovered, ultimately producing $500 million in gold.

Unlike the flamboyant Tabor, Stratton was an introvert and a neurotic. His fortune was twice the size of Tabor's, and it grew daily as the deflation of silver's value
boosted that of gold. But he invested most of it back in Cripple Creek, searching for
a fabulous mother lode that he never found. Ultimately, by the early 1900s, like silver, the overproduction of gold began to drive the price of the metal down.

Another turning point for Colorado occurred just after the turn of the century.
Theodore Roosevelt had visited the state in September 1900 as the Republican vice-
presidential nominee. Soon after he acceded to the presidency in September 1901,
after the assassination of President McKinley, he began to declare large chunks of the
Rockies as forest reserves. By 1907, when an act of Congress forbade the president
from creating any new reserves by proclamation, nearly one-fourth of Colorado was
national forest land—16 million acres in 18 forests. Another project that reached frui-
tion during the Roosevelt administration was the establishment in 1906 of Mesa
Verde National Park, in the state's southwest corner.

Tourism grew hand-in-hand with the setting aside of public lands. Easterners had
been visiting Colorado since the 1870s, when General William J. Palmer founded a
Colorado Springs resort and made the mountains accessible via his Denver & Rio
Grande Railroad.

Estes Park, northwest of Boulder, was among the first resort towns to emerge in the 20th century, spurred by a visit in 1903 by Freelan Stanley. With his brother Francis, Freelan had invented the Stanley Steamer, a steam-powered automobile, in Boston in 1899. Freelan Stanley shipped one of his steamers to Denver and drove the 40 miles to Estes Park in less than 2 hours, a remarkable speed for the day. Finding the climate conducive to his recovery from tuberculosis, he returned in 1907 with a dozen Stanley Steamers and set up a shuttle service to Estes Park. Two years later he built the luxurious Stanley Hotel, still a hilltop landmark today.

Stanley developed a friendship with Enos Mills, a young innkeeper whose property was more a workshop for students of wildlife than a business. A devotee of conservationist John Muir, Mills believed tourists should spend their Colorado vacations in the natural environment, camping and hiking. As Mills gained national stature as a nature writer and lecturer, he urged that the national forest land around Longs Peak, outside Estes Park, be designated a national park. In January 1915, the 400-square-mile Rocky Mountain National Park was created by President Woodrow Wilson, and today it is one of America's leading tourist attractions, with more than two million visitors each year.

The 1920s saw the growth of highways and the completion of the Moffat Tunnel, a 6.2-mile passageway beneath the Continental Divide that (in 1934) led to the long-sought direct Denver–San Francisco rail connection. Of more tragic note was the worst flood in Colorado history. The city of Pueblo was devastated when the Arkansas River overflowed its banks on June 1, 1921; 100 people were killed, and damage exceeded $16 million. The Great Depression of the 1930s was a difficult time for many Coloradans, but it had positive consequences. The federal government raised the price of gold from $20 to $35 an ounce, reviving Cripple Creek and other stagnant mining towns.

World War II and the subsequent Cold War were responsible for many of the defense installations that are now an integral part of the Colorado economy, particularly in the Colorado Springs area. The war also indirectly caused the other single greatest boon to Colorado's late 20th-century economy—the ski industry. Soldiers in the 10th Mountain Division, on leave from Camp Hale before heading off to fight in Europe, often crossed Independence Pass to relax in the lower altitude and milder climate of the 19th-century silver-mining village of Aspen. They tested their skiing skills, which were needed in the Italian Alps, against the slopes of Ajax Mountain.

In 1945, Walter and Elizabeth Paepcke—he the founder of the Container Corporation of America, she a devoted conservationist—moved to Aspen and established the Aspen Company as a property investment firm. Skiing was already popular in New England and the Midwest, but had few devotees in the Rockies. The Paepckes bought a 3-mile chair lift, the longest and fastest in the world at the time, and had it ready for operation by January 1947. Soon, Easterners and Europeans were flocking to Aspen—and the rest is ski history.

Colorado continued steady growth in the 1950s, aided by tourism and the federal government. The $200-million U.S. Air Force Academy, authorized by Congress in 1954 and opened to cadets in 1958, is Colorado Springs' top tourist attraction today. There was a brief oil boom in the 1970s, followed by increasing high-tech development and even more tourism.

Weapons plants that had seemed a good idea at the time began to haunt Denver and the state in the 1970s and 1980s. Rocky Mountain Arsenal, created during World War II to produce chemical weapons, was found to be creating hazardous conditions at home, contaminating land with deadly chemicals. A massive cleanup was begun in the early 1980s, and by the 1990s the arsenal was well on its way to accomplishing its goal of converting the 27-square-mile site into a national wildlife refuge. The story of Rocky Flats, a postwar nuclear weapons facility spurred on by the Cold War, is not so happy. Massive efforts to figure out what to do about contamination caused by nuclear waste have been largely unsuccessful. Although state and federal officials announced early in 1996 that they had reached agreement on means of removing some 14 tons of plutonium, their immediate plan calls for keeping it in Denver until at least the year 2010, and Department of Energy officials don't know what they'll do with it then. In the meantime, plans are underway to build storage containers that will safely hold the plutonium for up to 50 years.

In 1992, Colorado voters approved a constitutional amendment effectively banning laws currently in place to specifically protect gays and lesbians and preventing the enactment of new gay-rights legislation. Enforcement was put on hold while the matter made its way through the courts. Proponents of the amendment claimed that homosexuality is a lifestyle choice that doesn't warrant special legal protection; while opponents claimed that all gays and lesbians want is the same constitutional rights afforded all Americans, and that the amendment made this impossible.

The amendment's passage led gay rights and liberal activists to call for a nationwide boycott of Colorado tourism, although the result was somewhat limited, and many Colorado ski resorts posted record seasons. In May 1996, the U.S. Supreme Court struck down the measure in a 6-to-3 vote, saying that, if enforced, it would have denied homosexuals constitutional protection from discrimination in housing, employment, and public accommodations, making them unequal to other Americans.

As the state approaches the 21st century, thoughts have turned to controlling growth. With a growth rate in the early 1990s of nearly twice the national average, both residents and government leaders are questioning how this unabated influx of outsiders can continue without doing serious harm to the state's air, water, and general quality of life.

Planning a Trip to Colorado   3

The beauty of a vacation here is that there's truly something for everyone. Depending on where you choose to go, you can have an affordable vacation that's modest but fun, or you can spend a bit more and have a truly world-class experience. The more expensive resorts—Vail, Aspen, Steamboat, and Telluride—tend to fill up quickly, especially during ski season. You'll want to book as far in advance as possible to stay there. The same is true for the state's most popular attractions, such as the national parks—especially over busy school vacation periods. This chapter gives you all the tools you need to get started.

1 Visitor Information & Money

VISITOR INFORMATION

Start your trip planning by contacting **Colorado Travel & Tourism Authority,** P.O. Box 22005, Denver, CO 80222 (☎ **800/ COLORADO**) for a free copy of the official state vacation guide, which describes attractions, activities, and lodgings throughout the state. For more ideas on where to stay, the **Colorado Hotel and Lodging Association,** 999 18th St., Suite 1240, Denver, CO 80202 (☎ **800/777-6880**) is a good bet. It provides a reservation service for 1,700 properties, and can also arrange your air and ground transportation, as well as ski and golf packages.

If you prefer to stay in bed-and-breakfasts, the nonprofit **Bed and Breakfast Innkeepers of Colorado** has prepared a directory describing the group's more than 120 member bed-and-breakfasts across the state. Directories, which cost $3, can be obtained from the association at P.O. Box 38416, Colorado Springs, CO 80937-8416 (☎ **800/83-BOOKS**). Another source of information for those seeking unique lodging is the **Association of Historic Hotels of the Rocky Mountain West,** 1002 Walnut St., Suite 201, Boulder, CO 80302 (☎ **303/546-9040**). The association's free brochure describes about 2 dozen historic hotels in Colorado and other Rocky Mountain states.

If you plan to camp, the **Colorado Agency of Camping, Cabins, & Lodges,** 5101 Pennsylvania Ave., Boulder, CO 80303-2799 (☎ **303/499-9343;** fax 303/499-9333), is an invaluable resource. They publish a free annual booklet that describes commercial campgrounds, cabin facilities, and resorts throughout the state.

If it's a ranch vacation you're after, contact the **Colorado Dude & Guest Ranch Association,** P.O. Box 300, Tabernash, CO 80478 (☎ **970/887-3128;** fax 970/724-3449), which has information on more than 3 dozen dude and guest ranches in the state.

MONEY

ATM machines are everywhere, including many supermarkets. For the location of the nearest ATM, dial **800/424-7787** for the Cirrus network or **800/843-7587** for the Plus system (within the U.S.). Most ATMs will make cash advances against MasterCard and Visa, but make sure you have your personal identification number with you.

American Express cardholders can write a personal check, guaranteed against the card, for up to $1,000 in cash at any American Express office. The Denver branch is at 555 17th St., Anaconda Tower, Denver (☎ **303/298-7100**). It's open Monday through Friday from 8:30am to 5pm.

For those who prefer the extra security of **traveler's checks,** U.S. dollar traveler's checks and credit cards are accepted in almost all hotels, restaurants, shops, and attractions, plus many grocery stores; they can be exchanged for cash at banks and most check-issuing offices. However, be aware that smaller businesses may not be able to cash traveler's checks or even American currency in large denominations (over $50).

2 When to Go

Colorado essentially has two seasons—warm and cold. Those who want to wander through a few historic towns, take in a frontier museum or two, or ride the Pikes Peak Cog Railway will want to visit sometime between May and October. Obviously, if it's skiing or other winter sports you're after, you'll have to wait for winter, which generally gets underway in late November and continues through March or April.

The best way to avoid crowds at the more popular destinations like Rocky Mountain National Park, Garden of the Gods, and Pikes Peak, is to try to visit during the shoulder seasons of March through May and October through mid-December. Generally, those traveling without children will want to avoid visiting during school vacations.

To hear a Coloradan tell it, the state has perfect weather all the time. Although that's a bit of an exaggeration, the weather here is usually quite good, with an abundance of sun and relatively mild temperatures in most places—just avoid those winter snowstorms.

Along the Front Range, where Denver and Colorado Springs are located, summers are hot and dry, evenings pleasantly mild. Relative humidity is low, and temperatures seldom rise above the 90s. Evenings start to get cooler by mid-September, but even as late as November days can just as easily be warm and crisp. Winters are, surprisingly, warmer and less snowy than those of the Great Lakes or New England; Front Range golf courses, in fact, remain open year-round.

Most of Colorado is considered semiarid, and overall the state has an average of 296 sunny days a year, more sunshine than San Diego or Miami Beach. The prairies average about 16 inches of precipitation annually; the Front Range, 14 inches; the western slope, only about 8 inches. Rain, when it falls, is commonly a short deluge—a summer afternoon thunderstorm. However, if you want to see snow, simply head to the mountains, where snowfall is measured in feet instead of inches, and mountain peaks may still be white in July. Temperatures can be bitterly cold, especially if it's windy, but even here, at some of the nation's top ski resorts, you'll find plenty of sunshine.

Average Monthly High/Low Temperatures (°F) & Precipitation (inches)

	Denver	Grand Junction	Colorado Springs
elev.	5,280'	4, 586'	6,035'
Jan	43/16,0.5	36/15,0.6	41/16,0.3
Feb	47/20,0.6	45/24,0.5	45/20,0.4
Mar	52/26,1.3	56/32,0.9	49/24,0.9
Apr	62/35,1.7	66/38,0.8	60/33,1.2
May	71/44,2.4	76/48,0.9	69/43,2.2
June	81/52,1.8	88/57,0.5	80/52,2.3
July	88/59,1.9	94/64,0.7	85/57,2.9
Aug	86/57,1.5	91/62,0.8	82/56,3.0
Sept	77/48,1.2	81/54,0.8	75/47,1.3
Oct	66/36,1.0	68/42,1.0	66/37,0.8
Nov	53/25,0.9	51/29,0.7	50/25,0.5
Dec	45/17,0.6	66/40,0.6	44/19,0.5

COLORADO CALENDAR OF EVENTS

January

- **International Snow Sculpture Championships,** Breckenridge. Four-person teams transform 20-ton blocks of snow into works of art. ☎ **970/453-6018.** Second week.
- ✪ **Cowboy Downhill,** Steamboat Springs. Professional rodeo cowboys tame a slalom course, lasso a resort employee, and saddle a horse before crossing the finish line. ☎ **970/879-0740.** Mid-January.
- ✪ **National Western Stock Show and Rodeo,** Denver. World's largest livestock show and indoor rodeo. ☎ **303/297-1166.** Second and third weeks.
- **Colorado Indian Market,** Denver. Members of more than 90 tribes display, sell, and demonstrate arts and crafts and perform traditional dances. ☎ **303/892-1112.** Second and third weeks.
- **Ullrfest,** Breckenridge. A week-long festival honors Ullr, Norse god of snow, with ski competitions, a torchlight display, fireworks, and a parade. ☎ **970/453-6018.** Third week.
- **Boulder Bach Festival,** Boulder. Music of the master baroque composer is performed in back-to-back performances. ☎ **303/494-3159.** Last weekend.
- **Colorado MahlerFest,** Boulder. The only festival in the world devoted to the music of Gustav Mahler. The week-long celebration includes performances, films, discussions, and seminars. ☎ **303/494-1632.** January.
- ✪ **Aspen/Snowmass Winterskol,** Aspen. A 5-day event that includes a parade, fireworks, and torchlight skiing. ☎ **970/925-1940.** Late January.

February

- **Steamboat Springs Winter Carnival,** Steamboat Springs. Festivities include races, jumping, broomball, and ski joring street events. ☎ **970/879-0740.** First full week.

- **Loveland Valentine Remailing Program,** Loveland. Over 250,000 valentines are remailed from Loveland. ☎ 970/667-6311. Prior to February 14.
- **Buffalo Bill's Birthday Celebration,** Golden. Ceremonies and live entertainment commemorate the life of the legendary scout and entertainer. ☎ 303/526-0744. Last weekend in February.

March

- **Crystal Carnival,** Leadville. A celebration of winter, with a parade of lights, snow-mobile races, and hot-air balloon rides. ☎ 719/486-3900. Early March.
- **Crane Festival,** Monte Vista. Whooping and sandhill cranes return to the San Luis Valley for spring. There are crane-viewing expeditions, naturalist programs, and art exhibits. ☎ 719/852-2731. Mid-March.
- **Pow Wow,** Denver. More than 700 Native Americans, representing some 70 tribes from 22 states, perform traditional music and dances. Arts and crafts are also sold. ☎ 303/455-4575. Mid-March.

April

- ✪ **Easter Sunrise Service,** Colorado Springs. Worshippers watch the rising sun light red sandstone formations in the Garden of the Gods. Easter Sunday.

May

- ✪ **Boulder Kinetic Fest,** Boulder. In this wacky, crowd-pleasing event, some 70 teams race over land and water in a variety of imaginative human-powered con-veyances. Activities include the kinetic parade, kinetic concerts, kinetic kite flying, and the kinetic ball. ☎ 303/444-5600. Early May.
- **Bolder Boulder,** Boulder. A road race that attracts some 40,000 entrants each year; participants walk, jog, or run the 10-kilometer (6.2-mile) course. ☎ 303/444-RACE. Memorial Day.
- ✪ **Telluride Mountain Film Festival,** Telluride. Screenings and discussions of mountain and adventure films. ☎ 970/728-3041. Late May.
- ✪ **Alferd Packer BBQ Cookoff,** Lake City. A cooking contest, coffin races, and other odd activities recall the life of Colorado's cannibal, believed to have consumed his companions when stranded in a snowstorm. ☎ 970/944-2527. Memorial Day weekend.
- **Iron Horse Bicycle Classic,** Durango. Mountain bikers race the Durango & Silverton Railroad's historic steam train from Durango to Silverton. ☎ 800/525-8855. Memorial Day weekend.
- **Mountainfilm,** Telluride. Filmmakers, writers, and outdoor enthusiasts gather to celebrate mountains, adventure, and the environment with 4 days of films, semi-nars, and presentations. Recent guests have included Sir Edmund Hillary and David Brower. Memorial Day weekend.

June

- **Capitol Hill People's Fair,** Denver. One of Denver's most vibrant street festivals, with hundreds of booths offering arts, crafts, and food from local restaurants. There's also live entertainment. ☎ 303/830-1651. First weekend in June.
- **FIBArk Festival,** Salida. North America's longest and oldest downriver kayak race highlights this 4-day festival, which includes carnival rides, a parade, foot races, and live entertainment. ☎ 719/539-7254. Mid-June.
- **Strawberry Days,** Glenwood Springs. One of Colorado's oldest civic celebrations, events include a rodeo, talent show, music, dancing, an arts-and-crafts fair, a pa-rade, carnival, and foot races. ☎ 970/945-6589. Mid-June.

- **Colorado Music Festival,** Boulder. The single largest arts event in Boulder, features world-renowned musicians in its symphony orchestra and chamber music series. ☎ **303/449-1397.** Mid-June to early August.
- **Greeley Independence Stampede,** Greeley. One of the West's biggest rodeos, with top national entertainers. ☎ **970/352-3566.** Mid-June through early July.
- ✪ **Telluride Bluegrass Festival,** Telluride. A 4-day event featuring bluegrass, country, and acoustic music. ☎ **970/728-3041.** Late June.
- ✪ **Colorado Brewer's Festival,** Fort Collins. Colorado's numerous microbreweries set up tasting booths in Fort Collins's historic Old Town Square. ☎ **970/484-6500.** Late June.
- ✪ **Jazz Aspen,** Snowmass. Five-day jazz festival in Snowmass's town park. Recent performances have included Lou Rawls and the Neville Brothers. ☎ **970/920-4996.** Late June.
- ✪ **Colorado Shakespeare Festival,** Boulder. One of the top Shakespeare festivals in the country, performed in an outdoor theater. ☎ **303/492-0554.** Late June through mid-August.
- ✪ **Aspen Music Festival,** Aspen. Considered one of the finest summer music festivals in the country, featuring world-renowned artists. Indoor and open-air classical, chamber, and opera performances. ☎ **970/925-3254.** Late June to mid-August.
- **Breckenridge Music Festival,** Breckenridge. The Breckenridge Music Institute presents more than 50 classical music concerts performed by its instructors and students. ☎ **970/453-2120.** Late June to late August.
- **Bravo! Colorado Vail Valley Music Festival,** Vail and Beaver Creek. This young festival (since 1988) features music from virtually every genre—orchestral, chamber, vocal, jazz, and pops. ☎ **970/476-0206.** Late June to early August.

July

- **Pikes Peak Auto Hill Climb,** Colorado Springs. This "race to the clouds," held annually since 1916, takes drivers to the top of 14,110-foot Pikes Peak. ☎ **719/685-4400.** July 4.
- **Colorado State Mining Championship,** Creede. Entrants from six states compete in old-style hand steeling, hand mucking, spike driving, and newer methods of machine drilling and machine mucking. ☎ **800/327-2102.** July 4 weekend.
- **Cherry Creek Arts Festival,** Denver. Almost 200 artists display their work and give demonstrations. ☎ **303/355-2787.** July 4 weekend.
- **Brush Rodeo,** Brush. The world's largest amateur rodeo, with more than 400 participants. Traditional rodeo events, plus wild-cow milking, a parade, footrace, dance, and fireworks are all part of the festivities. ☎ **800/354-8659.** Early July.
- **Strings in the Mountains Festival of Music,** Steamboat Springs. Top-notch classical and jazz musicians give five performances a week during this 6-week festival. ☎ **970/879-5056.** Early July to mid-August.
- **Genuine Jazz in July,** Breckenridge. A showcase of Colorado jazz groups—from Dixieland to bebop to New Age. ☎ **970/453-6018.** Second weekend.
- **Pikes Peak Highland Games & Celtic Festival,** Colorado Springs. Sponsored by the Scottish Society of the Pikes Peak Region, with traditional games, Celtic music, a Highland dance competition, and Scottish foods. ☎ **719/578-6777.** Mid-July.
- **Denver Black Arts Festival,** Denver. Features the work of black artists and entertainers, plus a parade. ☎ **303/293-2559.** Mid-July.

- ✪ **DanceAspen Festival,** Aspen. One of the nation's leading summer dance festivals, featuring a broad spectrum of forms—classical ballet, modern, and jazz. ☎ 970/925-7718. July to August.
- **Colorado Dance Festival,** Boulder. Balletomanes from around the world flock to this 4-week event, including classes, lectures, film screenings, and panel discussions. ☎ 303/442-7666. July.

August

- **Pikes Peak or Bust Rodeo,** Colorado Springs. Largest outdoor rodeo in the state. ☎ 719/635-3547. Early August.
- **Boom Days,** Leadville. Events include a parade, a carnival, a street fair, live entertainment, a mine-drilling competition, and a 22-mile pack-burro race. ☎ 719/486-3900. First weekend.
- **Vail International DanceFest,** Vail. Features performances by the Bolshoi Ballet Academy at Vail (a satellite of the famous Russian company) as well as small ensembles comprised of dancers from renowned ballet companies from around the world. ☎ 970/479-1999. Early August.
- **Sculpture in the Park,** Loveland. Show and sale of sculpture, with demonstrations and an auction. ☎ 970/663-2940. Mid-August.
- ✪ **Rocky Mountain Wine and Food Festival,** Winter Park. Colorado's finest chefs and many of America's best-known vintners offer their creations to benefit the National Sports Center for the Disabled. ☎ 970/726-4118. Third weekend.
- **Colorado State Fair,** Pueblo. There's a national professional rodeo, carnival rides, food booths, industrial displays, horse shows, animal exhibits, and entertainment by top-name performers. ☎ 800/876-4567. Mid-August through Labor Day.

September

- **A Taste Of Colorado,** Denver. This is Denver's largest celebration, with an annual attendance of about 500,000. House specialties from local restaurants, crafts exhibits, and free concerts. ☎ 800/645-3446. Labor Day weekend.
- **Michael Martin Murphey's West Fest,** Copper Mountain. Music, art, and culture of the traditional American West. ☎ 970/668-0376. Labor Day weekend.
- **Steamboat Vintage Auto Race & Concours d'Elégance,** Steamboat Springs. Over 200 classic cars on a mountain course; vintage aircraft fly-in; rodeo series finals. ☎ 970/879-0880. Labor Day weekend.
- ✪ **Telluride Film Festival,** Telluride. An influential festival within the film industry that's premiered some of the finest independent films in recent years. Open-air screenings and seminars. ☎ 603/643-1255. Labor Day weekend.
- **Vail Fest,** Vail. An Oktoberfest-style weekend with street entertainment, yodeling contest, 5- and 10-kilometer (3.1- and 6.2-mile) runs, dancing, games, and sing-alongs. ☎ 970/476-1000. Second weekend.
- **Breckenridge Festival of Film,** Breckenridge. Attracts Hollywood power brokers and young directors to screen and discuss 2 dozen films of all genres. ☎ 970/453-6200. Third weekend.

October

- **Oktoberfest,** Ouray. Polkas, food, crafts, and an antique auto show. ☎ 800/228-1876. Early October.
- **Cowboy Gathering,** Durango. Cowboy poetry, western art, films, historical lectures, and demonstrations. ☎ 800/525-8855. Early October.

- **Great American Beer Festival,** Denver. Hundreds of American beers are available for sampling. ☎ 303/447-0816. Early October.
- **Vintage Six Wine Tasting,** Denver. Annual benefit for the Denver public television station. ☎ 303/620-5700. Mid-October.

November

- **Colorado Ski Expo,** Denver. Skiers and snowboarders get together at the Colorado Convention Center to check out the newest equipment and get information on the state's resorts, accommodations, and bargains. ☎ 303/837-0793. Early November.
- **Christmas Mountain USA,** Salida. Over 3,000 lights outline a 700-foot tree; also a parade of lights and a visit from Santa Claus. ☎ 719/539-2068. Day after Thanksgiving.

December

- **Parade of Lights,** Denver. A holiday parade winds its way through downtown Denver, with floats, balloons, and marching bands. ☎ 303/534-6161. Early December.
- **World's Largest Christmas Lighting Display,** Denver. The Denver City and County Building is illuminated by some 40,000 colored floodlights. All month.
- **Christmas in Old Town,** Burlington. Victorian carolers and Christmas music, plus other Victorian Christmas activities. Some events continue all month. ☎ 800/288-1334. Early December.

3 Health & Insurance

STAYING HEALTHY

Colorado's high elevation—about two-thirds of the state is more than a mile above sea level—means that there's less oxygen and less humidity than elsewhere in the West. Those in generally good health need not take any special precautions but can ease the transition to a higher elevation by changing altitude gradually. For instance, spend a night or two in Burlington (elevation 4,163 ft.) before going to Denver (elevation 5,280 ft.); or spend at least 2 or 3 nights in Colorado Springs (elevation 6,012 ft.) before driving or taking the cog railway to the top of Pikes Peak (elevation 14,110 ft.).

Lowlanders can also help their bodies adjust to higher elevations by taking it easy for their first few days in the mountains, cutting down on cigarettes and alcohol, and avoiding sleeping pills and other drugs. There is a drug, Diamox R, that can be taken to help prevent altitude problems and relieve the symptoms if they occur. You should consult medical professionals about its use. Individuals with heart or respiratory problems should consult their home physician before planning trips to the Colorado mountains.

Since the sun's rays are stronger in the thinner, high-altitude air, everyone should use a good quality sunblock and wear a hat and sunglasses with full ultraviolet protection.

If you plan to hike in the mountains, be sure to bring along plenty of water—at least one gallon per person, per day. Don't overexert yourself, as that makes you susceptible to acute mountain sickness, characterized in its early stages by headaches, shortness of breath, appetite loss and/or nausea, tingling in the fingers or toes, and lethargy or insomnia. Ordinarily, it requires no medical treatment, and can be alleviated by an aspirin and a slower pace. If it persists or worsens, descend to a lower altitude.

Less common but more serious is high altitude pulmonary edema, whose symptoms include a congested cough and shortness of breath. It looks and feels a lot like pneumonia. If you think you may have it, consult a doctor immediately.

Finally, there's Hantavirus, a rare but often fatal respiratory disease. First recognized in 1993, about half of the country's 100-plus confirmed cases have been reported in the Four Corners states of Colorado, New Mexico, Arizona, and Utah. The disease is believed to be spread by the urine and droppings of deer mice and other rodents. Campers should avoid areas with evidence of rodent droppings and thoroughly air out tents or cabins before use, especially if they've been unused for a period of time. The early symptoms of Hantavirus are similar to those of the flu, and quickly lead to breathing difficulties and shock.

INSURANCE

Before starting out, check your medical insurance policy to be certain you're covered away from home; if you aren't, consider purchasing a special traveler's policy, available from travel agents, insurance agents, and travel clubs. Traveler's policies are relatively inexpensive and can usually be purchased for the exact duration of your trip. It's also a good idea to carry a medical insurance identification card or other proof of insurance with you at all times when you're traveling.

In addition to being prepared for medical emergencies, it's wise to carry insurance in case of accidents, lost luggage, and trip cancellation (especially if you've prepaid a large portion of your vacation expenses). Again, check with your travel agent. Before you buy, though, check your homeowner's or renter's policy—off-premises theft and loss of your belongings may be covered there.

If you're planning to drive in Colorado, see "By Car" under "Getting Around," below for information on car insurance.

4 Tips for Travelers with Special Needs

FOR TRAVELERS WITH DISABILITIES

Travelers with physical disabilities should find Colorado relatively easy to get around. Some small towns aren't wheelchair-accessible, but the Front Range cities, and most major parks and historical monuments, are. To be safe, it's best to call ahead to make sure facilities are suitable.

If you're planning to visit Colorado's national parks and monuments, you can get the National Park Service's **Golden Access Passport,** available at all visitor centers. This lifetime pass is issued to any U.S. citizen or permanent resident who is medically certified as disabled or blind. The pass permits free entry and gives a 50% discount on park-service campgrounds and activities (but not on those offered by private concessions).

Mobility International USA, P.O. Box 10767, Eugene, OR 97440 (☎ voice and TDD **541/343-1284;** fax 541/343-6812), is a national nonprofit member organization that provides travel information and referrals, plus other services, for those with disabilities. It also provides educational programs on disability rights awareness and related issues.

Amtrak will, with 24-hour notice, provide porter service, special seating, and a 15% discount (☎ **800/USA-RAIL**) on most runs. If you're traveling with a companion, **Greyhound** will carry you both for a single fare (☎ **800/231-2222**).

FOR GAY & LESBIAN TRAVELERS

Colorado Springs, home of Focus on the Family and other conservative political organizations, isn't exactly gay-friendly (even if it does have one of the oldest gay bars in the West, **Hide 'n' Seek**), but Boulder, Denver, and the major ski resorts are all places where you'll feel right at home. In Denver, a good resource to know about is **the Gay and Lesbian Community Center of Colorado** (☎ **303/831-6268**).

FOR SENIORS

Many Colorado hotels, motels, restaurants, attractions, and public transportation systems offer discounts to senior citizens. You can save sightseeing dollars if you are 62 or over by picking up a **Golden Age Passport** from any federally operated park, recreation area, or monument. There is a one-time fee of $10 that entitles holders to free admission to parks and other federally managed fee areas plus a 50% savings on camping fees.

Amtrak will give a 15% discount on most fares to travelers 62 and older.

Membership in the following senior organizations offers a variety of travel benefits: The **American Association of Retired Persons (AARP),** 601 E. St. NW, Washington, DC 20049 (☎ **800/424-3410** or 202/434-2277); and the **National Council of Senior Citizens,** 1331 F. St. NW, Washington, DC 20004 (☎ **202/347-8800**).

FOR STUDENTS

Bring your student ID along, and ask about student discounts wherever you go. Joining **Hostelling International-American Youth Hostels,** Box 37613, Washington, DC 20013-7613 (☎ **202/783-6161**), will enable you to stay at inexpensive youth hostels throughout the state (a great way to meet other traveling students!). Ask for their free directory of U.S. hostels when you join, or purchase it for $1.50.

5 Getting There

BY PLANE

The state's two major airports are Denver International and Colorado Springs; you can fly directly to either airport from many cities in the United States and Canada. Fares to Colorado Springs are often lower, so it's wise to compare rates into both airports if cost is a factor for you.

Denver International, which opened in a new location in 1995, is 23 miles northeast of downtown Denver (about 35 to 45 min. by car). Airlines serving the airport include **American** (☎ 800/433-7300), **America West** (☎ 800/235-9292), **Continental** (☎ 800/525-0280), **Delta** (☎ 800/211-1212), **Frontier** (☎ 800/432-1359), **GP Express** (☎ 800/525-0280), **Martinair Holland** (☎ 800/366-4655), **Mexicana** (☎ 800/531-7921), **Northwest** (☎ 800/225-2525), **Sun Country** (☎ 800/359-5786), **TWA** (☎ 800/221-2000), **United** (☎ 800/241-6522), and **US Air** (☎ 800/428-4322). Regional and commuter airlines connect Denver with other points in the Rockies and Southwest; they include **Continental Connection** (☎ 800/525-0280), **Mesa Airlines** (☎ 800/637-2247), and **United Express** (☎ 800/241-6522).

An **airport information** line (☎ **800/AIR-2-DEN**), provides information about airport parking, ground transportation, current weather conditions, and even nearby accommodations.

Colorado Springs Airport, which completed an extensive expansion in 1994, is located in the southeast corner of the city, just a few minutes by car from downtown.

Airlines serving it include **American** (☎ 800/433-7300), **America West** (☎ 800/235-9292), **Delta** (☎ 800/221-1212), **Northwest** (☎ 800/225-2525), **Trans World** (☎ 800/221-2000), **United** (☎ 800/241-6522), and **Western Pacific** (☎ 800/930-3030). Intrastate connections are available on **Mesa** (☎ 800/637-2247), **Air 21** (☎ 800/FLY-AIR21), and **Reno Air** (☎ 800/736-6247).

BY CAR

Some 1,000 miles of interstate highways form a star on the map of Colorado, with its center at Denver. I-25 crosses the state from south to north, extending from New Mexico to Wyoming; over its 300 miles, it transits nearly every major city of the Front Range, including Pueblo, Colorado Springs, Denver, and Fort Collins.

I-70 crosses from west to east, extending from Utah to Kansas, a distance of about 450 miles; it enters Colorado near Grand Junction, passes through Glenwood Springs, Vail, and Denver, and exits just east of Burlington. I-76 is an additional 190-mile spur that begins in Denver and extends northeast to Nebraska, joining I-80 just beyond Julesburg.

Visitors entering Colorado from the southwest may take U.S. 160 (from Flagstaff, AZ) or U.S. 550 (from Farmington, NM). Both routes enter the state near Durango.

If you aren't already a member, it's a good idea to join the **American Automobile Association (AAA)** (☎ 800/336-4357), which has hundreds of offices nationwide. Members receive excellent maps and emergency road service; they'll even help you plan an exact itinerary.

BY TRAIN

Amtrak (☎ 800/USA-RAIL) has several routes through Colorado. One, which links San Francisco and Chicago, passes through Grand Junction, Glenwood Springs, Kremmling, Winter Park, Denver, Fort Morgan, Sterling, and Julesburg en route to Omaha, Nebraska. Another, which runs between Los Angeles and Chicago, travels from Albuquerque, New Mexico, via Trinidad, La Junta, and Lamar before crossing the southeastern Colorado border into Kansas. The third, which connects Chicago and Seattle, stops at Fort Morgan, Denver, and Greeley.

BY BUS

Greyhound (☎ 800/231-2222) has an extensive network that reaches nearly every corner of the state, with daily connections practically everywhere. Parts of southern Colorado are also served by **TNM&O Coaches** (Texas, New Mexico & Oklahoma Coaches), which can be booked through Greyhound.

ESCORTED TOURS

Travelers who want to avoid the hassles of planning, making reservations, renting cars, and the rest have some good options among escorted tours, including a few unique choices. An excellent compromise between doing your own thing and joining an organized tour is to work with **Colorado Reservation Service,** 3554 N. Academy Blvd., Colorado Springs, CO 80917 (☎ 800/777-6880; fax 719/591-7068). Tell the trip planners where you want to go, how long you want to stay, and how much you want to spend, and they will make lodging reservations for your entire trip. They can also take care of airline reservations and car rentals, and arrange rafting, mountain biking, horseback riding, and other activities. The company can make immediate or advance reservations.

Among the better companies that offer specialized tours to and within Colorado are:

American Dream Safari, P.O. Box 556, McPherson, KS 67460 (☎ **316/ 241-5656**). A unique and fun way to see parts of Colorado and nearby states, in groups of two to six people traveling in classic 1950s luxury automobiles, with appropriate lodging in 1950s-style motels or inns, or 1950s-era Airstream trailers.

Discover Colorado Tours, 2401 East St., Suite 204, Golden, CO 80401 (☎ **800/641-0129** or 303/277-0129). Offers personalized individual and group tours of half-day, full-day, or multidays throughout Colorado, including trips to gold mining areas, ghost towns, Rocky Mountain National Park, Pikes Peak, Mesa Verde, and the U.S. Air Force Academy.

Gray Line, 5855 E. 56th Ave. (P.O. Box 17527), Denver, CO 80217-0527 (☎ **303/289-2841**). Provides traditional bus and van tours to the U.S. Air Force Academy, Pikes Peak, Rocky Mountain National Park, and historic sites of Denver.

Maupintour, 1515 St. Andrews Dr., Lawrence, KS 66047 (☎ **800/255-4266**). Offers well-planned multiday tours that include Rocky Mountain National Park and other scenic and historic areas.

Sample Colorado Travel Club, P.O. Box 621906, Littleton, CO 80162-1906 (☎ **303/904-2376**). Offers scheduled and custom tours with a historic theme throughout the state, both day-trips from Denver and multiday excursions.

TCS Expeditions, 2025 First Ave., Suite 830, Seattle, WA 98123 (☎ **800/ 727-7477**). Among its tours on the *American Orient Express* train, with luxurious restored coaches from the 1940s and 1950s, is a 10-day trip to national parks of the West that includes stops at Rocky Mountain National Park, Estes Park, and Denver.

6 Getting Around

BY CAR

Driving is an excellent way to get around Colorado. The roads are well maintained and well marked, with interconnecting highways heading out in all directions, and a car is often the most economical and convenient way to get somewhere; in fact, if you plan to explore beyond the Denver, Boulder, or Colorado Springs areas, it's practically the only way to get to some places. However, visitors who drive their own cars around and to the state will find that steep mountain roads can put a severe strain on their vehicle, particularly on the cooling and braking systems. If you're planning to travel in winter, make sure you add plenty of antifreeze to your engine—most residents make sure there's enough to protect their cars to −35°—temperatures can get well below zero in the mountains. Tires rated for mud and snow are needed in most areas in winter, and are required on roads leading to most ski areas from November to March.

Car & R.V. Rentals   Rental cars are available in every sizable town and city in the state, usually at the local airport as well as downtown. Widely represented agencies include **Alamo** (☎ 800/327-9633), **Avis** (☎ 800/831-2847), **Budget** (☎ 800/ 527-0700), **Dollar** (☎ 800/800-4000), **Enterprise** (☎ 800/325-8007), **Hertz** (☎ 800/654-3131), **National** (☎ 800/227-7368), and **Thrifty** (☎ 800/ FOR-CARS). Campers, travel trailers, and motor homes are available in Denver from **Cruise America** (☎ 800/327-7778).

Driving Rules   Colorado law requires all drivers to carry proof of insurance, as well as a valid driver's license. Safety belts are required for drivers and all front-seat passengers; restraints are required for all children and teenagers age 15 and younger, regardless of where they're sitting. You must be 16 to drive in Colorado, period—

even if you have valid license from another state. The maximum speed limit on interstate highways is 75 miles per hour; 65 miles per hour on non-interstates, unless otherwise posted. Radar detectors are permitted. Colorado law allows drivers to make a right turn at a red signal after coming to a complete stop, unless posted otherwise.

Maps　A state highway map can be obtained from any state Welcome Centers or by mail (see "Visitor Information & Money," at the beginning of this chapter). Otherwise, maps can be purchased at bookstores, gas stations, and most supermarkets and discount stores. An excellent source for all kinds of maps and road atlases is **Maps Unlimited** in Denver (☎ **800/456-8703** or 303/623-4299).

Insurance　Be sure to carry proof of automobile liability insurance, and be certain that your policy includes protection from uninsured motorists. If you're renting a car, check your credit cards to see if any of them include a collision-damage waiver (CDW) when you rent with their card. If one of them does, it'll save you as much as $12 a day on the cost of your rental.

Roadside Assistance　In case of an accident or road emergency, contact the state patrol. American Automobile Association members can get free emergency road service by calling **AAA's emergency number** (☎ **800/AAA-HELP**). In Colorado, AAA headquarters is at 4100 E. Arkansas Ave., Denver, CO 80222-3491 (☎ **800/283-5222** or 303/753-8800).

Road Conditions & Winter Closings　A recorded **24-hour hot line** (☎ **303/639-1111**) provides information on road conditions statewide.

Two notable Colorado highways are closed in winter. U.S. 34 (the Trail Ridge Road through Rocky Mountain National Park) and Colorado 82 (over Independence Pass, east of Aspen), the main route between Denver and Aspen in the summer months.

In addition, the Mount Evans Road (Colo. 103 and Colo. 5) from Idaho Springs to the summit of Mount Evans is open from June to September only. The Eisenhower Tunnel through Loveland Pass (along I-70) is sometimes closed due to winter storms, but only for short periods.

FAST FACTS: Colorado

Area Codes　Colorado has three telephone area codes. In the immediate Denver area, it's 303. The south-central and southeastern parts of the state, including Colorado Springs, use 719; and the rest of the state uses 970.

Business Hours　Banks are typically open Monday through Thursday from 9am to 5pm, Friday 9am to 6pm, and sometimes Saturday. Most branches have automatic teller machines available 24 hours. Generally, stores are open 6 days a week, with many open on Sunday too; department stores usually stay open until 9pm at least 1 day a week. Discount stores and supermarkets are often open later than other stores, and some supermarkets in major cities are open 24 hours a day.

Embassies and Consulates　See Chapter 4, "For Foreign Visitors."

Emergencies　In almost all parts of Colorado, the number to dial for any emergency is **911,** and money is not required at pay phones. In a few rural areas, it will be necessary to dial "0" (zero) for the operator.

Liquor Laws　The legal drinking age is 21. Regarding package goods, you can buy 3.2% beer (a lesser-strength beer, see below) in supermarkets and convenience

Colorado Driving Times & Distances

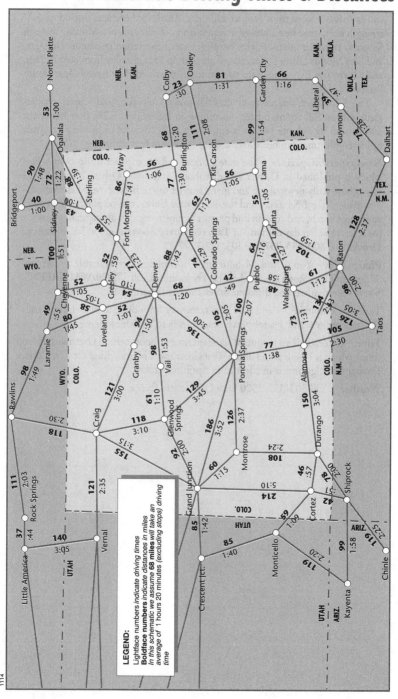

LEGEND:
Lightface numbers indicate driving times
Boldface numbers indicate distances in miles
In this schematic we assume **68 miles** will take an
average of 1 hours 20 minutes (excluding stops) driving
time

stores 7 days a week from 5am to midnight. Alcoholic beverages, including full-strength beer, must be purchased in liquor stores. These are open Monday through Saturday from 8am to midnight. Beverages may be served in restaurants, lounges, and bars Monday through Saturday from 7am to 2am, Sunday from 8am to 2am, and Christmas Day from 8am to midnight, provided they have proper liquor licenses.

The 3.2% beer, unique to Utah, Oklahoma, Colorado, and Kansas, has less alcohol than full-strength beer. According to Budweiser, 3.2% beer has about 4% alcohol by volume (which is equivalent to 3.2% alcohol by weight), while full-strength American beers have about 5% alcohol by volume.

Newspapers/Magazines   The state's largest daily newspaper is the *Denver Post,* which is published in Denver and distributed statewide. Other cities and large towns have daily newspapers, and many smaller towns publish weeklies. National newspapers like *USA Today* and the *Wall Street Journal* can be purchased in cities and major hotels, and you can find practically any newspaper or magazine you want (or at least the Sunday editions) at **Tattered Cover Bookstore,** 2955 E. First Ave., Denver (☎ **800/833-9327** or 303/322-7727).

Pharmacies   You'll find 24-hour prescription services available at selected Walgreens Drug Stores around the state. For locations, call ☎ **800/WALGREENS.** Many supermarkets and discount stores also have pharmacies.

Taxes   Combined city and state sales taxes vary from place to place but are usually between 6% and 9% for purchases, and 9% to 13% for lodging.

Time   Colorado is on mountain standard time (7 hours behind Greenwich mean time), which is 1 hour ahead of the West Coast and 2 hours behind the East Coast. Daylight savings time is in effect from April to October.

Weather   Call **303/337-2500** for a Denver area forecast.

For Foreign Visitors

4

American fads and fashions have spread across other parts of the world to such a degree that the United States may seem like familiar territory before your arrival. But there are still many peculiarities and uniquely American situations that you may find confusing or perplexing. This chapter tells you how to get to the United States as economically and effortlessly as possible, and explains how everyday basics work in Colorado—everything from receiving mail to making a local or long-distance telephone call.

1 Preparing for Your Trip

ENTRY REQUIREMENTS

Document Regulations   Canadian citizens may enter the United States without visas; they need only proof of residence. Citizens of the United Kingdom, New Zealand, Japan, and most western European countries traveling with valid passports may not need a visa for fewer than 90 days of holiday or business travel to the United States, provided that they hold a round-trip or return ticket and enter the United States on an airline or cruise line that participates in the visa-waiver program. (Note that citizens of these visa-exempt countries who first enter the United States may then visit Mexico, Canada, Bermuda, and/or the Caribbean Islands and then reenter the United States, by any mode of transportation, without needing a visa. Further information is available from any U.S. embassy or consulate.)

Citizens of countries other than those stipulated above must have two documents: a valid passport with an expiration date at least 6 months later than the scheduled end of the visit to the United States, and a tourist visa, available without charge from the nearest U.S. consulate.

To obtain a visa, the traveler must submit a completed application form (either in person or by mail) with a 1 1/2-inch square photo and provide evidence of a permanent residence abroad. Usually you can obtain a visa within 24 hours, but it may take longer during the summer rush from June to August. If you cannot go in person, contact the nearest U.S. embassy or consulate for instructions on applying by mail. Your travel agent or airline office may also be able to provide you with visa applications and instructions. The U.S. consulate or embassy that issues your visa will determine whether you will be issued a multiple- or single-entry visa and any restrictions regarding the length of your stay.

Medical Requirements   No inoculations are needed to enter the United States unless you are coming from or have stopped over in areas known to be suffering from epidemics, particularly cholera or yellow fever.

If you have a disease requiring treatment with medications containing narcotics or drugs requiring a syringe, carry a valid signed prescription from your physician to allay any suspicions that you are smuggling drugs.

Customs Requirements   Every adult visitor may bring into the United States free of duty: 1 liter of wine or hard liquor; 200 cigarettes or 100 cigars (but no cigars from Cuba) or 3 pounds of smoking tobacco; and $100 worth of gifts. These exemptions are offered to travelers who spend at least 72 hours in the United States and who have not claimed them within the preceding 6 months. It is altogether forbidden to bring into the country foodstuffs (particularly cheese, fruit, cooked meats, and canned goods) and plants (vegetables, seeds, tropical plants, and so on). Foreign tourists may bring in or take out up to $10,000 in U.S. or foreign currency with no formalities; larger sums must be declared to customs on entering or leaving.

INSURANCE

There is no national health-care system in the United States. Because the cost of medical care can be extremely high, it is recommended that every traveler obtain health coverage before setting out.

You may want to buy a comprehensive travel policy that covers sickness or injury costs (medical, surgical, and hospital); loss or theft of your baggage; trip-cancellation costs; guarantee of bail in case you are arrested; costs of accident, repatriation, or death. Such packages (for example, "Europe Assistance" in Europe) are sold by automobile clubs at attractive rates, as well as by insurance companies and travel agencies.

MONEY

Currency and Exchange   The U.S. monetary system has a decimal base: one American dollar ($1) = 100 cents (100¢). Dollar bills commonly come in $1 ("a buck"), $5, $10, $20, $50, and $100 denominations (the last two are not welcome when paying for small purchases and are often not accepted in taxis). There are also $2 bills (seldom encountered).

There are six denominations of coins: 1¢ (1 cent or "penny"), 5¢ (five cents or "a nickel"), 10¢ (ten cents or "a dime"), 25¢ (twenty-five cents or "a quarter"), 50¢ (fifty cents or "a half dollar"), and the rare $1 piece.

Exchange   The "foreign-exchange bureaus" so common in Europe are rare even at some airports in the United States, and nonexistent outside major cities. Try to avoid having to exchange foreign money or traveler's checks denominated in other than U.S. dollars at a small-town bank, or even a branch in a big city. Although some banks will exchange currency, your best choice is **Thomas Cook Currency Services, Inc.** The company has been in business since 1841 and offers a wide range of services. They buy and sell over 100 currencies, sell foreign and U.S. traveler's checks, foreign drafts, and wire transfers; the company also does check collections. Their rates are competitive, and their service is excellent. They maintain several offices in **New York City:** Fifth Avenue office (☎ 212/757-6915), at **JFK's International Arrivals Terminal** (☎ 718/656-8444), and at **La Guardia in the Delta terminal** (☎ 718/533-0784). (See "Currency Exchange," under the "Fast Facts: For the

Foreign Traveler" section later in this chapter for exchange services in Denver, Boulder, and Colorado Springs.)

Traveler's Checks   Traveler's checks denominated in U.S. dollars are readily accepted at most hotels, motels, restaurants, and large stores; however, the best place to exchange traveler's checks is at a bank. Do not bring traveler's checks denominated in other currencies.

Credit Cards   The method of payment most widely used in the United States is the credit card: Visa (BarclayCard in Britain), MasterCard (EuroCard in Europe, Access in Britain, Chargex in Canada), American Express, Diners Club, Discover, and Carte Blanche. You can save yourself trouble by using "plastic" rather than cash or traveler's checks in most hotels, motels, restaurants, and retail stores. A credit card can also be used as a deposit for a rental car, as proof of identity, or as a "cash card," enabling you to withdraw money from automatic teller machines (ATMs) that accept them.

SAFETY

General   Although Colorado has not seen the amount of crime against tourists that occurs in some U.S. cities, crime is on the increase, and even Colorado cities tend to be less safe than those in Europe or Japan. This is particularly true in some sections of Denver. It is wise to ask local visitor information centers if you're in doubt about which neighborhoods are safe. Avoid deserted areas, such as city parks, especially at night. Generally speaking, you can feel safe in areas where there are many people and many open establishments.

Be especially careful in national parks and other popular public lands. Recent years have seen an increase in crime at parks and national monuments, particularly thefts from campsites and parked vehicles.

Remember also that hotels are open to the public, and in a large hotel, security may not be able to screen everyone entering. Always lock your room door—don't assume that once inside your hotel you are automatically safe and no longer need be aware of your surroundings.

Driving   Safety while driving is particularly important. Question your rental agency about personal safety, or ask for a brochure of traveler safety tips when you pick up your car. Obtain written directions, or a map with the route marked in red, from the agency showing how to get to your destination.

Although Colorado does not have a lot of attacks against motorists, it is not unheard of. If you drive off a highway into a doubtful neighborhood, leave the area as quickly as possible. If you have an accident, even on the highway, stay in your car with the doors locked until you assess the situation or until the police arrive. If you are bumped from behind on the street or are involved in a minor accident with no injuries and the situation appears to be suspicious, motion to the other driver to follow you. Never get out of your car in such situations, but drive to the nearest police station, well-lighted service station, or all-night store.

If you see someone on the road who indicates a need for help, do not stop. Take note of the location, drive on to a well-lighted area, and telephone the police by dialing 911, or "0" (zero, not the letter "O").

Park in well-lighted, well-traveled areas if possible. Always keep your car doors locked, whether attended or unattended. Look around you before you get out of your car, and never leave any packages or valuables in sight. If someone attempts to rob you or steal your car, do not try to resist the thief/carjacker—report the incident to police immediately.

You may wish to contact the Colorado Travel & Tourism Authority (☎ **800/ COLORADO**) to discuss your plans and ask for advice.

2 Getting to the U.S.

Travelers from overseas can take advantage of the APEX (Advance Purchase Excursion) fares offered by all the major U.S. and European carriers. Aside from these, attractive values are offered by Virgin Atlantic Airways from London to New York/ Newark.

Airlines offering international flights into Denver through other American cities include: **American** (☎ **800/433-7300** in the U.S.; 0181/572-5555 in London), **Continental** (☎ **800/231-0856** in the U.S.; 4412/9377-6464 in London), and **TWA** (☎ **800/221-2000**; 0181/990-9900 in London). **British Airways** (☎ **081/ 897-4000** in London) has a code-sharing agreement with **America West** airlines. This means that you can fly to Phoenix on a British Airways aircraft, and then change to an America West plane for onward travel to Denver or Colorado Springs, all while retaining your original British Airways flight number. Miles for the entire itinerary can be accrued on either a British Airways or America West frequent-flyer account.

Visitors arriving by air, no matter what the port of entry, should cultivate patience and resignation before setting foot on U.S. soil. Getting through Immigration Control may take as long as 2 hours on some days, especially summer weekends. Add the time it takes to clear customs, and you'll see that you should allow extra time for delays when planning connections between international and domestic flights— an average of 2 to 3 hours at least.

In contrast, travelers arriving by car or by rail from Canada will find border-crossing formalities streamlined to the vanishing point. And air travelers from Canada, Bermuda, and some places in the Caribbean can sometimes go through customs and Immigration Control at the point of departure, which is much quicker and less painful.

3 Getting Around the U.S.

BY PLANE

Some large American airlines (TWA, American Airlines, Northwest, United, and Delta) offer travelers on their transatlantic or transpacific flights special discount tickets under the name **Visit USA,** allowing travel between various U.S. destinations at minimum rates. These tickets are not on sale in the United States and must, therefore, be purchased before you leave your foreign point of departure. This program is the best, easiest, and fastest way to see the United States at low cost. You should obtain information well in advance from your travel agent or the office of the airline concerned, since the conditions attached to these discount tickets can be changed without advance notice. With the recent completion of a new, larger Denver airport, international air traffic is expected to increase. Check with your travel agent or local airline.

Amtrak trains connect Denver to both the East and West coasts; however, there is no train service to Boulder or Colorado Springs. International visitors can buy a **USA Railpass,** good for 15 or 30 days of unlimited travel on Amtrak, available through many foreign travel agents. With a foreign passport, you can also buy passes at some Amtrak offices in the United States, including those in San Francisco, Los Angeles, Chicago, New York, Miami, Boston, and Washington, D.C. **Amtrak** (☎ **800/ USA-Rail** in the U.S.) also frequently has low-cost passes available for anyone, covering certain regions of the country. Reservations are generally required for train travel and should be made for each part of your trip as early as possible.

Be aware of the limitations of long-distance rail travel in the United States. With a few notable exceptions, service is rarely up to European standards, and routes are limited. Fares (especially with the inclusion of meals) are seldom cheaper than discount airfares.

BY BUS

The cheapest form of public transportation in the United States is usually the bus. **Greyhound** (☎ **800/231-7222** in the U.S.), the sole nationwide bus line, offers an **Ameripass** for various durations of unlimited travel; call for rates. Since bus travel in the United States can be slow and uncomfortable and routes are limited, this option is not for everyone.

BY CAR

Because much of Colorado is rural, with limited or nonexistent public transportation, the best way to explore the state is by car. Many car rental companies (see major city listings) offer unlimited-mileage weekly specials that can be quite affordable.

FAST FACTS: For the Foreign Traveler

Automobile Organizations   Auto clubs will supply maps, suggested routes, guide-books, accident and bail-bond insurance, and emergency road service. The major auto club in the United States is the **American Automobile Association** (**AAA**), with close to 1,000 offices nationwide, including offices in Denver, Boulder, Colorado Springs, Pueblo, Grand Junction, Fort Collins, and Greeley. If you belong to an auto club, inquire about reciprocal privileges before you leave home. AAA can provide you with an International Driving Permit validating your foreign license. You may be able to join AAA even if you are not a member of a reciprocal club. To inquire, call **800/222-4357** in the U.S. In addition, some automobile rental agencies now provide these services, so you should ask about their availability when you rent your car.

Automobile Rentals   To rent a car you need a major credit card and a valid driver's license, and usually must be at least 25 years old. Some companies will rent to younger drivers, but they add a surcharge. Be sure to return your car with the same amount of gas you started out with; rental companies charge excessive prices for gasoline. See also "Getting Around," in chapter 3.

Business Hours   Banks are usually open weekdays from 9am to 5pm, often until 6pm Friday, and sometimes Saturday. There's 24-hour access to the automatic teller machines (ATMs) at most banks, plus in shopping centers and other outlets. Generally, offices are open weekdays from 9am to 5pm. Stores are open 6 days a week, with many open on Sunday, too; department stores usually stay open until 9pm at least 1 day a week. Discount stores and supermarkets are often open later than other stores, and some supermarkets in major cities are open 24 hours a day.

Currency   See "Money" in "Preparing for Your Trip," above.

Currency Exchange   You will find currency-exchange services in most major airports with international service. Elsewhere, they may be quite difficult to come by.

In **Denver, Thomas Cook Currency Services** is located downtown in the **Adam's Mark Hotel,** at 1580 Court Place (☎ **303/571-0921;** fax 303/671-1504).

There's also a currency exchange booth at **Denver International,** and you can call (☎ 800/CURRENCY) for locations of other Thomas Cook offices.

In **Boulder,** currency exchange services are available at **Bank One,** at the corner of North Broadway and Canyon Blvd. (☎ **303/442-6770**); and in **Colorado Springs,** go to **Bank One,** 30 E. Pikes Peak Blvd. (☎ **719/471-5000**).

Electricity   The United States uses 110 to 120 volts, 60 cycles, rather than 220 to 240 volts, 50 cycles, as in most of Europe. In addition to a 100-volt converter, small appliances of non-American manufacture, such as hairdryers or shavers, will require a plug adapter with two flat, parallel pins.

Embassies/Consulates   Foreign visitors can obtain telephone numbers for their embassies and consulates by calling "Information" in Washington, D.C. (☎ 202/555-1212). The following countries have consulates in Denver: **Australia,** 999 18th St. (☎ 303/297-1200), **France,** 1420 Ogden St. (☎ 303/831-8616), **Germany,** 350 Indiana St. (☎ 303/279-1551), and **Italy,** 8820 W. 84th Ave., Arvada (☎ 303/431-1683).

Emergencies   Call **911,** or if that doesn't work dial "0" (zero, *not* the letter "O") to report a fire, call police, or get an ambulance.

Fax   See entry under "Telephone and Fax," below.

Gasoline (Petrol)   One U.S. gallon equals 3.75 liters, while 1.2 U.S. gallons equals 1 Imperial gallon. You'll notice there are several grades (and price levels) of gasoline available at most gas stations and that their names change from company to company. Unleaded gasoline with the highest octane is the most expensive, but most rental cars will run fine with the least expensive "regular" unleaded.

Holidays   On the following legal U.S. national holidays, banks, government offices, post offices, and some government-run attractions are closed: January 1 (New Year's Day), third Monday in January (Martin Luther King, Jr. Day), third Monday in February (Presidents' Day), last Monday in May (Memorial Day), July 4 (Independence Day), first Monday in September (Labor Day), second Monday in October (Columbus Day), November 11 (Veterans' Day/Armistice Day), fourth Thursday in November (Thanksgiving Day), and December 25 (Christmas). The Tuesday following the first Monday in November is Election Day and is a legal holiday in presidential-election years.

Stores and some restaurants often close only for New Year's Day, Easter, and Christmas.

Language   Major hotels sometimes have multilingual employees, with Spanish and German being the most common foreign languages spoken in Colorado.

Legal Aid   The foreign tourist, unless positively identified as a member of organized crime or a drug ring, will probably never become involved with the American legal system. If you are stopped for a minor infraction, such as speeding or some other traffic violation, never attempt to pay the fine directly to a police officer; you may be arrested on the much more serious charge of attempted bribery. Pay fines by mail or directly to the clerk of the court. If you are accused of a more serious offense, it's wise to say and do nothing before consulting a lawyer. Under U.S. law, an arrested person is allowed one telephone call to a party of his or her choice. Call your embassy or consulate.

Mail   If you want your mail to follow you on your vacation and you aren't sure of your address, your mail can be sent to you, in your name, c/o General Delivery at the main post office of the city or region where you expect to be. The addressee must pick it up in person and produce proof of identity (driver's license, passport, and so on).

Newspapers/Magazines National newspapers generally available in Colorado include the *New York Times, USA Today,* and the *Wall Street Journal.* National news magazines include *Newsweek, Time,* and *U.S. News & World Report.* The state's major daily newspaper is the *Denver Post.* Some 70 foreign newspapers, mostly Sunday editions, are available at the **Tattered Cover Bookstore,** 2955 E. First Ave., opposite Cherry Creek Shopping Center in Denver (☎ **800/833-9327** or 303/322-7727). These include major newspapers from the United Kingdom, Canada, Australia, New Zealand, Ireland, Switzerland, Germany, Norway, Finland, Denmark, Sweden, France, Italy, Spain, Russia, Japan, China, Greece, Israel, Columbia, Brazil, Chile, Mexico, and North Africa.

Radio/Television In Colorado, television viewers usually have a choice of at least a dozen channels via cable or satellite, although some of the major Denver hotels offer only five or six. PBS and the cable channel A&E broadcast a number of British programs. You'll also find a wide choice of local radio stations, each broadcasting particular kinds of talk shows and/or music—classical, country, jazz, pop—punctuated by news broadcasts and frequent commercials.

Rest Rooms Foreign visitors often complain that public rest rooms are hard to find in most U.S. cities. True, there are few on the streets, but the visitor can usually find one in a bar, restaurant, hotel, museum, department or discount store, or service station—and it will probably be clean (although service station facilities often leave much to be desired). Note, however, a growing practice in some restaurants and bars of displaying a sign Rest Rooms Are for Patrons Only. You can ignore this sign or, better yet, avoid arguments by paying for a cup of coffee or soft drink, which will qualify you as a patron.

Taxes In the United States, there is no VAT (value-added tax) or other indirect tax at a national level. Every state, as well as each city, has the right to levy its own local tax on all purchases, including hotel and restaurant checks, airline tickets, and so on. Sales taxes in Colorado vary, but usually total between 6% and 9%. An exception is the tax on lodging, which often runs 9% to 13%.

Telephone and Fax The telephone system in the United States is run by private corporations, so rates, especially for long-distance service, can vary widely—even on calls made from public telephones. Local calls in the United States usually cost 25¢ from pay telephones, and some of the more expensive hotels charge 50¢ to 75¢.

Most long-distance and international calls can be dialed directly from any phone. For calls to Canada and other parts of the United States, dial 1 followed by the area code and the seven-digit number. For international calls, dial 011 followed by the country code, city code, and the telephone number of the person you wish to call.

Generally, hotel fees on charged-to-your-room long-distance calls are astronomical. You can save money by calling collect, charging to a credit card, or using a public pay telephone, which in cities you will find clearly marked in many public buildings and private establishments, as well as on the street. Outside metropolitan areas, public telephones are more difficult to find; stores and gas stations are your best bet.

For **reversed-charge** or **collect calls,** and for person-to-person calls, dial "0" (zero, not the letter "O") followed by the area code and number you want; an operator will then come on the line, and you should specify that you are calling collect, or person-to-person, or both. If your operator-assisted call is international, ask for the overseas operator.

For **local directory assistance** ("information"), dial 411; for **long-distance information,** dial 1, then the appropriate area code and 555-1212.

Fax facilities are readily available in hotels, and 24-hour service is available at numerous copy centers, such as **Kinko's,** in larger cities.

Time   The United States is divided into four **time zones** (six, if Alaska and Hawaii are included). From east to west, these are: eastern standard time (EST), central standard time (CST), mountain standard time (MST), Pacific standard time (PST), Alaska standard time (AST), and Hawaii standard time (HST). Always keep time zones in mind if you are traveling (or even telephoning) long distances in the United States. For example, noon in New York City (EST) is 11am in Chicago (CST), 10am in Denver (MST), 9am in Los Angeles (PST), 8am in Anchorage (AST), and 7am in Honolulu (HST). Colorado is in the mountain time zone.

Daylight saving time (DST) is in effect in Colorado and most of the country, from the first Sunday in April through the last Saturday in October (actually, the change is made at 2am on Sunday). Daylight saving time moves the clock 1 hour ahead of standard time. Note that Arizona, Hawaii, part of Indiana, and Puerto Rico do not observe DST.

Tipping   This is part of the American way of life, based on the idea that you should expect to pay for any special service you receive (service personnel are usually paid low wages and therefore depend on tips for most of their income). Here are some rules of thumb:

In **hotels,** tip bellhops 50¢ to $1 per bag. Some people (but not all) believe a tip of $1 per night is appropriate for hotel maid service if you are staying more than a night or two. Tip the doorman or concierge only if he or she has performed some specific service for you (for example, calling a cab or obtaining difficult-to-get theater tickets).

In **restaurants, bars, and nightclubs,** tip service staff 15% to 20% of the check, tip bartenders 10% to 15%, tip checkroom attendants $1 per garment, and tip valet-parking attendants $1 per vehicle. Tip the doorman only if he has served you in some special way (such as calling a cab). Tipping is not expected in cafeterias and fast-food restaurants.

As for other service personnel, tip **redcaps** at airports or railroad stations at least 50¢ per bag, and tip **cab drivers** 15% of the fare. Hairdressers and barbers usually receive a 15% to 20% tip. Tipping gas-station attendants, and ushers in cinemas and theaters is not expected.

The Active Vacation Planner

The variety and sheer number of active sports and recreational activities Colorado offers is staggering. It's a place where you can easily arrange a week-long hard-core mountaineering expedition, but it's also a place where, just as easily, you can take one of the most scenic 2-hour bike rides of your life—right in downtown Boulder. Not to mention the superb winter activities—from dogsledding and downhill skiing to snowmobiling—that are open to travelers who visit during the colder months. This chapter outlines your choices, and offers a few tips for planning everything from an outfitted, multisport vacation to an afternoon's outing.

1 What You Need to Know Before You Go

Once you've picked the sport or activities you want to pursue, ask yourself a few questions: How physically fit am I really? How much skill in this particular activity do I have? How dangerous is this activity? How much money am I willing to spend? Answering these questions honestly can make the difference between a successful vacation with happy memories to last a lifetime and an unmitigated disaster you wish you could forget. There are some activities that require an outfitter, such as cattle drives, and others, such as cycling or mountain biking, camping, or hiking, that you can easily do on your own, provided you have some experience and are willing to travel with the necessary equipment or rent it after you arrive. Obviously, if you're attempting a dangerous sport in which you're inexperienced, such as rock climbing, it's best to go with someone who literally knows the ropes.

If money is an issue for you, prearranged escorted tour packages that include your lodging, equipment, and most of your meals can save you money and minimize the amount of planning you have to do. On the other hand, you'll be with a group, with limited freedom and flexibility to strike out on your own. Some people enjoy the convenience of having everything set up for them and the company of their fellow tour members; others can't stand it. It all depends on your temperament and personality.

Most outfitters and tour operators keep the size of their groups small and offer trips of different lengths for those of varying levels of ability. The best outfitters run well-organized trips in which

Active Colorado Online

If you have Web access, you may want to check out the Colorado section of **GORP** (the Great Outdoor Recreation Page), an online site that provides detailed information about hiking trails, fishing accesses, water sports, and other activities in Colorado's national and state parks, with links to related sites. You'll find it at **http://www.gorp.com/gorp/location/co/co.htm.**

Those interested in planning a midwinter ski break may find *Ski Magazine*'s website a useful tool. In addition to posting its annual reader resort survey in which North America's top ski resorts are rated by the magazine's readers on such factors as conditions, terrain, challenge, accessibility, food, and the après-ski scene, it offers a resort finder service that helps you select the ski area or resort that best fits your interests and budget. You'll find *Ski Magazine* at **http://www.skinet.com/ski/reports.**

every detail has been worked out in advance and is communicated to you. Operators should be responsive to your needs and willing to answer any and all questions you have, promptly and fully. They should have well-maintained equipment and be fully insured. If you have any doubts, ask for the name and phone number of a satisfied former customer, and call that person up and ask them about their experience. Something that's a decided asset in an outfitter, but isn't exactly common, is naturalist training. If you're rafting the Arkansas River, it's nice to be able to ask your guide questions about the ecology of the landscape through which you're paddling and get a coherent, knowledgeable response.

In most cases, the sections on individual activities that follow include at least one recommended outfitter through which you can arrange a packaged trip. Be sure to check the chapters that follow for more recommendations, particularly on local and regional operators. For activities that are easy to do on your own, we offer our picks for the best places to practice the activity, useful sources for information, and other facts to help you plan the perfect do-it-yourself active vacation.

There are several government agencies and other organizations that provide maps and information that can be extremely useful for a variety of activities. These include: **Colorado State Parks** (state park, boating, R.V., and snowmobile regulations), 1313 Sherman St., no. 618, Denver, CO 80203 (☎ **303/866-3437**); the **Colorado Outfitters Association** (for a list of licensed guides and outfitters in the state), P.O. Box 440021, Aurora, CO 80044-0021 (☎ **303/368-4731**); the **U.S. Bureau of Land Management** (for maps and information on activities on the vast amount of BLM land in the state), 2850 Youngfield St., Lakewood, CO 80215 (☎ **303/239-3600**); the **U.S. Forest Service** (for maps and information about hiking trails and campgrounds in national forests), Rocky Mountain Region, P.O. Box 25127, Lakewood, CO 80225 (☎ **303/236-9431**); the **U.S. Geological Survey** (for topographical maps), P.O. Box 25046, Federal Center, Mail Stop 504, Denver, CO 80225-0046 (☎ **303/236-5829**); and the **U.S. National Park Service** (for information on national parks, monuments, and recreation areas), P.O. Box 25287, Denver, CO 80225 (☎ **303/969-2000**).

Those looking to buy or rent equipment will find shops practically everywhere in the state, but particularly in resort towns. Check the regional chapters for our local recommendations. A convenient, statewide resource is **Gart Brothers,** the state's largest sporting-goods chain. It has numerous outlets in the Denver area, as well as in

Colorado Springs, Fort Collins, Vail, Grand Junction, and Glenwood Springs. For the location of the store nearest you, contact the **Gart Brothers Sports Castle,** a huge sales, repair, and rental facility, at 1000 Broadway in Denver (☎ **303/861-1122**).

2 Sports from A to Z

BALLOONING

You can take a hot-air balloon ride virtually anywhere in the state, but the most awe-inspiring scenery is in Vail, Montrose, and Ouray, where you get spectacular bird's-eye views of the surrounding mountains from aloft.

Generally, it's best to book a ballooning trip a few days in advance, although at particularly busy times, such as holiday weekends, make your reservations as early as possible. Hot-air ballooning is expensive, and it's one sport where you really don't want to cut corners. Although safer than some activities you might pursue, you'll literally be putting your life in the hands of a balloon pilot, and you want the best-trained operator and best-equipped balloon available. Choose an experienced and well-established balloon company, and if you have any qualms, ask about their safety record. As with most Colorado activities, you'll pay the highest rates at fancy resorts such as Vail. Prices in Crested Butte are usually quite reasonable, and the fields of wildflowers can be beautiful from the air. Prices are also good in Colorado Springs and Boulder, but are somewhat higher in Denver.

BICYCLING

Bicycling is popular throughout Colorado, but especially in Denver and what must be the state's road bike capital, Boulder, which has more bikes than people. Even in decidedly less sporty Fort Collins, bikes are ubiquitous enough that public buses have bike racks. Most larger cities are bike-friendly, with established bike paths that are sometimes completely off the highway and other times along roadways, but are usually wide and paved. Of course, bicyclists will occasionally find themselves surrounded by cars, or blocked by parked cars where they expected to find a bike path. Without a doubt, our favorite city bike path is the Boulder Creek Path, which meanders through 7 miles of Boulder parklands, with no cross streets or motor vehicle intrusion of any kind.

If an organized bike tour with nightly accommodations in charming inns sounds like your idea of the perfect week-long vacation, **Backroads,** 1516 5th St., Berkeley, CA 94710-1740 (☎ **800/GO-ACTIV**), is a great outfitter to know about. Among other annual cycling trips in the West, they offer a tour of the San Juan Mountains.

But as it's relatively easy to plan your own cycling vacation, we tend to recommend doing just that. To start your trip-planning, pick up the annual magazine *Bicycle Colorado* (for a free copy, call **800/997-2453**). It details the best spots for cycling in the state, and provides other useful tips.

BOATING

Those who take their powerboats along on their visit to Colorado will find lakes scattered across the state. Most have boat ramps, and some also have fuel and supplies. Boaters tend to gravitate to Bonny Lake near Burlington (known for water-skiing), Pueblo Reservoir, and Trinidad Lake State Park. Some of the larger lakes offer boat rentals—usually aluminum fishing boats, personal watercrafts, and large pontoon party boats. Navajo State Park in the Durango area gives access to a 35-mile-long reservoir straddling the New Mexico border, with a variety of boats available for rent, including fully equipped houseboats.

Colorado's Best Recreational Areas

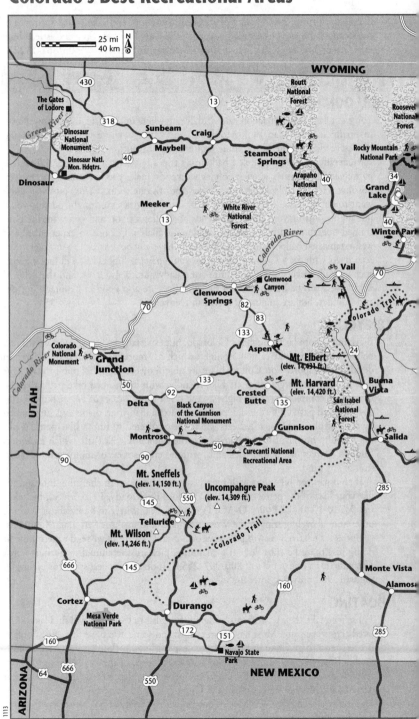

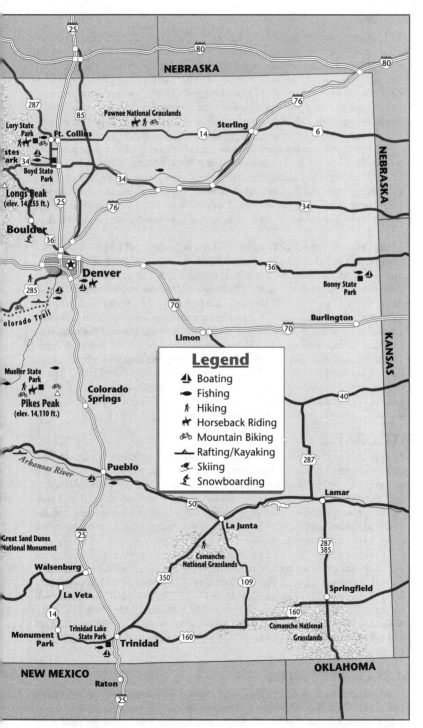

NEBRASKA

Pawnee National Grasslands

Lory State Park

Ft. Collins

Sterling

stes ark 34

Boyd State Park

Longs Peak
(elev. 14,255 ft.)

Boulder

Denver

Bonny State Park

Burlington

KANSAS

Limon

Legend

⛵ Boating
🐟 Fishing
🚶 Hiking
🏇 Horseback Riding
🚵 Mountain Biking
🛶 Rafting/Kayaking
🎿 Skiing
🏂 Snowboarding

Mueller State Park

Pikes Peak
(elev. 14,110 ft.)

Colorado Springs

Colorado Trail

Arkansas River

Pueblo

Lamar

Great Sand Dunes National Monument

La Junta

Comanche National Grasslands

Walsenburg

La Veta

Monument Park

Springfield

Trinidad Lake State Park

Trinidad

Comanche National Grasslands

OKLAHOMA

NEW MEXICO

Raton

CAMPING

With so many acres of public land, Colorado offers practically unlimited opportunities for R.V. or tent camping, especially in the mountains. In fact, it's one of the best and most economical ways to see the state during the summer months. More than 400 public campgrounds are maintained in the national forests alone, and camping is also allowed in Bureau of Land Management areas, national parks, national monuments, and state parks. In addition, most communities have commercially operated campgrounds with recreational vehicle hook-ups. If you plan to drive an R.V. into the state, one word of advice—get the mechanical system checked out thoroughly before you depart—there are some extremely steep grades in themountains.

One of the best places to camp in the state is Rocky Mountain National Park, but it is crowded, especially in summer. Visit in late September or early October, if possible. Backpackers will find numerous camping opportunities along the Colorado Trail—we especially like the area near Leadville—and in the Colorado State Forest west of Fort Collins. Mueller State Park, west of Colorado Springs, is tops for R.V. camping.

The **Colorado Agency of Camping, Cabins, & Lodges,** 5101 Pennsylvania Ave., Boulder, CO 80303-2799 (☎ **303/499-9343;** fax 303/499-9333) publishes a free annual booklet that describes commercial campgrounds, cabin facilities, and resorts throughout the state. A free copy of *Colorado State Parks,* which contains details on the state's 41 parks, is available from state park offices. A nationwide directory of Kampgrounds of America (KOA) franchise campgrounds (there are 30 in Colorado) is available free at any KOA, or by mail for $3 from **Kampgrounds of America, Inc.,** Executive Offices, Billings, MT 59114-0558; and members of the American Automobile Association can request the club's free *Southwestern CampBook,* which includes campgrounds and R.V. parks in Utah, Arizona, Colorado, and New Mexico. Several massive campground directories can be purchased in major bookstores, including our favorite, *Trailer Life Campground, R.V. Park & Services Directory,* published annually by TL Enterprises, Inc., P.O. Box 6060, Camarillo, CA 93011.

CATTLE DRIVES

As elsewhere in the West, opportunities abound for city slickers to play cowboy, riding and roping cattle on actual drives that last from a day to a week or more. You'll certainly get a feel for what it was like to be on a cattle drive 100 years ago, but the food will be a lot better, and the conditions a lot more comfortable. Each cattle drive is different, so you'll want to ask very specific questions about food, sleeping arrangements, and other conditions before plunking down your money. It's also a good idea to book your trip as early as possible.

The best places for joining a cattle drive are Steamboat Springs and Aspen, with their beautiful mountain scenery and fun towns—they're just perfect for relaxing at the end of the trail. Contact **Broken Skull Cattle Company,** 47080 Routt County Rd. 129, Steamboat Springs, CO 80487-9417 (☎ **970/879-0090**); or **Blazing Adventures,** P.O. Box 2127, Aspen, CO 81612 (☎ **800/282-7238** or 970/925-5651). **American Wilderness Experience,** P.O. Box 1486, Boulder, CO 80306 (☎ **800/ 444-0099** or 303/444-2622; fax 303/444-3999), can also arrange a cattle-drive vacation in Colorado.

CROSS-COUNTRY SKIING

Practically every major ski area also offers cross-country skiing—often on a nearby golf course. In addition, there are thousands of miles of trails throughout Colorado's national forests—often old mining and logging roads—that are perfect for cross-country skiing, and they're free. Among the state's top cross-country skiing destinations are Breckenridge, with a series of trails that wind through open meadows and a spruce forest; the beautiful San Juan Mountains in the Durango and Telluride areas; and Snow Mountain Ranch Nordic Center near Winter Park, with more than 100 kilometers (62 miles) of groomed trails, lighted trails for night skiing, and access to backcountry trail systems. Backcountry ski trips are offered by **Aspen Alpine Guides, Inc.,** P.O. Box 659, Aspen, CO 81612 (☎ **800/643-8621** or 970/ 925-6618); **Paragon Guides,** P.O. Box 130, Vail, CO 81658 (☎ **970/926-5299**); and **San Juan Hut Systems,** P.O. Box 1663, Telluride, CO 81435 (☎ **970/ 728-6935**).

A free directory of nordic centers, hut systems, guides, and guest ranches that cater to cross-country skiers is available from the **Colorado Cross Country Ski Association,** Box 1292, Kremmling, CO 80459 (☎ **800/869-4560**). Also contact the **U.S. Forest Service** (see above for address).

DOGSLEDDING

If your fantasy is to be a Canadian Mountie mushing across the frozen Yukon, save the airfare and head to the mountains of Colorado instead. Dogsled rides are offered at several ski resorts, but we like Steamboat Springs best, where dog-power takes you far from the crowds into the rugged backcountry. Some rides end with a fancy dinner. Spectators will want to go to Cortez in January for the annual dogsled races. Incidentally, those movies you've seen are wrong; the dogs almost never bark while running, just before and after.

FISHING

Many cold-water species of fish live in the state's mountains, lakes, and streams, including seven kinds of trout (native cutthroat, rainbow, brown, brook, lake, kokanee, and whitefish), walleye, yellow perch, northern pike, tiger muskie, and bluegill. Warm-water sport fish (especially in eastern Colorado and in large rivers) include catfish, crappie, and bass—largemouth, smallmouth, white, and wiper.

The most accessible lake fishing is at Bonny Lake (near Burlington), Boyd (near Loveland), and Vallecito (near Durango). There's also excellent fishing in the picturesque high-mountain lakes of the Colorado State Forest, west of Fort Collins. Our favorite places for stream fishing are the Big Thompson River near Fort Collins and the numerous streams and rivers in the national forests surrounding Steamboat Springs and Estes Park.

The fishing season is year-round, except in certain specified waters. A 1-year license costs $40.25 for an adult nonresident (15 and over), $20.25 for a resident; 5-day licenses are $18.25, 1-day licenses, $5.25 for nonresidents and residents alike. Children under 15 are restricted to half the daily bag limit without a license.

The **Colorado Division of Wildlife,** 6060 Broadway, Denver, CO 80216 (☎ **303/297-1192** or 303/291-7529) offers anglers several handy recorded messages. For general information on fishing, call 303/291-7533; for a list of fishing regulations, call 303/291-7299; for up-to-date fishing reports during the season (Apr–Sept), call 303/291-7534. Another good source for fishing information is **Colorado Trout Unlimited,** 7200 E. Dry Creek Rd., Suite G 201, Englewood, CO 80112 (☎ **303/ 270-7766**). Call or write for a copy of the organization's guide to fishing the upper Arkansas River ($3.95 including postage), or for contacts at the 27 Trout Unlimited chapters throughout the state for tips on the best fishing in their areas.

To arrange a guided hunting or fishing trip in the state, contact the **Colorado Outfitters Association,** P.O. Box 1304, Parker, CO 80134 (☎ **303/841-7760**) for recommended guides in the area you plan to visit.

4 X 4 = Four-Season Four-Wheeling

For years, experienced skiers have known that four-wheel–drive vehicles make getting to and from the slopes much easier in the dead of winter. Now that luxury Jeeps and 4X4s have virtually eclipsed cars in popularity, more and more travelers are choosing to see Colorado by four-wheel–drive vehicle during the spring and summer months as well.

If you own a Jeep or 4X4 and plan to drive it into the state, consider contacting the **Colorado Association of Four-Wheel–Drive Clubs** before you leave home at P.O. Box 1413, Wheat Ridge, CO 80034 (☎ **303/343-0646**). The association sells map-books of four-wheel–drive roads throughout Colorado and can direct you to local off-road clubs that welcome visitors on their trips.

Southwestern Colorado is an excellent place for off-roading—the San Juan Mountains offer scores of old mining trails that are just right for this kind of backcountry exploring. Ouray boasts three outfitters that lead Jeep tours into the high country: **Switzerland of America,** 226 Seventh Ave. (☎ **800/432-5337** or 970/325-4484), **San Juan Scenic Jeep Tours,** 480 Main St. (☎ **970/325-4444**), and **Colorado West Jeep Tours,** 630 Main St. (☎ **800/648-5337** or 970/325-4014).

Independent travelers can also rent their own four-wheeler upon arrival in the state from most major car rental companies. **Hertz** (☎ **800/654-3131**) rents Ford Explorers, Toyota 4 Runners, and Nissan Pathfinders out of their downtown Denver and Colorado Springs offices and can arrange rentals from other Colorado cities with 3 days advance notice; **Avis** (☎ **800/831-2847**) rents Jeep Cherokees and Nissan Pathfinders at their airport locations in Denver and Colorado Springs; and **Budget** (☎ **800/527-0700**) rents Ford Explorers and Isuzu Troopers at their Denver and Colorado Springs airport locations as well.

An environmental note: Anyone planning to explore the backroads on their own should first write to the **USDA Forest Service,** 324 25th St., Ogden, UT 84401, for a brochure entitled *Tread Lightly* that explains off-road driving procedures, with an emphasis on causing only minimal impact.

GOLF

Clear blue skies and beautiful scenery are hallmarks of Colorado golf courses, but don't think they're merely pretty faces—these courses can be as challenging as any in the country. Balls travel farther here than at sea level, and golfers tend to tire more quickly, at least until they've adapted to the higher elevation. The season is also considerably shorter, and the weather iffy. Be prepared for cool mornings and afternoon thunderstorms even at the height of summer. Courses at lower elevations, such as along the western slope, in the southwest corner, and around Denver, are often open year-round, however.

With a few notable exceptions—the Broadmoor in Colorado Springs, for instance—Colorado golf courses are not attached to exclusive resorts such as you'll find in Arizona and California. This makes all-inclusive packages and super-luxurious pampering hard to find, but you won't have to pay for it, either.

Particularly good golf resorts can be found in Crested Butte, Winter Park, Pueblo, and Alamosa. For high-altitude putting, try Leadville. For a directory of the state's major golf courses, contact the **Colorado Golf Resort Association,** 2110 S. Ash St., Denver, CO 80222 (☎ **303/699-4653**). Information is also available from the **Colorado Golf Association,** 5655 S. Yosemite St., Suite 101, Englewood, CO

80111 (☎ 303/779-4653). **The American Lung Association of Colorado,** 1600 Race St., Denver, CO 80206 (☎ 303/388-4327), offers a golf discount card with free or reduced greens fees at more than 700 courses in the western United States and British Columbia, including several dozen in Colorado. The cost is $25 per person.

HIKING, BACKPACKING & MOUNTAINEERING

Colorado is literally crisscrossed with hiking trails, and dotted with mountains begging to be climbed. The best opportunities, particularly for scenic beauty, are probably in Rocky Mountain National Park, but park hiking trails are among the most crowded in the state, especially in July and August. It is possible to get away from the crowds by taking longer hikes on lesser-used trails (ask rangers for suggestions), or by joining a climbing expedition. The highly respected **Colorado Mountain School,** based in nearby Estes Park, leads climbs up Longs Peak in the national park, and can also provide advice on mountaineering in other parts of the state.

The 500-mile Colorado Trail, which winds from Denver to Durango, crosses seven national forests and six designated wilderness areas. Scenery and terrain are varied, from grassy plains to snowcapped mountains. Although the entire trail can be hiked by those in excellent physical condition in 6 to 8 weeks, most hikers prefer excursions of a week or less, and many enjoy day hikes. Most of the trail is above 10,000 feet elevation (the highest point is at 13,334 ft.), and hikes of more than a day or two will inevitably include some steep climbs. However, most of the trail has grades of no more than 10%. You'll find the easiest sections of the trail in the first 90 miles from Denver, but other sections such as one 20-mile stretch near Salida, are also easy to moderate. In the Breckenridge and Winter Park areas, the trail is fairly rugged, and most sections below U.S. 50 are mountainous and at least somewhat strenuous.

The Colorado Trail's most crowded sections are near major population centers. There is much less trail use south of U.S. 50, where the trail winds through the San Juan Mountains. It's serenely peaceful here, but there are also fewer services, and if you're injured it could be a long wait for help. If you're really looking for serenity, consider climbing one of the fourteeners—peaks over 14,000 feet elevation—just off the Colorado Trail. Among the easiest is the climb to the summit of 14,420-foot Mount Harvard, the state's third highest peak. The trail branches off the Colorado Trail about 8 miles north of Buena Vista.

Those planning multiday hikes on the Colorado Trail should carry maps or the excellent official guidebook ($19.95 postpaid, address below), which includes maps and details of the entire trail—elevation changes, trail conditions, vehicle access points, closest services, and general descriptions. Contact the **Colorado Trail Foundation,** P.O. Box 260876, Lakewood, CO 80226 (☎ 303/526-0809) to purchase the book or obtain a free brochure with a general trail map and information on hiking the trail.

Although the Colorado Trail may be the state's most famous hike, there are plenty of other opportunities. We particularly like the hike to Long Lake in the Routt National Forest outside Steamboat Springs, a moderately difficult 12-mile round-trip hike that leads through a forest, past several waterfalls, to a peaceful, pristine alpine lake. Although hikers in the Denver area often head out on the Colorado Trail, another pleasant hike is the easy 9-mile walk around Barr Lake, 18 miles northeast of the city, which offers excellent viewing of wildlife and birds. For the best city hike, try the Boulder Creek Path, a 10-mile trail that leads from downtown Boulder into the nearby mountains, offering wildlife and bird watching and good views of the mountains and city. Those in Colorado Springs can hike among the beautiful red sandstone formations in Garden of the Gods; or head west about 30 miles to Mueller

State Park, with its 90 miles of trails through mountain scenery much like you'll find at Rocky Mountain National Park.

Even though you don't need to work with an outfitter to go on a hike, **American Wilderness Experience** (☎ **800/444-0099** or 303/444-2622; fax 303/444-3999) and **Backroads** (☎ **800/GO-ACTIV**) both offer guided hiking trips. For a backcountry trek, **Roads Less Traveled** (☎ **303/678-8750**) is a good bet, and if you're a bit more ambitiously minded, **Southwest Adventures** (☎ **800/642-5389**) runs guided mountaineering trips.

HORSEBACK RIDING

It's fun to see the Old West the way the pioneers of 100 years ago did—from a horse's saddle. There are plenty of stables and outfitters that lead rides lasting from 1 hour to several days, but we particularly recommend those near Estes Park, Steamboat Springs, Grand Junction, and Telluride. If you'd like to spend your entire vacation on horseback, the **Sylvan Dale Guest Ranch** just outside of Loveland is highly regarded (see chapter 10 for details). If you're staying in one of the Front Range cities and just want to go for an afternoon ride, the good news is that all three cities— Denver, Boulder, and Colorado Springs—have stables; but the best in-city ride has to be in Colorado Springs, where you can explore the Garden of the Gods on horseback.

MOUNTAIN BIKING

The town of Crested Butte claims to be the mountain biking capital of Colorado, but Telluride and Vail are also popular spots for fat-tire explorations. Those planning to go mountain biking in western Colorado can receive a free trail map by sending a stamped, self-addressed envelope to **Colorado Plateau Mountain Bike Trail Association,** P.O. Box 4602, Grand Junction, CO 81502.

The Colorado Trail, which runs some 500 miles from Denver to Durango, is also open to mountain bikers. Riding all the way across it is easily the state's top mountain bike adventure: It'll take at least 4 weeks, but you'll be traveling through Colorado's most scenic and rugged country—deep forests and high plains. You'll whiz alongside rushing rivers, surrounded by some of America's highest and most spectacular peaks. You'll also share the trail with hikers and horseback riders, and those with bikes must take detours around designated wilderness areas. Mountain bikers looking for a shorter trip can join or leave the trail at almost any point.

One easily accessible stretch runs 24 miles from Copper Mountain Ski Resort to Tennessee Pass, crossing 12,280-foot Elk Ridge and descending into the ghost town of Camp Hale. For information, contact the **Colorado Trail Foundation,** P.O. Box 260876, Lakewood, CO 80226 (☎ **303/526-0809**). You'll receive a brochure and general map of the trail, plus information on how to order detailed topographical maps, several books on the trail, T-shirts and other souvenirs. Also see "Hiking, Backpacking & Mountaineering," below.

In addition to the Colorado Trail, there are numerous trails on state land, in national forests, and in areas administered by the Bureau of Land Management. Our favorites are the many trails around Crested Butte and Winter Park, and the Colorado State Forest, located about 75 miles west of Fort Collins. These areas offer a variety of terrain, with trails for all levels of skill and physical condition.

Backcountry Bicycle Tours, P.O. Box 4029, Bozeman, MT 59772 (☎ **406/ 586-3556**) offers excellent multiday guided mountain-biking excursions, but **Roads Less Traveled** (☎ **303/678-8750**) is also a player.

ROCK CLIMBING

Although rock climbing is not as big here as in other parts of the West, such as Zion National Park in Utah, Colorado does attract its share of climbers. One of the best spots is the spectacular Glenwood Canyon in Glenwood Springs, but it is far too popular with rafters and sightseers to offer anything near a wilderness experience.

Somewhat more secluded and just as pretty is the Black Canyon of the Gunnison near Montrose, an extremely narrow canyon that sees very little daylight; and there are several good spots near Crested Butte. One area that is popular among rock climbers but practically unknown by the general population is Penitente Canyon, near the tiny community of La Garita, north of Alamosa. Although less magnificent than either Glenwood Canyon or Black Canyon of the Gunnison, it offers a challenge for climbers, good views of surrounding rock formations, and an abundance of peace and quiet. **Adventures to the Edge, Ltd.** (☎ **800/349-5219** or 970/349-5219), based in Crested Butte, offers instruction and guided trips for rock climbing in summer and ice climbing in winter.

ROCKHOUNDING & GOLD PANNING

The state's mining heritage continues in many areas among rock hounders, who search for semiprecious gemstones, petrified woods, and agatized fossil bones. Gold is found in most major mining areas, and gold panning is a popular pastime. The Salida area has some of the best rockhounding opportunities in the state. Those who want to try their hands at gold panning will enjoy Idaho Springs (near Denver) and Breckenridge, where they can receive instructions and rent pans.

A number of publications, including several free brochures, are available from **Colorado Geological Survey,** 1313 Sherman St., no. 715, Denver, CO 80203 (☎ **303/866-2611,** or 303/866-3340 for the publications office). You can get information on rock collecting, geology, fossils, and a list of rockhounding locations, as well as detailed guides and maps to rockhounding and gold-panning locations.

SKIING & SNOWBOARDING

The most popular winter sport in Colorado is, of course, downhill skiing. Since the state's first resort (Howelsen Hill in Steamboat Springs) opened in 1914, the word Colorado has been virtually synonymous with skiing in the western United States. Although the mountains are bigger and the slopes can be intimidating, there's rarely any ice. If you've got enough strength to turn on the several inches on fluffy dry powder, you may find it camouflages weaknesses in your technique better than the ice-encrusted stuff that passes for snow back East. But what truly sets Colorado skiing apart are the ski towns. It's hard to beat the vibrant atmosphere of these villages, each of which has its own distinct personality. With 30-plus ski areas, the state attracts more skiers per day than any other state, and its major resorts continue to win accolades from ski-magazine editors and readers.

The snowboarding craze has hit Colorado just as hard as it has other winter sports destinations, and after some initial resistance, it's been welcomed with open arms. Many resorts are starting to develop snowboarding parks as well as offering lessons and rentals. The only major ski area that does not permit snowboarders is Keystone, but nearby Arapahoe Basin, owned by the same company, has plenty of terrain set aside for boarders.

For **current ski conditions,** call **Colorado Ski Country USA** (☎ **303/ 837-0793**), 1560 Broadway, Suite 1440, Denver, CO 80202. The slopes are most crowded over Christmas and New Year's, as well as on the Martin Luther King, Jr.

and Presidents Day holiday weekends, when lodging rates are at their highest, some-times outrageously so. Those who can ski midweek will find more elbow room on the slopes, and the best time to ski to avoid crowds—assuming snow conditions are good—are at the beginning and end of the season.

Each of the state's ski areas has a variety of special events. Serious skiers are at-tracted by clinics and races, while party animals watch for the festivals and winter carnivals. Most resorts have at least one or two women's ski weeks, often in early December; there are almost always torchlight parades and other activities at Christ-mas and New Year's; and many have winter carnivals in early January or early Feb-ruary. Other notable events include Aspen's Gay Ski Week in late January, Girl Scout Cookie Days in late February at Silver Creek, God Bless Texas Week at Purgatory in early Match, National Disabled Veteran's Winter Sports Clinic at Crested Butte in late February, the Taste of Vail Food and Wine Event in early April, and the ever-popular Teenie Weenie Bikini Contest at Copper Mountain in mid-April.

Because not every ski area in Colorado is worth traveling to the state to ski, we've purposely chosen to cover only the 18 best areas in this guidebook. They can be divided into two categories: predominately day-use ski areas, with very little beyond a mountain with trails and a few lifts, such as Arapahoe Basin and Loveland, and actual ski villages or resorts, with accommodations in different price ranges, restau-rants, and nightlife all within a half-hour of the slopes. Of the latter category, we profile the behemoths against which all other resorts in Colorado are judged, Aspen and Vail, but also covered are the lesser constellations where the skiing is fabulous *and* there's a real community beyond the base lodge, such as Breckenridge, Crested Butte, Steamboat, and Telluride. The overview that follows describes the key moun-tains at these ski areas and resorts. Use it to choose the place that's right for you.

Arapahoe Basin (Summit County)   Arapahoe Basin, called "A-Basin" by its loyal fans, is the highest ski area in the state, and one of the oldest. Because of its high elevation, it gets a bit more snow than elsewhere, so some prefer to ski it during spring's warmer temperatures. Essentially one huge wide-open bowl, Arapahoe feels much larger than it actually is. It tends to attract better skiers and in-the-know lo-cals. See chapter 11.

Arrowhead (Vail)   A relatively new, very small family-oriented ski area of mostly beginner and intermediate terrain close to Beaver Creek. Owned and managed by Vail Associates. See chapter 11.

Aspen & Aspen Mountain (Aspen)   The village is here. With more than 100 restaurants and bars—from the most posh to the most down-to-earth—this is the heart of Colorado's most sophisticated resort. Aspen Mountain, formerly called Ajax, is the second most challenging of Aspen's four slopes (Aspen Highlands is the hard-est). Designed for advanced skiers, it has an abundance of expert-only trails. There is no easy terrain here. See chapter 11.

Aspen Highlands (Aspen)   An intense mountain for only the most skilled and athletic of skiers. If you're hot, this is the place to show off. The views from the top are spectacular. It's a quick shuttle ride from Aspen Village. See chapter 11.

Beaver Creek (Vail)   Once considered Vail's sister resort, Beaver Creek has come into its own. It's now considered to be the most refined—and possibly the most expensive—place to ski in Colorado. The scene is incredibly chic and much less flashy than the rest of Vail. The mountain has a good mix of runs for everyone but the super-expert, and lift lines are usually shorter than at Vail Mountain, especially on weekends. See chapter 11.

Breckenridge (Summit County)   Colorado's second most popular resort, Breckenridge is the crown jewel of Summit County's four ski areas. The only one that can properly be called a resort, its greatest charm is the genuine ski town in which it's located. Breckenridge has something to offer all levels of skiers and is especially kind to first-timers. It makes a great base camp for those who want to ski a different Summit County mountain every day. See chapter 11.

Buttermilk (Aspen)   The last of Aspen's four mountains, Buttermilk is a great place for affluent novices to practice their moves. There's a great ski school, and it's usually uncrowded. Located just outside the main village. See chapter 11.

Copper Mountain (Summit County)   With its five superb bowls and good variety of trails for all levels of ability, Copper is a great mountain for skiing, but its village, while less expensive than nearby Breckenridge, lacks amenities and charm. It's close enough to Breckenridge to make a good day-trip. See chapter 11.

Crested Butte (The Southern Rockies)   Dependable snow, good beginner and intermediate trails, and lots of extreme skiing, but very little expert terrain mark this increasingly talked-about resort. Earthy and somewhat funky, with a decidedly Old West feel (dogs in the back of pickup trucks), this is a great place for a winter vacation. See chapter 14.

Keystone (Summit County)   Of the four ski areas in Summit County, Keystone is the closest to Denver, about 90 miles west of the airport. Its three separate mountains, excellent snowmaking capability, and efficient lifts make it a good place for cruising, and its night skiing draws locals from miles around. The base village is small but well appointed. See chapter 11.

Loveland (North of Denver)   Less than an hour from Denver by car (it's just outside Summit County), Loveland is an old-fashioned day-ski area with mostly intermediate terrain. There's no village, just enough beginner and advanced trails to satisfy the average skier. If you're staying in Denver in winter, give it a whirl. See chapter 11.

Purgatory (Southwestern Colorado)   This small, low-key ski area is generally well liked. Its only drawback is its distance from Durango, the nearest town with amenities—a half-hour by car. Mostly intermediate, narrow, hilly trails meander through the trees amid the breathtakingly beautiful San Juan Mountains. Frequented by day skiers from Arizona. See chapter 13.

Silver Creek (Winter Park)   Geared to beginners and intermediates (but with some black diamond trails), Silver Creek is good for families, since it's nearly impossible to lose someone—all trails end at the same base area. There's also an excellent nursery and child-care center, several special full- or half-day ski programs for kids, and a children's ski park. See chapter 11.

Snowmass (Aspen)   The highlight of Aspen. With plenty of wide-open spaces and trails for absolutely every level of ability, Snowmass is perfect for well-heeled families. This is, by far, the largest mountain at Aspen. With its 5 high-speed detachable quad lifts, lines are blissfully short and quick. The base village has lots of beds, but not much nightlife. Most skiers head to Aspen village, 20 minutes down the road by free shuttle bus, once the day is over. See chapter 11.

Steamboat (North of Denver)   One of Colorado's three largest mountains (the other two are Vail and Snowmass), Steamboat offers near-perfect skiing. It's well laid out, and has gorgeous valley views. There's a small base village, but most skiers head for the authentic old ranching town of Steamboat Springs just a few miles away. It's not an Aspen or a Vail, but that suits its devotees just fine. See chapter 11.

Telluride (Southwestern Colorado)   Beautifully situated in an alpine valley, Telluride has changed dramatically over the past 25 years. If anything, the skiing—mostly advanced—has improved, but the scrappy old mining town at the mountain's base is now a polished, nationally known resort with its share of celebrity residents and chi-chi boutiques. The transition was accomplished with a fair degree of grace, to the point that Telluride may be the most romantic resort in the state. It's also popular among heliskiers. See chapter 13.

Vail (The Vail Valley)   Of Colorado's flashiest resorts, Aspen and Vail, Vail is the younger and brasher of the two. Its skiing is more diverse, and is spread out over a larger area. The ski school is top-notch and there are trails for everyone here. The completely self-contained alpine village at its base is flawlessly planned, and serviced by free shuttle buses. Needless to say, a ski vacation here doesn't come cheap. See chapter 11.

Winter Park (North of Denver)   Owned by the city of Denver, Winter Park is a unique place. It focuses on value, and offers an excellent skiing experience for the money. It's a large mountain with a variety of trails for all levels, and well-regarded programs for children and skiers with disabilities. Young and athletic in spirit, its amenities are somewhat bare-bones for a resort of its size. See chapter 11.

A WORD ABOUT RATES & STATISTICS

In the write-ups for each ski area in the regional chapters, we give exact daily lift-ticket rates. These are handy for comparison, but very few people actually pay these amounts. The vast majority of skiers buy packages that often include lift tickets for a certain number of days, plus lessons, but also might include rental equipment, lodging and/or meals, transportation, and lift tickets for other nearby ski areas. The possibilities are practically unlimited. Other than working with a reputable ski packager (see "Ski Packages & Tours," below), the best way to find out about current packages is to call the central reservation service for a particular resort as well as the reservation desks of nearby lodgings.

Although official lift ticket prices don't change much throughout the season, discounts are offered at slow times, and when combined with lodging, transportation, and other costs, choosing a less popular time to visit can save a bundle. Without a doubt the most expensive time to ski is during the Christmas season—from December 23 through January 1—followed by the Martin Luther King, Jr. and Presidents' Day holiday weekends. The "season," which lasts from February to March, is the next most expensive time to ski. "Value season," usually the month of January, is cheaper, but the low season—from Thanksgiving until mid-December and from April until ski areas close—is the least expensive time to ski. We prefer the last few weeks of the season since the snow's still great, the weather's nice, and the slopes are uncrowded (most skiers have turned their thoughts to golf and tennis by that time). But throughout the low season, lift tickets are often discounted and you're apt to find inexpensive lodging packages.

In addition to listing exact prices in this guide, we cite stats—peak elevation, vertical drop, acreage, number of lifts, and percentage of terrain that's marked beginner, intermediate, advanced, and expert. Because every mountain in Colorado (and the rest of North America, for that matter) bills itself as a complete skiing experience with trails intended to appeal to every level of skier, be wary of these statistics. One could easily write a dissertation on the ways in which these numbers are routinely fudged by a resort's marketing department in their favor, but here are just a few points to keep in mind. Easier mountains tend to overrate their trails. As this usually just results in an ego massage for the beginning- or intermediate-level skier, this is a relatively harmless example of false advertising. It's the opposite problem that can be dangerous—when a mountain underrates its trails, labeling what's really a black diamond trail blue. In general, be wary of a mountain with few green or blue trails unless you are an accomplished skier.

Another area of concern has to do with skiable acreage—a term that describes size. In theory, the more skiable acreage, the larger the resort. Since some resorts include the parking lot in this figure, it's not a particularly accurate gauge. What you really want to know is the number and length of an area's marked trails. The number of lifts a resort has can also be misleading. Just because a mountain has a large number of lifts doesn't necessarily guarantee short lift lines—lifts can be closed, or located in such an out-of-the-way location that they are virtually useless to the average skier.

Finally, be wary of the vertical—the difference in altitude from the top of the resort to its base. Is this entire area serviced by lifts or do skiers have to hike the last few feet to the top? Do you have to change lifts partway down the mountain to get all the way to the base? Just because a mountain has an impressive vertical doesn't guarantee long, continuous trails.

SKI PACKAGES & TOURS

While many skiers heading to Colorado's resorts find that planning their trip—lining up transportation, lodging, etc.—is part of the fun, others prefer making one call and letting a tour operator or trip planner take care of all the details. Not only do packages save time, but they're sometimes cheaper than doing it yourself. The key to picking a ski package is to make sure you get all the features you want, but that you don't end up paying for things you don't want. Packages often include air and ground transportation, lodging, and lift tickets. Trip cancellation insurance and some meals may also be included.

A good first step is to check with a ski club in your home town. These nonprofit organizations often offer some of the best deals, if they happen to be planning a trip to where you want to ski at a time when you want to go. Many travel agents can arrange ski vacations, and packages are also available through **Amtrak** (☎ **800/321-8684**), **Delta** (☎ **800/221-1212**), and **United** (☎ **800/525-2052**). Most of the individual ski-resort central reservation services can also arrange complete packages. Here are some respected national tour operators and trip planners that offer ski packages:

Any Mountain Tours, (☎ **800/296-2000**), is a good source for discount packages, especially at the last minute.

Damon-Nelson Travel, (☎ **619/235-6454**), offers a variety of packages to most major Colorado resorts.

K+M Tours, (☎ **800/233-2300**), has packages, including airfare, to most major Colorado resorts.

Moguls Ski & Sun Tours, (☎ **800/6MOGULS**), specializes in multi-resort ski vacations, including air and ground travel, lodging, and lift tickets.

Rocky Mountain Tours, (☎ **800/525-SKIS**), offers discount lodging and lift ticket packages, and can also arrange discount airfares and car rental rates.

SNOWMOBILING

If you've never been snowmobiling, the best places for a guided snowmobile tour are Vail, Aspen, and Steamboat Springs.

If you're an experienced snowmobiler, and you plan to bring your rig with you, national forest trails are prime snowmobiling spots. Some of the state's best and most scenic rides are in Roosevelt National Forest, about 50 miles west of Fort Collins (via U.S. 287 and Colo. 14) at Chambers Lake. Another particularly pretty ride is in the Routt National Forest several miles northwest of Steamboat Springs (via U.S. 40 and Forest Road 129), with spectacular mountain views. Because many of these trails are multiuse, snowmobilers should watch out for cross-country skiers and snowshoers, and slow down when passing them.

Colorado's light, dry snow is usually suitable for snowmobiling all winter long, although warm spring days can result in sticky snow, especially at lower elevations, that can gum up the works and make the going rough.

A comprehensive list of national forest trails open to snowmobilers is available for free from the **Colorado Snowmobile Association,** P.O. Box 1260, Grand Lake, CO 80447 (☎ **800/235-4480**).

WHITE-WATER RAFTING & KAYAKING

Rivers swollen with melted snow lure rafters and kayakers, especially from spring through midsummer, when rivers are at their fullest. The towns of Salida and Buena Vista, both located on the upper Arkansas River, have become famous rafting centers, and other popular destinations include Fort Collins, Estes Park, Grand Junction, Glenwood Springs, and Dinosaur National Monument.

Rivers are classified from I to VI, depending on the roughness of their rapids. Class I is an easy float trip, practically calm; class II has some rapids but is mostly calm; class III has some difficult rapids, with waves and boulders, and can be narrow in spots; class IV is considered very difficult, with long stretches of rough raft-flipping rapids; class V is extremely difficult with violent rapids and steep drops; and class VI is considered unrunnable in any type of raft or kayak. Rivers vary, though, so it is not unusual to float through a calm class I section, and just around the bend find an exciting class III section. The Arkansas River near Salida offers a good variety—from easy to almost unrunnable. The Colorado River through Glenwood Canyon is a particularly scenic class II–III river, wild enough for some thrills but with enough calm stretches to let you catch your breath and enjoy the view.

You'll find a variety of trips from numerous reliable outfitters, including **Dvorak's Kayak & Rafting Expeditions** (☎ **800/824-3795**) and **Wilderness Aware** (☎ **800/462-7238**). For a free directory of licensed river outfitters and tips on choosing a rafting company, contact the **Colorado River Outfitters Association,** P.O. Box 1662, Buena Vista, CO 81211 (☎ **303/369-4632**).

WILDLIFE WATCHING & BIRDING

There are numerous locations in Colorado to see animals and birds in the wild, including some that are close to the state's major cities. The South Platte River Greenway near Denver is a good spot to see ducks and other waterfowl, songbirds, deer, and beaver; and the U.S. Air Force Academy grounds in Colorado Springs offer opportunities to see deer, an occasional elk, peregrine falcons, and golden eagles. Other top spots to see wildlife include Durango, Glenwood Springs, Fort Collins, Vail, Rocky Mountain National Park, and Colorado National Monument.

A good national firm offering guided bird-watching tours to Colorado is **Victor Emmanuel Nature Tours** (☎ **800/328-VENT**), based in Texas.

3 Visiting Colorado's National Parks & Monuments

Some of the most beautiful parts of Colorado have been preserved within the federal government's national park system. These include the spectacular Rocky

Mountain National Park, near Estes Park; Mesa Verde National Park, near Cortez; Colorado National Monument, just outside Grand Junction; Black Canyon of the Gunnison National Monument, near Montrose; and Dinosaur National Monument, which isn't really near anything, but is closest to Grand Junction.

Rocky Mountain National Park, easily the most popular of the state's National Park Service properties in terms of number of visitors, is also the most beautiful. Because photos of its magnificent snowcapped peaks have graced so many calendars and coffee-table books, it is often the image of Rocky Mountain National Park that people imagine when they think of Colorado. The state's other national park, Mesa Verde, is entirely different. It's *raison d'être* is history, where you can see the best-preserved ancient Anasazi cliff dwellings in the Southwest.

The state's national monuments—Colorado, Black Canyon of the Gunnison, and Dinosaur—can't compare with Rocky Mountain National Park in terms of overall beauty, but each has its own charm and is well worth a visit. Colorado National Monument is similar to the national parks of southern Utah—a somewhat barren wasteland of spectacular red rock formations. Dinosaur National Monument should really be two parks; a scenic but arid canyon-lands section in Colorado and its namesake dinosaur quarry just across the border in Utah. And Black Canyon of the Gunnison is an extremely narrow rocky river canyon that's wild and beautiful, but difficult to explore because of its steep canyon walls.

To get the most from your visit, try to go during the off-season, but avoid school vacation periods and the dead of winter for the obvious reason that the high country of Rocky Mountain National Park and parts of Mesa Verde are inaccessible then and although the parks are beautiful under a frosting of snow, you won't be able to see as much.

If you're physically able, be prepared to hike. Even at the busiest times, most park visitors tend to stay on the beaten track, stopping at the same scenic vistas before rushing back to their cars. If you can spend even an hour or two on the trail, it's often possible to simply walk away from the crowds.

American parks and monuments are some of the biggest travel bargains in the world. With the special advance-purchase passes that are available, they become even more affordable. If you plan to visit a number of national parks and monuments within the calendar year, a **Golden Eagle Pass** for $25 will constitute a savings for you. It allows the bearer, plus everyone traveling with him or her in the same vehicle, free admission to all national parks and monuments (camping fees are extra). The **Golden Age Passport,** for those 62 and older, has a one-time fee of $10 and provides free admission to all national parks and monuments, plus a 50% discount on camping fees. Finally, there's the **Golden Access Passport,** free for permanently disabled U.S. citizens, which grants its bearer free access to all parks and monuments and 50% off on camping fees. All of the above passes can be purchased at park entrances.

6 Settling into Denver

It's no accident that Denver is called "the Mile High City." When you climb the State Capitol steps, you're precisely 5,280 feet above sea level. The fact that Denver happens to be at this altitude was purely coincidental; you see, Denver is one of the few cities that was not built on an ocean, lake, or navigable river, or even on an existing road or railroad.

In the summer of 1858, a few flecks of gold were discovered by eager Georgia prospectors where Cherry Creek empties into the shallow South Platte River. A tent camp quickly sprang up on the site (the first permanent structure was a saloon). When militia general William H. Larimer arrived in 1859, he claim-jumped the land on the east side of the Platte, laid out a city, and—hoping to gain political favors—named it after James Denver, governor of the Kansas Territory, to which this land belonged. Larimer didn't know that Denver had recently resigned from office.

Larimer's was one of several settlements on the South Platte; three others sought recognition. However, Larimer, a shrewd man, had a solution. For the price of a barrel of whiskey, he bought out the other founders, and the name Denver caught on.

Although the gold found in Denver was but a teaser for much larger strikes in the mountains nearby, the community grew as a shipping and trade center with a milder climate than the mining towns it served. With the establishment of rail links to the east and the influx of silver from the rich mines to the west, Denver's prominence grew. But it wasn't until the U.S. Mint was built in 1906 that Denver became the state's banking and financial center.

In the years following World War II, Denver mushroomed to become the largest city between the Great Plains and the Pacific Coast, with about 500,000 residents in Denver and more than 1.8 million in the metropolitan area.

Today, it's a sprawling, flat city, extending from the Rocky Mountain foothills on the west far into the plains to the south and east. Since the early 1980s, it, like the rest of the state, has been a mecca for young college graduates in search of a place where they can pursue an active lifestyle on weekends.

These well-educated newcomers have worked side-by-side with the city's longtime residents, revitalizing museums and performing-arts organizations and successfully luring major professional sports franchises to town, while at the same time starting intriguing new institutions of their own. They've also been the driving force behind the renovation of the lower downtown area. Now called LoDo, its lovingly restored old Victorian buildings house some of the city's more interesting jazz and blues clubs, art galleries, restaurants, and shops. So now, just as it has been historically, Denver continues to be one of the state's most important and vibrant places—the capital in both spirit and letter.

1 Orientation

ARRIVING

BY PLANE   **Denver International Airport,** which opened in a new location in February 1995, is 23 miles northeast of downtown, usually a 35- to 45-minute drive. Airlines serving the airport include **American** (☎ 800/433-7300), **America West** (☎ 800/235-9292), **Continental** (☎ 800/525-0280), **Delta** (☎ 800/211-1212), **Frontier** (☎ 800/432-1359), **GP Express** (☎ 800/525-0280), **Martinair Holland** (☎ 800/366-4655), **Mexicana** (☎ 800/531-7921), **Northwest** (☎ 800/225-2525), **Sun Country** (☎ 800/359-5786), **TWA** (☎ 800/221-2000), **United** (☎ 800/241-6522), and **US Air** (☎ 800/428-4322). Regional and commuter airlines connect Denver with other points in the Rockies and Southwest; they include **Continental Connection** (☎ 800/525-0280), **Mesa Airlines** (☎ 800/637-2247), and **United Express** (☎ 800/241-6522).

An **airport information** line (☎ **800/AIR-2-DEN**), provides information about airport parking, ground transportation, current weather conditions, and even nearby accommodations.

Getting to & from the Airport   Bus, taxi, and limousine services shuttle travelers between the airport and downtown, and most major car-rental companies have outlets at the airport. The cost of a **city bus** ride from the airport to downtown Denver is $6; from the airport to Boulder and suburban Park-n-Ride lots, it is about $8. The **Airporter** (☎ **303/333-5833**) provides door-to-door pickup and drop-off at rates from $20 to $40 one way. **Taxi** companies (see "Getting Around," below) are another option, with fares generally in the $30 to $50 range. However, you can often arrange to share a cab and split the fare by calling the cab company a day ahead. Because most major hotels are some distance from the airport, travelers should check on the availability and cost of hotel shuttle service when making reservations. The **Denver Airport Shuttle** (☎ **800/525-3177** or 303/342-5454) provides transportation to and from many hotels. Fares vary and may be paid in part or completely by the hotel.

BY CAR   The principal highway routes into Denver are I-25 from the north (Fort Collins, Cheyenne) or south (Colorado Springs, Albuquerque); I-70 from the east (Burlington, Kansas City) and west (Grand Junction); and I-76 from the northeast (Sterling). If you're driving into Denver from Boulder, take U.S. 36; from Salida and southwest, take U.S. 285.

BY TRAIN   **Amtrak** has several trains arriving daily from both coasts. Trains arrive at Union Station, 17th and Wynkoop streets (☎ **800/USA-RAIL** or 303/825-2583), in the lower downtown historic district.

VISITOR INFORMATION

The **Denver Metro Convention and Visitors Bureau** is located at 225 W. Colfax Ave., Denver, CO 80202 (☎ **800/645-3446** or 303/892-1112), across from the U.S. Mint. Ask for the *Denver Visitors Guide,* an impressive 150-plus–page full-color booklet with a comprehensive listing of accommodations, restaurants, and other visitor services in Denver and surrounding areas, as well as a good map. The information center is open in summer, Monday through Friday from 8am to 5pm and Saturday from 10am to 2pm; in winter, Monday through Friday from 8am to 5pm and Saturday from 9am to 1pm.

Visitor information is also available at the Denver International Airport.

CITY LAYOUT

You can never truly get lost in Denver, so long as you remember that the mountains—nearly always visible—are to the west. All the same, it can be perplexing to get around a city of half a million people. One element of confusion is that Denver has both an older grid system, which is oriented northeast-to-southwest parallel to the South Platte River, and a newer north-south grid system that surrounds the older one.

Main Arteries & Streets

It's probably easiest to get your bearings from Civic Center Park. From here, Colfax Avenue—U.S. 40—extends east and west as far as the eye can see. The same is true for Broadway, which reaches north and south.

Downtown Denver   North of Colfax and west of Broadway is the center of downtown Denver, where the streets follow the old grid pattern. **16th Street,** a mile-long pedestrian mall, cuts northwest off Broadway, just above this intersection. (The numbered streets parallel 16th to the northeast, extending all the way to 44th; and to the southwest, as far as 5th.) Intersecting the numbered streets at right angles are **Lawrence Street** (it runs one way northeast) and **Larimer Street** (it runs one way southwest), 12 and 13 blocks, respectively, from the Colfax-Broadway intersection.

I-25 skirts downtown Denver to the west, with access from Colfax or **Speer Boulevard,** which winds diagonally along Cherry Creek past Larimer Square.

Outside Downtown   Outside the downtown sector, the pattern is a little less confusing. But keep in mind that the numbered *avenues* that parallel Colfax to the north and south (Colfax is equivalent to 15th Ave.) have nothing in common with the numbered *streets* of the downtown grid. In fact, any byway labeled an "avenue" runs east to west, never north to south.

Finding An Address

North-South Arteries   The thoroughfare that divides avenues into "east" and "west" is Broadway, which runs one way south between 19th Street and I-25. Each block east or west adds 100 to the avenue address; thus, if you wanted to find 2115 E. 17th Ave., it would be a little over 21 blocks east of Broadway—just beyond Vine Street.

Main thoroughfares that parallel Broadway to the east include Downing Street (1200 block), York Street (2300 block; it becomes University Blvd. south of Sixth), Colorado Boulevard (4000 block), Monaco Parkway (6500 block), and Quebec Street (7300 block). Colorado Boulevard (Colo. 2) is the most significant artery, intersecting I-25 on the south and I-70 on the north. North-south cross streets that parallel Broadway west of Broadway include Santa Fe Drive (U.S. 85; 1000 block); west of I-25 are Federal Boulevard (U.S. 287 North, site of several sports arenas; 3000 block), and Sheridan Boulevard (Colo. 95; 5200 block), the boundary between Denver and Lakewood.

East-West Arteries   Denver streets are divided into "north" and "south" at Ellsworth Avenue, about 1 1/2 miles south of Colfax. Ellsworth is a relatively minor street, but it's a convenient dividing point because it's just a block south of First Avenue. With building numbers increasing by 100 each block, that puts an address like 1710 Downing Street at the corner of East 17th Avenue. First, Sixth, Colfax (1500 block), and 26th Avenues, and Martin Luther King, Jr., Boulevard (3200 block) are the principal east-west thoroughfares. There are no numbered avenues south of Ellsworth. Major east-west byways south of Ellsworth are Alameda (Colo. 26; 300 block), Mississippi (1100 block), Florida (1500 block), Evans (2100 block), Yale (2700 block), and Hampden Avenues (U.S. 285; 3500 block).

NEIGHBORHOODS IN BRIEF

Lower Downtown   Downtown Denver can be divided into three subdistricts. Lower Downtown or LoDo is the oldest part of the city. It extends northwesterly from Lawrence Street to Union Station and from the shops of Tivoli Denver northeast to 19th Street. Coors Field, the baseball stadium built for the Colorado Rockies, opened here in 1995. No skyscrapers are permitted in this historic district, most of which dates from the late 19th century.

Central Business District   This extends along 16th, 17th, and 18th streets between Lawrence Street and Broadway. Here, the ban on skyscrapers certainly does not apply.

Civic Center Park   This area is at the southeast end of 15th Street, where Broadway and Colfax Avenue meet. The two-square-block oasis of green is surrounded by state and city government buildings, the Denver Art Museum, the Colorado History Museum, the U.S. Mint, and the public library.

Capitol Hill   This area is located just southeast of downtown and extends roughly from the State Capitol (at Colfax and Lincoln) past the Governor's Mansion to East Sixth Avenue, and from Broadway to Cheesman Park (on Franklin Street). Here you'll find a great many Victorian mansions from the mining-boom days of the late 19th and early 20th centuries, including the Molly Brown House (see "Attractions" in chapter 7). But you'll see no old wooden buildings: after the disastrous fire of 1863, the government forbade the construction of wooden structures until after World War II.

Cherry Creek   Home to the Cherry Creek Shopping Center and Denver Country Club, this area extends north from East First Avenue to East Eighth Avenue, and east from Downing Street to Steele Street. You'll find huge, ostentatious stone mansions here, especially around Circle Drive (southwest of Sixth and University), where many of Denver's wealthiest families have lived for generations.

Historic Districts   There are 17 recognized historic districts in Denver, including Capitol Hill, the Clements District (around 21st and Tremont streets, just east of downtown), and Ninth Street Park in Auraria (off Ninth Street and West Colfax Avenue). **Historic Denver,** 821 17th St., Suite 500 (☎ **303/296-9887**), offers walking-tour maps of several of these areas.

Glendale   Denver fully surrounds Glendale, an incorporated city in its own right. It's a yuppie enclave straddling Cherry Creek on South Colorado Boulevard south of East Alameda Avenue.

Tech Center   At the southern end of the metropolitan area is Tech Center, along I-25 between Belleview Avenue and Arapahoe Road. In this district, about a 25-minute drive from downtown, you will find the headquarters of several international and national companies, high-tech businesses, and a handful of upscale hotels heavily oriented toward business travelers.

2 Getting Around

BY PUBLIC TRANSPORTATION

The **Regional Transportation District (RTD)** (☎ **800/366-7433** or 303/299-6000 for route and schedule information, 303/299-6700 for other business) calls itself "The Ride" for its bus routes and light rail system, with transfer tickets available free. It provides good service within Denver and its suburbs and outlying communities (including Boulder, Longmont, and Evergreen), as well as free parking at 50 **Park-n-Ride** locations throughout the Denver-Boulder metropolitan area. The light rail service, which began in late 1994, is designed to get buses and autos out of congested downtown Denver; many of the bus routes from outlying areas deliver passengers to light rail stations rather than downtown.

The local fare is $1 during peak hours (Monday through Friday 6–9am and 4–6pm) and 50¢ during off-peak hours. The express fare starts at $1.50; regional fares vary (for example, it is $2.50 between Denver and Boulder). Senior citizens pay only 15¢ off-peak, and children 5 and younger travel free. Exact change is required for buses, and train tickets can be purchased at vending machines beneath light rail station awnings.

Each route has its own schedule of frequency, including departure time of the last bus or train (it varies from 9pm to 1am). Maps for all routes are available at any time at the RTD Civic Center Station, 16th Street and Broadway; the Market Street Station, Market and 16th streets; and during regular business hours at the Denver Metro CVB, 225 W. Colfax Ave. RTD also provides special service to Colorado Rockies home baseball and Broncos home football games. All RTD buses and trains are completely wheelchair accessible.

Free buses run up and down the 16th Street Mall between the Civic Center and Market Street every 90 seconds during peak hours (less frequently at other times), daily from 6am to 1am.

Visitors like the **Cultural Connection Trolley** (☎ 303/299-6000), which runs daily in summer, with stops at Denver's most popular tourist attractions, including the State Capitol, Denver Botanic Gardens, Denver Zoo, U.S. Mint, and almost all major downtown museums. A full-day pass costs $3 (children 5 and younger ride free); detailed route information is available at the Denver Visitors Bureau.

From Memorial Day through Labor Day, plus weekends in winter (weather permitting), you can ride the **Platte Valley Trolley** (☎ 303/458-6255). Between 11am and 4pm daily there's a half-hour "Seeing Denver" ride ($2 adults, $1 seniors and children), which operates from 15th Street at Confluence Park, south to Decatur Street along the west bank of the Platte River. Another excursion leaves at noon, Monday through Friday, and 2pm Saturday and Sunday ($4 adults, $3 seniors, $2 children). This 1-hour trip takes visitors west of Decatur Street, following a portion of a historic tram line that ran to Golden until 1950.

BY TAXI

The main companies are **Yellow Cab** (☎ 303/777-7777), **Zone Cab** (☎ 303/444-8888), and **Metro Taxi** (☎ 303/333-3333). Taxis can be hailed on the street, though it's preferable to telephone for a taxi or wait for one at a taxi stand outside a major hotel.

BY CAR

Because cars are not really necessary downtown, visitors can save the cost of renting a car, as well as parking fees (some downtown hotels charge $5–$15 per night) by arranging to stay downtown the first few nights, and then renting a car when planning to leave the area.

Car Rentals   Most major car-rental agencies have outlets in or near downtown Denver, as well as at Denver International Airport. These include **Alamo,** 7400 E. 41st Ave. (☎ **800/327-9633** or 303/342-7373); **Avis,** 1900 Broadway (☎ **800/ 831-2847** or 303/839-1280); **Budget,** 1980 Broadway (☎ **800/527-0700** or 303/ 341-2277); **Dollar,** 23520 E. 78th Ave. (☎ **800/800-4000** or 303/342-9099); **Enterprise,** 5179 S. Broadway (☎ **800/325-8007** or 303/794-3333); **Thrifty,** 400 Quebec St. (☎ **800/327-7607** or 303/790-9220); **Hertz,** 2001 Welton (☎ **800/654-3131** or 303/297-9400); and **National,** 24200 E. 78th Ave. (☎ **800/ 227-7368** or 303/770-9900).

Per-day rentals range from $30 to $50 for midsize cars, although AAA and other discounts are often available, and weekend and multiday rates can also save money. Four-wheel–drive vehicles, trucks, and campers cost more.

Campers, travel trailers, motor homes, and motorcycles can be rented from **Cruise America,** 7450 E. 29th Ave. (☎ **800/327-7778** or 303/426-6699).

Parking   Downtown parking-lot rates vary from 75¢ per half hour to $10 per full day. Rates are higher in the vicinity of the 16th Street Mall and the central business district. Keep a handful of quarters, dimes, and nickels if you plan to use on-street parking meters.

FAST FACTS: Denver

American Express   **American Express** is located at 555 17th St. (☎ **303/298-7100**) and is a full-service travel agency. It's open Monday through Friday from 8:30am to 5pm.

Area Code   The area code for Denver is **303.**

Business Hours   Most banks are open Monday through Friday from 9am to 5pm, and some have Saturday hours, too. Major stores are open Monday through Saturday from 9 or 10am until 5 or 6pm, and often Sunday from noon until 5pm. Many large stores stay open at least one evening a week until 9pm.

Camera Repair   **Robert Waxman Camera and Video** has six Denver locations; its branch at 15th Street and California (☎ **800/525-3498** or 303/623-1155) may be the biggest single-floor camera store in the world.

Doctors & Dentists   For a doctor or dentist referral, call **Prologue** (☎ **303/ 443-2584**) or **Med-Search** (☎ **303/866-8000**). **Ask-A-Nurse** (☎ **303/777-6877**) provides free physician referrals and answers health questions 24 hours a day. The **Med-A-Kid** line (☎ **303/861-0123**) specializes in referrals to children's doctors and dentists.

Emergencies   For police, fire department, or medical emergencies call **911.**

Hospitals   Among Denver-area hospitals are **St. Joseph's,** 1835 Franklin St. (☎ **303/837-7111**), just east of downtown; **Rose Medical Center,** 4567 E. Ninth Ave. (☎ **303/320-2121**), five blocks east of Colorado Boulevard; and **St. Anthony's,** 4231 W. 16th Ave. (☎ **303/629-3511**), west of Mile High Stadium.

Hot Lines   For the **poison control center,** call 303/629-1123. For the **rape crisis hot line,** call 303/830-6800.

Maps   Denver's largest map store, **Maps Unlimited,** 899 Broadway, at Ninth Avenue (☎ **800/456-8703** or 303/623-4299), offers USGS and recreation maps, state maps and travel guides, raised relief maps, and globes.

Newspapers   The morning *Denver Post* is Colorado's largest daily newspaper. The afternoon *Rocky Mountain News* also covers the metropolitan area, and there's a widely read free weekly, *Westword,* known as much for its controversial jibes at local politicians as for its entertainment listings. National newspapers such as *USA Today* and the *Wall Street Journal* can be purchased at newsstands and at major hotels.

Pharmacies   Throughout the metropolitan area you will find Walgreens and Pay Less pharmacies, as well as Safeway and King Soopers grocery stores, which also have drugstores. The **Walgreens** at 2000 E. Colfax Ave. is open 24 hours a day (☎ **303/331-0917**). For the locations of other Walgreens, call **800/WALGREENS.** For an old-fashioned family-owned drugstore, there is **Watson's,** 900 Lincoln St. (☎ **303/837-1366**), open Monday through Thursday from 8am to 10pm, Friday from 8am to 11pm, and Saturday from 10am to 11pm.

Post Office   The main downtown post office is at 951 20th St. (☎ **303/296-2920**), open Monday through Friday from 7am to 6pm, Saturday from 9am to 1pm. For **24-hour postal service,** go to the General Mail Facility, 7500 E. 53rd Place (☎ **303/853-6456**).

Radio   A large variety of music, news, sports, and entertainment is presented on 4 dozen AM and FM radio stations in the Denver area, including KOA (850 AM) for news and talk, KKFN (950 AM) for all sports, KWBI (91.1 FM) for Christian ministry and music, KIMN (100.3 FM) for 1970s rock, KRFX (103.5 FM) for classic rock, KXPK (96.5 FM) for 1980s and 1990s rock, KBCO (97.3 FM) for alternative rock, KYGO (98.5 FM and 950 AM) for classic country, KZDG (92.5 FM) for new country, and KVOD (92.5 FM) for classical music.

Taxes   State and local sales tax in Denver is about 7%, (it varies slightly in neighboring counties and suburbs). The hotel tax is about 5%, bringing the total tax on accommodations to about 12%.

Television   Denver has 10 television stations, including KCNC (Channel 4), the CBS affiliate; KMGH (Channel 7), the ABC affiliate; KUSA (Channel 9), the NBC affiliate; and KDVR (Channel 31), the Fox affiliate. Other major stations include KWGN (Channel 2), an independent; and KRMA (Channel 6), the PBS affiliate. Cable or satellite service is available at most hotels.

Useful Telephone Numbers   For a **weather report,** the **time,** or the **temperature,** call **303/337-2500.** Statewide road condition reports are available by calling **303/639-1111.** For information on **possible road construction delays** in the Denver area, call **303/573-ROAD.**

3 Accommodations

Although most lodgings in the Denver area do not have seasonal rates (which are usually available elsewhere in Colorado), hotels that cater to business travelers, such as the Brown Palace and the Warwick, offer substantial discounts on weekends—sometimes as much as 50% off the regular rates.

Many of the major chains provide reasonably priced lodging in Denver. Moderate and lower-priced options downtown include: **Comfort Inn,** 401 17th St. (☎ **800/237-7431** or 303/296-0400), with a convenient location and rates of $75 to $105 double; **Ramada Inn—Mile High Stadium,** 1975 Bryant St., at I-25, Exit 210B (☎ **800/272-6232** or 303/433-8331), with rates of $82 to $90 double; **Holiday Inn DIA,** 15500 E. 40th St., at I-70, Exit 284 (☎ **800/HOLIDAY** or 303/371-9494), with rates of $115 to $120 double; and **La Quinta Inn Central,** 3500 Park Ave. W., at I-25, Exit 213 (☎ **800/531-5900** or 303/458-1222), which charges $75 to $92 double.

Outside downtown, chain lodgings include: **Hampton Inn,** 4685 Quebec St. (☎ **800/HAMPTON** or 303/388-8100), with rates of $68 to $73 double, $5 per additional person; **Quality Inn Denver South,** 6300 E. Hampden Ave. (☎ **800/ 647-1986** or 303/758-2211), with rates of $72 to $79 double (see "Family-Friendly Hotels"); and **Motel 6,** 6 W. 83rd Place, Thornton (☎ **800/466-8356** or 303/ 429-1550 for central reservations), which charges $32 to $40 double.

These are official, or "rack" rates, which do not take into consideration any discounts, such as those offered to members of AAA or AARP. Because a chain hotel's national reservation service may not be able to offer discounts, your best bet may be to call the hotel directly.

In these listings, the price range is categorized as follows: **very expensive,** more than $150 per night double; **expensive,** $100 to $150; **moderate,** $50 to $100; **inexpensive,** less than $50 per night double. These rates do not include the 12% tax that is added to all accommodation bills.

DOWNTOWN
VERY EXPENSIVE

✪ **Brown Palace Hotel.** 321 17th St., Denver, CO 80202. ☎ **800/228-2917** or 303/ 297-3111 in Colorado, 800/321-2599 elsewhere in North America. Fax 303/293-9204. 205 rms, 25 suites. A/C TV TEL. $185–$205 double; $245–$725 suite. Weekend rates start at $120. AE, CB, DC, DISC, ER, JCB, MC, V. Parking $14 per day.

A National Historic Landmark, the Brown Palace opened in August 1892 and has been operating continuously ever since. Designed with an odd triangular shape by the famous architect Frank Edbrooke, it is built of Colorado red granite and Arizona sandstone. The lobby's walls are paneled with Mexican onyx, and the floor is white marble. Elaborate cast-iron grillwork surrounds six tiers of balconies up to the stained-glass ceiling high above the lobby. During his presidency, Dwight Eisenhower (1953–61) maintained the Western White House here. The Eisenhower Suite is richly decorated, and a dent in the fireplace trim is reported to have been made by an errant golf ball.

The guest rooms, which were recently remodeled, have been uniquely decorated in either Victorian or art deco style. Each has a desk, remote-control TV (with Spectravision) hidden in an armoire, and its own heating and cooling control. The water's great here: the Brown Palace has its own artesian wells!

Dining/Entertainment: Excellent meals are served in the Palace Arms (see "Dining," below). Ellyngton's (nonsmoking) serves breakfast and lunch (light grills and pastas) and a champagne brunch on Sunday. The Ship Tavern, the hotel's oldest restaurant, is open daily for drinks and casual dining. The Churchill Bar, a sophisticated cigar bar with a library atmosphere, recently opened next to the Palace Arms. Luncheon tea (noon–2pm) is available in the lobby Monday to Friday, and afternoon tea (2–4pm) Monday to Saturday. The Brown Palace Club serves lunch for private members and hotel guests only.

Services: 24-hour room service, concierge, valet laundry, in-room massage, dual voice-modem lines and voice mail in all rooms, nightly turndown, robes, Crabtree-and-Evelyn amenities.

Facilities: Fitness center, business center, VCR rentals, boutiques, beauty salon, meeting facilities for up to 750.

Westin Hotel at Tabor Center. 1672 Lawrence St., Denver, CO 80202. ☎ **800/228-3000** or 303/572-9100. Fax 303/572-7288. 407 rms, 13 suites. A/C MINIBAR TV TEL. $114–$195 double; $150–$1,200 suite. Children under 18 stay free in parents' room. AE, CB, DC, DISC, MC, V. Parking $12–$14 per day.

The focal point of the two-square-block Tabor Center shopping-and-office complex, the 19-story Westin bridges the gap between the central business district and lower downtown, and is conveniently located near Coors Field. Its contemporary design incorporates architectural elements of nearby Victorian-era structures. The elegant second-floor lobby, reached by an elevator or long escalator, features three-dimensional murals and modern fountains.

The spacious guest rooms, three-quarters of which feature king-size beds, are beautifully appointed with modern, European-style furnishings. Every room is equipped with a remote-control color TV (with pay movie channels), clock radio, and two phones—one on a full-size working desk. There's a 50¢ charge for local calls or long-distance access, except for credit card calls. The Executive Club on the hotel's top three floors provides upgraded features and amenities, including continental breakfast, afternoon cocktails, and a resident concierge.

Dining/Entertainment: The award-winning Augusta is regarded by many as the finest hotel restaurant in Denver (see "Dining," below). A casual, contemporary bistro, the Tabor Grill serves three meals daily. There's live entertainment nightly Monday through Saturday in the Lobby Lounge.

Services: 24-hour room service, valet laundry, complimentary shoe-shine.

Facilities: Health club with indoor/outdoor swimming pool, hot tub, sauna, exercise and weight room, and racquetball courts. There's a business center, refreshment center, meeting space for 400, beauty salon, and gift shop.

EXPENSIVE

The Burnsley All Suite Hotel. 1000 Grant St. (at E. 10th Ave.), Denver, CO 80203. ☎ **800/231-3915** or 303/830-1000. 82 suites. A/C TV TEL. $99–$145 double. Weekend rates available. AE, CB, DC, MC, V. Free covered parking.

This small, elegant hotel offers suites with private balconies, and separate living, bedroom, dining, and fully stocked kitchen areas. The units are handsomely furnished, although slightly dated. There are a swimming pool and business center on the premises; guests have privileges at a nearby health club. The hotel is conveniently situated near the Cherry Creek shopping areas and only five blocks from downtown.

Denver Marriott-City Center. 1701 California St., Denver, CO 80202. ☎ **800/228-9290** or 303/297-1300. Fax 303/298-7474. 599 rms, 14 suites. A/C TV TEL. $139 double; $375–$800 suite. Children under 18 stay free in parents' room. AE, MC, V. Parking $15 per day.

This tall black tower in the center of the financial district is a good choice for both business and leisure travelers. The rooms are equipped with a king-size or two double beds, table and chairs, desk with a telephone (75¢ charge for local calls), a credenza with a color TV (and in-house movies), built-in radio, and a closet door with full mirror.

The restaurant offers a buffet for breakfast and lunch, and international cuisine for dinner. The lounge also serves light lunch fare. Room service, valet laundry, and upgraded concierge level are available. Facilities include guest laundry, game room, gift shop/newsstand, fitness center, aerobics classes, Jacuzzi, and meeting facilities for up to 2,000 people.

Oxford Hotel. 1600 17th St. (at Wazee St.), Denver, CO 80202. ☎ **800/228-5838** or 303/628-5400. Fax 303/628-5413. 79 rms, 2 suites. A/C TV TEL. $135–$160 double; $180 suite. Children under 18 stay free in parents' room. AE, CB, DC, DISC, MC, V. Valet parking $12 per day.

Designed by the architect Frank Edbrooke, this is one of Denver's few hotels that have survived from the 19th century. The facade is a simple red sandstone, but the interior boasts marble walls, stained-glass windows, frescoes, and silver chandeliers, all of which were restored between 1979 and 1983 using Edbrooke's original drawings. The hotel is listed on the National Register of Historic Places.

Antique pieces were imported from England and France to furnish the 81 large rooms that were created during the restoration from the 200 original small rooms. No two rooms are alike, but they are all equipped with stocked minibars, individual thermostats, hairdryers, dressing tables, and large closets. Although there is bedside lighting, the electrical outlets are limited. Local phone calls cost 75¢.

McCormick's Fish House & Bar (see "Dining," below) is open for three meals daily. The art deco Cruise Room Bar, famous for Angus beef, is open daily from 4:30 to 10pm. The Corner Bar has enormous stained-glass panels on its back bar. Twenty-four–hour room service and valet laundry are available. Facilities include a fitness center, health spa, meeting space for 110, and a beauty salon.

✪ **The Warwick.** 1776 Grant St. (at E. 18th Ave.), Denver, CO 80203. ☎ **800/525-2888** or 303/861-2000. Fax 303/839-8504. 142 rms, 49 suites. A/C TV TEL. $120–$160 double; $150–$800 suite. Weekend rate $79–$85 double. Rates include European-style buffet breakfast. Children under 18 stay free in parents' room. AE, CB, DC, DISC, JCB, MC, V. Self or valet parking $5 per day, underground.

One of four Warwicks in the United States (the others are in New York, San Francisco, and Seattle), this handsome midsize hotel is reminiscent of hotels in Paris, where the corporate office is located. The small marbled lobby is accented by richly upholstered antique chairs and couches. New elevators were installed in 1996.

Even the standard rooms provide a full private balcony, and all but a few rooms are equipped with a refrigerator, wet bar, and dining table. Room furnishings include one king-size or two queen-size beds, simple brass and mahogany furniture, antique hunting prints on the walls, cable TV (with Spectravision) in an armoire, a clock radio, and a telephone with two incoming lines—one for a modem connection. There's another phone in the bathroom. Local calls cost 60¢.

The Liaison Restaurant and Lounge serves breakfast daily; continental fare is offered for lunch and dinner Monday through Friday. twenty-four–hour room service and concierge, valet laundry, courtesy limousine service within a 5-mile radius, and complimentary newspaper are available; there is a charge for baby-sitting and secretarial services. Facilities include a rooftop swimming pool (seasonal), health club, meeting space for 300, and boutiques.

INEXPENSIVE

Denver International Youth Hostel. 630 E. 16th Ave. (Corner of Washington St. and 16th Ave.), Denver, CO 80203. ☎ **303/832-9996.** Fax 303/861-1376. 160 dormitory beds. $8.50 per person per day. Discounts for members of American Association of International Hostels (☎ 602/774-6731), and for helping with chores at certain times. No credit cards; traveler's checks accepted. Free parking.

This four-story brick building, four blocks east of the State Capitol, is perfect for those on a tight budget who don't mind sharing. In the hostel tradition, it provides friendly, relatively clean and safe accommodations in dormitory-style rooms, with shared bathrooms, kitchens (free food is often available), television room, laundry,

Denver Accommodations

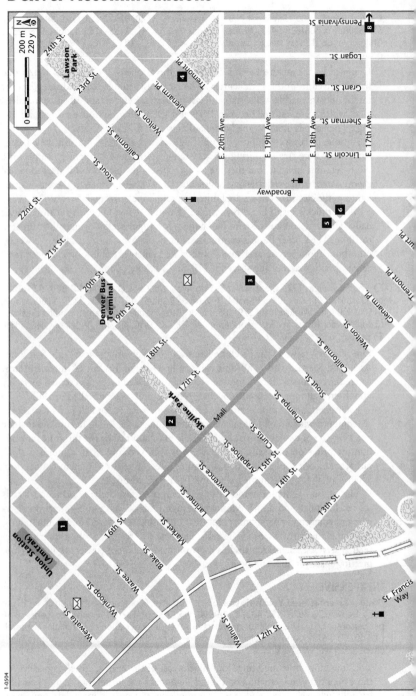

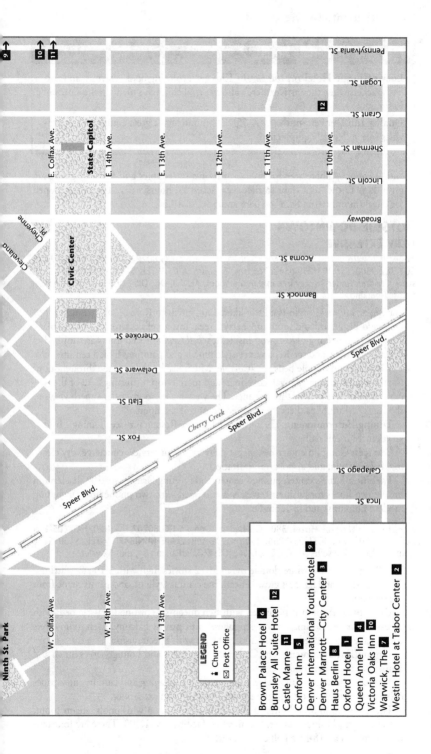

LEGEND
✝ Church
⊠ Post Office

Brown Palace Hotel **6**
Burnsley All Suite Hotel **12**
Castle Marne **11**
Comfort Inn **5**
Denver International Youth Hostel **9**
Denver Marriott—City Center **3**
Haus Berlin **8**
Oxford Hotel **1**
Queen Anne Inn **4**
Victoria Oaks Inn **10**
Warwick, The **7**
Westin Hotel at Tabor Center **2**

Family-Friendly Hotels

Loews Giorgio Hotel *(see this page)*   Kids get a coloring book, crayons, and animal crackers when they arrive; there's also a special children's menu in the Tuscany Restaurant.

Quality Inn Denver South *(see p. 65)*   This hotel has a great courtyard and provides free volleyball equipment.

---

and telephone. There are separate dorm rooms for couples and families; guests are given keys to the front door so they have access 24 hours a day. The office is open for check-in only from 8am to 10am and 5pm to 10:30pm.

OUTSIDE DOWNTOWN
VERY EXPENSIVE

Loews Giorgio Hotel. 4150 E. Mississippi Ave., Denver, CO 80222. ☎ **800/345-9172** or 303/782-9300. Fax 303/758-6542. 165 rms, 17 suites. A/C TV TEL. $195–$215 double; $250 suite. Children under 18 stay free in parents' room. AE, CB, DC, DISC, JCB, MC, V. Free valet and self-parking.

Staying at Loews Giorgio is a little like taking a trip to Rome. Located just east of Colorado Boulevard and south of Cherry Creek, this hotel's exterior is made of black steel with a reflecting-glass tower; inside, it's *bella Italia*. Its columns are finished in imitation marble, and the Renaissance-style murals and paintings look 5 centuries old.

King-size and double beds are available. Much use has been made throughout of floral patterns, Italian silk wall coverings, and marble-top furnishings. All of the spacious rooms have at least three phones. The west-facing rooms offer superb views of the Rocky Mountains. Pets are accepted on one of the floors.

Dining/Entertainment: The top-rated Tuscany Restaurant (see "Dining," below) serves three meals daily.

Services: Complimentary newspaper delivery, room service, concierge, dry cleaning, baby-sitting, and airport transportation.

Facilities: Fitness center, business center, and meeting facilities for 100. Each room on the two floors for business travelers is equipped with two phone lines (including modem hookups) and in-room fax.

Renaissance Denver Hotel. 3801 Quebec St., Denver, CO 80207. ☎ **800/HOTELS-1** or 303/399-7500. Fax 303/321-1966. 390 rms, 10 suites. A/C MINIBAR TV TEL. $150–$170 double; $195–$650 suite. AE, CB, DC, DISC, JCB, MC, V. Parking $4, plus $2 valet.

The Renaissance is a white double pyramid 12 stories high with a 10-story atrium. Tropical palms and fig trees grow beneath the central skylight, and plants drape from the balconies.

Each spacious room is furnished with two queen-size or one king-size bed, with an easy chair and ottoman, two telephones, and a private balcony. Each room offers coffeemakers, a stocked minibar, and cable TV with Spectravision.

Dining/Entertainment: The Concorde Restaurant and Lounge serves lunch and dinner (steak and seafood).

Services: 24-hour room service, a concierge, dry-cleaning and laundry, newspaper delivery, courtesy airport shuttle, express check-in, and fax service.

Facilities: Indoor and outdoor swimming pools, two whirlpools, steam room, exercise room, business center, and meeting facilities for 1,300. There are four tennis courts and an 18-hole golf course nearby.

MODERATE

Cherry Creek Inn. 600 S. Colorado Blvd., Denver, CO 80222. ☎ **303/757-3341.** Fax 303/756-6670. 323 rms. A/C TV TEL. $90 double; less expensive on weekends. AE, DC, DISC, MC, V. Free parking.

The Cherry Creek Inn is conveniently located in south-central Denver, 5 minutes from Cherry Creek shopping center, 10 minutes from downtown, and about 25 minutes from Denver International Airport. The spacious rooms are furnished with queen-size beds, minirefrigerators, coffeemakers, and cable TV. There's a seasonal outdoor swimming pool, access to a nearby health club, launderette, and beauty salon. Fax and photocopy services are available.

INEXPENSIVE

⑤ Cameron Motel. 4500 E. Evans Ave. (I-25, Exit 203), Denver, CO 80222. ☎ **303/757-2100.** Fax 303/757-0974. 33 rooms, 2 suites. A/C TV TEL. $43 double; $65 suite. AE, DISC, ER, MC, V.

A small mom-and-pop motel located about 10 minutes from downtown, the Cameron provides a clean, quiet alternative to some of the more expensive chains. Built in the 1940s, the property has been completely renovated. The walls of the rooms are of glazed brick; remote control color cable TVs offer 60 channels. Three rooms are equipped with kitchenettes. Fourteen rooms provide showers only, while 21 have tub/shower combinations. Pets are accepted, at an extra charge of $5 each per day. The owners live on-site, and their pride of ownership shows.

BED-AND-BREAKFASTS

Those seeking an alternative to the standard or even luxurious hotel or motel might consider one of Denver's many bed-and-breakfast inns. Often located in historic 19th-century homes, bed-and-breakfasts offer a more personalized lodging experience than you could expect in all but the very best hotels, simply because you rarely find more than 10 rooms in a bed-and-breakfast, and you are, quite literally, a guest in someone's home.

Castle Marne Bed & Breakfast. 1572 Race St., Denver, CO 80206. ☎ **800/92-MARNE** for reservations, or 303/331-0621. Fax 303/331-0623. 7 rms, 2 suites. A/C TEL. $85–$155 double; $180 suite. Rates include breakfast. AE, CB, DC, MC, V. Ample street parking.

A National Historic Landmark, Castle Marne is a massive stone fortress, designed and built in 1869 by the renowned architect William Lang for a contemporary silver baron. It is furnished with antiques, fine reproductions, and family heirlooms. It was so named because a previous owner's son had fought in the Battle of the Marne during World War I.

Two suites have Jacuzzi tubs for two; three rooms with private balconies are equipped with outdoor hot tubs for two; the old-fashioned bathrooms in three rooms contain both pedestal sinks and cast iron claw-footed tubs with shower rings. A gourmet breakfast is served in the original formal dining room (two seatings), and a proper afternoon tea is served daily in the parlor. The inn also provides a game room, library, gift shop, and an office for business travelers' use. Smoking is not permitted, and the inn is not suitable for children under 10.

Haus Berlin. 1651 Emerson St., Denver, CO 80218. ☎ **800/659-0253** or 303/837-9527. Fax 303/837-9527. 3 rms, 1 suite. A/C TV TEL. $85–$100 rooms; $130 suite. Rates include full breakfast. AE, DISC, MC, V. Parking on street.

A Victorian town house built in 1892, Haus Berlin is decorated with original art and collectibles gathered from around the world by the owners Christiana and Dennis

Brown. The rooms are furnished with queen- or king-size beds, fine linens, and down comforters. The suite, which encompasses the entire third floor, offers beautiful views of downtown Denver and is ideal for honeymooners and others celebrating special occasions. Smoking is not permitted, and this B&B is not suitable for children; the only pet permitted is the resident cat.

✪ **Queen Anne Bed and Breakfast Inn.** 2147–51 Tremont Place, Denver, CO 80205. ☎ **800/432-4667** or 303/296-6666. Fax 303/296-2151. 10 rms, 4 suites. A/C TEL. $75–$145 double, $135–$165 suite. Rates include breakfast. AE, DC, DISC, ER, MC, V. Parking in private lot.

A favorite of both business travelers and couples seeking a romantic getaway, the Queen Anne might be considered the perfect bed-and-breakfast in the perfect home. Actually it consists of two Victorian homes—one built by the well-known architect Frank Edbrooke in 1879, and the other built in 1886. Each room or suite is equipped with a telephone (free local calls) and a writing desk. Innkeeper Tom King also provides piped-in chamber music, fresh flowers, and fax services. Each of the 10 double rooms in the 1879 Pierce house is unique, decorated with period antiques. Each of the four two-room suites in the adjacent 1886 Roberts house is dedicated to a famous artist (Norman Rockwell, Frederic Remington, John Audubon, and Alexander Calder). The suites have deep soaking tubs, and the Remington suite has its own hot tub. The Rooftop Room has a two-person jetted spa on its outdoor deck and the Skyline Room a two-person jetted tub/shower in the bath.

Located in the Clements Historic District, the Queen Anne borders downtown Denver and is within easy walking distance of the State Capitol, 16th Street Mall, Convention Center, restaurants, theaters, and office buildings. Continental breakfast includes coffee, juice, fresh fruit, hot scones, granola, muffins, and a hot entree. Neither smoking nor pets are allowed.

Victoria Oaks Inn. 1575 Race St., Denver, CO 80206. ☎ **800/662-6257** or 303/355-1818. 9 rooms (7 with bath). A/C TEL. $55–$85 double. Rates include continental breakfast. AE, CB, DC, DISC, MC, V.

A European-style bed-and-breakfast, this circa-1896 Victorian home with handsome oak floors and leaded-glass windows is in fact a favorite of European travelers. This centrally located inn provides a continental breakfast of fruit, Danish, muffins, cereals, coffee, tea, and juice. Guests have kitchen and laundry privileges.

CAMPING

Chatfield State Park. 11500 N. Roxborough Park Rd., Littleton, CO 80125. ☎ **800/678-2267** for state park reservation service, or 303/791-7275. 193 sites. $7–$10, plus $3 day-use fee. MC, V only for advance reservations.

On the south side of Denver, 1 mile south of the intersection of Colo. 121 (Wadsworth) and Colo. 470, Chatfield offers a 1,550-acre reservoir that provides ample opportunities for boating, waterskiing, fishing, and swimming, plus 24 miles of horseback riding trails, mountain biking, and hiking. There are hot showers, picnic areas, a dump station, boat ramps and rentals, and electric hookups.

Delux R.V. Park. 5520 N. Federal Blvd., Denver, CO 80221. ☎ **303/433-0452.** 29 sites. $18 and up. MC, V.

This campground, with shaded sites, hot showers, laundry, and full hookups, provides the best Denver location for travelers who take their homes with them. It's convenient to buses (no. 31 RTD), shopping, and recreational facilities. Open year-round, the campground is located five blocks north of I-70 Exit 272, and two blocks south of I-76 Exit 3, on the east side of Federal Boulevard.

4 Dining

Denver has been inundated with chain and franchise eateries—mostly family restaurants—where the food is reliably good, but never great. The restaurants we've listed here are independently owned, unique to this area, and a cut above others in price range. The price categories can be defined as follows: **very expensive,** most dinner main courses are priced above $20; **expensive,** most dinner main courses are $15 to $20; **moderate,** dinner main courses run about $10 to $15; **inexpensive,** dinner main courses are generally under $10.

DOWNTOWN
VERY EXPENSIVE

The Broker Restaurant. 821 17th St. (near Champa St.) ☎ **303/292-5065.** Reservations recommended. Main courses $9–$16 at lunch, $18–$34 at dinner. AE, CB, DC, DISC, MC, V. Mon–Fri 11am–2:30pm; daily 5–11pm. STEAK/SEAFOOD.

The historic Denver National Bank building is the site of the Broker, with its circular 23-ton door still in place. Patrons sit in cherry-wood booths once used by bank customers to inspect safe-deposit boxes, and historic photos of Denver line the walls. Famous for its generous portions, the Broker's house favorites include New York and porterhouse steaks, beef Wellington, prime rib, Rocky Mountain trout, rack of lamb, roast duck, Alaskan king-crab legs, and blackened catfish. For vegetarians there is the vegetarian pasta medley. A large bowl of shrimp is served with all meals.

Buckhorn Exchange. 1000 Osage St. (at W. 10th Ave.) ☎ **303/534-9505.** Reservations recommended. Main courses $6.50–$14 at lunch, $17–$39 at dinner. AE, CB, DC, DISC, MC, V. Mon–Fri 11:30am–2pm; Sun–Thurs 5:30–10:30pm, Fri–Sat 5:30–11pm. ROCKY MOUNTAIN.

Thanks to Denver's new Light Rail system, this restaurant is just minutes from the 16th Street Mall, the Convention Center, and all downtown hotels. Still occupying the same premises since it was founded in 1893, the restaurant displays its Colorado Liquor License No. 1 over the 138-year-old hand-carved oak bar in the upstairs Victorian parlor and saloon. Try the Buckhorn's Rocky Mountain oysters, alligator tail, or smoked buffalo sausage for starters; then choose from among slow-roasted buffalo prime rib, lean and served medium rare, or elk or beef steaks. For dessert you might try the chocolate "moose."

☼ Cliff Young's. 700 E. 17th Ave. ☎ **303/831-8900.** Reservations recommended. Main courses $8–$16 at lunch, $20–$33 at dinner. AE, CB, DC, DISC, MC, V. Mon–Fri 11:30am–2pm; daily 6–9:30pm. NEW AMERICAN.

Cliff Young's is sophisticated but not pretentious—the ultimate upscale bistro. The dining room is spacious, elegant, and dimly lit, with a classical pianist playing nightly, joined by a violinist Wednesday through Sunday. The menu, which changes seasonally, includes seafood, game, and regional specialties. Typical dishes include rack of lamb with apricot mustard, filet mignon, or Atlantic salmon with a saffron scented tomato ragout. More than 300 wines are available in the wine cellar, and there is cigar service in the bar.

Palace Arms. In the Brown Palace Hotel, 321 17th St. ☎ **303/297-3111.** Reservations recommended. Jacket and tie required at dinner. Main courses $7.75–$16 at lunch, $20–$35 at dinner. AE, CB, DC, DISC, JCB, MC, V. Mon–Fri 11:30am–2pm; daily 6–10pm. INTERNATIONAL.

Despite a dramatic Napoleonic decor—antiques dating from 1670 include a dispatch case and a pair of dueling pistols that may have belonged to Napoleon—the cuisine is a combination of traditional American, new American, classical French, and southwestern. The fresh lobster enchilada, the Scottish smoked salmon, and smoked duck

Denver Dining

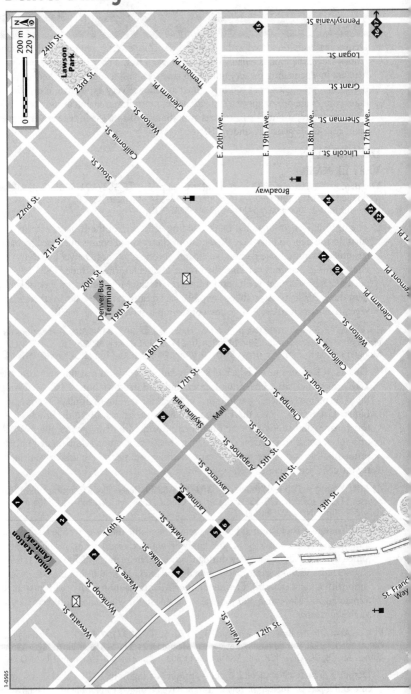

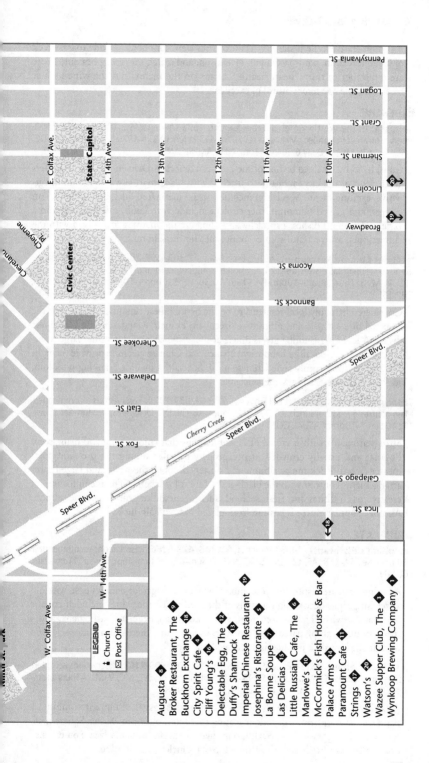

LEGEND

✝ Church
⊠ Post Office

Augusta ⑧
Broker Restaurant, The ⑨
Buckhorn Exchange ⑱
City Spirit Cafe ④
Cliff Young's ⑯
Delectable Egg, The ⑫
Duffy's Shamrock ⑬
Imperial Chinese Restaurant ⑲
Josephina's Ristorante ⑤
La Bonne Soupe ⑦
Las Delicias ⑮
Little Russian Cafe, The ⑥
Marlowe's ⑩
McCormick's Fish House & Bar ②
Palace Arms ⑭
Paramount Cafe ⑪
Strings ⑰
Watson's ⑳
Wazee Supper Club, The ③
Wynkoop Brewing Company ①

75

consommé are excellent starters. Main courses we recommend include roasted rack of Colorado lamb, pan-roasted loin of venison, and seared breast of pheasant. There are a number of tasty "heart healthy" items on the menu, and the wine list has received *Wine Spectator*'s award of excellence.

EXPENSIVE

Augusta. In the Westin Hotel at Tabor Center, 1672 Lawrence St. ☎ **303/572-9100.** Reservations recommended. Main courses $6.50–$13 at lunch, $11–$27 at dinner. AE, CB, DC, DISC, ER, JCB, MC, V. Daily 6:30am–11pm. NEW AMERICAN.

Considered by locals to be one of the best restaurants in Denver, the Augusta offers great views of the city, an art deco interior with black-marble walls, and an imaginative, exciting menu. Specialties include roasted marinated duck breast, tenderloin of beef, and grilled salmon. Other choices include veal, lamb, quail, pastas, and a variety of seafood dishes. Especially appealing are the many sauces served with the entrees, such as sweet-and-sour coconut sauce on the salmon.

Imperial Chinese Restaurant. 431 S. Broadway. ☎ **303/698-2800.** Reservations recommended. Individual dishes $8–$28. Complete multicourse dinners $15–$25. AE, CB, DC, MC, V. Mon–Thurs 11am–10pm, Fri 11am–10:30pm, Sat noon–10:30pm, Sun 4–10pm. CHINESE.

Considered by many local residents to be the best Chinese restaurant in Denver, the Imperial offers classic and innovative Szechuan, Hunan, Mandarin, and Cantonese dishes. A laughing Buddha greets diners at the entrance, and two rather large tropical fish tanks, an exquisite hand-carved panel, and Chinese ceramics provide the right atmosphere for a family-style Chinese meal. Specialties include Nanking pork loin, seafood bird's nest, and sesame chicken.

Strings. 1700 Humboldt St. (at E. 17th Ave.). ☎ **303/831-7310.** Reservations recommended. Main courses $7–$12 at lunch, $11–$21 at dinner. AE, CB, DC, DISC, MC, V. Mon–Sat 11am–11pm, Sun 5–10pm. CASUAL CONTEMPORARY.

Strings attracts a with-it crowd of 20-somethings that enjoy seeing and being seen. Popular and usually crowded, it is especially popular among the pre- and post-theater crowd. Rock music albums and posters decorate the walls, and large flower arrangements contrast with the black-and-white color scheme. The menu focuses on creative pasta dishes and fresh seafood, such as mesquite-grilled Atlantic salmon. Another popular entree is passion fruit–glazed roasted half duck.

MODERATE

Josephina's Ristorante. 1433 Larimer St. ☎ **303/623-0166.** Reservations recommended. Main courses $4–$18. AE, CB, DC, DISC, MC, V. Sun–Thurs 11am–1am, Fri–Sat 11am–2am. ITALIAN.

A Larimer Square institution, Josephina's invokes nostalgia for decades past, with old advertising signs decorating the walls of the bar. House specialties include fettucine Josephina's (with chicken, tomatoes, and wine sauce), eggplant parmigiana, and a specialty pizza, all prepared with northern Italian flair. There's also a nice selection of seafood. Live rock or blues is performed nightly.

✪ La Bonne Soupe. 1512 Larimer St. (Writer Sq.). ☎ **303/595-9169.** Reservations accepted. Main courses $5.95–$9.95 at lunch, $7.95–$18.95 at dinner. AE, DC, MC, V. Mon–Thurs 11am–10pm, Fri–Sat 11am–11pm, Sun 11:30am–9:30pm. FRENCH.

A faithful replica of a French sidewalk bistro, this casual restaurant combines a patio cafe atmosphere with indoor seating that looks out onto Writer Square mall. As the name suggests, the specialty soups here are meals in themselves. You can also order exotic sandwiches, fresh fish, beef, pasta, omelets, and fondue.

🧒 Family-Friendly Restaurants

Casa Bonita *(see p. 80)*   If the kids' attention isn't on the tacos, they'll be enthralled by puppet shows, high divers, a fun house, and a video arcade.

White Fence Farm *(see p. 80)*   Meals are served family-style, with Mom or Dad doling out the vegetables, but the best part is outside with the live farm animals and playground.

The Little Russian Cafe. 1424H Larimer St. ☎ **303/595-8600.** Lunch approximately $6.50, dinner $10–$15. AE, CB, DC, DISC, MC, V. Mon–Thurs 11:30am–2:30pm and 5:30–9:30pm; Fri 11:30am–10:30pm; Sat–Sun 5–10:30pm. RUSSIAN.

This quiet, charming cafe combines old-world atmosphere with authentic Russian cuisine. Russian paintings and posters decorate the dimly lit dining room; there's also an outdoor patio. In the Russian tradition you can, if you wish, begin your meal with a shot of ice-cold vodka and a bowl of borscht. Main dishes include beef Stroganoff, goulash, stuffed cabbage, lamb, and a variety of traditional Russian selections.

Marlowe's. 511 16th St. (at Glenarm St.) ☎ **303/595-3700.** Reservations recommended. Main courses $6.95–$10.95 at lunch, $8.95–$24.95 at dinner. AE, DC, MC, V. Mon–Thurs 11am–11pm, Fri 11am–midnight, Sat 5pm–midnight. STEAK/SEAFOOD.

This popular eatery and saloon occupies a corner of the 1891 Kittredge Building (listed in the National Register of Historic Places) and boasts an antique cherry-wood bar, granite pillars, and brass rails. It's a great spot for drinks and appetizers, especially in warm weather, when tables are set up outside. House specialties include a 20-ounce porterhouse steak, chicken marsala, almond crusted salmon, and live Maine lobster. There are also pasta platters, and several "heart healthy" choices.

McCormick's Fish House & Bar. In the Oxford Hotel, 1659 Wazee St. ☎ **303/825-1107.** Reservations recommended. Lunch and light dishes $4–$15; dinner $9–$24. AE, CB, DC, DISC, MC, V. Mon–Fri 6:30–10am and 11am–2pm; Sun–Thurs 5–10pm, Fri–Sat 5–11pm; Sat–Sun 7am–2pm. SEAFOOD.

Operating out of lower downtown's restored Oxford Hotel, McCormick's maintains a turn-of-the-century feel with stained-glass windows, oak booths, and a fine polished-wood bar. Seafood, which is flown in fresh daily, might include Dungeness crab from the Pacific Northwest, mussels from Maine, fresh yellowfin tuna from Hawaii, swordfish from California, rockfish from Oregon, and trout from Idaho. The menu also offers pasta, chicken, and a full line of certified Angus beef.

Wynkoop Brewing Company. 1634 18th St. (at Wynkoop St.) ☎ **303/297-2700.** Reservations required for large parties. Lunch $4–$7; dinner $5–$16. AE, CB, DC, DISC, MC, V. Mon–Sat 11am–midnight; Sun 10am–10pm. REGIONAL AMERICAN/PUB.

When the Wynkoop opened its doors in 1988 as Denver's first new brewery in more than 50 years, it started a minirevolution: since then, about 50 microbreweries have opened in Colorado. Wynkoop is located in a renovated warehouse across from Union Station and close to Coors Field. The menu offers pub fare, sandwiches, and pasta with a regional flair, for example, elk medallions, brewer's burger, and Pojoaque Valley green chile stew.

INEXPENSIVE

City Spirit Cafe. 1434 Blake St. ☎ **303/575-0022.** Reservations not accepted. Menu items $5–$7. AE, CB, DC, DISC, MC, V. Mon–Thurs 11am–midnight, Fri–Sat 11am–2am. ECLECTIC/VEGETARIAN.

This casual, friendly restaurant offers an unusual blend of Mexican, Mediterranean, Far Eastern, and American sandwiches, salads, main dishes, and pizza. Menu items include a home-style lamb sandwich, turkey and Swiss cheese sandwich, an organic tamale, vegetarian green chile, various pasta dishes, and Asian noodles with beef, shaved vegetables, and spices. There are various coffees and pastries, and a full bar.

⑤ The Delectable Egg. 1642 Market St. ☎ **303/572-8146.** Menu items $3–$6.25. AE, DC, DISC, MC, V. Daily 7am–2pm. AMERICAN.

Every city should have a cafe like this: more than 2 dozen egg dishes, pancakes, waffles, and French toast . . . plus, for the lunch crowd, a variety of salads and sandwiches. You can order eggs skillet-fried, baked in a frittata, scrambled into pita pockets, or smothered with chile or hollandaise. As a beverage, choose plain coffee, a latte, or an espresso.

Another Delectable Egg can be found at 1625 Court Place (☎ 303/892-5720).

✪ Duffy's Shamrock. 1635 Court Place. ☎ **303/534-4935.** Breakfast $1.75–$4.50; lunch $4–$7; dinner $5–$12. AE, CB, DC, MC, V. Daily 7am–1:30am. AMERICAN.

This traditional Irish bar and restaurant with fast, cheerful service has been thriving since the late 1950s. It specializes in Irish coffees and imported Irish beers. Daily specials may include prime rib, barbecued beef, fried prawns, or liver and onions. Sandwiches on practically every kind of bread include: corned beef, Reuben, Braunschweiger, and even a Dagwood.

Las Delicias. 439 E. 19th Ave. (at Pennsylvania St.) ☎ **303/839-5675.** Main courses $3–$9. AE, DISC, MC, V. Mon–Sat 8am–9pm, Sun 9am–9pm. MEXICAN.

Las Delicias, comprised of half a dozen red-brick-walled rooms, is known for its extensive menu of traditional Mexican dishes. Tamales, burritos, tacos, and fajitas are offered, along with generous portions of carne asada and carne de puerco adovado. Lots of fresh hot tortillas, chips, and salsa accompany each meal.

Paramount Cafe. 511 16th St. ☎ **303/893-2000.** Menu items $2.95–$7.95. AE, DC, DISC, MC, V. Mon–Thurs 11am–1am, Fri–Sat 11am–2am. AMERICAN.

Housed in the restored lobby of Denver's historic Paramount Theatre on the 16th Street Mall, this restaurant is popular, lively, and a bit noisy, with the jukebox playing both oldies and current pop music. In the pool room there are five tables plus darts and satellite trivia; outdoor seating is on the mall. The menu features exotic subs, half-pound burgers, numerous sandwiches, large salads, and Tex-Mex fare. Leave room for the margarita pie.

Watson's. 900 Lincoln St. ☎ **303/837-1366.** Menu items $2.25–$4.95. AE, DISC, MC, V. Mon–Thurs 8am–10pm, Fri 8am–11pm, Sat 10am–11pm. AMERICAN.

Established in 1951 as a soda fountain and pharmacy, Watson's evokes memories of that era. The walls are decorated with framed *Life* magazine covers and old-fashioned Coca-Cola advertising; water is served in conical paper cups, and the hand-dipped shakes and malts come with the "leftovers" in stainless steel mixers. Watson's specializes in such traditional American dishes as meat loaf and foot-long chile cheese dogs, together with a variety of sandwiches and daily lunch specials. About 200 microbrew beers are available for carry-out, and you can choose from among 1,200 different postcards! The full-service pharmacy is still in business, and there's an in-store U.S. Post Office; as you might expect, the jukebox plays hits of the 1940s and 1950s.

The Wazee Supper Club. 1600 15th St. (at Wazee St.) ☎ **303/623-9518.** Menu items $3.50–$7.95 (large pizzas cost more). AE, MC, V. Mon–Sat 11am–2am. PIZZA/SANDWICHES.

A former plumbing-supply store in lower downtown, the Wazee is a Depression-era relic with a black-and-white tile floor and a bleached mahogany back bar. A hangout for jazz and pizza lovers (some people believe the pizza here is the best in town), it also serves an array of sandwiches from kielbasa to corned beef, plus buffalo burgers. There are about a dozen draft beers. Don't miss the dumbwaiter used to shuttle food and drinks to the mezzanine floor—it's a converted 1937 garage-door opener.

OUTSIDE DOWNTOWN
VERY EXPENSIVE

Tuscany Restaurant. In Loews Giorgio Hotel, 4150 E. Mississippi Ave. ☎ **303/782-9300.** Reservations recommended. Main courses $8–$17 at lunch, $15–$26 at dinner. AE, CB, DC, DISC, MC, V. Mon–Sat 6:30–10:30am and 11am–2pm, Sunday 7–10am and 11am–2pm; daily 6–10:30pm. ITALIAN.

Under the creative eye of Tim Fields (one of Colorado's top chefs), the Tuscany has become one of Denver's premier restaurants. The elegant but comfortable dining room, which reflects the hotel's Italian theme, is decorated with a polished marble fireplace, fresh-cut flowers, and fine art. The food, which has tremendous visual and taste appeal, is Italian (or Italian style), and the service is excellent.

Breakfast includes a variety of egg dishes, pancakes, and waffles. On the lunch menu you'll find innovative sandwiches such as spicy chicken with grilled eggplant, and entrees such as grilled salmon. Dinner main dishes might include herb and goat cheese–crusted lamb chops or pepper-crusted tuna. A daily special might feature roast loin of rabbit with garlic potatoes.

EXPENSIVE

✪ **The Fort.** 19192 Colo. 8 (off W. Hampden Ave.—U.S. 285), Morrison. ☎ **303/697-4771.** Reservations recommended. Main courses $13.95–$34.95. AE, CB, DC, DISC, MC, V. Mon–Fri 5–10pm, Sat 5–11pm, Sun 5–8pm. Special holiday hours. ROCKY MOUNTAIN.

There are several reasons to drive the 18 miles southwest from downtown Denver to visit the Fort. First is the atmosphere: The building is a full-scale reproduction of Bent's Fort, Colorado's first fur-trading post, hand-built of adobe bricks in 1962. The interior is equally authentic, and the staff are dressed as 19th-century Cheyenne. A second reason is the owner Sam Arnold, a broadcast personality and master chef who opens champagne bottles with a tomahawk. He's had the menu translated into French, German, Spanish, Japanese, and braille.

The third (and best) reason to go is the food. The Fort built its reputation on high-quality, low-cholesterol buffalo, of which it claims to serve the largest variety and greatest quantity of any restaurant in the world. There's buffalo steak, buffalo tongue, broiled buffalo marrow bones, and even "buffalo eggs"—hard-boiled quail eggs wrapped in buffalo sausage. Other house specialties include Taos trout, broiled with fresh mint and orange marmalade; "The Bowl of the Wife of Kit Carson," a spicy-hot chicken stew; charbroiled quail; and elk medallions with wild huckleberry sauce. Diehards can get beefsteak.

MODERATE

Trail Dust Steak House. 7101 S. Clinton St., Tech Center, Englewood. ☎ **303/790-2420.** Reservations accepted for large groups only. Lunch $5–$15; dinner $8–$22. AE, CB, DC, DISC, MC, V. Mon–Fri 11am–2pm; Mon–Thurs 5–10pm, Fri 5pm–midnight, Sat 4pm–midnight, Sun noon–10pm. STEAK.

Country music lovers flock to the Trail Dust, which serves up live dance music along with mesquite-grilled steaks and ribs. Steaks range in size from 9 to 50 ounces; they are accompanied by salad, beans, and bread. Chicken and fish are also available. The

decor is made up of necktie tips, interspersed with large photos of Hollywood western villains and heroes.

To reach the Trail Dust, exit I-25 south at Arapahoe Road, drive one block east,
and turn onto Clinton Street. There's a second Trail Dust at the north end of
Denver: 9101 Benton St., Westminster (☎ 303/427-1446), next to the Westminster
Mall.

White Fence Farm. 6263 W. Jewell Ave., Lakewood. ☎ **303/935-5945.** Reservations
accepted for parties of 15 or more. Meals $10–$18. DISC, MC, V. Tues–Sat 5–9pm, Sun noon–
8pm. Closed January. AMERICAN.

Locals come here for the family-style fried-chicken dinners—a delicately fried half
chicken per person plus heaping bowls of potatoes, corn fritters, homemade gravy,
coleslaw, cottage cheese, pickled beets, and bean salad. Also available are T-bone
steaks, deep-fried shrimp, broiled whitefish fillet, and liver and onions. For dessert,
there are freshly baked pies. A children's menu is available, not to mention a
children's playground, farm animals, carriage rides, and a country store, all in a
beautiful country setting 20 minutes from downtown Denver.

INEXPENSIVE

Casa Bonita. In the JCRS Shopping Center, 6715 W. Colfax Ave., Lakewood. ☎ **303/
232-5115.** Reservations accepted for parties of 25 or more. Lunch or dinner $5.50–$8.50.
AE, CB, DC, DISC, MC, V. Daily 11am–9:30pm. MEXICAN/AMERICAN.

A west Denver landmark, Casa Bonita is more of a theme park than a restaurant. A
pink Spanish cathedral-type bell tower greets visitors, who will discover nonstop
action inside: divers plummeting into a pool beside a 30-foot waterfall, puppet shows,
a video arcade, fun house, and strolling mariachi bands. Food is served cafeteria
style—quite an undertaking for a restaurant that seats 1,100! There's standard Mexican fare—enchiladas, tacos, and fajitas—along with country-fried steak and fried
chicken. Hot sopaipillas, served with honey at your table, are included with each
meal.

⑤ Healthy Habits. 865 S. Colorado Blvd. ☎ **303/733-2105.** Lunch $5.50–$6.60, dinner
$6.50–$7.60. AE, DC, DISC, MC, V. Daily 11am–9pm. AMERICAN.

This award-winning cafeteria-style restaurant offers what may be Denver's best deal
for salad and pasta. The 70-item salad bar displays everything you'd expect and more,
including fresh fruit and a variety of pasta salads. A separate pasta bar offers a variety of pastas, fresh sauces, and pizza. The all-you-can-eat price includes fresh-baked
desserts. Beverages, including beer and wine, are extra. Additional Healthy Habits
restaurants can be found at 7418 S. University Blvd., Littleton (☎ 303/740-7044);
14195 W. Colfax Ave., Golden (☎ 303/277-9293); and 4760 Baseline Rd., Boulder (☎ 303/494-9177).

T-Wa Inn. 555 S. Federal Blvd. (near W. Virginia Ave.) ☎ **303/922-4584.** Lunch $4.50–$7.50;
dinner $5–$14. AE, CB, DC, DISC, MC, V. Daily 11am–10pm. VIETNAMESE.

Denver's first Vietnamese restaurant is still its best. The decor is simple but pleasant,
with Viet folk songs providing atmospheric background. Try the egg rolls, with
shrimp and crabmeat wrapped in rice paper; hearty meat-and-noodle soups; chicken
salad; or soft-shell crab.

What to See & Do
in Denver

7

An intriguing combination of modern American city and sprawling Old West town, Denver offers a wide variety of attractions, activities, and events. There is art, history, sports, recreation, and shopping, so it would be easy to spend a week here and never be bored. It's also a convenient base for side trips to Boulder, Colorado Springs, or up into the mountains.

1 Attractions

THE TOP ATTRACTIONS

Denver Art Museum. 100 W. 14th Ave. (at Civic Center Park). ☎ **303/640-4433.** Admission $3 adults, $1.50 students and seniors, children under 6 free; free for everyone Sat. Tues–Sat 10am–5pm, Sun noon–5pm. Bus: 7, 8, 50.

Founded in 1893, this 7-story museum is wrapped by a thin 28-sided wall faced with 1 million sparkling tiles designed by Gio Ponti of Italy and James Sudler Associates of Denver. Inside is the largest and oldest collection of Native American art of any museum in the United States, as well as a large collection of western and American art.

The Native American collection consists of more than 17,000 pieces from 150 tribes of North America, spanning nearly 2,000 years. The collection is growing not only through the acquisition of historic pieces, but by the commissioning of works by contemporary artists.

Other collections include African, Asian, oceanic, New World (pre-Columbian artifacts and Spanish colonial arts), painting and sculpture (featuring American and western art and a small collection of European art), and modern and contemporary art. A relatively new exhibit, "Architecture, Design & Graphics," ranks as one of the largest modern design galleries in the United States.

Overview tours are available (Tues–Sun at 1:30pm, plus 11am on Sat), and child-oriented educational activities are offered in a program called "Saturdays for Families." The Museum Shop sells replicas of art treasures and books on art and southwestern lore.

✪ **Denver Museum of Natural History.** City Park, 2001 Colorado Blvd. ☎ **800/925-2250** or 303/322-7009; 303/370-8257 for the hearing impaired. Admission to museum, $4.50 adults, $2.50 children 4–12 and seniors 65 and older; IMAX, $5 adults, $4 children and seniors; planetarium, $3.50

adults, $2.50 children and seniors; group rates available. Sat–Thurs 9am–5pm, Fri 9am–9pm. Closed Christmas Day. Bus: 24, 32, 40.

This rambling three-story museum is the fifth-largest natural history museum in the United States. Exquisitely fashioned human and animal figures in more than 90 dioramas depict the history of life on earth on four continents. There are displays on ancient old-world cultures, prehistoric American peoples, Colorado wildlife, North American bears and sea life, and Australian ecology. There are also rooms displaying artifacts of early Native American tribes from Alaska to Florida, and exhibits of South American wildlife and the habitats of Botswana, including a spectacular savannah diorama called "The Watering Hole."

In October 1995, the museum opened its most ambitious exhibit to date: the "Prehistoric Journey," which attempts to depict the history of life on earth through 3.5 billion years. Fossils, interactive exhibits, and dioramas of ancient ecologies make this the museum's most popular attraction, especially enticing for children.

The museum's **IMAX Theater** (☎ **303/370-6300**) presents science, nature, or technology-oriented films with sense-surround sound on a screen that measures $4^1/_2$ by $6^1/_2$ *stories;* and the **Charles C. Gates Planetarium** (☎ **303/370-6487**) schedules frequent multimedia star programs and laser light shows.

✪ **United States Mint.** 320 W. Colfax Ave. (between Cherokee and Delaware streets). ☎ **303/844-3582** or 303/844-3331. Free admission. Tickets available at the booth next to the visitors entrance on Cherokee St. Mon–Fri, 8am–2:45pm; tours every 10–20 min. depending on visitor volume. Reservations not accepted; June–Labor Day expect a 40–45 min. wait. Closed 2 weeks in summer for audit, call for exact date. Cultural Connection Trolley. Bus: 7.

Opened in 1863, the Mint originally melted gold dust and nuggets into bars. In 1904 the office moved to this site, and 2 years later began making gold and silver coins. Copper pennies were added a few years later. The last silver dollars (containing 90% silver) were coined in 1935. In 1970 all silver was eliminated from dollars and half dollars (today they're made of a copper-nickel alloy). The Denver Mint stamps more than 5 billion coins a year, and each has a small *D* on it.

Video monitors along the visitors' gallery through the mint provide a close view of the actual coin-minting process, and new displays are frequently being added. A shop at the end of the tour offers a variety of souvenirs.

✪ **Colorado State Capitol.** Broadway and E. Colfax Ave. ☎ **303/866-2604.** Free admission. 30-minute tours are offered year-round (more frequently in summer), Mon–Fri 9:30am–2:45pm (the dome is locked at 3:30pm). Bus: 2, 7, 8, 12, 15.

Built to last 1,000 years, the capitol was constructed in 1886 of granite from a Colorado quarry. The dome, which rises 272 feet above the ground, was first sheathed in copper, but it was replaced with 200 ounces of gold after a public outcry: Copper was not a Colorado product.

Murals depicting the history of water in the state adorn the walls of the first-floor rotunda, which offers a splendid view upward to the underside of the dome. The rotunda resembles the layout of the national Capitol in Washington, D.C. South of the rotunda is the governor's office, paneled in walnut and lighted by a massive chandelier.

On the first floor, the west lobby has a display case of dolls wearing ball gowns— miniature versions of those worn by various governors' wives. To the right of the main lobby is the governor's reception room. The second floor has main entrances to the House, Senate, and old Supreme Court chambers. Entrances to the public and visitor galleries for the House and Senate are on the third floor. The Colorado Hall of Fame is located near the top of the dome, with stained-glass portraits of Colorado pioneers; on clear days, the views from the dome are spectacular. Capitol memorabilia are available for purchase at the tour guide desk.

Larimer Square. 1400 block of Larimer St. ☎ **303/534-2367** or 303/446-9381 for the information booth. Bus: 2, 12, 15.

This is where Denver began. Larimer Street between 14th and 15th streets comprised the entire community of Denver City in 1858, with false-fronted stores, hotels, and saloons serving gold-seekers and other pioneers. In the mid-1870s it was the main street of the city and the site of Denver's first post office, bank, theater, and streetcar line. But by the 1930s this part of Larimer Street had deteriorated so much that it had become a "skid row" of pawnshops, gin mills, and flophouses. Plans had been made to raze these structures with a wrecking ball when the entire block was purchased by a group of investors in 1965.

The Larimer Square project became Denver's first major historic-preservation effort. All 16 of the block's commercial buildings, constructed in the 1870s and 1880s, were renovated, providing space for street-level retail shops, restaurants, and nightclubs, as well as upper-story offices. A series of inner courtyards and open spaces was created, and in 1973 Larimer Square was added to the National Register of Historic Places.

A free self-guided walking tour pamphlet is available at the Larimer Square information booth, on the southeast side of Larimer Street near 15th Street. Call for an appointment for a free guided tour.

MORE ATTRACTIONS
HISTORIC BUILDINGS

Byers-Evans House. 1310 Bannock St. (behind the Denver Art Museum). ☎ **303/620-4933.** Admission $3 adults, $2.50 seniors, $1.50 children 6–16, free for children under 6. Tues–Sun 11am–3pm. Closed state holidays. Bus: 8.

This elaborate Victorian home, built in 1883, has been restored to its 1912-to-1924 period, when it was owned by William Gray Evans, son of Colorado's second territorial governor. Guided tours describe the architecture and show a film about the home's early owners. Admission to the Byers-Evans House includes the renovated service wing and carriage house, which now houses the Denver History Museum. Here you will find artifacts relating to early Denver life, from the gold rush to World War II. There are also interactive video displays depicting historical events and issues, facts and figures, biographies of early Denverites, and historic photos.

✪ **Molly Brown House Museum.** 1340 Pennsylvania St. ☎ **303/832-4092.** Admission $5.00 adults, $3.50 seniors over 65, $1.50 children 6–12, free for children under 6. Year-round Tues–Sat 10am–4pm, Sun noon–4pm; June–Aug, also Mon 10am–4pm. Last tour of the day begins at 3:30pm. Closed major holidays. Bus: 2 on Logan St. to E. 13th, then one block east to Pennsylvania.

The property of Historic Denver, Inc., the Molly Brown House was designed by Denver architect William Lang and built in 1889 of Colorado lava stone with sandstone trim. From 1894 to 1932 it was the residence of James and Margaret (Molly) Brown. The "unsinkable" Molly Brown became a national heroine in 1912 when the *Titanic* sank: she took charge of a group of immigrant women in a lifeboat and later raised money for their benefit.

Restored to its 1910 appearance, the Molly Brown House has a large collection of turn-of-the-century furnishings and art objects, many of which had belonged to the Brown family. A carriage house at the rear is also open to visitors.

Downtown Denver Attractions

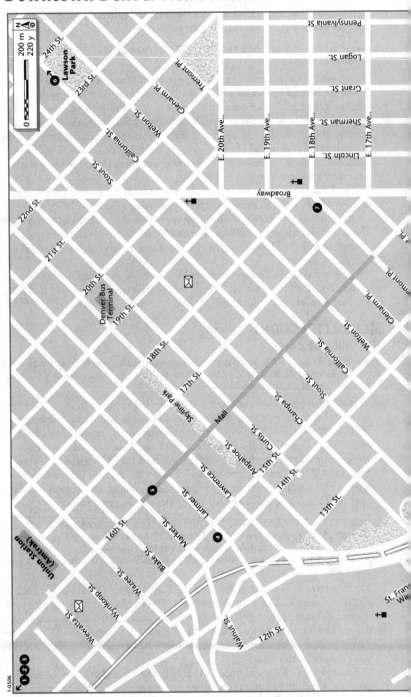

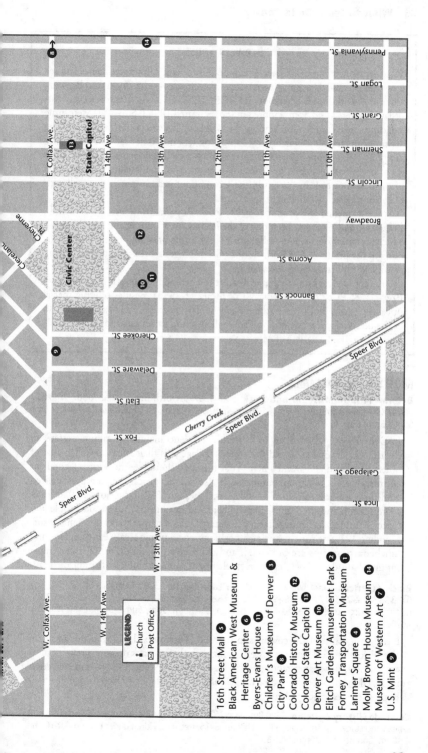

LEGEND
✝ Church
✉ Post Office

16th Street Mall **5**	
Black American West Museum &	
Heritage Center **6**	
Byers-Evans House **11**	
Children's Museum of Denver **3**	
City Park **8**	
Colorado History Museum **12**	
Colorado State Capitol **13**	
Denver Art Museum **10**	
Elitch Gardens Amusement Park **2**	
Forney Transportation Museum **1**	
Larimer Square **4**	
Molly Brown House Museum **14**	
Museum of Western Art **7**	
U.S. Mint **9**	

Brewery Tours

Whether or not you drink beer, it can be fun to look behind the scenes and see how beer is made. Denver's first modern microbrewery—the **Wynkoop Brewing Co.,** 1634 18th St. (at Wynkoop St.) ☎ **303/297-2700**—offers tours every Saturday between 1 and 5pm. Housed in the renovated 1898 J. S. Brown Mercantile Building across from Union Station, the Wynkoop is also a popular restaurant (see "Dining" in chapter 4). Six beers are always on tap; the "taster set" provides a nice sampling—six 4-ounce glasses of different brews. Half gallon and gallon containers of beer are available to go. For non–beer drinkers, the Wynkoop offers some of the best root beer in town. On the second floor is a top-notch pool hall with billiards, snooker, shuffleboard, and darts.

Since it opened in November 1991, **Rock Bottom Brewery,** 1001 16th St. (☎ **303/534-7616**) has been one of the leading brew pubs in the area. Tours—which are given on request—offer great views of the brewing process plus a sampling of the product. The Rock Bottom also has a good brew-pub menu, starting at $6; eight billiards tables are available.

Another Denver brewery that will escort you behind the scenes is the **Broadway Brewery & Pub,** 2441 Broadway (☎ **303/292-2555**). Besides offering special prices on its own house pints, the Broadway Brewery stocks perhaps a dozen or so of the best Colorado microbrews. You will also find calzones, sandwiches, handmade pizzas, and a variety of Mexican dishes.

MUSEUMS & GALLERIES

Belmar Village Museum and Park. 797 S. Wadsworth Blvd., Lakewood. ☎ **303/987-7850.** Free admission. Mon–Fri 10am–4pm, Sat 1–5pm, plus Memorial Day–Labor Day, Sun 1–5pm. Bus: 76.

In Denver's early days, many of its wealthy residents maintained summer estates in the rural Lakewood area, and this historic village tells their story, as well as that of others who lived and worked here. Your first stop should be the Visitor Center for an introduction to the museum; this is also where you can begin a personalized guided or self-guided tour. The village includes an 1880s farm house, 1920s one-room school, and the Barn Gallery. There's an exhibit on "Lakewood People and Places," antique and vintage farm machinery, guided nature walks through the surrounding 127-acre park, changing art exhibits, and a picnic area. Year-round lecture-luncheon programs are presented, and children's programs are scheduled most summer Saturdays. There's also an excellent gift shop with unique handmade items.

Black American West Museum and Heritage Center. 3091 California St. (at 31st St.). ☎ **303/292-2566.** Admission $3 adults, $2 seniors, $1 children 12–17, 50¢ children 3–11, free for children under 3. Wed–Fri 10am–2pm, Sat noon–5pm, Sun 2–5pm. Light Rail stop no. 1.

Nearly one-third of the cowboys in the Old West were blacks, and this museum chronicles their little-known history, along with that of black doctors, teachers, miners, farmers, newspaper reporters, and state legislators. The 35,000-item collection is lodged in the Victorian home of Dr. Justina Ford, the first black woman licensed to practice medicine in Denver.

Colorado History Museum. 1300 Broadway. ☎ **303/866-3682.** Admission $3 adults, $2.50 seniors and students with an ID, $1.50 children 6–16, free for children under 6. Mon–Sat 10am–4:30pm, Sun noon–4:30pm. Bus: 8.

The Colorado Historical Society's permanent exhibits include "The Colorado Chronicle," an 1800-to-1949 time line, incorporating biographical plaques and a remarkable collection of photographs, news clippings, and various paraphernalia from Colorado's past. Dozens of dioramas portray various episodes in state history including an intricate re-creation of 19th-century Denver, and there's a life-size display of early transportation and industry.

The museum hosts traveling exhibits and offers a series of lectures and statewide historical and archaeological tours. Its gift shop is also worth a visit.

Forney Transportation Museum. 1416 Platte St. ☎ **303/433-3643.** Admission $4 adults, $2 teens, $1 children under 12. Mon–Sat 10am–5pm, Sun 11am–5pm; opens an hour earlier in summer Mon–Sat. Take I-25, Exit 211 (23rd Ave.) and go east on Water St. Three-quarters of a mile to Platte St.

More than 100 antique and classic cars and trucks, plus some 350 other exhibits, fill a huge turn-of-the-century building and pour out onto the surrounding grounds. The collection includes a number of one-of-a-kind vehicles, including Amelia Earhart's "Gold Bug" roadster, a Rolls Royce that once belonged to Prince Aly Khan, and a 1909 French taxicab that transported World War I soldiers from Paris to the Battle of the Marne. Other displays include locomotives, wagons, music boxes, historic fashions, farm equipment, and a model train. The museum is housed (mostly) in the former Denver Tramway power building.

✪ **Four Mile Historic Park.** 715 S. Forest St. ☎ **303/399-1859.** Admission $3.50 adults, $2 seniors and children 6–15, children 5 and under free. Apr–Sept, Wed–Sun 10am–4pm; Oct–Mar, Thurs–Sat 11am–3pm. The park is 4 miles southeast of downtown Denver, at South Forest and Exposition Avenue.

The oldest log home (1859) still standing in Denver is the centerpiece of a 14-acre living-history facility. Everything is authentic for the period from 1859 to 1883— including the house (a former stagecoach stop), its furnishings, outbuildings, and farm equipment. There are draft horses and chickens in the barn and crops in the garden. Weekend visitors can enjoy stagecoach rides or observe costumed-volunteers engaged in various chores or crafts, from plowing and blacksmithing to quilting and cooking.

Museum of Western Art. 1727 Tremont Place. ☎ **303/296-1880.** Admission $3 adults, $2 seniors and students, free for children under 7. Tues–Sat 10am–4:30pm. Bus: 20.

This museum occupies a three-story Victorian brick house that was originally Denver's most notorious brothel and gambling casino. Among the more than 125 paintings and sculptures are classic western scenes by Frederic Remington and Charles Russell, as well as landscapes by Albert Bierstadt and Thomas Moran. The gift shop sells hard-to-find art books and prints.

The Turner Museum. 773 Downing St. ☎ **303/832-0924.** Admission $7.50, including a 30-minute personalized tour. Sun–Fri 2–5pm, and by appointment daily. Bus: 2, 12.

The Capitol Hill home of Douglas and Isis Graham houses one of the most outstanding private art collections in the United States. Permanent exhibitions include watercolors and engravings by the impressionist J.M.W. Turner as well as numerous landscapes by Thomas Moran, whose work inspired those who sought to establish the National Park Service. About 3,000 other works of art are exhibited on a revolving basis. There is a museum store, which focuses on items pertaining to J.M.W. Turner.

Open to the public is a dining room, where the Grahams serve three gourmet meals plus a "High Tea" daily (reservations are required), and there are regular classical music recitals.

Wings over the Rockies Air and Space Museum. 1750 E. Irvington Place in Lowry Air Force Base (entrances at Sixth Ave. and Dayton St., Quebec St. and First Ave., and Alameda Ave. between Havana and Monaco streets). ☎ **303/360-5360.** Admission $4 adults, $2 children 6–17 and seniors, free for children under 6. Group rates available. Mon–Sat 10am–4pm, Sun noon–4pm.

When Lowry Air Force Base closed in 1995, the Wings over the Rockies Museum moved into this massive hangar. Fifteen planes are now housed in the cavernous Hangar No. 1, including antique biplanes, a search-and-rescue helicopter, a massive B-1A bomber, and most of the F1 fighter series. Additional exhibits display a world-class World War I uniform collection, a pictorial history of the China-Burma-India Theater of World War II created by the veterans themselves, and the authentic Eisenhower Room—the dining room used by the First Couple when Lowry was nick-named the "Summer White House." New exhibits are planned for 1997. Once a month, the museum hosts "Open Cockpit Day," when children can climb into the planes' cockpits.

NEIGHBORHOODS

Far East Center. Federal Blvd., between W. Alameda and W. Mississippi aves.

Denver's Asian community is concentrated along this strip, which burgeoned in the aftermath of the Vietnam War to accommodate throngs of Southeast Asian refugees, especially Thais and Vietnamese. Look for authentic restaurants, bakeries, groceries, gift shops, and clothing stores. The Far East Center building at Federal and Alameda is built in Japanese pagoda–style.

Five Points. 20th to 38th sts., northeast of downtown.

The "five points" actually meet at 23rd Street and Broadway, but the cultural and commercial hub of Denver's black community covers a much larger area and incorporates four historic districts. Restaurants offer soul food, barbecued ribs, and Caribbean cuisine, while jazz and blues musicians and contemporary dance troupes perform in theaters and nightclubs. The Black American West Museum and Heritage Center is also in this area.

La Alma Lincoln Park/Auraria. Santa Fe Dr., between W. Colfax and W. Sixth aves.

Hispanic culture, art, food, and entertainment predominate along this strip, notable for its southwestern character and architecture. There are numerous restaurants, art galleries, and crafts shops. Denver's annual Cinco de Mayo celebration takes place here each May.

Lower Downtown. Wynkoop St. southeast to Market St. and 20th St. southwest to Speer Blvd.

A 22-block area surrounding Union Station, LoDo boasts numerous National Historic Landmarks and turn-of-the-century warehouses, many of which have been restored to accommodate galleries, shops, cafes, nightclubs, and at least one outstanding hotel (the Oxford Hotel). In addition, the 50,000-seat stadium, Coors Field, home of the Rockies baseball team, opened here in the spring of 1995.

Uptown. Broadway east to York St. (City Park) and 23rd Ave. south to Colfax Ave.

Denver's oldest residential neighborhood is best known today for two things: It's bisected by 17th Avenue's "Restaurant Row" (see "Dining" in chapter 4) and several of its classic Victorian and Queen Anne–style homes have been converted to bed-and-breakfasts (see "Accommodations" in chapter 6).

Parks and Gardens

City Park. E. 17th to E. 26th Ave., between York St. and Colorado Blvd. Free admission for park, although the zoo, museum, golf course, and other sites charge independently. Open 24 hours daily. Bus: 24, 32.

Denver's largest urban park covers 314 acres—96 square blocks—on the east side of Uptown. Established in 1881, and its Victorian touches still evident, it includes two lakes (with boat rentals), athletic fields, jogging and walking trails, playgrounds, tennis courts, picnic areas, and an 18-hole municipal golf course. In summer band concerts are performed in the park. It's also the site of both the Denver Zoo and the Denver Museum of Natural History (plus its planetarium and IMAX Theater).

✪ **Denver Botanic Gardens.** 1005 York St. ☎ **303/331-4000** or 303/331-4010 (24-hour recording). Admission May–Sept, $4 adults, $2 seniors and children 6–15; Oct–Apr, $3 adults, $1.50 seniors, $1 children; free for children under 6. Daily 9am–5pm. Cultural Connection Trolley. Bus: 2, 6, 10.

These outstanding 20-acre outdoor and indoor gardens display plants native to the desert, plains, mountain foothills, and alpine zones; there's also a traditional Japanese garden, scripture garden (relating plants to biblical history), herb garden, home-demonstration garden, water garden, and "wingsong" garden to attract songbirds.

Even in the cold of winter, the dome-shaped, concrete-and-Plexiglas Boettcher Memorial Conservatory houses more than 1,000 species of tropical and subtropical plants. Huge, colorful orchids and bromeliads share space with a collection of plants used for food, fibers, dyes, building materials, and medicines. The Botanic Gardens also include a gift shop, library, and auditorium.

✪ **Denver Mountain Parks.** Department of Parks and Recreation. ☎ **303/697-4545.** Free admission.

Formally established in August 1913, the Mountain Parks system immediately began acquiring land in the mountains near Denver to be set aside for recreational use by the city. Today's 31 mountain parks are great places for hiking, picnicking, bird watching, golfing, or lazing in the grass and sun.

The first and largest, Genesee Park, is 20 miles west of Denver off I-70; on its 2,400 acres can be found the Chief Hosa Lodge and Campground (the only such facility in the system), playgrounds, picnic areas with fireplaces, a softball field, scenic overlook, and an elk and buffalo enclosure. There is also Daniels Park, 23 miles south of Denver via I-25 to Castle Pines Parkway, west to the park, with similar facilities on 1,000 acres; and Dedisse Park, 2 miles west of Evergreen on Colo. 74, which provides picnic facilities; a golf course; facilities for ice-skating, fishing, and volleyball; a restaurant; and clubhouse. Echo Lake Park and Red Rocks Park are discussed later in this chapter (see "A Side Trip to Colorado's Gold Circle Towns").

Denver Zoo. City Park, 23rd Ave. and Steele St. ☎ **303/331-4110.** Admission $6 adults, $4 seniors, $3 children 4–12 (accompanied by an adult), free for children under 4. Summer, daily 9am–6pm; winter, daily 10am–5pm. (Hours change with daylight saving time.) Cultural Connection Trolley. Bus: 24, 32.

Six hundred species of animals (nearly 4,000 individual animals) live in this very spacious zoological park. Feeding times are posted near the zoo entrance so you can time your visit to see the animals at their most active. The Bear Mountain exhibit, when it was built in 1918, was the first animal exhibit in the United States to be constructed of simulated concrete rock-work. At the other end of the time line, Northern Shores (1987) allows underwater viewing of polar bears and sea lions; Tropical Discovery (1994) re-creates an entire tropical ecosystem under glass, complete with crocodiles, piranhas and king cobras, as well as an exhibit of the rare Komodo dragon. Exotic waterfowl inhabit several ponds, and 300 birds live in Bird World, which includes a hummingbird forest and a tropical aviary. The new Primate Panorama is a 5-acre world-class primate exhibit.

The zoo is home to the nation's only natural gas–powered zoo-train. The rubber-tired Zooliner tours all zoo paths from spring through fall. Full meals are served at the Hungry Elephant, a zoo cafeteria with an outdoor eating area. Many visitors bring picnic lunches to eat on the expansive lawns.

Rocky Mountain Arsenal National Wildlife Refuge. Quebec St. and 72nd Ave. ☎ **303/ 289-0467.** Free admission. Daylight hours. Bus: 48.

Once a site where the U.S. Army manufactured chemical weapons (for example, mustard gas and GB nerve agent), and later leased the facilities to a private enterprise for the production of pesticides, the Rocky Mountain Arsenal has become an environmental success story. The 27-square-mile Superfund cleanup site is comprised of open grasslands and wetlands west of DIA. The Arsenal is home to more than 200 species, including deer, coyotes, prairie dogs, and birds of prey. An estimated 100 bald eagles make this one of the largest eagle roosting locales during the winter months.

Visitors are invited to take part in the many programs sponsored by the U.S. Fish and Wildlife Service (for reservations, call 303/289-0232). For a guided tour, it is best to call a week in advance.

ESPECIALLY FOR KIDS

Denver abounds in child-oriented activities, and the listings below will probably appeal to young travelers of any age. In addition, some sights listed in the previous sections may appeal to families as well (the Colorado History Museum; Denver Art Museum; Denver Museum of Natural History; Denver Zoo; Four Mile Historic Park; and the U.S. Mint).

Adventure Golf. 9600 Sheridan Blvd. (at 96th Ave.). ☎ **303/650-7587.** Admission $4.95 adults, $4.45 seniors over 65 and children under 12. Easter–Halloween, Sun–Thurs 10am–10pm, Fri–Sat 10am–11pm, weather permitting. Hours may be shorter in spring and fall. Bus: 51.

Each hole at this 54-hole miniature golf course has a theme (for example, a haunted house, pirate battle, fairy castle, and Dutch windmill), or perhaps you'd prefer to visit The Lost Continent, with "deadly" piranha pools and quicksand pits.

Children's Museum of Denver. 2121 Children's Museum Dr. ☎ **303/433-7444.** Admission $4; $1.50 seniors 60 and over; free for children under 2. Tues–Sun 10am–5pm. Take Exit 211 (23rd Ave.) east off I-25; turn right on Seventh Street, and again on Children's Museum Drive.

This is Denver's best hands-on experience for children, with a computer lab where kids can log onto the Internet. In the Discovery Labs section, they can explore light, sound, electronics, and biology. There's a woodworking shop, TV weather forecasting studio, an exhibit where participants learn what it feels like to have various disabilities, and a gigantic mountain with year-round ski lessons. In another area, kids can examine size relationships by looking at the Denver Nuggets basketball team. Special events such as live theater are scheduled periodically; call for schedules.

Elitch Gardens Amusement Park. Speer Blvd. at I-25, Exit 212. ☎ **800/ELITCHS** or 303/ 595-4FUN. Gate admission with unlimited rides, $19.95 for ages 7–54; $15 for ages 55–69, $9.95 for children 3–6, and free for ages 2 and younger and 70–up. Memorial Day–Labor Day, Sun–Thurs 10am–10pm, Fri–Sat 10am–11pm. Call for off-season events.

A Denver tradition established in 1889, this amusement park moved to its present site in 1995. Close to 2 dozen rides include Twister II, a brand-new wooden roller coaster; Disaster Canyon, a raging river-rapids ride; the 300-foot Total Tower; and the newly renovated 1925 carousel with 67 hand-carved horses. The amusement park also has musical revues and other entertainment, games, food, shopping, a kiddieland, and beautiful flower gardens.

Lakeside Amusement Park. I-70, Exit 271 and Sheridan Blvd. ☎ **303/477-1621.** Gate admission, $1.50; unlimited rides, $9.75 Mon–Fri, $11.25 Sat–Sun and holidays. May: Sat–Sun and holidays noon–11pm; June–Labor Day: Mon–Fri 6–11pm, Sat–Sun and holidays noon–11pm. Call to check on late openings on summer Sats. Kiddie Playland, Mon–Fri 1–10pm, Sat–Sun and holidays noon–10pm. Closed Labor Day–Apr.

Among the largest amusement parks in the Rocky Mountains, Lakeside has close to 30 major rides, including a Cyclone roller coaster, a midway with carnival and arcade games, and a miniature train that circles the lake. There are also food stands and picnic facilities, plus a separate Kiddie Playland with 15 rides.

Water World. 88th Ave. and Pecos St., Federal Heights. ☎ **303/427-SURF.** Admission $16.95 adults, $15.95 children 4–12, free for seniors and children under 4. Memorial Day–Labor Day, daily 10am–6pm. Closed in winter. Take the Thornton exit (84th Avenue) off I-25 north.

This 60-acre complex, billed as America's largest family water park, has two oceanlike wave pools, river rapids for inner-tubing, twisting water slides, a small children's play area, as well as other attractions—32 in all.

WALKING TOUR
Downtown Denver

Start: Denver Information Center, Civic Center Park.
Finish: State Capitol, Civic Center Park.
Time: 2 to 8 hours, depending on how much time you spend shopping, eating, and sightseeing.
Best Times: Any Tuesday through Friday in late spring.

Start your tour of the downtown area at the Denver Information Center of the Denver Metro Convention & Visitors Bureau, opposite Civic Center Park on West Colfax Avenue at 14th Street. After collecting information about the city, cross to:

1. **Civic Center Park,** a two-square-block oasis featuring a Greek amphitheater, fountains, statues, flower gardens, and 30 different species of trees—two of which (it is said) were originally planted by Abraham Lincoln at his Illinois home.

Overlooking the park on its east side is the State Capitol. On its south side are the:

2. **Colorado History Museum,** a staircaselike building with exhibits that make the state's colorful history come to life; the Denver Public Library; and the:

3. **Denver Art Museum.** Designed by Gio Ponti of Milan, Italy, the art museum is a 28-sided, 10-story structure that resembles a medieval fortress with a skin of more than 1 million tiny glass tiles. Inside are 35,000 works of art, including a renowned Native American collection.

On the west side of Civic Center Park is the:

4. **City and County Building,** decorated in spectacular fashion with a rainbow of colored lights during the Christmas season.

A block farther west is the:

5. **U.S. Mint.** Modeled in the Italian Renaissance style, the building resembles the Palazzo Riccardi in Florence. More than 60,000 cubic feet of granite and 1,000 tons of steel went into its construction in 1904.

Cross back over Colfax to the information center, then turn diagonally northwest up 14th Street. Four blocks ahead, on the left, is the:

6. **Colorado Convention Center,** with its impressive, five-story, steplike white facade. Opened in June 1990, the million-square-foot building contains a 7-acre exhibit room and the largest ballroom between Chicago and Los Angeles.

   It's another two blocks up 14th to the:

7. **Denver Center for the Performing Arts,** covering four square blocks between 14th Street and Cherry Creek, and Champa Street and Arapahoe Street. The complex is entered under a block-long, 80-foot-high glass archway. The center includes seven theaters, a symphony hall in the round, a voice-research laboratory, and even a smoking solar fountain. Free tours are offered.

   Two more blocks up 14th past the arts center is:

8. **Larimer Square,** Denver's oldest commercial district. The 18 restored turn-of-the-century Victorian buildings accommodate more than 30 shops and a dozen restaurants and clubs. Colorful awnings, hanging flower baskets, and quiet open courtyards accent the square, once home to such notables as Buffalo Bill Cody and Bat Masterson. Horse-drawn carriage rides originate here for trips up the 16th Street Mall or through lower downtown. A new addition to Larimer Square is the Champion Brewing Company, with its unmistakable "Home Run Chewing Gum" wall mural.

   A walkway at the east corner of Larimer and 15th leads through:

9. **Writer Square,** another shopping-and-dining complex with quaint gas lamps, brick walkways, and outdoor cafes.

   At 16th Street, cross to the:

10. **Tabor Center,** a glass-enclosed shopping complex of 70 shops on three levels. In effect a two-block-long greenhouse (with the Westin Hotel rising from within), the Tabor Center was developed by the Rouse Company, the same firm that created the present-day Faneuil Hall in Boston, South Street Seaport in New York, and Harborplace in Baltimore.

    To the east, the Tabor Center is anchored by the:

11. **D & F Tower,** a city landmark patterned after the campanile of St. Mark's Basilica in Venice, Italy, in 1910. Here, begin a leisurely stroll down the:

12. **16th Street Mall,** with the State Capitol building to the southeast as your directional beacon. The $76-million pedestrian path is the finest people-watching spot in the city, from street entertainers to lunching office workers to travelers like yourself. Built of red and gray granite, it is lined with 200 red oak trees, a dozen fountains, festive banners, and a lighting system straight out of *Star Wars*—not to mention the outdoor cafes, restored Victorian buildings, modern skyscrapers, and hundreds of shops, restaurants, and department stores. Through it run sleek European-built shuttle buses, offering free transportation up and down the mall as often as every 90 seconds.

    You'll walk seven blocks down 16th Street from the Tabor Center before reaching Tremont Place. Turn left, go one block farther, and across the street, on your right, you'll see the:

13. **Brown Palace Hotel.** One of the most beautiful grande dame hotels in the United States, it was built in 1892 and features a nine-story atrium lobby topped by a Tiffany stained-glass ceiling. Step into the lobby for a look before continuing across Broadway on East 17th Avenue. Go two blocks to Sherman Street, turn right, and proceed two blocks south on Sherman to East Colfax Avenue.

Walking Tour—Downtown Denver

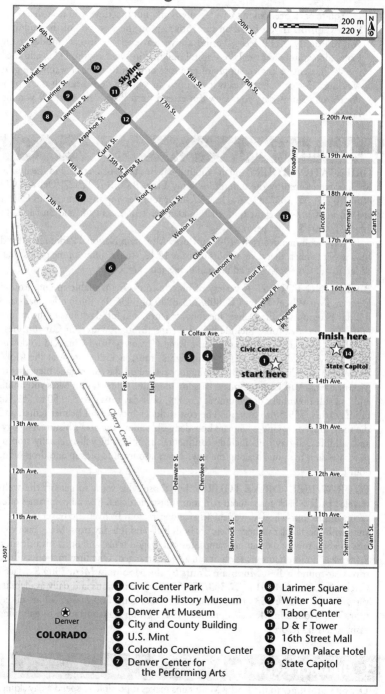

0 ___ 200 m
___ 220 y

N

16th St.
Blake St.
Market St.
Larimer St.
Lawrence St.
Arapahoe St.
Curtis St.
13th St.
14th St.
13th St.
Champa St.
Stout St.
California St.
Welton St.
Glenarm Pl.
Tremont Pl.
Court Pl.
Cleveland Pl.
Cheyenne Pl.
17th St.
18th St.
19th St.
20th St.
Skyline Park
E. 20th Ave.
E. 19th Ave.
E. 18th Ave.
E. 17th Ave.
E. 16th Ave.
Broadway
Lincoln St.
Sherman St.
Grant St.
E. Colfax Ave.
Civic Center
start here
14th Ave.
13th Ave.
12th Ave.
11th Ave.
E. 14th Ave.
E. 13th Ave.
E. 12th Ave.
E. 11th Ave.
Fax St.
Elati St.
Delaware St.
Cherokee St.
Bannock St.
Acoma St.
Broadway
Lincoln St.
Sherman St.
Grant St.
Cherry Creek
finish here
State Capitol

1-0507

Denver
COLORADO

- **1** Civic Center Park
- **2** Colorado History Museum
- **3** Denver Art Museum
- **4** City and County Building
- **5** U.S. Mint
- **6** Colorado Convention Center
- **7** Denver Center for the Performing Arts
- **8** Larimer Square
- **9** Writer Square
- **10** Tabor Center
- **11** D & F Tower
- **12** 16th Street Mall
- **13** Brown Palace Hotel
- **14** State Capitol

93

You're back overlooking Civic Center Park, but this time, you're at the:

14. **State Capitol.** If you stand on the 15th step on the west side of the building, you're exactly 5,280 feet (1 mile) above sea level. Architects modeled the Colorado capitol after the U.S. Capitol building in Washington, D.C., and used the world's entire known supply of rare rose onyx in its interior wainscoting. A winding, 93-step staircase leads to an open-air viewing deck beneath the capitol dome; on a sunny day, your view can extend from Pikes Peak to the Wyoming border.

2　Organized Tours

ORIENTATION TOURS　Half- and full-day bus tours of Denver and the nearby Rockies are offered by the ubiquitous **Gray Line,** P.O. Box 17527, Denver, CO 80217-0527 (☎ **303/289-2841**). A 3¹/₂-hour tour, leaving the Denver Bus Center at 19th and Curtis streets at 2pm, takes in Denver, Red Rocks Park, and Buffalo Bill's Grave. It costs $21 per person.

Highly recommended is the 10-hour Rocky Mountain National Park tour, offered June to September, that takes visitors over the 12,183-foot summit of the park's Trail Ridge Road. Cost is $39 for adults (children's rates are lower).

BICYCLING TOURS　A variety of bicycle tours are available in and around Denver. **Two Wheel Tours** (☎ **800/343-8940** or 303/798-4601) offers half- and full-day bike tours of the Denver metropolitan area, and full-day tours in the mountains. Denver area tours include half-day trips through Waterton Canyon, near Chatfield Reservoir; a ride on the Platte River Greenway from Chatfield to downtown Denver; and a "Denver City Highlights" tour, including stops at the Molly Brown House, City Park, and Washington Park. Full-day tours take bicyclists to Mount Evans, Vail Pass, or Squaw Pass for "downhill" rides (a van takes you uphill and you ride downhill); or to Summit County. Half-day trips cost $39.50 to $59.50; full-day trips, $59.50 to $89.50. The cost includes bicycle and helmet rental, and the tours are led by guides who are knowledgeable about the area's history, geology, and wildlife. All-day trips include continental breakfast; bicyclists usually stop to purchase their own lunch along the way. Tours also include pickup and drop-off at your hotel.

FOUR-WHEEL–DRIVE TOURS　For those who want to get off the well-traveled path, a back-roads mountain tour is just the ticket. Several companies offer excursions in four-wheel–drive vehicles that depart from Denver and travel to remote areas with spectacular scenery; there are both half- and full-day trips. Many take visitors to ghost towns, old mining camps, historic wagon trails, and other historic sites. Star treks on mountaintops at night can also be arranged. One firm that offers these trips year-round is **Best Mountain Tours by the Mountain Men,** 3003 S. Macon Circle, Aurora, CO 80014 (☎ **303/750-5200**). Destinations and daily availability vary. Typical rates are $35 per person for a 5-hour tour, $60 to $65 for an all-day tour. The Mountain Men also provide private group transportation to gambling casinos and ski resorts.

3　Outdoor Activities

Denver's proximity to the Rocky Mountains makes it possible to spend a day skiing, snowmobiling, horseback riding, hiking, river running, sailing, fishing, hunting, mountain climbing, or rockhounding—and return to the city by nightfall. There are more than 200 miles of jogging and bicycle paths, 100 or more free tennis courts, and more than 3 dozen public golf courses.

Campsites are easily reached from Denver, as are suitable sites for hang gliding and hot-air ballooning. Sailing is popular within the city at Sloans Lake and in Washington Park, and the Platte River is clear for many miles of river-running in rafts, kayaks, and canoes.

BALLOONING   You can't beat a hot-air balloon ride for viewing the magnificent Rocky Mountain scenery. **Looney Balloons** (☎ 303/979-9476) offers daily flights year-round, or you might try **Aero-Cruise Balloon Adventures** (☎ **303/469-1243**). **Life Cycle Balloon Adventures, Ltd.** (☎ **303/759-3907**), offers champagne flights for two. Cost is $175 per person for a 1½-hour flight.

BICYCLING   Denver is crisscrossed by paved bicycle paths, including a 12-mile scenic stretch along the bank of the South Platte River and along Cherry Creek beside Speer Boulevard. All told, the city has 85 miles of off-road trails for bikers and runners. Bike paths link the city's 205 parks, and many city streets are marked with bike lanes.

BOATING   Within the Denver city limits, Sloans Lake (West 17th Ave. from Newton St. to Sheridan Blvd.) is a popular spot for punting. Boaters enjoy the powerboat marinas at Cherry Creek State Park, 4201 S. Parker Rd., Aurora (☎ 303/690-1166), 11 miles from downtown off I-225; and Chatfield State Park, 11500 N. Roxborough Park Rd., Littleton (☎ 303/791-7275), 16 miles south of downtown Denver off Colo. 470; as well as the facilities at Barr Lake State Park, 13401 Picadilly Rd., Brighton (☎ 303/659-6005), 21 miles northeast of downtown via I-76. Boats with greater than 10-horsepower motors are not permitted on Barr Lake; boat rentals are not available there.

FISHING   A couple of good bets in the metropolitan area are Chatfield State Park, with trout, bass, and panfish, and Cherry Creek State Park, which boasts trout, walleye pike, bass, and crappie (see "Boating," above).

A number of sporting goods stores can provide further suggestions, including **Uncle Milty's Tackle Box,** 4811 S. Broadway, Englewood (☎ 303/789-3775). Another good source is **Flyfisher Ltd.,** 252 Clayton St. (☎ **303/322-5014**), particularly for recommendations of higher mountain lakes and streams. Flyfisher also offers lessons, seminars, and clinics, plus guided trips. Diehards may want to tune in at 6am Saturday morning for the 1-hour "Uncle Milty's Colorado Outdoors Show," on KHOW, 630 on the AM radio dial.

GOLF   Throughout the Front Range it's often said that you can play golf at least 320 days a year—the sun always seems to be shining, and even when it snows, the little snow that does stick melts quickly. With the resulting demand, the city of Denver operates seven municipal golf courses with greens fees ranging from $7 to $20: the **City Park Golf Course,** East 25th Avenue and York Street (☎ 303/295-4420); **Evergreen Golf Course,** 29614 Upper Bear Creek Rd., Evergreen (☎ 303/674-4128); **Harvard Golf Course** (par 3), E. Iliff Avenue and South Clarkson Street (☎ 303/698-4078); **Kennedy Golf Course,** 10500 E. Hampden Ave. (☎ 303/751-0311); **Mira Vista Golf Course,** First and Havana streets, (☎ 303/340-1520); **Overland Golf Course,** South Santa Fe Drive and W. Jewell Avenue (☎ 303/698-4975); **Wellshire Golf Course,** 3333 S. Colorado Blvd. (☎ 303/692-5636); and **Willis Case Golf Course,** 4999 Vrain St. near West 50th Avenue (☎ 303/458-4877).

For information on resorts and public courses, as well as other golf information, contact the Colorado Golf Association (☎ 303/779-4653).

HIKING/BACKPACKING   In addition to the Colorado Trail, which starts here and continues on to Durango (for tips on hiking it from Denver, call 303/526-0809), Mount Falcon Park offers excellent trails that are easy to moderate in difficulty, making this a good place for families with children. There are also picnic areas, shelters, and ruins of an old castlelike home. From Denver, go west on U.S. 285 and then south on Colo. 8; the park is open daily from dawn to dusk and admission is free. Mountain bikes and horseback riding are permitted, as are dogs on a leash.

Other relatively easy trails near Denver can be found in Roxborough State Park, 10 miles south of Littleton—the 1-mile Willow trail and the $2^1/2$-mile Fountain Valley Trail. Three other trails at Roxborough are more strenuous, but worth the effort if you enjoy beautiful red rocks and wildlife. To get to Roxborough Park, exit Colo. 470 south onto U.S. 85 and turn west on Titan Road, then south again at Roxborough Park Road to the main entrance. Admission is $3 per vehicle and the park is open daily from 8am to 8pm in summer, 8am to 6pm at other times. Dogs, bikes, and horseback riding are not permitted.

HORSEBACK RIDING   Equestrians can find a mount at **Stockton's Plum Creek Stables,** 7479 W. Titan Rd., Littleton (☎ **303/791-1966**), near Chatfield State Park, 15 miles south of downtown. Guided rides, by appointment only, are $15 per hour; children must be at least 8 years old. Stockton's also offers hayrides and barbecue picnics. **Paint Horse Stables,** 4201 S. Parker Rd., Aurora (☎ **303/690-8235**) at Cherry Creek State Park, also rents horses and provides riding lessons.

SKIING   Ski resorts closest to Denver include **Eldora** Mountain Resort, 45 miles west via Boulder (☎ **303/440-8700**); **Loveland** Basin and Valley, 56 miles west via I-70 (☎ **303/569-3203**); and **Winter Park,** 73 miles west via I-70 and U.S. 40 (☎ **303/726-5514**). Eldora and Winter Park boast Nordic as well as alpine terrain.

Some useful Denver telephone numbers for skiers: ski-area information (☎ 303/825-7669), weather report (☎ 303/398-3964), road conditions (☎ 303/639-1111).

TENNIS   The Denver Department of Parks and Recreation (☎ 303/964-2500) manages or owns 145 tennis courts, 60 of them lit for night play. The most popular are in City Park, Berkeley Park, Green Valley Park, Washington Park, and Sloan Lake Park. For more information on tennis, contact the Colorado Tennis Association, 1191 S. Parker Rd., Suite 101, Denver, CO 80231 (☎ 303/695-4116). Many public courts are free, and some charge $5 per hour. It's generally easier to find space at an outlying court than one in downtown Denver.

GREAT NEARBY OUTDOOR AREAS

BARR LAKE STATE PARK   About 25 miles northeast of Denver via I-76 in Brighton, this wildlife sanctuary of 2,500 acres comprises a prairie reservoir and surrounding wetlands. Boats with greater than 10-horsepower motors are not allowed, but you can sail, paddle, or row, as well as fish. A 9-mile hiking and biking trail circles the lake. A boardwalk from the nature center at the south parking lot leads to a good view of a heron rookery, and bird blinds along this trail allow wildlife observation and photography. Three picnic areas provide tables and grills; there's a commercial campground opposite the park. The entrance is at 13401 Picadilly Rd. Admission is $3 per vehicle. Call **303/659-6005** for more information.

CASTLEWOOD CANYON STATE PARK   Steep canyons, a meandering stream, a waterfall, lush vegetation, and considerable wildlife distinguish this 873-acre park. You can see the remains of Castlewood Canyon Dam, which was built for irrigation in 1890; it collapsed in 1933, killing two people. The park, 30 miles south of Denver on Colo. 83, east of Castle Rock in Franktown, provides picnic facilities and hiking trails. The entrance is at 2989 S. State Hwy.; admission is $3 per vehicle. Call **303/688-5242** for more information.

CHATFIELD STATE PARK   Just 8 miles south of downtown Denver via U.S. 85 in Littleton, this park occupies 5,600 acres of prairie against a backdrop of the steeply rising Rocky Mountains. Chatfield Reservoir, with a 26-mile shoreline, invites swimming, boating, fishing, and other water sports. The area also has 18 miles of paved bicycle trails, plus hiking and horseback-riding paths. In winter, there's ice fishing and cross-country skiing.

An observation area on the south side of the park permits you to view a 27-acre nature-study grove; it is closed during nesting season due to the heron population. The park also has a hot-air balloon launch pad.

There are 193 pull-through campsites with showers, laundry, and a dump station. Admission is $3 per vehicle; the camping fee is $7 to $10 daily. The entrance is at 11500 N. Roxborough Park Rd., Littleton (☎ 303/791-7275).

CHERRY CREEK STATE PARK   Because Cherry Creek, the central attraction of the park, used to flood Denver, Cherry Creek Dam was built in 1950. The resulting 880-acre reservoir has become a mecca for 1.5 million visitors a year. Located at the southeast Denver city limits (off Parker Rd. and I-225), the park comprises 3,900 acres.

Water sports include swimming, waterskiing, boating, and fishing. There's a nature trail, dog-training area, model airplane field with paved runways, rifle range, pistol range, and trap-shooting area. Six miles of paved bicycle paths and 10 miles of bridle trails circle the reservoir (horse rentals are available). Rangers offer guided walks on a 1¹/₂-mile nature trail, as well as evening programs in an amphitheater. Winter-sports enthusiasts enjoy skating, ice fishing, and ice boating.

Each of the park's 102 campsites provides showers, laundry, and a dump station, but no water or electric hookups. Many lakeshore sites are supplied with picnic tables and grills.

Admission is $4 per vehicle; the camping fee is $7 to $10 daily. Campgrounds may be closed in winter. The entrance is at 4201 S. Parker Rd. in Aurora. Call 303/690-1166 for general information or **800/678-2267** for camping reservations.

4 Spectator Sports

AUTO RACING   **Bandimere Speedway,** 3051 S. Rooney Rd., Morrison (☎ **303/697-6001,** or 303/697-4870 for a 24-hour recording), is the place to go for drag racing, with races scheduled from April through October. There are special events for high school students, motorcycles, pickup trucks, street cars, and sports cars, plus car shows, swap meets, and even volleyball tournaments.

Colorado National Speedway, at I-25, Exit 232, 20 minutes north of Denver (☎ **303/665-4173**), has NASCAR Winston Racing, superstocks, and RMMRA Midgets on a three-eighths–mile asphalt oval track every Saturday night from April through September.

BASEBALL   The Colorado Rockies, which began life as a National League expansion team in 1993, has taken over the Colorado sports scene with a vengeance. Rockies fever gripped the city in 1995 when the team played the Atlanta Braves in the National League playoffs. The team plays at Coors Field, which opened in the spring of 1995, in the historic lower downtown section of Denver. The 50,000-seat stadium, with its red brick exterior, was designed in the style of baseball stadiums of old. For information and tickets, call **ROCKIES** (☎ **800/388-7625** or 303/762-5437).

BASKETBALL   The Denver Nuggets (☎ 303/893-3865 for ticket information)
of the National Basketball Association play their home games at McNichols Sports
Arena, 1635 Bryant St. (☎ 303/640-7300). There are 41 home games a year between
November and April, with playoffs continuing into June.

The University of Denver (☎ 303/871-2336 for ticket office) plays a competitive college basketball schedule from late November to March, in addition to
women's gymnastics, men's hockey, and other sports.

FOOTBALL   The Denver Broncos (☎ 303/433-7466 for tickets) of the National
Football League make their home at Mile High Stadium, part of a sports complex
reached at Exit 210B of I-25. Tickets go on sale the third week of July, but the home
games are sold-out months in advance, so call early. Your best bet may be to find
someone hawking tickets outside the stadium entrance on game day.

You'll have better luck getting into a college game. The **University of Colorado
Buffaloes** in Boulder play in the Big Eight Conference. For ticket information, call
303/492-8337. Other top college football teams in the area can be found at **Colorado State University** in Fort Collins and at the **Air Force Academy** in Colorado
Springs.

HOCKEY   Denver's new National Hockey League team, the **Colorado Avalanche**
(☎ 303/893-6700 for ticket information), began playing in Denver during the
1995/1996 season, with games at McNichols Arena, 1635 Bryant St.

Coloradans went wild in June 1996 when the Avalanche surprised everyone by
winning the prestigious Stanley Cup, Colorado's first championship win in any major
league sport. The Avalanche had begun its season by beating the highly rated Detroit
Red Wings, and then, led by Most Valuable Player Joe Sakic, demolished the Florida
Panthers to bring the Stanley Cup home to Denver, where they were met by a
screaming throng of 450,000 fans and a ticker-tape parade.

RODEO   The National Western Stock Show and Rodeo (☎ 303/295-1660) is
held the second and third weeks of January at the Denver Coliseum, 46th and
Humboldt, and at the National Western Complex. With more than $400,000 avail-
able in prize money, this is one of the world's richest rodeos.

5 Shopping

THE SHOPPING SCENE

If you're exploring Denver on foot, you'll find the 16th Street Mall and adjacent
areas—including Larimer Square, The Shops at Tabor Center, Writer Square, and
(just slightly farther away) Tivoli Denver—most convenient.

For those with a car, there are more options—primarily the huge Cherry Creek
Shopping Center south of downtown. There are also many suburban shopping malls.

Business hours vary from store to store and from shopping center to shopping
center. In general, it's safe to assume that shops will be open Monday through
Friday from 10am to 9pm, Saturday from 10am to 6pm, and Sunday from noon
to 5pm.

SHOPPING A TO Z
ANTIQUES

Denver's main antiques area is the **1200 block of South Broadway,** between Arizona and Louisiana streets, with some 250 dealers selling all sorts of fine antiques,
collectibles, and junk. It's great fun wandering through the gigantic rooms, where

each dealer has his or her little space. Just remember that prices are often negotiable; unless you're quite knowledgeable about antiques, it wouldn't hurt to do some comparison shopping before making a major purchase. For information, contact the **Antique Guild,** 1298 S. Broadway (☎ **303/722-3358**). You'll find another 90 dealers at **Hampden Street Antique Market,** 8964 E. Hampden Ave. (☎ **303/ 721-7992**).

ARTS & CRAFTS

Camera Obscura. 1309 Bannock St. ☎ **303/623-4059.**

This highly respected photographic gallery exhibits vintage and contemporary photographs, including works by such renowned photographers as Henri Cartier-Bresson and Annie Liebowitz.

Core New Art Space. 1412 Wazee St. ☎ **303/571-4831.**

This lower downtown cooperative gallery features experimental art.

Inkfish Gallery. 949 Broadway. ☎ **303/825-6727.**

This gallery features museum-quality contemporary art in a wide range of prices.

Merrill Gallery of Fine Arts. 1401 17th St. (at Market St.). ☎ **303/292-1401.**

Established national and emerging regional artists are represented at this beautiful gallery in lower downtown.

Native American Trading Company. 1301 Bannock St. ☎ **303/534-0771.**

Weavings, ceramics, baskets, jewelry, and other Native American artifacts, as well as some contemporary paintings, are sold here. Appropriately, it's across the street from the Denver Art Museum.

The Squash Blossom. 1428 Larimer St. ☎ **303/572-7979.**

Southwestern-style paintings, Hispanic folk art and furniture, and jewelry, pottery, and weavings by Pueblo and Navajo peoples are available here at Larimer Square.

Turner Gallery. 301 University Blvd. ☎ **303/355-1828.**

Colorado's oldest gallery specializes in traditional art forms, including oils and Colorado landscapes by American and European painters. Its collection also includes etchings, engravings, and antique botanicals by early Colorado artists.

BOOKS

✪ **Tattered Cover Bookstore.** 2955 E. First Ave. (opposite Cherry Creek Shopping Center). ☎ **800/833-9327** or 303/322-7727.

This bookstore is so big that it supplies maps to help you find your way through its maze of shelves, which contain just about any book anyone could possibly want. There are comfortable chairs placed strategically throughout the building for those who want to check out the first chapter before buying or to rest up after a hike to the fourth floor. The store also provides a wide selection of newspapers and magazines, a bargain book section, free gift-wrapping, disabled access to all four floors via elevator, mail order, and out-of-print search services. There's also a full-service coffee bar, an enclosed rooftop restaurant specializing in new American cuisine, and storytelling in the children's section every Tuesday at 11am and Saturday at 10:30am. Open Monday through Saturday from 9am to 11pm and Sunday from 10am to 6pm. The Tattered Cover has a second location in lower downtown Denver at 1628 16th St. (☎ 303/436-1070).

CLOTHING

Applause. 2827 E. Third Ave. (at Detroit St.). ☎ **303/321-7580.**

Applause is filled with an eclectic collection of women's and children's clothing, accessories, shoes, and jewelry. It also sells art and hand-painted furniture.

Eddie Bauer Outlet. 3000 E. Cherry Creek Ave. (in the Cherry Creek Mall). ☎ **303/377-2100.**

This is the place to come for good deals on the famous Eddie Bauer line of upscale outdoor clothing. You'll find discontinued and overstocked items at reduced prices.

Lawrence Covell. 225 Steele St. (in Cherry Creek North). ☎ **303/320-1023.**

This upscale shop offers contemporary men's and women's fashions, including designer clothing by Ermenegildo Zegra, Vestimente, Claude Montana, and Yeohlee.

Sheplers. 8500 E. Orchard Rd., Englewood. ☎ **303/773-3311.**

Billing itself as the world's largest western clothing store, Sheplers sells boots, cowboy hats, western shirts, fancy skirts, belt buckles, scarves, jackets, plenty of jeans, and just about everything else western. This store is at I-25, Exit 198; there's another at 10300 Bannock St., at 104th Ave. (☎ 303/450-9999).

The Woolrich Store. 6900 W. 117th Ave., Broomfield. ☎ **303/469-5257.**

This outlet store, located at the factory off U.S. 36 between Denver and Boulder, sells top-quality woolens and other outdoor clothing, plus accessories and wool blankets.

FOOD & DRINK

Alfalfa's. 201 University Blvd. ☎ **303/320-0700.**

Already an institution in the Denver area, this huge natural-foods store—50,000 square feet in area—helps perpetuate Coloradans' healthy lifestyles. No food sold here contains artificial flavoring or preservatives, nor was any grown using pesticides, chemicals, or other additives. There's a juice and health-food bar as well. This Cherry Creek area store opened in 1990; others are scattered throughout the metropolitan area.

Applejack Liquors. 3320 Youngfield St. (in the Applewood Shopping Center), Wheat Ridge (I-70, Exit 264). ☎ **800/879-5225** or 303/233-3331.

This huge store, which claims to be Colorado's largest beer, wine, and liquor supermarket, offers some of the best prices in the area, as well as delivery. The wine selection is extensive, including a number of Colorado wines. Open Monday through Thursday from 8am to 10pm, and Friday and Saturday from 8am to 11pm.

Stephany's Chocolates. 4969 Colorado Blvd. (north of I-70). ☎ **303/355-1522.**

Denver's largest manufacturer and wholesaler of gourmet confections is best known for its Denver Mint and Colorado Almond Toffee. In business for more than 3 decades, it offers tours by appointment. There are retail outlets throughout the city.

GIFTS & SOUVENIRS

Colorado History Museum Store. 1300 Broadway. ☎ **303/866-4993.**

This museum shop carries unique made-in-Colorado gifts and souvenirs, including Native American jewelry and sand paintings, plus an excellent selection of western books.

Earth Works, Ltd. 1421-B Larimer Square. ☎ **303/825-3390.**

Handcrafted work by Colorado artisans is sold here, including pottery, jewelry, sculptures, photos, and clothing.

JEWELRY

John Atencio. 1440 Larimer St. (at Larimer Square). ☎ **303/534-4277.**

An award-winning designer, Atencio sells handcrafted gold jewelry. Many pieces are set with precious or semiprecious stones.

Shalako East. 3023 E. Second Ave. ☎ **303/320-5482.**

Authentic Native American jewelry is the specialty of Shalako East, which also carries pottery, kachinas, rugs, baskets, fetishes, and artwork.

MALLS & SHOPPING CENTERS

Cherry Creek Shopping Center. 3000 E. First Ave. (between University Blvd. and Steele St.). ☎ **800/424-6360** or 303/388-3900.

Saks Fifth Avenue, Neiman Marcus, Foley's, and Lord & Taylor anchor this deluxe million-square-foot mall, with more than 140 shops, restaurants, and services, including an eight-screen movie theater. Across the street is Cherry Creek North, an upscale neighborhood retail area. Open Monday through Friday from 10am to 9pm, Saturday from 10am to 7pm, and Sunday from 11am to 6pm.

Larimer Square. 1400 block of Larimer St. ☎ **303/534-2367** or 303/446-9381.

This restored quarter of old Denver (see "The Top Attractions" above) includes numerous art galleries, boutiques, restaurants, and nightclubs. Most shops are open Monday through Friday from 10am to 7pm, Saturday from 10am to 6pm, and Sunday from noon to 5pm. Restaurants and nightclubs vary.

The Shops at Tabor Center. 16th Street Mall (at Lawrence St.). ☎ **303/572-6868.**

Some 65 specialty shops are in this two-block, glass-enclosed galleria. You'll find upscale clothing, toys, books, gifts and collectibles, as well as more than a dozen dining opportunities. Open Monday through Saturday from 10am to 7pm and Sunday from noon to 5pm.

Tivoli Denver. 900 Auraria Pkwy. ☎ **303/556-6329** or 303/556-6330.

Transformed from a 19th-century brewery, this building is home to Auraria's Student Union. There are 29 outlets, including shops, cafes, restaurants, and movie theaters. Shops are open Monday through Saturday from 10am to 9pm and on Sunday from noon to 5pm.

SPORTING GOODS

Active travelers who want to pick up a few supplies may be pleased to discover that Denver has the world's largest sporting-goods store: **Gart Brothers Sports Castle,** on Broadway at 10th Avenue (☎ **303/861-1122**). There are a number of Gart Brothers outlets in the Denver area.

TOYS

✪ **Caboose Hobbies.** 500 S. Broadway. ☎ **303/777-6766.**

Model-train buffs should plan to spend at least half a day here. Billed as the world's largest train store, there are electric trains, accessories, books, and so much train-related stuff that it's hard to know where to start. Knowledgeable employees will help you choose whatever you need, and they seem just as happy to talk about trains as to sell them. Naturally, there are trains of every scale winding through the store, as well as test tracks so you can check out a locomotive before purchasing it. There are also mugs, patches, and decals from just about every railroad line that ever existed in North America.

The Wizard's Chest. 230 Fillmore St. ☎ **303/321-4304.**

The magical store design and legendary wizard out front alone are worth the trip, but make sure to go inside. The Wizard's Chest, located in Cherry Creek, is paradise for kids of all ages, specializing in games, toys, and puzzles. The costume department is fully stocked, from complete outfits to professional makeup.

6 Denver After Dark

Denver's performing arts and nightlife scene, an important part of this increasingly sophisticated western city, is anchored by the four-square-block, $80-million **Denver Performing Arts Complex,** located downtown just a few blocks from major hotels. The complex houses nine theaters, a concert hall, and what may be the nation's first symphony hall in the round; it is home to the Colorado Symphony, Colorado Ballet, Opera Colorado, and the Denver Center for the Performing Arts (an umbrella organization for resident and touring theater companies).

In all, Denver has some 30 theaters, more than 100 cinemas, and dozens of concert halls, nightclubs, discos, and bars. Clubs offer country-and-western music; jazz, rock, and comedy acts are also popular.

Current entertainment listings are presented in special Friday-morning sections of the two daily newspapers—the *Denver Post* and *Rocky Mountain News. Westword,* a weekly newspaper distributed free throughout the city every Wednesday, has perhaps the best listings of all since it focuses on the arts, entertainment, and local politics. Another free weekly, *Up the Creek,* found in racks around the city, primarily lists events at the southern end of the metropolitan area. The *Denver Post* provides information on movie show times and theaters; call 303/777-FILM.

Tickets for nearly all major entertainment and sporting events can be obtained from **TicketMaster** (☎ **303/830-TIXS** for information). Credit-card orders can be placed using American Express, Discover, MasterCard, or VISA. There are cash-only TicketMaster outlets at selected Gart Brothers sporting goods stores (including 10th Street and Broadway), Sound Warehouses, and Budget Tapes and CDs. The agency adds a $3 charge to every ticket, in addition to the city tax.

The **Ticket Bus,** an English double-decker on the 16th Street Mall at Curtis Street, sells tickets on a cash-only basis for many live theater performances as well as all events sold through TicketMaster. Half-price tickets may be available for some events. The Ticket Bus is open Monday through Friday from 10am to 6pm and Saturday from 11am to 3pm.

Discount tickets are often available for midweek and matinee performances.

THE CLUB & MUSIC SCENE
COUNTRY MUSIC
Cactus Moon. 1001 Grant St. (Thornton Town Center), Thornton. ☎ **303/451-5200.**

Advertising "the most fun you can have with your boots on," the Cactus Moon provides a 6,000-square-foot horseshoe-shaped dance floor, believed to be the biggest in Colorado. Free dance lessons are offered several nights a week, and Sunday is family night. The brave are invited to get their exercise with "Cactus Jack," a mechanical bull.

The Grizzly Rose. 5450 N. Valley Hwy. ☎ **303/295-1330.**

Named Club of the Year in 1993 by the Country Music Association, this huge dance hall is located at Exit 215 of I-25. Known to locals as "the Griz" or "the Rose," its 4,000-square-foot dance floor beneath a 1-acre roof draws such national acts as Garth

Brooks, Willie Nelson, and Tanya Tucker. Bands perform every night of the week. Free dance lessons are available, and Sunday is family night. The cafe serves a full-service menu.

ROCK

Herman's Hideaway. 1578 S. Broadway (near Iowa Ave.). ☎ **303/777-5840.** Cover $3–$15, depending on band.

Readers of the *Rocky Mountain News* named Herman's the best place to hear original rock music by bands on their way up. Open daily, there's live music usually Wednesday through Saturday nights; free valet parking is available.

I-Beam. 1427 Larimer St. ☎ **303/534-2326.** Cover free–$5, depending on band.

A downtown dance emporium on Larimer Square, the I-Beam features live and recorded rock, drink specials, and billiard tables. Open Wednesday through Sunday night.

Jimmy's Grille. 320 S. Birch St., Glendale. ☎ **303/322-5334.** Cover $4 after 8pm on weekends.

If you're looking for live reggae, this is the place to go—at least on Thursday, Friday, and Saturday nights. Other nights you might catch blues, jazz, or whoever happens to be in town, but it's always live. Jimmy's also has drinks, burgers, sandwiches, and Tex-Mex specials galore, plus special events such as the annual pig roast in May.

JAZZ, BLUES & MORE

El Chapultepec. 1962 Market St. ☎ **303/295-9126.** No cover.

There's live jazz nightly from 9pm, with top jazz stars as well as up-and-comers.

The Mercury Cafe. 2199 California St. (at 22nd St.). ☎ **303/294-9281.**

It's hard to classify the Mercury as specializing in any one genre of music. There's always live something Wednesday through Sunday, but the offerings range from avant-garde jazz to classical violin and harp to big band to progressive rock.

THE BAR SCENE

The first permanent structure built on the site of modern Denver was supposedly a saloon, and the city has been adding to that tradition ever since. Today there are sports bars, dance bars, lots of brew pubs, outdoor cafe bars, English pubs, Old West saloons, city-overlook bars, art deco bars, even bars that don't serve alcohol.

Glendale, an enclave completely surrounded by southeastern Denver where Colorado Boulevard crosses Cherry Creek, has long been recognized as after-hours headquarters for Denver's young professional crowd. An unusual zoning situation has led to more than a dozen drinking establishments built into a small, concentrated area. Other "strips" can be found along North and South Broadway, in lower downtown, and along East and West Colfax Avenue.

Bull & Bush Pub and Brewery. 4700 Cherry Creek Dr. S., Glendale. ☎ **303/759-0333.**

This re-creation of a famous London pub always offers good imported beer, as well as Sunday evening Dixieland jazz by regional groups.

Club Proteus. 1669 Clarkson St. ☎ **303/869-4637.**

A large gay club near downtown, Club Proteus features lots of drink specials, happy hour buffets, and dancing for the alternative gay crowd.

Cruise Room Bar. In the Oxford Hotel, 1600 17th St. (at Wazee St.). ☎ **303/825-1107.**

Modeled after a bar aboard the *Queen Mary* in the 1930s, this charming hotel lounge, recently restored to its art deco best, has all the atmosphere of an ocean-going cruise ship.

THE PERFORMING ARTS

Denver is more of a sports town, but its performing arts scene is steadily improving. The city's best-known venue is the immense, outdoor **Red Rocks Amphitheater** in Morrison (☎ **303/640-7300**), where John Tesh has performed to sold-out, televised crowds recently.

In downtown Denver, the largest multiuse facility is **the Denver Performing Arts Complex** ("the PLEX," to locals), at 14th and Curtis streets. This four-block-long structure has a concert hall as well as three separate theaters (☎ **303/893-4100**), and houses the **Denver Center for the Performing Arts,** an umbrella organization for resident and touring theater groups that also provides youth outreach and conservatory training. In addition to the **Denver Center Theatre Company** (see below), the Center sponsors **Robert Garner/Center Attractions,** which brings touring Broadway shows such as *Phantom of the Opera* and *Miss Saigon* to the Auditorium Theatre and Temple Hoyne Buell Theatre within the complex. Another downtown venue is the **Paramount Theatre** (☎ **303/534-8336**) at 1631 Glenarm Place, a historic, turn-of-the-century building that offers jazz concerts, pop and folk performances, lectures, and films.

The Museum of Outdoor Arts sponsors outdoor summer concerts by national and international rock, jazz, country music, and classical stars at **Fiddler's Green Amphitheatre** (☎ **303/741-5000**) in Englewood, just west of I-25 between Arapahoe and Orchard roads. You can purchase a reserved seat in the 7,500-seat theater or an unreserved ticket for the lawn. Also just outside the city, in Arvada, is the **Arvada Center for the Arts and Humanities** (☎ **303/431-3939**). This multidisciplinary arts center, with its own resident theater company, stages performances by local and visiting instrumental ensembles and dance troupes in its 500-seat indoor theater or 1200-seat outdoor amphitheater.

CLASSICAL MUSIC & OPERA COMPANIES

Colorado Symphony Orchestra. Denver Performing Arts Complex, 1031 13th St. ☎ **303/98-MUSIC.**

This international-caliber orchestra performs at Boettcher Concert Hall—perhaps the nation's first symphony hall in the round. The orchestra's classical concerts are interspersed with pops concerts featuring top touring musicians.

Opera Colorado. 695 S. Colorado Blvd., Suite 20. ☎ **303/778-1500.**

Each season three operas (12 performances) are staged—with English subtitles—at the Denver Performing Arts Complex. Internationally renowned singers and local favorites sing the lead roles. The typical schedule is three evening performances at 8pm (Sat, Tues, and Fri) and one matinee at 2pm Sunday. Contact the box office at 303/98-MUSIC for more information. Tickets are $15 and up.

THEATER COMPANIES

Denver's theater scene is limited. The most well known is the **Denver Center Theatre Company,** the largest professional resident theater company in the Rockies. The troupe performs 8 to 12 plays in repertory from late fall to early spring in all four theaters of the Helen G. Bonfils Theatre Complex (☎ **303/893-4100**) at the Denver Performing Arts Complex (see above).

Other theater companies include the **Avenue Theater** at 2119 E. 17th Ave. (☎ 303/321-5925), which mounts original and off-Broadway plays; the **Chicken Lips Comedy Theater** at 1360 17th St. (☎ 303/534-4440), whose productions include improvisational comedy, plays, and musicals, often with audience participation; **El Centro Su Teatro** at 4725 High St. (☎ 303/296-0219), a Hispanic theater and cultural center, presenting bilingual productions on a regular basis; and **Germinal Stage Denver** at 44th and Alcott streets (☎ 303/455-7108), which presents plays by Brecht, Albee, and Pinter, among other modern playwrights.

On the experimental side of things, check out **Hunger Artists Ensemble Theatre** (☎ 303/893-5438), an award-winning company that presents contemporary works. They perform at Jack's Theatre in the Zang Building, 1553 Platte St., just north of Larimer Square.

DANCE COMPANIES

Colorado Ballet. 1278 Lincoln St. ☎ **303/837-TUTU.**

The city's premier professional resident ballet company performs in the Auditorium Theatre at the Denver Performing Arts Complex. Its season always includes *The Nutcracker* at Christmastime.

Cleo Parker Robinson Dance Ensemble. 119 Park Ave. W. ☎ **303/295-1759.**

A highly acclaimed multicultural modern dance ensemble and school, the Cleo Parker Robinson group performs a varied selection of programs each year, many on tour.

8 A Side Trip to Colorado's Gold Circle Towns

Golden, Central City, Idaho Springs, and **Georgetown** comprise the fabled Gold Circle—those towns that boomed with the first strikes of the gold rush in 1859. We start this suggested side trip in Golden, the closest of the four towns to Denver, and perhaps best known today as the home of Coors, then move on to Idaho Springs and Georgetown. We don't cover Central City—between Golden and Idaho Springs—because it has few attractions to offer. (It's little more than a place for locals from Denver to gamble.) But as it was once the richest of these towns, you may want to stop there briefly to see its two major historical attractions—**Gilpin County Historical Museum** and the **Lost Gold Mine**—before moving on to Idaho Springs, where you can actively experience the area's past by panning for gold, riding a replica of a turn-of-the-century locomotive (the **Argo Express**), or donning a hard hat and following a working miner through the narrow tunnels of the **Phoenix Mine** to dig out your own ore sample.

GOLDEN

Golden, 15 miles west of downtown Denver via U.S. 6 or Colo. 58 off I-70, was for years, the territorial capital. In addition to Coors Brewery (founded in 1873), it is the home of the Colorado School of Mines (established in 1874).

For visitor information, contact the **Greater Golden Area Chamber of Commerce,** 507 14th St. (P.O. Box 1035), Golden, CO 80402-1035 (☎ 303/279-3113).

WHAT TO SEE & DO

Historic downtown Golden centers on the Territorial Capitol in the Loveland Building at 12th Street and Washington Avenue. Built in 1861, it housed the state's first legislature from 1862 to 1867. Today, it contains professional offices and a restaurant. Other historical buildings are the Armory at 13th and Arapahoe streets, probably the largest cobblestone structure in the United States; and the Rock Flour Mill Warehouse at Eighth and Cheyenne streets, which dates from 1863.

Boettcher Mansion and Open Space Nature Center. 900 Colorow Rd. (on Lookout Mountain). ☎ **303/526-0855.** Free admission. Mansion open Mon–Sat 8am–5pm or by appointment; grounds and trails, 8am–nightfall.

This Jefferson County estate was built by Charles Boettcher in 1917 as a summer home and hunting lodge. The historic home, now open to visitors, with changing art and history exhibits, also hosts conferences, weddings, and community events. A 1¹/₂-mile nature trail winds through the 110-acre property, among ponderosa pines and mountain meadows. A nature center (☎ 303/526-0594), which was being rebuilt at press time, is scheduled to reopen in early 1997. Call for hours.

Buffalo Bill Memorial Museum. 987¹/₂ Lookout Mountain Rd. ☎ **303/526-0747.** Admission $3 adults, $2 seniors, $1 children 6–15, free for children under 6. May–Oct, daily 9am–5pm; Nov–Apr, Tues–Sun 9am–4pm. Closed Christmas. I-70, Exit 260.

William Frederick Cody, the famous western scout, is buried atop Lookout Mountain, south of Golden. The adjacent museum has memorabilia from the life and legend of "Buffalo Bill," who rode for the Pony Express, organized buffalo hunts for foreign royalty, and toured the world with his Wild West Show. The museum, reached via I-70, Exit 256, is in 66-acre Lookout Mountain Park, a Denver municipal park popular for picnicking.

Colorado Railroad Museum. 17155 W. 44th Ave. ☎ **800/365-6263** or 303/279-4591. Admission $3.50 adults, $1.75 children under 16, $3 seniors over 60, $7.50 families. June–Aug, daily 9am–6pm; Sept–May, daily 9am–5pm. Closed New Year's morning, Thanksgiving, Christmas.

Housed in a replica of an 1880 railroad depot, this museum is a favorite of railroad buffs. On display are more than 4 dozen narrow- and standard-gauge locomotives and cars, plus other historic equipment and artifacts, historic photos and documents, and model trains. In fact, the exhibits cover 12 acres, including the two-story depot. You can climb up into many of the old locomotives and wander through the parlor cars. There's also an excellent gift and souvenir shop, selling hundreds of railroad-related items from coffee mugs to posters and T-shirts. The museum is located 2 miles east of Golden. Follow the signs from I-70, Exit 265 westbound, Exit 266 eastbound.

✪ Colorado School of Mines Geology Museum. 16th and Maple streets. ☎ **303/273-3815.** Free admission. School year, Mon–Sat 9am–4pm, Sun 1–4pm; closed for school holidays; summer, Mon–Sat 9am–4pm.

Exhibits include a replica of a gold mine, fine mineral and gem collections from around the world, displays of geology, earth history, paleontology, and some depicting Colorado's rich mining history. The Colorado School of Mines, founded in 1874, has an enrollment of about 3,000.

Coors Brewing Company. 13th and Ford streets. ☎ **800/443-8242** or 303/277-BEER. Free admission. Mon–Sat 10am–5pm. Closed holidays.

The world's largest single-site brewery, producing 1.5 million gallons of beer each day, Coors conducts free public tours of its brewery, followed by free samples of beer. Tours leave a central parking lot at 13th and Ford streets, where visitors pile onto a bus for a short drive through historic Golden before arriving at the brewery. There, a 40-minute walking tour covers the history of the Coors family and company, the barley-malting process, the 13,640-gallon gleaming copper kettles, and the entire process all the way to packaging. Children are welcome, and arrangements can be made for disabled and foreign-speaking visitors. There's also a gift shop.

Foothills Art Center. 809 15th St. ☎ **303/279-3922.** Free admission. Mon–Sat 9am–4pm, Sun 1–4pm.

Housed in an 1872 Gothic-style Presbyterian church (which is on the National Historic Register), this exhibition center developed from the annual Golden Sidewalk Art Show and features changing national and regional exhibits. A gift shop sells crafts by local artisans.

✪ **Hakushika Sake USA.** 4414 Table Mountain Dr. ☎ **303/279-7253.** Free admission. Mon–Fri 10am–noon and 1–4pm by reservation.

The Hakushika company, founded in 1662 and today one of Japan's foremost sake-makers, has opened a brewery in Golden that produces sake for distribution throughout the United States and Europe. Sake, considered the Japanese national drink, is made from fermented steamed rice, has an alcohol content of 16%, and is traditionally, but not exclusively, consumed with meals.

Guided tours, by reservation only, follow a glass-enclosed mezzanine that permits an excellent view of the entire brewing and bottling process. Visitors can also see displays of traditional sake-brewing techniques, and an exhibit of fine Japanese art from the 19th and early 20th centuries. There is also a tasting room and gift shop; children are welcome. The Hakushika Sake brewery is located in the Coors Technology Center. From Denver, take I-70, Exit 265, follow Highway 58 toward Golden to the McIntyre Street exit. Go 2 miles north on McIntyre, turn left onto Service Drive, and then left onto Table Mountain Drive, where Hakushika is located.

Heritage Square. U.S. 40. ☎ **303/279-2789.** Free admission, but individual activities impose their own charges. Memorial Day–Labor Day, Mon–Sat 10am–9pm, Sun noon–9pm; the rest of the year, Mon–Sat 10am–6pm, Sun noon–6pm. Bus: 17.

A shopping, dining, and entertainment village with a Wild West theme, Heritage Square features 30 Victorian specialty shops, a small museum, several fine restaurants, and a dinner theater. Warm weather rides include go-carts, bumper boats, a water slide, a bungee tower, mountain-bike rentals, white-water rafting, and a 2,350-foot alpine slide with bobsled-style carts. The Lazy H Chuckwagon serves dinner with a western-style show. Heritage Square Music Hall offers adult and children's shows, plus there's an ice-cream parlor and beer garden. It's located three-quarters of a mile south of the U.S. 6 and U.S. 40 interchange.

Mother Cabrini Shrine. I-70, Exit 259, Lookout Mountain. ☎ **303/526-0758.** Free admission, donations welcome. Summer, daily 7am–7pm; winter, daily 7am–5pm; gift shop, daily 9am–5pm.

A 22-foot statue of Christ stands at the top of a 373-step stairway, adorned by carvings representing the stations of the cross and mysteries of the rosary. Terra-cotta benches provide rest stops along the way. The shrine is dedicated to America's first citizen saint, St. Frances Xavier Cabrini, who founded the Order of the Missionary Sisters of the Sacred Heart. The order has a convent here with a gift shop, open 9am to 5pm daily.

National Earthquake Information Center. 1711 Illinois St. ☎ **303/273-8500.** Free admission. By appointment only, Mon–Fri 9–11am and 1–3pm.

The U.S. Geological Survey operates this facility to collect rapid earthquake information, transmit warnings via the Earthquake Early Alerting Service, and publish and disseminate earthquake data. Tours of 30 to 45 minutes can be scheduled.

WHERE TO STAY & DINE

La Quinta Inn—Golden, just off I-70 at Exit 264 at 3301 Youngfield Service Rd. (☎ **800/531-5900** or 303/279-5565), is a dependable choice for the night, with 129 units and rates of $69 to $79 double, $89 to $99 suite. **Table Mountain Inn** at 1310 Washington Avenue (☎ **800/762-9898** or 303/277-9898) is a slightly more expensive, if smaller alternative, with 29 rooms and 3 suites, and rates of $90 to $110 double; $140 suite. Open since 1992, it has southwest charm and beautiful views of the surrounding mesas.

For a good dinner, try the **Chart House** at 25908 Genesee Trail, just south of I-70 off Exit 254 (☎ **303/526-9813**). It offers grilled steak and seafood, a great salad bar with hearts-of-palm and caviar, and an incredible view of the mountains.

IDAHO SPRINGS

The "Oh My God" dirt road winds from Central City through Virginia Canyon to Idaho Springs, although most visitors prefer to take I-70 directly to this community, 35 miles west of Denver. Site of a major gold strike in 1859, Idaho Springs today beckons visitors to try their luck at panning for any gold that may still remain.

For visitor information, contact the **Idaho Springs Chamber of Commerce,** P.O. Box 97, Idaho Springs, CO 80452 (☎ **800/685-7785** or 303/567-4382).

WHAT TO SEE & DO

The **Argo Gold Mill and Museum,** 2350 Riverside Dr. (☎ **303/567-2421**), offers tours daily, year-round, from 10am to 6pm. Visitors can see the Double Eagle Gold Mine, relatively unchanged since the early miners first worked it more than 100 years ago, and the mill, where ore was processed into gold. Also at the mine and mill, you can ride the **Argo Express,** a one-half scale replica of a turn-of-the-century steam locomotive.

Still being worked is **Phoenix Mine** on Trail Creek Road (☎ **303/567-0422**), where you can don a hard hat, follow a working miner through narrow tunnels, and dig out your own ore sample. Open daily, the tours are informal and entertaining.

The Colorado School of Mines in Golden uses the **Edgar Experimental Mine,** less than a mile north of Idaho Springs on Eighth Avenue (☎ **303/567-2911**), as a research area and teaching facility for high-tech mining practices. Underground walking tours of 60 to 90 minutes are offered throughout the year: mid-June through August, Tuesday through Saturday at 9:30am and 1pm; other times by appointment. Tour rates: $4 adults, $2 ages 6 to 16, under 6 free, $3 over 60.

Just outside of town at 302 Soda Creek Rd. is **Indian Springs Resort** (☎ **303/567-2191**), a fine spot for a relaxing soak in the hot springs after a long day of skiing or hiking. There's a covered swimming pool as well as indoor and outdoor private baths. Lodging, meals, and weekend entertainment are also offered.

Idaho Springs is the starting point for a 28-mile drive to the summit of 14,260-foot **Mount Evans.** Colorado 103 winds through Arapahoe National Forest, along Chicago Creek, to **Echo Lake Park,** another Denver mountain park with fireplaces, hiking trails, and fishing. Take I-70, Exit 240. From here, Colo. 5—the highest paved auto road in North America—climbs to Mount Evans's summit. It is generally open from Memorial Day to Labor Day and is free.

Another way to see the country is by horseback. **A&A Historical Trails Stables,** 2380 Riverside Dr. (☎ **303/567-4808**), offers a variety of trail rides, including breakfast and moonlight rides, plus pony rides for children.

WHERE TO STAY & DINE

H&H Motor Lodge at 2445 Colorado Blvd. (☎ 800/445-2893 or 303/567-2838) is a mom-and-pop motel on the east side of town. It offers bright and cheery rooms with either two doubles or a queen bed, plus TV with HBO, a hot tub, sauna, and several larger family units. There are 19 rooms, pets are welcome, and rates are $38 to $65 double; kitchenettes $10 extra. Some rooms provide air-conditioning.

Beau Jo's Colorado Style Pizza at 1517 Miner St. (☎ 303/567-4376) offers a wide variety of so-called "mountain pizzas," including standard pepperoni, a Thai Pie with sweet-and-sour sauce, and a roasted garlic and veggie combo. Sandwiches are also available, plus a soup and salad bar set up in a pair of old claw-footed bathtubs. The entire restaurant is nonsmoking. Prices for menu items are $6 to $10.

GEORGETOWN

A pretty village of Victorian-era houses and stores, Georgetown, 45 miles west of Denver on I-70, at an elevation of 8,500 feet, is named for an 1860 gold camp. Among the best preserved of the foothills mining towns, Georgetown is one of the few that didn't suffer a major fire during its formative years. Perhaps to acknowledge their blessings, townspeople built eye-catching steeples on top of their firehouses, not their churches.

For information on attractions and travel services, contact the **Georgetown Chamber of Commerce,** P.O. Box 444, Georgetown, CO 80444 (☎ 303/569-2888), or Historic Georgetown, P.O. Box 667, Georgetown, CO 80444 (☎ 303/569-2840). There is a visitor information center, open in summer, at Sixth Street across from the Georgetown post office.

WHAT TO SEE & DO

The Georgetown-Silver Plume Mining Area was declared a National Historic Landmark District in 1966, and more than 200 of its buildings have been restored.

A convenient place to begin a **walking tour** is the Old County Courthouse at Sixth and Argentine streets. Now the Community Center and tourist information office, it was built in 1867. Across Argentine Street is the Old Stone Jail (1868); three blocks south, at Third and Argentine, is the Hamill House (see below).

Sixth Street is Georgetown's main commercial strip. Walk east from the Old Courthouse to, on your left, the Masonic Hall (1891), the Fish Block (1886), the Monti and Guanella Building (1868), and the Cushman Block (1874); and on your right, the Hamill Block (1881) and the Kneisel & Anderson Building (1893). The Hotel de Paris (see below) is at the corner of Sixth and Taos. Nearly opposite, at Sixth and Griffith, is the Star Hook & Ladder Building (1886), along with the town hall and marshal's office.

If you turn south on Taos Street, you'll find Grace Episcopal Church (1869) at Fifth Street, and the Maxwell House (1890) a couple of steps east on Fourth. Glance west on Fifth to see Alpine Hose Company No. 2 (1874) and the Courier Building (1875). North on Taos Street from the Hotel de Paris are the Old Georgetown School (1874), at Eighth Street; First Presbyterian Church (1874), at Ninth; Our Lady of Lourdes Catholic Church (1918), at Ninth; and the Old Missouri Firehouse (1870), at 10th and Taos.

If you turn west on Ninth at the Catholic church, you'll find two more historic structures—the Bowman-White House (1892), at Rose and Ninth and the Tucker-Rutherford House (circa 1860), a miner's log cabin with four small rooms on Ninth Street at Clear Creek, with a trapper's cabin in back.

Georgetown Loop Railroad. 1106 Rose St., Georgetown. ☎ **800/691-4FUN,** 303/569-2403, or 303/670-1686 in Denver. Admission $14.95 adults, $8.50 children 4–15, for train and mine tour; $11.95 adults, $7.50 children, for train ride only, no charge for children under 3 not occupying a seat; $4 adults, $2 children, for mine tour. Memorial Day–Labor Day, daily 9:20am–4pm; Labor Day–early Oct, full schedule on weekends, limited during the week. Departures from Georgetown and from Silver Plume. There's no mine tour on the final run.

An 1884 railroad bridge serves this restored narrow-gauge line, which runs daily trips in summer between Georgetown and Silver Plume. The steel bridge, 300 feet long and 95 feet high, was considered an engineering miracle a century ago. Though the direct distance between the terminals is 2.1 miles, the track covers 4.5 miles, climbing 638 feet in 14 sharp curves and switchbacks, crossing Clear Creek four times, and culminating with a 360° spiraling knot. Passengers may make a round-trip from either end: The whole trip takes about 2¹/₂ hours, including an optional walking tour of the Lebanon Mine and Mill, which can be reached only by train. In 1996 the "Taste of Tahoe" car, which serves meals, was added. The cost is slightly higher, since it offers English-style breakfast, lunch, and tea.

Mountain bikers might like to try a combination bike/train tour, priced from $45 to $85. This includes bicycling gear, uphill transportation, guided downhill tour, round-trip train ride, and lunch.

Hamill House. Third and Argentine streets. ☎ **303/569-2840,** or in Denver 303/674-2625. Admission $2.50 adults, $1.50 seniors, 50¢ children 12–16, under 12 free. Memorial Day–Sept 30, daily 10am–5pm; Oct–May, Sat–Sun noon–4pm.

Built in Country Gothic Revival style, this house dates to 1867, when it was owned by silver speculator William Hamill. When acquired by Historic Georgetown, Inc. (in 1971), the house had its original woodwork, fireplaces, and wallpaper. A delicately carved outhouse had two sections: one for the family with walnut seats, and the other for servants with pine seats.

Hotel de Paris. Sixth and Taos streets. ☎ **303/569-2311.** Admission $2.50 adults, $1.50 seniors, 50¢ children 12–16, under 12 free. Memorial Day–Oct 30, daily 10am–5pm; Nov–late May, Sat–Sun noon–4pm.

The builder of the hotel, Louis Dupuy, once explained his desire to build a French inn so far away from his homeland: "I love these mountains and I love America, but you will pardon me if I bring into this community a remembrance of my youth and my country." The hotel opened in 1875 and soon became famous for its French provincial luxury.

Today it's a historic museum run by the National Society of Colonial Dames of America, embellished with many of its original furnishings, including Haviland china, a big pendulum clock, paintings and etchings of the past century, photographs by William Henry Jackson, and carved walnut furniture. An antique stove and other cooking equipment are found in the kitchen; the wine cellar contains early wine barrels, with their labels still in place.

WHERE TO STAY & DINE

Colorado's oldest continually operating hotel, about 5 minutes from Georgetown, is the **Peck House Hotel and Restaurant** (☎ 303/569-9870; fax 303/569-2743), at 83 Sunny Ave. (on U.S. 40, just off I-70, exit 232). Established in 1862 as a stagecoach stop for travelers and immigrants from the East Coast, the hotel has an antique-filled parlor lined with photos of the Peck family and their turn-of-the-century guests. The rooms are comfortable and quaint (claw-footed tubs grace many bathrooms), and one of the best parts of a stay here is the wide veranda that offers a fine panoramic view of the Empire Valley. There are 11 rooms (9 with private bath), and rates are in the $50 to $110 range for two. The hotel's excellent **restaurant** serves fish and steak entrees and delicious hot-fudge cake and raspberries Romanoff.

Back in Georgetown, **The Happy Cooker,** at 412 Sixth Street (☎ **303/ 569-3166**), serves unusual soups, sandwiches on homemade breads, crêpes, quiches, and more substantial fare such as lasagna and barbecued beef, in a converted home in Georgetown's historic business district. **The Place,** at 715 Seventh Street (☎ **303/ 569-2552**), is a popular family restaurant offering burgers and sandwiches for lunch and steak, fish, chicken, pork, and pasta at dinnertime.

8 Colorado Springs

Magnificent scenic beauty, a favorable climate, and dreams of gold have lured visitors to Colorado Springs for well over 100 years.

Nearly 2 centuries ago—in 1806—army lieutenant Zebulon Pike led a company of soldiers on a trek around the base of an enormous mountain. He called it "Grand Peak," declared it unconquerable, and moved on. Today, the 14,110-foot mountain we now know as Pikes Peak has been conquered so often that an auto highway and a cog railway have been built to take visitors to the top.

Unlike many Colorado towns, neither mineral wealth nor ranching was the cornerstone of Colorado Springs' economy during the 19th century: Tourism was. In fact, when founded in 1871, Colorado Springs was the first genuine resort community west of Chicago. General William J. Palmer, builder of the Denver & Rio Grande Railroad, established the resort on his rail line, at an elevation of 6,035 feet. The state's growing reputation as a health center, with its high mountains and mineral springs, convinced him to build at the foot of Pikes Peak. In an attempt to lure affluent Easterners, he named the resort Colorado Springs, because most fashionable Eastern resorts were "springs." The mineral waters at Manitou were only 5 miles away, and soon Palmer exploited them by installing a resident physician, Dr. Samuel Solly, who exuberantly trumpeted the benefits of Manitou's springs in print and in person.

The 1890s' gold strikes at Cripple Creek, on the southwestern slope of Pikes Peak, added a new dimension to life in Colorado Springs. Among those who cashed in on the boom was Spencer Penrose, a middle-aged Philadelphian and Harvard graduate who came to the Springs in 1892, made some astute investments, and became quite rich. Penrose, who believed that the automobile would revolutionize life in the United States, promoted the creation of new highways. To show the effectiveness of motor cars in the mountains, he built (during 1913–15) the Pikes Peak highway, using more than $250,000 of his own money. Then, during World War I, at a cost of more than $2 million, he built the luxurious Broadmoor hotel at the foot of Cheyenne Mountain. World War II brought the military and defense industry to this area, and in 1958 the $200-million U.S. Air Force Academy opened.

Modern Colorado Springs is a growing city of 281,000. The majority of its residents are rather politically conservative (one-third of its residents are active or retired military personnel), and in recent years, it has developed a bit of a reputation for right-wing political activism. Focus on the Family, a key organization in the family values movement, is headquartered here, as are some of the country's largest nondenominational churches. But just when one thinks the entire city votes Republican, there is the decidedly liberal pocket of Manitou Springs to round out the picture. Despite being an incorporated city in its own right, Manitou is treated by many Colorado Springs residents as just another neighborhood. Here, Birkenstocks and morning espressos rule, and some of the area's most charming bed-and-breakfasts and intriguing restaurants can be found.

To many visitors, Colorado Springs and its immediate environs retain the feel of a small western town. Most come to see Colorado's most popular manmade attraction, the U.S. Air Force Academy, or to marvel at the natural scenery of the Garden of the Gods and Pikes Peak. They are rarely disappointed.

1 Orientation

ARRIVING

BY PLANE Major airlines offer some 100 flights a day to **Colorado Springs Airport,** located north of Drennan Road and east of Powers Boulevard in the southeastern part of the city (☎ **719/550-1900**). With a new terminal and runway completed in late 1994, the Colorado Springs Airport has the longest runway in the state (13,500 ft.). Encompassing 7,200 acres (3,000 are now in use, and the rest are available for future expansion), it's larger than Denver's new airport. At present, flights connect the Springs to most major U.S. cities.

Airlines serving Colorado Springs include **American** (☎ 800/433-7300), **America West** (☎ 800/235-9292), **Delta** (☎ 800/221-1212), **Northwest** (☎ 800/ 225-2525), **TWA** (☎ 800/221-2000 or 719/599-4400), **United** (☎ 800/241-6522), and **Western Pacific** (☎ 800/930-3030). Regional and commuter airlines include **Mesa** (☎ 800/637-2247 or 719/591-6211), with flights to Albuquerque; and **Reno Air** (☎ 800/736-6247), which connects Colorado Springs with Las Vegas.

Getting to & from the Airport The **airport shuttle service** (☎ **719/578-5232**) operates direct ground service from Colorado Springs airport to local hotels and the Denver airport.

BY CAR The principal artery to and from the north (Denver: 70 miles) and south (Pueblo: 42 miles), I-25 bisects Colorado Springs. U.S. 24 is the principal east-west route through the city.

Visitors arriving via I-70 from the east can take Exit 359 at Limon and follow U.S. 24 into the Springs. Arriving on I-70 from the west, the most direct route is Exit 201 at Frisco, then Colo. 9 through Breckenridge 53 miles to U.S. 24 (at Hartsel), and then east 66 miles to the Springs. This route is mountainous, so check road conditions before setting out in winter.

VISITOR INFORMATION

The **Colorado Springs Convention and Visitors Bureau** is located at 104 S. Cascade Ave., Colorado Springs, CO 80903 (☎ **800/DO-VISIT** or 719/635-7506; fax 719/635-4968). Ask for the free *Official Visitors Guide to Colorado Springs and the Pikes Peak Region,* a colorful booklet with a comprehensive listing of accommodations, restaurants, and other visitor services in the area, as well as a basic but efficient map. Inquire at the Visitor Information Center or local bookstores for more detailed maps (an excellent one is the Pierson Graphics Corporation's *Colorado Springs & Monument Valley* street map).

The **Visitor Information Center,** located in the same Sun Plaza Building at the corner of Cascade and Colorado avenues, is open in summer, daily from 8:30am to 6pm; in winter, Monday through Friday from 8:30am to 5pm. From I-25, take the Bijou Street exit, head east, and turn right at the second stoplight onto Cascade. Just past the Antlers Hotel, turn right onto Colorado Avenue, and almost immediately left into the parking lot for the Visitor's Center. The center also operates a weekly events line with a 24-hour recording (☎ **719/635-1723**).

Additional information on regional attractions plus accommodations, restaurants, and special events in the Manitou Springs area can be obtained from the **Manitou Springs Chamber of Commerce,** 354 Manitou Ave., Manitou Springs, CO 80829 (☎ **800/642-2567** or 719/685-5089). You can also contact the **Pikes Peak Country Attractions Association** at the same address (☎ **800/525-2250** or 719/685-5894).

CITY LAYOUT

It's easy to get around central Colorado Springs because it is laid out on a classic grid pattern.

If you focus on the intersection of I-25/U.S. 24, downtown Colorado Springs lies in the northeast quadrant—bounded on the west by I-25 and on the south by U.S. 24 (Cimarron St.). Boulder Street to the north and Wahsatch Avenue to the east complete the downtown frame. Nevada Avenue (U.S. 85) parallels the freeway for 15 miles through the city, intersecting it twice; Tejon Street and Cascade Avenue also run north-south through downtown between Nevada and the freeway. **Colorado Avenue** and **Platte Avenue** are the busiest east-west downtown cross-streets.

West of downtown, Colorado Avenue extends through the historic **Old Colorado City** district and the quaint foothill community of **Manitou Springs,** rejoining U.S. 24—itself a busy but less interesting artery—as it enters Pike National Forest.

South of downtown, Nevada Avenue intersects Lake Avenue, the principal boulevard into the Broadmoor, and proceeds south as Colo. 115 past Fort Carson.

North and east of downtown, Academy Boulevard (Colo. 83) is the street name to remember. From the south gate of the Air Force Academy north of the Springs, it winds through residential hills, crosses Austin Bluff Parkway, then runs without a curve 8 miles due south, finally bending west to intersect I-25 and Colo. 115 at Fort Carson. U.S. 24, which exits downtown east as Platte Avenue, and Fountain Boulevard, which leads to the airport, are among its cross streets. Austin Bluffs Parkway extends west of I-25 as **Garden of the Gods Road,** leading to that natural wonder.

City street addresses are divided by Pikes Peak Avenue into "north" and "south," and by Nevada Avenue into "east" and "west."

2 Getting Around

BY CAR

Although Colorado Springs has public transportation, most visitors prefer to drive. Parking and roads are good, and some of the best attractions, such as the Garden of the Gods, are accessible only by car. For regulations and advice on driving in Colorado, see "Getting Around," in chapter 3.

Car Rentals   Car-rental agencies in Colorado Springs—some of which have offices in or near downtown as well as at the airport—include: **Avis,** 7770 Drennan Rd. (☎ **800/831-2847** or 719/596-2751); **Budget,** 303 W. Bijou St. (☎ **800/527-0700** or 719/574-7400); **Dollar,** 3204 E. Platte Rd. (☎ **800/800-4000** or 719/447-8760); **Enterprise,** 803 W. Colorado Ave. (☎ **719/636-3900**); **Hertz,**

7770 Drennan Rd. (☎ **800/654-3131** or 719/596-1863); **National,** 7770 Drennan Rd. (☎ **800/227-7368** or 719/596-1519); **Payless,** 2870 S. Circle Dr. (☎ **800/ PAYLESS** or 719/576-RENT); and **Thrifty,** 4180 Center Park Dr. (☎ **800/ 367-2277** or 719/573-2613).

Parking   Most downtown streets have parking meters; the rate is 25¢ an hour. Look for city-run parking lots, which charge 25¢ per hour and also offer day rates. Outside of downtown, free parking is generally available on side streets.

BY PUBLIC TRANSPORTATION

City bus service is provided by **Colorado Springs Transit** (☎ **719/475-9733**). Buses operate 6am to 10pm Monday through Friday, and Saturday from 7am to 6pm, except holidays. Fares on in-city routes are 75¢ for adults; 35¢ for children 6 to 11, senior citizens, and the disabled; and free for children under 6. Fares for routes outside the city limits are 25¢ more. Bus schedules can be obtained at terminals, city libraries, and the Colorado Springs Convention and Visitors Bureau.

In Manitou Springs, the **Town Trolley** operates daily from Memorial Day to Labor Day and on a limited schedule in the weeks preceding Christmas and on weekends during April, May, September, and October, weather permitting. The open-sided trolleys provide 1-hour guided tours through Manitou Springs and a portion of Garden of the Gods. A $2 1-day pass allows riders to stop to see the sights and then resume the tour later. Children under 12, with their parents, ride free. During the summer, the trolleys run every half hour from 9am until 8pm.

BY TAXI

Call **Yellow Cab** (☎ **719/634-5000**) for taxi service and tours.

ON FOOT

Each of the main sections of town can easily be explored without a vehicle. It's fun, for instance, to wander the winding streets of Manitou Springs or explore the Old Colorado City strip. Between neighborhoods, however, distances are considerable. Unless you're particularly fit, it's wise to drive or take a bus or taxi.

FAST FACTS: Colorado Springs

Area Code   The telephone area code is **719.**

Business Hours   Most banks are open Monday through Friday from 9am to 5pm, and some have Saturday hours as well. Major stores are open Monday through Saturday from 9 or 10am until 5 or 6pm, and often Sunday from noon until 5pm. Stores that cater to tourists are usually open longer in the summer with shorter hours in winter. Some may close completely between October and April.

Camera Repair   For repairs, as well as camera and video supplies, go to **Robert Waxman Camera and Video,** 1850 N. Academy Blvd. (☎ **719/597-1575**), or **Shewmaker's Camera Shop,** downtown at 30 N. Tejon St. (☎ **719/636-1696**).

Dentists & Doctors   For 24-hour dental referrals, contact **Colorado Springs Dental Society Emergency and Referral Service,** 1870 Dublin Blvd. no. C (☎ 719/598-5161). For a physician referral, call **Memorial Hospital Physician Referral** (☎ 719/444-2273) or the **Colorado Springs Doctors Exchange** (☎ 719/ 632-1512).

Emergencies   For police, fire, or medical emergencies call **911.**

Hospitals Full medical services, including 24-hour emergency treatment, are offered by **Memorial Hospital,** 1400 E. Boulder St. (☎ **719/475-5000,** or 719/475-5221 for an emergency); and **St. Francis Hospital,** 825 E. Pikes Peak Ave. (☎ **719/776-8800**). Both are just east of downtown. **Penrose Hospital,** 2215 N. Cascade Ave. (☎ **719/776-5000,** or 719/776-5333 for an emergency), and **Penrose Community Hospital,** 3205 N. Academy Blvd. (☎ **719/776-3000,** or 719/776-3216 for an emergency), are on the north side.

Hot Lines To reach the **poison control center,** dial **800/332-3073.** The **rape crisis hotline** is **719/633-3819.**

Newspapers/Magazines The *Gazette Telegraph,* published daily in Colorado Springs, is the city's most widely read newspaper. Both Denver dailies—the *Denver Post* and *Rocky Mountain News*—are available at newsstands throughout the city. *USA Today* and the *Wall Street Journal* can be purchased on the streets and at major hotels. *Springs* magazine and *The Independent* are free arts-and-entertainment tabloids.

Post Office The **main post office** is downtown at 201 E. Pikes Peak Ave. (☎ **719/570-5343**), open Monday through Friday from 7:30am to 5pm. There are many other branches. For late-night pickup, you'll have to visit the **general mail facility,** 3655 E. Fountain Blvd. (☎ **719/570-5377**).

Prescriptions **Walgreens** has a 24-hour prescription service at 2727 Palmer Park Blvd. (☎ **719/473-9090**).

Radio More than a dozen AM and FM radio stations in the Colorado Springs area cater to all tastes in music, news, sports, and entertainment, including KCME (88.7 FM) for classical, KILO (94.3 FM) for album-oriented rock, KKFM (98.1 FM) for classic rock, KGFT (100.7 FM) and KCBR (1040 AM) for contemporary Christian, KCMN (1530 AM) for big band and hit parade, KKCS (101.9 FM) for country, KRDO (1240 AM) for sports talk, KKLI (106.3 FM) for adult contemporary, and KVOR (1300 AM) for all news.

Taxes The Colorado state sales tax is 3%. In Colorado Springs, the sales tax is about 7%, and the lodging tax is about 9%. Rates in Manitou Springs are about 7.5% for general sales tax and almost 10% for lodging.

Television Major television stations include Channel 5 (NBC), 8 (PBS), 11 (CBS), 13 (ABC), and 21 (FOX). Cable or satellite service is available at most hotels.

Useful Telephone Numbers **Road conditions and time** (☎ 719/630-1111); **ski conditions statewide** (☎ 303/831-SNOW); and **current weather reports** (☎ 719/475-7599).

3 Accommodations

You'll find a wide range of lodging possibilities here, from Colorado's fanciest resort—The Broadmoor—to a basic hostel. There are also several particularly nice bed-and-breakfasts, especially in Manitou Springs. The rates listed here are the officially quoted prices ("rack rates") and don't take into account any individual or group discounts.

In these listings, the price ranges, based on the summer rate for a double room, are: **very expensive,** more than $200; **expensive,** $120 to $200; **moderate,** $65 to $120; and **inexpensive,** less than $65. A lodging tax (about 8.5% in Colorado Springs, about 9.5% in Manitou Springs) will be added to all bills.

IN COLORADO SPRINGS
VERY EXPENSIVE

✪ **The Broadmoor.** Lake Circle, at Lake Ave. (P.O. Box 1439), Colorado Springs, CO 80901.
☎ **800/634-7711** or 719/634-7711. Fax 719/577-5779. 700 rms and suites. A/C TV TEL.
Summer, $230–$345 double; $375–$1,900 suite. Winter, $155–$195 double; $250–$1,350
suite. Winter packages may cost as little as $62.50 per person per night. AE, CB, DC, MC, V.
Free parking.

A Colorado Springs institution and a tourist attraction in its own right, the Broadmoor is a sprawling resort complex of pink Mediterranean-style buildings with modern additions, located at the foot of Cheyenne Mountain. Built in the Italian
Renaissance–style, the Broadmoor opened in 1918. Its marble staircase, chandeliers,
della Robbia tile, hand-painted beams and ceilings, and carved marble fountain
remain spectacles today, along with a priceless art collection featuring original work
by Toulouse-Lautrec and Ming dynasty ceramists. The first names entered on the
guest register were those of John D. Rockefeller, Jr. and his party.

The guest rooms are located in three separate buildings—Broadmoor Main,
adjacent Broadmoor South, and Broadmoor West across Broadmoor Lake—on the
3,000-acre grounds. The guest rooms, which are spacious and luxurious, are decorated with early 20th-century antiques and original works of art. Most rooms are furnished with two double beds or one king-size bed, desks and tables, plush seating,
secluded luggage areas, and excellent lighting. The service is impeccable: the hotel
staffs two employees for every room.

Dining/Entertainment: Charles Court (see "Dining," below), in Broadmoor
West, is the hotel's finest restaurant. The elegant Penrose Room, on the top floor of
Broadmoor South, offers continental cuisine and is open for dinner and a popular
Sunday brunch. The Tavern (see "Dining" below), in Broadmoor Main, serves steak
and seafood in an informal setting. The Lake Terrace Dining Room serves breakfast
daily. More casual are the Golden Bee (see "Colorado Springs After Dark" below),
an authentic English pub; Julie's, a sidewalk cafe and ice-cream shop on the west bank
of Cheyenne Lake; the Espresso cafe, with gourmet coffee and pastries; and the
Broadmoor Golf Club (members and hotel guests only). There are also six lounges,
each to fit a different mood. Across Lake Circle is the Broadmoor International
Theatre.

Services: 24-hour room service, full concierge service, in-room massage, valet
laundry, shuttle bus between buildings.

Facilities: Sports and recreational facilities include three 18-hole championship
golf courses, three swimming pools, 12 all-weather tennis courts, trap and skeet-
shooting grounds, bicycle rental, a state-of-the-art fitness center and full service
spa, aerobics classes, saunas, and a Jacuzzi. Horseback riding, paddle-boating on
Broadmoor Lake, and hot-air ballooning are also available. There are 28 shops (boutiques, galleries, jeweler, florist, pharmacy, hair salon, and gift shop), a cinema, car-
rental agency, and service station. There are nonsmoking rooms, and facilities for
those with disabilities. Up to 1,600 seats can be accommodated for meetings; there
are 46 meeting rooms and a conference center.

EXPENSIVE

The Antlers Doubletree Hotel. 4 S. Cascade Ave., Colorado Springs, CO 80903. ☎ **800/
222-TREE** or 719/473-5600. Fax 719/444-0417. 284 rms, 6 suites. A/C TV TEL. $125–$180
double; $300–$700 suite. AE, CB, DC, DISC, ER, JCB, MC, V. Parking $5 per day.

The Antlers has been a Colorado Springs landmark for more than a century—
although there have been three different Antlers on the same site. The first, a turreted

Colorado Springs Accommodations & Dining

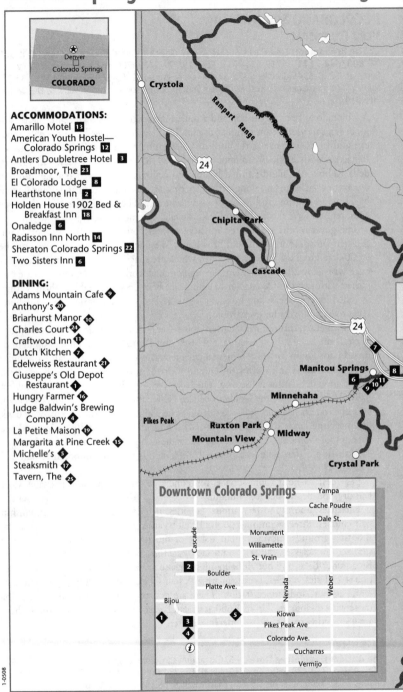

COLORADO
★ Denver
□ Colorado Springs

ACCOMMODATIONS:
Amarillo Motel **13**
American Youth Hostel—
  Colorado Springs **12**
Antlers Doubletree Hotel **3**
Broadmoor, The **23**
El Colorado Lodge **8**
Hearthstone Inn **2**
Holden House 1902 Bed &
  Breakfast Inn **18**
Onaledge **6**
Radisson Inn North **14**
Sheraton Colorado Springs **22**
Two Sisters Inn **6**

DINING:
Adams Mountain Cafe **9**
Anthony's **20**
Briarhurst Manor **10**
Charles Court **24**
Craftwood Inn **11**
Dutch Kitchen **7**
Edelweiss Restaurant **21**
Giuseppe's Old Depot
  Restaurant **1**
Hungry Farmer **16**
Judge Baldwin's Brewing
  Company **4**
La Petite Maison **19**
Margarita at Pine Creek **15**
Michelle's **5**
Steaksmith **17**
Tavern, The **25**

Crystola

Rampart Range

24

Chipita Park

Cascade

24

7

Manitou Springs
8
6
9 10 11

Minnehaha

Pikes Peak

Ruxton Park
Mountain View

Midway

Crystal Park

Downtown Colorado Springs

Yampa
Cache Poudre
Dale St.
Cascade
Monument
Williamette
St. Vrain
2
Boulder
Platte Ave.
Nevada
Weber
Bijou
1
3
5
Kiowa
4
Pikes Peak Ave
(i)
Colorado Ave.
Cucharras
Vermijo

1-0508

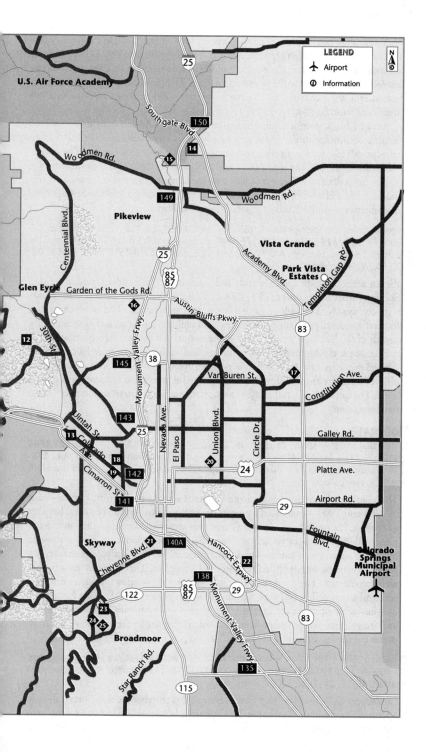

Victorian showcase built in 1883, was named for General William Palmer's collection of deer and elk trophies. After it was destroyed by fire in 1898, Palmer built an extravagant Italian Renaissance–style building that survived until 1964, when it was leveled to make room for the new Antlers Plaza. That, in turn, was closed for over a year after it was purchased by Doubletree Hotels—and reopened in October 1990 after a dramatic face-lift.

Antique black-walnut nightstands from the former Antlers provide a touch of historic continuity in the guest rooms, which also have armoires with TVs, two telephones (50¢ for local calls), coffeemakers, and ample closet space. The corner rooms are larger, and the west side rooms provide great views of the mountains.

The hotel offers a full range of facilities, including a beauty salon, fitness center, indoor pool, and whirlpool. It has two restaurants, including Colorado Springs' first microbrewery—Judge Baldwin's (see "Dining," below).

Sheraton Colorado Springs Hotel. 2886 S. Circle Dr. (I-25, Exit 138), Colorado Springs, CO 80906. ☎ **800/325-3535** or 719/576-5900 worldwide, 800/576-5470 direct. Fax 719/576-7695. 584 rms, 16 suites. A/C TV TEL. $88–$155 double; $310–$515 suites. AE, CB, DC, DISC, MC, V. Free parking.

Eleven acres of landscaped grounds and a beautiful skylit indoor garden set this Sheraton apart from others. The grounds feature trees, waterfalls, and three plaza-style courtyards. The indoor garden has a pool and Jacuzzi. The outdoor garden features a second pool, sunbathing area, and children's play area. There are also a health club, business center, and game room. All rooms are equipped with coffeemakers, clock radios, full-size mirrors, and vanities. Some have balconies and stocked minibars, and many offer views of the indoor or outdoor pool. A half-dozen bi-level suites are furnished with a king-size bed in a loft and a sleeper sofa downstairs. The hotel offers a full range of services, including courtesy airport shuttle and two restaurants.

MODERATE

✪ **Hearthstone Inn.** 506 N. Cascade Ave., Colorado Springs, CO 80903. ☎ **800/521-1885** or 719/473-4413. Fax 719/473-1322. 25 rms and suites, 2 rms with shared bath. A/C. $78–$130 private bath, $62–$65 shared bath; $130–$148 suite. Rates include full breakfast. AE, MC, V. Free parking.

This comfortably elegant small downtown inn is actually two historic homes—built in 1885 and 1900—connected by a carriage house. Listed on the National Register of Historic Places, and the winner of numerous preservation awards, the inn is decorated with old photographs and antiques, plus reproduction king- and queen-size brass beds. Each room has its own distinct personality. The Study, for instance, is a parlor-style room with built-in bookcases and a fireplace. The Solarium has an open-air latticed porch. The third-floor Loft has three dormer windows, a queen-size brass bed, and a tiny child's bed with a child-size rocking chair. Breakfasts are fantastic—imaginative variations of the standard eggs, cheese, and meat, plus home-baked breads and fruit dishes. There are no televisions or telephones in the rooms. A common parlor has games, a piano, and fresh coffee. No pets or smoking.

✪ **Holden House 1902 Bed & Breakfast Inn.** 1102 W. Pikes Peak Ave., Colorado Springs, CO 80904. ☎ **719/471-3980.** 6 rms. A/C TEL. $80–$115 double. Rates include full breakfast. AE, CB, DC, DISC, MC, V. Free parking.

Innkeepers Sallie and Welling Clark restored this storybook colonial revival–style Victorian house and its adjacent 1906 carriage house, and filled the rooms with antiques and family heirlooms. Located near Old Colorado City, the inn has a

---

🎠 Family-Friendly Hotels

Radisson Inn North *(see this page)*   Kids like the 24-hour pool and video games; for teens who want to hang out, Chapel Hills Mall is right across the street.

Sheraton Colorado Springs Hotel *(see p. 120)*   Two swimming pools, a separate children's pool, shuffleboard, and a putting green should keep most kids occupied.

---

living room with a tile fireplace, a front parlor with a television, and verandas. Guests enjoy a 24-hour coffee/tea service with a bottomless cookie jar, and a gourmet breakfast in the formal dining room. Smoking, children, and pets are not permitted—the two resident cats, Mingtoy & Muffin, claim prior tenancy. Each guest room, which is named after a Colorado mining area, contains memorabilia of that district. All have queen-size beds, three have fireplaces, and several have tubs for two. The newest room, Independence Suite, in the adjacent building, is accessible to the disabled and is cat-free for those with allergies.

Radisson Inn North. 8110 N. Academy Blvd. (I-25, Exit 150A), Colorado Springs, CO 80920. ☎ **800/333-3535** or 719/598-5770. Fax 719/598-3434. 193 rms, 7 suites. A/C TV TEL. $80–$120 double, $149–$249 suite. AE, CB, DC, DISC, ER, JCB, MC, V. Free parking.

The nearest full-service hotel to the Air Force Academy has a large and beautiful atrium, with fountains beneath a skylight. Guest rooms are outfitted with king or double beds, light-wood furnishings, dressing tables, and TV with in-house movies. Facilities include a restaurant, indoor pool, fitness center, whirlpool, sauna, guest laundry, gift shop, and game room. There is a complimentary airport shuttle. Chapel Hills Mall is within easy walking distance.

INEXPENSIVE

⑤ Amarillo Motel. 2801 W. Colorado Ave., Colorado Springs, CO 80904. ☎ **800/216-8539** or 719/635-8539. Fax 719/473-2609. 30 rms. A/C TV TEL. $30–$45 double. MC, V. Free parking.

If you're looking for a clean, basic, reasonably priced motel, try the Amarillo. Well-maintained rooms have all the usual amenities, and many have kitchenettes. There is cable television, a coin-operated laundry, and free local phone calls. The motel is located on the west side of Old Colorado City, close to Garden of the Gods and other attractions. It does not have a swimming pool.

American Youth Hostel—Colorado Springs. 3704 W. Colorado Ave., Colorado Springs, CO 80904. ☎ **800/345-8197** or 719/475-9450. Fax 719/475-9450. 48 dormitory beds. $10 for AYH members. MC, V. Closed mid-Sept–mid-May.

Located in the Garden of the Gods Campground, this hostel—comprised of a series of streamside cabins—is blessed with a remarkably beautiful location. As with all hostels, the bathrooms are shared, and there's a laundry and telephone. This hostel also has a huge swimming pool and whirlpool. It's open only in summer, and only to AYH and IYH members.

IN MANITOU SPRINGS
MODERATE

Onaledge. 336 El Paso Blvd., Manitou Springs, CO 80829. ☎ **800/530-8253,** or 719/685-4265 (voice and fax). 3 rms, 2 suites. A/C. $80–$90 double; $109–$130 hot tub suite. Rates include breakfast. AE, DISC, MC, V. Directions: Take U.S. 24 west, turn onto Manitou Ave. west for two blocks and then right on Mayfair St.; go to the top of the hill to El Paso Blvd., and Onaledge will be directly in front of you.

Highlights of this handsome English Tudor stone mansion include a copper fireplace hood, two player pianos, hardwood floors, and eight natural rock terraces outside. The rooms and suites are opulently comfortable. The Craftwood Room is furnished with a brass bed and wicker furniture; the large windows of the Onaledge Room frame Pikes Peak; the Rockledge Suite offers a king-size canopy bed and a hot tub for two; and the Fireplace Suite features a private hot tub. The new carriage house boasts a private patio with a hot tub for two just outside the door. A full gourmet breakfast is served outdoors under a vine arbor when the weather allows.

✪ **Two Sisters Inn.** 10 Otoe Place, Manitou Springs, CO 80829. ☎ **719/685-9684.** 4 rms (2 with bath), 1 cottage with bath. $63 with shared bath, $75 with private bath; $95 cottage. Rates include full breakfast. DISC, MC, V. Free parking.

Built by two sisters in 1919 as a boardinghouse, this award-winning bed-and-breakfast is still owned and operated by two women—sisters in spirit if not actually in blood. Wendy Goldstein and Sharon Smith have furnished the four bedrooms and separate honeymoon cottage with family heirlooms and photographs, in a style best described as informal elegance. The rooms in the main house feature Victorian frills and furnishings, such as quilts and claw-footed bathtubs. The cottage, with a separate bedroom and living room, has a feather bed, gas-log fireplace, refrigerator, and shower with skylight. There are fresh flowers in each room, and homemade chocolates and baked goods are served in the evenings. Well-supervised children over 10 years of age are accepted, but smoking and pets are not permitted.

INEXPENSIVE

El Colorado Lodge. 23 Manitou Ave., Manitou Springs, CO 80829. ☎ **800/782-2246** or 719/685-5485. 26 cabins (8 with kitchen). A/C TV TEL. Summer, $44.50–$96.50. Winter rates up to 30% off. AE, CB, DC, DISC, MC, V.

Most of the cabins in this southwestern-style lodge have fireplaces and beamed ceilings. Each cabin has from one to three clean, well-appointed rooms and can accommodate from two to six people. The lodge boasts the largest outdoor swimming pool in Manitou Springs, an outdoor pavilion for groups, and fully equipped kitchenettes. Pets not allowed.

CAMPING

Garden of the Gods Campground. 3704 W. Colorado Ave., Colorado Springs, CO 80904. ☎ **800/345-8197** or 719/475-9450. $22–$25 for two people. Extra person $2. AE, DISC, MC, V. Closed mid-Oct–mid-Apr.

Near the park, this large, tree-shaded campground offers 250 full R.V. hookups, an adults-only section, and additional tent sites. Facilities include tables, a barbecue pit, bathhouses, a grocery, laundry, heated swimming pool, Jacuzzi, playground, and game room.

Mueller State Park. P.O. Box 49, Divide, CO 80814. ☎ **800/678-2267** for reservations, or 719/687-2366. 90 sites. $3 per vehicle park entrance fee, plus camping fee of $7 for walk-in sites, $10 for drive-in sites with electricity. MC, V for reservations, cash only at the park.

Located on the west slope of Pikes Peak, this park is ideal for campers who want to get away from it all but still enjoy a hot shower and modern rest room at the end of the day. To reach the park entrance, take U.S. 24 west from Colorado Springs to Divide (25 miles), then go 3½ miles south on Colo. 67.

4 Dining

Colorado Springs and the tiny neighboring community of Manitou Springs have, between them, an excellent variety of above-average restaurants. For some reason, almost all of them put a lot of effort into creating exciting desserts. The restaurant price categories given below refer to most dinner main courses: **very expensive,** over $20; **expensive,** $15 to $20; **moderate,** $10 to $15; and **inexpensive,** under $10.

IN COLORADO SPRINGS
VERY EXPENSIVE

Charles Court. Broadmoor West, in the Broadmoor, Lake Circle. ☎ **719/634-7711.** Reservations recommended. Breakfast $7.75–$15.50, main courses $18–$36. CB, DC, MC, V. Daily 7–10am and 6:30–9:30pm. CONTEMPORARY AMERICAN.

The English country-manor atmosphere of this outstanding restaurant, with picture windows looking across Broadmoor Lake to the renowned Broadmoor Hotel, lends itself to a fine dining experience complete with attentive service.

The creative menu changes seasonally, but you'll usually find such delicacies as Colorado lamb chops, beef tenderloin, salmon fillet, and a wild-game selection such as Colorado elk. The wine list includes more than 600 selections, and the desserts are extraordinary.

EXPENSIVE

✪ **La Petite Maison.** 1015 W. Colorado Ave. ☎ **719/632-4887.** Reservations recommended. Main courses $15–$22. AE, CB, DC, DISC, MC, V. Tues–Sat 5–10pm. CONTEMPORARY.

This delightful 1894 Victorian cottage houses a gem of a restaurant, providing a blend of classic French and modern southwestern cuisine, served in a friendly, intimate setting to the strains of chamber music. The food is top rate and the service impeccable. This is where locals go to celebrate special occasions. Our recommendations include lamb chops dijonnaise and sautéed beef tenderloin with Danish bleu-cheese sauce. The menu also includes the evening's pasta selection, sautéed duck breast, and fresh fish.

The Margarita at Pine Creek. 7350 Pine Creek Rd. ☎ **719/598-8667.** Reservations recommended. Fixed-price dinner $19–$23. AE, DISC, MC, V. Lunch Tues–Fri 11:30am–2pm; dinner Tues–Sat 6–9pm; brunch Sun 10:30am–2pm. INTERNATIONAL.

A delightful spot to sit and watch the sun setting over Pikes Peak; the Margarita, at the north end of the city, is decorated in southwestern style with tile floors and stuccoed walls. A tree-shaded outdoor patio is open in summer. Lunches feature a choice of soup (usually a beef barley and a seafood or mushroom bisque), salad, and homemade bread. There is also a southwestern special. Six-course dinners offer three choices of entree, usually fresh fish, veal, steak, pasta, lamb, or duckling, and a Mexican dish weeknights.

Steaksmith. 3802 Maizeland Rd. (at Academy Blvd.). ☎ **719/596-9300.** Reservations recommended. Main courses $12–$35. AE, CB, DC, MC, V. Mon–Sat 5:30–10pm, Sun 4–9pm. Open for cocktails from 4pm daily. STEAK/SEAFOOD.

Reputed to serve some of the best steaks and seafood in Colorado Springs, the Steaksmith works hard to maintain its reputation. In addition to a wide choice of top-quality beef, the restaurant offers excellent seafood, including Alaskan king crab, Australian lobster tails, and large Gulf shrimp. Be warned that the prime rib and fresh seafood specials often sell out early in the evening—a sure sign of success. The menu also features baby-back ribs, chicken entrees, a variety of appetizers, homemade soups, and desserts (for example, homemade caramel piñon nut ice cream).

✪ **The Tavern.** Broadmoor Main, at the Broadmoor, Lake Circle. ☎ **719/634-7711.** Reservations recommended. Appetizers $5–$9.50; main courses $7.50–$17 at lunch, $10–$35 at dinner. Children's menu $3.25–$4.25. AE, CB, DC, MC, V. Daily 11:30am–4pm, 5–11pm. STEAK/SEAFOOD.

Original Toulouse-Lautrec lithographs on the walls mark the Tavern as a restaurant with unusual ambiance. The main dining room features live background music at night, while the adjoining Garden Room has luxuriant tropical foliage. In both rooms the service is impeccable—and this is the Broadmoor's *informal* dining spot!

The lunch menu features London broil au jus, seafood crêpes Louise, Welsh rarebit, and a variety of sandwiches and salads. Dinners are more elaborate: choose from slow-roasted prime rib, filet mignon, blackened or broiled salmon or swordfish, or half a roast duck or chicken.

MODERATE

Anthony's. 1919 E. Boulder St. ☎ **719/471-3654.** Reservations recommended for groups of 5 or more. Main courses at dinner $11–$20; at lunch $5–$10. AE, DISC, MC, V. Mon–Fri 11am–2pm; Tues–Thurs and Sun 5–9pm, Fri–Sat 5–10pm. ITALIAN.

Situated in a quiet eastside neighborhood, Anthony's is a tranquil escape from a hectic day. In summer, there is an outdoor patio for dining; in winter, a blazing fire keeps you warm. All pastas, from manicotti to fettuccine, are homemade. Regulars often choose chicken parmigiana and saltimbocca alla Romana. All dinners come with soup, salad, and garlic bread, and a plate of linguine accompanies meat dishes.

Edelweiss Restaurant. 34 E. Ramona Ave. ☎ **719/633-2220.** Reservations recommended. Main courses at dinner $7.75–$16.50; at lunch $4.10–$6.95. AE, DC, DISC, MC, V. Mon–Fri 11:30am–2pm; Sun–Thurs 5–9pm, Fri–Sat 5–9:30pm. GERMAN.

An impressive stone building with red trim, a big fireplace inside, and a patio outside, the Edelweiss underscores its Bavarian atmosphere with strolling folk musicians on weekends. Located southwest of I-25, just west of Nevada Avenue, it offers a hearty menu of *Jägerschnitzel,* Wiener schnitzel, sauerbraten, bratwurst, and other old-country specials—as well as New York strip steak, fresh fish, and chicken. The fruit strudels are excellent.

Giuseppe's Old Depot Restaurant. 10 S. Sierra Madre St. ☎ **719/635-3111.** Menu items $3.95–$18.95. AE, CB, DC, DISC, MC, V. Sun–Thurs 11am–10pm, Fri–Sat 11am–midnight. ITALIAN/AMERICAN.

Lodged in a restored Denver & Rio Grande train station, glass ticket windows line the walls, and a garden room has been added. The same menu is served all day, offering a wide variety. Spaghetti, lasagna, and stone-baked pizza are house specialties. American dishes include baby-back ribs, prime rib, fried chicken, and Louisiana shrimp Creole.

The Hungry Farmer. 575 Garden of the Gods Rd. ☎ **719/598-7622.** Reservations accepted. Main courses at dinner $10.95–$15.95; at lunch $4.75–$10.95. AE, CB, DC, DISC, MC, V. Mon–Fri 11:30am–2pm; Mon–Thurs 5–9pm, Fri 5–10, Sat 4–10, Sun 11:30am–9pm. AMERICAN.

Locally famous for its generous portions and slow-cooking prime rib, this restaurant has a farm atmosphere, complete with bales of hay, which makes it a favorite among kids. There's a large selection of steak, chicken, seafood, ribs, and veal, and all dinners include a bottomless bucket of soup, corn on the cob, salad, potato, and hot homemade muffins and rolls. Children have their own menu, and there's a full-service bar.

> ### 🙂 Family-Friendly Restaurants
>
> **Edelweiss Restaurant** *(see p. 124)*   Kids will enjoy the strolling musicians who play German folk music on weekends, and they'll love the apple and cherry strudels.
>
> **The Hungry Farmer** *(see p. 124)*   With their own menu, kids will feel special here. They'll also enjoy the farm-like atmosphere, complete with bales of hay.
>
> **Giuseppe's Old Depot Restaurant** *(see p. 124)*   An original locomotive stands outside this old Denver & Rio Grande Railroad station. Most kids adore the spaghetti and the pizza.

INEXPENSIVE

Judge Baldwin's Brewing Company. The Antlers Doubletree Hotel, 4 S. Cascade Ave. ☎ **719/473-5600.** Menu items $3.95–$8.95. AE, CB, DC, DISC, MC, V. Sun–Thurs 11am–11pm; Fri–Sat 11am–midnight. AMERICAN.

Judge Baldwin's, like many good brew pubs, takes just as much pride in its food as it does in its handcrafted beer. The great-tasting burgers are made from one-half pound of fresh ground beef, charbroiled to order. If you don't want red meat, you can get a burger made with ground turkey. There's also a pasta of the day, black-bean chile, a huge club sandwich, beer-batter shrimp, a turkey sandwich, pizza, and the highly recommended killer quesadillas (flour tortillas filled with Monterey Jack and Cheddar cheeses and jalapeno peppers). The menu also lists a variety of soups and salads; everything here goes well with Judge Baldwin's excellent beers (see "The Bar Scene," below).

Ⓢ **Michelle's.** 122 N. Tejon St. ☎ **719/633-5089.** Reservations not accepted. Breakfast $2.50–$5; lunch and dinner $4–$7. AE, DB, DC, DISC, MC, V. Mon–Thurs 9am–11pm, Fri–Sat 9am–midnight, Sun 10am–11pm. AMERICAN/GREEK/SOUTHWEST.

The menu is eclectic, but it's amazing how many different dishes Michelle's prepares well—and at such reasonable prices. Since it opened in 1952, this restaurant has been known for its excellent handmade chocolates, fresh churned ice cream, and Greek specialties such as gyros and spanakopita. But it also has great burgers, croissant sandwiches, a half-dozen different salads, numerous omelets, and a delicious breakfast burrito. A three-page ice-cream menu includes everything from a single scoop of vanilla to the "Believe It or Not Sundae," featured in *Life* magazine in November 1959; it weighed 42 pounds and included every flavor of ice cream Michelle's makes.

There's also a Michelle's in the Citadel Shopping Center, at East Platte Avenue and North Academy Boulevard (☎ 719/597-9932).

IN MANITOU SPRINGS
EXPENSIVE

Briarhurst Manor. 404 Manitou Ave., Manitou Springs. ☎ **719/685-1864.** Reservations suggested. Main courses $10.50–$29.50. Lower prices for seniors' and children's portions. AE, CB, DC, MC, V. Mon–Sat 6–10:30pm; May–Labor Day Sun 11am–3pm. CONTINENTAL/AMERICAN.

The original 1876 stone home of Manitou Springs founder Dr. William Bell, this magnificent Tudor mansion has all the style you'd expect to find in an English country house. Scheduled for demolition in 1975, the building was purchased by chef Sigi Krauss, an East German who came to Colorado Springs after 10 years in Vail. Krauss restored its rich wood interior, including a Gothic oak staircase, and turned it into a world-renowned restaurant.

The Briarhurst features meticulously prepared selections ranging from Rocky Mountain rainbow trout to Colorado lamb chops to a vegetarian platter. There are also homemade pastas, chicken and seafood, and a variety of beef dishes. A special treat is the Wednesday night all-you-can-eat candlelight buffet, with a marvelous array of delicacies from around the world—from appetizers to dessert.

✪ **Craftwood Inn.** 404 El Paso Blvd., Manitou Springs. ☎ **719/685-9000.** Reservations recommended. Main courses $10–$30. DISC, MC, V. Daily 5–10pm. COLORADO CUISINE.

Ensconced in an English Tudor building with beamed ceilings, stained-glass windows, and a copper-hooded fireplace, the Craftwood Inn, built in 1912, was originally a coppersmith's shop. Today this excellent restaurant specializes in regional game—dishes such as juniper venison, grilled piñon trout, and roast pheasant—plus seafood, chicken, and vegetarian dishes. Save room for one of the superb desserts—such as jalapeno white-chocolate mousse with raspberry sauce and prickly pear sorbet.

To reach the Craftwood Inn, turn north off Manitou Avenue onto Mayfair Avenue; go uphill one block, and turn left onto El Paso Boulevard.

INEXPENSIVE

Adams Mountain Cafe. 110 Cañon Ave., Manitou Springs. ☎ **719/685-1430.** Breakfast $2.50–$6.95; lunch $2.50–$6.95; dinner $5.95–$12. MC, V. Tues–Sat 7:30am–3pm, 5–9pm; Sun 7:30am–3pm. INTERNATIONAL/NATURAL FOODS.

This cafe has a country French/Victorian setting, with exposed brick and stone, antique tables and chairs, fresh flowers, and original watercolors. The menu includes grilled items and fresh fish, although the restaurant focuses on vegetarian offerings made with the freshest ingredients. Many entrees are prepared in a decidedly Mediterranean style. Homemade chocolate cake is a specialty.

Dutch Kitchen. 1025 Manitou Ave., Manitou Springs. ☎ **719/685-9962.** Lunch main dishes $3.40–$5.15; dinner main dishes $5.50–$7.25. Sat–Thurs 11:30am–3:30pm and 4:30–8pm. Closed Dec, Jan, and Feb. AMERICAN.

Good, homemade food served in a casual, friendly atmosphere is what you'll find at this relatively small restaurant which has been owned and operated by the Flynn family since 1959. The corned beef, pastrami, and ham sandwiches have been popular since the restaurant opened, and if you're there in summer be sure to try the fresh rhubarb pie. Other house specialties include buttermilk pie and homemade soups.

5 Attractions

The attractions of the Pikes Peak region can be placed in two general categories: natural, such as Pikes Peak, Garden of the Gods, and Cave of the Winds; and historic and educational, including the Air Force Academy, Olympic Training Center, museums, historic homes, and art galleries. And there are also the gambling houses of Cripple Creek. If you have just arrived in Colorado from a sea-level area, you might want to schedule any mountain excursions, such as the cog railway to the top of Pikes Peak, for the end of your stay; this will allow your body to adapt better to the lack of oxygen at higher elevations.

THE TOP ATTRACTIONS

United States Air Force Academy. Off I-25, Exit 156B. ☎ **719/472-2555.** Free admission. Daily 9am–5pm in winter, 9am–6pm in summer; additional hours for special events.

Colorado Springs' pride and joy got its start in 1954, when Congress authorized the establishment of a U.S. Air Force Academy and chose this 18,000-acre site—on a broad mesa buffered on the west by the Rockies, 12 miles north of downtown—from among 400 prospective sites. The first class of cadets enrolled in 1958. Each year since, about 4,000 cadets have enrolled for the 4 years of rigorous training required to become Air Force officers.

Approach the academy through the North Gate, off I-25, Exit 156B. Soon after entering the grounds, at the intersection of North Gate Boulevard and Stadium Boulevard, you'll see an impressive outdoor B-52 bomber display. Where North Gate Boulevard becomes Academy Drive (in another mile or so), look to your left to see the Cadet Field House, where basketball and ice hockey games are played (see "Outdoor Activities," below), and the Parade Ground, where cadets can sometimes be spotted marching.

Academy Drive soon curves to the left. Six miles from the North Gate, signs mark the turnoff to the Barry Goldwater Air Force Academy Visitor Center. Open daily, it offers a variety of exhibits and films on the academy's history and cadet life, extensive literature and self-guided tour maps, and the latest information and schedules on academy activities. There's also a large gift shop, coffee shop, public telephones, and rest rooms.

A short trail from the Visitor Center leads to the Cadet Chapel. Its 17 gleaming aluminum spires soar 150 feet skyward, and within the building are separate chapels for the major Western faiths as well as an "all-faiths" room. The public can visit Monday through Saturday from 9am to 5pm and on Sunday from 2 to 5pm; Sunday services at 9 and 11am are also open to the public. The chapel is closed for 5 days around graduation and during special events.

Also within easy walking distance of the Visitor Center are the Academy Planetarium, a classroom for astronomy, physics, and navigation classes that offers periodic free public programs; Arnold Hall, the social center that houses historical exhibits, a cafeteria, and a theater featuring a variety of public shows and lectures; and Harmon Hall, the administration building, where prospective cadets can obtain admission information.

After leaving the Visitor Center, continue south, then east, on Academy Boulevard to Stadium Boulevard, where you will see Falcon Stadium on your left. Turn right on Stadium Boulevard, and follow it out to South Gate Boulevard, which leaves the academy grounds at I-25, Exit 150B. En route, you'll pass the Thunderbird Airmanship Overlook, where you might be lucky enough to see cadets parachuting, soaring, and practicing their takeoffs and landings in U.S. Air Force Thunderbirds.

For specific information about the academy, write Visitor Services Division, Directorate of Public Affairs, U.S. Air Force Academy, Colorado Springs, CO 80840.

Pikes Peak Cog Railway. 515 Ruxton Ave., Manitou Springs. ☎ **719/685-5401.** Admission $23 adults, $11 children under 12 (but those under 5 held on an adult's lap are free). June–Aug, eight departures daily; in late Apr and Sept–Oct, two to six departures daily. Definite late Apr–Oct departures from Manitou Springs at 9:20am and 1:20pm. Reservations recommended. I-25, Exit 141 west on U.S. 24 for 4 miles, turn onto Manitou Ave. west 1 1/2 miles to Ruxton Ave., and turn left for about half a mile.

The first passenger train climbed 14,110-foot Pikes Peak on June 30, 1891, and diesel slowly replaced steam power between 1939 and 1957. Four custom-built Swiss twin-unit rail cars, each seating 216 passengers, were put into service in 1989. The 9-mile route, with grades up to 25%, takes 75 minutes to traverse, and the round-trip requires 3 hours and 10 minutes (including a 40-min. stopover at the top).

The journey is exciting from the start, but passengers really begin to "ooh" and "ahh" when the track leaves the forest, creeping above the timberline at about 11,500 feet. The view from the summit takes in Denver, 75 miles north; New Mexico's Sangre de Cristo range, 100 miles south; the Cripple Creek mining district, on the mountain's western flank; wave after wave of Rocky Mountain subranges to the west; and the seemingly endless sea of Great Plains to the east. The Summit House at the top of Pikes Peak has a restaurant and gift shop.

Take a jacket or sweater because it can be cold and windy on top. If you have cardiac or respiratory problems, this trip is not advisable.

Pikes Peak Highway. Off U.S. 24 at Cascade. ☎ **719/684-9383.** Admission $5 adults, $2 children 6–11, free for children under 6. Memorial Day–Labor Day, daily 7am–7pm; the rest of the year daily 9am–3pm, except closed Tues–Wed, Jan.–Feb. I-25, Exit 141 west on U.S. 24 about 10 miles.

There is perhaps no view in Colorado to equal the 360° panorama from the 14,110-foot summit of Pikes Peak. Whether you go by cog railway (see above) or private vehicle, the ascent is a spectacular and exciting experience, although not for those with heart or breathing problems or a fear of heights. This 19-mile toll highway (paved for 7 miles, all-weather gravel thereafter) starts at 7,400 feet, some 4 miles west of Manitou Springs. There are numerous photo stops as you head up the mountain; deer, mountain sheep, and other animals can often be seen on the slopes, especially above the timberline (around 11,500 feet). This 156-curve toll road is the site of the annual July Fourth Pikes Peak Auto Hill Climb, the Pikes Peak Marathon footrace in August, and the New Year's Eve climb and fireworks show.

✪ **Colorado Springs Pioneers Museum.** 215 S. Tejon St. ☎ **719/578-6650.** Free admission. Tues–Sat 10am–5pm; plus May–Sept Sun 1–5pm. I-25, Exit 141 east to Tejon St., left two blocks.

Housed in the former El Paso County Courthouse, which was built in 1903 and is now listed on the National Register of Historic Places, this museum is an excellent place to begin your visit to Colorado Springs. Exhibits depict the community's history including its beginning as a fashionable resort, the railroad and mining eras, and its growth and change into the 20th century. There's also the Victorian home of writer Helen Hunt Jackson, a section on the history of blacks in the region, plus turn-of-the-century toys, quilts, and clothing.

You can ride an 80-plus-year-old Otis bird-cage elevator to the restored original courtroom, where several Perry Mason episodes were filmed. The renovation uncovered gold and silver images of goddesses, painted on the courtroom walls as a protest when the country was changing from a gold to silver monetary standard. There are also murals depicting three periods in the history of the Pikes Peak Region, each represented by 12 panels.

✪ **Garden of the Gods.** Ridge Rd., I-25, Exit 146. ☎ **719/634-6666.** Free admission. Park: May–Oct, daily 5am–11pm; Nov–Apr, daily 5am–9pm. Visitor Center: summer, daily 7am–9pm; rest of year 9am–6pm. Take Garden of the Gods Rd. west off I-25 (Exit 146), and turn south on 30th Street, or follow Ridge Rd. north off U.S. 24 or Colorado Ave.

One of the West's unique geological sites, the Garden of the Gods is a beautiful giant rock garden, composed of spectacular red sandstone formations sculpted by rain and wind over millions of years. Located where several life zones and ecosystems converge, the park harbors a variety of plant and animal communities. Oldest survivors are the ancient, twisted junipers, some 1,000 years old. The strangest

---

Impressions

The air is so refined that you can live without much lungs.

—Shane Leslie, *American Wonderland*, 1936

animals are honey ants, which gorge themselves on honey in the summer and fall, thus becoming living honey pots to feed their colonies during winter hibernation.

Hiking maps for the 1,300-acre city-run park are available at the **Visitor Center,** which also offers an 8-minute geology show; displays on the history, geology, plants, and wildlife of the park; a cafeteria; and other conveniences. In the summer, park naturalists lead 45-minute walks through the park and conduct afternoon interpretive programs. You may spot technical rock climbers on some of the park spires (they are required to register at the Visitor Center).

Also in the park is the **Rock Ledge Ranch Historic Site** (see "More Attractions," below).

United States Olympic Complex. 1 Olympic Plaza, corner of Boulder St. (entrance) and Union Blvd. ☎ **719/578-4618.** Tour reservations required for groups of 10 or more. Free admission. Summer, Mon–Sat 9am–5pm, Sun 10am–4pm; Winter, Mon–Sat 9am–4pm, Sun noon–4pm. Take I-25, Exit 143.

This 36-acre site in the middle of Colorado Springs houses a sophisticated training center for more than half of the 41 U.S. Olympic sports, providing a training ground for some 17,000 athletes of all ages each year. Make your first stop the **Visitor Center** for a free guided tour, starting every 30 minutes in summer and every hour during the winter. Tours begin with a film depicting the U.S. Olympic effort, and then take in the **Sports Center,** with five gymnasiums and a weight-training room; the **Indoor Shooting Center,** with two 50-meter ranges; a new gymnasium that can accommodate 14 different sports; and a swimming complex with a 50-meter ten-lane pool. A gift shop next to the Visitor Center sells Olympic-logo merchandise; the proceeds help to support athlete training programs. One mile south of the Olympic Complex, in Memorial Park off Union Boulevard, is the **7-Eleven Velodrome,** with a banked track for bicycle and roller speed-skating.

MORE ATTRACTIONS
ARCHITECTURAL HIGHLIGHTS
The Broadmoor. Lake Circle, at Lake Ave. ☎ **719/634-7711.** Free admission. Open daily, year-round.

This famous Italian Renaissance–style resort hotel has been a Colorado Springs landmark since it was built by Spencer Penrose in 1918. (See "Accommodations," above.)

Miramont Castle Museum. 9 Capitol Hill Ave., Manitou Springs. ☎ **719/685-1011.** Admission $3 adults, $1 children 6–11, free for children under 6. Memorial Day–Labor Day, daily 10am–5pm; Apr–Memorial Day and Labor Day–mid-Dec, daily 11am–4pm; rest of year, daily noon–3pm. Located just off Ruxton Ave., en route from Manitou Ave. to the Pikes Peak Cog Railway.

Built into a hillside by a wealthy French priest as a private home in 1895, and converted by the Sisters of Mercy into a sanatorium in 1907, this unique Victorian mansion has always aroused curiosity. At least nine identifiable architectural styles are incorporated into the structure, which has four stories, 28 rooms, 14,000 square feet of floor space, and 2-foot-thick stone walls. One room is a miniature museum, and there's a model railroad museum in a separate building outside the castle. During the summer, light meals and tea are served from 11am to 4pm in the Queen's Parlour.

HISTORIC BUILDINGS
McAllister House. 423 N. Cascade Ave. (at St. Vrain St.). ☎ **719/635-7925.** Admission $3 adults, $2 seniors and students, $1 children 6–16, free for children under 6. Summer, Wed–Sat 10am–4pm, Sun noon–4pm; winter, Thurs–Sat 10am–4pm. I-25, Exit 141 east to Cascade Ave., left about six blocks.

Colorado Springs Attractions

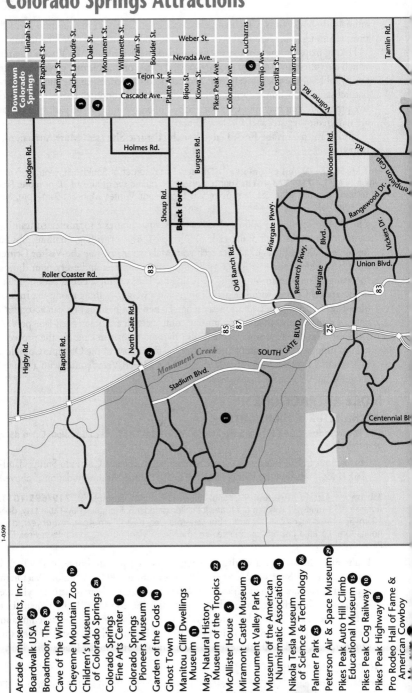

Downtown Colorado Springs

Uintah St.
San Raphael St.
Yampa St.
Cache La Poudre St.
Dale St.
Monument St.
Willamette St.
Vrain St.
Boulder St.
Weber St.
Nevada Ave.
Cucharras
Tejon St.
Platte Ave.
Bijou St.
Kiowa St.
Pikes Peak Ave.
Colorado Ave.
Vermijo Ave.
Costilla St.
Cimmaron St.
Cascade Ave.
Tamlin Rd.
Vollmer Rd.

Holmes Rd.
Burgess Rd.
Hodgen Rd.
Shoup Rd.
Black Forest
Woodmen Rd.
Briargate Pkwy.
Rangewood Dr.
Rd.
Templeton Gap
Vickers Dr.
Roller Coaster Rd.
Old Ranch Rd.
Research Pkwy.
Briargate Blvd.
Blvd.
Union Blvd.
North Gate Rd.
Monument Creek
Higby Rd.
Baptist Rd.
SOUTH GATE BLVD.
Stadium Blvd.
Centennial Bl

1-0509

Arcade Amusements, Inc. ⑬
Boardwalk USA ㉗
Broadmoor, The ⑳
Cave of the Winds ⑨
Cheyenne Mountain Zoo ⑲
Children's Museum
    of Colorado Springs ㉘
Colorado Springs
    Fine Arts Center ③
Colorado Springs
    Pioneers Museum ⑥
Garden of the Gods ⑭
Ghost Town ⑰
Manitou Cliff Dwellings
    Museum ⑪
May Natural History
    Museum of the Tropics ㉒
McAllister House ⑤
Miramont Castle Museum ⑫
Monument Valley Park ㉓
Museum of the American
    Numismatic Association ④
Nikola Tesla Museum
    of Science & Technology ㉖
Palmer Park ㉕
Peterson Air & Space Museum ㉙
Pikes Peak Auto Hill Climb
    Educational Museum ⑮
Pikes Peak Cog Railway ⑩
Pikes Peak Highway ⑧
Pro Rodeo Hall of Fame &
    American Cowboy

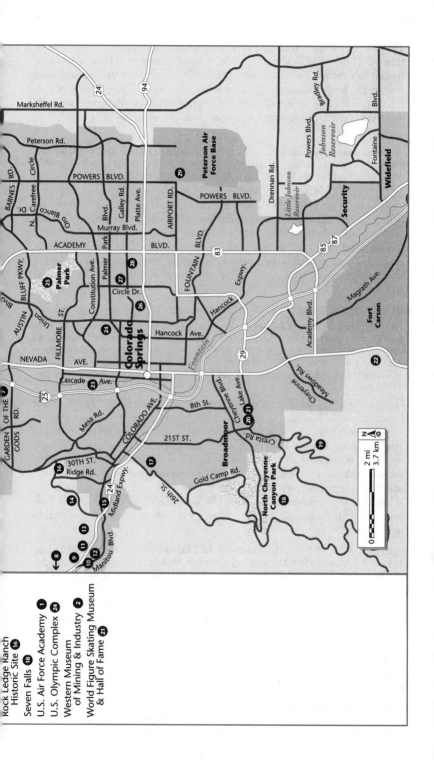

Rock Ledge Ranch
Historic Site **16**

Seven Falls **18**

U.S. Air Force Academy **1**

U.S. Olympic Complex **24**

Western Museum
of Mining & Industry **2**

World Figure Skating Museum
& Hall of Fame **21**

Marksheffel Rd.

Peterson Rd.

POWERS BLVD.

Peterson Air
Force Base

POWERS BLVD.

AIRPORT RD.

ACADEMY BLVD.

Murray Blvd.

Galley Rd.

Platte Ave.

Park Blvd.

BARNES RD.

N. Carefree Circle

Oro Blanco Dr.

25 Palmer Park

BLUFF PKWY.

Constitution Ave.

Palmer

27

28

26

AUSTIN

Union BLVD.

FILLMORE ST.

24

Circle Dr.

Hancock Ave.

Hancock Ave.

Colorado Springs

FOUNTAIN BLVD.

83

Drennan Rd.

Powers Blvd.

Bradley Rd.

Johnson Reservoir

Blvd.

Fontaine

Widefield

Little Johnson Reservoir

Security

85 **87**

Academy Blvd.

Magrath Ave.

Fort Carson

29

NEVADA AVE.

25

Cascade Ave. **23**

Fountain

29

Cheyenne Meadows Rd.

22

GARDEN OF THE GODS RD.

Mesa Rd.

COLORADO AVE.

8th St.

21ST ST.

16 30TH ST.
Ridge Rd.

14

15 **24** Midland Expwy.

17

Manitou Blvd.

8

9

10 **12**

11

13

26th St.

Cheyenne Blvd.

Lake Ave.

20 **21**

Cresta Rd.

Broadmoor

Gold Camp Rd.

North Cheyenne Canyon Park

18

19

N

2 mi

3.7 km

0

131

This Gothic cottage, listed in the National Register of Historic Places, was constructed of brick in 1873 when the builder, an army major named Henry McAllister, learned that the local wind was so strong that it had blown a train off the tracks nearby. The house has many original furnishings, including three marble fireplaces. It is now owned by the Colonial Dames of America, whose knowledgeable volunteers lead guided tours. Tea is served on certain holidays, and croquet is available on summer Sundays.

Rock Ledge Ranch Historic Site. Gateway Rd., Garden of the Gods. ☎ **719/578-6777.** Admission $3 adults, $2 seniors, $1 children 6–12, free for children under 6. June–Aug, Wed–Sun 10am–5pm; Sept to late Dec, Sat 10am–4pm, Sun noon–4pm. Closed Jan–May. I-25, Exit 146, follow signs west to Garden of the Gods.

The history of three different pioneer eras can be appreciated at this living-history farm at the east entrance to Garden of the Gods park. Visitors can see how Coloradans lived during the homestead era (1867–74), the working-ranch era (1874–1900), and the estate period (1900–09). Guides in period costumes compare the lifestyles of the three eras, and there are a working blacksmith shop and demonstrations of historical agricultural techniques. Visitors can also see a homestead cabin and general store.

MUSEUMS & GALLERIES

Colorado Springs Fine Arts Center. 30 W. Dale St. (west of N. Cascade Ave.). ☎ **719/ 634-5581.** Admission to galleries and museum, $3 adults, $1.50 seniors and students, $1 children 6–12, free for children under 6. Free for everyone Sat 10am–noon. Separate admission for performing arts events. Galleries and museum, Tues–Fri 9am–5pm, Sat 10am–5pm, Sun 1–5pm. Closed federal holidays. I-25, Exit 143 east to Tejon St., turn right to Dale St., and then turn right again.

Georgia O'Keeffe, John James Audubon, John Singer Sargent, Charles Russell, Albert Bierstadt, Nicolai Fechin, and other famed painters and sculptors are represented in the permanent collection, including a world-class collection of Native American and Hispanic works. Opened in 1936, the center also houses a 450-seat performing arts theater, 32,000-volume art research library, the Bemis Art School offering visual arts and drama classes, a tactile gallery for those who are visually impaired, and a delightful sculpture garden. Changing exhibits in two galleries showcase local collections, as well as touring international exhibits. Designed by renowned Santa Fe architect John Gaw Meem, the art-deco–style building reflects southwestern mission and pueblo influences.

Ghost Town. 400 S. 21st St., Old Colorado City. ☎ **719/634-0696.** Admission $4.50 adults, $2 children 6–16, under 6 free. Memorial Day–Labor Day, Mon–Sat 9am–6pm, Sun noon–6pm; Labor Day–Memorial Day, Mon–Sat 10am–5pm, Sun noon–5pm. Just west of I-25, Exit 241 on U.S. 24 at 21st St.

Comprised of authentic 19th-century buildings relocated from other parts of Colorado, this ghost town is sheltered from the elements in Old Colorado City. There's a sheriff's office, jail, saloon, general store, livery stable, blacksmith shop, rooming house, and assay office. Animated frontier characters tell stories of the Old West, while a shooting gallery, antique arcade machines, and nickelodeons provide additional entertainment. The Taming of the West Theater presents a short film on frontier ghost towns.

✪ **Manitou Cliff Dwellings Museum.** U.S. 24, Manitou Springs. ☎ **719/685-5242.** Admission $6 adults, $5 seniors, $4 children 7–11, free for children under 7. June–Aug, daily 9am–8pm; Mar–May and Sept–Oct, daily 9am–6pm; Nov–Feb, Sat–Sun 10am–5pm. I-25, Exit 141 west on U.S. 24 about 5 miles.

The cliff dwelling ruins here are real, although originally they were located elsewhere. In the early 1900s, archaeologists, who saw such dwellings being plundered by treasure hunters, dismantled some of the ancient buildings, gathered together artifacts found there, and hauled them away. Some of them may now be seen in this relocated 12th-century village, built by archaeologists in Phantom Cliff Canyon around 1900. Native American dancers perform during the summer.

May Natural History Museum of the Tropics. 710 Rock Creek Canyon Rd. ☎ **719/ 576-0450.** Admission $4.50 adults, $2.50 children. May–Sept, daily 9am–6pm. Closed Oct– Apr. Take Colo. 115, and drive southwest out of Colorado Springs for 9 miles; watch for signs.

One of the world's best public collections of giant insects and other tropical invertebrates is presented here. James F. May (1884–1956) spent more than half a century exploring the world's jungles while compiling this illustrious collection of about 7,000 arthropods. A new Museum of Space Exploration is also located at the museum center, adjacent to the Golden Eagle Ranch R.V. park and campground.

Museum of the American Numismatic Association. 818 N. Cascade Ave. ☎ **719/ 632-2646.** Free admission, but donations are welcome. Mon–Fri 8:30am–4pm. I-25, Exit 143 east to Cascade Ave., then turn left for about six blocks.

The largest collection of its kind west of the Smithsonian Institute consists of eight galleries of coins, tokens, medals, and paper money from around the world. There's also a collectors' library, a gallery for the visually impaired, and an authentication department.

Nikola Tesla Museum of Science and Technology. 2220 E. Bijou St. ☎ **719/475-0918.** Admission $5 adults, $3 youths 13–17, $2 children 12 and under and seniors. Mon–Fri 10am– 4pm, Sat 11am–4pm. I-25, Exit 142 east to Cascade, turn left one block, then right onto Platte Ave. After about 2 miles, turn right onto Union Blvd. and left at the first block onto Bijou St. It's about three blocks down.

Science buffs will love this small but fascinating collection of early electronics and related gadgets. The museum's primary purpose is to display and demonstrate some of the many inventions of Nikola Tesla (1856–1943), who was awarded more than 100 U.S. patents and is believed responsible for accidentally throwing all of Colorado Springs into darkness during one of his many experiments. Tesla, a contemporary of Thomas Edison, perfected alternating current and invented the Tesla coil, a transformer used to produce high-frequency power. Guided hands-on tours are usually given Tuesday, Thursday, and Saturday at 2pm during the summer; Saturdays only in winter. The museum has an extensive science and technology bookstore.

Peterson Air and Space Museum. Peterson Air Force Base main gate, off U.S. 24. ☎ **719/ 556-4915.** Free admission. Tues–Fri 8:30am–4:30pm, Sat 9:30am–4:30pm. Closed Sun, Mon, and holidays and occasionally during military exercises. I-25, Exit 141, then follow U.S. 24 east about 7¹/₂ miles.

Through its exhibits, this museum traces the history of Peterson Air Force Base, NORAD, the Air Defense Command, and Air Force Space Command. Of special interest are 17 historic aircraft, including P-47 Thunderbolt and P-40 Warhawk fighters from World War II, plus four missiles and jets from the Korean War to the present. For the USAF 50th Anniversary, a Memorial Grove of 58 trees honoring the USAF Medal of Honor Recipients was planted. There's also a small gift shop.

Pikes Peak Auto Hill Climb Educational Museum. 135 Manitou Ave., Manitou Springs. ☎ **719/685-4400.** Admission $4 adults, $3 seniors, free for children under 12 accompanied by an adult. Mid-May–Oct 1, daily 9am–5pm; remainder of year, Mon–Fri 9am–4pm, Sat 9am– 3pm. I-25, Exit 141 west 4 miles on U.S. 24 to Manitou Ave., east one block.

Commemorating the nation's second-oldest auto race (the oldest is the Indianapolis 500), this museum displays nearly a century of memorabilia and historic photos, plus almost 2 dozen race cars from the 1920s to today. Racing legends including Mario Andretti, Parnelli Jones, and Al and Bobby Unser have competed in the annual July Fourth race—156 turns on a gravel highway to the summit of Pikes Peak—14,110 feet above sea level.

✪ **Pro Rodeo Hall of Fame and American Cowboy Museum.** 101 Pro Rodeo Dr. (off Rockrimmon Blvd.). ☎ **719/528-4764.** Admission $6 adults, $3 children 5–12, free for children under 5. Daily 9am–5pm. Closed New Year's Eve and Day, Easter, Thanksgiving, and Christmas. Just off I-25, Exit 147.

The development of Rodeo, from its origins in early ranch work to major professional sport, is featured in two multimedia presentations. The newly expanded Heritage Hall showcases cowboy and rodeo gear and clothing, and rodeo greats are honored in the Hall of Champions. There is a replica rodeo arena and live rodeo animals, as well as a display of western art.

✪ **Western Museum of Mining and Industry.** Gleneagle Drive, at I-25, Exit 156A. ☎ **719/488-0880.** Admission $5 adults, $4 seniors 60 and older and students 13–17, $2 children 5–12, and free for children under 5. Mar–Nov, Mon–Sat 9am–4pm, Sun noon–4pm; call for hours Dec–Feb. The 27-acre site is located just east of the north gate of the U.S. Air Force Academy.

Historic hard-rock mining machinery and other equipment from Cripple Creek and other turn-of-the-century Colorado gold camps form the basis of this museum's 3,000-plus item collection. There's an operating Corliss steam engine with a 17-ton flywheel, a life-size underground mine reconstruction, and an exhibit on mining-town life showing how early western miners and their families lived. Visitors can also pan for gold—there's a wheelchair-accessible trough—and view an 18-minute multi-projector slide presentation on life in the early mining camps. In 1995, a new exhibit opened: "What's Mined is Yours," explaining the use of minerals in the production of everyday items such as makeup and insulation.

World Figure Skating Museum and Hall of Fame. 20 First St. ☎ **719/635-5200.** Free admission. June–Aug, Mon–Sat 10am–4pm; Sept–May, Mon–Fri and the first Sat of each month 10am–4pm. I-25, Exit 138 west on Lake Ave.; just before the Broadmoor, turn right onto First St.

This is the only museum of its kind in the world, exhibiting 1,200 years of ice skates—from early skates of bone to highly decorated cast-iron examples and finally the skates of today. There are skating costumes, medals, and other memorabilia, changing exhibits, films, a library, and gift shop. A gallery displays skating-related paintings, including works by the 17th-century Dutch artist Pieter Brueghel and Americans Winslow Homer and Andy Warhol.

NATURAL ATTRACTIONS

Cave of the Winds. U.S. 24, Manitou Springs. ☎ **719/685-5444.** Admission $10 adults, $5 children 6–15, free for children under 6. May–Labor Day, daily 9am–9pm; Labor Day–Apr, daily 10am–5pm. Adventure Tours depart every 15 min.; in summer, Lantern Tours ($12 adult, $6 child 6–15; not recommended for those under 6) are conducted four times daily and Explorer Tours ($60 per person, children 13–17 must be accompanied by parent or guardian; under 13 not permitted) three times daily, other times by reservation. Visitors with heart conditions, visual impairment, or other physical limitations are advised not to take the Lantern Tour, and may not take the Explorer Tour. Take I-25, Exit 141, and go 6 miles west on U.S. 24.

Discovered by two boys on a church outing in 1880, this impressive underground cavern has offered public tours for well over a century. The 40-minute Discovery

Tour takes visitors along a well-lit three-quarter-mile passageway through 20 subterranean chambers, complete with classic stalagmites, stalactites, crystal flowers, and limestone canopies. In the Adventure Room, modern lighting techniques return visitors to an era when spelunking was done by candle and lantern. The 1 1/4-hour Lantern Tour follows unpaved and unlighted passageways and corridors, is rather strenuous with some stooping required in areas with low ceilings, and might muddy your shoes, but not your clothes. There's also a physically demanding, 4-hour Explorer Tour that's guaranteed to get participants dirty: armed only with flashlights and helmets, adventurers slither and scramble through remote tunnels.

Seven Falls. At the end of South Cheyenne Canyon Rd. ☎ **719/632-0765.** Admission $6.50 adults, $3.50 children 6–15, free for children under 6. Memorial Day–Labor Day, daily 8am–11pm; reduced hours in other months. I-25, Exit 140, head south to Cheyenne Blvd., turn right for about 3 miles to S. Cheyenne Canyon Rd., and then turn left.

A spectacular 1-mile drive through a box canyon takes you between the Pillars of Hercules, where the canyon narrows to just 42 feet, ending at these cascading falls. Seven separate waterfalls dance down a granite cliff, illuminated each summer evening by colored lights. An elevator takes visitors to the Eagle Nest viewing platform. A mile-long trail atop the plateau passes the grave of 19th-century author Helen Hunt Jackson (*Ramona*) and ends at a panoramic view of Colorado Springs.

NEIGHBORHOODS

Manitou Springs. Manitou Ave. off U.S. 24 W.

Actually a separate town with its own government, Manitou Springs is one of the country's largest National Historic Districts. Legend has it that Utes named the springs Manitou, their word for "Great Spirit," because they believed that the Great Spirit had breathed into the waters to create the natural effervescence of the springs.

Today, the community offers the breathtaking sight of Pikes Peak, plus a step back in history to magnificent Victorian buildings, many housing fascinating shops, galleries, and restaurants. An effort is under way to reestablish the lure of the mineral springs by restoring and preserving the spring houses and many of the 28 original mineral springs.

Old Colorado City. Colorado Ave., between 21st and 31st sts.

Founded in 1859, before Colorado Springs itself, Colorado City boomed in the 1880s after General Palmer's railroad came through. Tunnels led from the respectable side of town to this saloon- and red-light district so that the city fathers could carouse without being seen going or returning—or so the legend goes. Today this historic district has an interesting assortment of shops, galleries, and restaurants.

PARKS & ZOOS

✪ **Cheyenne Mountain Zoo.** Cheyenne Mountain Zoo Rd. above the Broadmoor. ☎ **719/633-9925.** Admission $6.50 adults, $5.50 senior citizens 65 and up, $3.50 children 3–11, free for children under 3. Summer, daily 9am–6pm; rest of year, daily 9am–5pm. Take I-25, Exit 140A, and head south on Colo. 115 to Lake Ave., which you follow west to Cheyenne Mountain Zoo Rd.; watch for a sign.

Located on the lower slopes of Cheyenne Mountain at 6,800 feet above sea level, this medium-sized zoo claims to be the country's only mountain zoo. Animals, many in "natural" environments, include Siberian tigers, lions, black leopards, elephants, hippos, otters, monkeys, giraffes, reptiles, snakes, and lots of birds. Rocky cliffs have been created for the mountain goats; there's a pebbled beach for penguins and an animal-contact area for children. Three Mexican gray wolves (an endangered species) are at home in mountainside "wolf woods." The zoo also has a colorful antique carousel. A new exhibit, "Asian Highlands," is the home of Siberian tigers, amur leopards, and red pandas.

Admission to the zoo includes road access to the **Will Rogers Shrine of the Sun,** a tall wooden tower built in 1937 where you will find photos and other information on the American humorist. It also provides a great view of the city and surrounding countryside.

Memorial Park. Between Hancock Ave. and Union Blvd. (south of Pikes Peak Ave.). ☎ **719/ 578-6640.** Free admission. Open daily, year-round.

One of the largest parks in the city, Memorial is home to the Mark "Pa" Sertich Ice Center and the Aquatics and Fitness Center (see "Outdoor Activities," below) as well as the famed 7-11 Velodrome, which is used for world-class bicycling events. There are baseball/softball fields, volleyball courts, tennis courts, a bicycle criterium, and jogging trails. At the south side of the park is Prospect Lake, where fishing and swimming (summer, 10am–5pm, $2.50 adults, $1 children) are permitted and paddleboats can be rented (approximately $8 an hour). The park also hosts a terrific fireworks display on Independence Day.

Monument Valley Park. Monument Creek from Bijou St. north to Fontanero St. ☎ **719/ 578-6640.** Free admission. Open daily, year-round.

This long, slender park follows Monument Creek through downtown Colorado Springs. At its south end are formal zinnia, begonia, and rose gardens, and in the middle are demonstration gardens of the Horticultural Art Society. There are softball/baseball fields, a swimming pool (open daily in summer, $2 adults, $1 children), volleyball and tennis courts, children's playgrounds, picnic shelters, and two trails—the $4^1/_4$-mile Monument Creek Trail for walkers, runners, and cyclists, and the 1-mile Monument Valley Fitness Trail at the north end of the park, beside Bodington Field.

✪ **Mueller State Park.** P.O. Box 49, Divide, CO 80814. ☎ **719/687-2366.** Admission $3 per vehicle for day use. Daily 6am–10pm.

Somewhat like a junior version of Rocky Mountain National Park, Mueller has 12,000 acres of prime scenic beauty along the west slope of Pikes Peak. There are 90 miles of trails, designated for hikers, horseback riders, and mountain bikers, with opportunities to observe elk, bighorn sheep, and the park's other wildlife. The best times to spot wildlife are spring and fall, just after sunrise and just before sunset. There are ranger-led hikes and campfire programs in an 80-seat amphitheater. To reach the park entrance, take U.S. 24 west from Colorado Springs to Divide (25 miles), then go $3^1/_2$ miles south on Colo. 67. (Also see "Camping," above.)

North Cheyenne Cañon Park. 2120 S. Cheyenne Cañon Rd. (west of 21st St.). ☎ **719/ 578-6146.** Free admission. Park, May–Oct, daily 5am–11pm; Nov–Apr, daily 5am–9pm. Starsmore Discovery Center, early June–Labor Day, daily 9am–10pm; Labor Day–early June, Wed–Sun 10am–4pm. Helen Hunt Falls Visitor Center, May–Sept, daily 9am–5pm; Sept–Oct, Sat–Sun 10am–4pm, closed Nov–Apr.

Entirely within the city limits of Colorado Springs, this city park includes North Cheyenne Creek, which drops 1,800 feet over the course of 5 miles in a series of cascades and waterfalls. There are picnic areas, hiking trails, and a seasonal tram. The Visitor Center at the foot of Helen Hunt Falls has exhibits on history, geology, flora, and fauna. The Starsmore Discovery Center, at the entrance to the park, has maps, information, tram tickets ($5.75 adults, $3.25 children), and interactive exhibits for both kids and adults, including audiovisual programs and a climbing wall where you can learn about rock climbing.

Palmer Park. Maizeland Rd. off Academy Blvd. ☎ **719/578-6640.** Free admission. Open daily, year-round.

Deeded to the city in 1899 by Colorado Springs' founder Gen. William Jackson Palmer, this 722-acre preserve permits hiking, biking, and horseback riding across a mesa overlooking the city. It boasts a variety of minerals (including quartz, topaz, jasper, and tourmaline), rich vegetation (including a yucca preservation area), and considerable wildlife. The Edna Mae Bennet Nature Trail is a self-guided excursion; there are numerous other trails, including those shared with riders from the adjoining Mark Reyner Stables. The park also includes 12 separate picnic areas, softball/baseball fields, and volleyball courts.

ESPECIALLY FOR KIDS

In addition to the listings below, children will probably enjoy the following, described above: **May Natural History Museum, Miramont Castle Museum, Cheyenne Mountain Zoo,** and **Ghost Town.**

Arcade Amusements, Inc. 930 Block Manitou Ave., Manitou Springs. ☎ **719/685-9815.** Free admission; arcade games range from 1¢ to 75¢. First weekend in May–Labor Day, daily 10am–midnight. In winter, open on nice weekends 11am–6pm; call first.

Among the West's oldest and largest amusement arcades, this game complex just might be considered a hands-on arcade museum as well as a fun place for kids of all ages. There are some 250 machines, from original working penny pinball machines to modern video games, skee-ball, and 12-player horse racing.

Boardwalk USA. Pioneer Plaza Mall at Circle Dr. and Galley Rd., ☎ **719/637-PLAY.** Admission $5 for 1 hour plus $1 more for each additional hour; $10 for all day. School days 11am–10pm; school holidays, weekends, and summer, 9am–midnight.

This entertainment center provides lots of activities for kids of all ages, including bumper cars, an 18-hole miniature golf course, large video-game room, virtual reality, and an indoor theme park just for younger children (under 4 ft. tall).

Children's Museum of Colorado Springs. 750 Citadel Dr. (in the Citadel Mall). ☎ **719/574-0077.** Admission $2.50. Summer: Mon–Sat 10am–5pm, Sun noon–5pm; school year: Wed–Thurs 11:30am–5pm, Sun noon–5pm, Mon–Tues and Fri–Sat 10am–5pm. Off Academy Blvd. north of Platte Ave., in the mall upstairs next to J.C. Penney.

Kids create laser light designs, play in a mock hospital, improvise on the stage, and enjoy many more hands-on activities at this nonprofit art and science museum. A major renovation was under way in 1996.

6 Organized Tours

SIGHTSEEING TOURS   Half- and full-day bus tours of Colorado Springs, Pikes Peak, the Air Force Academy, and other nearby attractions are offered by **Pikes Peak Tours,** 3704 W. Colorado Ave. (☎ **800/345-8197** or 719/633-1181). A variety of other tours are offered from May through October, including an excursion to Royal Gorge and white-water rafting trips. Prices range from $15 to $60 per person.

WALKING TOURS   Historic walking tours, as well as customized individual and group tours are available from **Talk of the Town,** 1313 Sunset Rd. (☎ **719/633-2724**); they also publish a book of walking tours, *Trips on Twos,* and a book of driving tours, *Trips on Wheels,* both of which are available at local bookstores.

A free downtown **Walking Tour** brochure, with a map and descriptions of more than 30 historic buildings, is available at the Colorado Springs Convention and Visitors Bureau as well as at local businesses. Another free brochure, titled **"Old**

Colorado City," not only shows the location of more than a dozen historic buildings, but also lists shops, galleries, and other businesses.

During the summer months, the Town Trolley provides tours and transportation through Manitou Springs and into part of Garden of the Gods (see "Getting Around," above, for details).

Visitors to Manitou Springs can pick up a self-guided walking tour map to that community's **Mineral Springs** at the Manitou Springs Chamber of Commerce, 354 Manitou Ave. (☎ **800/642-2567** or 719/685-5089), along with a cup to sample the waters. The chamber also has a brochure pointing the way to a variety of outdoor sculptures located throughout the community as part of the **Manitou Art Project.** Works can be purchased through the chamber.

7 Outdoor Activities

AERIAL SPORTS   The Black Forest Soaring Society, 24566 David Johnson Loop, Elbert, CO 80106 (☎ **303/648-3623**), some 30 miles northeast of the Springs, offers glider rides, rentals, and instruction. Rides cost about $50, with rentals $30 to $40 per hour.

Those wanting to rise above it all in a **hot-air balloon** can contact several commercial ballooning companies for tours, champagne flights, and weddings, including **High But Dry Balloons,** P.O. Box 49006, Colorado Springs, CO 80949 (☎ **719/260-0011**). A 2-hour champagne flight costs $130 per adult. On Labor Day weekend, the **Colorado Springs Balloon Classic** sees more than 100 hot-air balloons launched from the city's Memorial Park. Admission is free. (☎ **719/471-4833**).

BICYCLING   Aside from the $4^{1}/_{4}$-mile loop trail around Monument Valley Park (see "Parks & Zoos" under "Attractions," above), there are numerous other urban trails for bikers. Inquire at the city's Visitor Information Center, 104 S. Cascade Ave. (☎ **719/635-1632**), for the Colorado Springs Area Bicycle Access Map. **The Criterium,** 326 N. Tejon (☎ **719/475-0149**) in Memorial Park offers rentals for about $25 per day.

FISHING   Most serious Colorado Springs anglers drive south 40 miles to the Arkansas River, or west to the Rocky Mountain streams and lakes, such as Eleven Mile State Park and Spinney Mountain State Park on the South Platte River west of Florissant. Bass, catfish, walleye pike, and panfish are found in the streams of eastern Colorado; trout is the preferred sport fish of the mountain regions.

Angler's Covey, 917 W. Colorado Ave. (☎ **800/753-4746** or 719/471-2984), is a specialty fly-fishing shop and a good source of general fishing information for southern Colorado. It offers guided half- and full-day trips ($110–$160), as well as licenses, rentals, flies, tackle, and so forth.

Just half an hour from Colorado Springs, **Rainbow Falls Park,** P.O. Box 9062, Woodland Park, CO 80866 (☎ **719/687-9074**), offers a relaxing family fishing vacation with no state licenses required ($13 adults, $6.50 children). There are also horseback trail rides, hay-wagon rides, tent and R.V. camping ($12 to $15), cabins, and chuck-wagon suppers ($6–$15).

GOLF   Public courses include: **Cherokee Ridge Golf Club,** 1850 Tuskegee Place (☎ **719/597-2637**); **Patty Jewett Golf Course,** 900 E. Española St. (☎ **719/ 578-6827**); **Pine Creek Golf Club,** 9850 Divot Trail (☎ **719/594-9999**); and **Valley Hi Municipal Golf Course,** 610 S. Chelton Rd. (☎ **719/578-6351**). Greens fees range from $17 to $24 for 18 holes. Call to reserve tee times.

The Springs' finest golf resorts are private. Guests of the Broadmoor hotel can enjoy the 54-hole **Broadmoor Golf Club** (☎ **719/577-5790**).

HIKING   Opportunities abound in municipal parks (see "Parks & Zoos" under "Attractions," above) and Pike National Forest, which borders Colorado Springs to the west.

Especially popular are the $7^1/_2$-mile **Waldo Canyon Trail,** with its trailhead just east of Cascade off U.S. 24; the 10-mile **Mount Manitou Trail,** starting in Ruxton Canyon above the hydroelectric plant; and the 12-mile **Barr Trail** to the summit of Pikes Peak. **Mueller State Park** (☎ **719/687-2366**), $3^1/_2$ miles south of Divide en route to Cripple Creek, has 90 miles of hiking and backpacking paths.

HORSEBACK RIDING   The **Academy Riding Stables,** 4 El Paso Blvd., near the Garden of the Gods (☎ **719/633-5667**), offers guided trail rides for children and adults by reservation ($20–$40). About 20 miles northwest of the city is **Woodman Stables West,** 1997 Rampart Range Rd., Woodland Park (☎ **800/842-7615** out of state, or 719/687-3732), which offers lessons and rentals.

ICE-SKATING   The **Mark "Pa" Sertich Ice Center** at **Memorial Park** (☎ **719/578-6883**) is open daily, offering prearranged instruction and rentals. In 1995, the United States Olympic Complex opened the **Colorado Springs World Arena Ice Hall,** located at 3205 Venetucci Blvd. (☎ **719/579-8014**), with public sessions daily (admission $1–$4). To get there, take I-25, Exit 138, go west on Circle Drive to Venetucci Boulevard, and south to the arena.

MOUNTAIN BIKING   From May through early October, **Challenge Unlimited,** 204 S. 24th St. (☎ **800/798-5954** or 719/633-6399), hosts fully equipped, guided rides for every level of experience. Your guide on the 19-mile ride down the Pikes Peak Highway, from the summit at 14,110 feet to the toll gate at 7,000 feet, presents an interpretation of the nature, history, and beauty of the mountain. To participate, you must be at least 10 years old; advance reservations are advised. Rates are $60 to $80 for a 5-hour trip.

RIVER RAFTING   Colorado Springs is only 40 miles from the Arkansas River near Cañon City. Among the licensed white-water outfitters who tackle the Royal Gorge is **Echo Canyon River Expeditions,** P.O. Box 1002, Colorado Springs, CO 80901 (☎ **800/748-2953** or 719/275-3154). Trips ranging from a half-day to 3 days on "mild to wild" stretches of river are offered. The company uses state-of-the-art equipment, including self-bailing rafts. Costs range from $28 to $295.

SWIMMING   If your accommodation doesn't have a pool of its own, visit the **Aquatics and Fitness Center** in **Memorial Park,** 270 Union Blvd. (☎ **719/578-6634**). Admission is $2 adults, $1 children. Call for seasonal hours.

TENNIS   Many city parks have tennis courts, including **Memorial Park,** at the corner of Hancock and Pikes Peak avenues (☎ **719/578-6676**). The city courts are free.

8 Spectator Sports

The Air Force Academy Falcons (the football team) dominate the sports scene here, although there are also competitive baseball, basketball, hockey, and soccer teams. For schedules and ticket information, call **800/666-USAF** or 719/472-1895.

AUTO RACING   The annual **Pikes Peak Auto Hill Climb** (☎ **719/685-4400**), known as "the Race to the Clouds," is held annually on July 4. An international field of drivers negotiate the winding, hairpin turns of the final 12.4 miles of the Pikes Peak Highway to the top of the 14,110-foot mountain.

BASEBALL   The Colorado Springs Sky Sox of the Pacific Coast League, the Colorado Rockies AAA farm team, play a full 144-game season, with 72 home games at Sky Sox Stadium, 4385 Tutt Ave. (☎ **719/597-3000**). The season begins the second week of April and runs through Labor Day. Games are played afternoons and evenings. Tickets cost $6 for reserved seating, $4 for general admission. Call the stadium or check the newspaper sports pages for schedule information.

RODEO   The Pikes Peak or Bust Rodeo, held annually (since 1941) in early August, is a major stop on the Professional Rodeo Cowboys Association circuit. Its purse of more than $150,000 makes it the second-largest rodeo in Colorado (after Denver's National Western Stock Show), 15th in North America. Events are held at Penrose Stadium, 1045 W. Rio Grande Ave. off Fountain Creek Boulevard (☎ **719/635-3547** or 719/520-6710). Various events around the city, including a parade, observe rodeo week.

9 Shopping

Five principal areas attract shoppers in Colorado Springs. The Manitou Springs and Old Colorado City neighborhoods are best for souvenir hunting and arts-and-crafts galleries. The Citadel and Chapel Hills malls combine major department stores with a variety of fashionable boutiques. Downtown Colorado Springs, of course, also has numerous fine shops.

SHOPPING A TO Z
ANTIQUES
The Antique Emporium at Manitou Springs. 719 Manitou Ave., Manitou Springs. ☎ **719/685-9195.**

The shop's 4,000 square feet of floor space amply displays furniture, china, glassware, books, collectibles, and primitives.

The Villagers. 2426 W. Colorado Ave., Old Colorado City. ☎ **719/632-1400.**

Here you will find a diverse array of quality antiques and collectibles. All proceeds go to Cheyenne Village, a community of adults with developmental disabilities.

ART GALLERIES
Business of Art Center. 513 Manitou Ave., Manitou Springs. ☎ **719/685-1861.**

This renovated historic building is home to numerous artists' studios (open for viewing by visitors); a gallery featuring renowned Colorado artists in 2-month-long exhibits; juried, ongoing monthly exhibits of regional art; a sales gallery with a varied selection of regional artwork including prints, photographs, jewelry, sculpture, ceramics, wearable art, hand-blown glass, carved wood objects and more; and a coffee house where visitors can view regional black-and-white photography. Occasionally they offer theater, music, and dance performances in the afternoon or evening ($3 donation requested).

Michael Garman's Gallery. 2418 W. Colorado Ave., Old Colorado City. ☎ **719/471-9391.**

A showcase for Garman's sculptures and casts depicting urban and western life, plus "Magic Town," a large model of an inner city with sculptures and holographic actors. Admission to "Magic Town" is $3 for adults, $2 for children 7 to 12, free for children under 7.

The Flute Player Gallery. 2511 W. Colorado Ave., Old Colorado City. ☎ **719/632-7702.**

This gallery offers contemporary and traditional Native American jewelry, Pueblo pottery, Navajo weavings, and Hopi kachina dolls.

BOOKS

The Chinook Bookshop. 210 N. Tejon St. ☎ **800/999-1195** or 719/635-1195.

This is a gem of a bookstore, with 75,000 titles, including an extensive western Americana collection. There's an entire room devoted to maps and globes, and the Children's Room is a large, sunny area with a two-story playhouse and a carpeted and cushioned reading platform.

CRAFTS

The Candle Shoppe. 2421½ W. Colorado Ave., Old Colorado City. ☎ **719/633-4856.**

Candles in all shapes, scents, and sizes are offered in this unique shop. Among the 25,000 candles offered for sale here, there are a 20-pound wax grizzly bear and religious and historic figures that are much too beautiful to burn.

Van Briggle Art Pottery. 600 S. 21st St., Old Colorado City. ☎ **719/633-7729.**

Founded in 1900 by Artus Van Briggle, who applied Chinese matte glaze to Rocky Mountain clays and imaginative art nouveau shapes, this is one of the oldest active art potteries in the United States. Today artisans demonstrate their craft, from "throwing on the wheel" to glazing and firing. Free tours are available, 8:30am to 4:30pm, Monday through Saturday. Finished works are sold in the showroom.

JEWELRY

All That Glitters. 2518 W. Colorado Ave., Old Colorado City. ☎ **719/475-7160.**

This well-established Colorado Springs jeweler is known for beautiful custom gold work and one-of-a-kind designer jewelry.

Manitou Jack's Jewelry & Gifts. 742 Manitou Ave., Manitou Springs. ☎ **719/685-5004.**

Black Hills gold, 10- and 14-karat, is the specialty here. There's also an extensive collection of Native American jewelry, pottery, sand paintings, and other art. The shop will create custom jewelry and make repairs.

Megel & Graff Jewelers Ltd. 12 E. Pikes Peak Ave. ☎ **719/632-2552.**

A downtown institution since 1949, this well-respected shop offers full-service jewelry repair, often while you wait, plus a large selection of diamonds and gems.

MALLS & SHOPPING CENTERS

Chapel Hills Mall. 1710 Briargate Blvd. (N. Academy Blvd. at I-25, Exit 150A). ☎ **719/594-0111.**

Joslins, Sears, Mervyn's, J.C. Penney, and K-Mart are among the 135-plus stores here. There's also a Gart Bros. sporting goods store, a Fashion Bar, a cinema complex, and a dozen food outlets from Greek to Chinese.

The Citadel. 750 Citadel Dr. E. (N. Academy Blvd. at E. Platte Ave.). ☎ **719/591-2900.**

This is southern Colorado's largest regional shopping mall, with Dillard's, Foley's, J.C. Penney, Mervyn's, and more than 170 other stores and restaurants.

SPORTING GOODS

Leading sporting-goods dealers in the city include **Grand West Outfitters,** 3250 N. Academy Blvd. (☎ **719/596-3031**) and **Mountain Chalet,** 226 N. Tejon St. (☎ **719/633-0732**).

WINE & LIQUOR

Cheers Liquor Mart. 1105 N. Circle Dr. ☎ **719/574-2244.**

A liquor supermarket with a huge selection of beer and wine, including Colorado wines, at good prices.

Pikes Peak Vineyards. 3901 Janitell Rd. (I-25, Exit 138). ☎ **719/576-0075.**

This small, award-winning winery produces 8 to 10 moderately priced red, white, and blush wines. Tours and tastings are offered. Call for hours.

10 Colorado Springs After Dark

The Colorado Springs entertainment scene is spread throughout the metropolitan area. Pikes Peak Center, the Colorado Springs Fine Arts Center, City Auditorium, Colorado College, and the various facilities at the U.S. Air Force Academy are all venues for the performing arts. The city also supports dozens of cinemas, nightclubs, bars, and other after-dark attractions.

Current weekly entertainment schedules can be found in the Friday edition of the *Gazette Telegraph.* Also look at the listings in *Springs* magazine and *The Independent,* free entertainment tabloids. Or call the city's weekly events hot line (☎ **719/ 635-1723**).

Tickets for nearly all major entertainment and sporting events can be obtained from **TicketMaster** (☎ **719/520-9090**).

THE CLUB & MUSIC SCENE

COUNTRY & ROCK

Cowboys. 3910 Palmer Park Blvd. ☎ **719/596-1212.** Cover $3–$5.

Two-steppers and country-and-western music lovers flock to this eastside club, where dance lessons and drink specials are available; open daily from 4pm to 2am.

The Club House Restaurant and Underground Pub. 130 E. Kiowa St. ☎ **719/633-0590.** Live music $2–$3; no cover otherwise.

This popular hangout for college students and recent graduates offers progressive and alternative rock on its basement stage, either live or recorded. Open Monday to Saturday from 11am to 2am, Sunday 5pm to 2am.

Metro. 5917 N. Academy Blvd. ☎ **719/528-6097.**

The Metro is a large dance club in northern Colorado Springs, playing the latest hot dance sounds. The bar offers many drink specials; free drinks often available from 7 to 9pm.

JAZZ, BLUES & FOLK

Poor Richard's Restaurant. 324^1/$_2$ N. Tejon St. ☎ **719/632-7721.** Usually no cover. Daily 11am–10pm.

An eclectic variety of performers appears here several nights each week, presenting everything from acoustic folk to Celtic melodies and jazz to bluegrass.

THE BAR SCENE

Beckett's. 128 S. Tejon St. ☎ **719/633-3230.**

Fourteen different handcrafted ales and stouts highlight the drink menu at this casually elegant spot.

The Golden Bee. Lower level entrance of the Broadmoor International Center, Lake Circle. ☎ **719/634-7111.**

An opulent English pub was disassembled, shipped from Great Britain, and reassembled piece by piece to create this delightful drinking establishment. You can have imported Bass Ale by the yard if you choose, while enjoying a beef-and-kidney pie or other English specialties.

Hide 'n' Seek. 512 W. Colorado Ave. ☎ **719/634-9303.**

The Hide 'n' Seek, which opened in 1972, is one of the oldest and largest gay bars in the West. It has four bars, with country, sports, and dance areas, plus a restaurant.

Judge Baldwin's Brewing Company. In the Antlers Doubletree Hotel, 4 S. Cascade Ave. ☎ **719/473-5600.**

Although Judge Baldwin's offers more than a dozen designer beers from all over the United States, look around this cheery bar and you'll see that practically everyone is drinking the Judge's own. And with good reason. The most popular is amber ale (served with a pretzel), but those who prefer a richer brew might want to try the nut brown ale. Or order a sampler, and try all four beers.

The Ritz Grill. 15 S. Tejon St. ☎ **719/635-8484.**

Especially popular with young professionals after work and the chic clique later in the evening, this restaurant-lounge, with a large central bar, brings an art-deco feel to downtown Colorado Springs. On the weekends, live rock and blues are played, such as Gyzunglasus and Stray Cats.

THE PERFORMING ARTS

As a large, growing city, Colorado Springs receives its share of visiting performers—from nationally renowned classical artists and modern-dance troupes to the latest rock acts—and even has resident music and theater companies of its own. Perhaps most tellingly, though, it's a place that hasn't forsaken its western roots: dinner theater and hokey melodramas are still being performed here, and this is as good a place as any in the state to check out one of these offerings.

Pikes Peak Center, 190 S. Cascade Ave. (☎ **719/520-7469**), is the area's primary performing-arts facility. This 2,000-seat concert hall in the heart of downtown has been acclaimed for its acoustics, and the city's symphony orchestra and dance theater call it home. Top-flight touring entertainers, Broadway musicals, and symphony orchestras make appearances here as well. Other major concert halls and all-purpose auditoriums include: the **Arnold Hall Theater** at the U.S. Air Force Academy (☎ **719/472-4499**), where everything from plays and lectures to concerts by top-name national and international performers—all open to the public—take place; the **City Auditorium,** 221 E. Kiowa St. (☎ **719/578-6652**), where concerts (as well as conventions and trade shows) are regularly scheduled in the main hall, and a resident theater troupe, **Star Bar Players,** walks the boards at the **Lon Chaney Theatre;** and the historic **Colorado Springs Fine Arts Center,** 30 W. Dale St. (☎ **719/634-5581,** or 719/634-5583 for the box office), which, in addition to hosting a children's theater program and a repertory theater company, mounts concerts and dance programs, and screens classic films.

THE FESTIVAL SCENE

Colorado Springs has just one major festival.

Colorado Opera Festival. 17 S. Tejon St. ☎ **719/473-0073.** Tickets $10.50–$55.50.

Every year in late July, one opera is staged at the Pikes Peak Center. This past year, Puccini's *Turandot* received rave reviews and drew capacity crowds at its four performances. Original language productions with English subtitles feature nationally known opera singers.

CLASSICAL MUSIC & OPERA COMPANIES

Colorado Springs Symphony Orchestra. 619 N. Cascade Ave. ☎ **719/633-4611,** or 719/520-7469 for ticket information. Tickets free–$38.

This fine professional orchestra annually performs 2 dozen classical concerts, as well as youth, pops, chamber, holiday, and free summer concerts. Most performances are held at the Pikes Peak Center.

THEATER COMPANIES

Bluebards. Arnold Hall Theater, U.S. Air Force Academy. ☎ **719/472-4499.**

The Air Force Academy's cadet theater group performs to appreciative townspeople and visitors as well as fellow cadets.

Star Bar Players. Lon Chaney Theatre, City Auditorium, 221 E. Kiowa St. ☎ **719/578-6855.**

Each year this resident theater company presents four full-length plays, two studio productions, and a children's Christmas show.

DANCE COMPANIES

Colorado Springs Dance Theatre. 7 E. Bijou St., Suite 213, Colorado Springs, CO 80903. ☎ **719/630-7434.** Tickets $13–$30, with discounts for students and seniors.

This nonprofit organization presents dance companies from around the world in a September to May season at Pikes Peak Center, Colorado College's Armstrong Hall, and other venues. Notable recent performances have included Mikhail Baryshnikov, Alvin Ailey Repertory Ensemble, Ballet Folklorico of Mexico, and other traditional, modern, ethnic, and jazz dance programs. Each year three to five performances are scheduled, and there are often master classes, lectures, and other programs coinciding with the performances. Request a brochure listing forthcoming events.

Rocky Mountain Cloggers. 806 Cardinal St., Colorado Springs, CO 80911. ☎ **719/392-4791.**

The eight members of this national exhibition clog-dance team perform some 3 dozen shows in the Colorado Springs area each year. Ask for a current schedule.

DINNER THEATERS

About Town Dinner Theatre. The Broadmoor Hotel, Lake Ave., Colorado Springs, CO 80906. ☎ **719/579-9000.** Tickets $18.

Entertaining comedies and musicals are the specialty of this theater troupe, whose performances have included Neil Simon's *Last of the Red Hot Lovers* and *The Odd Couple,* as well as *Murder at the Howard Johnson's,* by Ron Clark and Sam Bobrick.

Flying W Ranch. 3330 Chuckwagon Rd. ☎ **800/232-FLYW** or 719/598-4000. Reservations strongly recommended. Admission: chuck-wagon dinners, $14 adults, $7 for children 8 and younger; winter steak house, $18 adults, $8 for children 8 and younger.

This working cattle and horse ranch just north of the Garden of the Gods treats visitors to a western village of a dozen restored buildings and a mine train. A western stage show features bunkhouse comedy, cowboy balladry, and foot-stompin' fiddle, mandolin, and guitar music. From mid-May through September the ranch opens each afternoon at 4:30pm; a chuck-wagon dinner is served ranch style at 7:15pm, and the show begins at 8:30pm. The winter steak house is open October to December and March to May on Friday and Saturday evenings, with seatings at 5 and 8pm.

Iron Springs Chateau Melodrama. 444 Ruxton Ave., Manitou Springs. ☎ **719/685-5104** or 719/685-5572. Tickets, dinner and show, $20 adults, $19 seniors, $11 children; show only, $10 adults, $9 seniors, $6.50 children.

Located near the foot of the Pikes Peak Cog Railway, this popular comedy/drama dinner theater urges patrons to boo the villain and cheer the hero. Past productions have included *Farther North to Laughter or Buck of the Yukon, Part Two,* and *When the Halibut Start Running or Don't Slam the Door on Davy Jones' Locker.* A family-style dinner, served Monday through Saturday from 6 to 7:15pm, offers all you can eat of oven-baked chicken and barbecued ribs. You'll need reservations. Show time is 8:30pm, followed by a sing-along intermission and a vaudeville-style olio show. The theater is closed the last 2 weeks of January and first 2 weeks of February.

11 A Side Trip to Florissant Fossil Beds National Monument

Approximately 35 miles west of Colorado Springs on U.S. 24 is the small village of Florissant, which means "flowering" in French. It couldn't be more aptly named—every spring its hillsides are virtually ablaze with wildflowers. And just 3 miles south is one of the most spectacular, yet relatively unknown, collections of fossil beds in the world, Florissant Fossil Beds National Monument (from Florissant, follow the signs along Teller County Road 1).

The fossils in this 6,000-acre National Park Service property are preserved in the rocks of ancient Lake Florissant, which existed 26 to 38 million years ago. Volcanic eruptions spanning half a million years trapped plants and animals under layers of ash and dust; the creatures were fossilized as the sediment settled and became shale.

The detailed impressions, first discovered in 1874, offer the most extensive record of its kind in the world today. Some 80,000 specimens have been removed by scientists, including 1,100 separate species of insects. Dragonflies, beetles, ants; every known species of fossil butterfly in the New World; plus spiders, fish, some mammals and birds—all are perfectly preserved from as long as 35 million years ago. Leaves from birches, willows, maples, beeches, and hickories, and needles of fir trees and sequoias, are plentiful. The finding of palm-tree fossils shows how the climate has changed over the centuries.

Mud flows also buried forests during this long period of time, petrifying the trees where they stood. Nature trails pass petrified sequoia stumps; one is 10 feet in diameter and 11 feet high. There's a display of carbonized fossils at the Visitor Center, which also offers interpretive programs. An added attraction within the monument is the homestead of Adeline Hornbek, who pioneered the area with her children in 1878. The national monument also has some 14 miles of hiking trails.

Admission is $2 per person, up to a maximum of $4 per family, making a visit here an incredibly affordable outing. It's open from June to September, daily 8am to 7pm; during the rest of the year, daily 8am to 4:30pm. Closed New Year's Day, Thanksgiving, and Christmas. Contact **Florissant Fossil Beds National Monument,** P.O. Box 185, Florissant, CO 80816 (☎ **719/748-3253**) for further information.

9

Boulder

Set at the foot of the Flatirons of the Rocky Mountains, just 30 miles northwest of downtown Denver and only 74 feet higher in elevation, Boulder was settled by hopeful miners in 1858 and named for the large rocks in the area. Welcomed by Chief Niwot and the resident southern Arapahoe, the miners struck gold in the nearby hills the following year. By the 1870s Boulder had become a regional rail-and-trade center for mining and farming. The university, founded in 1877, became the economic mainstay of the community after mining collapsed around the turn of the century.

Since the 1950s Boulder has grown as a center for scientific and environmental research. The National Center for Atmospheric Research and the National Institute of Standards and Technology are located here, as are IBM, Storage Tek, and Ball Aerospace.

Today's residents are a mix of students attending the University of Colorado (called C.U. by locals); employees of the many computer, biotech, and research firms in the area; and others who were attracted by the casual, environmentally aware, and hip lifestyle that prevails here. Whatever differences exist among the residents, they are joined by a common love of the outdoors. Boulder has 25,000 acres of open space within its city limits, 56 parks, and 150 miles of trails. On any given day, seemingly three-quarters of the population is outside, making great use of this land, generally from the vantage point of a bike seat. With an estimated 93,000 bicycles—more than one per resident—in town, it's the preferred mode of transport in Boulder.

1 Orientation

ARRIVING

BY PLANE Boulder doesn't have its own commercial airport. Air travelers must fly into Denver International, then make ground connections to Boulder. See chapter 6, "Arriving," for information about flights into Denver International from major U.S. cities.

Getting To & From the Airport The **Boulder Airporter** limo van (☎ **303/444-0808**) leaves Denver hourly from 8am to 11pm, and Boulder hourly from 5am to 9pm; there are fewer departures on holidays. Scheduled pickups in Boulder are made from the University of Colorado campus and from certain hotels; pickups are made on call from other hotels. The one-way fare from a scheduled pickup point to the airport is $14 per person ($26 round-trip), or $16 ($30 round-trip) for door-to-door pickup service from other points.

International Boulder Limousine Airport Express (☎ 303/449-5466) charges $76 plus 20% gratuity to take two people from Boulder to Denver Airport in a sedan limousine; $90 plus 20% gratuity for up to six people in a stretch limousine.

Boulder Yellow Cab (☎ 303/442-2277) charges $50 one way to the airport for up to five passengers.

Buses operated by the **Regional Transportation District (RTD)** (☎ 303/299-6000) charge $8 for a one-way trip to the airport (exact change required). Buses leave from (and return to) the main terminal at 14th and Walnut streets daily every hour from 6am to 11pm.

BY CAR   The Boulder Turnpike (U.S. 36) branches off from I-25 north of Denver and passes through the suburbs of Westminster, Broomfield, and Louisville before reaching Boulder some 25 minutes later.

If you're arriving from the north, take the Longmont exit from I-25 and follow Colo. 119 all the way. Longmont is 7 miles due west of the freeway; Boulder is another 15 miles southwest via the Longmont Diagonal Highway.

VISITOR INFORMATION

The **Boulder Convention and Visitors Bureau,** 2440 Pearl St. (at Folsom Street), Boulder, CO 80302 (☎ 800/444-0447 or 303/442-2911), is open Monday through Friday from 9am to 5pm, and can provide excellent maps, brochures, and general information on the city.

From Memorial Day to Labor Day, there is a **visitor information center** at the **Davidson Mesa overlook,** several miles southeast of Boulder on U.S. 36. Brochures are available at the overlook year-round.

CITY LAYOUT

The north-south streets increase in number going from west to east, beginning with Third Street. (The eastern city limit is at 61st Street, although the numbers continue to the Boulder County line at 124th Street in Broomfield.) Where U.S. 36 enters Boulder (and does a 45° turn to the north), it becomes 28th Street—a major commercial artery. The Longmont Diagonal Highway (Colo. 119 east), entering Boulder from the northeast, intersects 28th Street at the north end of the city.

To reach downtown Boulder from U.S. 36, turn west on Canyon Boulevard (Colo. 119 west) and north on Broadway, which would be 12th Street if it had a number. It's two blocks to the Pearl Street Mall, a four-block pedestrians-only strip from 11th to 15th streets, which constitutes the historic downtown district. Boulder's few one-way streets circle the mall: 13th and 15th streets are one-way north; 11th and 14th are one-way south; Walnut Street (a block south of the Mall) is one-way east; and Spruce Street (a block north) is one-way west.

Broadway continues across the Mall, eventually joining U.S. 36 north of the city. South of Arapahoe Avenue, Broadway turns to the southeast, skirting the University of Colorado campus and becoming Colo. 93 (the Foothills Hwy. to Golden) after crossing Baseline Road. Baseline follows a straight line from east Boulder, across U.S. 36 and Broadway, past Chautauqua Park and up the mountain slopes. To the south, Table Mesa Drive takes a similar course.

The Foothills Parkway (not to be confused with the Foothills Hwy.) is the principal north-south route on the east side of Boulder, extending from U.S. 36 at Table

Mesa Drive to the Longmont Diagonal; Arapahoe Avenue, a block south of Canyon Boulevard, continues east across 28th Street as Arapahoe Road.

2 Getting Around

BY PUBLIC TRANSPORTATION

Regional Transportation District (RTD) buses provide service throughout the city as well as the Denver greater metropolitan area. Fares within the city are 60¢ for adults and children (15¢ for seniors during off-peak hours); schedules are available at the Boulder Transit Center, 14th and Walnut streets (☎ **303/299-6000**), open Monday through Friday from 5am to midnight and on Saturday and Sunday from 6am to midnight, at the Chamber of Commerce, and at other locations around the city. All buses are wheelchair-accessible.

The city of Boulder runs a shuttle bus service, called **HOP,** which connects downtown, at University Hill, the University of Colorado, and Crossroads Mall. It operates between 7am and 7pm Monday through Wednesday, 7pm to 10pm Thursday and Friday, and 9am to 10pm Saturday. While the University of Colorado is in session, the night HOP runs 10pm to 2:30am Thursday through Saturday to every destination except Crossroads Mall. Buses run about every 10 minutes, and fares are 25¢, 15¢ for seniors, or free with any RTD pass. For more information, call **303/447-8282.**

BY TAXI

Boulder Yellow Cab (☎ **303/442-2277**) offers 24-hour service. Rates in town are $2.70 for the first mile and $1.20 for each additional mile; the out-of-town fare is $1.20 per mile. There are no taxi stands, and taxis won't stop for you on the street; you need to call for service.

BY CAR

If you're staying downtown, you don't really need a car to get around (it can even be a hindrance, particularly near the Pearl Street Mall). But, if you're planning to do some serious exploring, especially outside the city, it'll come in handy.

Car Rentals   Car-rental agencies in Boulder include: **Avis,** 4800 Baseline Rd. (☎ **800/831-2847** or 303/499-1136); **Budget,** 1345 28th St. (☎ **800/222-6772** or 303/341-2277); **Hertz,** 2990 Diagonal Hwy. (☎ **800/654-3131** or 303/413-8023); and **National,** 2960 Center Green Court S. (☎ **800/227-7368** or 303/442-5110).

Parking   Most downtown streets have parking meters, with rates of about 25¢ per half hour. Downtown parking lots get about 35¢ for 3 hours before 5pm. Parking is hard to find around the Pearl Street Mall. Outside downtown, free parking is generally available on side streets.

BY BICYCLE

Boulder is a wonderful place for bicycling; there are bike paths throughout the city, as well as an extensive trail system leading for miles beyond Boulder's borders (see "Outdoor Activities," below).

At the following shops, you can rent mountain and touring bikes (and also buy a copy of the very useful *Boulder Bicycling Map* for $3): **Doc's Ski and Sports,** 627 S. Broadway (☎ **303/499-0963**) and **Full Cycle,** 1211 13th St., near the C.U. campus (☎ **303/440-7771**). Bike rentals cost $16 to $24 daily. Maps are also available at the **Boulder Chamber of Commerce,** 2440 Pearl St. (☎ **303/442-1044**) and **Go Boulder** (☎ **303/441-4260**).

ON FOOT

Most of what's worth seeing in Boulder can be reached by pure foot power, especially around the Pearl Street Mall and University of Colorado campus.

FAST FACTS: Boulder

Area Code The area code is **303.**

Baby-sitters Boulder's **Child Care Referral Service** (☎ **303/441-3180**), open Monday through Friday from 1 to 5pm, can help arrange a sitter, if someone at the front desk of your hotel cannot.

Business Hours Most banks are open Monday through Friday from 9am to 5pm, and some have Saturday hours, too. Major stores are open Monday through Saturday from 9 or 10am until 5 or 6pm, and often Sunday from noon until 5pm.

Camera Repair For repairs, as well as equipment and supplies, contact **Mike's Camera,** 2500 Pearl St. (☎ **303/443-1715**).

Emergencies For police, fire, or medical emergencies, call 911.

Hospitals Full medical services, including 24-hour emergency treatment, are available at **Boulder Community Hospital,** 1100 Balsam Ave. (at N. Broadway) (☎ **303/440-2273**).

Hot Lines The **poison control center** can be reached at (☎ **800/332-3073** or 303/629-1123), and the **rape crisis hot line** is (☎ **303/443-7300**).

Newspapers/Magazines Boulder's *Daily Camera* is an award-winning daily newspaper. Many townspeople also read the campus paper, the *Colorado Daily,* available all over town. Both Denver dailies—the *Denver Post* and *Rocky Mountain News*—are available at newsstands throughout the city. You can also find *The New York Times, Wall Street Journal,* and *Christian Science Monitor* at many newsstands. The free *Boulder* magazine, published three times a year, lists seasonal events and other information on restaurants and the arts.

Pharmacies Reliable prescription services are available at the Medical Center Pharmacy in the **Boulder Medical Center,** 2750 N. Broadway (☎ **303/440-3111**), and **Jones Drug and Camera Center,** 1370 College Ave. (☎ **303/443-4420**). The pharmacy at **King Soopers Supermarket,** 1650 30th St. (in Sunrise Plaza), is open 24 hours (☎ **303/444-0164**).

Post Office The main downtown post office is at 15th and Walnut streets (☎ **303/938-1100**).

Radio Boulder radio stations include KBCO (1190 AM and 97.3 FM) for alternative rock; KBKS (1490 AM) for news, sports, and contemporary rock; and KGNU (88.5 FM) for Boulder public radio. Boulder is also within reception range of most Denver stations.

Taxes State and city sales tax total almost 7%.

Television The following Denver television stations can be received in Boulder: Channels 2 (KWGN-independent), 4 (CBS), 6 (PBS), 7 (ABC), 9 (NBC), and 31 (FOX). Boulder has two independent stations: Channels 20 (KTVD) and 59 (KUBD). Cable or satellite service is available at many motels.

Useful Telephone Numbers   Road conditions (☎ 303/639-1111); ski reports (☎ 303/825-7669); current weather conditions (☎ 303/398-3964).

3 Accommodations

You'll find a good selection of comfortable lodgings in Boulder, with a wide range of rates to suit almost every budget. Be aware, though, that the town literally fills up during the popular summer season, making advance reservations essential. It's also almost impossible to find a place to sleep during any major event at the University of Colorado, particularly graduation. Those who do find themselves in Boulder without lodging can check with the Boulder Convention and Visitors Bureau (see "Visitor Information" above), which keeps track of availability. Of course, you can usually find a room in Denver, a half-hour away.

Major chains and franchises that provide reasonably priced lodging in Boulder include: **Holiday Inn Boulder,** 800 28th St. (☎ **800/465-4329** or 303/443-3322), with 165 rooms and rates of $85 to $99 double; **Best Western Golden Buff Lodge,** 1725 28th St. (☎ **800/999-BUFF** or 303/442-7450), charging $80 to $91 double; and **Super 8,** 970 28th St. (☎ **800/525-2149,** 800/800-8000, or 303/443-7800), with rates of $60 to $95 double.

For the accommodations listed here, the price categories have been defined as follows: **expensive,** more than $100 per night double; **moderate,** $70 to $100 per night double; **inexpensive,** less than $70 per night double. These rates do not include the 9.5% sales tax that will be added to all hotel bills.

EXPENSIVE

✪ **The Alps.** 38619 Boulder Canyon Dr., Boulder, CO 80302. ☎ **800/414-2577** or 303/444-5445. Fax 303/444-5522. 12 rms. TEL. $75–$205. Rates include full breakfast. AE, CB, DC, DISC, MC, V. Free parking.

A stagecoach stop in the late 1800s, this historic log lodge has been turned into a beautiful bed-and-breakfast by its owners Jeannine and John Vanderhart. Sitting on a mountainside about 7 minutes west of downtown Boulder, the Alps is decorated with antiques. Each room is different, but all have functional fireplaces with Victorian mantels, queen beds with down comforters, individual thermostats, and clock radios. Most are spacious, with either a claw-footed or double Jacuzzi tub, with shower. Many rooms have private porches. There's a beautiful lounge with a huge rock fireplace, and a shared television with VCR. Smoking and pets are not permitted.

The Briar Rose. 2151 Arapahoe Ave., Boulder, CO 80302. ☎ **303/442-3007.** Fax 303/786-8440. 9 rms. A/C TEL. May–Dec, $109–$139 double. Dec–Apr, $90–$120 double. Rates include continental breakfast. AE, DC, MC, V.

A country-style brick home set amid a lovely garden, every room within is furnished with antiques—from the bedrooms and the parlor to the back sun porch. Amenities have been added to several rooms to accommodate the business traveler—modem hookup, large work table, and super lighting. Fax and copy machine are available.

Five rooms are in the main house, four in a separate cottage. Two in the main house have fireplaces, all are furnished with feather comforters, and the cottage rooms come with either a patio or balcony. The continental breakfast is gourmet quality: croissants, granola, fresh nut breads, yogurt with fruit, and much more.

Clarion Harvest House. 1345 28th St., Boulder, CO 80302. ☎ **800/545-6285** or 303/443-3850. Fax 303/443-1480. 264 rms, 5 suites. A/C TV TEL. $128–$169 double, $175–$395 suite. AE, CB, DC, DISC, MC, V. Free parking.

Harvest House is exceptional in that it is a downtown hotel and yet has spacious and lovely grounds. Located on the west side of U.S. 36, the Harvest House looks like almost any other four-story hotel from the front. But its backyard melts into a park that surrounds the east end of the 10-mile Boulder Creek Path.

All rooms are furnished with one king-size or two double beds, a lounge chair and ottoman, remote-control cable TV, and direct-dial phone. Spacious VIP Tower accommodations provide upgraded amenities such as hairdryers and bathrobes, daily newspapers, and an extra phone jack for a computer modem.

Continental breakfast and cocktail hour are served in the VIP Tower's Club Room. The hotel's restaurant serves three meals daily, from 6:30am to 10pm, and there's a popular sports bar with a big fireplace, also open daily. Room service, valet and self-service laundry, masseur, airport shuttle are available. Facilities include 15 tennis courts (5 indoors), indoor lap pool and hot tub, outdoor swimming pool and hot tub, baby pool, fitness center, bicycle rentals at Boulder Creek Path, playground, volleyball, business center, nonsmoking rooms, facilities for the disabled, and meeting space for 200.

✪ **Hotel Boulderado.** 2115 13th St. (at Spruce St.), Boulder, CO 80302. ☎ **800/433-4344** or 303/442-4344. Fax 303/442-4378. 133 rms, 27 suites. A/C TV TEL. $141–$201 double. Extra person $12. AE, CB, DC, DISC, JCB, MC, V. Free parking.

Opened on January 1, 1909, this elegant and historic hotel still has the same Otis elevator that wowed visiting dignitaries on opening day. The colorful leaded-glass ceiling and cantilevered cherry-wood staircase are other reminders of days past, along with the rich woodwork of the balusters around the mezzanine and the handsome armchairs and settees in the main-floor lobby. Their Christmas tree, a 24-footer with 1,000 white lights, is a Boulder tradition.

The original five-story hotel, just a block off the Pearl Street Mall, has 42 bright and cozy guest rooms, every one a little bit different. Although all rooms have recently been renovated down to the wiring and plumbing, they retain a Victorian flavor. The construction of a spacious North Wing a few years ago almost quadrupled the number of rooms, while continuing the turn-of-the-century feel in the wallpaper and reproduction antiques. Some units have refrigerators.

The hotel offers a full range of services and dining and other facilities.

MODERATE

🆂 **Days Inn Boulder.** 5397 S. Boulder Rd., Boulder, CO 80303. ☎ **800/329-7466** or 303/499-4422. Fax 303/494-0269. 72 rms, 2 suites. A/C TV TEL. $89 double, suites $20 additional. Rates include continental breakfast. AE, CB, DC, DISC, MC, V. Free parking.

One of the best values around, this four-story lodging offers great views of the mountains. Perhaps the reason it looks and feels as if it should cost a lot more is because, unlike many franchise lodgings, the owner is also the manager. The rooms are large, with night tables on each side of the beds. Each room has cable television, desks, and modem hookups; fax and photocopy services are available at the front desk. The continental breakfast is excellent; there's a seasonal outdoor heated pool, and they accept small pets.

University Inn. 1632 Broadway (near Arapahoe Ave.), Boulder, CO 80302. ☎ **800/258-7917** or 303/442-3830. Fax 303/442-1205. 39 rms. A/C TV TEL. $62–$105 double. AE, DC, DISC, MC, V. Free parking.

Conveniently located between the University of Colorado campus and the Pearl Street Mall (and within walking distance of both), this two-story motel has simple, cozy rooms equipped with king, queen, or double beds, light-wood furnishings,

Boulder Accommodations & Dining

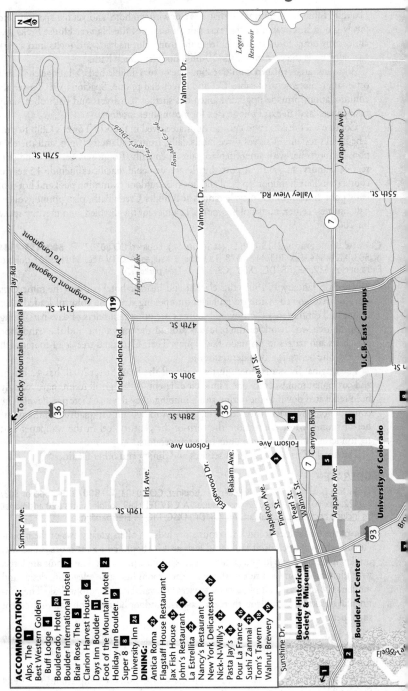

ACCOMMODATIONS:
Alps, The **1**
Best Western Golden
Buff Lodge **4**
Boulderado, Hotel **20**
Boulder International Hostel **7**
Briar Rose, The **5**
Clarion Harvest House **6**
Days Inn Boulder **11**
Foot of the Mountain Motel **2**
Holiday Inn Boulder **9**
Super 8 **8**
University Inn **24**

DINING:
Antica Roma **23**
Flagstaff House Restaurant **10**
Jax Fish House **15**
John's Restaurant **3**
La Estrellita **22**
Nancy's Restaurant **13**
New York Delicatessen **17**
Nick-N-Willy's **12**
Pasta Jay's **14**
Pour La France **16**
Sushi Zanmai **21**
Tom's Tavern **18**
Walnut Brewery **19**

152

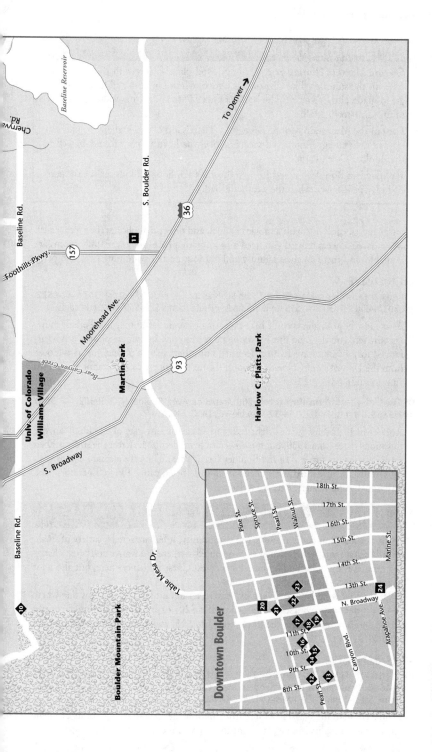

Baseline Reservoir

Cherryvale Rd.

To Denver →

S. Boulder Rd.

36

Baseline Rd.

157

Foothills Pkwy.

11

Moorehead Ave.

Bear Canyon Creek

Martin Park

93

Harlow C. Platts Park

Univ. of Colorado
Williams Village

S. Broadway

Baseline Rd.

Table Mesa Dr.

Boulder Mountain Park

Downtown Boulder

18th St.

17th St.

Pine St.

Spruce St.

Pearl St.

Walnut St.

16th St.

15th St.

14th St.

Marine St.

13th St.

24

N. Broadway

20

21

22

23

17

18

29

16

11th St.

14 15

10th St.

Pearl St.

12

23

9th St.

8th St.

Canyon Blvd.

Arapahoe Ave.

Family-Friendly Hotels

Clarion Harvest House *(see p. 150)*   A good place to stay with the kids, especially in the summer. The Clarion has a nice swimming pool and lots of nearby green space; also, it's next to the Boulder Creek Path and within walking distance of the Crossroads Mall.

Foot of the Mountain Motel *(this page)*   There's lots of space where the kids can expend their energy. Across the street is a lovely park with a playground, as well as the Boulder Creek Path.

Holiday Inn Boulder *(see p. 150)*   At the inn's "Holidome," kids can use the pool and play inside even when the weather is bad.

refrigerators, cable TV with a movie channel, and direct-dial phones (free local calls). Most have showers only; if you need a room with a bathtub, ask. Family rooms are available, and there's a guest laundry and outdoor heated swimming pool. No pets.

INEXPENSIVE

Boulder International Hostel. 1107 12th St., Boulder, CO 80302-7029. ☎ **303/442-0522.** Fax 303/442-0523. 50 rms. $15 for dorm beds; private rooms $25–$50. No credit cards.

As at most hostels, guests come here expecting to share—and they do. Toilets, showers, kitchen, laundry, and the TV room are communal. Individual phones can be arranged for private rooms (with a deposit), but others share a phone. Just two blocks from the University of Colorado campus, the hostel is open for registration daily from 7am to midnight.

ⓢ Foot of the Mountain Motel. 200 Arapahoe Ave., Boulder, CO 80302. ☎ **303/442-5688.** 18 rms. TV TEL. $55–$70 double. AE, DISC, MC, V.

A series of log cabins (with bright-red trim) near the east gate of Boulder Canyon, this motel dates from 1930, but it has been fully modernized. Across the street is Eben Fine Park, at the top end of the Boulder Creek Path. The very pleasant cabins with pine walls are furnished with queen or double beds, cable TV, refrigerators, and individual water heaters. Pets are welcome.

4 Dining

Partly because Boulder is a young, hip community, it has attracted a variety of small, with-it restaurants—chef-owned and -operated—where innovative and often changing cuisine is the rule. You'll find a lot of West Coast influences here, but also a lot of top-notch chefs doing their own thing.

In the following listing, a **very expensive** restaurant is categorized as one where most dinner main courses are priced above $20; **expensive,** the dinner courses are $15 to $20; **moderate,** the prices are $7 to $15; and **inexpensive,** they cost less than $7.

VERY EXPENSIVE

✪ Flagstaff House Restaurant. 1138 Flagstaff Rd. (west up Baseline Rd.). ☎ **303/442-4640.** Reservations recommended. Main courses $21–$39. AE, DC, MC, V. Sun–Fri 6–10pm, Sat 5–10pm. NEW AMERICAN/REGIONAL.

People come to the Flagstaff House from all over the state to partake of its excellent cuisine and enjoy its spectacular nighttime view of the lights of Boulder, spread out

1,000 feet below. A local institution since 1951, the restaurant has an elegant, candlelit dining room with glass walls that maximize the view.

The menu, which changes daily, offers an excellent selection of seafood and Rocky Mountain game, all prepared with a creative flair. Typical appetizers include smoked rabbit or duck, oysters, wild mushrooms, and cheeses. Entrees, many of which are seasonal, might include Colorado buffalo, Australian lobster tail, Canadian halibut, and soft-shell crabs. There are dessert soufflés, a spectacular wine cellar, and an impressive selection of after-dinner drinks.

EXPENSIVE

John's Restaurant. 2328 Pearl St. ☎ **303/444-5232.** Reservations recommended. Main courses $15.50–$22. AE, DC, DISC, MC, V. Daily from 5pm until closing. CONTINENTAL/ AMERICAN.

This small, charming restaurant was top-rated by the *Denver Post* and *Westword* newspapers in 1994 and 1995, but that's no surprise; John's has been winning awards and raves since it opened in 1974. Chef-owned, the restaurant serves the classic dishes of France, Italy, and Spain, along with contemporary American cuisine. Entrees include medallions of lamb chilindron, lobster ravioli, filet mignon with Stilton ale sauce, Louisiana seafood gumbo, chicken with juniper berry gravy, and shrimp Nancy (named for John's wife). The menu also includes vegetarian items, such as wild mushroom ravioli. Homemade desserts include John's Chocolate Intensity. There's a well-chosen wine list, microbrewery and other beers, and cocktails.

Sushi Zanmai. 1221 Spruce St. ☎ **303/440-0733.** Reservations requested for groups of four or more. Lunch $6–$10; dinner $12–$20. AE, MC, V. Mon–Fri 11:30am–2pm; daily 5–10pm. JAPANESE.

For years local newspaper readers have rated Sushi Zanmai as Boulder's best Japanese restaurant. All of the food is traditionally prepared in Japanese cookware while you watch—at the hibachi steak table, the sushi bar, or tableside. There are lunch specials as well as sushi happy-hour specials during lunch and dinner. Karaoke sing-along takes place every Saturday from 10pm to midnight.

MODERATE

Antica Roma. 1308 Pearl St. (on the Mall). ☎ **303/442-0378.** Reservations accepted. Main courses $6–$18; pizza $7.50–$8.95. DISC, MC, V. Lunch daily 11:30am–3:30pm; dinner, Mon–Thurs 5–10pm, Fri–Sat 5–11pm. ROMAN ITALIAN.

Walking into the Antica Roma is like entering a piazza in Rome—there's a lovely little fountain at the entrance, and the brick walls are finished like the outside of Roman homes—they even have laundry hanging on the balcony. The food is equally authentic, with all the pasta made on the premises, hand-thrown pizza baked in a wood-burning oven, and crusty Italian bread. Particularly popular are the salmon Mediterranean, pesto, and the award-winning lasagna. There's a full bar and a large selection of Italian wines.

Jax Fish House. 928 Pearl St. (one block west of the Mall). ☎ **303/444-1811.** Reservations not accepted. Main courses $6–$16. MC, V. Mon–Thurs 4–10pm; Fri–Sat 4–11pm; Sun 4–9pm. SEAFOOD.

This small restaurant has clean lines and open space with brick walls and seating either at the counter or a table. The menu includes shrimp, Atlantic salmon, Rocky Mountain trout, South American sea bass, Hawaiian tuna, Mississippi catfish, and Prince Edward Island mussel stew; for those who prefer meat, there is New York strip steak and hamburgers. No smoking.

Nancy's Restaurant. 825 Walnut St. ☎ **303/449-8402.** Breakfast $4–$8, lunch $6–$8, dinner $8–$20. AE, MC, V. Daily 7:30am–2pm, Tues–Sat 5:30–9pm. CONTINENTAL.

Nancy's is a delightful local favorite, set in a handsome and comfortable Victorian home. The food is excellent, and the menu varied and imaginative. Breakfast offerings include omelets and other egg dishes, along with waffles, blintzes, and yogurt. For lunch, you might enjoy quiche, a choice of pastas, or one of several chicken breast dishes. For dinner there are a number of chicken dishes, plus steaks, tenderloin seasoned with cracked pepper, fresh seafood, and several pasta dishes. Your main course comes with an appetizer or soup, salad, vegetables, rice or polenta, and bread with herb cheese.

Nick-N-Willy's. 8th and Pearl St. (two blocks west of the Mall). ☎ **303/444-2934.** Medium (12") pizza $6.50–$14.50. Mon–Fri 11:30am–9pm, Sat–Sun 11:30am–9:30pm. PIZZA.

This tiny place is a favorite of pizza-loving locals. The dough and sauces are homemade, and the cheese is grated fresh daily. They'll even create your pizza and let you take it home to bake it fresh yourself. You can also order a sandwich or salad. There's a second location in south Boulder at 4800 Baseline Rd. (☎ 303/499-9898).

✪ **Pasta Jay's.** 925 Pearl St. ☎ **303/444-5800.** Main courses $6–$11.50. MC, V. Mon–Thurs 11am–10:30pm, Fri–Sun 11am–11pm. ITALIAN.

Expect a long line when you arrive at this Mediterranean boutique, with its red-checked tablecloths indoors and its outdoor patio facing Pearl Street. The big attractions are good food, generous portions, and low prices. The menu includes manicotti, gnocchi, tortellini, rigatoni, eggplant or chicken parmigiana, and other Italian classics. Jay's also has good pizza and sandwiches. Try an ice-cream pie for dessert. No smoking is permitted; beer and wine are served.

Pour La France. 1001 Pearl St. ☎ **303/449-3929.** Breakfast $1.50–$8; lunch $5–$8; dinner $7–$14. AE, MC, V. Mon–Wed 7am–10:30pm; Thurs–Sat 7am–midnight, Sun 8am–10pm. FRENCH BISTRO.

A cafe and bistro on the mall, Pour La France is like a Paris brasserie—a casual sidewalk cafe with an awning that shades outdoor diners and big windows that provide the same view to those inside. You can start your day with any of a variety of specialty coffees and an exotic omelet; a few hours later you can return for a gourmet salad or imaginative sandwich, such as grilled chicken with melted Gruyère cheese and French herbs. Dinners feature a number of pasta dishes (many with chicken or seafood), plus daily specials, and the desserts are a chocolate lover's dream.

Walnut Brewery. 1123 Walnut St. (near Broadway). ☎ **303/447-1345.** Lunch $4.50–$8.95; dinner $6.25–$17.95. AE, CB, DC, DISC, MC, V. Sun–Thurs 11am–11pm, Fri–Sat 11am–midnight. AMERICAN.

This establishment looks as a brewery should—brick walls, prominent brew tanks, warehouselike decor, big beer-label signs. Order an appetizing taster of the brewery's six handcrafted beers, but don't ignore the food. Lunches feature the "brewtus" salad, the brew burger, and the brewer's club, as well as excellent beer-batter fish-and-chips. The dinner menu includes the same brewery favorites and pasta, plus such entrees as brown ale chicken, chile-crusted salmon, tenderloin with roasted garlic, and baby-back ribs.

INEXPENSIVE

La Estrellita. 2037 13th St. ☎ **303/939-8822.** Meals $3–$10. AE, DISC, MC, V. Mon–Thurs 11am–10pm, Fri–Sat 11am–11pm, Sun noon–10pm. MEXICAN.

👪 Family-Friendly Restaurants

Sushi Zanmai *(see p. 155)*   Flashing knives and tableside cooking give kids a lot to watch.

New York Deli *(this page)*   Fifteen varieties of burgers are offered here, plus pizza, Coney Island hot dogs, and Dagwood-style sandwiches. Take-out and delivery service are available.

Using recipes developed by his parents at the original La Estrellita in Fort Lupton in the 1950s and 1960s, John Montoya established this restaurant in 1986. You'll find all the standard tacos, tostadas, enchiladas, tamales, and chile rellenos, in generous portions, as well as a few surprises: *costillas adobadas* (Mexican-style ribs), Indian tacos, and stuffed sopaipillas. Fajitas are also a big seller. In recent years *Hispanic Magazine* chose La Estrellita as one of the 50 Best Mexican Restaurants in the United States.

New York Delicatessen. 1117 Pearl St. ☎ **303/447-DELI.** $2–$8.95. AE, CB, DC, DISC, MC, V. Daily 8am–10pm. DELI.

Remember television's *Mork and Mindy?* Back in the 1970s, Robin Williams and Pam Dawber made their home-away-from-home at this authentic New York–style deli on the Pearl Street Mall. You can join the local college and business crowd as they enjoy Dagwood-style sandwiches, Coney Island hot dogs, or Reuben sandwiches. Soups, salads, and pastries are prepared fresh daily. The extensive menu also includes pizza and 15 different burgers. There's booth seating and a sunny outside deck, take-out service, and free delivery.

😊 **Tom's Tavern.** 1047 Pearl St. ☎ **303/443-3893.** $5–$10. AE, CB, DC, DISC, MC, V. Mon–Sat 11am–midnight, Sun 1–9:30pm. AMERICAN.

Boulder's most popular place for a good hamburger, Tom's has been a neighborhood institution for almost 40 years. Located in a turn-of-the-century building that once housed an undertaker, the tavern has vinyl-upholstered booths and patio seating outdoors. Besides the one-third-pound burgers and other sandwiches, Tom's serves dinner anytime: a 10-ounce steak, fried chicken, or a vegetarian casserole—all in the $6 range.

JAVA JUNCTION: ESPRESSO BARS, CAFES & COFFEE HOUSES

Espresso fans will have no problem finding a decent espresso, cappuccino, or latte, since there are outlets of **Starbucks** and **Brio,** as well as independent coffee bars, throughout Boulder. Many of the indies, located in the vicinity of the Pearl Street Mall, provide outdoor seating in nice weather. One of our favorites is **Bookend Cafe,** 1115 Pearl Street Mall (☎ **303/440-6699**); besides a variety of coffee drinks, it offers a delightful array of baked goods and egg dishes for breakfast; soups, salads, and sandwiches for lunch; plus ice cream floats and shakes. At the east end of the mall is the somewhat bohemian **Penny Lane** (☎ **303/443-9516**), a gathering place for talking, playing chess, or reading, while sipping regular coffee, espresso, cappuccino, or a latte, and munching a bagel or muffin. There's a wide variety of newspapers and often live music. The **Caffe Mars,** 1425 Pearl St. (☎ **303/938-1750**) has live entertainment Wednesday through Saturday evenings.

5 Attractions

THE TOP ATTRACTIONS

✪ **Boulder Creek Path.** 55th St. and Pearl Pkwy. to the mouth of Boulder Canyon. ☎ **303/441-3400.** Free admission. Daily 24 hours. Bus: HOP.

Following Boulder Creek, this nature corridor provides about a 10-mile-long oasis and recreation area through the city and west into the mountains. With no street crossings (there are bridges and underpasses instead), the path is popular with Boulder residents, especially on weekends, when you'll see numerous walkers, runners, bicyclists, and in-line skaters. Walkers should stay to the right since the left lane is for faster traffic. The C.U. campus and several city parks are linked by the path, as are local office buildings. Near the east end, watch for deer, prairie dog colonies, and wetlands, where some 150 species of birds have been spotted. You may see Canada geese, mallard ducks, spotted sandpipers, owls, and woodpeckers.

At 30th Street, south of Arapahoe Road, the path cuts through Scott Carpenter Park (named for Colorado's native-son astronaut), with swimming in summer and sledding in winter. Just west of Scott Carpenter Park you'll find Boulder Creek Stream Observatory, which is adjacent to and maintained by the Clarion Hotel. In addition to observing trout and other aquatic wildlife, you're invited to feed the fish with trout food purchased from a vending machine (25¢). Central Park, at Broadway and Canyon Boulevard, preserves some of Boulder's history with a restored steam locomotive. The Boulder Public Library is also in this area.

Traveling west, watch for the Charles A. Heartling Sculpture Garden (with the stone image of local Indian Chief Niwot) and the Kids' Fishing Ponds; these ponds are stocked by the Boulder Fish and Game Club and are open only to children under 12, who can fish for free and keep what they catch. Near Third Street and Canyon Boulevard you'll find the Xeriscape Garden, where drought-tolerant plants are tested for reduced water intake.

The Eben G. Fine Park is named for the Boulder pharmacist who discovered Arapahoe Glacier on nearby Arapahoe Peak. To the west, Red Rocks Settlers' Park marks the beginning of the Boulder Canyon Pioneer Trail, which leads to a continuation of Boulder Creek Path. The park is named for Missouri gold-seekers who camped at this spot in 1858 and later found gold about 12 miles farther west. Watch for explanatory signs along the 1.2-mile path. The Whitewater Kayak Course has 20 slalom gates for kayakers and canoeists to use free; to the west, Elephant Buttresses is one of Boulder's more popular rock-climbing areas. The path ends at Four Mile Canyon—the old town site of Orodell.

Note: Although the path is generally well populated and quite safe, Boulderites warn against using it late at night if you are alone; one of the problems is the number of transients who take refuge there.

✪ **Pearl Street Mall.** Pearl St. from 11th to 15th streets Bus: HOP.

This four-block-long tree-lined pedestrian mall marks at once Boulder's downtown core and its center for dining, shopping, strolling, and people-watching. Musicians, mimes, jugglers, and other street entertainers hold court on the landscaped mall day and night, year-round; you'll find everyone watching the shows. Buy your lunch from one of the many vendors, and sprawl on the grass in front of the courthouse to rest and eat. Locally owned businesses and galleries share the mall with trendy boutiques, sidewalk cafes, and major chains including Esprit, Peppercorn, Banana Republic, and Pendleton. There's a wonderful play area for youngsters, with climbable boulders set in gravel. Don't miss the bronze bust of Chief Niwot (of the southern Arapahoe) in front of the Boulder County Courthouse between 13th and 14th streets. Niwot, who welcomed the first Boulder settlers, was killed in southeastern Colorado during the Sand Creek Massacre of 1864.

University of Colorado. East side of Broadway, between Arapahoe Ave. and Baseline Rd. ☎ **303/492-1411.** Bus: HOP.

The largest university in the state, with 25,000 students (including 4,000 graduate students) and covering 786 acres, the University of Colorado dominates the city. Its student population, cultural and sports events, and intellectual atmosphere have helped to shape Boulder into the city it is today. Colorado is one of only 12 universities in the United States that has a NASA program.

Old Main, on the Norlin Quadrangle, was the first building erected after the university was established in 1876; at that time, it housed the entire school. Later, pink sandstone Italian Renaissance–style buildings came to predominate on campus. Visitors may want to take in the university's Heritage Center, on the third floor of Old Main; the University of Colorado Museum (see "More Attractions," below), a natural-history museum in the Henderson Building on Broadway; the Mary Rippon Outdoor Theatre, behind the Henderson Museum, site of the annual Colorado Shakespeare Festival; the Fiske Planetarium and Science Center, between Kittredge Loop Drive and Regent Drive on the south side of campus; and the Norlin Library, on the Norlin Quadrangle, the largest research library in the state, with extensive holdings of American and English literature. Prospective students and their parents can arrange campus tours by contacting the admissions office (☎ 303/492-6301).

Tours are available weekdays at the Laboratory for Atmospheric and Space Physics (☎ 303/492-6412), on the east campus, with at least 1 week's advance notice. The Sommers-Bausch Observatory (☎ 303/492-5002) offers tours and Friday evening open houses. Among the telescopes there are 16-, 18-, and 24-inch Cassegrain reflectors and a 10-inch aperture heliostat.

National Center for Atmospheric Research. 1850 Table Mesa Dr. ☎ **303/497-1174.** Free admission. Self-guided tours, Mon–Fri 8am–5pm, Sat–Sun and holidays 9am–3pm; guided tours, June–Sept, Mon–Sat at noon; rest of year, Mon and Wed at noon. Take Broadway heading southeast out of town to Table Mesa Dr., and follow it west to the center.

I. M. Pei designed this striking pink sandstone building, which overlooks Boulder from high atop Table Mesa in the southwestern foothills. Scientists here study such phenomena as the greenhouse effect, wind shear, and ozone depletion to gain a better understanding of the earth's atmosphere. Among the technological tools on display are satellites, weather balloons, interactive computer monitors, robots, and supercomputers that can simulate the world's climate. There are seven hands-on weather-oriented exhibits from the San Francisco Exploratorium Museum, now on permanent display. The center also hosts a changing art exhibit.

MORE ATTRACTIONS
INDUSTRIAL TOURS

✪ **Celestial Seasonings.** 4600 Sleepytime Dr. (off Spine Rd. at Colo. 119—Longmont Diagonal). ☎ **303/581-1202.** Free Admission. Mon–Sat, with tours on the hour from 10am to 3pm. Gift shop, Mon–Sat 9am–6pm, Sun noon–5pm. Reservations are required for groups of eight or more. Bus: J.

The nation's leading producer of herbal teas, housed in a modern new building in northeastern Boulder, offers tours that are an experience for the senses. The company, which began in a Boulder garage in the 1970s, now produces more than 50 varieties of tea from more than 100 different herbs and spices, imported from 35 foreign countries. You'll understand why they invite you to "see, taste, and smell the

Boulder Attractions

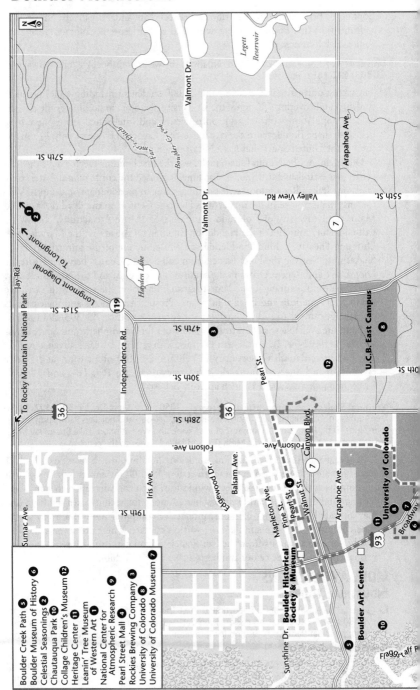

Boulder Creek Path **5**
Boulder Museum of History **6**
Celestial Seasonings **2**
Chautauqua Park **10**
Collage Children's Museum **12**
Heritage Center **11**
Leanin' Tree Museum
  of Western Art **1**
National Center for
  Atmospheric Research **9**
Pearl Street Mall **4**
Rockies Brewing Company **3**
University of Colorado **8**
University of Colorado Museum **7**

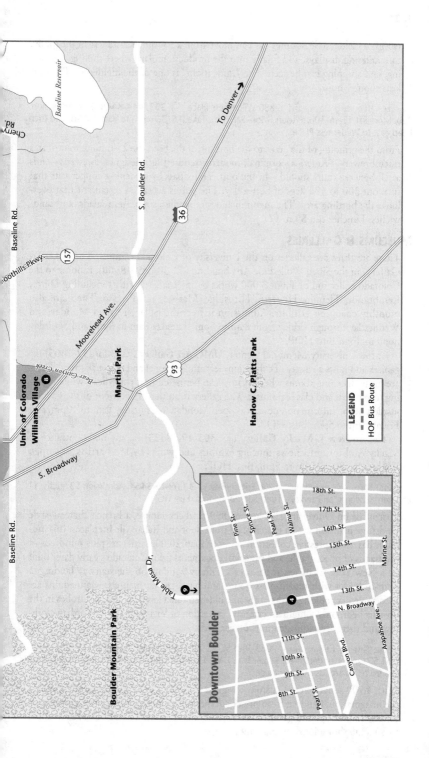

world of Celestial Seasonings" as you move from a consumer taste test in the lobby, to marketing displays, and finally into the production plant where milling, packaging, and shipping can be seen. The "mint room" is one of the highlights. The tour lasts about 1 hour.

Rockies Brewing Company. 2880 Wilderness Place. ☎ **303/444-8448.** Free Admission. Pub, Mon–Sat 11am–10pm; tours, Mon–Sat 2pm. Take U.S. 36 north to Valmont Rd. and then head east to Wilderness Place.

From the grinding of the grain to the bottling of the beer, the 25-minute tour of this microbrewery—America's original, modern trendsetting "designer" brewery—ends as all brewery tours should—in the pub. Tours pass by glistening copper vats that turn out 300 to 400 kegs of beer a day. The pub is actually a restaurant that overlooks the bottling area. The menu includes munchies, soup, fresh salads, and sandwiches. Lunches run $5 to $7.

MUSEUMS & GALLERIES

There are three art galleries on the University of Colorado campus. **The C.U. Art Gallery,** in the Sibell Wolle Fine Arts building (☎ **303/492-8300**), is home to the Colorado collection of about 3,000 works by international artists including Dürer, Rembrandt, Tiepolo, Hogarth, Hiroshige, Matisse, and Picasso. There are also monthly changing exhibits. Admission is free; the gallery is open Monday and Wednesday through Friday from 8am to 5pm, Tuesday 8am to 8pm, and Saturday noon to 4pm. Bus: HOP.

At the University Memorial Center, **UMC Art Gallery** (☎ **303/492-7465**) organizes and hosts a variety of exhibitions featuring regional and national artists. There are music-listening rooms where visitors can peruse current periodicals while listening to modern and classical music. The gallery is on the second floor of the Center, just left of the information desk; it is open Monday to Thursday 9am to 10pm, and Friday 9am to 5pm. Bus: HOP.

The **Andrew J. Macky Gallery** (☎ **303/492-8423**), at the main entrance of Macky Auditorium, shows touring exhibits and works by local artists. It's open Wednesday from 10am to 5pm. Bus: HOP.

Boulder Museum of History. 1206 Euclid Ave. ☎ **303/449-3464.** Admission $2 adults, $1 children, students, and seniors. Tues–Sun noon–4pm. Bus: HOP.

Ensconced on University Hill in the 1899 Harbeck House, a French château–style sandstone mansion with a Dutch-style front door and Italian tile fireplaces, this museum has an impressive collection of more than 20,000 artifacts, plus hundreds of thousands of photographs and historical documents from Colorado's early days. Built by a New York financier, it features a Tiffany window on the stairway landing, a built-in buffet with leaded-glass doors, and hand-carved mantels. Mannequins are used to depict cooking in the authentic old-fashioned kitchen. The wardrobes in the upstairs bedrooms contain an extensive collection of Victorian and Edwardian clothing, and there are exquisite quilts on the beds.

Collage Children's Museum. 2065 30th St. ☎ **303/440-9894.** Admission $2.50 per person, $1.50 seniors, under 2 free, $8 per family. Wed 2–5pm, Thurs–Sat 10am–5pm, Sun 1–5pm. Across from Crossroads Mall, east side.

With 4,700 square feet of custom-designed interactive exhibits created to stimulate the imagination, children from preschool through elementary grades are encouraged to touch, dress up, and get involved here. Children under 12 must be accompanied by an adult, but adults can play, too.

Heritage Center. Third floor of Old Main, University of Colorado. ☎ **303/492-6329.** Free Admission. Tues–Fri 10am–4pm; and preceding most home football games. Bus: HOP.

Located in the oldest building on campus, this museum reflects the history of the university. Within seven galleries are exhibits depicting the early history of student life, together with a complete set of yearbooks, C.U.'s contributions to space exploration, campus architecture, photographs of distinguished C.U. alumni, and an overview of the university's history.

Leanin' Tree Museum of Western Art. 6055 Longbow Dr. (off Spine Rd. and Longmont Diagonal). ☎ **303/530-1442.** Free Admission. Mon–Fri 8am–4:30pm, Sat 10am–4pm. Bus: 205.

You may know Leanin' Tree as the world's largest publisher of western-art greeting cards. What's not so well known is that here in the company's headquarters is an outstanding collection of original paintings and bronze sculptures by contemporary artists—all depicting scenes from the Old or New West, including a collection of humorous cowboy art. Some of the works have been reproduced on the company's greeting cards that are offered for sale in the gift shop.

University of Colorado Museum. University of Colorado, Henderson Bldg., Broadway at 15th St. ☎ **303/492-6892.** Free Admission, but donations accepted. Mon–Fri 9am–5pm, Sat 9am–4pm, Sun 10am–4pm. Bus: HOP.

The natural history and anthropology of the Rocky Mountains and Southwest are the focus of this campus museum, founded in 1902. Featured exhibits include Anasazi pottery and dinosaurs; there are also collections in geology, paleontology, botany, entomology, and zoology. A children's area has interactive exhibits, and the main gallery is devoted to special displays that change throughout the year.

ESPECIALLY FOR KIDS

City parks (see "Outdoor Activities," below), **Collage Children's Museum** (see above), and the **University of Colorado's Fiske Planetarium** offer the best diversions for children.

On the **Boulder Creek Path** (see "The Top Attractions," above), youngsters are fascinated by the underwater fish observatory behind the Clarion Harvest House. They can feed the huge trout (25¢ machines cough up handfuls of fish food) swimming behind a glass barrier on the creek. Farther up the path, on the south bank around Sixth Street, fishing ponds, stocked by the Boulder Fish and Game Club, are open to children under 12. There's no charge for either activity.

The Fiske Planetarium (☎ 303/492-5002) has an after-school and summer Science Discovery Program as well as a special Saturday event called "Stories Under the Stars." On some Friday nights the planetarium presents a light show followed by an opportunity to look at the stars through the telescope. Visitors can take a half-hour walk through a scale model of the solar system (☎ 303/492-5001). Dedicated to the memory of C.U. alumnus Ellison Onizuka and the six other astronauts who died in the space shuttle *Challenger,* the tour begins at the entrance to the planetarium with the sun and inner planets, and continues across Regent Drive to the outer planets, located along the walkway to the Engineering Center. Bus: HOP.

6 Outdoor Activities

Boulder is clearly one of the leading spots for outdoor sports in North America. The city manages 8,555 acres of park lands, including more than 100 miles of hiking trails and long stretches of bicycle paths. Several canyons lead down from the Rockies directly into Boulder, attracting mountaineers and rock climbers. Families enjoy picnicking and camping in the beautiful surroundings. It seems that everywhere you look, men and women of all ages are running, walking, biking, skiing, or engaged in other active sports.

The **Boulder Convention and Visitors Bureau** has developed four self-guided, active tours of the city, called *Circle Tours*. **Tour no. 1,** titled **Beauty & Beasts,** is a fairly long (about 85 miles) driving and/or biking loop; the brochure presents historical information about the towns you'll go through, plus the flora and fauna you can see along the way. **Tour no. 2,** for both bikers and hikers, is called **Bolder Biking;** it presents several trails in and around Boulder, with pertinent information on each one so that you can decide whether or not it's for you. **Tour no. 3, Mines & Minerals,** is another driving/biking loop, taking you through some of the lesser known mining towns of the area. **Tour no. 4,** called **Take a Hike,** lists about 30 hikes in Boulder, Lyons, Allenspark, Peaceful Valley, and Nederland—all beginning within a half-hour drive through Boulder.

The **Boulder Parks and Recreation Department** (☎ 303/441-3400) schedules many activities for children as well as adults year-round. Seasonal booklets on activities and city parks are available free from the Chamber of Commerce office. Although many of the programs last for several weeks or months, some are half- or one-day activities that visiting children can join, although usually at a slightly higher price than charged for city residents. The department sponsors hikes, horseback rides, fitness programs, ski trips, water sports, special holiday events, and performances in local parks.

In addition, there are two outdoor nature areas to keep in mind: Chautauqua Park and Eldorado Canyon State Park. The former dates from the late 19th and early 20th centuries, when more than 400 Chautauquas—adult education and cultural entertainment centers—sprang up around the United States. This 26-acre **Chautauqua Park** in Boulder, on a hillside west of downtown, is one of the few remaining in the country. In summer, it hosts a wide-ranging program of music, dance, theater, and film, including the Colorado Music Festival (see "Boulder After Dark," later in this chapter). There are playgrounds, picnic grounds, tennis courts, and hiking trailheads. The historic Chautauqua Dining Hall, which first opened on July 4, 1898, serves three meals daily at moderate prices, Memorial Day through Labor Day. Reservations are not accepted. Some accommodations are available in cottages and two lodges; the cost ranges from $50 to $100 per night for 4-night stays (lower rates for 7 days or more). The entrance is at Ninth Street and Baseline Road (Bus: 203). For further information, call **303/442-3282** or 303/440-3776 (for the restaurant).

Eldorado Canyon State Park, just 8 miles southwest of Boulder in Eldorado Springs, is a favorite of technical rock climbers, but the 850-foot-high canyon's beauty makes it just as popular among hikers, picnickers, and others who want to get away from it all. The 845-acre park includes 12 miles of hiking and horseback trails, plus 9 miles of trails suitable for mountain bikes; fishing is permitted, but not camping. Exhibits at the Visitor Center describe the canyon's geologic formations. Admission is $3 per vehicle; open daily 5am–10pm. For further information, contact Eldorado Canyon State Park, c/o Colo. 170, Box B, Eldorado Springs, CO 80025 (☎ 303/494-3943).

BALLOONING Float above the ground in a hot-air balloon, watching as the early morning light gradually brightens to full day. Flights often include complimentary champagne and a continental breakfast. Call **Fair Winds, Inc.** (☎ 303/939-9323) or **Air Boulder** (☎ 303/442-5253). Prices range from $125 to $150 per person.

BICYCLING   On some days you can see more bikes than cars in Boulder. Paths run along many of the city's major arteries, and local racing and touring events are scheduled year-round. Bicyclists riding at night are required to have lights; perhaps because of the large number of bicyclists in Boulder, the local police actively enforce traffic regulations that apply to bicyclists. Generally, bicyclists must obey the same laws that apply to operators of motor vehicles.

For current information on biking events, the best places to ride, and equipment sales and repairs, check with **University Bicycles,** 839 Pearl St. (☎ **303/444-4196**). The shop also provides bike rentals for about $20 per day.

For maps of the city's 80 miles of bike lanes, paths, and routes, stop at University Bicycles or contact the city's alternative transportation program, **Go Boulder,** P.O. Box 791, Boulder, CO 80306 (☎ **303/441-4260**). Each June, the city, county, and university cosponsor **Boulder Bike Week,** which includes races, a kids' bike rodeo, a safety forum, and maintenance clinics. For a city bike map, send $2 and a self-addressed stamped envelope to Go Boulder. Free wallet-sized bike and bus maps are also available.

FISHING   Favored fishing areas near Boulder include **Boulder Reservoir** (run by the Boulder Parks & Recreation Dept., ☎ **303/441-3400**), North 51st Street, 1¹/₂ miles north of Jay Road, northeast of the city off the Longmont Diagonal; **Lagerman Reservoir,** west of North 73rd Street off Pike Road, about 15 miles northeast of the city, where only nonmotorized boats can be used; **Barker Reservoir,** just east of Nederland on the Boulder Canyon Drive (Colo. 119), for bank fishing; and **Walden Ponds Wildlife Habitat,** about 6 miles east of downtown on North 75th Street.

GOLF   Local courses include **Coal Creek Golf Course,** 585 W. Dillon Rd., Louisville (☎ **303/666-PUTT**); **Flatiron Golf Course** (run by Boulder Parks & Recreation Dept.), 5706 Arapahoe Ave. (☎ **303/442-7851**); and **Lake Valley Golf Course,** 4400 Lake Valley Dr., 2 miles north of Boulder off Neva Road (☎ **303/444-2114**). Greens fees for 18 holes range from $20 to $25.

HIKING & BACKPACKING   From Chautauqua Park, Ninth Street and Baseline Road, rangers (with the Boulder Parks & Recreation Dept., ☎ **303/441-3408**) lead hikes and offer advice on trips into Boulder Mountain Parks. The mountain parks system includes 4,625 acres bordering the Boulder city limits to the west and south, including the Flatirons and Flagstaff Mountain. You can obtain a *Boulder Mountain Parks Trail Map* ($4) from the city Chamber of Commerce, 2440 Pearl St. (☎ **303/442-1044**). A very popular hike is the **Enchanted Mesa Trail,** which leaves from Chautauqua Park, joins the longer Mesa Trail, and follows the ridge of the Flatirons for about 6 miles to Eldorado Springs.

Numerous Roosevelt National Forest trailheads leave the Peak to Peak Scenic Byway (Colo. 72) west of Boulder. Check with the U.S. Forest Service, Boulder Ranger District, 2995 Baseline Rd., Room 110 (☎ **303/444-6600**). West of Boulder, on the Continental Divide, is the Indian Peaks Wilderness Area (☎ **303/444-6003**). More than half of the area is fragile alpine tundra; permits are required from June 1 to September 15. North of Boulder, via Estes Park, is Rocky Mountain National Park, one of the state's prime destinations for hikers and those seeking beautiful mountain scenery (see chapter 11).

HORSEBACK RIDING   Several area ranches offer day rides and pack trips, including **Lazy Ranch Riding Stables,** Eldorado Springs (☎ **303/499-4940**), which charges $15 per hour.

GLIDER FLYING & SOARING   The atmospheric conditions generated by the peaks of the Front Range are ideal for year-round soaring and gliding. **The Cloud**

Base, 5534 Independence Rd. (☎ **303/530-2208**), offers rides and lessons from Boulder Municipal Airport, 2 miles northeast of downtown. Rides cost from $50 to $110.

ROCK CLIMBING   If you would like to tackle the nearby mountains and cliffs with ropes and pitons, contact **Boulder Mountaineer,** 1335 Broadway (☎ **303/ 442-8355**), or the **Colorado Athletic Training School,** 2800 30th St. (☎ **303/ 939-9699**).

The Flatiron Range (easily visible from downtown Boulder) and nearby Eldorado Canyon are two favorite destinations among expert rock scalers.

RUNNING   The best place to get information about running or walking is the **Runners Roost,** 1129 Pearl St. (on the Mall) (☎ **303/443-9868**); besides selling shoes and apparel, this shop serves as headquarters for numerous race events in the city. Most of these are untimed fun runs, varying in distance from 5 kilometers (3.1 miles) to a half marathon (13 miles). **The Bolder Boulder** (☎ **303/444-RACE**), held every Memorial Day, attracts 40,000 runners who circle its 10-kilometer (6.2-mile) course.

SKIING   Friendly **Eldora Mountain Resort,** P.O. Box 1697, Nederland, CO 80466 (☎ **303/440-8700**), is just 21 miles (about a 40-min. drive) west of downtown Boulder via Highway 119 through Nederland. RTD buses leave Boulder for Eldora four times daily, beginning at 8:10am, during ski season. Recently, the resort added a large ski-school building and expanded the area's snowmaking capacity for a longer season.

For cross-country skiers, Eldora has 45 kilometers (28 miles) of groomed and backcountry trails, and an overnight hut available by reservation. Trail fee is $10, or $7 for seniors 65 to 69.

You can rent all your ski and snowboard equipment at the ski-rental center, and Nordic equipment at the Eldora Nordic Center. A free base area shuttle runs throughout the day from the Lodge to the Little Hawk area and the Nordic Center.

In Boulder, downhill and cross-country equipment, snowboards, snowshoes, and car racks can be rented at **Crystal Ski Shop,** 3216 Arapahoe Ave., Suite (☎ **303/ 449-7669**), open daily 7am–8pm. **Mountain Sports,** 821 Pearl St. (☎ **303/ 443-6770**) offers cross-country, telemark, and touring skis.

SWIMMING   There are five public pools within the city. Indoor pools, all open daily year-round, are at the **North Boulder Recreation Center,** 3170 Broadway (☎ **303/441-3444**), the **East Boulder Community Center,** 5660 Sioux Dr. (☎ **303/441-4400**), and the **South Boulder Recreation Center,** 1360 Gillaspie Dr. (☎ **303/441-3448**). Swimming fees are $4 adults, $1.50 children, and $2.50 seniors. There are two outdoor pools (both open daily Memorial Day–Labor Day)— **Scott Carpenter Pool,** 30th Street and Arapahoe Avenue (☎ **303/441-3427**), and **Spruce Pool,** 21st and Spruce streets (☎ **303/441-3426**).

TENNIS   There are more than 30 public courts in the city. The North and South Boulder Recreation Centers (see "Swimming," above) each have four lighted courts, accept reservations, and charge $4 per person. Free courts are available at **Arapahoe Ridge Park** on Eisenhower Drive south of Arapahoe Street; **Chautauqua Park,** Ninth Street and Baseline Road; **Columbine Park,** 20th Street and Glenwood Street; and **Martin Park,** 36th Street and Eastman Street. Contact the Boulder Parks and Recreation Department (☎ **303/441-3400**) for more information.

WATER SPORTS   For boating, sailboard instruction, or swimming at a sandy beach, head for the 1400-acre **Boulder Reservoir** (☎ **303/441-3456**) on North 51st

Street off the Longmont Diagonal northeast of the city. Boats and canoes can be rented for $5 an hour, with sailboards at $10 an hour.

7 Spectator Sports

The major attraction is **University of Colorado football, women's volleyball,** and **men's and women's basketball.** For tickets, contact the Ticket Office, Campus Box 372, Boulder, CO 80309 (☎ **303/49-BUFFS**). Football tickets sell out early, particularly for Homecoming and games with Nebraska, Texas A&M, and Oklahoma, so it would be wise to make reservations far in advance, perhaps even months ahead.

BEACH VOLLEYBALL   Although volleyball may seem out of place here in the mountains, each June there is the **José Cuervo Doubles Volleyball Tournament,** a professional beach-volleyball tournament that attracts the best two-person teams in the nation. It takes place at Boulder Reservoir, 5565 N. 51st St. (☎ **303/441-3468**). There's a separate division for amateurs, played at the South Boulder Recreation Center, 1360 Gillaspie Dr. (☎ 303/441-3410).

8 Shopping

SHOPPING A TO Z

The best shopping in Boulder is the Pearl Street Mall (see "Top Attractions" above), where you'll find not only shops and galleries galore, but street entertainers as well.

If you are more interested in a suburban-style shopping mall, head to **Crossroads Mall** (☎ **303/444-0722**), located between 28th and 30th streets off Arapahoe Road. It has more than 150 stores, including major chains such as Sears, J.C. Penney, Foley's, and Mervyn's.

ARTS & CRAFTS

Art Source International. 1237 Pearl St. ☎ **303/444-4080.**

Natural-history prints, maps, and rare books on western Americana—all from the 18th and 19th centuries—are the specialty here, along with a collection of turn-of-the-century Colorado photographs. Featured artists include Thomas Moran, George Catlin, Karl Bodmer, Basil Besler, John James Audubon, and Daniel Giraud Elliot.

Boulder Arts and Crafts Cooperative. 1421 Pearl St. ☎ **303/443-3683.**

This shop, owned and operated by its artist members since 1971, features a wide variety of original handcrafted work by more than 100 artists in the Rocky Mountain region.

Handmade in Colorado. 1426 Pearl St. ☎ **303/938-8394.**

This cooperative gallery offers pottery, glass, wood, quilts, photographs, jewelry, dried flower arrangements, and other unique items made by more than 20 artists.

Maclaren/Markowitz Gallery. 1011 Pearl St. ☎ **303/449-6807.**

Works by nationally known artists in a variety of mediums and styles are presented here, including metal sculpture, Southwest jewelry, and ceramics.

CLOTHING

Alpaca Connection. 1326 Pearl St. ☎ **303/447-2047.**

Natural fiber clothing from around the world, including alpaca-and-wool sweaters from South America, are featured at this shop.

Zippety Doo-Da. 2425 Canyon Blvd. ☎ **303/449-2522.**

Everything here is for kids—children's clothing and accessories, including such lines as Flapdoodles, Mousefeathers, and Monkeywear, sized for newborns to size 14. There's a play area to keep kids busy while their parents shop.

FOOD & DRINK

Alfalfa's. 1651 Broadway. ☎ **303/442-0997.**

The original Alfalfa's—a natural-foods supermarket—sells excellent produce (much of it certified organic) and chemical-free groceries; there's also a deli, soup-and-salad bar, juice-and-espresso bar, hot food case, and a sit-down cafe.

Boulder Wine Merchant. 2690 Broadway. ☎ **303/443-6761.**

This store has a solid wine collection with more than 2,000 varieties from around the world, plus knowledgeable sales people who can help you make the right choice.

Liquor Mart. 1750 15th St. (at Canyon Blvd.). ☎ **303/449-3374.**

Here you'll find a huge selection of discounted wine and liquor, with more than 5,000 wines and 900 beers, including a wide choice of imported and microbrewed beers.

GIFTS & SOUVENIRS

Nature's Own Imagination. 1133 Pearl St. Mall. ☎ **303/443-4430.**

This shop has a unique collection of birdhouses, garden statuary and ornaments, jewelry, picture frames, T-shirts, wall hangings, mobiles, fossils, minerals, and geodes.

Traders of the Lost Art. 1429 Pearl St. ☎ **303/440-9664.**

Here you'll find incense, candles, cards, jewelry, and colorful clothing and accessories from Asia, Africa, South America, and elsewhere.

HARDWARE

✪ **Mcguckin Hardware.** 2525 Arapahoe Ave. ☎ **303/443-1822.**

Mcguckin's claims to have the world's largest hardware selection, with 250,000 items in stock. But in addition to more nuts, bolts, brackets, paints, tools, and assorted whatchamacallits than you've ever seen, the store carries sporting goods, kitchen gizmos, automotive supplies, stationery, some clothing, electronics, outdoor furniture, and a whole lot of other stuff.

JEWELRY

Florence Bear Jewelry & Antiques. 2014 Broadway. ☎ **303/443-6311.**

In business for 2 decades, this shop focuses on Native American jewelry, including many hard-to-find pieces; gold and silver work is also available.

KITCHENWARES

Peppercorn. 1235 Pearl St. ☎ **800/447-6905** or 303/449-5847.

From cookbooks to pasta makers, you can find virtually everything for the kitchen here, along with china, glassware, flatware, and table linens. This vast store has hundreds of kitchen gadgets and appliances—everything you might need to prepare, serve, and consume the simplest or most exotic meal.

MUSIC

✪ **Boulder Early Music Shop.** 2010 14th St. ☎ **303/499-9231.**

Musicians and music lovers from across North America rely on this shop for sheet music, recordings, books, musical gifts, and instruments (including recorders, flutes, harpsichords, dulcimers, and viols). Browsing is loads of fun, and the musician-shopkeepers are the friendly, highly knowledgeable sort of folks who obviously enjoy their work.

SPORTING GOODS

There are a number of well-established sporting goods stores in the city. **Mountain Sports,** 821 Pearl St. (☎ **800/558-6770** or 303/443-6770), which claims to be Boulder's oldest mountaineering shop, specializes in equipment, clothing, and accessories for backpacking, camping, rock and ice climbing, backcountry and telemark skiing, ski skating, and snowshoeing. Equipment-rentals include sleeping bags, tents, backpacks, and snowshoes; backcountry and telemark ski packages are available. **Doc's Ski and Sport,** 627 S. Broadway (☎ **303/499-0963**), sells, rents, and repairs skis, mountain bikes, and in-line skates. **Boulder Army Store,** 1545 Pearl St. (☎ **303/442-7616**), can supply you with simple camping or fishing equipment (or perhaps a disarmed hand grenade or pair of fatigues). **Gart Brothers,** 2525 Arapahoe Ave. (☎ **303/449-6180**), is a good all-purpose sporting goods source.

9 Boulder After Dark

Boulder has one of Colorado's better music and live performing arts scenes. It's especially noted for its summer music, dance, and Shakespeare festivals, although major events take place here year-round, both downtown and on the University of Colorado campus.

There's also a wide choice of nightclubs and bars—but it hasn't always been so. Boulder was dry for 60 years, from 1907 (13 years before national prohibition) until 1967. The first new bar in the city (in the Hotel Boulderado) opened in 1969.

Entertainment schedules can be found in the *Daily Camera's* weekly "Friday Magazine"; in either of the Denver dailies, the *Denver Post* or the *Rocky Mountain News;* in *Westword,* the Denver weekly; or the free *Boulder Weekly.*

THE PERFORMING ARTS

Perhaps the city's most unique venue is the **Chautauqua Auditorium,** at 900 Baseline Rd. (☎ **303/442-3282**), in the city's historic Chautauqua Park. First opened on Independence Day, 1898, this all-wooden building is notable for its excellent acoustics. Home of the **Chautauqua Summer Festival,** the auditorium hosts popular concerts, lectures, and dance and theater performances throughout the summer. Also in the historic park is the **Community House,** which features a more intimate program.

The **Guild Theatre** at 4840 Sterling Dr. (☎ **303/449-5151**) is the home of the **Upstart Crow** theater company, which performs four classic plays from early autumn through spring; the children's theater troupe, **Boulder Conservatory Theatre** (☎ **303/444-1885** or 303/499-1059), for kids aged 5 to 18; and the **Actors Ensemble** (☎ **303/449-3296**), which presents contemporary plays. Finally, there's the **Mary Rippon Outdoor Theatre** at the University of Colorado, situated on Broadway between 15th and 16th streets (☎ **303/492-0554**), between the Hellems and Henderson buildings. The official birthplace of the **Colorado Shakespeare Festival** (1958), this beautiful garden theater (which seats 1,000) was built by the Works Progress Administration in 1936 and named for the university's first woman professor. Then there's the Macky Auditorium Concert Hall, also at the University of Colorado.

THE FESTIVAL SCENE

In addition to the Colorado Shakespeare Festival, summer brings the longstanding **Colorado Dance Festival** and the **Colorado Music Festival** to Boulder. As if that weren't enough to establish the city's high-culture credentials, Boulderites have gone on in recent years to found January's **Mahler festival,** and the practically year-round **Bach festival,** in addition to more modest efforts.

✪ **Boulder Bach Festival.** P.O. Box 1896, Boulder, CO 80306. ☎ **303/494-3159.**

First presented in 1981, this celebration of the music of Johann Sebastian Bach includes not only a late-January festival, but also concerts and other events year-round. Individual tickets cost $22 to $50, students $11 to $12.50; a three-concert series is $59 to $95.

Colorado Dance Festival. P.O. Box 356, Boulder, CO 80306. ☎ **303/442-7666.**

Dancers from around the world flock to Boulder for this 4-week event each July. Varied performances are interspersed with classes, workshops, lectures, film and video screenings, and panel discussions.

Colorado MahlerFest. P.O. Box 1314, Boulder, CO 80306. ☎ **303/494-1632.**

Begun in 1986, this international festival is the only one of its kind in the world. It celebrates the work of Gustav Mahler for a week each January with a performance of one of his symphonies, as well as films, discussions, seminars, and other musical concerts.

Colorado Music Festival. 1525 Spruce St., Boulder, CO 80302. ☎ **303/449-1397.**

Begun in 1976, this is the single biggest annual arts event in Boulder, lasting 7 weeks—from mid-June to early August. There is both a symphony orchestra and chamber music series, with musicians from around the world performing at the acoustically revered Chautauqua Auditorium. There's also a children's concert in late June and a holiday concert on the Fourth of July.

✪ **Colorado Shakespeare Festival.** Campus Box 460, University of Colorado, Boulder, CO 80309. ☎ **303/492-1527,** or 303/492-0554 for the box office.

Considered one of the top three Shakespearean festivals in the United States, this $7^{1}/_{2}$-week annual event attracts more than 40,000 theatergoers between late June and mid-August. Held since 1958 in the University of Colorado's Mary Rippon Outdoor Theatre, and indoors at University Theatre, it offers 14 performances of each of four Shakespearean plays. Actors, directors, designers, and everyone associated with the productions are fully schooled Shakespearean professionals. Tickets run $12 to $36 for a single performance, $36 to $108 for a four-play package. During the festival, company members conduct 45-minute backstage tours before each show; the cost is $3.

CLASSICAL MUSIC & JAZZ COMPANIES

Artist Series. Macky Auditorium Concert Hall, University of Colorado. ☎ **303/492-8008.**

For more than a half-century, the Artist Series has brought world-class performers to Boulder. Each season features an outstanding lineup of classical soloists, jazz artists, dance companies, and multidisciplinary events designed to inspire and intrigue audiences.

Boulder Philharmonic Orchestra. Macky Auditorium Concert Hall, University of Colorado. ☎ **303/449-1343.**

This acclaimed community orchestra performs an annual fall-to-spring season, with world-class artists such as singer Marilyn Horne, guitarist Carlos Montoya, and violinist Pinchus Zuckerman. Tickets are $9 to $31.

DANCE COMPANIES

Visiting dance companies can be seen as part of the **Artist Series** at the University of Colorado (see above); to check out the homegrown talent, attend a performance of the **Boulder Ballet Ensemble** (☎ **303/442-6944**), which dances on the stage at Macky Auditorium Concert Hall, University of Colorado. This community group, established in 1984, is best known for its production of *The Nutcracker,* performed with the Boulder Philharmonic each Thanksgiving weekend.

THE CLUB & MUSIC SCENE
ROCK

Fox Theatre. 1135 13th St. ☎ **303/447-9848** or 303/447-0095.

Live bands perform in this converted movie theater 7 nights a week. The talent is a mix of local, regional, and national acts. There are three separate bars, plus a cafe.

Tulagi. 1129 13th St. ☎ **303/442-1369.**

An informal college bar on the Hill off-campus, Tulagi features live bands most nights.

JAZZ, BLUES & FOLK

Brillig Works Cafe and Bakery. 1322 College Ave. ☎ **303/443-7461.** No cover.

This college hangout evokes the atmosphere of Greenwich Village coffee houses in the 1960s. There's music every Thursday evening, plus an extensive selection of coffees, teas, and homemade baked goods. The Brillig also serves vegetarian lunches and dinners.

The Catacombs. In the basement of the Hotel Boulderado, 13th and Spruce streets. ☎ **303/443-0486.** Cover: minimal.

This popular bar attracts a crowd to listen to blues and jazz nightly. The loud, raucous atmosphere makes this a favorite of C.U. students.

Mezzanine Lounge. In the Hotel Boulderado, 13th and Spruce sts. ☎ **303/442-4344.** No cover.

Light jazz combos or soloists perform in Victorian surroundings—this is a great place to have a conversation with friends without being overwhelmed by loud music.

DANCE CLUBS

Bentley's. In the Broker Inn, 30th St. and Baseline Rd. ☎ **303/449-1752.** Cover: $3 on comedy night.

There's dance music at this meat-markety singles bar that tends to attract young professionals rather than college students. There are happy-hour specials Monday through Friday from 4 to 7pm; Tuesday night is comedy night.

Potter's. 1207 Pearl St. ☎ **303/444-3100.** No cover.

The Pearl Street Mall's most popular dance club features recorded music. There's also a big-screen TV for major sports, and two pool tables.

THE BAR SCENE

The Barrel House. 2860 Arapahoe Rd. ☎ **303/442-4594.**

Voted the number one sports bar in Boulder 3 years running, The Barrel House offers a choice of 28 beers on tap, most of which are Colorado microbrews. There are close to 2 dozen television sets and a menu that ranges from buffalo burgers to jambalaya to Maine lobster. The Barrel House also boasts Boulder's longest happy hour—3 to 7pm and 10pm to closing every day.

✪ **The Corner Bar.** In the Hotel Boulderado, 13th and Spruce streets. ☎ **303/442-4344.**

Probably the best Boulder bar for people-watching, the Corner Bar serves sandwiches, soups, a fresh-oyster bar and an extensive list of wines by the glass.

J. J. McCabe's Cafe. 945 Walnut St. ☎ **303/449-4130.** Cover: $1–$4.

This casual downtown cafe bar, which serves a variety of soups, sandwiches, and burgers, is an ideal place to view sports, with its 17 television sets.

Mountain Sun Pub & Brewery. 1535 Pearl St. (east of the Mall). ☎ **303/546-0886.**

An English-style neighborhood pub and microbrewery, Mountain Sun produces 35 barrels of beer each week and provides tours on request. The menu features soups, salads, burgers, sandwiches, and a few Mexican dishes, and there's live folk and bluegrass Sunday nights (no cover). Half-gallon jugs of its brew are available to go.

The Sink. 1165 13th St. ☎ **303/444-SINK (7465).**

This off-campus establishment has been open since 1949, but has been updated with new spacey wall murals that help make this one of Boulder's funniest—as well as fun—nightspots. There's a full bar with 14 regional microbrews, live music, Sinkburgers and "ugly crust" pizza.

Walnut Brewery. 1123 Walnut St. (near Broadway). ☎ **303/447-1345.**

This large microbrewery, popular with the after-work crowd—both young and old—has its restaurant/bar/brewery in a historic brick warehouse a block from the Pearl Street Mall. Six beers, from a pale ale to a stout, are always available, including two cask-conditioned ales. Several seasonal specials are also brewed here.

West End Tavern. 926 Pearl St. (between 9th and 10th streets.). ☎ **303/444-3535.**

The West End seems to have a lock on the annual best neighborhood bar balloting conducted by the *Daily Camera*. Sunny afternoons find dozens of Boulderites on the tavern's roof garden, and evenings see them tuned into a wide-ranging selection of jazz, blues, or other live music in the trendy bar. Fare includes hot chile, pizza, and charbroiled sandwiches.

The Yard. 2690 28th St., Unit C. ☎ **303/443-0486.**

A gay bar that attracts a diverse crowd, The Yard features dancing on Fridays and Saturdays, as well as pool, darts, and a daily happy hour from 4 to 7pm.

Here are the spacious skies, stretching without obstacle or interruption hundreds of miles eastward from the foot of the Rocky Mountains. Here are the golden, rolling, irrigated fields of wheat and corn, spreading along the valleys of the South Platte and Republican rivers and their tributaries.

The western edge of this magnificent country is defined by the regal Rockies themselves. Impressive geological features mark the foothills, where the mountains meet the Great Plains at Fort Collins and Loveland.

A different Colorado exists on the sparsely populated plains, one that inspired James Michener's novel *Centennial*. Alive are memories of the Comanche buffalo hunters who first inhabited the region; trailblazers and railroad crews who opened up the area to white settlement; hardy pioneer farmers who endured drought, economic ruin, and so many other hardships; and ranchers like John W. Iliff, who carved a feudal empire built on longhorn cattle. Pioneer museums, frontier forts, old battlefields, and preserved downtown districts won't let history die. Vast open stretches—wetlands swollen with migrating waterfowl, the starkly beautiful Pawnee National Grassland—remain to remind us that Colorado wilderness is not the sole domain of the Rockies.

1 Fort Collins

A bustling college town, Fort Collins began in 1862 as a trading post on the Cache la Poudre River, named for a powder cache left by French fur trappers. A stage station and army camp, commanded by Lieutenant Colonel William O. Collins, followed. The fort was abandoned in 1867, but the settlement prospered, first as a quarrying and farming center, and by 1910 with sugar-beet processing.

Today Fort Collins is regarded as one of the fastest-growing cities in the United States, with an average annual growth rate of 3.5%. Population leaped from 43,000 in 1970 to 65,000 in 1980 to 97,000 today, not including the many Colorado State University students. C.S.U. was established in 1870; today it is nationally known for its forestry and veterinary medicine schools, and its research advances in space engineering and bone cancer.

ESSENTIALS

GETTING THERE   By Car   Coming from south or north, take I-25, Exit 269 (Mulberry St., for downtown Fort Collins), Exit 268 (Prospect Rd., for Colorado State University), or Exit 265 (Harmony Rd., for south Fort Collins). From Rocky Mountain National Park, follow U.S. 34 to Loveland, then turn north on U.S. 287. The drive takes about 1¼ hours from Denver or Estes Park, about 40 minutes from Cheyenne.

By Plane   Many visitors to Fort Collins fly into **Denver International** (see chapter 6 for a listing of airlines that service that airport). **Fort Collins Municipal Airport,** 4900 Earhart Rd., (☎ **970/962-2850**), off I-25 Exit 259, 7 miles northeast of downtown Loveland, is served by **United Express** (☎ **800/241-6522** or 970/663-4614) to and from Denver. **Western Pacific** (☎ **800/930-3030**) was scheduled to begin flights from Colorado Springs and other cities in late 1996. Rental-car agencies at the airport include **Hertz** (☎ **800/654-3131** or 970/962-9323) and **Dollar** (☎ **800/800-4000** or 970/663-3503). **Airport Express** (☎ **970/482-0505**) provides shuttle services between Denver and Fort Collins, but does not serve Fort Collins Municipal Airport.

ORIENTATION   Fort Collins is located at the foot of the Rockies on the Cache la Poudre River, a major tributary of the South Platte. Downtown "Fort" is 4 miles due west of I-25. College Avenue (U.S. 287) is the main north-south artery and the city's primary commercial strip; Mulberry Street (Colo. 14), which crosses I-25 at Exit 269, the major Fort Collins interchange, is the main east-west thoroughfare.

Downtown Fort Collins extends north of Mulberry Street on College Avenue to Jefferson Street; Old Town is contained in a triangle bounded by College Avenue, Jefferson Street, and Mountain Avenue, which parallels Mulberry four blocks to the north. The main Colorado State University campus is in the mile-square sector bounded by Mulberry Street on the north, Prospect Road on the south, College Avenue on the east, and Shields Street on the west. Drake Road, Horsetooth Road, and Harmony Road cross College Avenue at 1-mile intervals south of Prospect. Taft Hill Road and Overland Trail parallel College Avenue at 1-mile intervals west of Shields; Lemay Avenue and Timberline Road are at 1-mile intervals east.

VISITOR INFORMATION   **The Fort Collins Convention & Visitors Bureau** has a visitor information center at 420 S. Howes St., Suite 101 (P.O. Box 1998), Fort Collins, CO 80522 (☎ **800/274-FORT** or 970/482-5821; fax 970/493-8061). That's two blocks west of the intersection of College Avenue and Mulberry Street.

GETTING AROUND   By Public Transportation   The city bus system, known as **Transfort** (☎ **970/221-6620**), operates ten routes throughout Fort Collins Monday through Saturday from 6:30am to 6:30pm, except major holidays. All buses are accessible to those with disabilities, and all have bike racks; call for information. Fares are 85¢ for adults, 40¢ for seniors and those with disabilities, and youths 17 and under ride free; exact change is required. A 10-ride ticket is $6.

By Taxi   Taxi service is provided 24 hours a day by **Shamrock Yellow Cab** (☎ **970/224-2222**).

By Bicycle   Bicycling is a popular and viable means of transportation in Fort Collins. Just about the only place you can't ride them is College Avenue. See "Sports & Outdoor Activities," below for information about bike rentals.

Northeastern Colorado

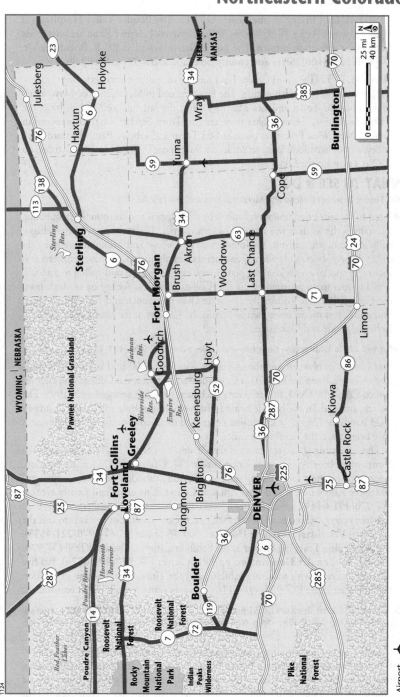

Airport ✈

FAST FACTS   In case of **emergency,** call **911.** The **Poudre Valley Hospital** is at 1024 S. Lemay Ave. (☎ **970/495-7000**), between Prospect Road and Riverside Avenue just east of downtown. The **post office** is located at 301 E. Boardwalk Dr. (☎ **970/225-4100**). **State and county taxes** add about 9% to hotel bills.

SPECIAL EVENTS   Fort Collins has a number of special events occurring throughout the year that are worth noting. The first weekend in May, Cinco de Mayo is celebrated in Old Town and Lee Martinez Park; the last full weekend in June, the Colorado Brewers' Festival takes place on Old Town Square; the third weekend in August, New West Fest takes place in Old Town and Library Park; the third week in September is Balloon Fest, on Mulberry Street near I-25; and in mid-October, go to Old Town for the Oktoberfest.

WHAT TO SEE & DO

Old Town. Between College and Mountain aves and Jefferson St.

A red-brick pedestrian walkway, flanked by street lamps and surrounding a bubbling fountain, is the focus of this restored historic district. The main plaza extends diagonally to the northeast from the intersection of College and Mountain avenues; on either side are shops and galleries, restaurants and nightspots. Outdoor concerts and a string of special events keep the plaza lively, especially from mid-spring to mid-fall. Walking-tour maps prepared by the Fort Collins Historical Society are available from the Convention and Visitors Bureau, individual merchants, and city offices. You'll find public rest rooms open 8am to 9pm daily, just east of the intersection of South College Avenue and Oak Street.

Colorado State University. University and College aves. ☎ **970/491-1101.**

Fort Collins revolves around the university, with its 22,000 students and 4,500 faculty and staff. Founded in 1870 as Colorado State Agricultural College, and later renamed Colorado A&M, the university celebrated its 125th anniversary in 1995. The "A" constructed on the hillside behind Hughes Stadium by students and faculty in 1923 stands for "Aggies" and remains a cherished tradition even though athletic teams have been called the Rams for decades.

   Those wanting to see the campus should stop first at the Visitors Center, at the corner of College Avenue and Pitkin Street (☎ 970/491-6222) for information, maps, and parking passes. Among stops are the Administration Building, on the Oval where the school began, and **Lory Student Center,** University and Center avenues (☎ **970/491-6444**), which houses a food court, bookstore, art gallery, floral shop, activities center, ballroom, and other facilities. Appointments can be made to visit the renowned **Veterinary Teaching Hospital,** 300 W. Drake Rd. (☎ **970/221-4535**), and the **Equine Teaching Center** at the Foothills Campus, Overland Trail (☎ **970/491-8373**). The **Art Department,** on Pitkin Street (☎ **970/491-6774**), has five different galleries with revolving exhibits; and the **University Theatre** in Johnson Hall, on East Drive (☎ **970/491-5116**), presents student productions year-round.

✪ Anheuser-Busch Brewery. 2351 Busch Dr. (I-25 exit 271). ☎ **970/490-4691.** Free admission. May–Oct, daily 9:30am–5pm; Nov–Apr, Wed–Sun 10am–4pm. Closed some major holidays.

One of Fort Collins's leading employers—and its top tourist attraction—Anheuser-Busch brews some six million barrels of beer each year, distributed to 10 western states. The 1¼-hour tours leave from the visitors center and gift shop, and include exhibits on the history of the Anheuser-Busch company, displays of great old ads from the 1950s, and a complete look at the brewing process, from the huge brew kettles to the high-speed packaging plant that fills 2,000 cans per minute. You can also visit the barn that's home to the giant Clydesdale draft horses used to promote Budweiser and other Busch beers since 1933, and stop at the tasting room for a free sample.

Avery House. 328 W. Mountain Ave. ☎ **970/221-0533.** Admission by donation. Sun and Wed 1–3pm except Easter, Christmas, and New Year's Day.

Custom-built in 1879 for banker-surveyor Franklin Avery and his wife, Sara, this Victorian home at the corner of Mountain Avenue and Meldrum Street was constructed of red-and-buff sandstone from the quarries west of Fort Collins. The city purchased the house in 1974, and the Poudre Landmarks Foundation was formed to restore it to its original Victorian splendor—from furniture to wallpaper to wall-papered ceilings. The Foundation holds an Annual Historic Homes Tour in September and celebrates a Victorian Christmas in December to help raise funds for the restoration, which is nearing completion. The grounds, with a gazebo, carriage house, and fountain, are popular for weddings and receptions.

The Farm at Lee Martinez Park. 600 N. Sherwood St. ☎ **970/221-6665.** Free admission. Wed–Sat 10am–5:30pm, Sun noon–5:30pm; hours change seasonally.

Early 20th-century farm machinery is on display; crafts are sold in the Silo Store; and oats are available to feed the animals. The Farm Museum has exhibits depicting farming techniques from the turn of the century. Special programs are scheduled year-round, and there are weekend pony rides ($2) for the kids from mid-March through October.

Brewery Tours

One might say that Fort Collins is a beer town. Not only is it home to the giant ✪ **Anheuser-Busch Brewery,** with its famous Clydesdale horses (see above), but it is fast becoming a center for microbreweries and brew pubs in Colorado. **Coopersmith's Pub & Brewing Co.** (see "Where to Dine" below) provides patrons a view of the brewing process from inside the restaurant, as well as offering guided tours Saturdays from 1 to 4pm. Using English malted barley and hops from the Pacific Northwest, Coopersmith's brews from 6 to 10 ales. For those who don't like beer, the brewery also makes its own root beer, ginger ale, and cream soda. Just northeast of Old Town, across the railroad tracks, **New Belgium Brewing Company,** 500 Linden St. (☎ **970/221-0524**), concentrates on beer-making only, producing top-quality Belgian-style ales. The brewery is open Monday through Thursday 10am to 6pm, Friday 10am to 7pm, and Saturday 10am to 5pm. Tours are offered on the hour, with self-guided tours anytime. Bottles—22-ounce and 6-packs of 12-ounce—can be purchased, along with glasses, caps, T-shirts, and other souvenirs. You'll find **Odell's Brewing Company** at 800 E. Lincoln Ave. (☎ **970/ 498-9070**). Specializing in English-style ales, Odell's produces draft and bottled beers, which are available in restaurants and bars in Colorado, Kansas, and Wyoming. Tours are given Monday through Saturday between 11am and 1pm, and by appointment; and the tasting room is open Monday through Thursday from 9am to 6pm, Friday 9am to 7pm, and Saturdays from 10am to 7pm. Bottles and half-gallon brewery jugs are available. **H.C. Berger Brewing Company,** 1900 E. Lincoln Ave. (☎ **970/493-9044**), produces handcrafted German-style ales using a cold-maturation process. Up-close personalized brewery tours are offered Saturdays from 1 to 5pm and by appointment, and the tasting room is open Monday through Saturday from 8am to 5pm. Ales can be purchased at the brewery in brewery jugs and kegs, and in smaller bottles at local stores.

Fort Collins Municipal Railway. Oak & Roosevelt, at City Park. ☎ **970/224-5372.** Admission $1 adults, 75¢ seniors, 50¢ children 12 and under. May–Sept, weekends and holidays only, noon–5pm.

One of the few remaining original trolley systems in the nation, this restored 1919 Birney streetcar runs on its original route, along Mountain Avenue for 1½ miles from City Park to Howes Street. It's certainly more for fun than practical urban transport.

Fort Collins Museum. 200 Mathews St. ☎ **970/221-6738.** Free admission, donations accepted. Tues–Sat 10am–5pm, Sun noon–5pm.

Located in the 1904 Carnegie Library Building just a block south of Old Town, this museum boasts the largest collection of Folsom points of any western museum, plus military artifacts from Fort Collins, and pioneer and Victorian objects. There is an 1850s cabin, the 1864 log officers' mess hall known locally as "Auntie Stone's cabin," and a log one-room schoolhouse built in 1905. The renovated Overland Trail Room reopened in March 1996 for traveling exhibits. Annual events include a Rendezvous and Skookum Day, a living-history day.

✪ **Swetsville Zoo.** 4801 E. Harmony Rd. ☎ **970/484-9509.** Free admission, but donations appreciated. Year-round, daily dawn–dusk. The zoo is one-quarter mile east of I-25 exit 265.

Don't come to Bill Swets' zoo expecting to find animals—not live ones, that is. The Sculpture Park is a constantly growing menagerie of about 150 dinosaurs and other real and imaginary animals, flowers, and windmills—all constructed from car parts, farm machinery, and other scrap metal. There's also a miniature three-quarter-mile steam train visitors can ride summer weekends and holidays, and an outdoor exhibit of old farm equipment and a 10-seat bicycle.

SPORTS & OUTDOOR ACTIVITIES

With its prime location, nestled in the foothills of the Rockies, Fort Collins is ideally situated for those who want to get out and experience nature. Major Fort Collins parks include: **City Park,** 1500 W. Mulberry St. (☎ 970/484-6686), with boat rentals, miniature train rides, a nine-hole golf course, and an outdoor swimming pool; **Edora Park,** 1420 E. Stuart St. (☎ 970/221-6679), with the excellent Edora Pool Ice Center, combination indoor swimming pools and ice rink; and **Rolland Moore Park,** 2201 S. Shields St. (☎ 970/221-6667), which features an outdoor complex for racquetball and handball players. You'll find picnic grounds, tennis courts, and softball fields at all four parks. For additional information on the city's park system, call the administration office (☎ 970/221-6640).

Among the most popular areas for outdoor recreation is **Horsetooth Reservoir,** about 15 minutes west of downtown, just over the first ridge of the Rocky Mountain foothills. The 6.5-mile-long, man-made lake is named for the distinctive tooth-shaped rock that has long been an area landmark. It's reached via County Road 44E or 42C, both off Overland Trail, or County Road 38E off Taft Hill Road (☎ **970/226-4517**). At the reservoir and nearby **Horsetooth Mountain Park,** located several miles west via County Road 38E (same phone as the reservoir), you'll find a wide array of outdoor activities from fly-fishing to rock climbing to water-skiing. **Lory State Park,** just west of Fort Collins along the northwest edge of Horsetooth Reservoir (☎ **970/493-1623**), is known for its scenic beauty and extensive trail system. To get to the park, take U.S. 287 north from Fort Collins through the village of LaPorte, turn left (west) at the Bellvue exit onto County Road 52E, go 1 mile and turn left (south) onto County Road 23N, which you follow about 1½ miles to County Road 25G, where you turn right and drive about 1½ miles to the park entrance. ✪ **Colorado State Forest,** about 75 miles west of Fort Collins via

Colo. 14 (☎ **970/723-8366**), covers 70,000 acres with spectacular mountain scenery, alpine lakes, an abundance of wildlife, camping, and numerous trails. See below for details on activities at these areas.

BICYCLING   There are more than 75 miles of designated bikeways in Fort Collins, including the 5-mile Spring Creek Trail and the 6-mile Poudre River Trail. Bicyclists, hikers, and joggers use two asphalt trails through the city: Poudre River Trail, southeast from North Taft Hill Road to East Prospect Road, and Spring Creek Trail, west from East Prospect Road to West Drake Road. There's also a dirt trail: Foothills Trail, parallel to Horsetooth Reservoir from Dixon Reservoir north to Campeau Open Space and Michaud Lane. For bike rentals ($18–$25 per day), repairs, accessories, maps, and tips on where to ride, stop at **Lee's Cyclery,** 202 W. Laurel St. (☎ **970/ 482-6006**), or at its second location at 931 E. Harmony St. (☎ 970/226-6006). Also see "Mountain Biking," below.

FLY-FISHING   Guided fly-fishing trips and clinics are available from **Rocky Mountain Adventures,** P.O. Box 1989, Fort Collins, CO 80522 (☎ **800/858-6808** or 970/493-4005). They access the Big Thompson, Cache la Poudre, and North Platte rivers, plus waters on two private ranches. Guided trips start at $80 for a half-day. Those who'd like to strike out on their own might try nearby Roosevelt National Forest. For further information, contact the U.S. Forest Service Information Center, 1311 S. College Ave., (☎ 970/498-2770); and the Colorado Division of Wildlife, 317 W. Prospect Rd. (☎ 970/484-2836). Those heading out to Colorado State Forest have a good chance of catching a variety of trout species; only artificial flies and lures are permitted in some lakes there.

GOLF   Fort Collins has three municipal courses: **Collindale Golf Course,** 1441 E. Horsetooth Rd. (☎ **970/221-6651**), **City Park Nine,** 411 S. Bryan Ave. (☎ **970/221-6650**), and **Southridge Golf Club,** 5750 S. Lemay Ave. (☎ **970/ 226-2828**). Rates range from $5 per nine holes for junior golfers to $17 per 18 holes for adult golfers during prime time, and tee times should be reserved 3 days in advance.

HIKING   The Comanche Peak Wilderness area, 67,500 acres of pine and spruce-fir forests below expanses of alpine tundra, offers scenic hiking trails along the north and east sides of Rocky Mountain National Park. Contact the U.S. Forest Service Information Center, 1311 S. College Ave., (☎ 970/498-2770).

Colorado State Forest has miles of hiking trails and even gives overnight visitors the opportunity to stay in a yurt (see "Skiing," below); and there are 26 miles of trails at Horsetooth Mountain Park that are shared by hikers, mountain bikers, and horseback riders. Finally, Lory State Park has about 25 miles of hiking trails, where the top of Arthur's Rock—a hike of 2 miles—offers a marvelous view across Fort Collins and the northeastern Colorado plains.

HORSEBACK RIDING   For the most part, riding is permitted anywhere on the Estes-Poudre District of the National Forest without special permit or license. Horsetooth Mountain Park, Colorado State Forest, and Lory State Park have horse trails as well. Lory State Park has the added advantage of the **Double Diamond Stable** (☎ **970/224-4200**), which offers horse rentals, guided rides, hayrides, chuckwagon dinners, and sleigh rides when there's enough snow. Prices for trail rides start at about $15 per hour, and hay rides and sleigh rides are about $5 per person.

KAYAKING   **Rocky Mountain Adventures,** P.O. Box 1989, Fort Collins, CO 80522 (☎ **800/858-6808** or 970/493-4005) offers kayaking classes covering the Eskimo roll, paddling techniques, and white water skills. 1996 prices were $45 for the roll, $75 for paddling, and $165 to $199 for white water.

MOUNTAIN BIKING   The Foothills Trail for mountain bikers runs along the east side of Horsetooth Reservoir from Dixon Dam north to Michaud Lane. Horsetooth Mountain Park, Lory State Park, and Colorado State Forest have excellent trails appropriate for mountain biking as well. In addition, there are yurts for overnighting at Colorado State Forest (see "Skiing," below). Also see "Bicycling," above.

OFF-ROADING   Horsetooth Reservoir has a small area set aside for motorcycles and similar small, all-terrain vehicles, located north of the lake. There are also miles of marked trails open to four-wheelers in Colorado National Forest.

RIVER RAFTING   River-rafting enthusiasts have ample opportunities for boating the Cache la Poudre, a nationally designated wild and scenic river. **Rocky Mountain Adventures,** P.O. Box 1989, Fort Collins, CO 80522 (☎ **800/858-6808** or 970/493-4005) offers half-day, full-day and overnight trips on the Cache la Poudre. Costs range from $33 to $49 for half a day, $73 for a full day, and to $155 for overnight. For 1- or 2-day trips on the pristine, high altitude (8,000 ft.) North Platte River, expect to pay $73 to $169. **A Wanderlust Adventure,** 3500 Bingham Hill Rd., Fort Collins, CO 80521 (☎ **800/745-7238** or 970/484-1219), offers half-day trips on the Cache la Poudre River for $33 to $49, and full-day trips for $79.

ROCK CLIMBING   There are plenty of opportunities for rock climbing on the northwestern shore of Horsetooth Reservoir in Lory State Park.

SKIING & OTHER WINTER SPORTS   Cross-country skiers will find plenty of trails and rolling hills at Lory State Park, surrounding national forests (☎ 970/498-2770), and in Colorado State Forest, where they can stay overnight in a backcountry yurt system owned by **Never Summer Nordic, Inc.,** P.O. Box 1983, Fort Collins, CO 80522 (☎ **970/482-9411**). The yurts, which are circular, tentlike canvas and wood structures on a high wood deck, have wood-burning stoves, padded bunks, and complete kitchens, and are located in Colorado State Forest. Most sleep up to six, and one sleeps at least 10. Winter rates for the entire yurt are $75 to $95 for the six-person yurts and $95 to $115 for the large unit. In summer, rates are $45 to $55 and $65 to $75, respectively. Colorado National Forest also has an extensive system of snowmobile trails, either groomed or packed, that is separate from its cross-country ski trail system.

There's year-round **ice-skating** at Edora Park's pool and ice center (EPIC), 1801 Riverside Dr. (☎ 970/221-6683). Call for rates and hours.

SWIMMING   **Edora Pool Ice Center** (EPIC), at 1801 Riverside Dr. in Edora Park, (☎ **970/221-6683**), has swimming and water exercise programs and diving. It is open afternoons and evenings. (Admission: $1.35 youth, $2 adults, discounts for seniors.) The indoor **Mulberry pool,** 424 W. Mulberry St. (☎ **970/221-6659**), has lap lanes, a diving area, and "Elrog the Frog," a poolside slide. The pool is open all afternoons and most evenings. The **City Park Outdoor Pool,** 1599 City Park Ave. (☎ **970/484-6686**), is open afternoons during warm weather, and there's also swimming at Horsetooth Reservoir (see below).

WATER SPORTS   **Inlet Bay Marina,** 4314 Shoreline Dr. (☎ **970/223-0140**) at Horsetooth Reservoir, is a full-service marina open from April through September. There's a boat launching ramp and boat rentals. Fishing boats, with 10-horsepower motors, cost $10 per hour or $50 per day; personal watercraft cost $50 per hour or $150 per half-day; and ski boats (with skis) rent for $50 per hour or $200 per day. Fuel is extra. There's also a swimming beach and snack bar.

WILDLIFE WATCHING   Although you'll see some wildlife and water birds at Lory State Park and Horsetooth Reservoir, go to Colorado State Forest to try to catch a glimpse of the state's largest moose population, along with elk, mule deer, mountain lions, and black bears.

SHOPPING

Visitors enjoy shopping in **Old Town Square,** at Mountain and College avenues, with numerous shops, galleries, and restaurants. Also downtown is **One West Art Center,** 201 S. College Ave. (☎ 970/482-ARTS), housed in a 1911 Italian Renaissance–style building that for 6 decades was the Fort Collins post office. The visual-arts complex now has two galleries and a gallery shop. It's open Tuesday through Saturday from 10am to 5pm, year-round. Admission is $2 adults, $1 students and seniors, free for children under 6, and free for everybody on Saturdays.

Northern Colorado's largest enclosed shopping mall is the **Foothills Fashion Mall,** 215 E. Foothills Pkwy., at South College Avenue and Horsetooth Road (☎ 970/226-5555). Anchored by four department stores—Foley's, J.C. Penney, Sears, and Mervyn's—it has more than 100 specialty stores and a food court, and is open Monday through Saturday from 10am to 9pm and on Sunday from noon to 5pm (closed major holidays).

WHERE TO STAY
MODERATE

Elizabeth Street Guest House. 202 E. Elizabeth St., Fort Collins, CO 80524. ☎ **970/493-BEDS.** Fax 970/493-6662. 3 rms (1 with bath). $45 single without bath, $65 single with bath; $65 double without bath, $85 double with bath. Rates include full breakfast. AE, MC, V.

This 1905 American Foursquare brick home, just a block from C.S.U. at Elizabeth and Remington streets, is furnished with antiques, handmade crafts, and old quilts, setting off the handsome leaded windows and oak woodwork. All three guest rooms have new wallpaper and curtains. Smoking is not permitted in the rooms. Guests have access to a TV, phone, and refrigerator.

Helmshire Inn. 1204 S. College Ave., Fort Collins, CO 80524. ☎ **970/493-4683.** 25 rms. A/C TV TEL. May–Sept $95 double; Oct–Apr $79 double. Discounts for stays over 5 days. Rates include breakfast. AE, DC, MC, V.

A three-story custom-built inn across from the C.S.U. campus, the Helmshire has a lobby like a living room and a lovely adjoining dining room. Guest rooms are individual, but each has a kitchenette and is furnished with antiques and reproductions. Ask for a back room—they're quieter. Guests have privileges at a health club in town. Infants or one child are welcome, and the building has an elevator. There's no smoking indoors, but there are spacious covered porches for smokers.

Holiday Inn University Park. 425 W. Prospect Rd., Fort Collins, CO 80526. ☎ **800/HOLIDAY** or 970/482-2626. Fax 970/493-6265. 259 rms and minisuites. A/C TV TEL. $99 double; $99–$109 minisuites. AE, CB, DC, DISC, JCB, MC, V. Free parking.

Conveniently located across the street from the Colorado State University main campus and adjacent to the Spring Creek trail for bikers and runners, this is the city's largest hotel. It's built around a beautiful central atrium with a three-story waterfall, trees, and standing plants.

Standard rooms have one king or two oversize double beds and all standard hotel furnishings, including a credenza with remote-control TV, direct-dial phone (local calls 75¢), and attractive serigraphs on the walls. The hotel offers a full range of concierge services, limited room service, fitness center, indoor pool, and restaurant.

INEXPENSIVE

Budget Host Inn. 1513 N. College Ave., Fort Collins, CO 80524. ☎ **800/825-4678** or 970/484-0870. Fax 970/224-2998. 29 rms, 1 suite. A/C TV TEL. Mid-May–Sept, $36–$52 double; Oct–mid-May, $32–$42 double. Rates include continental breakfast. AE, DISC, MC, V.

At the north end of town on U.S. 287 near Willox Lane, this motel has been owned and operated by Tom and Karen Weitkunat since 1975. Kids enjoy the playground, while adults like the outdoor hot tub. Eight units have kitchenettes; all have coffeemakers and queen or double beds. Half of the rooms have a shower only, so if you need a tub, request it. The suite was completely renovated in 1996.

Mulberry Inn. 4333 E. Mulberry St., Fort Collins, CO 80524. ☎ **800/234-5548** or 970/493-9000. Fax 970/224-9636. 116 rms, 4 suites. A/C TV TEL. $40–$85 double; suites $75–$115; Jacuzzi units $56–$100. AE, DC, DISC, MC, V.

Most rooms in this pleasant motel have queen beds, a desk, and other standard furnishings. VCRs and movies are available for rent. There are hot tubs in 35 rooms; some suites have wet bars and large private decks. There's a heated, seasonal outdoor swimming pool and a restaurant serving Italian cuisine daily from 4 to 10pm.

CAMPING

Nearby Arapahoe and Roosevelt National forests have a number of established campgrounds, most with rest rooms, water, and picnic tables. Cost is $9 per site per night. Call **970/498-2770** for more information. There's also camping at Colorado State Forest (☎ **303/723-8366**), 75 miles west of Fort Collins via Colo. 14.

WHERE TO DINE
EXPENSIVE

Nico's Catacombs. 115 S. College Ave. ☎ **970/482-6426.** Reservations recommended. Main courses $14.50–$30. AE, CB, DISC, DC, MC, V. Mon–Sat 5–10pm. CONTINENTAL.

A classic, dimly lit cellar restaurant, with a richly decorated lounge separated from the main dining room by a stained-glass partition, Nico's features tableside service and daily specials (including fresh seafood) announced on blackboards. You might start with a shellfish dish such as mussels Marseilles, or perhaps the Galantine de foie gras, then move on to steak Diane flambé, shrimp parmesan, or one of the house specialties, such as rack of lamb paloise or chateaubriand bouquetiére for two. The lounge offers a bar menu including baked brie and oysters Rockefeller plus desserts and cappuccinos.

MODERATE

✪ **Bisetti's.** 120 S. College Ave. ☎ **970/493-0086.** Reservations not accepted. Main courses $4.25–$6.95 at lunch, $6.50–$15.95 at dinner. AE, DISC, MC, V. Mon–Fri 11am–2pm; Sun–Thurs 5–9pm, Fri–Sat 5–10pm. ITALIAN.

The first thing you notice upon entering this long-standing family business is the ceiling: from one end to the other dangle empty Chianti bottles signed by over a decade of patrons. This is a dark, candlelit room; two adjoining rooms are brighter and more modern. The menu features a variety of homemade pastas, from spaghetti and lasagna to rigatoni and manicotti. Full main courses include veal saltimbocca, basil fettucine with chicken, and smoked salmon Alfredo. Arrive before 6:30pm Monday through Saturday for early-bird dinner specials.

Coopersmith's Pub & Brewing Co. 5 Old Town Sq. ☎ **970/498-0483.** $6–$13. MC, V. Fri–Sat 11am–2am, Sun–Thurs 11am–midnight. BRITISH PUB.

This modern brew pub isn't just a place for knocking back a few. Within its brick walls is an open kitchen that prepares such traditional pub specialties as fish-and-chips, bangers and mash, and Highland cottage pie. You can also get hamburgers, sandwiches, salads, and soups. Breads, rolls, and desserts are prepared in Coopersmith's in-house bakery. Portions are generous, and the outdoor patio is a favorite in good weather. There's also a children's menu.

Jay's American Bistro. 151 S. College Ave. ☎ **970/482-1876.** Main courses $4–$8 at lunch, $9–$19 at dinner. AE, DC, DISC, MC, V. Mon–Fri 11am–10pm; Sat 5–10pm. CREATIVE AMERICAN.

An eclectic menu and a friendly, casual atmosphere are what you'll find at Jay's. Appetizers include crab cakes, and there's a decidedly southwestern influence in many of the main entrees, such as seafood enchiladas, or chipotle pasta: a smoked jalapeno pasta with tequila lime sauce. Other choices include northern Italian–style pastas, wild game, a variety of fresh seafood, steak, veal, and California-style pizza.

INEXPENSIVE

⑤ The Egg & I. 2809 S. College Ave. ☎ **970/223-5271.** $3.25–$5.95. AE, DISC, MC, V. Mon–Sat 6am–2pm; Sun 7am–2pm. AMERICAN.

Voted by locals as offering the best breakfast in town, The Egg and I creates a number of imaginative egg dishes such as scrambled eggs with shrimp, a Wisconsin scramble with four types of cheese, and several variations on eggs Benedict. There are also omelets, fritattas, skillet breakfasts, huevos rancheros, and other Mexican dishes. Pancakes, French toast, sandwiches, and salads round out the menu.

El Burrito. 404 Linden St. ☎ **970/484-1102.** $3.50–$9.95. AE, MC, V. Daily, 11am–2pm and 5–10pm. MEXICAN.

The Godinez family has been concocting authentic Mexican specialties at this tiny north-of-downtown restaurant for about 30 years, and year-in, year-out, Fort Collins residents have been filling up on the restaurant's popular burritos. It also serves good tacos, enchiladas, and chile rellenos, and you can eat in or order your food to go.

✪ Silver Grill Cafe. 218 Walnut St., Old Town. ☎ **970/484-4656.** $3–$8. DISC, MC, V. Mon–Sat 6am–2pm, Sun 7am–1pm. AMERICAN.

Continually operated since 1933, this working-man's cafe attracts blue- and white-collar types, as well as seniors, students, and families. When there's a line outside, as there often is on weekends, coffee is served to those waiting. Come for the giant cinnamon rolls or standard American fare: eggs, pancakes, and biscuits 'n' gravy for breakfast; burgers and other sandwiches for lunch; "noontime dinners" like chicken-fried steak and roast beef. Everything's prepared fresh daily. Grilling and frying are done in salt-free and cholesterol-free vegetable oil.

FORT COLLINS AFTER DARK

The college crowd does much of its drinking and hanging out at **Fort Ram,** a large dance club near the railroad tracks at 450 N. Linden St. (☎ **970/482-5026**), with live country music Monday nights and a variety of recorded music the rest of the week. There's live music a few blocks away in Old Town at **Linden's Bourbon Street,** 214 Linden St. (☎ **970/482-9291**), the spot for jazz, blues, zydeco, and occasional comedy. You might also try **Avogrado's Number,** 605 S. Mason St. (☎ **970/493-5555**) for live bluegrass and acoustic music. Country-and-western fans head to the big dance floor at the **Sundance,** 2716 E. Mulberry St. (☎ **970/484-1600**), for live country music and country swing dance lessons.

Many Fort Collins folk head 24 miles up the Poudre River to the **Mishawaka Amphitheatre & Restaurant,** 13714 Poudre Canyon, (☎ **970/482-4420**), where top regional bands—and occasional national acts—perform summers in an outdoor amphitheater on the banks of the Poudre River. Concert tickets range from $9 to $18, and you can also dine on an outside deck over the river or inside with a view of the river.

When you just want to have cool beer at the end of the day, **Coopersmith's Pub & Brewing Co.,** 5 Old Town Sq. (☎ **970/498-0483**), may be the best place in town. It attracts everyone from students to business executives with its pub menu and custom beers. Nearby **Old Chicago,** 147 S. College Ave. (☎ **970/482-8599**), is another good bet, with its international list of 125 beers.

Fort Collins's principal venue for the performing arts is **Lincoln Center,** 417 W. Magnolia St., at Meldrum Street (☎ **970/221-6730**). Built in 1978, the center includes the 1,180-seat Performance Hall and the 220-seat Mini-Theatre, as well as three art galleries and an outdoor sculpture and performance garden. It is home to the Fort Collins Symphony, Opera Fort Collins, Canyon Concert Ballet, Larimer Chorale, OpenStage Theater, and the Children's Theater. Annual concert, dance, children's, and travel film series are presented. The center is wheelchair accessible and has an infrared sound system for the hearing impaired. The box office is open Monday to Saturday from noon to 6pm, with tickets ranging from $5 to $26.

Fort Collins Symphony (☎ **970/482-4823**), established in 1948, performs both classical and pops music plus special events with guest performers. For those who enjoy a casual atmosphere with their classical music, there's the popular *Beethoven in Blue Jeans* concert each January, which concludes with a party.

The **OpenStage Theatre Company** (☎ **970/484-5237**) is the leading professional stage group. It offers six contemporary productions annually, as well as various popular, classical, operatic, and musical pieces. Recent productions have included *Becket* and *Arsenic and Old Lace.* Tickets are $12 to $16, with discounts for students, senior citizens, and matinee performances.

Notable **summer concert programs** include the Concert Under the Stars series (☎ **970/484-6500**), with free concerts in Old Town Square each Thursday evening from early June through early August, featuring rock, bluegrass, country, jazz, and swing.

Broadway musicals are presented year-round at **Carousel Dinner Theatre,** 3509 S. Mason St. (☎ **970/225-2555**), each Thursday through Saturday at 6pm and Sunday at noon. A choice of three entrees is offered, and prices are $25 to $29, which include dinner, show, and tax, but not beverages or dessert. Recent productions have included *Hello Dolly, Annie Get Your Gun,* and *Forever Plaid.* The company also stages weekend matinee children's shows and children's theater workshops; call for details.

The **Colorado State University** Department of Music, Theater, and Dance (☎ **970/491-5116** or 970/491-5529) presents a variety of dramas and musicals, plus concerts by music faculty ranging from jazz to classical during the school year at Johnson Hall on the C.S.U. campus. Live performances and movies are also presented at Lory Student Center (☎ **970/491-5402**).

2 Loveland

Named for Colorado Central Railroad President W. A. H. Loveland in the 1870s, this former trading post now calls itself the "Sweetheart City," because every February some 300,000 Valentine's Day cards are remailed from here with a Loveland postmark. Established as a trading post in the late 1850s, the community grew around a flour mill in the late 1860s, before being platted on a wheat field near the railroad tracks in 1877. Today the city is a shipping and agriculture center with a population of just over 37,000. It also has a growing arts community, and several foundries. Loveland is on the banks of the Big Thompson River, at the foot of the Rockies.

ESSENTIALS

GETTING THERE   By Car   Loveland is at the junction of U.S. 287 and U.S. 34. Coming from south or north, take I-25 exit 257. From the west (Rocky Mountain National Park) or east (Greeley), follow U.S. 34 directly to Loveland. The drive takes about 1 hour from Denver.

By Airport Shuttle   Visitors who fly into Denver International can reach Loveland with **Airport Express** (☎ **970/482-0505**).

By Plane   If you'd prefer to fly in from Denver, the closest airport is **Fort Collins Municipal Airport** (☎ **970/962-2850**), 7 miles northeast of downtown Loveland, just off I-25 at exit 259. **United Express** (☎ **800/241-6522** or 970/663-4614) offers regular flights to and from Denver. **Western Pacific** (☎ **800/930-3030**) was scheduled to begin flights from Colorado Springs and other cities in late 1996. Rental-car agencies at the airport include **Hertz** (☎ **800/654-3131** or 970/ 962-9323) and **Dollar** (☎ **800/800-4000** or 970/663-3503).

ORIENTATION   The city is notable for more than a dozen lakes within or just outside the city limits—including Lake Loveland, just west of city center. U.S. 34, known as Eisenhower Boulevard, the main east-west thoroughfare, does a slight jog around the lake. Lincoln Avenue (one-way northbound) and Cleveland Avenue (one-way southbound) comprise U.S. 287 through the city. The downtown district is along Lincoln and Cleveland south of Seventh Street, seven blocks south of Eisenhower.

VISITOR INFORMATION   Contact the **Loveland Chamber of Commerce,** 541 Lincoln Ave. (P.O. Box 7058), Loveland, CO 80537 (☎ **800/258-1278** or 970/ 667-6311).

GETTING AROUND   Taxi service is provided by **Shamrock Yellow Cab** (☎ **970/667-6767**).

FAST FACTS   In case of **emergency,** call **911.** The hospital is **McKee Medical Center,** 2000 Boise Ave. (☎ **970/669-4640**) in the northeastern part of the city. The **post office** is at 446 E. 29th St. (☎ **970/667-0344**), just off Lincoln. **State and county taxes** add about 9% to hotel bills.

SPECIAL EVENTS   Loveland features the Annual Rotary Sweetheart Sculpture Show and Sale in February, Ethnic Food Fest in June, Corn Roast Festival and Larimer County Fair and Rodeo in August, and a Pumpkin Festival in October.

SENDING YOUR VALENTINES FROM LOVELAND

To get your Valentine's Day cards remailed from Loveland before February 14, address and stamp each one individually, making sure to leave room in the lower-left-hand corner of the envelopes for the special Loveland stamp, and mail them in a large envelope to the Postmaster, Attn.: Valentines, Loveland, CO 80538. Mark SPECIAL HANDLING on the outer envelope. To ensure delivery by Valentine's ᴦ mail for the United States must be received in Loveland by February 9, and ᶠ mail should be received by February 3.

FOUNDRY TOURS

Several foundries will provide tours by appointment. **Art Castings of Colorado** (☎ 970/667-1114) gives foundry tours several weekday mornings, at a charge of $4 per person. **Loveland Sculpture Works** (☎ 970/667-0991) offers tours several times each week to groups of at least four people, all older than twelve. Cost is $5 per person.

SPORTS & OUTDOOR ACTIVITIES

Loveland has more than 2 dozen city parks, a mountain park, three golf courses, a trail system, and a recreation center. Full information on all city-run recreation sites is available from **Loveland Parks and Recreation Department,** 500 E. Third St. (☎ 970/962-2727).

In addition, ○ **Boyd Lake State Park** (☎ 970/669-1739) is located just a mile east of downtown Loveland via Madison Avenue and County Road 24E. One of the largest lakes in the northern Front Range, with 1,800 surface acres when full, Boyd Lake State Park is geared to water sports, including water-skiing (on the south end of the lake only), sailing, and windsurfing. There are sandy beaches for swimming, 148 campsites ($7), showers, a dump station, picnic areas, a children's playground, a paved walking/biking trail that connects to the city's path system, two paved boat ramps, and excellent fishing (especially for walleyes). Visitors often see foxes, beavers, coyotes, great-horned owls, hawks, eagles, and other wildlife. A commercially run **marina** (☎ 970/663-2662) is open from 8am until 8pm during the summer, with boat slips and moorings, a full-service gas dock, boat rentals from May to September, bait, groceries, and other supplies. Rentals are $10 per hour or $50 per day for fishing boats, including gas; $45 per hour or $175 per day for ski boats, including skis but not fuel; and $50 per hour for personal watercraft, plus gas. A **restaurant** at the **swimming beach** (☎ 970/663-3314) is open 10am to 6pm in summer, with hot food, snacks, and rentals of beach toys, chairs, and umbrellas.

BICYCLING/JOGGING A combination **biking/jogging/walking path** that will eventually circle the city, joining with a 3-mile path at Boyd Lake State Park, is gradually being constructed. For a map showing completed sections, stop at the Loveland Chamber of Commerce (see above).

GOLF Golfers can enjoy two 18-hole municipal golf courses: **Loveland** and **Marianna Butte,** with greens fees of $12 to $15 for nine holes and $18 to $28 for 18 holes; and the nine-hole **Cattail Creek Golf Course,** which charges $7 for nine holes. For tee times, current rates, and directions to all three courses, call **970/669-5800.**

HIKING The city-run **Viestenz-Smith Mountain Park,** in Big Thompson Canyon 8 miles west of Loveland along U.S. 34 (☎ 970/962-2727), is one of your best bets for hiking, with two trails. **The Summit Adventure Trail,** a moderately difficult 4³/₄-mile (one-way) hike, climbs 2,750 feet to offer scenic views of the mountains to the west and plains to the east. Those not interested in that much exercise will enjoy the easy 1-mile (one-way) **Foothills Nature Trail.** The park, which is open year-round, also has picnic tables, a playground, and a fishing stream.

LLAMA PACKING Loveland's proximity to Rocky Mountain National Park offers many hardier challenges. One outfit taking advantage is the **Buckhorn Llama Co.** (☎ 970/667-7411), based in Masonville, a small community about 10 miles northwest of Loveland via County Road 27. A day hike and lunch with a llama runs $35 to $50 per person; wilderness pack trips of 3 to 5 days are also arranged at an average cost of $150 per person. Or you can do it yourself and rent a llama for $25 to $30 per day.

SOFTBALL The **Barnes Park Softball Complex,** 405 S. Cleveland Ave. (☎ **970/ 667-0495**), has a seven-station batting cage with both softball and baseball pitching machines.

SWIMMING **North Lake Park,** at 29th Street and Taft Avenue, has a free swimming beach, fishing, tennis and racquetball courts, a playground, and a miniature narrow-gauge train. The **Winona Outdoor Swimming Pool** (☎ 970/669-6907), in Osborn Park on S.E. First Street, is open in summer and has a pool, water slide, diving area, bathhouse, and children's wading pool and children's water play area. There's also swimming at Boyd Lake State Park (see above).

IN-TOWN ATTRACTIONS

Benson Park Sculpture Garden. 29th St. between Aspen and Beech streets. ☎ **970/ 663-2940.**

A large number of sculptures are permanently displayed among the trees and plants at this city park, where "Sculpture in the Park," one of the largest outdoor sculpture shows in the United States, takes place each August. The event features work by more than 160 sculptors.

Loveland Museum and Gallery. 503 N. Lincoln Ave. at E. Fifth St. ☎ **970/962-2410.** Free admission. Tues–Wed and Fri 10am–5pm, Thurs 10am–9pm, Sat 10am–4pm, Sun noon–4pm.

Changing exhibits of local historical subjects and the work of regional, national, and international artists fill this fine, small museum. A "Life on Main Street" exhibit area depicts Loveland at the turn of the 20th century. The museum also sponsors programs on art and history, workshops, concerts, and poetry readings.

WHERE TO STAY

Best Western Coach House Resort. 5542 E. U.S. 34, Loveland, CO 80537. ☎ **800/ 528-1234** or 970/667-7810. Fax 970/667-1047. 90 units. A/C TV TEL. $38–$91 double, $92 suite. AE, CB, DC, DISC, MC, V.

Nestled beside U.S. 34 as it enters Loveland from the east, this expansive, modern motel features indoor and outdoor swimming pools, a tennis court, whirlpool bath, barbecue area, moderately priced restaurant (serving three meals daily), and lounge. Rooms have king, queen, or double beds, TVs with VCRs, and direct-dial phones. Small pets are accepted.

Budget Host Exit 254 Inn. 2716 S. E. Frontage Rd., I-25, Loveland, CO 80537. ☎ **800/ 825-4254** or 970/667-5202. 30 units. A/C TV TEL. $38–$53 double, hot-tub room $58. AE, CB, DC, DISC, MC, V.

An inexpensive alternative beside the freeway, this motel has individually heated rooms with king or queen beds, 25-inch TVs, in-room coffee, and direct-dial phones (free local calls). One room has a hot tub. There's a coin-operated laundry, a playground for the kids, and a restaurant nearby. Small pets are permitted with deposit.

Lovelander Bed-and-Breakfast Inn. 217 W. Fourth St., Loveland, CO 80537. ☎ **800/ 459-6694,** or 970/669-0798 reservations. Fax 970/669-0797. 11 rms. A/C TEL. $83–$125 double. Rates include full breakfast. AE, DISC, MC, V.

Bob and Marilyn Wiltgen's rambling 1902 Victorian, just west of downtown, is considered Loveland's most charming accommodation. Every room has period antiques, including vintage iron or hardwood beds, writing tables, and claw-footed bathtubs.

All rooms have private baths; one has a steam shower for two; and two have whirlpools. Breakfast is served in the dining room or on the terrace, and complimentary fruit, homemade cookies, and beverages are offered. Outside, guests can enjoy rose and herb gardens. Neither pets nor smoking are permitted; children over 10 are welcome.

✪ **Sylvan Dale Guest Ranch.** 2939 N. County Rd. 31D, Loveland, CO 80537. ☎ **970/ 667-3915.** Fax 970/635-9336. 14 rms, 11 cottages. Mid-June–Aug, 6-night packages only, $798 per adult, $637 per youth (ages 6–12), $458 per child (ages 1–5). Sept–mid-June, $75– $105 double; $85–$105 cottage; $13 extra person. No credit cards (personal and traveler's checks accepted).

A working cattle-and-horse ranch on the banks of the Big Thompson River, 7 miles west of Loveland via U.S. 34, the Jessup family urges guests to join in with daily ranch chores and roundups. There's horseback riding ($15 for a 1-hour ride), an outdoor pool, tennis, basketball and volleyball courts, lakes stocked with rainbow trout, trophy fly-fishing, hayrides, guided nature walks, an indoor recreation room, square dancing, and a kids' play area. Summer guests must schedule 6-day full-board stays; the rest of the year, overnight guests are welcome. The ranch offers complimentary van service from Loveland for packages. Pets are not accepted, and smoking is not permitted inside any buildings.

WHERE TO DINE

✪ **The Peaks Cafe.** 425 E. Fourth St. ☎ **970/669-6158.** Reservations not accepted. Breakfast $1.75–$3.50; lunch $3–$5. AE, MC, V. Mon–Fri 7am–4pm, Sat 8am–3pm. Closed Saturdays in winter. NATURAL FOODS.

Come to this cheery little cafe in the morning for breakfast burritos, porridge, yogurt parfait, or the weekly Wednesday pancake fest. Lunch offers salads, soups, a healthy spinach lasagna, build-your-own deli sandwiches, and other health-conscious foods. The cafe also serves excellent home-baked goods, ice cream, and espressos.

The Summit. 3208 W. Eisenhower Blvd. (U.S. 34). ☎ **970/669-6648.** Reservations recommended. Main courses $5–$8 at lunch, $8–$25 at dinner. AE, DC, DISC, MC, V. Tues–Fri 11:30am–2pm; Sun–Thurs 4:30–9:30pm, Fri–Sat 4:30–10pm; Sun 10am–2pm. STEAK/ SEAFOOD.

The Summit offers magnificent views of the Rockies through south-facing windows and from the back deck in warm weather. The interior is a bit dark, but the large wood-beams and different dining levels add interest. The menu includes three cuts of prime rib, New York and sirloin steaks, tenderloin of elk, chicken piccata or chipeta, fresh fish, shrimp Diane, and Alaskan snow crab. There are daily specials, wines by the glass, homemade pies, and a children's menu.

LOVELAND AFTER DARK

Outdoor concerts and presentations are staged all summer long at **Foote Lagoon,** in **Civic Center Park,** and at **Peters Park,** next to the Loveland Museum and Gallery. Call the museum (☎ 970/962-2410) or the Chamber of Commerce (☎ 800/258-1278 or 970/667-6311) for information on performances by the community's chamber orchestra, choral society, concert band, theater orchestra, and community theater group.

3 Greeley

Greeley is one of the few cities in the world that owes its existence to a newspaper. It was founded in 1870 as a sort of prairie Utopia by Nathan C. Meeker, farm columnist for the *New York Tribune.* Meeker named the settlement—first known as

Union Colony—in honor of his patron, *Tribune* publisher Horace Greeley. Through his widely read column, Meeker recruited more than 100 pioneers from all walks of life and purchased a tract on the Cache la Poudre from the Denver Pacific Railroad. Within a year, the colony's population was at 1,000, and it's been growing steadily ever since, to just over 60,000 today. Greeley's economy is supported almost exclusively by agriculture, with more than 96% of Weld County's 2.5 million acres devoted to either farming or raising livestock. A combination of irrigated and dry-land farms produce grains, including oats, corn, and wheat, and root vegetables that include sugar beets, onions, potatoes, and carrots.

ESSENTIALS

GETTING THERE   By Car   Greeley is located at the crossroads of U.S. 34 (east to west) and U.S. 85 (north to south), midway between Denver and Cheyenne, Wyoming—both of which are more directly reached by U.S. 85 than by I-25. U.S. 34 heads west 17 miles to I-25, beyond which are Loveland and Rocky Mountain National Park. To the east, U.S. 34 connects Greeley to Fort Morgan via I-76, 37 miles away.

By Airport Shuttle   Visitors who fly into **Denver International** can travel on to Greeley with **Rocky Mount Shuttle** (☎ 970/356-3366) or **Airport Express** (☎ 970/352-0505).

ORIENTATION   Greeley is located on the Cache la Poudre River just west of the point where it joins the South Platte. Laid out on a standard grid, it's an easy city in which to find your way around—provided you don't get confused by the numbered streets (which run east to west) and numbered avenues (which run north-south). It helps to know which is which when you're standing at the corner of 10th Street and 10th Avenue. Eighth Avenue (U.S. 85 north) and 11th Avenue (U.S. 85 south) are the main north-south streets through downtown. Ninth Street is U.S. 34 Business, jogging into 10th Street west of 23rd Avenue. The U.S. 34 Bypass joins U.S. 85 in a cloverleaf just south of town.

VISITOR INFORMATION   Contact the **Greeley Convention & Visitors Bureau,** 1407 Eighth Ave., Greeley, CO 80631 (☎ 800/449-3866 or 970/352-3566).

GETTING AROUND   The city bus system, called simply **The Bus,** provides in-town transportation. For route information, call **970/350-9287.** All buses are lift-equipped, but those who cannot use them because of mobility impairments can call for information on paratransit service (☎ 970/350-9290). For a taxi call **Shamrock Yellow Cab** (☎ **970/352-3000**).

FAST FACTS   In case of **emergency,** call **911.** The hospital, **North Colorado Medical Center,** is at 1801 16th St. (☎ **970/352-4121**), just west of downtown. The **post office** is at 925 11th Ave. (☎ **970/353-0398**). **State and county taxes** add about 7% to retail sales and hotel bills.

SPECIAL EVENTS   The Colorado Farm Show is held in late April; UNC Jazz Festival is held on the last weekend of April at the University of Northern Colorado; in late June and early July the Independence Stampede is held; and Potato Day is held in early September.

SPORTS & OUTDOOR ACTIVITIES

Beginning about 25 miles northeast of Greeley and extending 60 miles east, the **Pawnee National Grassland** is a popular destination for hiking, mountain biking, birding, wildlife viewing, and horseback riding. Nomadic tribes lived in this desertlike area until the late 19th century; farmers subsequently had little success in culti-vating the grasslands. Today the region is administered by the U.S. Forest Service. Although primarily grassland, the dramatic Pawnee Buttes, in the eastern section, are a pair of sandstone formations that rise some 250 feet. The most popular springtime activity is bird watching, when you're apt to see lark buntings, meadowlarks, thrushes, orioles, and burrowing owls among the 200-plus species known to frequent the area. Antelope, coyotes, mule deer, prairie dogs, and short-horned lizards are among the prolific wildlife.

There are many ways to the grasslands; one is to follow U.S. 85 north 11 miles to Ault, then east on Colo. 14 toward Briggsdale, 23 miles away. Those planning to explore the grasslands are advised to pick up a map at the U.S.F.S. office in Greeley before setting out.

SPECTATOR SPORTS

FOOTBALL   The **Denver Broncos** of the National Football League hold their preseason training camp at the University of Northern Colorado for 6 weeks during July and August. For practice and scrimmage information, call **970/351-2007.**

RODEO   The **Greeley Independence Stampede** comes to town for 2 weeks, start-ing in late June. Hundreds of professional cowboys compete for over $150,000 in prize money at Greeley's Island Grove Park. Festivities include concerts by top coun-try-western stars, art shows, a carnival, children's rodeo, fun-runs, barbecues, and a parade and fireworks display. For information and tickets, call **800/982-BULL** or 970/356-BULL.

IN-TOWN ATTRACTIONS

Historic Centennial Village Museum. 1475 A St. at N. 14th Ave., adjacent to Island Grove Park. ☎ **970/350-9224.** Admission $3.50 adults, $3 seniors (60 and older), and $2 children 6–12, children under 6 are free. Memorial Day–Labor Day, Tues–Sat 10am–5pm, Sun 1–5pm; mid-Apr–Memorial Day and Labor Day–mid-Oct, Tues–Sat 10am–3pm.

This collection of almost 30 structures on $5^1/_2$ acres depicts life on the High Plains of Colorado between 1860 and 1920. Visit the blacksmith shop, print shop, and fire station of the commercial district, and stroll through Hannah Square surrounded by elegant Victorian homes, a school, depot, and church. Living-history demonstrations and other special events bring the past alive.

Meeker Home Museum. 1324 Ninth Ave. ☎ **970/350-9221.** Admission $3.50 adults, $3 seniors (60 and older), $2 children 6–12, children under 6 are free. Memorial Day–Labor Day, Tues–Sat 10am–5pm, Sun 1-5pm; Labor Day to mid-Oct and mid-April to Memorial Day, Tues–Sat 10am–3pm.

This two-story adobe brick residence, built in 1870 for Greeley founder Nathan Cook Meeker, is on the National Register of Historic Places. Full restoration was completed in 1995, and the museum is furnished with original Meeker family belongings and 19th-century antiques. Interpretive panels discuss the history of Greeley and north-eastern Colorado, with emphasis on the Meeker family and their struggle for survival after Nathan's death in the 1897 Meeker Massacre.

THINGS TO SEE & DO SOUTH OF GREELEY

South from Greeley, U.S. 85 travels south-southwest to Denver. There are interest-ing stops en route in **Platteville,** 16 miles from Greeley; **Fort Lupton,** 25 miles; and **Brighton,** 32 miles.

Just 1 mile south of Platteville on U.S. 85 is **Fort Vasquez** (☎ **970/785-2832**), an adobe reconstruction of a fur trader's fort from the 1830s, with exhibits on

Colorado's fur trading days. There's a museum store and Visitor Center. It's open daily from 10am to 5pm in summer, with limited hours and days at other times. The **Fort Lupton Museum,** at 453 First St. (Colo. 52), Fort Lupton (☎ **303/857-1634**), is a small museum featuring south Weld County artifacts. It's usually open weekdays; call for hours.

The **Adams County Museum Complex,** 9601 Henderson Rd., Brighton (☎ **303/659-7103**), has three galleries: the Cultural Center offers art and cultural displays; the Patio Galleries display restored agricultural equipment; and the Earth Science Section has a fully operational blacksmith shop from the 1930s and 1940s, and a 1930s Conoco gas station. Open Tuesday through Saturday, 10am to 4:30pm; admission is free, but donations are appreciated.

WHERE TO STAY

Fairfield Inn. 2401 W. 29th St., Greeley, CO 80631. ☎ **800/228-2800** or 970/339-5030. Fax 970/339-5030. 54 rms, 8 suites. A/C TV TEL. $69 double; $77 suites. Rates include continental breakfast. AE, DC, DISC, MC, V.

This handsome three-story hotel is part of the Marriott's economy line. The spacious, modern rooms have either king or queen beds and wood-grain furnishings, while suites have a king plus a hide-a-bed, small refrigerator, and microwave oven. There are an indoor heated swimming pool and hot tub. Laundry service is available. Pets are permitted in smoking rooms only.

Greeley Inn. 721 13th St., Greeley, CO 80631. ☎ **970/353-3216.** 38 rms. A/C TV TEL. $45–$55 double. AE, CB, DISC, MC, V.

This downtown motel offers attractive, comfortable rooms with remote-control cable television and a heated outdoor swimming pool in summer. Some rooms have small refrigerators, microwave ovens, and coffeemakers. Nonsmoking rooms are available; pets are not accepted.

WHERE TO DINE

The Armadillo. 111 S. First St., La Salle. ☎ **970/284-5565.** $3–$8.25. AE, DC, MC, V. Sun–Thurs 11:30am–9pm, Fri–Sat 11:30am–10pm. MEXICAN.

Occupying a large brick building beside the Union Pacific tracks in La Salle, 5 miles south of Greeley, this popular Mexican restaurant offers an extensive menu. Many of the recipes come from the family that has run this restaurant since 1970. Specialties include the "Mexican Turnover," a deep-fried meat pie, and the "Burrito Supreme." Fajitas are also very popular.

Cable's End. 3780 W. 10th St. ☎ **970/356-4847.** $6–$14. AE, DISC, MC, V. Mon–Sat 11am–1am, Sun 11am–11pm. ITALIAN.

Locally popular for its homemade pastas, including spaghetti and ravioli, Cable's End also offers fresh seafood, prime rib, steaks, chicken, and pizza. There's a seafood-and-pasta special Friday night and a prime-rib-and-pasta special on Saturday. Kids eat for $1 from the children's menu on Sunday, and there are luncheon pasta specials weekdays.

Potato Brumbaugh's Restaurant & Saloon. 2400 17th St. ☎ **970/356-6340.** Reservations recommended. Lunch $5–$8; dinner $9–$21. AE, DC, DISC, MC, V. Mon–Fri 11:15am–2pm; Mon–Sat 5–10pm. AMERICAN.

Named for a character in James Michener's *Centennial,* this casually elegant restaurant in the Cottonwood Square shopping center follows the novel's theme in its western decor. The menu features steaks, prime rib, poultry, seafood, and a variety of light dishes.

GREELEY AFTER DARK

Greeley's cultural focus is the **Union Colony Civic Center,** 701 10th Ave., at Seventh Street (☎ **970/356-5000**), which hosts national touring and regional productions. It is the performance home for local theater and music groups, including a children's chorale and the Greeley Philharmonic Orchestra, the oldest continually performing orchestra west of the Mississippi River. The **University Garden Theater** is the scene of Concerts Under the Stars in July and August. For information or tickets, call the University of Northern Colorado box office at **970/351-2200.** Other cultural programs scheduled by the university are also open to the public (for information call 970/351-2265).

Among Greeley's more popular **nightspots** are the Smiling Moose Bar & Grill, 2501 11th Ave. (☎ 970/356-7010) and Potato Brumbaugh's Restaurant & Saloon, 2400 17th St. (☎ 970/356-6340). The college crowd particularly enjoys the Union Colony Brewery, 1412 8th Ave. (☎ 970/356-4116), offering fresh, locally brewed beer, billiards, and darts. There's dancing Thursday through Saturday nights to live country music at The Gambler, 618 25th St. (☎ 970/351-7575).

4 Fort Morgan

A laid-back city of some 9,000 people, Fort Morgan may be best known as the childhood home of famed big-band leader Glenn Miller, who graduated from Fort Morgan High School in 1921 and formed his first band, the Mick-Miller Five, in the city. Established as a military outpost in 1864, the original Fort Morgan housed about 200 troops who protected stagecoaches and pioneers traveling the Overland Trail from marauding Cheyenne and Arapahoe warriors. The threat had passed by 1870, and the fort was dismantled, but the name stuck when the city was founded in 1884. The town grew in the 20th century with the establishment of the Great Western Sugar Company for sugar-beet processing and with a pair of oil discoveries in the 1920s and 1950s. Cattle ranching has always been important here, and continues to be today.

ESSENTIALS

GETTING THERE   By Car   Fort Morgan is located on U.S. 34 at I-76, the main east-west route between Denver and Omaha, Nebraska. U.S. 34 proceeds west to Greeley and Estes Park, east to Wray and southern Nebraska. Colorado 52 is the principal north-south route through Fort Morgan.

By Plane   Denver International is less than 90 minutes away (see chapter 6 for a listing of airlines servicing this airport).

By Train   Amtrak trains make daily stops on the Denver-to-Chicago route at the Fort Morgan depot, located on Ensign Street south of Railroad Avenue (☎ **800/ 872-7245**).

ORIENTATION   Situated in the South Platte River valley is Fort Morgan's appropriately named principal east-west thoroughfare, Platte Avenue (U.S. 34). The north-south artery, Main Street, divides it and other streets into east and west designations. I-76 exits onto Main Street north of downtown.

VISITOR INFORMATION   Contact the **Fort Morgan Area Chamber of Commerce,** 300 Main St. (P.O. Box 971), Fort Morgan, CO 80701 (☎ **800/354-8660** or 970/867-6702). The chamber is located in a handsome old stone bank building that's listed on the National Register of Historic Places.

FAST FACTS   In case of **emergency,** call **911.** The **Colorado Plains Medical Center** is located at 1000 Lincoln St. (☎ **970/867-3391**). The **post office** (☎ **970/867-7111**) is at 300 State St. **State and county taxes** add just under 7% to hotel bills.

SPECIAL EVENTS   The Fort Morgan area offers the following: the Brush Antique Show, in early April in Brush; Huck Finn & Becky Thatcher Days, in June in Fort Morgan; the Brush Rodeo in early July in Brush; Festival in the Park in mid-July in Fort Morgan; and the Morgan County Fair, in August in Brush.

WHAT TO SEE & DO

✪ Fort Morgan Museum. City Park, 414 Main St. ☎ **970/867-6331.** Free admission. Mon–Fri 10am–5pm, plus Tues–Thurs 6–8pm, and Sat 11am–5pm.

An impressive collection of northeastern Colorado Native American artifacts, beginning with Clovis points 13,000 years old, is the highlight of this museum—the smallest one in Colorado to be accredited by the American Association of Museums. Other permanent exhibits focus on farming, ranching, and the railroad history of Morgan County, plus a display on the life of native son Glenn Miller and a fully restored 1920s soda fountain.

Oasis on the Plains Museum. 6877 County Rd. 14. ☎ **970/432-5200.** Free admission (donations appreciated, including items for exhibit). Sun noon–4pm, or by appointment.

This working-ranch museum about 15 miles southwest of Fort Morgan displays artifacts, antiques, collectibles, and other items from the northeastern Colorado plains pioneer days.

Sherman Street National Historic District. 400 and 500 blocks of Sherman St. ☎ **970/867-6331.**

Four Victorian mansions built between 1886 and 1926 are of special interest. Located around the intersection of Sherman Street and East Platte Avenue, they include the Warner House, an 1886 Queen Anne home; the Curry House, an 1898 Queen Anne Victorian home with decorative spindlework porches, a barn, carriage house, and water tower; the Graham House, a 1914 American Foursquare home; and the Bloedorn House, a 1926 brick Georgian revival–style house. Each is associated with a prominent city pioneer and are still private homes, not open to the public.

The Fort Morgan Museum publishes a walking-tour brochure both for Sherman Street and for the 9-block downtown district, the latter noting 44 buildings that comprised the early town. These are available at the Chamber of Commerce and the museum.

SPORTS & OUTDOOR ACTIVITIES

The main outdoor recreational areas here are **Riverside Park,** off Main Street between I-76 and the South Platte River, with a large children's playground and free admission; and **Jackson Lake State Park,** which has a $3 day-use fee. To get to Jackson Lake, follow Colo. 144 northwest for about 22 miles; the park is about 2¹/₂ miles north of the community of Goodrich via County Road 3.

ARCHERY/TENNIS   You'll find tennis courts and an archery range at Riverside Park.

FISHING   Anglers fish year-round (ice-fishing in winter) at Jackson Lake State Park for trout, walleye, bass, catfish, and perch, except when fishing is prohibited during the migratory waterfowl season. **Jackson Lake Marina** (☎ **970/768-6011**) has supplies and services. See "Water Sports," below.

HIKING   There's a half-mile nature trail at Jackson Lake State Park.

WATER SPORTS   Water-skiing, sailboarding, and boating are the most popular activities on the 2,700-acre reservoir at Jackson Lake State Park, which has sandy beaches and boat ramps. A **marina** (☎ 970/768-6011) has fuel, fishing and boating supplies, a snack bar, and boat rentals from May through September. Fishing boats cost $18 per hour; personal watercraft and 18-foot pontoon boats are $45 per hour; and ski boats cost $65 per hour (skis are extra). Those who prefer traveling under their own power can rent paddle boats for $15 per hour. The lake is closed to motorized boats from November until all the ice is gone in spring.

In town, Riverside Park offers facilities for swimming during the summer months.

WILDLIFE AND BIRDING   At Jackson Lake State Park, watch for eagles, deer, coyotes, beaver, and turkeys—especially in the mornings.

WINTER SPORTS   Ice fishermen, skaters, and cross-country skiers share Jackson Lake State Park during winter. In town, Riverside Park is open to ice-skating in the winter months as well.

SPECTATOR SPORTS

RODEO   The Brush Rodeo, the world's largest amateur rodeo, is held in the town of Brush, 10 miles east of Fort Morgan, over the Fourth of July weekend, with all the usual rodeo events, plus wild-cow milking, a parade, footrace, dance, and fireworks. Call **800/354-8659.**

STOCK-CAR RACING   Fans head to Fort Morgan's I-76 Speedway (☎ 970/867-2101), where they can see late-model, street stocks, minisprints, dwarves, and IMCA modifieds race on a quarter-mile, high-banked dirt oval track from April through October.

WHERE TO STAY

Best Western Park Terrace Inn. 725 Main St., Fort Morgan, CO 80701. ☎ **800/528-1234** or 970/867-8256. Fax 970/867-8357. 24 rms. A/C TV TEL. $47–$56 double. AE, CB, DC, DISC, MC, V.

Family-owned since 1980, this attractive Best Western is four blocks south of I-76. Rooms have queen-size beds, individual heating, and coffeemakers. There's a swimming pool and a Jacuzzi. The restaurant, decorated with antiques and collectibles, serves three meals daily from an extensive menu: Mexican, Italian, steaks, seafood, and American dishes. The motel accepts preapproved pets in smoking rooms only, with a deposit required.

ⓢ Budget Host Empire Motel. 1408 Edison St., Brush, CO 80723. ☎ **800/BUD-HOST** or 970/842-2876. 18 rms. A/C TV TEL. $34–$43 double. AE, DISC, MC, V.

A comfortable, clean, small roadside motel in Brush, about 10 miles from Fort Morgan, this mom-and-pop operation provides small but adequate rooms with at-your-door parking and cable TV. Pets are accepted.

CAMPING

Jackson Lake State Park has 250 campsites with electric hookups, showers, and a dump station. Fees are $7 to $10 per night.

WHERE TO DINE

Country Steak Out. 19592 E. Eighth Ave., Fort Morgan. ☎ **970/867-7887.** $4.95–$19.95. AE, MC, V. Tues–Sat 11am–9pm, Sun 11am–2pm. STEAK/SEAFOOD.

This open and airy restaurant, with high ceilings and lots of wood and brick, is a favorite of locals. In addition to the popular steaks and prime rib, there's salmon, halibut, and trout, plus homemade soups, daily luncheon specials, and an extensive salad bar at both lunch and dinner.

🟢 **Stroh's Inn.** 901 W. Platte Ave., Fort Morgan. ☎ **970/867-6654.** Breakfast $2.25–$5.25; lunch and dinner $3.25–$11.95. AE, MC, V. Mon–Sat 6am–9pm, Sun 6am–2pm. AMERICAN.

This family-owned and -operated restaurant is known for its generous portions of homemade food, with an extensive menu that includes eight different burgers, 18 sandwiches, a half dozen Mexican dishes, plenty of salads, and a variety of steaks, pork, roasted chicken, and seafood. An all-you-can-eat shrimp dinner is served Tuesdays and Fridays, and pies are baked fresh daily. The breakfast menu offers all the American standards. There's a children's menu and full bar service.

5 Burlington

As the first major community motorists traveling I-70 from the east hit in Colorado, Burlington is an excellent place to overnight and spend some time at the beginning of a Colorado vacation. It's the largest community in east-central Colorado, with a population of about 3,000, and has preserved its turn-of-the-century heritage with an impressive Old Town and famous carousel (see "What to See & Do," below). Dryland farmers established Burlington and other "Outback" communities along the Kansas City–Denver rail line in the 1880s, and while wheat is very much the dominant crop today, you'll also find corn and dry beans.

ESSENTIALS

GETTING THERE   By Car   Burlington is located on east-west I-70, 13 miles from the Kansas border. U.S. 385, which runs the length of Colorado's eastern frontier, makes a north-to-south pass through the town.

ORIENTATION   The town lies on the north side of I-70. Rose Avenue (U.S. 24) runs east to west through the center of Burlington. Main north-south streets are Eighth Street (U.S. 385 north) on the east side of town; 14th Street (which locals call Main Street); and Lincoln Street (U.S. 385 south) on the west side of town.

VISITOR INFORMATION   The Colorado Welcome Center is on I-70 beside Burlington Old Town (☎ 719/346-5554). For information specifically on Burlington, contact the **Burlington Chamber of Commerce,** 480 15th St., (☎ 719/346-8070).

FAST FACTS   In case of **emergency,** call **911.** The **Kit Carson County Memorial Hospital** is at 186 16th St. (☎ 719/346-5311). The **post office** (☎ 719/346-8964) is at 259 14th St. For **weather and road conditions,** call 719/346-8778. Tax adds about 7% to lodging bills.

SPECIAL EVENTS   In August the Kit Carson County Fair takes place; in September Old Town's Outback Hoedown is held; and in December, Old Town Christmas and Parade of Lights are scheduled.

SPORTS & OUTDOOR ACTIVITIES

As soon as the winter snows are gone the folks in Burlington and other eastern Colorado communities head to the beach, and that means **Bonny State Park,** 23 miles north of Burlington on U.S. 385, then east on County Roads 2 or 3 for about

1^1/$_2$ miles (☎ **970/354-7306**). Built as a flood control project in 1951, the reservoir contains 1,900 surface-acres of relatively warm water, perfect for swimming, water-skiing, windsurfing, and fishing.

There are two swimming areas (no lifeguards); four campgrounds with a total of 200 campsites ($6 to $10 per night), with electric hookups, rest rooms, and showers; picnic areas; a self-guided nature trail (not handicapped-accessible); and a fish cleaning station. Fishing is good for walleye, northern pike, and a variety of bass.

There are boat launching ramps, and the **Bonny Dam Marina** (☎ **970/354-7339**) sells fuel, groceries, and boating and fishing supplies. The marina also rents boats between mid-May and mid-September. Aluminum fishing boats cost $40 per half-day or $70 per day; 20- to 24-foot pontoon boats cost $100 to $125 per day; and personal watercraft rent for $45 per hour. Gas is extra. The 5,000-acre park also provides opportunities to see wildlife, with some 250 species of birds, mule and white-tail deer, coyotes, badgers, muskrats, bobcats, beavers, and rabbits.

If you're traveling this way in winter, stop by for an afternoon of cross-country skiing, ice-skating, or ice-fishing, but don't forget your long underwear—winter winds are bone-chilling out here on the plains.

WHAT TO SEE & DO

✪ **Kit Carson County Carousel.** County Fairgrounds, 15th St. at Colorado Ave. ☎ **719/346-8070.** Admission 25¢ per ride. Memorial Day–Labor Day, daily 1–8pm. Private tours given at other times: write P.O. Box 28, Stratton, CO 80836, with 2 weeks advance notice.

This is the town's pride and joy, the only National Historic Landmark in eastern Colorado. Carved in 1905 by the Philadelphia Toboggan Company, it is fully restored and operational, and is one of the few wooden carousels left in America that still wears its original coat of paint. The 46 stationary animals—mostly horses, but also including giraffes, zebras, camels, a hippocampus (sea horse), lion, tiger, and others—march counterclockwise around three tiers of oil paintings, representing the lifestyles and interests of the American Victorian middle class. A Wurlitzer Monster Military Band Organ, one of only two of that size and vintage in operation today, provides the music.

✪ **Old Town.** 420 S. 14th St. ☎ **800/288-1334** or 719/346-7382. Admission $4 adults, $2 youths 12–18, $1 children 3–11, $3.50 for seniors 60 and older. Memorial Day–Labor Day, daily 8:30am–7pm; the rest of the year, Mon–Sat 9am–6pm and Sun noon–6pm.

Close to 2 dozen turn-of-the-century–style Old West buildings make up this living-history museum, where you're likely to see a gunfight, melodrama, or a can-can show in the Longhorn Saloon during summer months. Ten of the buildings are original historic structures, moved to Old Town, and the rest are reproductions, all furnished with turn-of-the-century artifacts to show what it was like in the Wild West 100 years ago.

Visit the blacksmith shop, bank, law office, newspaper office and operating print shop, general store, school house, and barn. The depot, built in 1889 in Bethune, Colorado, contains the conductor's uniform worn by Keppel Disney, a relative of Walt Disney, who worked in this area. Of course there's the saloon, where you're likely to find the local madam during the summer, or perhaps you'd prefer to stop at the church, built in 1921 and still used for weddings.

The doll house is home to a number of unique dolls, and you'll see tools over 100 years old in the wood shop. The original Burlington town jail cells are here; the two-story six-bedroom Manor house was built in the early 1900s. Belgian draft horses pull the "Old Town Express" through the village, and special events and celebrations are scheduled throughout the year. Heritage Hall contains a large collection of 45 wagons, guns, and other exhibits. There's also a 2,000-square-foot gift shop, with handcrafted items and other souvenirs.

WHERE TO STAY

Burlington Inn. 450 S. Lincoln St., Burlington, CO 80807. ☎ **719/346-5555.** Fax 719/346-5555. 108 rms, 4 suites. A/C TV TEL. $36–$46 double; from $51 suite. AE, CB, DC, DISC, MC, V.

This conveniently located motel offers spacious rooms with cable TV, and dances almost every weekend. There's a swimming pool, lounge, and dining room serving three meals daily. A child under 16 stays free with parent. Pets are accepted at $5 per day.

Ⓢ **Sloan's Motel.** 1901 Rose Ave., Burlington, CO 80807. ☎ **800/362-0464** or 719/346-5333. Fax 719/346-9536. 27 rms. A/C TV TEL. Memorial Day–Labor Day $36 double. Labor Day–Memorial Day $32 double. Family units $39–$45. AE, CB, DC, DISC, MC, V.

A well-kept, comfortable establishment, this motel has a children's playground and enclosed swimming pool. All rooms have queen or double beds, 27-channel cable TV, and clock radios. One family unit has two rooms.

WHERE TO DINE

Mr. A's Interstate House Restaurant. 415 S. Lincoln St., at I-70 Exit 437. ☎ **719/346-8010.** Breakfast $1.50–$8; lunch and dinner $3–$15. AE, DC, DISC, MC, V. Daily 6am–10pm. AMERICAN/MEXICAN.

Called the "Yellow Top" by locals because of its distinctive bright yellow roof, this family restaurant is a favorite because of its good home-cooked food, quick service, and low prices. Particularly popular are the chicken fried steak, spaghetti with meat sauce (especially when it's the all-you-can-eat Thursday night special), and hamburgers. There are also seafood selections, pork chops, tacos, burritos, chile, and steaks charbroiled to order. Breakfasts, most of which are available all day, feature the standard egg and pancake selections, and you can get a giant hot cinnamon roll for just $1.25.

11 The Northern Rockies

Literally and figuratively, this is the mother lode. It's where scrappy silver and gold miners struck it rich time and time again in the late 19th century (and you might still find an ore deposit while hiking or fishing here today); yet it's also where Colorado's rugged beauty is shown off to fullest effect.

The northern Rockies begin just outside of Denver, and extend on either side of the meandering Continental Divide down sawtooth ridgelines, through precipitous river canyons, and across broad alpine plains. Here, snowfall is measured in feet, not inches; it's where you'll find Colorado's hottest ski resorts—Aspen, Vail, and Steamboat—as well as a few smaller areas that are making headlines, such as Winter Park. One of the few municipally run ski areas in the world (it's owned by the city of Denver), Winter Park offers a great, and affordable, bare-bones ski vacation for families, and it's miles closer to the Front Range than other leading resorts.

And then there's Summit County, with possibly more major ski areas within a half-hour's drive than anywhere else in the country. If you're easily bored, rent a condo or take a room in Breckenridge and spend your days skiing a different mountain every day. With Copper, Keystone, Arapahoe Basin, and even tiny Loveland Basin all within a few miles' drive, you've got plenty of choices.

When spring's sun finally melts away the walls of white, a whole new world opens up amid the brilliantly colored alpine wildflowers. You can head to any of the area's ski resorts and shop their stores, and hike or cycle their trails, or you can visit the state's largest national park, Rocky Mountain National Park, where there are a wide variety of activities to entertain the whole brood.

1 Estes Park & Grand Lake: Gateways to Rocky Mountain National Park

Estes Park is the eastern gateway to Rocky Mountain National Park, and Grand Lake is the closest town to the park's western entrance. Of the two, Estes Park is more developed. It has more lodging and dining choices, as well as a few noteworthy sights that are worth visiting if you have time. If you're driving to Rocky Mountain National Park via Boulder or Denver, you'll want to make Estes Park your base camp.

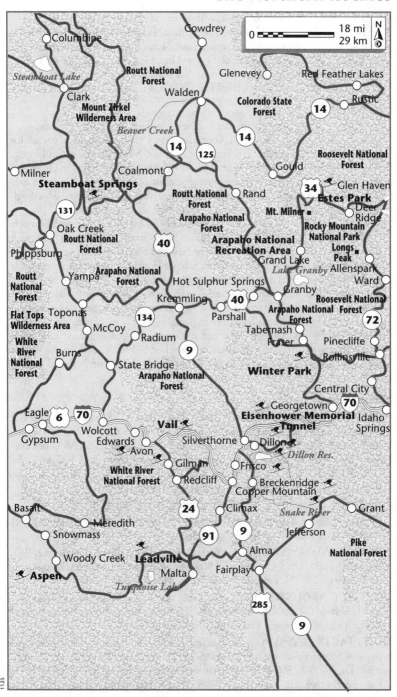

Columbine

Cowdrey

Steamboat Lake

Routt National Forest

Glenevey

Red Feather Lakes

Clark

Walden

Colorado State Forest

Rustic

Mount Zirkel Wilderness Area

Beaver Creek

14

Milner

Coalmont

125

Gould

Roosevelt National Forest

Steamboat Springs

Routt National Forest

Rand

34

Glen Haven

Estes Park

131

Mt. Milner

Deer Ridge

Oak Creek

Arapaho National Forest

Rocky Mountain National Park

Phippsburg

Routt National Forest

40

Arapaho National Recreation Area

Longs Peak

Yampa

Arapaho National Forest

Grand Lake

Allenspark

Routt National Forest

Hot Sulphur Springs

Lake Granby

Granby

Ward

Kremmling

40

Roosevelt National Forest

Flat Tops Wilderness Area

Toponas

134

Parshall

Arapaho National Forest

72

McCoy

Radium

Tabernash

Pinecliffe

White River National Forest

9

Fraser

Rollinsville

Burns

State Bridge

Arapaho National Forest

Winter Park

Central City

Eagle

6

70

Georgetown

70

Gypsum

Wolcott

Vail

Eisenhower Memorial Tunnel

Idaho Springs

Edwards

Silverthorne

Dillon

Avon

Gilman

Frisco

Dillon Res.

White River National Forest

Redcliff

Breckenridge

Copper Mountain

Basalt

24

Climax

Snake River

Grant

Meredith

91

9

Jefferson

Snowmass

Alma

Pike National Forest

Woody Creek

Leadville

Fairplay

Aspen

Malta

Turquoise Lake

285

9

0   18 mi
  29 km

N

Grand Lake is a more rustic spot, with plenty of places to camp, several motels, and a few guest ranches. If you're coming from Steamboat Springs or Glenwood Springs, Grand Lake is a more convenient base. At any time of year, you can get there via U.S. 34. In summer, you can also get to Grand Lake by taking the Trail Ridge Road through Rocky Mountain National Park from Estes Park. Both routes are scenic, although the national park route (usually closed in winter) is definitely prettier.

ESTES PARK

Unlike most Colorado mountain communities, which got their starts in mining, Estes Park has always been a resort town. Long known by Utes and Arapahoes, it was "discovered" in 1859 by rancher Joel Estes. He soon sold his homestead to Griff Evans, who built it into a dude ranch. One of Evans's guests, the British Earl of Dunraven, was so taken by the region that he purchased most of the valley and operated it as his private game reserve, until thwarted by such settlers as W. E. James, who developed a ranch on a portion of the land to supply fish to Denver restaurants.

The recent history of Estes Park is inextricably linked with the accomplishments of two individuals: Freelan Stanley and Enos Mills. Stanley, a Bostonian who, with his brother Francis, invented the kerosene-powered Stanley Steamer automobile in 1899, settled in Estes Park in 1907. Once here, he launched a Stanley Steamer shuttle service and built the landmark Stanley Hotel, ushering in an era of mass tourism to the region. Mills, an innkeeper-turned-conservationist, was the prime advocate for the creation of Rocky Mountain National Park. Although much less well known than John Muir, Mills is an equally important figure in the history of U.S. conservation. His tireless efforts as an author and stump speaker increased sentiment nationwide for preserving our national wild lands, and resulted in President Woodrow Wilson signing a bill to set aside 400 square miles for Rocky Mountain National Park in 1915.

ESSENTIALS

GETTING THERE   By Car   The most direct route is U.S. 36 from Denver and Boulder. At Estes Park, that highway joins U.S. 34, which runs up the Big Thompson Canyon from I-25 and Loveland, and continues through Rocky Mountain National Park to Grand Lake. An alternative scenic route to Estes Park is Colo. 7, the "Peak-to-Peak Scenic Byway" that transits Central City (Colo. 119), Nederland (Colo. 72), and Allenspark (Colo. 7), under different designations.

By Plane   The closest airport is Denver International Airport, 80 miles away.

By Bus   Charles Tour and Travel Services (☎ **800/586-5009** or 970/586-5151) connects Estes Park with Boulder and Denver.

VISITOR INFORMATION   The **Estes Park Area Chamber of Commerce,** P.O. Box 3050, Estes Park, CO 80517 (☎ **800/44-ESTES** or 970/586-4431), has a Visitor Center on U.S. 34, just east of its junction with U.S. 36.

GETTING AROUND   There's year-round **taxi** service with **Charles Tour and Travel Service** (☎ **800/586-5009** or 970/586-5151), which also provides tours into Rocky Mountain National Park during the summer.

FAST FACTS   Call **911** for **emergencies.** The hospital, **Estes Park Medical Center,** is at 555 Prospect Ave. (☎ **970/586-2317**). The **post office** is at 215 W. Riverside Dr. (☎ **970/586-8177**). For statewide **road conditions,** call 303/639-1111. For a **current weather report,** call 970/586-5555. **State and local taxes** add about 8% to hotel bills.

SPECIAL EVENTS   Notable special events include: the Stanley Steamer Tour in May; Scandinavian Mid-Summer Festival, on the weekend closest to the summer solstice; the Rooftop Rodeo and Western Heritage Days, during the third week of July; the Estes Park Music Festival, during July and August; and the Scottish-Irish Highland Festival on the second weekend of September.

THINGS TO SEE & DO

Enos Mills Cabin and Gallery. Colo. 7 opposite Longs Peak Inn. ☎ **970/586-4706.** Memorial Day–Labor Day, Tues–Sun 11am–4pm. By appointment in other seasons.

The 1885 cabin and homestead of the late 19th- and early 20th-century conservationist is open to the public, operated by Mills's family. There's a 5-minute walk down a nature trail to the cabin, where Mills's daughter Enda Mills Kiley discusses her father's life and work. Memorabilia in the cabin includes copies of Mills's 15 books and the cameras he used to take thousands of photos of the mountains he loved. There's also a bookshop, photo gallery, and nature center.

Estes Park Aerial Tramway. 420 E. Riverside Dr. ☎ **970/586-3675.** Admission $8 adults, $4 children under 12. Summer, daily 9am–6:30pm.

Panoramic views of Longs Peak and the Continental Divide, plus Estes Park village itself, are afforded by this lift. Its lower terminal is one block south of the post office. Its upper terminal has a gift shop and snack bar. Numerous trails converge atop the mountain.

Estes Park Area Historical Museum. 200 Fourth St. at Colo. 36. ☎ **970/586-6256.** Admission $2.50 adults, $1 children 12 and under, $10 maximum for families. May–Oct, Mon–Sat 10am–5pm, Sun 1–5pm; Nov–Apr, Fri–Sat 10am–5pm, Sun 1–5pm; extended Dec holiday hours.

The lives of early homesteaders in Estes Park are depicted in this excellent, small museum, which includes a completely furnished turn-of-the-century log cabin, old ranch wagons, an original Stanley Steam Car, a changing exhibit gallery, and a discovery room for children with hands-on activities, all housed in the original headquarters of Rocky Mountain National Park. In addition, the museum publishes a self-guided historical walking tour of Estes Park that's available at the entrance.

Estes Park Brewery. 470 Prospect Village Dr. (P.O. Box 2161), Estes Park, CO 80517. ☎ **970/586-5421.** Daily 11am–late evening.

This is the only brewery in Estes Park, and it produces up to 6,000 barrels of beer and ale a year, using water from the headwaters of the Big Thompson River, high in the snowcapped mountains of Rocky Mountain National Park. The brewery specializes in fresh, clean beer and Belgian-style ales, the most popular of which is Longs Peak Raspberry Wheat. Free tours and samples are offered, and beer is available for purchase in 22-ounce bottles, half-gallon jugs, or kegs. Souvenir glasses, caps, and posters are also sold, and you can eat lunch or dinner here (pizzas, burgers, and sandwiches), if you like; billiard tables, darts, and other games keep those who feel like lingering entertained. A beer garden was added in summer 1995.

Michael Ricker Pewter Casting Studio and Museum. 2050 Big Thompson Ave. ☎ **800/373-9837** or 970/586-2030. Admission free. Summer, Mon–Sat 9am–9pm, Sun 9am–6pm; winter, Mon–Sat 9am–6pm, Sun noon–6pm.

Ricker is an internationally recognized artist and sculptor, whose works have been displayed in the Great Hall of Commerce in Washington, D.C. and at both Disneyland and Disney World. There are over 1,000 pewter sculptures in the museum and gallery, including Ricker's masterpiece, "Park City," claimed to be the world's largest pewter sculpture. Free guided tours are available daily.

SHOPPING

The **Art Center of Estes Park** in the Stanley Village Shopping Center, 517 Big Thompson Ave. (☎ **970/586-5882**), is a community visual-arts center featuring changing exhibits of local and regional art, classes, and other programs. It's open daily from 11am to 5pm in summer; call for winter hours.

Among the galleries and gift shops that are worth a look are those in the **Old Church Shops,** 157 W. Elkhorn Ave., and **Sundance Center for the Arts,** 150 E. Riverside Dr. Also look for **The Glassworks,** 323 W. Elkhorn Ave. (☎ **970/586-8619**), with hand-glass-blowing demonstrations; **Serendipity Trading Company,** 117 E. Elkhorn Ave. (☎ **970/586-8410**), traders in Native American arts and crafts; and **Wooden Things, Etc.** in Park Place Mall at 145 E. Elkhorn Ave. (☎ **970/586-5144**), featuring home accessories, puzzles, sculpture, and toys.

Ten miles south of Estes Park is **Eagle Plume's** store & museum, 9853 Colo. 7, Allenspark (☎ **303/747-2861**). A University of Colorado graduate (now deceased), Charles Eagle Plume was one-quarter Blackfoot and a true entertainer and entrepreneur. His fascinating collection of museum-quality artifacts is not for sale, but the trading post has much that is, including crafts, pottery, jewelry, baskets, and rugs. It's open daily April through December from 9am to 5pm, and weekends-only from January through March.

WHERE TO STAY

For help finding accommodations, call the **Estes Park Area Chamber of Commerce Lodging Referral Service** (☎ **800/44-ESTES** or 970/586-4431). National chains with lodgings here include: **Best Western Lake Estes Resort,** 1650 Big Thompson Hwy. (☎ **800/292-8439** or 970/586-3386), with rates of $92 to $115 for a double room, and $145 to $200 for a suite from mid-June to mid-September (rates drop at other times of the year); and **Holiday Inn of Estes Park,** U.S. 36 and Colo. 7 (☎ **800/80-ESTES** or 970/586-2332), charging $59 to $100 for a double room, and $100 to $200 for a suite in summer (lower rates in winter).

Expensive

✪ **Boulder Brook.** 1900 Fall River Rd., Estes Park, CO 80517. ☎ **800/238-0910** or 970/586-0910. Fax 970/586-8067. 16 suites. TV TEL. $89–$135 double; $139–$175 spa suites. AE, DISC, MC, V.

It would be hard to find a more beautiful setting for a lodging than this. Surrounded by tall pines, all suites face the Fall River, have private riverfront decks, and either full kitchens or wet bars. Spa suites contain two-person spas, fireplaces, sitting rooms with cathedral ceilings, and king-size beds. One-bedroom suites offer king-size beds, window seats, two televisions, and baths with whirlpool tub and shower combinations. There's also a year-round outdoor hot tub. VCRs and in-room movies are available, and special occasion packages can be arranged year-round.

Castle Mountain Lodge. 1520 Fall River Rd., Moraine Rte., Estes Park, CO 80517. ☎ **970/586-3664.** 28 cabins. TV. Mid-June–Sept, $83–$95 double; $115–$280 two- and three-bedroom cabins. $8 per person extra for three or more in cabin. Fall and spring rates about 20% less; winter rates, about 40% less. AE, DISC, MC, V.

These modern but rustic cabins on the Fall River, situated in a wooded tract facing Castle Mountain, offer guests a wide choice of options. No two cabins are alike, and they range in size from studio cottages to three-bedroom units. Most have full kitchens, fireplaces, hide-a-bed sofas, barbecues, and outdoor furniture. There are lawn games, and pets are allowed ($10 a day) by prior arrangement.

Romantic Riversong Inn. Lower Broadview Dr. off Mary's Lake Rd. (P.O. Box 1910), Estes Park, CO 80517. ☎ **970/586-4666.** Fax 970/586-0417. 9 rms. $135–$250 double. Rates include breakfast. MC, V.

A 1920 Craftsman mansion on the Big Thompson River, this elegant bed-and-breakfast has 27 forested acres with hiking trails and a trout pond, as well as prolific wildlife. It's at the end of a country lane, the first right off Mary's Lake Road after it branches off U.S. 36 south. The cozy bedrooms are decorated with a blend of antique and modern country furniture. Some have ornate brass beds and claw-footed tubs; several have jetted tubs for two; and all have fireplaces. Smoking is not permitted. Hosts Sue and Gary Mansfield prepare gourmet candlelight dinners by advance arrangement.

✪ **Stanley Hotel.** 333 Wonderview Ave. (P.O. Box 1767), Estes Park, CO 80517. ☎ **800/976-1377** or 970/586-3371. Fax 970/586-3673. 129 units. TV TEL. $99–$169 double, $159–$199 suite. AE, DISC, JCB, MC, V.

F. O. Stanley, inventor of the Stanley Steam Car, built this elegant, white-pillared hotel in 1909. The equal of European resorts of the time, it was constructed into solid rock. Today the handsome hotel is a registered National Historic District. As is often the case in historic hotels, each room is different in size and shape, with assorted views of Longs Peak, Lake Estes, and surrounding hillsides. Facilities include a heated outdoor swimming pool, whirlpool, exercise room, gift shop, and business center. New owners have been renovating the entire property, and the lobby has been restored to its original dark-wood splendor.

Streamside Cabins. 1260 Fall River Rd., Moraine Rte. (P.O. Box 2930), Estes Park, CO 80517. ☎ **800/321-3303** or 970/586-6464. Fax 970/586-6272. 19 units. TV. $115–$165 double; $145–$175 suite; $15 additional person. AE, DISC, MC, V.

These cabins, on 16 acres along the Fall River, about a mile west of Estes Park on U.S. 34, are surrounded by woods and meadows rife with wildflowers. Deer, elk, and occasional bighorn sheep are such regular visitors that many have been given names.

Everything is top drawer in these solid-wood cabins. Most have beamed cathedral ceilings, skylights, and southwestern country decor. Furnished like condominiums, they have king- or queen-size beds, Jacuzzi tubs or steam baths, fireplaces, cable TV, VCRs, decks or patios with gas grills, and most have full kitchens. Guests also have use of an indoor hot tub/swim spa.

Moderate

Allenspark Lodge. Colo. 7 Business Loop (P.O. Box 247), Allenspark, CO 80510. ☎ **303/747-2552.** 12 rms (6 with bath), 3 cabins. $45–$90 double. Rates include an elaborate continental breakfast. Call for cabin rates. MC, V.

There's a historic ambiance to this three-story lodge, built in 1933 of native stone and hand-hewn ponderosa pine logs. Located 16 miles south of Estes Park, in a tiny village at the southeast corner of the national park, all lodge rooms have mountain views and original handmade 1930s pine furniture. At the top end is the Hideaway Room, with a brass bed, bear-claw–footed tub, and fine linens. Guests share the stone fireplace in the great room, Ping-Pong and pool tables in the game room, and books in the library. Complimentary afternoon and evening coffee, tea, and cookies are served. There's also a hot tub and gift shop.

☼ Baldpate Inn. 4900 S. Colo. 7 (P.O. Box 4445), Estes Park, CO 80517. ☎ **970/586-6151.**
13 rms (4 with bath), 3 cabins. $70 shared bath; $85 private bath; $125 cabin. Rates include
full breakfast. DISC, MC, V. Closed Oct–Apr.

Built in 1917, the Baldpate was named for the novel *Seven Keys to Baldpate*, a murder mystery in which seven visitors believe they possess the only key to the hotel. In
1996 the Baldpate was added to the National Register of Historic Places. Guests today can watch several movie versions of the story, read the book, and add their keys
to the inn's collection of more than 20,000 keys.

The inn is adjacent to Rocky Mountain National Park, just 7 miles south of Estes
Park. It sits at an impressive elevation of 9,000 feet. The lobby has a stone fireplace
and VCR with a collection of videos guests can watch free of charge. Each of the
early-20th-century–style rooms is unique, with handmade quilts on the beds. An excellent soup and salad buffet is served for lunch and dinner daily during summer (see
"Where to Dine" below). Pets and smoking are not permitted.

☼ Estes Park Center/YMCA of the Rockies. 2515 Tunnel Rd., Estes Park, CO 80511-2550.
☎ **970/586-3341,** or 303/623-9215 from Denver. 565 rms (450 with bath), 201 cabins.
Lodge rooms, summer $45–$84, winter $30–$56; cabins, year-round $51–$207. No credit
cards.

Extremely popular, this family lodge makes an ideal base for exploring the Estes Park
area. Lodge units are basic. The spacious mountain cabins have two to four bedrooms
that sleep up to 10, complete kitchens, and telephones. Some have fireplaces. YMCA
membership is required and is sold at a nominal charge. The center occupies 860
wooded acres, and offers hiking, horseback riding, miniature golf, a heated swimming
pool, fishing, bicycling, three tennis courts, and cross-country skiing. Pets are permitted in cabins, but not in lodge rooms.

Glacier Lodge. Hwy. 66 (P.O. Box 2656), Estes Park, CO 80517. ☎ **800/523-3920** or 970/
586-4401. 3 rms, 23 cottages. TV. June–Labor Day, $55–$85 rooms; $92–$145 cottages. Late
May–early June and Sept, $48–$75 rooms; $82–$120 cottages. Oct–late May, $40–$44 rooms;
$78–$95 cottages. MC, V.

Deer and elk frequently visit these lovely cottages, spread across 15 acres of woodland along the Big Thompson River. Poolside chalets sleep up to six; cozy, homey
river duplexes have outside decks overlooking the stream; and river triplexes are similar, ranging from earthy to country quaint in decor. Almost all have kitchens and fireplaces, with a bundle of wood delivered daily. There's a swimming pool, sport court,
playground, fishing, lending library, and stables. There are weekly steak cookouts and
kids' evenings in summer, at an extra charge.

Inexpensive

H-Bar-G Ranch Hostel. 3500 H-Bar-G Rd., off Dry Gulch Rd. (P.O. Box 1260), Estes Park, CO
80517. ☎ **970/586-3688.** Fax 970/589-5004. 100 beds (20 with bath). Memorial Day–
Labor Day, $8 per bed. Hostelling International membership required. Closed Labor Day–
Memorial Day. MC, V.

Bring a sleeping bag to throw on your dorm bunk, and be prepared to pitch in with
daily chores—that's the hosteler's way. There are separate accommodations for men
and women, and family cabins with private baths, by advance reservation. Everyone
shares the kitchen and game room. Hiking trails lead into the national forest; you'll
also find tennis and volleyball courts, barbecues, and a fireplace. The hostel is located
5¹/₂ miles northeast of Lake Estes, in the national forest at an elevation of 8,200 feet,
with easy access to the national park. Check-in is between 5:15 and 9pm. A van takes
guests to the hostel from the Estes Park Tourist Information Center at 5pm daily;
call to arrange a pickup.

CAMPING

In addition to campgrounds in the park (see "Rocky Mountain National Park," below), there are a few commercial campgrounds in the Estes Park area.

Mary's Lake Campground. 2120 Mary's Lake Rd. (P.O. Box 2514), Estes Park, CO 80517. ☎ **800/445-6279** or 970/586-4411. 150 sites. $19–$23 per campsite for two people. Extra person $2. DISC, MC, V. May 15–Sept 30.

Amid a backdrop of mountain views, there are campsites for everything from tents to 40-foot recreational vehicles with full hookups here. Facilities include bathhouses, a laundry, dump station, playground, basketball court, small store, heated swimming pool, and game room. Fishing licenses and bait and tackle can be obtained here for shore fishing at the lake and stream fishing in the national park.

National Park Resort. 3501 Fall River Rd., Estes Park, CO 80517. ☎ **970/586-4563.** 100 sites. $19–$22 per campsite for two people. Extra person $2. DISC, MC, V. May–Sept.

This wooded campground can accommodate both tents and R.V.s. Full hookups include electric, water, sewer, and cable TV. Facilities include bathhouses and a laundry. Cabins, available year-round, cost $80–$120.

Spruce Lake R.V. Park. Rte. 36 and Mary's Lake Rd. (P.O. Box 2497), Estes Park, CO 80517. ☎ **970/586-2889.** 110 sites. $15–$25 with hookups. MC, V. Apr–Oct 15.

Spruce Lake has a heated pool, free miniature golf, a large playground, a stocked private fishing lake, large sites, and spotless rest room/shower facilities. There are Sunday pancake breakfasts and weekly ice-cream socials. Ground tents are not permitted, but pets are, as long as you walk them within your campsite and carry or drive them out of the park. Reservations are strongly recommended, especially in summer.

WHERE TO DINE

Expensive

The Fawn Brook Inn. Colo. 7 Business Loop, Allenspark. ☎ **303/747-2556.** Reservations required. Main courses $23–$39.50. AE, MC, V. May 1–Oct 15, Tues–Sun 5–8:30pm. Call for winter hours. CONTINENTAL.

While a bit frumpy in appearance, this establishment, 16 miles south of Estes Park, serves what many consider to be the finest food, with the best service in the area. The continental dishes have a German flair. A great way to start is with a wild-game pâté, langoustine rémoulade, or Caesar salad prepared tableside. Then move on to a wide choice of main dishes, such as sweetbreads Monte Carlo, chateaubriand, sole meunière, or fresh seafood.

Moderate

The Dunraven Inn. 2470 Colo. 66. ☎ **970/586-6409.** Reservations highly recommended. Main courses $7.50–$21.95. AE, DISC, MC, V. Sun–Thurs 5–10pm, Fri–Sat 5–11pm; closes slightly earlier in winter. ITALIAN.

The decor is eclectic, to say the least: Images of the *Mona Lisa* are scattered about, everything from a mustachioed lady to opera posters, and autographed dollar bills are posted in the lounge area. Recently, a separate smoking room has been added, leaving the main dining room entirely nonsmoking. House specialties are scampi, linguini with white clam sauce, veal parmigiana, chicken cacciatore, and Dunraven Italiano: a charbroiled sirloin steak in a sauce of green, red, and yellow peppers, with black olives, mushrooms, and tomatoes. There are vegetarian plates and a children's menu.

Gazebo, Restaurant on the Park. 225 Park Lane. ☎ **970/586-9564.** Reservations recommended. Lunch $5–$15; Sun brunch $5–$15; dinner $10–$30. 20% dinner discount for seniors. AE, CB, DC, DISC, MC, V. Daily 11:30am–9pm; Nov–May closed Wed–Thurs. INTERNATIONAL.

This handsome restaurant in the heart of Estes Park, best suited for adults, offers seasonal outdoor seating and spectacular views. A variety of specialty gourmet dishes are offered, such as spuntini: a hollowed-out *boule* of homemade bread, filled with chile, beef stew, or a seafood or chicken casserole, and served with a salad. Other dishes include Khyber chicken or cubed beef, marinated overnight in yogurt and spices, broiled, and served with a chutney relish.

Inexpensive

Baldpate Inn. 4900 S. Colo. 7. ☎ **970/586-6151.** Reservations recommended. Buffet $8.75 adults, $5.25 children under 10. DISC, MC, V. Memorial Day–Oct 1, daily 11:30am–7pm. SOUP & SALAD.

Don't be misled by the simple food—the buffet is deliciously filling and plentiful. Everything is freshly prepared daily, with the cooks barely staying one muffin pan ahead of the guests. Soups include hearty stews, chile, a marvelous chicken rice, garden vegetable, and classic French onion—with a choice of two offered each day. The salad bar provides fresh greens and an array of toppings, plus chunks of cheese, and fruit and vegetable salads. Honey wheat bread is a staple, plus wonderful rolls, muffins, and cornbread. To top off the meal there are fresh homemade pies and cappuccino. The Baldpate, on the National Register of Historic Places, is entirely nonsmoking.

La Casa del Estorito. 222 E. Elkhorn Ave. ☎ **970/586-2807.** Reservations recommended. Main courses $4.95–$14.95. AE, DC, DISC, MC, V. Daily 11am–9:30pm; Sun Champagne Brunch 10:30am–1:30pm. MEXICAN/CAJUN/AMERICAN.

One thing that Mexican and Cajun cuisines have in common, besides the Gulf of Mexico, is a high level of spiciness—and that's the emphasis at the Estorito family's restaurant in downtown Estes Park. Try blackened redfish, mesquite chicken, or a spicy beef burrito. There are also burgers and sandwiches. In summer, there's seating in a lovely outdoor garden.

Molly B's. 200 Moraine Ave. ☎ **970/586-2766.** Reservations recommended for dinner. Breakfast $2.95–$6.25; lunch $3.95–$5.75; dinner $8.95–$16.95. AE, MC, V. Daily 6:30am–3pm, 5–10pm. AMERICAN.

The friendly staff makes you feel right at home in this casual, popular restaurant. Menu items include vegetarian, fresh seafood, pasta, prime rib, and steak. In summer there's patio seating. A children's menu is available.

ESTES PARK AFTER DARK

The Fine Arts Guild of the Rockies, P.O. Box 1165, Estes Park, CO 80517 (☎ 970/586-5035) sponsors a musical and two plays during the year. Recent productions have included *South Pacific, Mame,* and *Cinderella.* The Guild also produces arts-and-crafts shows and festivals.

Estes Park Music Festival, P.O. Box 4290, Estes Park, CO 80517 (☎ 970/586-9203), presents seven Monday night classical concerts at 8pm beginning in early July, with the Young Philharmonic of Munich, Germany. Tickets start at $18. The **Chamber Music Society of Estes Park** (☎ 970/586-9203) presents three concerts in early October, with tickets costing $12 per concert, or $30 for all three.

The historic **Stanley Hotel** (see "Where to Stay," above), 333 Wonderview Ave. (☎ 800/ROCKIES or 970/586-3371), offers free concerts Sunday afternoons from September to May, and dinner theater during summer and holidays.

Nine miles south of Estes Park off Colo. 7, **Rocky Ridge Music Center,** 465 Longs Peak Rd. (☎ 970/586-4031), offers concerts Sunday afternoons from late June through August.

The **Lazy B Ranch,** 1915 Dry Gulch Rd. (☎ **800/228-2116** or 970/586-5371), offers a chuck-wagon supper and western show. There's also a program on the history of western music. To reach Lazy B, take U.S. 34 east from Estes Park about 1¹/₂ miles, turn left at Sombrero Stables, and follow the signs. Open early June to Labor Day.

For live music and dancing, check out **Lonigan's Saloon,** 110 W. Ave. (☎ **970/ 586-4346**).

GRAND LAKE

The western entrance to Rocky Mountain National Park is at the picturesque little town of Grand Lake, in the shade of Shadow Mountain at the park's southwestern corner.

Here, in the crisp mountain air at 8,370 feet above sea level, you can stroll down an old-fashioned boardwalk while a local resident parallels you on horseback along adjoining Grand Avenue. Located within the Arapahoe National Recreation Area, Grand Lake is surrounded by three lakes—Grand Lake, Shadow Mountain Reservoir, and Lake Granby—each with a marina that offers boating (with rentals), fishing, and other water sports. Throughout the recreation area you'll also find miles of trails for hiking, horseback riding, four-wheeling, and mountain biking that become cross-country skiing and snowmobiling trails in winter.

The town's namesake lake, which reaches a depth of 400 feet, is the largest natural lake in Colorado. It's linked by channels to the two other larger lakes—both dammed portions of the Colorado River. Water from the three is pumped east 13 miles under the mountains to the Big Thompson River and Lake Estes, where it is channeled to the plains for irrigation. To see how this is all accomplished, drop by **Farr Pumping Plant** for a tour.

Visitors can also stop at the **Kaufman House,** 407 Pitkin Ave. (☎ **970/ 627-3351**), an early log structure that serves as the museum of the Grand Lake Historical Society. Golfers may want to test their skills at the 18-hole championship **Grand Lake Golf Course** (☎ **970/627-8008**), altitude 8,420 feet.

The Grand Lake Yacht Club hosts the **Grand Lake Regatta** and **Lipton Cup Races** every August. The club was organized in 1902, and the regatta began 10 years later. Sailboats from around the world compete to win the prestigious Lipton Cup, given to the club by Thomas Lipton in 1912. Other summer events include an enormous Fourth of July fireworks display; Western Week, with a buffalo barbecue and mountain man rendezvous, in mid-July; and the Grand Festival of Arts and Crafts, which includes a food and wine event, in late August.

For further information on these and other activities, stop at the Visitor Information Center on U.S. 34 at the turnoff into town; or contact the **Grand Lake Area Chamber of Commerce,** P.O. Box 57, Grand Lake, CO 80447 (☎ **800/531-1019** or 970/627-3402).

There are plenty of places to stay and eat in Grand Lake. Lodging possibilities include the **Inn at Grand Lake,** 1103 Grand Ave. (☎ **800/627-9234** or 970/ 627-9234), a well-maintained motel with rates of $40 to $95 for a double room; and the **Daven Haven Lodge,** 604 Marina Dr. (☎ **970/627-8144;** fax 970/627-5098), with a variety of cabins that cost $60 to $120 for two. Among our choices for a bite to eat are **Chuck Hole Cafe,** 1131 Grand Ave. (☎ **970/627-3509**), open daily for breakfast and lunch ($3–$7); and **EG's Garden Grill,** 1000 Grand Ave. (☎ **970/ 627-8404**), which is also open daily, and serves light, healthy lunches and dinners ($5–$18).

2 Rocky Mountain National Park

With its high elevation (even the lush valleys are 8,000 ft. above sea level), Rocky Mountain National Park presents a stunning scenery of the sky to visitors. There are 17 snow-covered peaks above 13,000 feet and several shimmering alpine lakes, many of which can be seen from the park's primary east-west roadway, Trail Ridge Road, which has the distinction of being the highest continuously paved highway in the United States.

But what really sets the park apart (after all, this sort of eye-popping beauty is not unusual in the Rockies) are its three distinct ecological zones. As you rise and descend in altitude, the landscape of the park changes dramatically. In relatively low areas, about 7,500 to 9,000 feet, a lush forest of ponderosa pine and juniper cloaks the sunny southern slopes, with Douglas fir on the cooler northern slopes. Thirsty blue spruce and lodgepole pine cling to streamsides, with occasional groves of aspen. Elk and mule deer thrive. On higher slopes a subalpine ecosystem exists, dominated by forests of Engelmann spruce and subalpine fir, but interspersed with wide meadows alive with wildflowers during spring and summer. This is where bighorn sheep, unofficial mascots of the park, reside. Above 10,500 feet, the trees become increasingly gnarled and stunted until they disappear altogether and alpine tundra takes over. Fully one-third of the park is in this bleak, rocky world, and many of the plants are identical to those found in the Arctic.

Entering the park from Estes Park, it's wise to stop first at **Park Headquarters,** U.S. 36 west of Colo. 66 (☎ **970/586-1206**). There's a good interpretive exhibit here, including a relief model of the park, an audiovisual program, a wide choice of books and maps for sale, and knowledgeable people to answer questions and give advice. In summer, it's open daily from 8am to 9pm; in winter, daily from 8am to 5pm.

JUST THE FACTS

ENTRY POINTS   Entry into the park is from either the east (through Estes Park) or west (through Grand Lake). East and west sides of the park are connected by the Trail Ridge Road, open during summer and early fall, but closed to all motor vehicle travel by snow the rest of the year. Most visitors enter the park from the Estes Park side. The Beaver Meadows Entrance, west of Estes Park via U.S. 36, is the national park's main entrance and the best way to get to the Visitor Center and headquarters. It is also the most direct route to Trail Ridge Road. U.S. 34 west from Estes Park takes you to the Fall River Entrance (north of the Beaver Meadows Entrance), and from there you can access Old Fall River Road or Trail Ridge Road. Heading south from Estes Park on Colo. 7 you can access two trailheads in the southeast corner of the national park, but there are no connecting roads to the main part of the park from those points. These are Longs Peak trailhead—the turnoff is 9 miles south of Estes Park and the trailhead about another mile; and Wild Basin trailhead—another 3^1/$_2$ miles south to the turnoff and then 2^1/$_2$ miles to the trailhead. Those entering the park from the west should take U.S. 40 to Granby and then follow U.S. 34 north to the community of Grand Lake and the park entrance.

FEES   Park admission is $5 per week per vehicle, $3 for bicyclists and pedestrians.

VISITOR CENTERS & INFORMATION   In addition to the park headquarters office (detailed above), there are four visitor centers in the park, all excellent sources

Rocky Mountain National Park

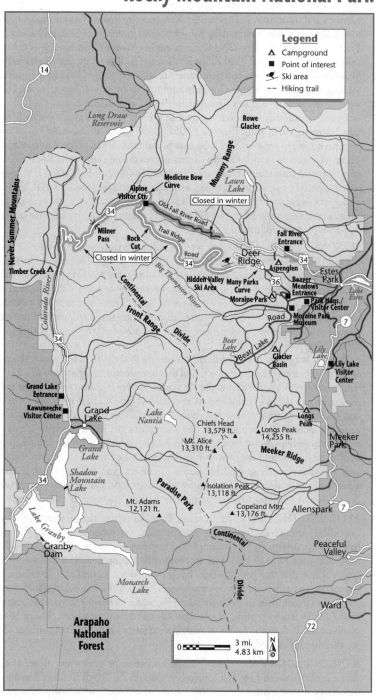

Legend
△ Campground
■ Point of interest
⚡ Ski area
--- Hiking trail

14

Long Draw Reservoir

Rowe Glacier

Mummy Range

Medicine Bow Curve

Alpine Visitor Ctr.

Old Fall River Road

Closed in winter

Lawn Lake

Never Summer Mountains

34

Milner Pass

Rock Cut

Trail Ridge

Road 34

Fall River Entrance

34

Deer Ridge

Closed in winter

Big Thompson River

Hidden Valley Ski Area

Many Parks Curve

Aspenglen

36

Beaver Meadows Entrance

Estes Park

Lake Estes

Timber Creek △

Colorado River

Continental

Front Range

Divide

Moraine Park

Park Hdqs./ Visitor Center

Moraine Park Museum

7

Road

Bear Lake

Bear Lake

△ Glacier Basin

Lily Lake

Lily Lake Visitor Center

Grand Lake Entrance ■

Kawuneeche Visitor Center ■

Grand Lake

Lake Nantia

Chiefs Head 13,579 ft.

Mt. Alice 13,310 ft.

▲ Longs Peak 14,255 ft.

Longs Peak △

Meeker Park

Grand Lake

Shadow Mountain Lake

34

Paradise Park

Mt. Adams 12,121 ft.

▲ Isolation Peak 13,118 ft.

Meeker Ridge

▲ Copeland Mtn. 13,176 ft.

Allenspark

7

Lake Granby

Granby Dam

Continental

Peaceful Valley

Monarch Lake

Divide

Ward

72

Arapaho National Forest

0 3 mi.
   4.83 km

N

for maps and information. They are the **Kawuneeche Visitor Center** (open in summer, daily 7am–7pm; winter, daily 8am–4:30pm), located at the Grand Lake end of Trail Ridge Road (☎ **970/627-3471**); the **Alpine Visitor Center** (open in summer, daily 9am–5pm), just off Trail Ridge Road near Fall River Pass; the **Moraine Park Museum** (open mid-June–mid-September, daily 9am–5pm) on Bear Lake Road; and the **Lily Lake Visitor Center** (open in summer, daily 9am–4:30pm), along Highway 7, 7 miles south of Estes Park near the Wild Basin entrance.

To receive information about the park before you depart, contact **Rocky Mountain National Park,** Estes Park, CO 80517-8397 (☎ **970/586-1206**) for a complete packet of information, including a map, and information on current conditions. Those who want more detailed trip-planning tools should contact the **Rocky Mountain Nature Association** at the park (☎ **800/816-7662** or 970/586-1258), which sells a variety of maps, guides, books, and videos (including some in PAL format). Those who want to help the nonprofit association, and get a 15% discount on purchases at this and many other national parks and monuments, can join. Memberships start at $15 for individuals.

SEASONS   Even though the park is technically open year-round, Trail Ridge Road, the main east-west thoroughfare through the park, is almost always closed in winter. It's safest to assume that you will not be able to drive clear across the park from mid-October until Memorial Day, and even into June it's quite possible that the road will be closed for hours or even a day or more by snow. That's not to say that intrepid travelers can't enjoy the park in winter. All park entrances are open, and roads are plowed to a number of good viewing points and areas for cross-country skiing and snowshoeing.

Weather is a key factor that will affect your trip to the park in any season. Because of its range of high elevations, you'll find that temperatures vary greatly. In summer, temperatures typically climb into the 70s during the day and drop to the 40s at night; the higher into the mountains you go, the cooler it gets. Winters see highs in the 20s and 30s and lows from 10 below zero to 20 above. Spring and fall temperatures are generally midway between summer and winter, but can just as easily be pleasantly warm or bitterly cold and snowy. For this reason, spring and fall are also when you need to be flexible and adjust your itinerary to suit the current conditions. Particularly at higher elevations, windchill factors can be extreme, and hypothermia can be a problem at any time, even in summer when afternoon thunderstorms sometimes occur without warning, often dropping temperatures dramatically and suddenly.

AVOIDING THE CROWDS   Because large portions of the park are hard (if not impossible) to reach during half the year, practically everyone visits during the other half of the year—spring and summer. The very busiest time in the park, though, is from mid-June through mid-August—essentially during school vacations—so just before or just after that period is best. For those who don't mind chilly evenings, late September and early October are less crowded and can be beautiful, although there's always the chance of an early winter storm. Regardless of when you visit, the best way to avoid crowds is by putting on a backpack or climbing onto a horse. Rocky Mountain National Park has 355 miles of trails leading into all corners of the park (see "Seeing the Highlights," below).

RANGER PROGRAMS   Campfire talks and other programs are offered at each visitor center between June and September. Consult the "High Country Headlines" newsletter (free at visitor centers) for scheduled activities, which vary from photo walks to fly-fishing and orienteering.

SEEING THE HIGHLIGHTS

Although Rocky Mountain National Park is generally considered the domain of hikers and climbers, it's surprisingly easy to thoroughly enjoy the park without working up too much of a sweat.

Begin in Estes Park. Drive approximately 4 miles south on U.S. 36 to Bear Lake Road and the **Moraine Park Museum** (open mid-June–mid-September, daily 9am–5pm). Spend a half-hour looking at their excellent natural history exhibits covering the park's geology and botany. This is a good way to learn something about the park before you begin to see it in depth. If, however, capturing calendar-quality photos of the park's spectacular snowcapped mountains and glaciers is your top priority, skip the museum, and start your tour as early in the day as possible. Most of the best views face east, and early morning light is usually best. (There's also less traffic on the roads.)

Continue (or start) along **Bear Lake Road,** one of the few paved roads in the Rockies that leads to a high mountain basin. It's a winding 9-mile-long journey to **Bear Lake,** but well worth it. Along the way, you'll pass glistening waterfalls and have excellent views of Longs Peak (Colorado's highest mountain) and the snowy glaciers ringing the lake.

Once you've had your fill of these sights, head west along Trail Ridge Road to Grand Lake. Built in 1932, Trail Ridge Road is undoubtedly one of America's most scenic highways, providing expansive and sometimes dizzying views in all directions. Allow at least 3 hours for driving its entire 48-mile length, so you can savor it fully. You'll be afforded spectacular vistas of snowcapped peaks, meadows of wildflowers where bighorn sheep, elk, and deer browse, and deep forests.

When you reach Fall River Pass, be sure to stop at the **Alpine Visitor Center** to learn about life on the tundra. The permanent exhibit will explain much of what you're seeing around you. A good place to pull off the road is the **Rock Cut** parking area (elevation 12,110 ft.), just beyond the Visitor Center. The views of glacially carved peaks along the Continental Divide are spectacular, and a short nature trail (1-mile loop) with close-up views of the tundra leaves from here.

If you don't have the time to drive across the park on Trail Ridge Road, consider taking the shorter but scenic **Fall River Road** from Estes Park. The original park road, it leads to Fall River Pass and the Alpine Visitor Center via Horseshoe Park Junction. (Note that west of the Endovalley picnic area, the road is one-way uphill and closed to trailers and motor homes.) As you negotiate Fall River Road's gravelly switchbacks, you'll get a clear idea of what early auto travel was like in the West. Once you've checked out the Alpine Visitor Center, you can return to Estes Park via Trail Ridge Road, a loop that easily can be completed in a couple hours.

WALKS & HIKES   One particularly easy trail is the **Alberta Falls Trail** from the Glacier Gorge parking area (0.6 mile one-way), which only climbs 160 feet. Another easy and scenic walk is the 0.6-mile loop around Bear Lake.

A slightly more difficult option is the **Bierstadt Lake Trail** from the Bear Lake parking area (1.6 miles one-way), which climbs 245 feet in elevation. Yet more challenging (but still only moderately difficult) is the trail from Bear Lake to **Emerald Lake,** which passes Nymph and Dream Lakes en route. The half-mile hike to Nymph Lake is easy, climbing 225 feet; it's the second 0.6 miles to Dream Lake and the final 0.7 miles to Emerald Lake that's more challenging, as you'll have climbed 605 feet from the trailhead by the time you reach Emerald Lake.

Another moderately challenging hike is the relatively uncrowded **Ouzel Falls Trail,** which leaves from Wild Basin Ranger Station and climbs about 950 feet to a picture-perfect waterfall (2.7 miles). Among our favorite hikes in the park is the **Mills Lake**

Trail, a 2.5-mile hike (one-way), with an elevation change of about 700 feet. Starting from Glacier Gorge Junction, it leads to a picturesque mountain lake, nestled in a valley among towering mountain peaks. This is among the best spots for photographing dramatic Longs Peak, and it's the perfect place for a picnic.

A note about the altitude: Don't underestimate how the park's high altitude can wind you. Unless you're in tip-top physical condition, all trails (even the easiest ones) threading from parking areas) take some time for your body to adjust to.

SUMMER AND WARM-WEATHER SPORTS & ACTIVITIES

In addition to what's available within the park, Estes Park and the nearby Roosevelt National Forest are great places for outdoor recreation. To obtain information on hiking, horseback riding, fishing, and other activities in these areas, contact the **Estes-Poudre Ranger District Office,** 148 Remington St. (P.O. Box 2747), Estes Park, CO 80517 (☎ **970/586-3440**).

BACKPACKING & BACKCOUNTRY CAMPING   In summer, the most popular trails are crowded. Ask about lesser-used trails at any ranger station, or pick up one of the several specialized hiking guidebooks for sale at the visitor centers. The visitor centers also carry topographical maps.

The 4.8-mile **Timber Lake Trail** in the western part of the park offers stunning views of timberline lakes and alpine tundra. On it, you'll climb to an elevation of 2,060 feet. Another strenuous trail—only for experienced mountain climbers in top physical condition—is the 8-mile (one-way) **East Longs Peak Trail,** which climbs some 4,855 feet along steep ledges and through narrows to the top of Longs Peak.

Backcountry permits are required for all overnight hikes. They're free at park headquarters and ranger stations; for information, call **970/586-1242.** There is a 7-night backcountry camping limit from June to September, with no more than 3 nights of camping allowed in any one spot. Tents are not permitted in the backcountry in summer.

BICYCLING   Bicyclists share the park's major roadways with motor vehicles. If you're planning a bike trip to the park, bear in mind that these are narrow roads with 5 to 7% grades, and the park is choked with traffic in the peak summer months. As in most national parks, bikes are not permitted off established roads. One popular 16-mile bike ride is the Horseshoe Park/Estes Park Loop, which goes from Estes Park west on U.S. 34 past Aspenglen Campground and the park's Fall River entrance, and then back east at the Deer Ridge Junction, following U.S. 36 through the Beaver Meadows park entrance. There are plenty of beautiful mountain views; allow from 1 to 3 hours to complete this loop. A free park brochure, available at all visitor centers and at park headquarters, provides information on safety and bicycling regulations, in addition to other suggested routes. Tours, rentals, and repairs are available at **Colorado Bicycling,** 184 E. Elkhorn Ave., Estes Park (☎ **970/586-4241**).

BOATING   Small Lake Estes, a half-mile east of Estes Park along U.S. 34, has a marina (☎ **970/586-2011**) that's popular with boaters and fishermen (see also "Fishing," below), although a bit cool for swimming. It's open from Memorial Day to mid-September. Canoe rentals are $10 per hour; paddle boats, $12 per hour; small sport boats, $17 per hour. Seven-person pontoon boats rent for $28 per hour.

FISHING   With a state fishing license, you can fish for four species of trout—brown, rainbow, brook, and cutthroat—in certain streams and lakes in the park. Only artificial lures or flies are permitted. A number of lakes and streams in the national park are closed to fishing, including Bear Lake; a free park brochure, available at all visitor centers, lists all open and closed waters and fishing regulations.

Local trout fishermen also head to Lake Estes. The marina there sells fishing licenses, tackle, gear, and groceries, and rents fishing boats with small outboard motors for $14 per hour.

GOLF There are two nearby courses: **Estes Park Golf Course** (18 holes), 1080 S. St. Vrain St. (☎ **970/586-8146**), which is just off Colo. 7 and charges $30 for 18 holes; and **Lake Estes Executive Golf Course** (nine holes), 690 Big Thompson Hwy. (☎ **970/586-8176**), which is along U.S. 34 east of downtown Estes Park and charges $11 for nine holes.

HORSEBACK RIDING Many of the national park's trails are open to those on horseback, and a number of outfitters provide guided rides, both in and outside the park, ranging from 1 hour (about $17) to all day (about $70). There are also breakfast and dinner rides and multi-day pack trips. Recommended companies include: **Sombrero Ranch Stables,** opposite the Lake Estes dam at 1895 Big Thompson Hwy. (U.S. 34) (☎ **970/586-4577**); **The National Park Village Stables** at the Fall River entrance of the national park on U.S. 34 (☎ **970/586-5269**); and the **Cowpoke Corner Corral,** at Glacier Lodge 3 miles west of town, 2166 Colo. 66 (☎ **970/ 586-5890**). **Hi Country Stables** operates two stables inside the park—call for reservations (**Glacier Creek Stables,** ☎ **970/586-3244;** and **Moraine Park Stables,** ☎ **970/586-2327**).

RIVER RAFTING Although there aren't any major navigable rivers in the immediate vicinity of Rocky Mountain National Park, rafters often head out for trips down the Colorado (to the southwest) and the Poudre (to the northeast). **Rapid Transit Rafting,** P.O. Box 4095, Estes Park, CO 80517 (☎ **970/586-8852**), provides half-day and full-day river trips with transportation from Estes Park, starting at about $40 per person. It's about a 2¹/₂-hour drive to the Colorado River put-in point and about 1¹/₂ hours to the Poudre put-in point.

ROCK CLIMBING **Colorado Mountain School,** P.O. Box 2062, Estes Park, CO 80517 (☎ **970/586-5758**), is a year-round guide service and a national-park–sanctioned technical climbing school that caters to all ages. The most popular climb is Longs Peak (the highest mountain in the park). It can be ascended by novice climbers in good physical condition via the "Keyhole," but its north and east faces are for experts only. Rates vary, and the larger the group the less per person, but base rate for one person for a 1-day excursion is about $200. The school also operates a small store and offers lodging in a hostel-type setting for about $17 per night per person.

WILDLIFE WATCHING Rocky Mountain National Park is a premier wildlife viewing area, and fall, winter, and spring are the best times. Large herds of elk and bighorn sheep are often seen in meadows and on mountainsides. In addition you may see mule deer, beavers, coyotes, and river otters. Watch for moose among the willows on the west side of the park. In the forests there is an abundance of songbirds and small mammals; particularly plentiful are gray and Steller's jays, Clark's nutcrackers, chipmunks, and golden-mantled ground squirrels. There's a good chance of seeing bighorn sheep, marmots, pikas, and ptarmigan along Trail Ridge Road. For detailed and current wildlife viewing information, stop by one of the park's visitor centers, and look into the many interpretive programs, including bird walks.

CROSS-COUNTRY SKIING & OTHER WINTER ACTIVITIES

A popular place for **cross-country skiing** and **snowshoeing** in the park is Bear Lake, south of the Beaver Meadows entrance. A lesser-known but beautiful area is Wild Basin, south of the park's east entrances off Colo. 7, about 1 mile north of the community of Allenspark. On weekends, the Colorado Mountain Club often opens a warming hut near the trailhead, and rangers often lead guided snowshoeing walks. It's possible to explore the high country; just be aware that instant storms and avalanches can occur. Before you set forth, stop by park headquarters for maps, information on where the snow is best, and a permit if you plan to stay out overnight. Ski rentals, instruction, and guide service are available from **Colorado Mountain School,** P.O. Box 2062, Estes Park, CO 80517 (☎ **970/586-5758**).

Snowmobiling is permitted on the west side of the park only, accessible only from Grand Lake in winter. Register at the **Kawuneeche Visitor Center** (☎ **970/ 627-3471**). The park's speed limit for snowmobiles is 25 m.p.h.

CAMPING

The park has five campgrounds with a total of 589 sites. Nearly half (247) are at **Moraine Park;** another 150 are at **Glacier Basin. Moraine Park, Timber Creek** (100 sites), and **Longs Peak** (26 tent sites) are open year-round; Glacier Basin and **Aspenglen** (54 sites) are seasonal. Camping is limited to 3 days at Longs Peak and 7 days at other campgrounds. Moraine Park and Glacier Basin require reservations if you're visiting between Memorial Day and early September. Contact **Destinet,** 9450 Carroll Park Dr., San Diego, CA 92121-2256, or call **800/365-2267** up to 5 months in advance. Arrive early in summer if you hope to snare one of the first-come, first-served campsites. Campsites cost $10 to $12 per night during the summer; $6 in the off-season. No showers or R.V. hookups are available.

3 Steamboat Springs

A resort town that effectively fuses two very different worlds—a state-of-the-art ski village with a genuine western ranching center—Steamboat is where ranchers still go about their business in cowboy boots and Stetsons, seemingly unaware of the fashion statement they are making to city-slicker visitors.

Numerous mineral springs and abundant wild game made this a summer retreat for Utes centuries before the arrival of white settlers. Mid–19th-century trappers swore they heard the chugging sound of "a steamboat comin' round the bend" until investigation revealed a bubbling mineral spring. Prospectors never thrived here as they did elsewhere in the Rockies, though coal mining has proven profitable. Ranching and farming—cattle and sheep, hay, wheat, oats, and barley—were the economic mainstays until tourism arrived, yet agriculture remains of key importance today.

But this area is perhaps best known as the birthplace of organized skiing in Colorado. Although miners, ranchers, and mail carriers used primitive skis as a means of transportation as early as the late 1880s, it wasn't until a Norwegian ski-jumping and cross-country champion, Carl Howelsen, built a ski jump here in 1914 (Howelsen Hill) that skiing began to be considered a recreational sport in Colorado. In 1963, a nearby mountain, Storm Mountain, was developed for skiing, and Steamboat's future as a modern ski resort was ensured. Renamed Mount Werner after the 1964 avalanche death in Europe of Olympic skier Buddy Werner, a Steamboat Springs native and staunch supporter of developing Storm Mountain into a full-fledged resort, today the mountain is managed by the Steamboat Ski & Resort Corporation and, more often than not, is called simply Steamboat. Howelsen Hill continues to operate primarily as a facility for ski jumpers, but is owned by the city of Steamboat Springs.

ESSENTIALS

GETTING THERE   By Car   The most direct route to Steamboat Springs from Denver is to take I-70 west 68 miles to Silverthorne, Colo. 9 north 38 miles to Kremmling, and U.S. 40 west 52 miles to Steamboat. (*Note:* Rabbit Ears Pass, 25 miles east of Steamboat, can be treacherous in winter.) If you're traveling east on I-70, exit at Rifle, proceed 88 miles north on Colo. 13 to Craig, then take U.S. 40 east 42 miles to Steamboat. For statewide road-condition reports, call 303/639-1234.

By Plane   The **Steamboat Springs Airport,** 3 miles northwest of town on Elk River Road (☎ **970/879-9042**), serves charter and private flights. The **Yampa Valley Regional Airport,** 22 miles west of Steamboat Springs near Hayden (☎ **970/ 276-3669**), is served by **Mesa Airlines/United Express** (☎ **800/241-6522** or 970/ 276-4116). Ground transportation is provided by **Alpine Taxi-Limo** (☎ **800/ 343-7433** or 970/879-8294), **Steamboat Express** (☎ **970/879-3400**), and **Western Coach Limousine Service** (☎ **970/870-0771**). Local car-rental agencies include **Avis** (☎ **970/879-3785**) and **Alamo** (☎ **800/327-9633**). At Yampa Valley Regional Airport (see below), look for **Avis** (☎ **970/276-4377**) and **Dollar** (☎ **970/ 276-3702**).

By Airport Shuttle   **Steamboat Express,** 1401 Lincoln Ave. (☎ **800/525-BOAT** or 2628 or 970/879-3400), a service of Panorama Coaches, travels daily December through April between Denver International and Steamboat Springs.

ORIENTATION   There are really two Steamboats. The ski resort, known as Steamboat Village, is about 2 miles southeast of the historic Steamboat Springs, a division that seems to work well for everyone. If you're coming from Denver, U.S. 40 approaches Steamboat from the south and parallels the Yampa River through town. Mount Werner Road, which turns east off U.S. 40, leads directly to the resort community, centered around Mount Werner Circle and Ski Time Square. U.S. 40 is known as Lincoln Avenue through the town of Steamboat, where it is crossed by Third through 13th streets. You'll cross the Yampa River to Howelsen Hill and River Road if you turn left on Fifth Street, wind uphill to the Strawberry Park Hot Springs if you turn right on Seventh Street, and find your way to the Steamboat Springs Airport and Steamboat Lake if you turn right on Elk River Road (County Rd. 129), half a mile beyond 13th.

VISITOR INFORMATION   The **Steamboat Springs Chamber Resort Association,** 1255 S. Lincoln Ave. (P.O. Box 774408), Steamboat Springs, CO 80477 (☎ **970/879-0880**), provides visitor information.

GETTING AROUND   **Steamboat Springs Transit** (☎ **970/879-5585**) provides free rides throughout the area. During ski season, buses run every 15 minutes during peak hours; during the rest of the year, buses run less frequently, about once every half hour during peak travel times. **Steamboat Express** (☎ **970/870-0771**) and **Alpine Taxi-Limo** (☎ **970/879-8294**) provide taxi service.

FAST FACTS   In case of **emergency,** call **911. Routt Memorial Hospital,** 80 Park Ave., off Seventh Street (☎ **970/879-1322**), provides 24-hour medical service. The **post office** is at 200 Lincoln Ave. (☎ **970/879-0363**). For **road information,** call 970/879-1260. **State and local taxes** add about 9% to hotel bills.

SPECIAL EVENTS   Area events include the Cowboy Downhill, during the second week of January; the Winter Carnival, in early February; the Yampa River Festival, in early June; Western Heritage Weekend, in mid-June; Cowboy Roundup Days, over the Fourth of July weekend; the Vintage Auto Race, over the Labor Day weekend; Fall Foliage Festival, in late September; and the Torchlight Parade, on New Year's Eve.

SKIING & OTHER WINTER ACTIVITIES

STEAMBOAT   When devoted skiers describe Steamboat, they practically invent adjectives to describe its incredibly light powder.

Four peaks comprise Mount Werner. Christie Peak, the lower mountain area, is ideal for beginners. Thunderhead Peak, served by a silver-bullet gondola, is mainly suitable for intermediate skiers. Three separate restaurants, not including the ski-school cafeteria, are located at the gondola terminal. Storm Peak accesses the extreme "Chutes" area, advanced mogul runs and powder bowls, as well as "Buddy's Run," one of the Rockies' great intermediate cruisers. The most famous tree runs—"Shadows" and "Twilight"—are on Sunshine Peak, along with more bump runs and cruising slopes. In Rendezvous Saddle, midmountain at the foot of "High Noon," are two more restaurants. New for the 1996-to-1997 season, Morningside Park includes 179 acres on the back of Storm Peak, with intermediate to advanced terrain served by a new triple chair.

The vertical drop here is among the highest in Colorado: 3,668 feet from the 10,568-foot summit. Skiable terrain of 2,679 acres (61% groomable) includes 113 named runs, served by 21 lifts—the eight-passenger gondola, one quad chair, two express quad chairs, seven triple chairs, seven double chairs, and three surface lifts.

At press time, lift tickets were $44 per day for adults; $25 per day for youths; seniors 70 and over ski free. Rates are subject to change. Lessons and rentals are available, and the resort also has cross-country skiing and snowboarding.

Steamboat is open from Thanksgiving to Easter, daily 8:30am to 4pm. For further information, contact **Steamboat Ski & Resort Corporation,** 2305 Mt. Werner Circle, Steamboat Springs, CO 80487 (☎ **800/922-2722** or 970/879-6111). For daily ski reports, dial 970/879-7300; fax 970/879-4757.

HOWELSEN HILL   In addition to Steamboat, there's Howelsen Hill (☎ **970/ 879-8499**), which has remained open every winter since it first opened in 1915. The first accredited public-school ski classes in North America were taught on this slope. It offers both day and night skiing on its 30 acres of terrain served by a double chair, a poma lift, and a pony tow. Its rises 440 feet to a 7,136-foot summit elevation. Tickets (1995–96 rates) were $10 for adults, $5 for children 12 and under (11am–10pm Mon–Fri, Sat–Sun 9am–10pm).

Howelsen Hill has bred more North American skiers for international competition than any other—primarily because of its ski-jumping complex. The U.S. ski-jumping team trains each year on the 20-, 30-, 50-, 70-, and 90-meter jumps.

CROSS-COUNTRY SKIING   Seasoned cross-country skiers swear by the **Steamboat Ski Touring Center** at the Sheraton Steamboat Resort and Conference Center, Clubhouse Road (☎ **970/879-8180**). Some 25 kilometers (15 miles) of groomed cross-country trails are set across the fairways beside Fish Creek, near the foot of the mountain. Fees start at $8 for a half-day (beginning at 1pm) to $10 for a full day; equipment rentals and lessons are also available.

Popular cross-country skiing trails in nearby national forest land include **Rabbit Ears Pass,** 25 miles east of Steamboat on U.S. 40, and **Dunkley Pass,** 25 miles south on Colo. 131. For trail maps and information, contact **Medicine Bow-Routt National Forest,** Hahns Peak/Bears Ears Ranger Station, 57 10th St. (P.O. Box

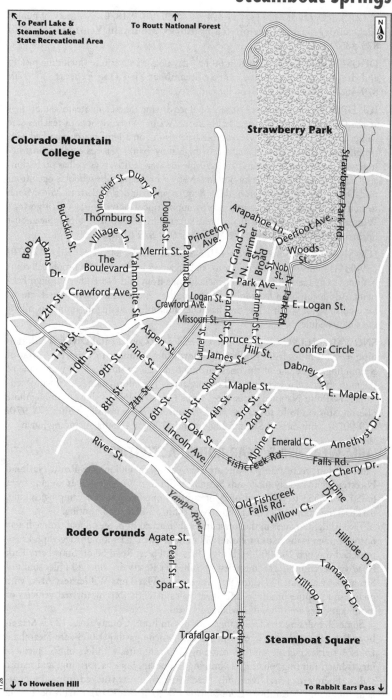

Steamboat Springs

To Pearl Lake &
Steamboat Lake
State Recreational Area

To Routt National Forest

N

Strawberry Park

Colorado Mountain
College

Strawberry Park Rd.

Uncochief St. Duary St.

Douglas St.

Thornburg St.

Buckskin St.

Village Ln.

Bob
Adams
Dr.

The
Boulevard

Merrit St.

Pawintab

Princeton Ave.

Arapahoe Ln.

Deerfoot Ave.

Woods St.

N. Grand St.

N. Larimer St.

Broad St.

Nob St.

N. Park Rd.

Yahmonite St.

Crawford Ave.

Crawford Ave.

12th St.

Logan St.

Park Ave.

N. Grand St.

Larimer St.

E. Logan St.

Missouri St.

Spruce St.

Hill St.

Conifer Circle

11th St.

10th St.

9th St.

8th St.

Aspen St.

Pine St.

7th St.

Laurel St.

James St.

Short St.

Dabney Ln.

E. Maple St.

Maple St.

6th St.

5th St.

4th St.

3rd St.

2nd St.

Oak St.

Lincoln Ave.

Alpine Ct.

Emerald Ct.

Amethyst Dr.

Fishcreek Rd.

Falls Rd.

Cherry Dr.

River St.

Lupine Dr.

Old Fishcreek
Falls Rd.

Willow Ct.

Yampa River

Rodeo Grounds

Agate St.

Hillside Dr.

Pearl St.

Spar St.

Tamarack Dr.

Hilltop Ln.

Lincoln Ave.

Trafalgar Dr.

Steamboat Square

1126

To Howelsen Hill

To Rabbit Ears Pass

217

771212), Steamboat Springs, CO 80477 (☎ **970/879-1870**). A variety of guided backcountry ski tours are offered by **Rocky Mountain Ventures** (☎ **970/ 879-4857**).

DOGSLEDDING   For a delightful half-day dogsled adventure (including pickup and drop-off at your hotel), contact **Steamboat Sled Dog Express** (☎ **970/ 879-4662**), which charges $165 for one or two people.

ICE DRIVING   America's first school of ice driving is based in Steamboat Springs at the foot of Mount Werner. Bridgestone Winter Driving School teaches safe winter driving the smartest way possible—hands-on, on a 1-mile circuit packed with frozen water and snow, and guarded by high snow banks. Classes combine instruction with on-track practice, and are available for average drivers as well as professionals. Classes range from $120 for 3 hours to $695 for 2 days. The school is open from mid-December to mid-March, daily 8am to 5pm, and closed from Mid-March to mid-December. Course admission by appointment only. Contact **Bridgestone Winter Driving School,** 1850 Ski Time Square Dr. (P.O. Box 774167), Steamboat Springs, CO 80477 (☎ **800/WHYSKID** or 970/879-6104).

ICE-SKATING   **The Howelsen Ice-Skating Rink,** 243 River Rd. (☎ **970/ 879-0341**), rents skates, offers lessons, and organizes ice-hockey and broomball competitions. The ice-skating season generally runs from mid-November through February. Admission is $3 for adults, $2 for youths 17 and under; skate rentals are $2 for adults, $1 for youths. The rink has roller and in-line skating in summer. Call for the rink schedule.

SNOWMOBILING   Snowmobilers consider the **Continental Divide Trail,** running over 50 miles from Buffalo Pass north of Steamboat to Gore Pass, west of Kremmling, to be one of the finest maintained trails in the Rockies, with some of the most spectacular scenery you'll see anywhere. For information, check with Medicine Bow-Routt National Forest (see "Cross-Country Skiing," above). Among those offering **snowmobile tours** are **High Mountain Snowmobile Tours** (☎ **970/ 879-9073**), with rates of $65 for 2 hours and $100 for 4 hours, including lunch.

WARM-WEATHER & YEAR-ROUND ACTIVITIES

Most outdoor recreation pursuits are enjoyed in 1.1-million-acre **Routt National Forest,** which virtually surrounds Steamboat Springs. With elevations ranging from 6,750 to 13,553 feet, the national forest offers opportunities for camping, hiking, backpacking, mountain biking, horseback riding, fishing, and hunting.

Two wilderness areas in the forest are easily reached from Steamboat. Immediately north of town is the **Mount Zirkel Wilderness Area,** a region of rugged peaks approached through 10,800-foot Buffalo Pass, on Forest Road 60 off Strawberry Park Road via Seventh Street. Southwest of Stillwater Reservoir, some 40 miles south of Steamboat via Colo. 131 through Yampa, is the **Flat Tops Wilderness Area,** with picturesque alpine meadows and sheer volcanic cliffs. No motorized vehicles or mountain bikes are allowed in wilderness areas.

Some 28 miles north of Steamboat Springs on Routt County Road 129 is **Steamboat Lake State Park** (☎ **970/879-3922**), encompassing 1,053-acre Steamboat Lake. Activities include summer camping (183 campsites with fees of $6), picnicking, fishing, hunting, boating, swimming, canoeing, horseback riding, and nature walks. There's an attractive sandy beach (the sand was trucked in) and a boat-launching ramp. **Steamboat Lake Marina** (☎ **970/879-7019**), usually open from mid-May through September, has a small store, boat fuel, and boat rentals. Canoes and paddle boats start at $12 for 2 hours; small fishing boats cost $25 for 2 hours; and pontoon boats cost $50 for 2 hours. In winter, there's ice fishing, cross-country skiing, snowmobiling, and snowshoeing. Day-use fee is $3 per vehicle.

BICYCLING & MOUNTAIN BIKING   The 5-mile, dual-surface **Yampa River Trail** connects downtown Steamboat Springs with Steamboat Village, and links area parks and national forest trails. The **Mount Werner Trail** links the river to the ski area, which has numerous slopes open to mountain bikers in summer. **Spring Creek Trail** climbs from Yampa River Park into Routt National Forest. Touring enthusiasts can try their road bikes on the 110-mile loop over Rabbit Ears and Gore passes, rated one of the 10 most scenic rides in America by *Bicycling* magazine.

Stop at **Sore Saddle Cyclery,** 1136 Yampa St. (☎ **970/879-1675**), for information on the best local trails (maps are on display), accessories, repairs, and rentals ($12 for a half-day, $18 for a full day). This full-service bike shop also has a manufacturing plant for Moots Cycles, handmade titanium road and mountain bikes that are sold worldwide (about $4,500). Ask for a free tour of the facility.

BOATING   See description of Steamboat Lake State Park above.

CATTLE DRIVES   **Broken Skull Cattle Company,** 47080 Routt County Rd. 129, Steamboat Springs, CO 80487-9417 (☎ **970/879-0090**), is a working cattle ranch—not some Hollywood-style dude ranch—that offers a genuine Old West experience. Each July its herd of longhorns is taken some 50 miles into the mountains to summer pasture, and in September the herd is brought back to the Steamboat Springs ranch. On each 9-day trip, up to 10 greenhorns ride and work alongside seasoned cowboys, sleep in tents, and eat chuck-wagon grub. Cost is $1,300 for the entire 9 days or $150 per day for those who want to join for only part of the drive.

FISHING   There are nearly 150 lakes and reservoirs and almost 600 miles of streams in Routt County. Trout—rainbow, brown, brook, and cutthroat—are prolific. Contact **Straightline Outdoor Sports,** 744 Lincoln Ave. (☎ **800/354-5463** or 970/879-7568), for information, licenses, and either rental or purchase of equipment. Straightline also offers guide services—a half-day float on the Yampa costs $175 for two people—and schedules free casting classes several evenings each week.

Visitors are welcome year-round at the **Finger Rock Fish-Rearing Unit** of the Colorado Department of Wildlife, 5 miles south of Yampa on Colo. 131 (☎ **970/638-4490**). This hatchery has exhibits on fish-raising, and visitors can feed the fish and examine the raceways, tanks, and other facilities. There's also a public fishing pond on the property, stocked with rainbow trout, that is open during daylight hours from late spring through fall.

GOLF   The course at **Sheraton Steamboat Resort and Conference Center,** Clubhouse Drive (☎ **970/879-2220**), designed by Robert Trent Jones, Jr. in 1972, is considered one of the Rockies' finest. The 18-hole, 6,906-yard course offers spectacular scenery and challenging fairways. Greens fees from mid-May through September are $55 for Sheraton guests, $80 for the public; from April to mid-May, and October until it's closed by snow, it's $40 for Sheraton guests, $55 for the public. There are discounts for late-afternoon tee times. Call for information on lessons, clinics, and packages.

HIKING & BACKPACKING   There are numerous trails in the **Mount Zirkel Wilderness Area,** immediately north of Steamboat, and the **Flat Tops Wilderness Area,** 48 miles southwest. An especially scenic 4-hour hike in the Flat Tops area takes you from Stillwater Reservoir to the Devil's Causeway, with unforgettable views. Contact the U.S. Forest Service for maps and additional information.

HORSEBACK RIDING   Several area ranches offer trail rides by the hour, half day, full day, or overnight, including **Del's Triangle 3 Ranch,** 55675 County Rd. 62 in Clark (☎ **970/879-3495**); and **Sunset Ranch,** 42850 County Rd. 129 (☎ **970/879-0954**). Typical adult rates are $18 for a 1-hour ride, $55 for a half day, and $85 for a full day, including lunch. Also see "Cattle Drives," above.

HOT SPRINGS   More than 150 mineral springs are located in and around the Steamboat Springs area. Black, Heart, Iron, Lithia, Soda, Sulphur, and Steamboat—the springs for which the town was named—are located in city parks. Their healing and restorative qualities were recognized for centuries by Utes, and James Crawford, the area's first white settler, regularly bathed in Heart Spring and helped build the first log bathhouse over it in 1884.

Today, Heart Spring is part of the **Steamboat Springs Health & Recreation complex,** 136 Lincoln Ave. (☎ **970/879-1828**), in downtown Steamboat Springs. In addition to the man-made pools into which the spring's waters flow, there's a lap pool, water slide, spa, whirlpool, weight room, and massage therapy. Pool admission is $5 for adults, $3.50 for youths 13 to 17, and $2 for children under 13 and seniors 62 and over. Suit and towel rentals are available. It's open year-round, Monday to Friday from 6:30am to 9:45pm, and Saturdays and Sundays from 8am to 9:45pm. The slide is open noon to 6pm in summer and 4 to 8pm in winter. The complex also has tennis courts ($6 per hour).

The **Hot Springs at Strawberry Park,** 44200 County Rd. 36 (☎ **970/879-0342**), are 7 miles north of downtown. It's a wonderful experience to spend a moonlit evening in a sandy-bottomed, rock-lined soaking pool, kept between 102° and 104°, with snow piled high around you. Follow Strawberry Park Road, off Park Avenue via Seventh Street. Open daily from 10am to midnight, daytime admission is $5; Sunday through Thursday nights are $7; and Friday and Saturday it's $10. Massages are available, and cabins can be rented year-round at $40 per night; tent sites at $30 per night.

A free city parks department brochure, "The Springs of Steamboat: A Walking Tour," will acquaint you with other local mineral springs.

KAYAKING   **Mountain Sport Kayak School** offers kayaking lessons—from beginner to advanced—starting at $45 (including all equipment) for a half-day. The school, in business since 1980, conducts a number of children's programs, is affiliated with the Yampa River Festival, and rents and sells equipment.

MOUNTAINEERING   There's plenty of year-round action here. **Backdoor Sports of Steamboat,** 811 Yampa St. (☎ **970/879-6249**), may be your best resource. You can schedule a guided climb with them or ask for a recommendation. They also provide maps and equipment rentals.

RODEO   The **Steamboat Springs PRCA Summer Prorodeo Series** (☎ **970/879-1818**) takes place each year from mid-June to Labor Day at Howelsen Park. Professional rodeo cowboys and cowgirls compete in bull riding, bareback and saddle bronco riding, steer wrestling, calf roping, team roping, and barrel racing. In the Wrangler Calf Scramble, children are invited to try to pluck a ribbon from the tail of a calf. Admission costs $9 for anyone over age 12; free for those 12 and younger.

SWIMMING   See "Hot Springs," above.

THE FESTIVAL SCENE

Summer is a busy time for the performing arts in Steamboat. **Strings in the Mountains Festival of Music,** P.O. Box 774627, Steamboat Springs, CO 80477 (☎ **970/879-5056**), offers five performances a week (daily except Wed and Sun) for 6 weeks, from early July to mid-August, in the Performing Arts Tent at Torian Plum Plaza, featuring award-winning classical and jazz musicians. Tickets for the Monday and Tuesday evening concerts cost $5 to $17; admission to the Thursday night chamber music concerts costs $11 to $14; Friday night programs of jazz, country, bluegrass or other genres cost $17; and Saturday night chamber music concerts cost $12 to $15. Wednesday at noon there is a free lecture, and Monday at 1pm are Youth Concerts for ages 4 to 18 with $1 admission.

Strings in the Mountains overlaps with the **Perry-Mansfield Performing Arts Camp,** at 40755 County Rd. 36 (☎ **970/879-7125**), whose alumni include actors Dustin Hoffman and Lee Remick and dancer José Limon. The camp, for youths 10 through college age, has operated continually since 1913. There are programs offering classes in ballet, modern and jazz dance, repertoire, acting, musical theater, voice, art, English and western horseback riding, and creative writing. The public is invited to various performances, including the "Perry-Mansfield Follies" and "An Evening of Dance."

OTHER THINGS TO SEE & DO

You can learn about Steamboat's history at the **Lodge at Howelsen Hill** (☎ **970/ 879-4300**), where there's an informative exhibit on the building of the ski jump (open daily 8am–10pm, free admission); and the ✪ **Tread of Pioneers Museum** (800 Oak St., ☎ **970/879-2214**), a beautifully restored Victorian home that features exhibits on pioneer ranch life, the Utes, and 100 years of skiing history. Museum admission is $2.50 for adults, $2 for seniors, and $1 for children 6 to 12; open daily from 11am to 5pm. While there, ask for a copy of the **Steamboat Springs self-guided historical walking tour.** Among other places, it directs you to **The Eleanor Bliss Center for the Arts at the Depot** (13th St. and Stockbridge Rd. between the Yampa River and the railroad tracks, (☎ **970/879-9008**), a pleasant art gallery and gift shop located in a historic (1908) train depot. Home of the Steamboat Arts Council, which coordinates music, dance, theater, and visual-arts activities in the upper Yampa Valley, the Depot Gallery has changing exhibits and shows of local and regional artists. Performances take place in the community auditorium in the newly remodeled baggage room. Admission is free; hours are Monday to Friday 9am to 5pm and some weekends.

Just 4 miles from downtown in Routt National Forest is a breathtaking 283-foot waterfall, **Fish Creek Falls**—perfect for a picnic. To reach the short footpath that leads to the falls, turn right off Lincoln Avenue onto Third Street; go one block; and turn right again onto Fish Creek Falls Road. Follow the signs.

If you've got kids in tow, a visit to the **nature center at Casey's Pond** will give them a better understanding of the natural and cultural history of the Yampa Valley. It's run by the Steamboat Springs Parks & Recreation Department; call 970/ 879-4300 for further information.

SHOPPING

Lincoln Avenue, between 5th and 9th streets, is where most of the more interesting shops and galleries are located. You won't find many bargains here, but a number of shops sell memorable merchandise. Art lovers will enjoy **Artisans' Market of Steamboat** (☎ **970/879-7512**), 626 Lincoln Ave., a nonprofit cooperative of local artists; and **Steamboat Art Company** (☎ **970/879-3383**), 903 Lincoln Ave., which offers western art, jewelry, and crafts in wood, glass, and pottery. **The Homesteader,** 821 Lincoln Ave. (☎ **970/879-5880**), is a delightful kitchen shop with gourmet coffee, espresso, and cappuccino.

If you forgot to pack your cowboy hat, there's a tremendous selection of Stetsons, plus just about everything else a Westerner wears, at **F. M. Light & Sons,** 826 Lincoln Ave. (☎ **970/879-1822**). And while hardware stores might not be on everyone's list of tourist sites, take a few minutes to stop at **Bogg's Hardware,** established in 1939, at 730 Lincoln Ave. (☎ **970/879-6250**), where you'll find snowshoes, art and antiques, and just about every kitchen gizmo ever made.

Lyon's Corner Drug & Soda Fountain, at the corner of Ninth and Lincoln (☎ **970/879-1114**), is not only a drugstore and card shop; it also has a great old Wurlitzer jukebox spinning golden oldies and an old-time soda fountain where you can get real malts, ice-cream sodas, egg creams, phosphates, sundaes, and fresh-squeezed lemonade.

WHERE TO STAY

As at all Colorado ski resorts, rates are highest during the Christmas holiday season: mid-December through New Year's Day. Next highest are the rates charged during February and March (the season). Value season is usually January, and the low season runs from Thanksgiving until mid-December and from April until the ski areas close. Rates are normally much lower during the summer, from Memorial Day to mid-October. Because vacancy rates are so high during shoulder seasons—April to May and October to November—many accommodations close at these times.

Steamboat Reservation Services (☎ **800/922-2722**) can book your lodging and make other travel arrangements.

VERY EXPENSIVE

Château Chamonix. 2340 Apres Ski Way, Steamboat Springs, CO 80487. ☎ **800/833-9877** or 970/879-7511. Fax 970/879-9321. 27 units. TV TEL. Two-bedroom (double), $140–$150 summer, $495–$520 winter; three-bedroom (double), $170–$190 summer, $600–$630 winter. Holiday rates higher; discounts possible between seasons. AE, MC, V. Free parking, covered lot.

Located a few steps from the base of the Silver Bullet gondola, this is one of the most convenient accommodations at Steamboat Village. Two buildings have condominium units with private decks facing the slopes. All have fireplaces, fully equipped kitchens with refrigerators, washers and dryers, wet bars, VCRs, and furnishings of pine, walnut, or oak. Most units are two-bedroom suites, with twin beds in one room, a king bed in the master bedroom, and a whirlpool tub in the adjoining bathroom. Local calls are free. There are a swimming pool, outdoor hot tub, sauna, ski lockers, and conference facilities for 70.

Torian Plum at Steamboat. 1855 Ski Time Square Dr., Steamboat Springs, CO 80487. ☎ **800/228-2458** or 970/879-8811. Fax 970/879-8485. 47 units. TV TEL. One to three bedroom units, $120–$195 summer, $195–$365 early and late ski season, $415–$780 regular ski season, $520–$920 holiday season. AE, MC, V. Free parking in underground lot.

These slope-side ski-in/ski-out condominiums have handsome light-wood furnishings, a fully equipped tile kitchen (with microwave and dishwasher), washer/dryer, whirlpool tub, gas fireplace, private balcony, cable TV with VCR, and ski locker.

The manager is Steamboat Premier Properties, Ltd., which also operates the neighboring Bronze Tree and Trappeur's Crossing condominium developments, with equivalent facilities.

Services during ski season include concierge, shuttle van, bell staff, and 24-hour front desk; more limited services at other times. There's an outdoor heated swimming pool, outdoor and indoor hot tubs, sauna, four tennis courts, and VCR and video rentals.

EXPENSIVE

The Ranch at Steamboat. 1 Ranch Rd. (off Clubhouse Dr.), Steamboat Springs, CO 80487. ☎ **800/525-2002** or 970/879-3000. Fax 970/879-5409. 88 units. TV TEL. Rates are $110–$195 double summer; $120–$175 regular ski season. Higher rates on winter holidays. AE, MC, V. Free parking, private garages.

Spread across a 36-acre hillside on Burgess Creek, not far from Ski Time Square, these impressive condominiums offer a peaceful, quiet location. The two-story condo units have full kitchens (including microwaves), large fireplaces, private barbecue decks, and washer/dryer facilities. There's a direct entrance from the private garage into the kitchen. Local phone calls cost 50¢.

There are shuttle vans during ski season. Facilities include a swimming pool, hot tub, sauna, recreation center, four tennis courts, game room, and meeting facilities for 200.

✪ **Sheraton Steamboat Resort.** 2200 Village Inn Court, Steamboat Springs, CO 80477. ☎ **800/848-8878** or 970/879-2220. Fax 970/879-7686. 270 rms, 29 suites and condos. A/C TV TEL. Late May–mid-Oct, $89–$109; winter, low-season $99–$179, value season $179–$259, Christmas and regular season $209–$289. Children under 17 stay free in parents' room in summer. AE, CB, DC, MC, V. Free parking in underground lot. Closed 1 month in spring and fall.

Steamboat Springs' premier hotel is located in the heart of Ski Time Square, at the foot of the Silver Bullet gondola. The Sheraton opens directly onto the ski slopes, and every room has a view of the mountain, valley, or slopes. In summer, sports lovers enjoy its golf club, one of the finest in the Rockies.

Opened in the mid-1970s, the hotel was fully renovated in 1994 in a combination western and alpine decor. Most rooms have one king or two queen beds, a private balcony, in-room movies, and a large closet with full mirror doors. All have coffeemakers, humidifiers, and minirefrigerators.

Remington's restaurant has a view straight up the Headwall chair lift. Breakfast (6:30–11am) and dinner (5:30–10pm) are served daily. The restaurant has Steamboat's largest soup-and-salad bar; steak, seafood, and poultry dishes run $11.75 to $18.95. Buddy's Run, open winters only, serves breakfast and lunch from 8am to 5pm; in the early evening, it's a comedy club. The hotel also has a sports bar and a pastry shop. Room service (7am–10pm), a concierge (8am–6pm), valet and guest laundry services, and a children's summer day-camp program are available. Facilities include a cross-country ski course and golf club (see "Skiing & Other Winter Activities" and "Warm-Weather & Year-Round Activities," respectively, above), year-round heated swimming pool, hot tubs, saunas, massage, game room, gift-and-sundry shop, ski storage and rental, and meeting facilities for 600.

MODERATE

✪ **The Harbor Hotel.** 703 Lincoln Ave. (P.O. Box 774109), Steamboat Springs, CO 80477. ☎ **800/543-8888** out of state, 800/334-1012 within Colorado or 970/879-1522. Fax 970/879-1737. 65 units. TV TEL. $55–$100 double Easter–Thanksgiving, $58–$107 in low ski season, $95–$169 in value and regular seasons, $163–$285 holiday season; $90–$120 condos in summer and low-season, $145–$215 in value and regular seasons, $266–$338 holiday season. Rates include continental breakfast. AE, CB, DC, DISC, MC, V. Free off-street parking.

A European-style hotel built in 1939, the Harbor has expanded in recent years with an adjoining motel and condominium complex. Guests enter the hotel through polished bronze doors from a turn-of-the-century London bank, and register in a small, antique-filled lobby.

Each of the 15 hotel guest rooms has a different decor, with period furnishings; motel units are basic and economical; and the condos have well-equipped kitchens with stoves, microwaves, and refrigerators. Local phone calls cost 50¢.

Services and facilities include free winter shuttle pass, ski and bicycle storage, two Jacuzzis, sauna, steam room, coin-operated laundry, gift shop, and boutique. Pets are accepted in the summer, with some restrictions.

Sky Valley Lodge. 31490 E. U.S. 40 (P.O. Box 3132), Steamboat Springs, CO 80477. ☎ **800/ 538-7519** or 970/879-7749. Fax 970/879-7752. 24 rms. TV TEL. Late May–Thanksgiving, $68– $98 double. Winter, $108–$168 double. Extra person $10. Rates include breakfast—full in ski season, continental the rest of the year. AE, CB, DC, DISC, MC, V. Free parking. Closed mid-Apr–late May.

Located below Rabbit Ears Pass with a spectacular view of the upper Yampa River Valley, this lodge—actually two rustic lodges, 8$\frac{1}{2}$ miles east of Steamboat Springs— offers country-manor charm in a woodsy setting, where guests can relax around a big fireplace in the lobby.

Each room is a bit different, but all have an old-fashioned ski-lodge atmosphere. Only four units have full baths; others have showers only, and sinks are in the bedroom. There are king and queen brass beds, wood beds, and several daybeds; floral decor predominates. Guests snuggle into feather beds in winter. Local calls cost 50¢.

Gourmet family-style dinners are served Wednesday through Sunday in winter, with a choice of three main courses each night. A full bar opens at 3pm daily. Services and facilities include a shuttle to the Ptarmigan Inn at the foot of the ski slopes, where equipment can be stored; outdoor hot tub; coed saunas; and game room. Pets are permitted, with restrictions. The lodge is nonsmoking.

INEXPENSIVE

The Inn at Steamboat Bed & Breakfast. 3070 Columbine Dr. (P.O. Box 775084), Steamboat Springs, CO 80477. ☎ **800/872-2601** or 970/879-2600. Fax 970/879-9270. 31 rms, 1 suite. TV TEL. Double, $69–$85 summer, $69–$139 winter; additional person $10, children under 13 free. AE, DISC, MC, V. Free parking.

A large ranch-style bed-and-breakfast, the inn is one of the least expensive accommodations in the Steamboat Village area. Etched-pine decor and a large stone fireplace add flair. The inn has an outdoor swimming pool, sauna, service bar, self-serve laundry, VCR and video rental, and game room, and offers ski-tuning and a private ski shuttle.

Rooms are spacious, with queen and double beds, and sliding glass doors lead to private decks. Local phone calls are free. Rates include an extensive continental breakfast spring through fall and a full breakfast in winter, served in the quaint dining room. The entire inn is nonsmoking.

Steamboat Bed & Breakfast. 442 Pine St. (P.O. Box 775888), Steamboat Springs, CO 80477. ☎ **970/879-5724.** 7 rms. Mid-Apr–mid-Nov, $75–$85 double. Mid-Nov–mid-Apr $105–$135 double. Rates include full breakfast. AE, DISC, MC, V. Off-street parking.

Steamboat Springs' first house of worship, an 1891 Congregational Church that lost its steeple and top floor to a lightning strike, is now a fine bed-and-breakfast with many stained-glass windows. There are beautiful antiques in every room, reproduction antique beds, hardwood floors in the common areas and baths, and carpeting in the bedrooms. Guests share a huge living/dining room with a stone fireplace and complimentary fresh fruit and baked goods, an upstairs library, hot tub, sun deck, and a music conservatory with piano, television, VCR, and video rentals. Smoking and pets are not allowed.

Steamboat Valley Guest House. 1245 Crawford Ave. (P.O. Box 773815), Steamboat Springs, CO 80477. ☎ **800/530-3866** or 970/870-9017. Fax 970/879-0361. 4 rooms. Queen $75–$115, king $100–$135. Rates include full breakfast. AE, DISC, MC, V. Free covered parking.

This western-style log house has spectacular views of the ski area and town. The four guest rooms are all individually decorated with antiques and family heirlooms; the honeymoon suite has a king bed and ceramic fireplace. Homemade breakfasts are different each day and might include Swedish pancakes or a green chile cheese soufflé. A common room has a fireplace, baby grand piano, and TV, and guests have access to a cordless phone (some rooms have phones). There is a sun deck and seasonal hot tub. Smoking and pets are not permitted.

WHERE TO DINE
EXPENSIVE

Hazie's. 2305 Mt. Werner Circle, Thunderbird Terminal, Silver Bullet Gondola. ☎ **970/879-6111, ext. 465.** Reservations recommended for lunch, required for dinner. Lunch main courses $8–$14; four-course fixed-price dinner $50, including round-trip gondola ride. AE, CB, DC, DISC, MC, V. Daily 11:30am–2:30pm; Tues–Sat 6:30–9:30pm. Summer hours may be shorter. CREATIVE CONTINENTAL.

Steamboat Springs' most exciting dining experience can be found at the top of the gondola, midway up Mount Werner. The views of the upper Yampa River valley are spectacular by day and romantic by night, as the lights of Steamboat Springs spread out at the foot of the mountain. Lunch features a variety of salads and sandwiches, plus pasta, seafood, and meat specials daily. But it's at dinner that Hazie's really struts its stuff. They offer a fixed-price four-course meal that includes round-trip gondola transportation for $50 per person. The menu features seafood, poultry, and beef. Evening child-care is available.

MODERATE

La Montaña. Village Center Shopping Plaza, 2500 Village Dr. at Apres Ski Way. ☎ **970/879-5800.** Reservations recommended. Main courses $9–$23. AE, DISC, MC, V. Daily 5–10pm (bar daily 4:30pm–midnight). May close Sun–Mon in spring and fall. MEXICAN/SOUTHWESTERN.

This isn't your everyday Mexican restaurant; it's a gourmet experience. The festive decor sets the mood, with greenhouse dining and handsome photos by owner Tom Garrett on the stuccoed walls. You might want to start with the restaurant's award-winning braided sausage: a mesquite-grilled combination of elk, lamb, and chorizo sausage, and then choose from among sizzling fajitas (with chicken, pork, shrimp, beef, or elk), enchiladas, or chile rellenos.

Steamboat Brewery & Tavern. 435 Lincoln Ave. ☎ **970/879-2233.** Reservations not accepted. Main courses $5.95–$7.95 at lunch, $8.75–$12.95 at dinner. AE, CB, DC, DISC, MC, V. Daily 11:30am–10pm, pizza available until 11pm, bar open until midnight. AMERICAN.

This modern brew pub has a long bar, polished wood trim, and white stucco walls decorated with early-20th-century–style prints and metal advertising signs. It offers a full bar, with about a dozen wines available by the glass, and five or six microbrewed beers on tap. There's a wide selection of soups, sandwiches, burgers, and salads, vegetarian meals, plus hand-twirled pizza and their own bread baked on the premises. Tours of the brewery are available by request.

INEXPENSIVE

🆂 **Cugino's Pizzeria, Inc.** 825 Oak St. ☎ **970/879-5805.** Reservations not accepted. Pizzas $4.75–$15.65; entrees $3.30–$12.50. No credit cards. Daily 11am–10pm. Delivery available 5–9:30pm Mon–Sat, 11am–9:30pm Sun. ITALIAN.

Local families pack this restaurant in downtown Steamboat Springs, and with good reason—good food, generous portions, and low prices. The decor is simple—posters of Italian operas. The extensive menu includes pizza, of course, plus hoagies and steak sandwiches, pasta, seafood, and calzones. Those with healthy appetites might want to try a stromboli—fresh-baked pizza dough stuffed with mushrooms, onions, peppers, mozzarella and provolone cheeses, ham, Genoa salami, and capacola. A vegetarian version is also served. Beer and wine are available.

The Tugboat Saloon & Eatery. Ski Time Sq. ☎ **970/879-7070.** Reservations not accepted. Breakfast $2.95–$7.95; lunch/dinner $5–$14. AE, MC, V. Winter, daily 7:30am–10pm; summer, daily 11am–10pm (bar open Mon–Sat to 1:30am, Sun to midnight). Closed April 15–May. AMERICAN.

Oak floors and rough barn-wood walls cloaked with game and fishing trophies, sports memorabilia, and celebrity photographs are the trademark of this foot-of-the-slopes establishment. The hand carved cherry-wood bar, circa 1850, came from the Log Cabin Saloon in Baggs, Wyoming, a Butch Cassidy hangout; look for the bullet hole in one of the columns. The fare includes omelets, huevos rancheros, and pancakes for breakfast; a variety of burgers, burritos, deli sandwiches, fish favorites, soups and salads for lunch and dinner. Many folks sup on nachos, teriyaki wings, and other generous appetizer plates. Live music starts nightly at 9:30pm.

STEAMBOAT SPRINGS AFTER DARK

Nightlife in Steamboat, while never dull, comes especially alive in winter. At Steamboat Village, the **Inferno,** Gondola Square (☎ **970/879-5111**), is a hot dance club with live music; the rustic **Tugboat Saloon & Eatery,** Ski Time Square (☎ **970/879-7070**), attracts more of a local crowd for rock music and dancing; and **Buddy's Run,** in the Sheraton Steamboat Resort (☎ **970/879-2220**), does a quick change from a foot-of-the-slopes bar to a comedy club in the early evening. Other happening nightspots include **Mather's Bar,** 420 Yampa Ave., Craig (☎ **970/824-9946**), with live music weekends, video games, pool, and shuffleboard; and **Dos Amigos,** at 1910 Mount Werner Rd. (☎ **970/879-4270**), a friendly neighborhood Mexican restaurant and bar.

In downtown Steamboat, the **Old Town Pub & Restaurant,** Sixth Street and Lincoln Avenue (☎ **970/879-2101**), has big-screen ski movies; and **Buffalo Wild Wings and Weck** ("BW-3"), 729 Lincoln Ave. (☎ **970/879-2431**), has live music weekends.

4 Winter Park

Originally an Ute and Arapahoe hunting ground, today most of the hunting is for the best ski runs. First settled by whites in the 1850s, the laying of a rail track over Rollins Pass in 1905 and the completion of the 6.2-mile Moffat Tunnel in 1928 opened forests here to logging, which long supported the economy while providing Denver with raw materials for its growth.

The birth of the Winter Park ski area in January 1940, at the west portal of the Moffat Tunnel, helped induce the Colorado ski boom. Although it hasn't yet achieved the notoriety of Vail or Aspen, Winter Park still manages to attract more than a million skier visits per season. One of its draws is the Winter Park Ski Train, the last of its kind in the West. While skiers should find enough lodgings and restaurants to meet their needs, shoppers accustomed to the bounty in Aspen may be disappointed—at least for now. Plans for the development of a major base village were announced in February 1996.

ESSENTIALS

GETTING THERE   By Car   From Denver or other points east or west, take I-70, Exit 232, at Empire and climb 24 miles north on U.S. 40 over Berthoud Pass to Winter Park. U.S. 40 links Winter Park directly to Steamboat Springs, 101 miles northwest, and, via U.S. 34 (at Granby) through Rocky Mountain National Park, to Estes Park, 84 miles north.

By Plane   Visitors fly into **Denver International Airport** and can continue to Winter Park with **Home James Transportation Service** (☎ **800/451-4844** or 970/726-5060).

By Train   Winter Park Resort is the only ski area in the western United States to have rail service directly to the slopes. The dramatically scenic **Winter Park Ski Train** between Denver and Winter Park has been making regular runs over the same route since 1940, stopping just 50 yards from the foot of the lifts. On its 2-hour run, the train climbs almost 4,000 feet and passes through 29 tunnels (including the 6.2-mile Moffat Tunnel). The train, which operates weekends from late-December to early April (but not Christmas), departs Denver's Union Station at 7:15am and leaves Winter Park for the return trip at 4:15pm. For ticket information, call **303/296-ISKI** (303/296-4754).

The **Amtrak California Zephyr** (☎ **800/USA-RAIL**) stops daily in Fraser, 2 miles north of Winter Park, on its Chicago–West Coast run.

By Bus   The **Winter Park Grayline Express** bus provides daily round-trip service for day skiers from Denver to Winter Park (☎ **800/348-6877** during ski season).

ORIENTATION   U.S. 40 (Winter Park Drive) runs almost directly north to south through the community. Coming from Denver, you first cross Berthoud Pass; 15 miles later, the Winter Park Resort is on your left. About 1 mile farther is downtown Winter Park; Vasquez Road, one of the few side roads with accommodations, is the first major left turn as you arrive. Two miles farther on U.S. 40 is Fraser, site of the Amtrak terminal and several condominium developments.

VISITOR INFORMATION   Main sources of visitor information are the **Winter Park/Fraser Valley Chamber of Commerce,** P.O. Box 3236, Winter Park, CO 80482 (☎ **800/903-PARK** or 970/726-4118 for general information, or for lodging call **800/722-4118**), and the **Winter Park Resort,** P.O. Box 36, Winter Park, CO 80482 (☎ **970/726-5514**). The chamber of commerce's Visitor Center, on the east side of U.S. 40 in the center of town, is open daily from 8am to 5pm year-round.

GETTING AROUND   The Lift (☎ **970/726-4163**), a free local shuttle service, runs between most accommodations and the ski area in winter. **Home James Transportation Service** (☎ **970/726-5060**) provides taxi service. **Car rentals** are available from **Hertz** (☎ **800/654-3131** or 970/726-8993).

FAST FACTS   In case of **emergency,** call **911.** The hospital, **Seven Mile Medical Clinic,** at the Winter Park Resort (☎ **970/726-8066**), can handle most medical emergencies. The **post office** (☎ **970/726-5495**) is in the heart of Winter Park on U.S. 40. For **road information,** call 970/639-1111. **State, county, and city taxes** add 9% to hotel bills.

SPECIAL EVENTS   Annual events include the National Women's Ski and Snowboard Week in late January; High Country Stampede Rodeo, every Saturday night from early July through August; the Alpine Art Affair, in late July; Rocky Mountain Wine and Food Festival, in early August; King of the Rockies Mountain Bike Festival, in late August; Fallfest Lumberjack Show, in mid-September; and the Torchlight Parade, on Christmas Eve.

SKIING & OTHER WINTER ACTIVITIES

Winter Park is one of those rare resorts that seems to have something for everyone. Experts rave about the chutes and steep mogul runs on Mary Jane Mountain, but intermediates and beginners are well-served on other slopes. Moreover, Winter Park is noted for wide-ranging programs for children and those with disabilities.

The resort includes three interconnected mountain areas totaling 121 trails on 1,414 acres of skiable terrain. Twenty lifts include 7 high-speed express quads, 5 triples, and 8 double chairs.

Winter Park Mountain has 12 lifts and 46 trails, with mostly beginner and intermediate terrain. **Discovery Park** encompasses over 20 acres of prime beginner terrain served by three lifts.

Mary Jane Mountain has 7 chair lifts and 50 trails on intermediate and expert terrain. **Vasquez Ridge,** the resort's third mountain area, offers primarily intermediate terrain on 13 trails. All are served by one quad lift. Fans of tree-line skiing will like **Parsenn Bowl,** more than 200 acres of open-bowl and gladed-tree skiing that fan out from the summit at North Cone and merge with Mary Jane's Backside.

Annual snowfall at Winter Park averages 30 feet. The vertical drop is 3,060 feet, from the 12,060-foot summit off North Cone. There are 11 restaurants and three bars, including The Lodge at Sunspot, a mountaintop restaurant.

Winter Park's 32,000-square-foot **Children's Center** includes a play area, a rental shop, rest rooms, and a children's instruction hill. The **National Sports Center for the Disabled,** founded in 1970, is one of the largest programs of its kind in the world. Each year, more than 2,500 children and adults take over 23,000 lessons. Cost for a half-day lift ticket, private lesson, and adaptive equipment was $40 at press time; and the cost of a lift ticket and equipment only was $27.

The 1995/1996 adult lift tickets were $42 per day, $18 per day for children 6 to 13 and seniors 62 to 69, free for those under 5 and over 70. Full-rental packages are available, as are alpine, telemark, and snowboard lessons. On-mountain snowshoe tours are scheduled daily and cost $25 per person (1995–96 rate), including equipment.

Winter Park is open from mid-November to mid-April, Monday to Friday 9am to 4pm; Saturday, Sunday, and holidays 8:30am to 4pm. It is open for summer operations from early June through September. For more information, contact **Winter Park Resort,** P.O. Box 36, Winter Park, CO 80482 (☎ **970/726-5514,** or 303/892-0961 in Denver). For lodging information, call **800/453-2525.** For daily ski reports, call **303/572-7669.**

Rental equipment for downhill or cross-country skiing and snowmobiling can be obtained from more than a dozen outlets in the Winter Park area, including **Winter Park Sports Shop** in Kings Crossing Shopping Center, at the intersection of Winter Park Drive and Kings Crossing Road; **Winter Park Ski Shop, Ltd.,** at the foot of the ski slopes (☎ **800/222-7547,** or 970/726-5554 for both); and **Flanagan's Ski Rentals,** U.S. 40, Winter Park (☎ **800/544-1523** or 970/726-4412).

CROSS-COUNTRY SKIING   The outstanding cross-country skiing in the Winter Park area is highlighted by what the *Denver Post* calls "the best touring center in Colorado." **The Devil's Thumb Cross-Country Center at Devil's Thumb Ranch Resort** (see "Where to Stay," below) has more than 100 kilometers (67 miles) of groomed trails. Full rentals and instruction are available.

Snow Mountain Ranch-YMCA Nordic Center, on U.S. 40 between Tabernash and Granby (☎ **970/887-2152**) features 100 kilometers (60 miles) of groomed trails for all abilities, including 3 kilometers (2 miles) of lighted track for night skiing.

ICE-SKATING   There's ice-skating at **Snow Mountain Ranch-YMCA of the Rockies,** near Tabernash (☎ **970/887-2152**), and in downtown Winter Park.

SLEIGH RIDES   Opportunities abound for horse-drawn sleigh rides. **Jim's Sleigh Rides** (☎ **970/726-0944**) takes you through woods and meadows along the Fraser River on a 1¹/₄-hour trip. The cost is about $15 per person, which includes a hot drink in front of a roaring fire in the woods. Sleigh rides and dinner sleigh rides are also provided at **Devil's Thumb Ranch** and its exceptional **Ranch House Restaurant** (☎ **970/726-5632**).

SNOWMOBILING   Guided tours by snowmobile are offered by **Trailblazer Snowmobile Tours** (☎ **800/669-0134** or 970/726-8452). Rates are about $40 an hour.

WARM-WEATHER & YEAR-ROUND ACTIVITIES

There are plenty of recreational opportunities in the **Arapahoe National Forest** and **Arapahoe National Recreation Area.** Maps and brochures on hiking, mountain biking, and other activities are available at the Sulphur Ranger District office, 62429 U.S. 40 (P.O. Box 10), Granby, CO 80446 (☎ **970/887-4100**). The **Devil's Thumb Ranch Resort** (see "Where to Stay," below) is famous for its numerous recreation packages, including rafting, hiking, mountain biking, and fly-fishing.

ALPINE SLIDE   Colorado's longest alpine slide, at 1¹/₂ miles long, cools summer visitors. Rates are about $7 for adults; $6 for children 6 to 13 and seniors 62 to 69. Those under 6 and over 69 are admitted free. For information, contact Winter Park Resort (☎ **970/726-5514**).

FISHING   Fraser Valley and surrounding Grand County are renowned among anglers. Head to Williams Fork Reservoir and the Three Lakes District for kokanee salmon, lake trout, brookies, and browns. Fishing ponds stocked with various species are in Fraser, across from the Fraser Valley Center on U.S. 40. The upper pond is reserved for children and people in wheelchairs; the lower pond is open to everyone. Ponds are generally open and stocked by mid-May.

GOLF   **Pole Creek Golf Club,** 10 miles northwest of Winter Park on U.S. 40 (☎ **970/726-8847**), considered among the finest mountain courses in the state, continues to be highly rated by *Golf Digest* magazine. Mountain views on the Ron Kirby/Gary Player–designed course are terrific. There's also a full-service pro shop, driving range, lessons, club rentals, and a restaurant. The course usually opens by Memorial Day (or as soon as the snow melts) and remains open until the middle of October. Rates in midsummer are $35 for nine holes and $55 for 18 holes Monday through Thursday; $40 for nine holes and $60 for 18 holes Friday through Sunday. Rates are lower at the beginning and end of the season.

HIKING & BACKPACKING   Check with Arapahoe National Forest (☎ **970/ 887-4100**) for trail maps and other information. Beautiful Rocky Mountain National Park is less than an hour's drive north.

MOUNTAIN BIKING   Winter Park and the Fraser Valley have won national recognition for their expansive trail system and established race program. Many off-road bike trails connect to the 600 miles of backcountry roads and trails in the adjacent national forest. The King of the Rockies Off-Road Stage Race and Festival, held each year in August, is one of the top professional mountain-bike races in America; part of it is run on the 30-mile Tipperary Creek Trail, among Colorado's best mountain-bike trails.

For advice, information, and maps, talk to the knowledgeable folks at **Winter Park Sports Shop** in Kings Crossing Shopping Center, at the intersection of Winter Park Drive and Kings Crossing Road (☎ **800/222-7547** or 970/726-5554). In business almost 50 years, the shop is open 7 days a week year-round, providing mountain-and road-bike sales, repairs, and rentals (about $15 per day). For specific information on trails and races, and to pick up a free trail map, call the **Winter Park/Fraser Valley Chamber of Commerce** (☎ **800/903-7275, ext. 1**).

RIVER RAFTING   Half-day, full-day, and multiday trips on the Colorado, Arkansas, Eagle, North Platte, and other rivers are offered by numerous local outfitters, including **Colorado River Runs** (☎ **800/826-1081**), **Mad Adventures** (☎ **800/359-7530** or 970/726-5290), and **Raven Adventure Trips** (☎ **800/332-3381** or 970/887-2141). Half-day trips are about $30.

RODEOS   Every Saturday night for about 8 weeks beginning in July, the **High Country Stampede Rodeos** hold forth at John Work Arena in nearby Fraser (☎ **800/903-7275**). Professional and top amateur cowboys compete in bronco riding, calf roping, and other events. A barbecue precedes the rodeo.

TUBING   The Fraser Valley Tubing Hill, Fraser (☎ **970/726-5954**), offers a return to childhood for many adults, where, for a fee of $8 to $10 per hour you can slide down a steep hill in a big inner tube in winter.

OTHER THINGS TO SEE & DO

Amaze 'N Winter Park. At the base of Winter Park Resort. ☎ **970/726-0214.** Admission $4 adults, $3 children 5–12, free for children under 5. Additional maze runs $2. Memorial Day weekend–Sept only. Call for hours.

A human maze by Amaze 'n Colorado, this two-level labyrinth of twists and turns offers prizes to participants who can "beat the clock." The maze is constructed in such a way that it can be easily changed, which is done weekly to maintain interest for repeat customers. An observation deck (free) gives a bird's-eye view of the maze, as well as the surrounding scenery.

Cozens Ranch House Restoration Museum. U.S. 40 between Winter Park and Fraser. ☎ **970/726-5488.** Admission $2 adults, $1 children. Dec 15–Mar, Tues–Sun 11am–4:30pm; June 15–Sept, daily 11am–4:30pm.

A series of 1870s ranch buildings, including a family residence, small hotel, stage stop, and the original Fraser Valley post office, have been restored by the Grand County Historical Association, presenting a glimpse into Colorado's pioneer past.

Rio Grande Caboose Museum. Ski Train Terminal, Winter Park Resort. ☎ **970/726-5514.** Admission free. Nov–Apr and June–Aug, daily 9am–5pm. Closed May, Sept, and Oct.

A vintage 1945 caboose has been converted to a ski museum, with a display of ski memorabilia and historical photos showing the half-century development of Winter Park Ski Area. It doubles as a visitor information center and has a small bookstore. Outside are exhibits on ski patrol, ski lifts, and snowmaking technology.

WHERE TO STAY

There are more than 100 accommodations in the Fraser Valley, including hotels, condominiums, family-style mountain inns (serving breakfast and dinner daily), bed-and-breakfasts, lodges, and motels. Bookings can be made by **Winter Park Central Reservations,** P.O. Box 36, Winter Park, CO 80482 (☎ **800/453-2525** or 970/726-5587; fax 970/726-5993). The agency can also book air and rail tickets, rental cars, airport transfers, lift tickets, ski-school lessons, ski rentals, and other activities.

There's some gray area from lodge to lodge about where one season ends and another begins, so confirm rates when making your reservations.

MODERATE

Gästhaus Eichler. 78786 U.S. 40 at Vasquez Creek (P.O. Box 3303), Winter Park, CO 80482. ☎ **800/543-3899** or 970/726-5133. Fax 970/726-5175. 15 rms. TV TEL. Summer, $30–$40 per person per unit, double occupancy. Winter, $55–$75 per person per unit, double occupancy. AE, DC, MC, V.

The charm of this small inn is exactly what you'd expect to find at a European resort. Lace curtains and down comforters grace each room, and each has its own Jacuzzi. The restaurant offers innovative specials, fresh fish, and lighter fare, three meals daily.

The Inn at Silver Creek. U.S. 40 (P.O. Box 4222), Silver Creek, CO 80446. ☎ **800/926-4386** or 970/887-2131. Fax 970/887-2350. 200 rms, 11 suites. TV TEL. Summer, $69 double; $169 suite. Peak season, from $89 double; $199 suite. Christmas, from $159 double; $300 suite. Low season, $59 double; $129 suite. AE, DC, DISC, MC, V.

This outstanding resort is located 15 miles north of Winter Park and 2 miles southeast of Granby. It's becoming a popular conference location with its meeting area, all-season athletic facilities, and a wide range of in-season activities.

Every room is luxurious, with a whirlpool and steam cabinet in the bath. Each unit has a deck or balcony and cable TV with in-room movies. Third-floor rooms and suites have vaulted ceilings, skylights, and lofts. Suites and studios have fireplaces, wet bars (with minirefrigerator and microwave), and dining-and-living areas.

Snowblaze. U.S. 40 (P.O. Box 66), Winter Park, CO 80482. ☎ **800/525-2466** or 970/726-5701. Fax 970/726-4208. 73 units (studio, two- and three-bedroom). Double: low-season $77–$180; value season $109–$290; pre-Christmas $124–$316; Christmas $196–$506; summer $70–$130 (additional summer discounts certain months). AE, MC, V.

One of Winter Park's more prestigious condominiums, Snowblaze features the Fraser Valley's leading athletic club on site. The units are in downtown Winter Park, 1 1/2 miles from the ski area by shuttle. All have full baths (one per bedroom), fully equipped kitchens, electric stoves and/or microwaves, and color TVs. Two- and three-bedroom units also have fireplaces (with wood provided) and private dry saunas. All have simple but handsome decor, with big picture windows and rich wood furnishings. Winter Park Adventures, the property management firm for Snowblaze, also manages 14 other area properties.

The Vintage. 100 Winter Park Dr. (P.O. Box 1369), Winter Park, CO 80482. ☎ **800/472-7017** or 970/726-8801. Fax 970/726-9230. 118 rms, 20 suites. A/C TV TEL. Summer, $65–$95 double; $150–$200 suite. Winter, $85–$195 double; $235–$475 suite. AE, DC, DISC, MC, V.

Château-like, the Vintage rises five stories above the foot of Winter Park's ski slopes, not far from the Mary Jane base facilities. A full-service resort hotel, it offers convenient access, excellent dining and atmosphere, and luxury accommodations. Every room in the hotel has a view of either the ski slopes or the Continental Divide, and many have balconies. Some have fireplaces, kitchens, and whirlpool tubs. There's an outdoor heated pool, sauna, small exercise room, game room, self-serve laundry, and on-site ski rentals.

INEXPENSIVE

✪ **Devil's Thumb Ranch Resort.** Grand County Rd. 83 (P.O. Box 750, Winter Park, CO 80482), Tabernash, CO 80478. ☎ **800/933-4339** or 970/726-5632. Fax 970/726-9038. 14 rms (about half with private bath), 6 cabins, 1 dormitory. Winter, $20–$60 per person; summer, $20–$48 per person. Meal plans available. MC, V.

This is the sort of place that attracts outdoor sports freaks in droves. Established in 1937, the ranch—8 miles north of Winter Park—is as famous today for its cross-country skiing in winter (see "Skiing & Other Winter Activities," above) as for its horseback riding and fly-fishing in summer. Accommodations are available for all pocketbooks, from a honeymoon cabin with a fireplace to dormitory beds in the bunkhouse. Most guests stay in one of the cozy rooms in the log Elk Lodge, where they have access to a spa, sauna, TV, and billiards room. The Ranch House Restaurant and Saloon (open daily 7am–11pm) lures Winter Park residents for creative country cuisine and seasonal specialties.

Engelmann Pines. 1035 Cranmer Ave. (P.O. Box 1305), Winter Park, CO 80482. ☎ **800/992-9512** or 970/726-4632. 7 rms (5 with bath). Winter, $75–$85 shared bath; $95–$115 private bath. Summer, $65–$75 shared bath; $85–$95 private bath. Rates include full breakfast. AE, DISC, MC, V.

Antique furnishings add an elegant touch to this contemporary home outside Winter Park. Heinz and Margaret Engel serve Swiss confections and other treats around their large fireplace in winter. Some rooms have balconies and fireplaces, and all have whirlpool tubs. There's a free shuttle to the ski resort or Amtrak station. In summer, mountain bikers and hikers appreciate the same trailhead across the street that cross-country skiers use in winter. Guests have full use of the kitchen. No smoking or pets are allowed, and children are welcome.

WHERE TO DINE

Crooked Creek Saloon & Eatery. U.S. 40, Fraser. ☎ **970/726-9250.** Breakfast $1.95–$5.95; lunch $2.95–$7.95; dinner $3.95–$14.95. DISC, MC, V. Daily 7am–10pm (bar open until 2am). AMERICAN/MEXICAN.

The Fraser Valley's favorite drinking spot, the Crooked Creek offers breakfasts of biscuits and gravy, frittatas, breakfast burritos, and steak and eggs. You can get an Awesome Fatboy Burger (10 oz. of ground beef), a variety of sandwiches, and Mexican dishes most anytime, or St. Louis–style ribs, New York strip steak, pan-fried trout, and London broil after 5pm. Especially popular are the hot wings and the Friday night prime-rib specials. There's live music Tuesday, Friday, and Saturday evenings.

Deno's Mountain Bistro. U.S. 40, downtown Winter Park. ☎ **970/726-5332.** Burgers and sandwiches $3.95–$7.95; main courses $7.95–$16.95. AE, CB, DC, DISC, MC, V. Daily 11am–11pm; bar open later. BISTRO.

A favorite of locals and visitors alike, this self-proclaimed mountain bistro on Winter Park's main street has a casual atmosphere and impressive bar, with 75 national and international beers and an award-winning wine list of more than 300 selections. The gourmet cuisine includes such dishes as angel hair pomadora, with fresh basil and rock shrimp; aged New York strip steak; and prime rib. There are fresh seafood specials nightly, and burgers, sandwiches, salads, and pizzas.

The Last Waltz. King's Cross Shopping Center, U.S. 40. ☎ **970/726-4877.** Breakfast $2.95–$6.95; lunch $2.95–$6.95; dinner $6.50–$15.95. AE, DC, DISC, MC, V. Daily 7am–2pm; 5–9pm. Sun breakfast is available until 2pm. AMERICAN/MEXICAN.

A favorite of those who enjoy good home-style cooking, this cafe treads the line between cultures at every meal: flapjacks, cheese blintzes, or migas (a south-of-the-border egg scramble) for breakfast; Cajun-blackened ham, Rocky Mountain Reuben, or quesadilla (Mexican cheese) sandwiches for lunch. In the evening, you can choose between crabmeat enchiladas, honey-and-pecan fried chicken, pork chops, fish-and-chips, or a 12-ounce rib-eye steak. Children's and senior's portions available.

WINTER PARK AFTER DARK

With Denver so close by, there's not much nightlife in Winter Park. If you're too lazy to hit the road but feel like hearing a local band, head for the **Slope,** half a mile from the ski area on U.S. 40 (☎ **970/726-5727**); or the **Crooked Creek Saloon** in downtown Fraser (☎ **970/726-9250**).

5 Breckenridge & Summit County

By and large, Summit County is a modern creation. The mountain towns that surround its excellent ski areas—Arapahoe Basin, Breckenridge, Copper, Keystone, and Loveland—were barely on the map in the 1880s, when the rest of the state was laying claim to its stake of history. Breckenridge was a prosperous mining town circa 1887 when the largest gold nugget ever found in Colorado, 13 pounds, 7 ounces, was unearthed here, and Copper Mountain gained a modest reputation for the copper ore it produced around the same time, but both towns had fallen on comparatively hard times before their respective ski areas opened in 1961 and 1972.

Today, Summit County is a major recreational sports center, with skiing in winter, and fishing, hiking, and mountain biking in summer. Though skiers began coming to Arapahoe Basin and Loveland in the immediate postwar period, Summit County wasn't known for its ski areas until Breckenridge opened, and its reputation was only enhanced with the openings of Keystone and Copper a few years later.

ESSENTIALS

GETTING THERE   By Car   I-70 runs through the middle of Summit County. For Keystone, exit on U.S. 6 at Dillon; the resort is 6 miles east of the interchange. For Breckenridge, exit on Colo. 9 at the county seat of Frisco; the resort town is 10 miles south. Copper Mountain is right on I-70 at the Colo. 91 interchange.

By Airport Shuttle   Most visitors fly into **Denver International** or **Colorado Springs** and continue to Breckenridge, Frisco, Keystone, and/or Copper Mountain via shuttle. **Resort Express** (☎ **800/334-7433** or 970/468-7600), and **Vans to Breckenridge** (☎ **800/222-2112** or 970/668-5466) offer shuttles; **People's Choice Transportation** (☎ **800/777-2388** outside Colorado, or 303/659-7780) offers luxury transport to Summit County resorts. (For listings of airlines servicing Denver and Colorado Springs, see chapters 6 and 8, respectively.)

ORIENTATION   At the heart of Summit County is Dillon Reservoir, its arms reaching like an octopus to the southwest, where the county seat, Frisco, is located; to the south, pointing directly up the Blue River toward Breckenridge; to the north, site of the town of Dillon; and to the east, up U.S. 6, the artery to Keystone, Arapahoe Basin, and Loveland Pass. I-70 follows the western shore of the lake, separating Dillon from Silverthorne at the top end and swinging past Copper Mountain (6 miles south of Frisco) before climbing over Vail Pass.

VISITOR INFORMATION   The main source of visitor information for the entire region is the **Summit County Chamber of Commerce,** P.O. Box 214, Frisco, CO 80443 (☎ **970/668-0376** or 970/668-5800). The chamber has an information center at the junction of Colo. 9 and U.S. 6 (Summit Blvd. at Main St.), en route from I-70 to Breckenridge.

For additional information on Breckenridge, contact the **Breckenridge Resort Chamber,** with an information center at 309 N. Main St. and administrative offices at 311 S. Ridge St. (P.O. Box 1909), Breckenridge, CO 80424 (☎ **800/221-1091** or 970/453-6018); for information about activities in Breckenridge, contact the

Activity Center (☎ 970/453-5579). For other communities, contact the following: the **Copper Mountain Resort Chamber,** P.O. Box 3003, Copper Mountain, CO 80443 (☎ 970/968-6477); **Keystone Resort,** P.O. Box 38, Keystone, CO 80435 (☎ 800/222-0188 within CO, 800/525-1309 outside CO, or 970/468-2316); or the **Lake Dillon Resort Association,** P.O. Box 446, Dillon, CO 80435 (☎ 800/ 365-6365 or 970/468-6222).

GETTING AROUND   Summit Stage (☎ 970/453-1241 or 970/453-1339) provides free year-round service between Frisco, Dillon, Silverthorne, Keystone, Breckenridge, and Copper Mountain daily 6am–11:30pm from late November to mid-April; shorter hours the rest of the year. The Stage runs until 1:30am on peak ski-holiday weekends.

For a cab, call **Ridge Taxi Service** (☎ 970/453-8294) in Breckenridge. You can get around Breckenridge on the free **Town Trolley** (☎ 970/453-2251), and there's also free shuttle service at Keystone Resort (☎ 970/453-5241).

FAST FACTS   In case of emergency, call **911.** Hospitals include the **Provenant Medical Center at Summit,** Colo. 9 at School Rd., Frisco (24-hours ☎ 970/ 668-3300 for emergencies); the **Breckenridge Medical Center,** Village at Breckenridge Resort, 555 S. Park St., Plaza II, Breckenridge (☎ 970/453-9000); and **Mountain Medical Center,** 130 Ski Hill Rd., Breckenridge (☎ 970/453-7600). **Post offices** are at 300 S. Ridge St., Breckenridge (☎ 970/453-2310); and 65 W. Main St., Frisco (☎ 970/668-5505). **State and county taxes** add about 9.5% to hotel bills. For **weather and road conditions,** call 970/453-1090.

**SPECIAL EVENTS   Highlights include: the International Snow Sculpture Championships, second week in January; Ullr Fest, the third week of January, in Breckenridge; Ski Fiesta, on the fourth Saturday of February, in Keystone; the John Elway Celebrity Ski Race and Teenie Weenie Bikini Contest, over the first weekend of April, in Copper Mountain; Taste of Breckenridge, in early April; Beachin' at the Basin Spring Skiing Blowout, over Memorial Day weekend, in Arapahoe Basin; the Breckenridge Music Festival from late June through late August; Michael Martin Murphey's West Fest, over Labor Day weekend, in Copper Mountain; the Breckenridge Festival of Film, in the third week of September; and Frisco Founders Day, on the third weekend of September.

SKIING & OTHER WINTER ACTIVITIES

One of the highlights of alpine skiing in Summit County is the Breckenridge-Keystone alliance lift ticket, called KAB. It includes eight mountains: Breckenridge's Peaks 7, 8, 9, and 10 of the Ten Mile Range; Keystone's North Peak, Keystone Mountain, and the Outback; and Arapahoe Basin, where skiers have been seen for nearly half a century. Skiers have their choice of 276 trails, 4,142 acres of terrain, 41 lifts, both day and night skiing, nearly 20 on-mountain and base-area dining possibilities, and express shuttle buses running between the resorts from 8am until 11pm.

The adult **KAB ticket** (1995/96 season) costs $44 a day; $25 for seniors 60 to 69; $20 for children 6 to 12; seniors 70 and up and children 5 and under ski free. There are also multiday rates. Equipment rentals at Summit County resorts average $17 a day; 2¹/₂-hour class lessons start at $34. Skiers should also inquire about the Ski the Summit Pass, which includes Copper Mountain.

ARAPAHOE BASIN   Arapahoe Basin, on U.S. 6, between Keystone and Loveland Pass, is one of Colorado's oldest ski areas, having opened in 1945. It is now operated by **Keystone Resort, P.O. Box 38, Keystone, CO 80435 (☎ 800/222-0188

Breckenridge & Summit County

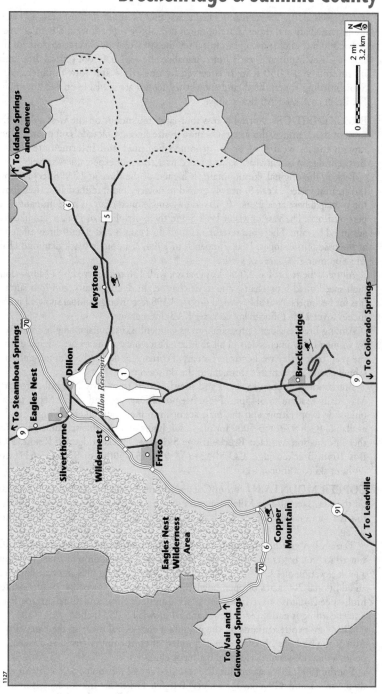

or 970/468-2316). Several features make Arapahoe exceptional. Most of its 490 acres are intermediate and expert terrain, much of it above timberline, and with an average of 360 inches of snow a year, it is often the last Colorado ski area to close for the season—usually not until early June. Arapahoe offers a 1,650-foot vertical drop from its summit at 13,050 feet. It is served by one triple and four double chairs. Snowboarding is permitted, and snowboard rentals are available on the mountain. For ticket cost, see KAB ticket above.

BRECKENRIDGE   Spread across four large mountains on the west side of the town of Breckenridge, this area ranks third in size among Colorado's ski resorts. Once known for its wealth of open, groomed beginner and intermediate slopes, Breckenridge in recent years has expanded its acreage for expert skiers as well.

Peak 8, the original ski mountain, is highest of the three at 12,998 feet and has the greatest variety. Peak 9, heavily geared to novices and intermediates, rises above the principal base area. Peak 10, served by a single quad chair, is predominantly expert territory. The vast bowls of Peak 8 and the North Face of Peak 9, are likewise advanced terrain. There are restaurants high on Peaks 8 and 9 and three cafeterias at the base of the slopes. Peak 7, opened in 1994, is a double black diamond challenge on over 1,200 feet of vertical.

All told, the resort has 2,028 skiable acres, with 136 trails served by 17 lifts—four high-speed quad superchairs, one triple chair, eight double chairs, and four surface lifts for beginners. Available vertical drop is 3,398 feet; average annual snowfall is 255 inches (over 21 ft.). For ticket cost, see KAB ticket above.

Among Breckenridge's programs are its women's ski seminars, taught exclusively by women for women skiers of all abilities. Three such seminars are offered during the year, over 3-day weekends in January, February, and March. Women-only ski-school classes are available throughout the ski season.

Breckenridge is open to skiers and snowboarders from early November to early May, daily 8:30am to 3:45pm. From Memorial Day weekend to late Sept., the alpine slide is operating, and the trails are open to mountain bikers; minigolf is also available. (Call 970/453-5000 for off-season hours and chairlift schedule.) For further information, contact: **Breckenridge Ski Area,** Breckenridge Ski Resort, P.O. Box 1058, Breckenridge, CO 80424 (☎ **970/453-5000,** or 970/453-6118 for 24-hour ski conditions).

COPPER MOUNTAIN   From Copper Mountain village, the avalanche chutes on the west face of Ten Mile Mountain seem to spell out the word SKI. Though this is a natural coincidence, locals like to say the mountain has terrain created for skiing.

Terrain is about half beginner and intermediate, with the rest ranging from advanced to "you better be really good." The area has a vertical drop of 2,601 feet from a peak elevation of 12,313 feet. There are 1,370 skiable acres plus snowcat skiing on an additional 700 acres of open bowl. The 101 trails are served by 19 lifts—three high-speed quads, six triple chairs, six double chairs, and four surface lifts. Snowboarding is permitted. Average annual snowfall is 255 inches.

There are two restaurants on the mountain and several more in the base village. Also at the base are 25 kilometers (15 miles) of cross-country track, an ice-skating pond, and a full-service racquet and athletic club.

For the 1995/1996 season, lift tickets started at $42 for adults, $19 a day for children 4 to 12, and $29 a day for seniors 60 to 69. Tickets are free for seniors over 70 and children 3 and under. Equipment rentals average $25 a day; full-day class lessons start at $42.

Copper Mountain is open from mid-November to late April, Monday to Friday 9am to 4pm, Saturday and Sunday 8:30am to 4pm. For information, contact **Copper Mountain Resort,** P.O. Box 3001, Copper Mountain, CO 80443 (☎ **970/ 968-2882**). For reservations, call **800/458-8386;** for a snow report, call **800/ 789-7609.**

KEYSTONE   Keystone is not only a superb mountain for intermediate skiers, it's also one of the best spots for night skiing in America. It's possible to take the gondola to dinner in the Summit House atop 11,640-foot Keystone Mountain, then ski until 9pm.

Spacious Keystone Mountain offers some 600 acres of intermediate terrain and ample beginner slopes. Over its back side are North Peak and the Outback region, both with advanced intermediate and expert runs. A second gondola connects the Summit House with the Outpost, a new restaurant atop 11,660-foot North Peak.

From its peak elevation of 12,200 feet, Keystone's vertical drop is 2,340 feet; the North Peak/Outback complex has 1,740 feet of its own. Together, they offer 1,737 acres of skiing, 90 trails, and 19 lifts—including two connecting high-speed gondolas, three high-speed quads, one quad chair, three triple chairs, six double chairs, and four surface lifts. Average annual snowfall is 230 inches (about 19 ft.). Snowboarding is not permitted. For lift ticket costs, see above.

Keystone is open from late October to early May, daily 8:30am to 9pm. For further information, contact **Keystone Resort,** P.O. Box 38, Keystone, CO 80435 (☎ **800/222-0188** or 970/468-2316). During ski season, call 970/468-4111 for a daily snow report.

LOVELAND   Just across the county line, on the east side of I-70's Eisenhower Memorial Tunnel, is **Loveland Ski Area,** P.O. Box 899, Georgetown, CO 80444 (☎ **800/736-3754** or 303/569-3203 for information, 800/225-LOVE for reservations). Comprised of Loveland Basin and Loveland Valley, it was created in the late 1930s by a Denver ski club wanting to take advantage of the area's heavy snowfall (385 in., more than 31 ft., annually). You can still see the original rope-tow cabins from 1942, when all-day tickets cost $2. Tickets for the 1995/1996 season cost $32 for adults, $22 for seniors 60 to 69, and $15 for children 6 to 12; children under 6 ski free.

There's good beginner–intermediate terrain, with 836 skiable acres, and a vertical drop of 1,680 feet from a top elevation of 12,280 feet. Lifts include one quad chair, two triples, five doubles, one poma, and one mighty mite. Snowboarders are welcome, and Loveland's snowboard park offers an 80-foot sidewinder quarter-pipe. The resort is usually Colorado's first to open, in mid-October, and it generally remains open until mid-May.

CROSS-COUNTRY SKIING   The **Frisco Nordic Center,** on Colo. 9 east of Frisco (☎ **970/668-0866**), sits on the shores of Dillon Reservoir. Its trail network includes 37 kilometers (22 miles) of set tracks and groomed skating lanes, and access to backcountry trails. There are trails for beginning, intermediate, advanced, and expert skiers. The lodge has a snack bar and a shop with rentals and retail sales; instruction is also offered. The master plan for the Nordic Center was developed by Olympic silver medalist Bill Koch, who is considered America's greatest Nordic skier of the last 50 years. Open November to April, daily from 9am to 4pm, the center charges $10 a day for adult tickets, $6 for seniors or children. Group lessons cost $20 and private are $35. Backcountry and snowshoe tours are available.

Peak's Trail connects the Frisco Nordic Center to the **Breckenridge Nordic Ski Center,** on Willow Lane near the foot of Peak 8 (☎ **970/453-6855**), and trail tickets are interchangeable. In addition, both centers have their own groomed trails, 28 kilometers (17.4 miles) at Breckenridge and 37 kilometers (23 miles) at Frisco.

The **Copper Mountain Cross-Country Center** has 25 kilometers (15.5 miles) of track and skating lanes through the wooded valley and is adjacent to 1,200 acres of alpine skiing terrain (☎ 800/458-8386, ext. 5 or 970/968-2882, ext. 6342).

Ski tours to the 1880 Sallie Barber Mine are offered by the Summit Historical Society Saturdays at 1pm. Tours start at the **Edwin Carter Museum,** 111 N. Ridge St. in Breckenridge (☎ 970/453-9022), take about 2 hours, and cost $8 for adults and $4 for children ages 4 through 12. Call for reservations.

For information on the numerous cross-country skiing trails in the area's national forests, contact the **Dillon Ranger District,** located in the town of Silverthorne at 680 Blue River Pkwy., half a mile north of I-70 exit 205 (P.O. Box 620, Silverthorne, CO 80498; ☎ 970/468-5400).

SNOWBOARDING   Snowboarding is permitted at all local resorts except Keystone. Enthusiasts can get equipment and lessons from the **Breckenridge Ski Resort** (☎ 800/789-7669 or 970/453-3250), where snowboarding has been popular since the early eighties. They offer both class and private lessons. **Pioneer Sports** rents boards in three locations: 203 N. Main St. in Breckenridge (☎ 970/453-0132); on Colo. 9 next to Wal-Mart in Frisco (☎ 970/668-3668); and in the main lobby of the Hampton Inn in Silverthorne (☎ 970/468-1632).

SNOWMOBILING   Snowmobilers can join guided tours from **Eagles Nest Snowmobile Center,** Colo. 9, 3 miles north of Silverthorne (☎ 970/468-0677); **Good Times, Inc.,** 216 S. Main St., Breckenridge (☎ 800/477-0144 or 970/453-7604); or **Tiger Run Tours,** 85 Tiger Run Rd., Breckenridge (☎ 800/321-1357 or 970/453-9690). Tours vary considerably, but often include stops at ghost towns and old mining camps, and may include lunch or dinner. Rates usually start in the $50 to $75 range for one person on a snowmobile and $75 to $100 for two, for a 2-hour trip.

ICE-SKATING   All three major resort communities have groomed ponds for ice-skating, with rentals and lessons available.

WARM-WEATHER & YEAR-ROUND ACTIVITIES

Two national forests—**Arapahoe** and **White River**—overlap the boundaries of Summit County. These recreational playgrounds offer opportunities not only for downhill and cross-country skiing and snowmobiling in winter, but also for hiking and backpacking, horseback riding, boating, fishing, hunting, and bicycling in summer. White River National Forest encompasses the **Eagles Nest Wilderness Area** and Arapahoe National Forest includes **Green Mountain Reservoir,** both in the northern part of the county.

The **U.S. Forest Service's Dillon Ranger District,** located in the town of Silverthorne at 680 Blue River Pkwy., half a mile north of I-70 exit 205 (☎ 970/468-5400, or write P.O. Box 620, Silverthorne, CO 80498), has an unusually good selection of information on outdoor recreation possibilities, including maps and guides to hiking and mountain-biking trails, jeep roads, cross-country skiing, snowmobiling, fishing, and camping. You can also get information on a wide variety of outdoor activities from the **Breckenridge Activity Center** at ☎ 970/453-5579.

BICYCLING   There are more than 40 miles of paved bicycle paths in the county, including a path from Breckenridge (with a spur from Keystone) to Frisco and

Copper Mountain, continuing across Vail Pass to Vail. This spectacularly beautiful two-lane path is off-limits to motorized vehicles of any kind.

BOATING   Dillon Reservoir, a beautiful mountain lake along I-70 between Dillon and Frisco, is the place to go. Also called Lake Dillon, the 3,300-acre reservoir, which provides drinking water to Denver, is about 190 feet deep. At 9,017 feet elevation, it claims to have America's highest altitude yacht club and holds colorful regattas most summer weekends plus the popular Dillon Open, a huge sailboat race the first weekend in August. Swimming is not permitted.

The **Dillon Marina,** 150 Marina Dr. (☎ 970/468-5100), is a full-service marina, open from the last weekend of May through the last weekend of October, with boats available for 2-hour, half-, or full-day rental, sailing instruction, and charter cruises. Boat rental fees for a half-day are $45 for small fishing boats, $105 for runabouts, and $160 for 24-foot pontoon boats. Fuel is extra. Sailboats cost $95 to $150 for a half-day for boats ranging from 18 to 23 feet. There's also a store, repair shop, restaurant and bar.

FISHING   Popular for brook, brown, cutthroat, lake, and rainbow trout, as well as kokanee salmon, are the Blue River, Ten Mile River, Snake River, and Straight Creek. For lake fishing, try Dillon Reservoir, Green Mountain Reservoir, and Pass Lake. The Blue River, from Lake Dillon Dam to its confluence with the Colorado River at Kremmling, is rated a gold medal fishing stream.

Mountain Angler, 311 S. Main St. in the Main Street Mall, (P.O. Box 467) Breckenridge 80424 (☎ 800/453-4669 or 970/453-4665), offers year-round guide service. Fly-fishing instruction is given weekends in July (4-hour lessons cost $110–$180, 2-days cost $279). Guided fly-fishing trips, on both public and private waters, are $125 to $195 for a half-day; $180 to $280 for a full day, including lunch. A float-fishing guided trip, limited to two anglers, costs $275 for one and $325 for two and includes transportation, lunch, and gear. The shop is open 8am to 9pm in summer, 9am to 9pm in winter.

GOLF   Summit County has four public golf courses. The **Breckenridge Golf Club,** 200 Clubhouse Dr., Breckenridge (☎ 970/453-9104), was designed by Jack Nicklaus. Greens fees range from $25 (nine holes in low season) to $70 (18 holes in high season, mid-June–mid-Sept). The **Copper Creek Golf Club,** 104 Wheeler Place, Copper Mountain Resort (☎ 970/968-2339), claims to be the highest 18-hole course in North America, at 9,650 feet. The **Keystone Ranch Golf Course,** Keystone Ranch Road, Keystone (☎ 970/468-4250), designed by Robert Trent Jones, Jr., has been rated the leading resort course in Colorado and one of the top 50 in the United States by *Golf Digest.* The **Eagles Nest Golf Club,** Colo. 9, 3 miles north of Silverthorne (☎ 970/468-0681), is another 18-hole public course.

HIKING & BACKPACKING   The Colorado Trail cuts a swath through Summit County. It enters from the east across Kenosha Pass, follows the Swan River to its confluence with the Blue River, then climbs over Ten Mile Mountain to Copper Mountain. The trail then turns south toward Tennessee Pass, north of Leadville.

There are myriad hiking opportunities in the national forests. Consult the **U.S. Forest Service** (☎ 970/468-5400), the **Breckenridge Activity Center** (☎ 970/453-5579), or a visitor information center for maps and details.

The Adventure Company, 101 Ski Hill Rd., Breckenridge (☎ 970/453-0747); offers guided hikes for all ages and physical abilities. Rates begin at $15.

HORSEBACK RIDING   One of the most popular rides in Summit County is the 7am breakfast ride offered by **Breckenridge Stables,** located just above the Alpine

Super Slide parking area, 1700 Ski Hill Rd., Breckenridge (☎ **970/453-4438**). Cost for the 2-hour ride with a breakfast of eggs, sausage, and all the pancakes you want is $30. The company also offers a 1-hour ride for $18, a 2-hour afternoon ride for $30, and dinner rides (choice of rib-eye steak or trout) for $38. The rides follow some of Breckenridge's ski runs, offering magnificent views of the mountains, and are suitable for all family members. Call for reservations.

MOUNTAIN BIKING   Numerous trails beckon mountain bikers. Some of them retrace 19th-century mining roads and burro trails, often ending in ghost towns.

Energetic fat-tire fans can try the Devil's Triangle, a difficult 80-mile loop that begins and ends in Frisco after climbing four mountain passes (including 11,318-foot Fremont Pass). If you'd like to watch a few talented riders go at it, Summit County's premier race event for mountain bikers is the annual Fall Classic, a 2-day, three-stage race in mid-September, the final event in the Colorado Off-Road Points Series (☎ **970/453-5548**). Several Summit Mountain Challenges are organized as recreational races for beginners as well as experts.

Rentals and general information can be obtained from the **Knorr House,** 303 S. Main St., Breckenridge (☎ **970/453-2631**); **Kodi Rafting & Bikes,** Bell Tower Mall, Breckenridge (☎ **970/453-2194**); and **Wilderness Sports,** 171 Blue River Pkwy., Silverthorne (☎ **970/468-8519**). For repairs, try **Mountain Outfitters,** 112 S. Ridge St., Breckenridge (☎ **970/453-2201**). Excursions into the high country can be arranged with **The Adventure Company,** 101 Ski Hill Rd., Breckenridge (P.O. Box 3876, Breckenridge, CO 80424, ☎ **800/497-7238** or 970/453-0747).

RIVER RAFTING   Trips through the white water of the Blue River—which runs through Breckenridge to Frisco—as well as longer journeys on the Colorado and Arkansas rivers are offered by various companies. These include the **Adventure Company,** 101 Ski Hill Rd., Breckenridge (☎ **970/453-0747**); **Kodi Rafting & Bikes,** Bell Tower Mall, Breckenridge (☎ **800/525-9624** or 970/453-2194); and **Performance Tours,** 110 Ski Hill Rd., Breckenridge (☎ **800/328-7238** or 970/453-0661).

THE FESTIVAL SCENE

Breckenridge has a number of festivals that draw visitors in large numbers every year. The **Breckenridge Music Festival** is held each summer in the $2.7 million Riverwalk Center. Presented by the Breckenridge Music Institute and National Repertory Orchestras, the event includes more than 50 classical music concerts performed by the institute's professional musicians and young students. Concerts take place from late June through late August, and tickets cost from $10 to $22, with discounts for seniors and students under 18. There is also a free Fourth of July concert. Contact the Breckenridge Music Festival, P.O. Box 1254, Breckenridge, CO 80424 (☎ **970/453-2120**).

Genuine Jazz in July, on the second weekend of the month, showcases Colorado jazz ensembles with styles ranging from Dixieland to bebop to New Age. Local bars and nightclubs host Friday- and Saturday-night performances. Free Saturday- and Sunday-afternoon concerts are outdoors at Maggie Pond, at the base of Peak 9. Call **970/453-6018** for schedules.

The **Breckenridge Festival of Film,** held the third full weekend of September, attracts Hollywood directors and actors to town to discuss some 2 dozen films in all genres. Contact the Breckenridge Festival of Film office for information (☎ **970/453-6200**).

Every Labor Day weekend, Copper Mountain is the scene of country singer **Michael Martin Murphey's West Fest.** The 3-day event focuses on the art, culture, and music of the American West with a full slate of guest appearances. For information, contact Copper Mountain Resort (☎ **970/968-2882**).

OTHER THINGS TO SEE & DO

Amaze 'N Breckenridge. 710 S. Main St., Breckenridge. ☎ **970/453-7262.** Admission $4 adults, $3 children 5–12, free for children under 5. Additional maze runs $2. Memorial Day weekend–Sept. Call for hours.

Colorado's largest human maze, this is the original one by Amaze 'n Colorado. The two-level labyrinth of twists and turns offers prizes to participants who can "beat the clock." The maze is constructed in such a way that it can be easily changed, which they do weekly to maintain interest for repeat customers. An observation deck (free) gives a bird's-eye view of the maze, as well as the surrounding scenery.

Breckenridge National Historic District. Breckenridge. ☎ **970/453-9022.** Admission to tours, $3–$5 adults, $2 ages 4–12. June–Aug, Mon–Sat 10am–4pm by appointment.

The entire Victorian core of this 19th-century mining town has been carefully preserved. Colorfully painted shops and restaurants occupy the old buildings, most dating from the 1880s and 1890s. The Summit Historical Society conducts guided 2-hour walking tours beginning from the Breckenridge Activity Center, in the Riverwalk Center at 105 W. Adams Ave. Most of the historic district focuses on Main Street, and extends east on either side of Lincoln Avenue. Among the 254 buildings in the district are the 1875 **Edwin Carter Museum,** 200 E. Lincoln Ave.; and the **1896 William Harrison Briggle House,** 104 N. Harris St., which houses the historical society's decorative-arts museum. The society also leads tours to the outskirts of town to visit the underground shaft of the hard-rock **Washington Gold Mine** and the gold-panning operation at **Lomax Placer Gulch.**

Country Boy Mine. 0542 French Gulch Rd., P.O. Box 8569, Breckenridge. ☎ **970/453-4405.** Admission $10 adults, $5 children 4–12, under 4 free. Special rates and hours are available for families and groups. MC, V. Daily 10am–5pm.

The hundred-year-old Country Boy Mine was opened for tours in July 1994. Take a guided tour 1,000 feet underground, pan for gold in Eureka Creek, explore the mining exhibit and the five-story 75-year-old mill, and listen to the legends. The mine is a constant 55°F year-round, so take a jacket even in August. Future plans include the addition of a train ride into the mine.

Frisco Historic Park. 120 Main St. (at Second St.), Frisco. ☎ **970/668-3428.** Free admission. Summer, Tues–Sun 11am–4pm; winter, Tues–Sat 11am–4pm.

Nine historic buildings, including the town's original 1881 jail, a one-room schoolhouse, log chapel, and homes dating to the 1880s, comprise this beautifully maintained historic park. The schoolhouse contains displays and artifacts from Frisco's early days, and a trapper's cabin has a hands-on exhibit of animal pelts. Artisans sell their wares in several buildings, and a variety of events are scheduled during the summer. A self-guided walking tour of historic Frisco can be obtained at the park.

Summit Historical Museum. 403 LaBonte St., Dillon. ☎ **970/453-9022.** Admission by donation. Museum, Memorial Day–Labor Day, Tues–Sat 1–5pm; or by appointment. Montezuma Schoolhouse, July 4–mid-Aug, Sat only.

A one-room country school—filled with such artifacts of early Colorado education as desks with inkwells, McGuffey readers, and scientific teaching apparatus—is the highlight of Dillon's historic park. Also on the site are the 1885 Lula Myers ranch house and the depression-era Honeymoon Cabin. All buildings were moved from Old Dillon (now beneath the waters of the reservoir) or Keystone. Tours are conducted to the 1884 Montezuma Schoolhouse, located at 10,200 feet elevation in the 1860s mining camp of Montezuma.

SHOPPING

Breckenridge is the place. A variety of shops and galleries occupy the historic buildings along Main Street.

For contemporary art and sculpture, check out **Breckenridge Gallery,** 124 Main St. (☎ **970/453-2592**); western art in a variety of media and techniques can be found at **Paint Horse Gallery,** 226 S. Main St. (☎ **970/453-6813**). Art glass and jewelry, plus glass blowing demonstrations, are offered at **Fineline Studios Inc.,** 306¹/₂ S. Ridge St. (☎ **970/453-2116**). For beautiful photos of Colorado, stop at **Colorado Scenics,** 124 S. Main St. (☎ **970/453-4922**). Photographer Steve Tohari has been photographing his adopted state (he's originally from London) since 1983.

If you're in the market for a special hat, try the **Sundance Hat Co.,** Four Seasons Plaza, 411 S. Main St. (☎ **800/383-HATS** or 970/453-2737). Traditional and contemporary Native American jewelry can be found at **Southwest Designs,** 101 S. Main St. (☎ **800/887-6008** or 970/453-6008). The **Silverthorne Factory Stores** has over 4 dozen outlet shops—from fashion and athletic wear to home accessories, including **9 West, Tommy Hilfiger,** and **Eddie Bauer.** Take I-70 exit 205.

WHERE TO STAY

Thousands of rooms are available in Summit County resorts at any given time. Even so, during peak seasons, finding accommodation may be difficult. In many cases it will be best to simply call one of the reservation services, tell them when you plan to visit and how much you want to spend, and ask for their suggestions. As a general rule, lodging in Breckenridge is the most expensive. Throughout the county condominiums prevail. While they often offer the best value, they're sometimes short on charm. If you're planning to spend much time in one, it pays to ask about views and fireplaces before booking. Local reservation services include: **Summit County Central Reservations** (☎ **800/842-8069**); **Breckenridge Central Reservations** (☎ **800/221-1091** or 800/800-BREC); **Keystone Central Reservations** (☎ **800/ 222-0188**), which can also help with Arapahoe Basin; and **Copper Mountain Resort** (☎ **800/458-8386**).

IN BRECKENRIDGE

Those planning to stay in Breckenridge may want to consider **The Village at Breckenridge,** 655 S. Park St. (P.O. Box 8329), Breckenridge, CO 80424 (☎ **800/ 800-7829** or 970/453-2000), which, as the name implies, is a complete village with its own hotels, condominiums, restaurants, lounges, health clubs, and shops. Rates range from under $100 per night in the slow seasons to close to $1,000 per night for the larger, more luxurious lodgings at Christmas.

✪ **Allaire Timbers Inn Bed & Breakfast.** 9511 Colo. 9 (P.O. Box 4653), Breckenridge, CO 80424. ☎ **800/624-4904** or 970/453-7530. Fax 970/453-8699. 8 rms, 2 suites. TEL. $120–$185 double; $185–$245 suite. Rates include full breakfast. AE, DISC, MC, V.

This is a lovely contemporary log lodge, with a stone wood-burning fireplace in the living room, an outside hot tub, and magnificent views of the mountains and town. All rooms are named for and decorated around the motif of a Colorado mountain pass. There are tiled showers—no tubs—in standard rooms, but suites have hot tubs and stone fireplaces with gas-burning logs. All units have private decks, sprinklers, robes, and fuzzy fleece socks. Located just outside the town limits, there is an easy path that takes you right into town. The homemade gourmet breakfast includes a choice of a meat or vegetarian entree, plus fruit and muffins. In the afternoon guests can enjoy homemade hot citrus cider (an old family recipe), beer, or wine; and the coffee bar is available 24 hours. Smoking and pets are not allowed.

East West Resorts. 465 4 O'Clock Rd. (P.O. Box 2009), Breckenridge, CO 80424. ☎ **800/525-2258** or 970/453-2222. Fax 970/453-0463. 130 units. TV TEL. Summer, $85–$550; winter, $135–$700. Weekly and monthly rates in summer. AE, DISC, MC, V. Free parking in underground lot.

There are several condominium complexes to choose from here, offering everything from a studio to four-bedroom units. Most have mountain views or are nestled among tall pines, provide ski lockers, and have a fireplace and access to a pool and hot tub; many are ski-in and -out.

Little Mountain Lodge Bed & Breakfast. 98 Sunbeam Dr. (P.O. Box 2479), Breckenridge, CO 80424. ☎ **800/468-7707** or 970/453-1969. Fax 970/453-1919. 8 rms, 2 suites. TV TEL. $110–$200 double; $150–$230 suite. Rates include full breakfast. AE, MC, V.

This handsome, whitewash-stained log lodge is nestled among the trees above Breckenridge, with breathtaking views of the mountains from the front rooms and the aspen forest from the back. All rooms are open and airy, and have a balcony or deck, handmade log furnishings, ceiling fans, TV-VCR combo (there's a video library available), and clock radios. Some rooms have whirlpool tubs, and back rooms have cathedral ceilings. There's one handicapped-accessible room with a roll-in shower.

The living room has a huge fireplace made from river rock, with overstuffed sofa and chairs comfortably arranged around it, and a game room has a gas fireplace, pool table, and TV. There's also a ski storage room with a boot dryer. The inn is entirely nonsmoking, and pets are not allowed.

The Lodge at Breckenridge. 112 Overlook Dr. (P.O. Box 391), Breckenridge, CO 80424. ☎ **800/736-1607** or 970/453-9300. Fax 970/453-0625. 45 suites. TV TEL. Mid-Nov–mid-April (except holidays), $135–$250 double; Christmas, $175–$250 double; May–mid-Nov, $105–$200 double. Rates include continental breakfast. AE, DISC, MC, V.

From below, this refurbished log building—a European-style spa with a Rocky Mountain atmosphere—looks like a mountaintop Tibetan monastery. Once you've entered through the landscaped garden, you'll find a superb view. Stone fireplaces and deer-antler chandeliers add a regional touch. Rooms, decorated in different themes, have hardwood floors, Southwest decor and artwork, balconies (or views), and two queen beds. The Longs Peak Room has colorful floral prints in a rustic setting, pedestal sinks, and other antique touches. Suites have sitting areas and kitchens.

The Top of the World Restaurant & Bar, named the community's best during the 1995 Taste of Breckenridge food and wine-tasting event, serves American dinners with a regional and southwestern flair ($15–$25). Room service, 24-hour front desk, ski and boot storage, and a complimentary shuttle for skiers and dinner guests are available. Facilities include a health club, free weights and nautilus equipment, indoor pool, four Jacuzzis, sauna, steam room, spa treatments, wellness programs, and meeting space for 110.

Ridge Street Inn Bed & Breakfast. 212 Ridge St. (P.O. Box 2854), Breckenridge, CO 80424. ☎ **800/452-4680** or 970/453-4680. 6 rms (4 with bath). Summer, $70–$80 with private bath, $65 with shared bath; winter season, $100–$115 with private bath, $90 with shared bath; early and late season, $80–$90 with private bath, $70 with shared bath. Holiday, $115–$135 with private bath, $98 with shared bath. Rates are for double occupancy and include full breakfast. MC, V.

This 1890 Victorian-style inn, located in the heart of the Breckenridge Historic District, is close to restaurants, shops, the town trolley, and shuttle services. The star of the inn is Parlor Suite, furnished with butter-print antiques. It has bay windows, a queen bed and queen sofa sleeper, large private bath, TV, and private entrance. Rooms with private baths also have TVs; the two rooms that share a bath also share a TV lounge. Home-cooked breakfasts might include waffles, fresh strawberry crêpes, or omelets. Children over five are welcome. Neither smoking nor pets are permitted.

CAMPING

✪ Tiger Run R.V. & Chalet Resort. 85 Tiger Run Rd. (3 miles north of Breckenridge off Colo. 9), Breckenridge, CO 80424. ☎ **970/453-9690.** 200 sites. Apr–mid-Nov $30–$35; mid-Nov–Mar $33–$35. Rates include water, sewer, electric, and cable TV. Weekly rates available. DISC, MC, V.

Named for a historic mine in the area, Tiger Run is both conveniently and beautifully located. There is a full-time activities director, with skiing and snowmobiling available in the winter, and live music Friday and Saturday nights in summer. The clubhouse lodge, in the middle of the park, is open year-round, with an indoor swimming pool, hot tubs, game room, TV room, laundry facilities, rest rooms with showers, and telephones. There are tennis, volleyball, and basketball courts, a children's playground, and other sports equipment available at the office, including bicycles for rent. In addition, there is a convenience store at the office, and pets are welcome. There are also 50 chalet-style cabins on the property, with rates of $80 double plus $5 per additional person in summer and $125 double plus $10 for each additional person in winter.

AT COPPER MOUNTAIN

Most lodging at Copper Mountain is in condominium-type units, ranging from efficiencies to four-bedroom suites. **Copper Mountain Resort,** I-70 exit 195 (P.O. Box 3001), Copper Mountain, CO 80443 (☎ **800/458-8386** or 970/968-2882), has 525 units, most with fireplaces, available through its Copper Mountain Lodging Services, with rates starting at about $130 double, although off-season discounts may be available. Rates during the Christmas holidays will be considerably higher.

Club Med Copper Mountain. 50 Beeler Place, Copper Mountain, CO 80443. ☎ **800/ CLUB-MED** or 970/968-2161. Fax 970/968-2166. $150–$230 per day; $970–$1,580 per week. Rates are per person, double occupancy and include three meals daily, lift tickets and instruction, and a children's program. Highest rates and minimum stay requirement at Christmas and other holidays. Special packages available in early winter. Closed mid-Apr–Nov. AE, MC, V.

One of only two American entries in this famed international chain of resorts (the other is in Florida), Club Med occupies a modern seven-story lodge near the west end of Copper Mountain village. The main doors open to a central cocktail lounge beside a cozy fireplace, creating an immediate atmosphere of leisure. Guest rooms are simple but adequate. All have twin beds or a king on request, full bathrooms, and attractive appointments. Many have mountain views. One of the main draws is the 40-instructor Club Med ski school, among the few programs in the United States that offer the highly respected French method of teaching. Lessons for adults and children, as well as snowboarding instruction, are offered.

The main dining room serves three buffet-style meals daily. On the lower level are a more intimate restaurant for private dining and a nightclub which often features live entertainment. Transportation from Denver International Airport can be arranged for a fee. Facilities include four outdoor Jacuzzis, two saunas, exercise and aerobics classes, a game room, big-screen TV, theater, boutique, ski-rental shop, and guest laundry.

IN FRISCO

Relatively easy to get to from Summit County's five ski areas, Frisco is where you'll find the area's least expensive lodging.

Holiday Inn-Summit County. I-70 exit 203 (P.O. Box 4310), Frisco, CO 80443. ☎ **800/ 782-7669** or 970/668-5000. Fax 970/668-0718. 213 rms, 1 suite. A/C TV TEL. Dec–Apr, $89– $195 double; spring and fall, $69–$79 double; summer, $79–$109 double. Children 19 and under stay free in parents' room. AE, DC, DISC, MC, V.

Located beside the shoreline wetlands of Dillon Reservoir, this Holiday Inn maintains the feel of a ski lodge. Many second-floor rooms have balconies with views across the lake. All have standard hotel furnishings; most feature two double beds or a queen bed. Local phone calls cost 50¢.

The restaurant serves three meals daily and offers home-style meals such as pot roast and chicken-fried steak, plus an all-you-can-eat soup-and-salad bar.

Services and facilities include room service, dry cleaning, and refreshments in the lobby; HoliDome with indoor swimming pool, Jacuzzi, sauna, sun deck, access to nearby health club, game room, and video arcade; ski rentals and repairs; guest laundry; and meeting space for 250. Pets are not allowed.

Twilight Inn. 308 Main St. (P.O. Box 397), Frisco, CO 80443. ☎ **800/262-1002** or 970/ 668-5009. 12 rms (8 with bath). Winter, $90 double without bath, $103–$128 double with bath; summer, $50 double without bath, $60–$75 double with bath. Rates include continental breakfast. AE, DISC, MC, V. Private off-street parking.

Most rooms in this modern country bed-and-breakfast inn, located in downtown Frisco, have private decks or balconies and antique furnishings. Guests can relax around the fireplace in the large living room or in front of the television in the cozy library. Amenities include an indoor hot tub and steam room, laundry room, kitchen use, and locked storage area. Children are catered to with cribs and high chairs, and pets are accepted.

AT KEYSTONE

At **Keystone Resort,** U.S. 6 (P.O. Box 38), Keystone, CO 80435 (☎ **800/258-9553**), there are more than 1,100 units, including 152 rooms at the highly rated **Keystone Lodge,** where rates are about $140 to $150 for two people in spring and fall, ranging up to $200 to $230 double during peak holiday seasons.

WHERE TO DINE
IN BRECKENRIDGE
Expensive

Briar Rose Restaurant. 109 E. Lincoln St. ☎ **970/453-9948.** Reservations recommended. Main courses $10–$26. AE, DISC, MC, V. Daily 5–10pm. REGIONAL/STEAK/SEAFOOD.

Located uphill from the Main Street traffic light, the Briar Rose is among the town's most elegant restaurants. Classical paintings, fine music, and white-linen service underscore Briar Rose's sophisticated atmosphere. The adjoining trophy lounge has big-game heads, a few paintings, and a hundred-year-old bar. You can start with escargot, crab-stuffed mushrooms, or homemade soup. Dinners feature game when available— usually elk, moose, buffalo, and caribou. Other popular choices include slow-cooked prime rib, veal, steaks, duck, and seafood. Vegetarian meals are also available, plus a children's menu and an extensive wine list.

Hearthstone Casual Dining. 130 S. Ridge St. ☎ **970/453-1148.** Reservations recommended. Main courses, lunch $4.95–$7.95, dinner $12.50–$24.95. AE, MC, V. Daily 5:30– 10pm; plus in summer 11:30am–3pm. REGIONAL/STEAKS.

This restaurant in the 1886 Kaiser House is among Breckenridge's favorites. Blue on the outside, with white trim and wrought iron, it has a rustic yet elegant interior. There are fine views across the Ten Mile Range from the upstairs lounge. You can get great lunches here—jalapeno-wrapped shrimp, turkey-and-avocado sandwiches, half-pound burgers—but dinner is what the Hearthstone is known for. Start with baked Brie or steamed mussels. Then choose from fresh seafood, such as Hearthstone shrimp (with garlic and ginger) or yellowfin tuna; chicken; and a variety of steaks and wild game, or slow-roasted prime rib. Vegetarian choices are also offered.

Moderate

Breckenridge Brewery and Pub. 600 S. Main St. ☎ **970/453-1550.** Reservations not accepted. Lunch $4.75–$8.25; dinner $6.95–$16.95. AE, DISC, MC, V. Daily 11am–midnight, bar open until 2am. AMERICAN/SOUTHWEST.

This brew pub was designed around its brewery, giving diners a first-hand view of the brewing process. Try the India Pale Ale or the Avalanche—a local favorite. Lunch choices include fish-and-chips, half-pound burgers, charbroiled chicken sandwiches, chicken or vegetable burritos, soups and salads, lasagna and calzones. The dinner menu adds ravioli marinara, Colorado elk medallions, baby-back ribs, Mama T's meat loaf, New York sirloin, and North Atlantic grilled salmon. Desserts are homemade, and this brew pub also caters to abstainers—they brew their own root beer.

Horseshoe II Restaurant. 115 S. Main St. ☎ **970/453-7463.** Breakfast $2.75–$5.95; lunch $3.95–$6.50; dinner $9.50–$17.50. AE, MC, V. Daily 7:30am–10pm. Hours may be shorter in spring. AMERICAN.

A family-style restaurant in a historic 19th-century building, the Horseshoe II (yes, there was once a I) is set in the heart of downtown Breckenridge. It has two outdoor patios, ornate walls and ceilings, lace curtains, and mounted horseshoes. The bar is equally popular for espressos and alcoholic beverages, with over 15 varieties of draft beer, including microbrewed choices.

You can get three meals a day here, starting with breakfasts such as the Breck-Mex Express and the HAB (high-altitude breakfast), consisting of two eggs, two pancakes, breakfast meat, and juice. Lunch offers salads, burgers, and sandwiches. Dinners are more elaborate and feature the likes of pecan-and-chicken stir-fry, chicken-fried steak, fresh grilled Colorado trout, prime rib, and baby-back pork ribs.

Poirrier's Cajun Café. 224 S. Main St. ☎ **970/453-1877.** Reservations recommended. Main courses $6–$11 at lunch, $13–$20 at dinner. AE, CB, DC, DISC, MC, V. Daily 11:30am–2:30pm; 5:30–10pm. CAJUN/CREOLE.

This brownstone is straight out of New Orleans, with sidewalk cafe seating behind a wrought-iron railing. Two rooms inside display harlequin masks and photos of Louisiana. Indeed, owners Bobby and Connie Poirrier are native Cajuns. For lunch, order a po-boy, New Orleans–style red beans and rice, or seafood gumbo. At dinnertime, there's poisson Hymel (a catfish filet surrounded with crayfish étoufée, served with steamed rice and gumbo), blackened catch of the day, chicken à la Poirrier (with a mushroom sauce), and rib-eye steak. Finish your meal with Lafayette bread pudding. A children's menu is available.

Inexpensive

Mi Casa. 600 Park Ave. ☎ **970/453-2071.** Reservations not accepted. Main courses $4.95–$14.95. AE, MC, V. Daily 11:30am–3pm, 5–10pm (bar open 11:30am to closing). MEXICAN.

A large room with stuccoed walls, a tile floor, wooden furniture, and baskets of silk flowers hanging from a beamed ceiling, Mi Casa is considered Breckenridge's best Mexican restaurant. Its popular adjoining cantina offers margaritas by the liter. In addition to the standard burritos, tostadas, fajitas, and enchiladas, there is a fine selection of beef, lamb, seafood, chicken, pasta, and vegetarian dishes.

At Copper Mountain

O'Shea's Copper Bar. Copper Junction Bldg. opposite Mountain Plaza. ☎ **970/968-2882, ext. 6504.** Reservations not accepted. Main courses $7–$15. AE, CB, DC, MC, V. Late Nov–late Apr, daily 10:30am–midnight. AMERICAN/MEXICAN.

There are two floors to this restaurant—a casual, mountain-style cafe on the main level, and a sports bar in the basement. There are buffets, including Mexican dishes at lunch and prime rib at dinner. Or order off the menu: salads and burgers at midday, mesquite chicken or buffalo shrimp at night. There's also a children's menu.

In Frisco

Charity's. 307 Main St., Frisco. ☎ **970/668-3644.** Reservations not accepted. Main courses $3.95–$7.95 at lunch, $5.95–$14.95 at dinner. AE, MC, V. Daily 11:30am–10pm. STEAK/SEAFOOD.

Charity's offers a wide selection of pastas, charbroiled steaks, fresh seafood, and a variety of Colorado microbrewed beers, including eight on tap. Fresh seafood selections might include grilled salmon and trout Grand Marnier, and you'll also find roast chicken, burgers, and miner's stew on the menu.

At Keystone

Keystone Ranch. Keystone Ranch Rd. ☎ **970/468-4161.** Reservations required. Six-course dinner $62. AE, CB, DC, DISC, MC, V. Daily 6pm–midnight, two seatings. CREATIVE REGIONAL.

A working cattle ranch for over 3 decades until 1972, the Keystone Ranch now boasts riding stables, a fine golf course, and this outstanding gourmet restaurant in the 1940s ranch house. The six-course menu offers a choice of appetizer, followed by soup, salad, and fruit sorbet. Main dishes, which vary seasonally, might include rack of lamb, beef, fresh seafood, elk or other regional game. There's valet parking and a full bar.

SUMMIT COUNTY AFTER DARK

Breckenridge has the greatest selection of bars and clubs in Summit County, but every community has its watering holes.

Popular bars in Breckenridge include **Breckenridge Brewery & Pub,** 600 S. Main St. (☎ **970/453-1550**), whose microbrews include Avalanche, a full-bodied amber ale billed as "the one you can't get away from"; and **JohSha's,** 500 S. Park St. (☎ **970/453-4146**), a popular live-music dance club. For live blues and jazz, try **Alligator Lounge,** 318 S. Main St. (☎ **970/453-7782**); and for both live and recorded dance music, there's **Eric's Underground** at **Downstairs at Eric's,** a bar and restaurant at 111 S. Main St. (☎ **970/453-1401**).

In Frisco, **Moose Jaw Food & Spirits,** 208 Main St. (☎ **970/668-3931**), is a burgers, pool, and darts hangout. Silverthorne's **Old Dillon Inn,** 321 Blue River Pkwy. (☎ **970/468-2791**), serves delicious Mexican food, margaritas, and ice-cold beer in an 1870s Old West–style bar, along with live country music and dancing. In Dillon, the **Snake River Saloon,** 23074 U.S. 6 (☎ **970/468-2788**), is a noisy skier hangout, with live rock music nightly all winter, weekends in summer.

6 Vail & Beaver Creek

Consistently ranked the country's most popular ski resort by skiers and ski magazines almost since its inception, Vail is it. In fact, it's hard to imagine a more celebrated spot to schuss. Off the slopes, Vail is an incredibly compact Tyrolean village, frequented by almost as many Europeans as Americans, a situation which lends its restaurants, lodgings, and trendy shops a more transatlantic feel than other Colorado resorts. But the size of the mountain and the difficulty and excitement of its trails are still what draw the faithful.

Historically speaking, there was very little in the town's past to indicate that Vail would become the mega-destination it has. No substantial amount of gold was found in the Gore Valley, as it was then known, and until U.S. 6 was built through Vail Pass in 1939, the only inhabitants were a handful of sheep ranchers. Dropping farther back into history, it's worth noting that the resort could never have been possible if it weren't for the reaction members of the Ute tribe had to the first incursions into this valley by white gold-seekers in the 1850s and 1860s. In response to the disturbance these profiteers caused to their way of life, the Utes set the valley's forests alight in "spite fires"—burnings that created the wide-open ridges and back bowls that make skiers the world over quiver in their boots.

It was only when veterans of the Tenth Mountain Division, who trained during World War II at Camp Hale, 23 miles south of the valley, returned in the 1950s that the reality of skiing the Rockies was realized. One of them, Peter Siebert, urged development of this mountain land in the White River National Forest. His investment company began construction in 1962, and the entire ski resort—immediately among the three largest ski areas in the United States—was completed and ready to open in December 1963. Additional ski-lift capacity made Vail America's largest ski resort by 1964.

Beaver Creek, built in 1980, has quickly built a reputation as an elegant, if expensive, place to vacation. Like Vail, it is a fully equipped four-season resort that offers golf (the course was designed by Robert Trent Jones, Jr.), hot-air ballooning, mountain biking, fishing, and horseback riding, in addition to skiing. Its atmosphere is a bit more formal than the surrounding area, and its nightlife tends more toward refined piano bars than rowdy saloons, but the exclusivity of its après-ski spots isn't reflected on the slopes. At Beaver Creek, there's a trail for everyone. Experts are challenged but beginners aren't left out—they too can head straight to the top and then ski all the way down on a trail that matches their skill level.

ESSENTIALS

GETTING THERE   By Car   Vail is right on the I-70 corridor, so it's exceedingly easy to find your way there. Just take exit 176, whether you're coming from the east (Denver) or the west (Grand Junction). A more direct route from the south may be U.S. 24 through Leadville; this Tennessee Pass road joins I-70 5 miles west of Vail.

By Plane   From mid-December to early April visitors can fly directly into **Eagle County Jet Center,** 35 miles west of Vail between I-70 exits 140 and 147 (☎ 970/524-7700). **Delta** (☎ 800/221-1212) lands here, and **American** (☎ 800/433-7300) offers a flight from Dallas. Call the jet center for possible availability of flights at other times.

By Airport Shuttle   Most visitors fly into **Denver International Airport** and continue on to Vail aboard any of four shuttle services: **Airport Transportation Service** (☎ 800/247-7074 or 970/476-7576), in winter only; **Colorado Mountain Express** (☎ 800/525-6363 or 970/949-4227); **Vail Valley Transportation** (☎ 800/882-8872 or 970/476-8008); or **Vans to Vail** (☎ 800/222-2112 or 970/476-4467). Visitors can also fly into Colorado Springs Airport and then take Vans to Vail.

ORIENTATION   Narrow Vail Valley, hemmed in on the south and north by steep mountains, is in a long strip along Gore Creek. In fact, as you come in from the east across Vail Pass, you'll find a series of separate communities: East Vail (exit 180), Vail (exit 176), West Vail (exit 173), Minturn (exit 171), Avon and Beaver Creek (exit 167), and Edwards (exit 163).

The town of Vail is mostly on the south side of the interstate, which you exit onto Vail Road. The two main skiing areas are Vail Village, slightly to the east, and Lionshead, to the west. Because much of Vail is open to pedestrians only, it's wise to park in one of the major parking structures off South Frontage Road, then get hold of one of several available tourist maps to find your way through the network of lanes.

VISITOR INFORMATION   For information or reservations in the Vail Valley, contact the **Vail Valley Tourism and Convention Bureau,** 100 E. Meadow Dr., Vail, CO 81657 (☎ **800/525-3875** or 970/476-1000); or **Vail Associates, Inc.,** P.O. Box 7, Vail, CO 81658 (☎ **800/525-2257** or 970/476-5601). The CVB's information guide is also available in Spanish.

Information centers are located at the parking structures in Vail and Lionshead on South Frontage Road.

GETTING AROUND   Vail is one of only a few Colorado communities where you really don't need a car. The Town of Vail runs a **free shuttle-bus service** between 7am and 2am daily, although hours may be shorter in shoulder seasons. Shuttles in the Vail Village–Lionshead area run every 3 to 5 minutes, and there are regularly scheduled trips to West Vail and East Vail (☎ 970/479-2172). There's also free transportation between Beaver Creek Resort and the village of Avon (☎ 970/949-1938). Buses between Vail and Beaver Creek, an 11-mile trip, run daily from 5:30am to 2am for a nominal fee (☎ 970/949-6121).

Vail Valley Taxi (☎ **970/476-TAXI**) operates throughout the area, around-the-clock.

For **car rentals,** try **Hertz** (☎ **800/654-3131** or 970/524-7177) at the Eagle County Jet Center in Eagle, **Thrifty** (☎ **800/367-2277,** 970/476-8718 in Vail, or 970/949-7787 in Beaver Creek), or **Enterprise Rent-A-Car** (☎ **800/325-8007** or 970/845-8393). For four-wheel–drive vehicles, call **Crazy Horse 4-Wheel Drive Rentals** (☎ 800/888-7320).

FAST FACTS   In case of an **emergency,** call **911.** The hospital, **Vail Valley Medical Center,** is at 181 West Meadow Drive between Vail Road and East Lionshead Circle (☎ **970/476-2451,** or 970/476-8065 for 24-hour emergency department). The **post office** is on North Frontage Road West, opposite Donovan Park (☎ **970/476-5217**). For **road information,** call 970/479-2226. **State, county, and city taxes** add about 8% to hotel bills in Vail, and about 9.5% in Beaver Creek.

SPECIAL EVENTS   The Vail area holds the following annual events: Taste of Vail, over the first weekend of April; Vail America Days, on July 4 valley-wide; the Bravo! Colorado Music Festival, from early July to early August in Vail and Beaver Creek; the Eagle County Fair and Rodeo, on the second weekend of August in Eagle; the Beaver Creek Arts Festival, over the third weekend of August in Beaver Creek; Oktoberfest, in mid-September in Vail/Lionshead; Minturn Jazz and Blues Fest, weekends of October and November in Minturn; and the Torchlight Parade in Vail, December 31st.

SKIING & OTHER WINTER ACTIVITIES

VAIL   In his *Skiing America* guide, author Charles Leocha writes, "Vail comes closest of any resort in America to epitomizing what many skiers would call perfection."

It's hard to disagree. You can arrive at the base village, unload and park your car, and not have to drive again until it's time to go. You'll find all the shops, restaurants, and nightlife you could want within a short walk of your hotel or condominium.

Ski area boundaries stretch 7 miles from east to west along the ridge top, from Outer Mongolia to Game Creek Bowl, and the skiable terrain is measured at 4,014 acres. Virtually every lift on the front (north-facing) side of the mountain has runs for every level of skier, with a predominance of novice and intermediate terrain. The world-famous Back Bowls are decidedly *not* for beginners, and there are few options for intermediates. The seven bowls—from west to east: Sun Down, Sun Up, Tea Cup, China, Siberia, Inner Mongolia, and Outer Mongolia—are strictly for advanced and expert skiers; snow and weather conditions determine just *how* expert you ought to be. They are served by four lifts, one of them a short surface lift to access the Mongolias. One trip down the Slot or Rasputin's Revenge will give you a fair idea of just how good you are.

From Mongolia Summit, at 11,450 feet, Vail has a vertical drop on the front side of 3,250 feet; on the back side, 1,850 feet. Average annual snowfall is 334 inches (nearly 28 ft.). All told, there are 121 named trails served by 26 lifts—a gondola, 11 quad chairs, three triple chairs, five double chairs, and six surface lifts. "Meet the Mountain" tours begin at Lionshead and Vail Village daily at 9am. Snowboarders are welcome, and there's a 400-foot half-pipe at Golden Peak.

Eleven **mountain restaurants** include two that ask for reservations: the **Cook Shack** (☎ **970/479-2030**), with creative American cuisine, at the Summit, and the **Wine Stube** (☎ **970/479-2034**) at Eagle's Nest, with international cuisine atop the Lionshead Gondola. **Two Elk Restaurant** on the Far East summit has southwestern cuisine and pasta, and baked potato and salad bars. **Wok 'n' Roll,** in China Bowl, is a ski-by pagoda with Asian fast food; **the Dog Haus** offers ski-by hot dogs at the foot of the Northwoods Express; **Wildwood Shelter** specializes in smoked or barbecued foods; **Eagle's Nest** has salad, potato, and pasta bars. And Mid-Vail has two levels of cafeterias: **Golden Peak** and **Trail's End** serve breakfast, lunch, and après-ski drinks. **Salsa's** has Mexican fast food at Eagle's Nest.

Vail has a highly respected children's program. **The Golden Peak Children's Skiing Center and the Lionshead Children's Skiing Center** (☎ **970/476-3239** for both) are under the aegis of the Ski School. Call 970/476-9090 for recorded information on a wide range of day and night family activities. There are daily NASTAR races at the Black Forest Race Arena.

At press time, lift tickets cost $48 per day for adults, $35 per day children 12 and under, $37 per day seniors 65 to 69; free for seniors 70 and older. Rates are subject to change.

Vail is open from early November to the third week of April, daily from 8:30am to 3:30pm. For further information, contact **Vail Mountain,** Vail Associates, Inc., P.O. Box 7, Vail, CO 81658 (☎ **800/525-2257** or 970/476-5601; snow reports 970/476-4888; fax 970/845-5729).

BEAVER CREEK   Vail's other mountain is an outstanding resort in its own right, one with a more secluded atmosphere than its better-known neighbor. Located in a valley $1^1/_2$ miles off the I-70 corridor, Beaver Creek combines European château–style elegance in its base village with expansive slopes for novice and intermediate skiers. The Grouse Mountain lift reaches expert terrain.

From the village, the Centennial Express lift to Spruce Saddle reaches wide-open northwest-facing midmountain slopes and the Stump Park beginners' area.

Vail

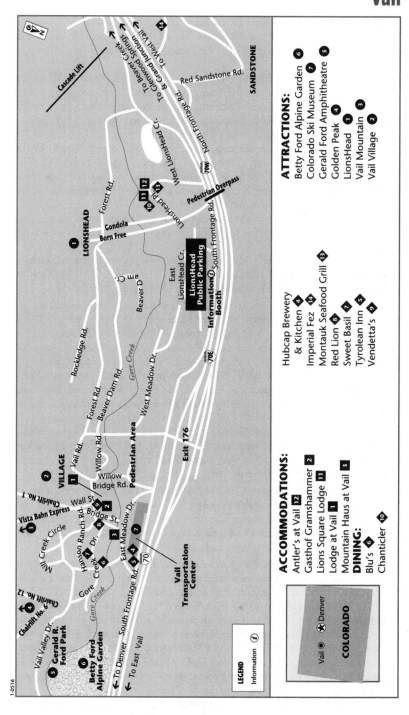

ATTRACTIONS:
Betty Ford Alpine Garden **6**
Colorado Ski Museum **7**
Gerald Ford Amphitheatre **5**
Golden Peak **4**
LionsHead **1**
Vail Mountain **3**
Vail Village **2**

ACCOMMODATIONS:
Antler's at Vail **12**
Gasthof Gramshammer **2**
Lions Square Lodge **11**
Lodge at Vail **1**
Mountain Haus at Vail **3**

DINING:
Blu's **6**
Chanticler **10**
Hubcap Brewery & Kitchen **4**
Imperial Fez **14**
Montauk Seafood Grill **13**
Red Lion **8**
Sweet Basil **7**
Tyrolean Inn **5**
Vendetta's **9**

LEGEND
Information **ⓘ**

COLORADO
Vail ● ★ Denver

251

Opposite, the Strawberry Park lift accesses Larkspur Bowl and the McCoy Park cross-country area at 9,840 feet. Three other lifts—Larkspur, Grouse Mountain, and Westfall (serving the expert Birds of Prey area)—leave from Red-Tail Camp at midmountain.

Beaver Creek's vertical drop is 3,340 feet from the 11,440-foot summit. There are 1,414 developed acres, though Vail Associates are licensed to develop up to 5,600; plans are on the drawing board. Currently, 11 lifts (three quad chairs, four triples, and four doubles) serve 61 trails and the average annual snowfall is 330 inches. Snowboarding is permitted, and there is a snowboarding park.

There are six **mountain restaurants,** including the highly praised **Beano's Cabin** (see "Where to Dine," below). Others include **Rafters,** at Spruce Saddle (☎ 970/ 845-5528 for reservations), the **Spruce Saddle Cafeteria,** the **Red-Tail Camp** fast-food stop, **McCoy's,** offering breakfast, lunch, and après-ski entertainment at the base, and **Tater's,** at the top of Strawberry Park Express.

At press time, lift tickets cost $48 per day for adults, $35 per day children 12 and under, $37 per day seniors 65 to 69; free for seniors 70 and older. Rates are subject to change.

Beaver Creek is open daily 8:30am to 3:30pm. For more information, contact **Beaver Creek Resort,** Vail Associates, Inc., P.O. Box 7, Vail, CO 81658 (☎ 800/ 525-2257 or 970/949-5750; snow reports 970/476-4888; fax 970/845-5729).

ARROWHEAD For those who want to give the glitterati wide berth, there's another ski resort in Eagle County: Arrowhead Mountain, P.O. Box 7, Vail, CO 81658 (☎ 970/926-3029; fax 970/926-2321). Located 2 miles west of Beaver Creek on U.S. 6, it's a small family-oriented area, with one high-speed quad chairlift and a beginners' surface lift serving 15 runs, nearly all of them for intermediates or novices. A new lift is planned for the 1996/1997 season which will connect Arrowhead Mountain with Beaver Creek Resort. The mountain has a 1,700-foot vertical drop, from the 9,100-foot summit. Additional snowmaking equipment was installed in 1995 to supplement the annual snowfall of 115 inches (almost 10 ft.). Snowboarding is permitted. Arrowhead is open mid-December to early April, daily from 9am to 3:30pm. Full-day tickets (1995/1996 rates) cost $32 for adults, $20 for children 16 and under, $26 for seniors 65 to 69; free for seniors 70 and over.

BACKCOUNTRY SKI TOURS **Paragon Guides,** P.O. Box 130, Vail, CO 81658 (☎ 970/926-5299; fax 970/926-5298), is one of the country's premier winter guide services and the oldest guide service on the Tenth Mountain Trail & Hut System, with over 15 years experience. They offer a wide variety of trips designed for all ability levels, from 3 to 6 days, and limited to eight persons with two guides. Costs start at $530 per person (1995/1996 rate).

CROSS-COUNTRY SKIING Cross-country skiers won't feel left out at any of Vail's ski areas. Each of the resorts has ample Nordic terrain set aside, and there's a tremendous system of winter trails through the surrounding mountains.

Vail's Nordic Center, 458-X Vail Valley Dr., Vail, CO 81657 (☎ 970/ 845-5313), has 33 kilometers (20 miles) of trails, part of them on the Vail Golf Course, and offers guided tours, lessons, and snowshoeing. **Beaver Creek** has a Nordic skiing center on its golf course, and a 32-kilometer (21-mile) mountaintop track system with a skating lane in 9,840-foot McCoy Park (☎ 970/949-5750). Most of the high-altitude terrain here is intermediate, though there's some for both beginners and advanced cross-country skiers; telemarking lessons are available.

For general information on the network of backcountry trails in the Vail area, contact the **Holy Cross Ranger District Office,** White River National Forest, P.O. Box

190, Minturn, CO 81645 (☎ 970/827-5715). Of particular note is the system of trails known as the **Tenth Mountain Division Hut System,** 1280 Ute Ave., Aspen, CO 81611 (☎ 970/925-5775). Generally following the World War II training network of the Camp Hale militia, the trails cover 273 miles and link Vail with Leadville, Aspen, and Arrowhead. There are 14 overnight cabins, and hikers and mountain bikers also use this trail.

SNOWCAT SKIING Adventurous downhillers who want to get away from the crowded slopes can try snowcat tours with **Nova Guides** (☎ 970/949-4232).

BOBSLEDDING The Vail Bobsled (☎ 970/476-5601) runs a 3,200-foot course beginning just below Mid-Vail near the Short Cut run. The ride lasts about 1 minute and costs about $15, including helmet.

ICE-SKATING There's year-round public skating at the **John A. Dobson Ice Arena,** East Lionshead Circle (☎ 970/479-2270); call for hours and admission fees. **Nottingham Lake** in Avon (☎ 970/949-5648) has free afternoon and evening skating in winter, as well as a hockey rink and speed-skating lane. Skate rentals are available at both.

SLEIGH RIDES Horse-drawn sleigh rides, including dinner rides, are offered by several companies in the Vail area, including **Steve Jones' Sleigh Rides** (☎ 970/476-8057) and **4 Eagle Ranch** (☎ 970/926-3372). Rates for a sleigh ride with dinner are about $50 for adults and $25 for children, and rates for sleigh rides alone start at about $25 for a 1-hour ride.

SNOWMOBILING You can see a lot of beautiful country in a short amount of time on a snowmobile. Among companies offering guided trips are **Piney River Ranch,** Red Sandstone Road (☎ 970/476-3941), **Nova Guides** (☎ 970/949-4232), and **Timberline Tours** (☎ 970/476-1414). Rates are usually about $100 for one person on a snowmobile or $150 for two for a 2-hour ride.

WARM-WEATHER & OTHER YEAR-ROUND ACTIVITIES

Vail doesn't shut down once the skiers go home, although lodging rates drop dramatically. Instead, visitors and locals alike trade their skis for mountain bikes and hiking boots, and hit the trails again. The resort closes parts of the mountain to access from early May to late June to protect elk calving habitats, but other than that, warm-weather activities cover the mountains.

The town of Avon's **Nottingham Lake** (☎ 970/949-4280) has fishing and paddle boats in summer. Contact **Vail Recreation District** (☎ 970/479-2294) for information on various activities, including the town's children's programs.

BALLOONING Camelot Balloons (☎ 800/785-4743 or 970/926-2435) and **Mountain Balloon Adventures** (☎ 970/476-2353) fly year-round, with rides lasting from a half-hour to 45 minutes to well over an hour, and usually concluding with a champagne toast. Rates start at $125.

CATTLE DRIVES For a taste of the Old West, join a cattle drive at **4 Eagle Ranch,** which can be reached via I-70. Take exit 157, and drive 4 miles north on Colo. 131 (☎ 970/926-3372). Chuck-wagon dinners and hayrides are also offered.

FISHING The streams and mountain lakes surrounding Vail are rich with rainbow, brook, brown, and cutthroat trout, and mountain whitefish. Gore Creek through the town of Vail is a popular anglers' venue, especially toward evening from its banks along the Vail Golf Course. Also good are the Eagle River, joined by Gore Creek 5 miles downstream near Minturn; the Black Lakes near the summit of Vail

Pass; and 60-acre Piney Lake (see directions under "Mountain Biking," below). At the latter site, the **Piney River Ranch,** c/o Vail Associates, P.O. Box 7, Vail, CO 81658 (☎ 970/476-3941), rents canoes and small boats for fishing and will also supply fly rods and waders.

For a guided fishing trip from a boat or the shore, both lake and river, call **Nova Guides,** P.O. Box 2018, Vail, CO 81658 (☎ 970/949-4232). Boat trips run about $200 for a half day and $295 for a full day for two persons. For fishing supplies, stop at **Gore Creek Fly Fisherman, Inc.,** 183 E. Gore Creek Dr., Vail (☎ 970/ 476-3296). Ask about the company's guided fishing trips, 3-day fishing school, boat trips, and horseback fishing trips.

GOLF The season for golf varies in the Vail valley, depending on snow conditions, but courses are usually open from mid-May to mid-October. Generally considered the best course in the area is the **Beaver Creek Resort Golf Course,** 75 Offerson Road, Beaver Creek (☎ 970/949-7123), designed by Robert Trent Jones, Jr., with greens fees of about $100 for 18 holes, including cart. The **Vail Golf Course,** 1778 Vail Valley Dr., Vail (☎ 970/479-2260), charges about $45 for nine holes and $70 for 18; and the **Eagle-Vail Golf Course,** 0431 Eagle Dr., Avon (☎ 970/949-5267), is a challenging course that charges about $60 for 18 holes.

HIKING & BACKPACKING The surrounding White River National Forest has a plethora of trails leading to pristine lakes and spectacular panoramic views. The Holy Cross Wilderness Area, southwest of Vail, encompasses 14,005-foot Mount of the Holy Cross and is an awesome region with over 100 miles of trails. Eagle's Nest Wilderness Area lies to the north, in the impressive Gore Range. For information on these and other hiking areas, consult the **Holy Cross Ranger District Office,** 24747 U.S. 24 (P.O. Box 190), Minturn, CO 81645 (☎ 970/827-5715).

Among the less strenuous walks in the immediate Vail area is the 11-mile Two Elk Trail, a national scenic trail. It starts in East Vail, just south of the Gore Circle Campground on old U.S. 6, and ends in Minturn.

For supplies and more information, visit **Vail Mountaineering,** 500 Lionshead Mall, Vail (☎ 970/476-4223).

HORSEBACK RIDING One of the best ways to explore this beautiful and rugged mountain country is on the back of a horse, and there are a number of outfitters and stables willing and able to help.

The **Spraddle Creek Ranch,** 100 N. Frontage Rd. E., Vail (☎ 970/476-6941), is geared for family day outings. Located across I-70 from the Vail interchange, it features a pony ring for children. Also providing horseback rides, including multiday pack trips, are **Beaver Creek Stables** at the Beaver Creek Resort (☎ 970/845-7770) and **Piney River Ranch,** 15 miles north of Vail via Red Sandstone Road (☎ 970/ 476-3941).

A. J. Brink Outfitters, at Sweetwater Lake Resort, 3406 Sweetwater Rd., Gypsum (☎ 970/534-9301), about 60 miles west of Vail, offers half-day rides for $50 and full-day trips starting at $75, plus overnight pack trips, photo rides, and horseback fishing trips. The resort also has cabins ($85–$130), several motel units ($50), camping ($9), boat rentals ($25 per day), and a restaurant that serves three meals daily.

JEEP TOURS The mountains are accessible to virtually anyone in four-wheel–drive vehicles. Contact **Nova Guides, Inc.,** P.O. Box 2018, Vail 81658 (☎ 970/ 949-4232), for guided Jeep Tours ($50–$60).

LLAMA TREKKING   **Paragon Guides,** P.O. Box 130, Vail, CO 81658 (☎ **970/ 926-5299;** fax 970/926-5298), offers llama trekking trips, which can be custom designed to each group or family. They range from 3 to 6 days, June through September, and are limited to eight persons for camping, slightly larger groups for hut trips.

MOUNTAIN BIKING   Summer visitors can take the Lionshead Gondola to Eagle's Nest on Vail Mountain, rent mountain bikes (and helmets) there, and cruise downhill on what had been ski runs to return their bikes at the base of the gondola.

There are many choices for avid bikers, both on backcountry trails and road tours. The 13½-mile Vail Pass Bikeway connects the mountain village to Copper Mountain, from which additional bike paths lead to Breckenridge and Keystone. Another popular trip is the 15-mile Red Sandstone Road to Piney Lake, beginning from North Frontage Road West a mile west of the Vail exit from I-70.

Mountain bike rentals are available at a number of shops, including **Vail Bike Tech,** in the Lift House Lodge (☎ **970/476-5995**); **Base Mountain Sports,** at the Vail Village Inn Plaza Store (☎ **970/476-4515**); and the **Vail 21 Store** in Lionshead (☎ **970/476-3600**). Rates are about $7 for the first hour and $2 for each additional hour.

Paragon Guides, P.O. Box 130, Vail, CO 81658 (☎ **970/926-5299;** fax 970/ 926-5298), offers a 5-day fall foliage mountain biking and hiking tour from late July into late September, along old logging and mining roads in the backcountry. Rentals are available starting at $18 per day, and they will also custom design a trip for a group.

RIVER RAFTING   The Eagle River, just a few miles west of Vail, offers excellent white water during the summer, especially during the May to June thaw. Families can enjoy the relatively gentle (Class II–IV) lower Eagle, west of Minturn; the upper Eagle, above Minturn, is significantly rougher (Class IV–V rapids). Area rafting companies also take trips on the Colorado River, which they access about 35 miles northwest via Colo. 131, at State Bridge.

One respected company that has been running area rivers for close to 25 years is **Colorado River Runs,** Star Route, Box 32, Bond, CO 80423 (☎ **800/826-1081** or 970/653-4292). Although the company offers all types of trips, from calm to rough, it specializes in the easier trips, suitable for families. Rates for half-day trips are in the $26 to $36 range, while full-day trips, including lunch, are usually $45 to $65. Other companies offering raft trips include **Nova Guides,** P.O. Box 2018, Vail, CO 81658 (☎ **970/949-4232**), and **Lakota River Guides,** (☎ **970/476-RAFT**), with similar rates, although trips on rougher white water will be higher.

TENNIS   There are many public courts in the Vail valley, including nine at Golden Peak, at the foot of Lift 6, and six at Ford Park, on South Frontage Road east of Vail Village.

THE FESTIVAL SCENE

The summer season's big cultural event is the **Bravo! Colorado Vail Valley Music Festival,** from late June through early August. Established in 1988, the festival features everything from classical orchestra and chamber music to vocal and pops, baroque to modern jazz, ethnic performances to contemporary youth concerts. In residence are the Detroit Symphony and Rochester Philharmonic Orchestras. Performance days and times vary, but there are typically chamber-music concerts Tuesdays at 6pm at the Chapel at Beaver Creek (tickets $20); open-air concerts Fridays, Saturdays, and Sundays at 6pm at the Gerald R. Ford Amphitheatre in Ford Park, Vail (tickets $10–$27); and more intimate presentations at various mountain residences. For tickets and information, contact the festival office at 953 S. Frontage Rd., Vail, CO 81657 (☎ 970/476-0206; fax 970/479-0559).

The **Vail International DanceFest** features both classes and performances. The Bolshoi Ballet Academy at Vail is the satellite school of the famous Bolshoi of Moscow and teaches the Russian style of artistic expression to 30 dancers aged 15 to 19. The Vail International Workshop gives 50 dancers, ages 11 to 14, the opportunity to study different international dance styles and techniques, while the International Ballet Teachers Conference brings public and private dance instructors from around the world together to share ideas, philosophies, and techniques. In early August is the new Ensemble Series, offering performances with eight-to-twelve-member ensembles comprised of artists and principal dancers from several renowned ballet companies from around the world. The Paul Mitchell International Evenings of Dance, in mid-August, features an array of world-class couples. For information, contact the Vail Valley Foundation, P.O. Box 309, Vail, CO 81658 (☎ 970/479-1999; fax 970/949-9265).

Vail's Ford Amphitheatre hosts **Hot Summer Nights** concerts of contemporary rock or jazz Friday evenings in July and August.

NEARBY MUSEUMS & OTHER ATTRACTIONS

Betty Ford Alpine Gardens. Ford Park, east of Vail Village, Vail. ☎ 970/476-0103. Free admission. Snowmelt to snowfall, daily dawn–dusk.

At 8,200 feet, these alpine gardens are the highest public botanical gardens in North America. The alpine display, perennial garden, and mountain meditation garden together represent about 2,000 varieties of plants, demonstrating the wide range of choices to be grown at high altitudes.

Colorado Ski Museum—Ski Hall of Fame. Vail Transportation Center, Level 3, P.O. Box 1976, Vail, CO 81658. ☎ 970/476-1876. Free admission. Tues–Sun 10am–5pm. Closed May and Oct, except by appointment.

The history of more than a century of Colorado skiing—from the boards that mountain miners first strapped on their feet, to the post–World War II resort boom, to Coloradans' success in international racing—is depicted in this popular showcase. Also included are the evolution of ski equipment and fashions, and the role of the U.S. Forest Service. There's one room devoted to the Tenth Mountain Division, the only division of the military trained in ski warfare. A theater presents historical and current ski videos. The museum incorporates the Colorado Ski Hall of Fame with plaques and photographs honoring Vail founder Peter Seibert, filmmaker Lowell Thomas, Olympic skier Buddy Werner, and others.

Minturn Cellars. 107 Williams St., Minturn. ☎ 970/827-4065. Summer daily noon–6pm; winter, Wed–Sat noon–6pm. Minturn is located between Vail and Beaver Creek on U.S. 24, just a few miles south of I-70 exit 171.

A small winery, Minturn cellars produces red, white, blush, and dessert wines, with up to a half dozen on hand at any given time for free tastings. Free tours of the winery are available on request. Prices start at $8 and go as high as $65, but most are in the $12 to $14 range. June through August, the winery offers a light menu of fruits, salads, cheeses, and grilled fare.

SHOPPING

There are a wide variety of shops and galleries in Vail and Beaver Creek, but this is not a place for bargain-hunters.

Among art galleries of note are **Knox Galleries,** 100 E. Meadow Dr. (☎ **970/ 476-5171**), with beautiful bronze sculptures and impressionist paintings, and additional galleries in Beaver Creek and Denver; and **Gotthelf's Gallery,** 122 E. Meadow Dr. (☎ **970/476-1777**), featuring glass and innovative jewelry. You can get a complete listing of galleries and information on evening art walks from the Vail Valley Arts Council, P.O. Box 1153, Vail, CO 81658 (☎ 970/476-4255).

Other interesting shops include **Kitchenworks,** 100 E. Meadow Dr. (☎ **970/ 476-2817**), which carries fine cookware, cookbooks, and a multitude of handy gadgets; **The Christmas Store,** in Gateway Plaza (☎ **970/479-0232**) with lovely music boxes, chocolates, and myriad ornaments; **Gore Creek Gold,** 183 E. Gore Creek Dr. (☎ **970/476-0900**), which offers gold jewelry and Southwest-style silver and beaded jewelry; and **Menzel,** in Gateway Plaza (☎ **970/476-9238**), which sells beautiful wooden lamps with unusual and lovely fabric shades, plus furniture, sculpture, and other unusual and handsome wooden items.

WHERE TO STAY

Like most of Colorado's ski resorts, Vail has a lot of condominiums, and it seems that more are built every day. Many are individually owned and available for rent when the owners aren't in town, so you'll find that they have more individuality and homey touches than you would find in a hotel. Still, a condo is a condo, and after you've been in three or four they begin to look a lot alike. We discuss some of the better condominium developments below (along with other lodging choices), and there are scores more. Contact the Vail Valley Tourism and Convention Bureau, 100 E. Meadow Dr., Vail, CO 81657 (☎ 800/525-3875 or 970/476-1000), which can provide additional lodging information or make your reservations for you, as well as provide information on skiing and other activities.

IN VAIL

Reliable chain properties in Vail include: **Best Western Vailglo Lodge,** 701 W. Lionshead Circle (P.O. Box 189), Vail, CO 81658-0189 (☎ **800/541-9423** or 970/ 476-5506; fax 970/476-3926), with rates for two of $225 mid-November through January, $200 the rest of the ski season, and considerably lower rates the rest of the year; and the **Holiday Inn Chateau Vail,** 13 Vail Rd., Vail, CO 81657 (☎ **800/ HOLIDAY** or 970/476-5631; fax 970/476-2508), which charges $125 to $299 per double from late November to March, and less at other times.

Expensive

The Lodge at Vail. 174 E. Gore Creek Dr., Vail, CO 81657. ☎ **800/331-LODG** or 970/ 476-5011. Fax 970/476-7425. 60 rms, 40 suites. TV TEL. Winter (includes full breakfast) $355– $480 double; $525–$1,800 suite. Summer, $160–$195 double; $225–$750 suite. 2-week minimum stay over Christmas holidays. AE, DC, MC, V. Free valet parking.

Vail's original deluxe hotel—owned by Venice Simplon Orient Express—sits at the base of the Vista Bahn Express in the heart of Vail Village. (Follow Vail Rd. south from the main Vail interchange, through two stop signs and around a curve to the left, to the end of the road.) As with most Vail properties, everything you need is within a few steps of your room: winter and summer recreation, restaurants, lounges, boutiques, galleries, and stunning views.

The lodge offers hotel rooms and one-, two-, and three-bedroom suites. All have private balconies, mahogany furnishings and paneling, minirefrigerators, and full-view mirrors. The bathrooms, finished with marble, have hair dryers and heated towel racks. All rooms were recently refurbished and now include two-poster beds with duvet covers, armoires, leather-covered chairs, and dining tables. Suites, each with a fireplace and full kitchen, are individually owned and decorated.

The Wildflower Inn serves creative American cuisine in a garden atmosphere. The Cucina Rustica, a Tuscan grill, offers smoked salmon, crab salad, pasta dishes, and grilled meats on winter evenings. Mickey's piano bar has featured the well-regarded Mickey Poage for almost 20 years. Twenty-four–hour room service, a concierge, valet laundry, international currency exchange, business center, baby-sitting, and ski storage are available. Facilities include a heated swimming pool, Jacuzzi, sauna, exercise room, gift shop, and meeting space for 200.

Moderate

Antlers at Vail. 680 W. Lionshead Place, Vail, CO 81657. ☎ **800/843-VAIL** or 970/476-2471. Fax 970/476-4146. 69 suites. TV TEL. Winter, $205–$755; summer, $105–$220. AE, DC, DISC, MC, V.

These luxurious condominium units near the foot of the Lionshead Gondola have a reputation for friendly service and unobstructed views of Vail Mountain. Units range in size from studios to three-bedroom suites; each has a full-size, fully equipped kitchen, a fireplace, and private balcony. Facilities include a heated outdoor swimming pool, Jacuzzi, sun deck, two saunas, guest laundry, and ski storage. There's meeting space for 150.

Gasthof Gramshammer. 231 E. Gore Creek Dr., Vail, CO 81657. ☎ **800/610-7374** or 970/476-5626. Fax 970/476-8816. 24 rms, 4 suites. TV TEL. Winter, $195–$260 single or double; $270–$595 suite. Summer, $85–$120 single or double; $135–$310 suite. Children under 9 stay free in parents' room; $40 extra person. AE, CB, DC, MC, V.

Austrian natives Pepi and Sheika Gramshammer built this Tyrolean lodge over 3 decades ago and watched Vail Village grow around it. The lodge still maintains a deluxe European-style ambiance all the way to the goose-down comforters. There's a wide choice of rooms: standard (two double beds), deluxe (two queen or one king bed), deluxe with kitchenette, studio apartment, studio suites with connecting bedroom, one-bedroom apartment, two-bedroom suite, and family suite. The restaurant serves continental cuisine plus wild game for lunch and dinner.

Lion Square Lodge. 660 W. Lionshead Place, Vail, CO 81657. ☎ **800/525-5788** or 970/476-2281. Fax 970/476-7423. 28 rms, 75 suites. TV TEL. Winter $125–$315 double; $280–$1,100 suites. Summer $74–$103 double; $95–$215 suite. Children under 17 stay free in parents' room; $25 extra person. AE, CB, DC, DISC, MC, V. Free parking, valet available.

A ski-in, ski-out property on Gore Creek at the base of the Lionshead Gondola, the Lion Square offers deluxe lodge rooms or one-, two-, and three-bedroom condominiums. All condo units have mountain views, spacious living rooms with balconies and fireplaces, and fully equipped kitchens.

There are complimentary coffee, cookies, and newspapers in the lobby each morning, and the restaurant serves steak and seafood dinners. The lodge offers a concierge, valet laundry, and a free local shuttle van. Facilities include a heated outdoor swimming pool, hot tubs, sauna, ski and bicycle storage, guest laundry, and meeting space for 300.

Mountain Haus at Vail. 292 E. Meadow Dr., Vail, CO 81657. ☎ **800/237-0922** or 970/476-2434. Fax 970/476-3007. 10 rms, 64 condos. TV TEL. Winter, $120–$225 double lodge room; $205–$1,210 condominium. Summer, $95 double lodge room; $125–$280 condominium. AE, DISC, MC, V. Parking free in summer, $12 in winter.

Located in Vail Village on East Meadow Drive at Bridge Street, at the covered bridge across Gore Creek, the Mountain Haus offers guests the choice of handsome hotel rooms or spacious one- to four-bedroom condo units. All have gas fireplaces, VCR's, private balconies, and fully equipped kitchens. Two-bedroom units sleep six; there's a sleeper sofa in the living room, two bathrooms, and a ski room at the entrance.

The property has a heated outdoor swimming pool, indoor and outdoor Jacuzzis, men's and women's steam rooms and saunas, a guest laundry, and valet laundry service. There is a twenty-four-hour desk, concierge, and breakfast discount program.

Inexpensive

Park Meadows Lodge. 1472 Matterhorn Circle, Vail, CO 81657. ☎ **970/476-5598.** Fax 970/476-3056. 28 units. TV TEL. Winter, $59–$225; summer, $49–$85. Weekly rates available; children 12 and under stay free in parents' room. MC, V.

Located in West Vail, adjacent to the bicycle path, and an 8-minute walk from the Cascade Village Lift and terminus of the free Vail shuttle, the Park Meadows is one of the few family-style economy lodges left in the Vail valley. A condominium property, units range from efficiency studios to one- and two-bedrooms, and each has a full kitchen and a hide-a-bed. There's a common area with a large fireplace, board games, and pool and Ping Pong tables, a hot tub in an outdoor courtyard, and a coin laundry. There's basic cable TV with pay-per-view movies. Pets are not allowed.

⑤ The Roost Lodge. 1783 N. Frontage Rd. W., Vail, CO 81657. ☎ **800/873-3065** or 970/ 476-5451. Fax 970/476-9158. 72 rms. TV TEL. Winter, $69–$136; summer, $49–$69. Rates include continental breakfast and après-ski. AE, DC, DISC, MC, V.

Personal attention in a country-inn atmosphere is the boast of the Roost, a family-run ski lodge on the north side of I-70 in West Vail. Rooms are cozy and homey, and most have either king or queen beds. They offer basic cable TV with pay-per-view movies. The lodge has an enclosed swimming pool, outdoor Jacuzzi, and sauna. There are nature trails nearby, and bicycle rentals are available. The free Vail shuttle bus runs to Vail Village every 15 minutes, and the lodge provides supplementary service.

WEST OF VAIL & BEAVER CREEK

Expensive

✪ Hyatt Regency Beaver Creek. P.O. Box 1595, Avon, CO 81620. ☎ **800/233-1234** or 970/949-1234. Fax 970/949-4164. 295 rms and suites. TV TEL. Winter, $390–$575; $1,005– $2,290 suite. Spring, $95–$345; $340–$855 suite. Summer, $200–$315; $425–$1,050 suite. Fall, $125–$245; $340–$940 suite. Rates are for double occupancy. Children 18 or under stay free in parents' room. AE, CB, DC, DISC, JCB, MC, V. Valet parking $15.

An architecturally unique hotel at the foot of the Beaver Creek lifts, this ski-in/ski-out Hyatt blends features of medieval European alpine monasteries with Rocky Mountain styles and materials. The exterior is native stone, offset with stucco and rough timbers. The interior is of rough-hewn pine and sandstone; wall-size fireplaces enhance numerous cozy alcoves furnished with overstuffed chairs and sofas. Elk-antler chandeliers and works by contemporary artisans lend a western ambiance.

Guest rooms have a European country elegance, with knotty-pine furnishings. The raised beds have dust ruffles, pillow shams, and quilted comforters. The TV is in an armoire. Most rooms have private balconies. The bathroom features a marble-top vanity, hair dryer, heated towel rack, and coffeemaker.

The Patina, open for three meals daily, has an open fireplace for cold days and an outdoor terrace for warm ones. The menu offers everything from gourmet continental cuisine to light snacks. The Crooked Hearth, open only in winter, serves prime rib, fish, and other selections around another large fireplace and offers live entertainment most nights. The Double Diamond Deli has all manner of snacks and sandwiches, and prepares picnic baskets for mountain hikes and rides. McCoy's Slopeside Café, open in winter only, offers quick meals and a daily après-ski party. Room service, a concierge, complimentary ski valet, and children's program are available. Facilities include an indoor/outdoor swimming pool; six open-air Jacuzzis; saunas; weight-and-exercise room; aerobics and water aerobics classes; facials and massages; six tennis courts; retail boutiques, including jewelry and sportswear; coin-operated laundry rooms scattered throughout the hotel; and meeting space for 750.

The Lodge at Cordillera. 2205 Cordillera Way (P.O. Box 1110), Edwards, CO 81632. ☎ **800/877-3529** or 970/926-2200. Fax 970/926-2486. 28 rms and suites. A/C TV TEL. $255–$450 double; $480–$600 suites; children under 12 stay free in parents' room; $20 extra person. AE, CB, DC, JCB, MC, V. Free valet parking.

Like a mountain château in the Pyrenees of southwestern France, this luxurious hideaway nestles in 3,200 acres of private forest 13 miles west of Vail, and about 3 miles from Beaver Creek.

Rocky Mountain timber and stone, along with elegant wrought iron, are prominent in the handsome, residential-style guest rooms. More than half the rooms feature wood-burning fireplaces; all have king or queen beds with down comforters, and most have private balconies or decks with views of the New York Range of the Rockies. All bathrooms have bidets. Smoking and pets are not permitted.

The Restaurant Picasso is one of the Vail Valley's better restaurants. The Lobby Lounge presents piano music Wednesday through Sunday during ski season. Room service, a concierge, and valet laundry are available. Facilities include an outdoor swimming pool, indoor lap pool, indoor and outdoor Jacuzzis, steam room, sauna, weight-and-exercise room, aerobics, massage, hydrotherapy; 18-hole golf course; 15 miles of Mountain Biking/cross-country skiing trails, Nordic ski center; bicycle rentals, two tennis courts, volleyball; and meeting facilities for 80.

Moderate
✪ **Black Bear Inn of Vail.** 2405 Elliott Rd. in West Vail, Vail, CO 81657. ☎ **970/476-1304.** Fax 970/476-0433. 12 rooms. TEL. $100–$170 double; Christmas $200. $25 per additional person. Rates include full breakfast. DISC, MC, V.

This is an overgrown log cabin, with huge ceiling timbers, all Engelmann spruce. Most of the furniture is solid pine and made in Colorado. Rooms have down comforters on the beds and quilts and watercolors by local artists on the walls. Two rooms have two twin beds each; the others have queens, and most have a hide-a-bed. Breakfast and afternoon refreshments are served in the main room. Downstairs is a game room with pool table, pinball machine, books, TV, video player and movies. There is one handicapped-accessible room; kids are welcome, but pets are not. The entire inn is nonsmoking, and there's a meeting room for 12.

Eagle River Inn. 145 N. Main St. (P.O. Box 100), Minturn, CO 81645. ☎ **800/344-1750** or 970/827-5761. Fax 970/827-4020. 12 rms (all with three-quarter bath). TV. Winter $180–$200; Summer $95–$100; $20 extra person. Rates are for double occupancy and include breakfast. AE, MC, V.

Built in 1894 when the Denver & Rio Grande Railroad first made the village of Minturn a stop on its route, the picturesque Eagle River Inn has had many incarnations. Its latest makeover, in 1986, turned it into a fine bed-and-breakfast. It feels like Santa Fe throughout, from the sala-style lobby (complete with kiva fireplace, bancos, and other southwestern-style appointments) to the bright and breezy second- and third-story guest rooms, with tiled three-quarter baths and down comforters.

Breakfast includes homemade granola, fresh fruit, and baked goods. The hot tub on a deck overlooking the Eagle River is always available. Smoking and pets are not permitted. The inn usually closes for about 5 weeks between the end of ski season and Memorial Day.

Inexpensive

Comfort Inn. 161 W. Beaver Creek Blvd. (P.O. Box 5510), Avon, CO 81620. ☎ **800/ 423-4374** or 970/949-5511. Fax 970/949-7762. 142 rms, 4 studios. A/C TV TEL. Winter, $89– $249 double. Summer, $79–$109 double. Rates include continental breakfast; children under 18 stay free in parents' room. AE, DC, DISC, ER, JCB, MC, V.

A four-story lodging just off the I-70 Avon/Beaver Creek interchange, this comfortable establishment has a big stone fireplace in its lobby lounge and a southwestern decor. Most of the spacious rooms have two queen beds; a few have king beds, plus comfortable chairs. There's indoor ski storage and a free shuttle to Beaver Creek Resort, a heated outdoor pool, Jacuzzi, and guest laundry.

CAMPING

Sylvan Lake State Park. Take I-70 exit 147 to Eagle, drive south through town on Main St. to West Brush Creek Rd., turn right, and go 16 miles to the park entrance. ☎ **800/678-2267** for reservations, or 970/625-1607 for park information. 50 sites. $6 per site, plus $3 state parks pass. MC, V for reservations; cash only at the park.

Two separate campgrounds on this beautiful 115-acre park put visitors close to trout fishing and boating on a 40-acre lake in the White River National Forest. The park has flush toilets, fire pits, and water, but no showers, R.V. hookups, or dump station.

WHERE TO DINE
VERY EXPENSIVE

Beano's Cabin. Foot of Larkspur Lift, Beaver Creek Resort. ☎ **970/949-9090.** Reservations required. Fixed-price, $80 adults, $46 children under 12. AE, DISC, MC, V. Daily 5–9:30pm (departures from Rendezvous Cabin). REGIONAL.

One splurge that every Beaver Creek visitor should make is the sleigh-ride dinner trip (or in summer, the horse-drawn wagon ride) to Beano's. This isn't the log homestead that Chicago lettuce farmer Frank "Beano" Bienkowski built on Beaver Creek Mountain in 1919—it's far more elegant. Diners board the 42-passenger, snowcat-driven sleighs at the base of the Centennial Lift, arriving 15 minutes later for a candlelit six-course dinner around a crackling fire with musical entertainment.

There's a choice of eight different entrees, which always include beef, seafood, chicken, and pasta. Vegetarian meals may be requested. A full bar, extensive wine list, and a children's menu are also available.

EXPENSIVE

Chanticler. 710 W. Lionshead Circle. ☎ **970/476-1441.** Reservations recommended. Main courses $17.50–$29. AE, CB, DC, DISC, MC, V. Daily 6–10pm. INTERNATIONAL/REGIONAL.

The over-stressed will find instant solace in the relaxed elegance of this excellent restaurant in the Vail Spa decorated in French country–style. Pewter antiques and fine artwork grace the shelves and walls, and beautiful brass chandeliers hang over the candlelit tables. Service is attentive but not intrusive.

Fresh fish, fowl, game, and steaks are the chef's forte, and house specialties include grilled salmon with orange hollandaise, oven-roasted duck, and chicken breast stuffed with lobster. Only fresh ingredients are used, and many of the sauces are made with wine or liqueur. Desserts are all homemade. The wine list includes over 140 wines from around the world.

The Golden Eagle Inn. Village Hall, Beaver Creek Mall. ☎ **970/949-1940.** Main courses $8.50–$13.95 at lunch, $15.95–$27.95 at dinner. AE, MC, V. Daily 11:30am–10pm. CREATIVE AMERICAN.

Sidewalk tables on the Beaver Creek promenade are the outstanding feature of this restaurant, owned by Austrian Pepi Langegger of Vail's Tyrolean Inn. Appetizers might include herbed peppered ahi or black bean soup. Main courses feature seafood, game, pastas, roast loin of elk, rack of lamb, and filet mignon.

Imperial Fez. 1000 Lions Ridge Loop. ☎ **970/476-1948.** Reservations recommended. Fixed-price dinner $30–$36. AE, DC, MC, V. Dec–Mar daily 6–9:30pm; Apr–Nov daily 5–10pm. MOROCCAN.

You'll find yourself in a giant Moroccan tent when you walk through the door. Owner Rafih Benjelloun will seat you on cushions at a low, round table, then spread white towels across your laps to protect your clothes while eating with your fingers. (Finger bowls are provided.) Belly dancers and sword dancers add to the atmosphere. Main courses cover a wide range of foods and preparations, such as apricot lamb, fresh fish tajine, beef brochette, or lamb M'shui. There are also poultry, prawns, and vegetarian offerings. For dessert, consider a cup of mint tea and a chocolate b'stella.

Sweet Basil. 193 E. Gore Creek Dr. ☎ **970/476-0125.** Reservations recommended. Main courses $7–$9.50 at lunch, $21–$29 at dinner. AE, MC, V. Daily 11:30am–2:30pm and 5:30–10pm. CREATIVE AMERICAN.

Simple modern decor with contemporary art and the tasteful use of mirrors and large windows is the earmark of this pleasant restaurant. A deck looks out on the Lodge Promenade in the center of Vail Village. Diners can sit at private tables or be served at the wine bar.

Menus change seasonally but include items such as almond-crusted rack of lamb, honey-baked pork chop, and grilled New York steak; creative seafood dishes are the specialty, such as seared tuna with portabello mushroom Napoleon, crispy potatoes, and merlot sauce.

Tyrolean Inn. 400 E. Meadow Dr. ☎ **970/476-2204.** Reservations recommended. Main courses $14.95–$29.95. AE, MC, V. Daily 6–10pm. REGIONAL/CONTINENTAL.

The Langegger family is proud of its Old World roots. Pepi established this Vail landmark more than 2 decades ago, and the ambiance today remains decidedly alpine, with gracious, friendly service and authentic Tyrolean decor. In summer, there's dining on an outdoor patio beside Gore Creek.

Wild game is the house specialty: venison sauerbraten, pheasant Kroatzbeere—or for the total experience, the wild-game medley of wild boar, elk, and caribou. You'll also find such items as grilled chicken with artichokes and olives, Wiener schnitzel, and Muscovy duck.

Vendetta's. 291 Bridge St. ☎ **970/476-5070.** Reservations recommended. Main courses $5.95–$8.95 at lunch, $13.95–$24.95 at dinner. AE, MC, V. Daily 11am–10:30pm. NORTHERN ITALIAN.

Located on busy Bridge Street in the heart of Vail Village, Vendetta's is a casual, friendly spot as famous for its après-ski (on a sunny deck) as for its fine Italian cuisine. Pasta lovers may enjoy such dishes as manicotti Veneziana (baked with four cheeses), and lasagna pasticciate verde (baked with beef and sausage). Osso bucco and pollo D'Angelo (chicken sautéed with artichoke hearts, garlic, mushrooms, and pimiento) are favorites, and seafood specials range from linguine al salmone to cioppino to fettucine frutti di mare.

MODERATE

Blu's. 193 E. Gore Creek Dr. ☎ **970/476-3113.** Reservations not accepted. Breakfast/lunch $4.50–$9, main courses $9–$18.95. AE, CB, DC, MC, V. Daily 9am–11pm. AMERICAN/ CONTINENTAL.

This eatery, located downstairs from the Children's Fountain by Gore Creek, off Willow Bridge Road, is a local favorite—in no small part because it offers breakfasts daily until 5pm. There's a wide selection of breakfast/lunch items, including green eggs and ham, omelets, vegetarian specialties, pasta dishes, salads, sandwiches, and burgers. Dinner entrees include fresh seafood, pasta, mustard pepper steak, and Spanish paella; and there's an extensive wine list.

Hubcap Brewery and Kitchen. 143 E. Meadow Dr., Crossroads Shopping Center ☎ **970/ 476-5757.** Reservations not accepted. Main courses $4.75–$9 at lunch, $6.95–$14.95 at dinner. AE, MC, V. Daily 11:30am–1am. AMERICAN.

A state-of-the-art brew pub with a glass-enclosed brew house, the Hubcap serves unfiltered, unpasteurized beer. Sandwich offerings include grilled chicken, BLTs, steak, and tuna. There are also burgers, chicken pot pie, meat loaf, salads, and soups. Dinner selections, which come with homemade beer bread, include barbecued chicken, New York strip steak, a vegetarian platter, and fish-and-chips. During ski season, grilled quail, barbecued ribs, and fresh seafood are also offered. Apple pie tops the dessert selections.

Montauk Seafood Grill. 549 Lionshead Mall. ☎ **970/476-2601.** Reservations recommended. Main courses $15.95–$21.95. AE, MC, V. Daily 5–10pm. SEAFOOD.

Gary Boris, managing partner of this seafood grill, grew up around the harbors of Montauk Point, New York. Now that he's landlocked, he flies fresh fish in daily from both coasts, as well as from Hawaii and the Gulf of Mexico; all are grilled with a sampling of sauces. Steak, chicken, and pasta are also available. The area's only raw bar is stocked not only with oysters, but with clams, shrimp, and crab as well.

The Red Lion. 304 Bridge St. ☎ **970/476-7676.** $8–$18.95. AE, DISC, MC, V. Daily 11am– midnight. BURGERS/BARBECUE.

Established soon after the village of Vail was incorporated, the Red Lion has been a popular spot for some 3 decades. Food here is traditional but good and filling: the Red Lion's hallmark is hickory-smoked barbecue, but their burgers, specialty salads, and sandwiches are also popular, as is their children's menu. Beer drinkers are drawn by the Around the World Beer Club (over 50 varieties); and there's live entertainment nightly in winter (weekends in summer), as well as 14 TVs for sporting events.

VAIL AFTER DARK

Vail's greatest concentration of late-night haunts can be found in a 1¹/₂-block stretch of Bridge Street from Hanson Ranch Road north to the covered bridge over Gore Creek. From mountainside to creek, they include the **Club** (☎ 970/479-0556), the **Red Lion** (☎ 970/476-7676), **Vendetta's** (☎ 970/476-5070), and **Nick's** (☎ 970/476-3433).

Just off Bridge Drive on Gore Creek Drive is **Sheika's,** a hot disco at Gasthof Gramshammer (☎ 970/476-5626). Another popular place for hanging out is **Garton's Saloon,** 143 E. Meadow Dr. (☎ 970/479-0607).

Country music enthusiasts find swing and two-step on the dance floor at the **Sundance Saloon,** Sunbird Lodge, 675 Lionshead Place (☎ 970/476-3453); or the **Jackalope,** 2161 N. Frontage Rd. West (☎ 970/476-4314).

Piano bars draw quieter types to **Mickey's,** in the Lodge at Vail, 174 E. Gore Creek Dr. (☎ **970/476-5011**); and **Ludwig's** in the Sonnenalp Hotel, 20 Vail Rd. (☎ **970/476-5656**). Acoustic guitarists soothe nerves at **Hong Kong Café,** 227 Wall St. (☎ **970/476-1818**).

Vail's first brew pub, **Hubcap Brewery and Kitchen,** at the Crossroads Shopping Center, East Meadow Drive at Willow Bridge Road (☎ **970/476-5757**), invites beer connoisseurs to relax on its large deck and sip White River Wheat Ale and Rainbow Trout Stout. In Beaver Creek, the place to go is the **Beaver Trap Tavern,** St. James Place (☎ **970/845-8930**).

7 Leadville

There was a time, not much more than a century ago, when Leadville was the most important city between St. Louis and San Francisco. It was the stopping point for Easterners with nothing to lose and everything to gain from the promise of gold and silver. Today, Leadville is one of the best places to rediscover the West's mining heritage.

Founded in 1860 on the gold that glimmered in prospectors' pans, the Oro City site quickly attracted 10,000 miners who dug $5 million in gold out of a 3-mile stretch of the California Gulch by 1865. When the riches were gone, Leadville was deserted, although a smaller lode of gold-bearing quartz kept nearby Oro City alive for another decade. Then in 1875 two prospectors discovered that the lead ore in the valley's heavy black soil contained 15 ounces of silver to the ton, and located the California Gulch's first paying silver lode. Over the next 2 decades, Leadville grew to an estimated 30,000 residents—among them Horace Tabor, who parlayed his mercantile-and-mining investments into unimaginable wealth; and "the Unsinkable" Molly Brown, whose husband made his fortune here before moving to Denver, where the family lived at the time of Molly's *Titanic* heroism.

Many buildings of the silver boom (which produced $136 million between 1879 and 1889) have been preserved in one of Colorado's most complete National Historic Districts. So for those who want to take a break from playing outdoors to explore Colorado's frontier past, Leadville's just the place to do it.

A final notable fact: Leadville has the highest elevation of any incorporated city in the United States: 10,430 feet, nearly 2 miles above sea level.

ESSENTIALS

GETTING THERE   By Car   Coming from Denver, leave I-70 at exit 195 (Copper Mountain), and proceed south 24 miles on Colo. 91. From Grand Junction, depart I-70 at exit 171 (Minturn), and continue south 33 miles on U.S. 24. From Aspen, in the summer take Colo. 82 east 44 miles over Independence Pass (closed in winter), then turn north on U.S. 24 for another 15 miles; in winter return to I-70, and follow directions from Grand Junction, above. There's also easy access from the south via U.S. 24.

By Plane   Leadville Airport, 915 County Rd. 23 (☎ **719/486-2627**), 2 miles south of downtown, at 9,927 feet elevation, is said to be America's highest airport. Air service is limited to air-taxi, charter, sightseeing, and training flights.

ORIENTATION   U.S. 24 is Leadville's main street. Entering from the north, the highway is known as Poplar Street; it staggers west one block at Ninth Street. To stay on U.S. 24, turn left onto Harrison Avenue. The next seven blocks south, to Second Street, are the heart of this historic town. Leadville's stoplight is at the intersection of Harrison Avenue and Sixth Street, which proceeds west to civic and recreational complexes. A block north, Seventh Street climbs east to the old train depot and 13,186-foot Mosquito Pass, among America's highest, open to four-wheel–drive vehicles in summer.

VISITOR INFORMATION   Contact **The Greater Leadville Area Chamber of Commerce,** 809 Harrison Ave. (P.O. Box 861), Leadville, CO 80461 (☎ **800/ 933-3901** or 719/486-3900; fax 719/486-8478).

GETTING AROUND   Car rentals are available through **Leadville Leasing** at the airport (☎ **719/486-2627**). **Dee Hive Tours,** 506 Harrison Ave. (☎ **719/ 486-2339**), offers **taxi** service plus year-round charter service.

FAST FACTS   In case of **emergency,** call **911. Leadville Medical Center** is at 825 W. Sixth St. (☎ **719/486-1264**). The **post office** is at West Fifth and Pine streets, a block west of Harrison Avenue (☎ **719/486-1667**). The Lake County Sheriff's office (☎ 719/486-1249) provides **road reports.** Taxes add just under 9% to lodging bills.

PLACES TO EXPERIENCE LEADVILLE'S PAST

If you're visiting Leadville in summer, begin your explorations with a **horse-drawn surrey tour.** This seven-passenger carriage departs from the chamber of commerce office daily from 10am to 4pm. Along the way, your guide will point out Leadville's most notable historical landmarks.

A great many of these are former residences of successful mining operators, engineers, and financiers. Most are brick-and-masonry structures, but there are also some wood-frame houses. They're preserved within the **Leadville National Historic District,** which stretches along seven blocks of Harrison Avenue and part of Chestnut Street, where it intersects Harrison at the south end of downtown. The chamber of commerce sells self-guided walking tour and driving tour maps of this district for $2 each.

An informative 30-minute film, **The Earth Runs Silver: Early Leadville,** is shown at the New Fox Theater, 115 W. Sixth St. (☎ **800/933-3901** or 719/486-3900). It gives a good overview of Leadville's place in American mining history. Admission: $3 adults, $2 children 2 to 12; group rates available. Call for the times of daily showings or ask at the chamber of commerce, which also sells tickets.

At the ✪ **National Mining Hall of Fame and Museum,** 120 W. Ninth St. (☎ **719/486-1229**), you'll find working models of mining machinery and dioramas giving an episode-by-episode history of Colorado gold mining. There are dioramas of individual mines, including the Climax molybdenum mine, and displays of crystals and luminescent minerals. There's a life-size model of a blacksmith shop and hard-rock mine, a priceless collection of gold nuggets, and a wonderful display of period photos. Admission: $4 adults, $3.50 seniors, $2 children 6 to 12, free for children under 6. Open May through October, daily from 9am to 5pm; November through April, Monday to Friday 10am to 2pm.

Now that you understand how mines work, the surface view of Horace Tabor's immense mine at the **Matchless Mine Museum,** 1¼ miles east up Seventh Street, may make more sense. The museum also gives guided tours of the cabin where Tabor's widow, Baby Doe, spent the final 36 years of her life, hoping to strike it rich once more. Admission: $2 adults, $1 for children 6 to 12, under age 6 free. Open June–Labor Day, daily 9am–5pm.

To get an up-close look at where a few fortunate miners were able to escape the rough-and-tumble atmosphere of the mines, if only for an evening, visit **Healy House and Dexter Cabin,** 912 Harrison Ave. (☎ **719/486-0487**). Healy House was built by mining engineer August Meyer in 1878, who threw frequent parties and developed a reputation as a refined and gracious host. Daniel Healy purchased the house in 1888, and turned it into a boardinghouse. The adjacent Dexter Cabin was built of logs in 1879 by mining magnate James Dexter, who used the building as his Leadville residence. Admission: $3 adults, $2 children 6 to 16, $2.50 seniors over 65, free for children under 6. Open Memorial Day weekend to Labor Day, daily 10am to 4:30pm; in September, Saturday and Sunday 10am to 4:30pm; other times by appointment.

The **Tabor Opera House,** 308 Harrison Ave. (☎ **719/486-1147**) is where Leadville's mining magnates and their wives kept up with cultural happenings back East. Over its 75-year history operation, the Opera House hosted everything from the Ziegfeld Follies and the Metropolitan Opera, to prizefighter Jack Dempsey (a Colorado native) and magician Harry Houdini (whose vanishing square is still evident on the stage floor). Autographed photographs of many of the entertainment greats who performed here line the walls of the foyer. Guided and self-guided tours of the 880-seat theater are available every day in summer; you're encouraged to wander the aisles, visit the original dressing rooms, and study many of the original sets and scenery. Tour admission: $4 adults, $2 children 6 to 11, free for children under 6. A melodrama is offered Wednesday, Thursday, and Saturday evenings at 8pm (tickets $10, theater opens 7:30pm).

Another place worth stopping at is the **Western Hardware Museum & Emporium,** 431 Harrison Ave. (☎ **719/486-2213**), which operated as a hardware store from 1880 until 1985. Today, it's a museum-cum-antique shop with lots of original detail, including a wall lined with 1,000 drawers and a ladder on rollers that clerks used to retrieve items from them. The emporium also sells espresso and candy to keep up your strength.

OTHER THINGS TO SEE & DO

Leadville, Colorado & Southern Railroad. 326 E. Seventh St. at Hazel St. ☎ **719/486-3936.** Admission $22.50 adults, $12.50 children 4–12, free for children 3 and under. Daily, Memorial Day–early Oct, call for schedule.

This spectacularly scenic ride, in a modern diesel train, departs the 1893 C&S Depot, three blocks east of U.S. 24, and follows the old "high line" to the headwaters of the Arkansas River, stopping near the molybdenum mining camp of Climax, from which there's a splendid view of Fremont Pass. The return takes you to the French Gulch Water Tower for a dramatic look at Mount Elbert, Colorado's tallest mountain, at 14,431 feet. The ride lasts about $2^{1}/_{2}$ hours, and because of the high elevations, jackets or sweaters are recommended even on the hottest summer days.

Leadville National Fish Hatchery. 2844 Colo. 300 (4 miles southwest of Leadville off U.S. 24). ☎ **719/486-0189.** Free admission. Summer, daily 7:30am–5pm; rest of the year, daily 7:30am–4pm.

Established in 1889, this is the second-oldest hatchery operated by the U.S. Fish and Wildlife Service. Rainbow, brook, brown, and cutthroat trout are raised here, at an elevation of 10,000 feet on the east side of Mount Massive. In addition to the hatchery operation, visitors can enjoy the self-guided nature trails, which not only provide breathtaking views of the surrounding mountains and sometimes deer and elk, but one trail passes by the remains of a late-1800s resort, the Evergreen Hotel. They also connect to the Colorado Trail. In winter, take cross-country skis or snowshoes.

SPORTS & OUTDOOR ACTIVITIES

FISHING   There's good trout and kokanee fishing at Turquoise Lake, Twin Lakes, and other small high-mountain lakes, as well as at beaver ponds located on side streams of the Arkansas River. There's also limited stream-fishing.

Licenses, supplies, and information can be obtained from **Buckthorn Sporting Goods,** 616 Harrison Ave. (☎ **719/486-3944**), and other local stores. Huck Finn Pond at City Park, West Fifth Street at Leiter Street, is open for free children's fishing in summer.

GOLF   The Mount Massive Golf Course, 3¹/₂ miles west of Leadville at 259 County Rd. 5 (P.O. Box 312, Leadville, CO 80461, ☎ **719/486-2176**), claims to be North America's highest golf course, at 9,700 feet. Greens fees are $12 for nine holes and $20 for 18, and views of surrounding mountain peaks are magnificent.

HIKING & MOUNTAINEERING   The U.S. Forest Service, San Isabel National Forest office, 2015 Poplar St. (☎ 719/486-0749), has detailed maps. The adventurous can attempt an ascent of Mount Elbert (14,433 ft.) or Mount Massive (14,421 ft.); either can be climbed in a day without technical equipment, though altitude and abruptly changing weather conditions are factors that should be weighed.

HORSEBACK RIDING   There are stables, open late May through Labor Day, at **Pa and Ma's Guest Ranch,** 4 miles west of Leadville on U.S. 24 at East Tennessee Road (☎ **719/486-3900**). Rates start at about $15 per hour.

RIVER RAFTING   Expeditions on the Arkansas River, including thrilling Browns Canyon, are organized by **Twin Lakes Expeditions** (P.O. Box 70, Twin Lakes, CO 81251; ☎ **800/288-0497** or 719/486-3928). A full-day trip costs about $65, including lunch.

SKIING   Ski Cooper, P.O. Box 896, Leadville, CO 80461 (☎ **719/486-3684,** or 719/486-2277 for snow reports), began as a training center for Tenth Mountain Division troops from Camp Hale during World War II. Located 10 miles north of Leadville on U.S. 24 near Tennessee Pass, it offers numerous intermediate and novice runs, and hosts backcountry Chicago Ridge Snowcat Tours for experts. The lifts— a triple chair, double chair, T-bar, and beginners' poma—serve 26 runs on a 1,200-foot vertical. The Piney Creek Nordic Center (☎ 719/486-1750), at the foot of the mountain, has a 25-kilometer (15.5-mile) skate and classic cross-country track, plus rentals and lessons.

WHERE TO STAY

Apple Blossom Inn. 120 W. Fourth St., Leadville, CO 80461. ☎ **800/982-9279** or 719/486-2141. 8 rms (3 with bath). $59–$99 double; $118 and up, suite. Rates include breakfast. AE, MC, V.

An 1879 Victorian structure on Leadville's millionaires' row, this inn features the original handcrafted woodwork, detailed mantels, and crystal lights installed by its original owners. Rooms range from warm and cozy to large and sunny. Estelle's Room has a large fireplace, brass queen feather bed, and sitting area; while the Library has a 14-foot ceiling, five stained-glass windows, parquet floor, and a four-poster queen feather bed. Full breakfasts are served on request, and special diets can be accommodated. Children are welcome, but pets are not. Smoking is not permitted.

✪ **Delaware Hotel.** 700 Harrison Ave., Leadville, CO 80461. ☎ **800/748-2004** or 719/486-1418. Fax 719/486-2214. 36 rms and suites. TV TEL. $65–$75 double; $90–$100 family rooms; $100–$110 suite. Rates include breakfast. Inquire about the special weekend packages for skiing, golfing, and theme weekends. AE, DC, DISC, MC, V.

Built in 1886, this hotel was restored in 1985 and is once again a Victorian gem. The lobby is beautiful in the style of grand old hotels, with a turn-of-the-century player piano, crystal chandeliers, and magnificent Victorian furnishings. Guest rooms have brass or iron beds, quilts, and lace curtains. Rooms have private baths with showers but no tubs; suites have full baths with tubs. The hotel also has a Jacuzzi. A restaurant serves three meals daily, featuring steaks and continental cuisine. There is also a full bar.

Pan Ark Lodge. 5827 U.S. 24, Leadville, CO 80461. ☎ **800/443-1063** or 719/486-1063. 48 rms. $49–$54 double. DISC, MC, V.

Located 9 miles south of Leadville, this comfortable motel has spacious rooms, all with natural moss-rock fireplaces, kitchenettes, and beautiful mountain views. Some rooms have televisions. There's a coin-operated laundry. Pets are not permitted.

CAMPING

Sugar Loafin' Campground. 303 Colo. 300, Leadville, CO 80461. ☎ **719/486-1031.** $19–$22 for two. MC, V. Closed Oct–mid-May.

Located 3¹/₂ miles northwest of downtown Leadville via West Sixth Street, this campground has spectacular mountain views and clean bathhouses with plenty of hot water. There are tent and full-hookup R.V. sites. An ice-cream social and a slide show of area attractions takes place nightly, and campers are invited to try their luck panning for gold. Located at a 9,696-foot elevation, the campground provides a playground, self-service laundry, telephone, and a general store selling fishing tackle. Pets are welcome. There's a public golf course nearby.

WHERE TO DINE

The Grill. 715 Elm St. ☎ **719/486-9930.** Main courses $4.75–$9.75. MC, V. Daily 11am–10pm. MEXICAN.

The Grill serves authentic south-of-the-border food and what many think are the best margaritas in Colorado's mountains. You can get one or two tacos, enchiladas, tamales, and burritos, or complete dinners such as the house specialty: sopapillas stuffed with a variety of items. Vegetarian and children's plates are available.

The Prospector. 2798 Colo. 91. ☎ **800/844-2828** or 719/486-3955. Reservations recommended. Main courses $9–$20. MC, V. Tues–Sun 5–9pm. STEAK/SEAFOOD.

Lodged in a spacious log cabin with a stone entrance, 3 miles north of town in a picturesque mountain setting, the Prospector has long been considered one of Leadville's finest restaurants. Dinners include steaks, baby-back ribs, rack of lamb, chicken, pasta, and seafood, plus prime rib on Fridays and Saturdays. There are daily specials, plus a salad bar, and menus for children and light appetites. There's also a full bar.

Steph & Scott's Columbine Cafe. 612 Harrison Ave. ☎ **719/486-3599.** Reservations not accepted. Main courses $3–$6. Daily 5:30am–3:30pm. AMERICAN DINER.

This is a simple cafe with historic tools and some old wooden skis on the walls. Breakfasts range from traditional eggs and pancakes to more exotic dishes such as malted Belgian waffles and Steph's eggs Benedict, which can be prepared with avocados or tomatoes for vegetarians. Lunches include basics such as home-style roast beef, sandwiches, and burgers plus more unique items like the spicy Cajun burger.

LEADVILLE AFTER DARK

Leadville is on the quiet side. If it's lively anywhere, it will be the **Pastime Saloon,** 120 W. Second St. (☎ **719/486-9986**), with an original Chinese bar from Oro City;

or the **Silver Dollar Saloon,** 315 Harrison Ave. (☎ **719/486-9914**), an Irish-style bar decorated with pictures of "Baby Doe" Tabor. The **Delaware Hotel** (see above) has an oak lobby bar, with piano entertainment.

8 Aspen

Like Vail, Aspen's reputation precedes it. Anyone with a pulse knows that, come winter, it's more than likely to wind up in the tabloids when two celebrities—who are married to other people—are captured on film sharing a chairlift together; and, yes, we guess it's possible that Hunter S. Thompson may serve you a drink downtown, if he happens to be tending bar somewhere as a favor to the owner, but that's not particularly likely.

If you take the time to dig beneath the media hype, you may be surprised by what you find. Aspen is a real town with a fascinating history, some great old buildings, and spectacular mountain scenery. If you're a serious skier, you owe yourself at least a few days' worth of hitting the slopes (as if you need us to tell you that); but if you've never strapped on boards, and you're thinking of visiting in summer, you'll be doubly pleased: Prices are significantly lower, and the crowds thin out. Many of its fabulous restaurants are still open, the surrounding forests are teeming with great trails for hiking, biking, and horseback riding, and it becomes one of the best destinations in the U.S. for summer music and dance festivals.

Aspen was "discovered" when silver miners from nearby Leadville wandered a bit further afield. When the Smuggler Mine produced the world's largest silver nugget (1,840 lb.), prospectors started heading to Aspen in droves. The city soon had 12,000 citizens—but just as quickly the population dwindled to one-tenth that number after the 1893 silver crash.

It took almost 50 years for Aspen to begin its comeback, which came as a result of another natural resource—snow. Shortly before World War II, a small ski area with a primitive boat tow was established on Aspen Mountain. During the war, Tenth Mountain Division ski-soldiers training near Leadville spent weekends in Aspen and were enthralled with its possibilities. An infusion of money in 1945 by Chicago industrialist Walter Paepcke, who moved to Aspen with his wife, Elizabeth, resulted in the construction of what was then the world's longest chairlift. The Aspen Skiing Corporation (now Company) was founded the following year, and in 1950 Aspen's status as an international resort was confirmed when it hosted the alpine world skiing championships. Then came the opening in 1958 of Buttermilk Mountain and Aspen Highlands, and in 1967, the birth of Snowmass.

The Paepckes' vision of the resort was not exclusively commercial, however. They saw Aspen as a year-round intellectual and artistic community that would nourish the minds and spirits as well as the bodies of those who visited. Chief among their accomplishments was the establishment of the Aspen Institute for Humanistic Studies and the Aspen Music Festival.

Their love of ideas and high-minded discourse attracted the likes of Thornton Wilder, Ortega y Gasset, and Albert Schweitzer to the Paepckes' resort, and the couple became important promoters of Walter Gropius's Bauhaus design movement in America. The Paepckes believed in discipline, individual rights and responsibilities, and hard work. After Walter's death in 1960, Elizabeth strived to continue this tradition but found a less receptive audience among those who moved to Aspen in the 1960s and 1970s. By the 1980s, relatives reported that Elizabeth was disillusioned with the excesses that 2 decades of new, free-wheeling money had brought, but she remained—in many respects Aspen's conscience—living out her ideals with purpose, but also grace and élan, until her death in 1994. The continuing success—and critical praise—of the Institute's programs ensures that the Paepckes' vision for Aspen has not been forgotten.

ESSENTIALS

GETTING THERE   By Car   Aspen is located on Colo. 82, halfway between I-70 at Glenwood Springs (42 miles northwest) and U.S. 24 south of Leadville (44 miles east). In summer, it's a scenic 3¹/₂-hour drive from Denver: Leave I-70 West at exit 195 (Copper Mountain); follow Colo. 91 south to Leadville, where you pick up U.S. 24; turn west on Colo. 82 through Twin Lakes and over 12,095-foot Independence Pass. In winter, the Independence Pass road is closed, so you'll have to take I-70 to Glenwood Springs, and head east on Colo. 82. In optimal winter driving conditions, it'll take about 4 hours from Denver.

By Plane   Visitors who wish to fly directly into Aspen can arrange to land at **Pitkin County Airport-Sardy Field,** 3 miles northwest of Aspen on Colo. 82 (☎ **970/920-5384**). Operating year-round flights are **United Express** (☎ **800/241-6522**) with connecting service from Denver, and **Lone Star** (☎ **800/877-3932**), with flights from Dallas-Fort Worth. Other airlines sometimes operate during ski season.

Another option is the **Eagle County Jet Center** near Vail (☎ **970/524-7700**).

Ground transportation from both of these airports is provided by **Airport Shuttle Colorado** (☎ **800/222-2112**) and **Colorado Mountain Express** (☎ **800/525-6363**).

By Airport Shuttle   Those who choose to fly into **Denver International** can take one of two shuttle van services to Aspen: **Skier Connection** (☎ **800/824-1104**) or **Airport Shuttle Colorado** (☎ **800/222-2112**).

By Train   En route from San Francisco or Chicago, **Amtrak** (☎ **800/USA-RAIL**) stops in Glenwood Springs (passenger station ☎ **970/945-9563**), 42 miles northwest of Aspen. Taxis, as well as rental cars, are available at the depot, and the Aspen bus system also provides transportation (see "Getting Around," below).

ORIENTATION   Located in the heart of White River National Forest, Aspen is in the relatively flat valley of the Roaring Fork River, a tributary of the Colorado River. It's lodged at the northern foot of Aspen Mountain, facing Smuggler Mountain to the north and the peaks of the Elk Mountain Range to the east.

Entering town from the northwest on Colo. 82, the arterial jogs right (south) two blocks on Seventh Street, then left (east) at Main Street. "East" and "West" street numbers are separated by Garmisch Street, the next cross street after First Street. Mill Street is the town's main north-south street. Monarch Street marks the west boundary of downtown Aspen, and Original Street marks the east. Colo. 82 turns south on Original then east again toward Independence Pass on Cooper Avenue. Durant Avenue, one block south of Cooper, sits at the foot of Aspen Mountain. There are several pedestrian malls downtown, which throw a curve into the downtown traffic flow.

VISITOR INFORMATION   For information, contact the **Aspen Chamber Resort Association,** 425 Rio Grande Place, Aspen, CO 81611 (☎ **970/925-1940**), or drop by the **Aspen Visitor Center** at the Wheeler Opera House, Hyman Avenue and Mill Street.

GETTING AROUND   By Shuttle Bus   Free bus service is available within the Aspen city limits, beyond which you can get connections west as far as Carbondale. The fare from Aspen to Snowmass is $2 adults, $1 children 6 to 16, and free for

Aspen

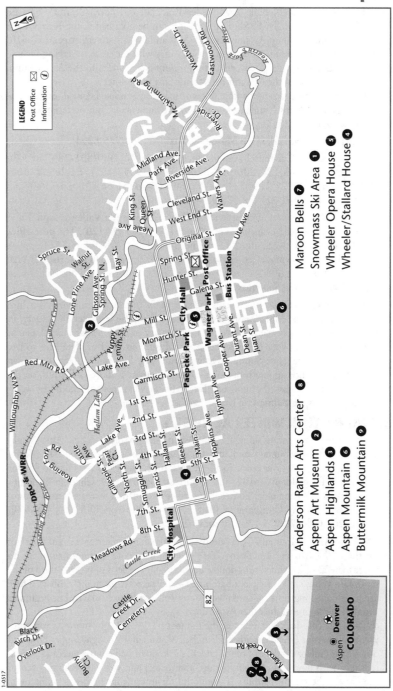

Anderson Ranch Arts Center ⑧
Aspen Art Museum ②
Aspen Highlands ③
Aspen Mountain ⑥
Buttermilk Mountain ⑨

Maroon Bells ⑦
Snowmass Ski Area ①
Wheeler Opera House ⑤
Wheeler/Stallard House ④

COLORADO
Denver ★
Aspen

LEGEND
Post Office ☒
Information ⓘ

children under six and seniors 65 and older. Exact fare is required. Normal hours are 6:15am to 2:15am daily. Further information can be obtained at the **Rubey Park Transit Center,** Durant Avenue between Mill and Galena streets, Aspen (☎ 970/925-8484). Schedules, frequency, and routes vary with the seasons; services include free ski shuttles in winter between all four mountains, shuttles to the Aspen Music Festival, and tours to the Maroon Bells scenic area in summer.

Free shuttle transportation within Snowmass Village is offered daily during ski season and on a limited schedule in summer, by the Snowmass Transportation Department (☎ 970/923-2543).

By Taxi   For a cab, call **High Mountain Taxi** (☎ **970/925-8294**).

By Rental Car   Car-rental agencies include **Avis** (☎ **800/831-2847** or 970/925-2355), **Budget** (☎ **800/527-0700** or 970/925-2151), **Eagle** (☎ **800/282-2128** or 970/925-2128), **Hertz** (☎ **800/654-3131** or 970/925-7368), and **Thrifty** (☎ **800/367-2277** or 970/920-2305).

FAST FACTS   In case of **emergency,** call **911.** The **Aspen Valley Hospital** is at 401 Castle Creek Rd., near Aspen Highlands (☎ **970/925-1120**). The **post office** is at 235 Puppy Smith St., off Mill Street north of Main (☎ **970/925-7523**); there's another in the Snowmass Center (☎ 970/923-2497). For **road reports,** call 970/920-5454. **Sales tax** of 8.2% is added to hotel bills, with an additional civic assessment of 4% added in Snowmass.

SPECIAL EVENTS   Annual events include: the Wintersköl Carnival, in the third week of January, in Aspen/Snowmass; Gay Ski Week, the last week in January, in Aspen; the Snowmass Mardi Gras, in late February or early March; Jazz Aspen at Snowmass, the last week of June; the Aspen Music Festival, from late June to late August; the DanceAspen Summer Festival, from July 5 to mid-August; the Aspen Writers Conference, in late June or July; the Snowmass Children's Festival, on the first weekend of August; the Snowmass International Music Fest, on Labor Day weekend; and the Aspen Filmfest, in late September.

SKIING & OTHER WINTER ACTIVITIES

Skiing Aspen really means skiing the four Aspen Valley resorts—Aspen, Aspen Highlands, Buttermilk Mountain, and Snowmass. All are managed by Aspen Skiing Company, and one ticket gives access to all. At press time, lift tickets were $39 to $52 for adults; $30 for children 7 to 12; and $36 for seniors 65 to 69. Children 6 and under and seniors 70 and older ski free. For further information, contact **Aspen Mountain,** Aspen Skiing Company (P.O. Box 1248), Aspen, CO 81612 (☎ **970/925-1220**). Call 970/925-1221 for snow reports.

ASPEN   Aspen Mountain—previously called Ajax for an old miner's claim—is not for the timid. It is the American West's original hard-core ski mountain, with no fewer than 23 of its named runs double diamond—for experts only. One-third of the mountain's runs are left forever ungroomed—sheer ecstasy for bump runners. There are mountain-long runs for intermediates as well as advanced skiers, but beginners should look to one of the other Aspen areas.

From the **Sundeck** restaurant at the mountain's 11,212-foot summit, numerous intermediate runs extend on either side of Bell Mountain—through Copper Bowl and down Spar Gulch. To the east of the Gulch, the knob of Bell offers a mecca for mogul mashers, with bump runs down its ridge and its east and west faces. To the west of the Gulch, the face of Ruthie's is wonderful for intermediate cruisers, while more mogul runs drop off International. Ruthie's Run extends for over 2 miles down the west ridge of the mountain, with an extension via Magnifico Cut Off and Little Nell to the base.

Mid-mountain restaurants include **Bonnie's,** at Tourtelotte Park near the top of Ruthie's Lift, and **La Baita,** at the bottom.

Aspen Mountain has a 3,267-foot vertical drop, with 75 trails on 631 skiable acres. There are eight lifts—the high-speed Silver Queen gondola, three quad chairs, and four double chairs—and snowcats deliver advanced-and-expert skiers to an additional 1,500 acres of powder skiing in back bowls. Average annual snowfall at the 11,212-foot summit is 300 inches (25 ft.).

Aspen is open from Thanksgiving through mid-April, daily from 9am to 3:30pm.

ASPEN HIGHLANDS   Highlands has the most balanced skiable terrain—novice to expert, with lots of intermediate slopes—in the Aspen valley.

It takes two lifts to reach the 11,800-foot Loge Peak summit, where most of the advanced expert runs are found in the Steeplechase area and 199 acres of glades in the Olympic Bowl. Kandahar, Golden Horn, and Thunderbowl give the intermediate skier a long run from top to bottom, and novices are best served mid-mountain on trails like Red Onion and Apple Strudel. There are two restaurants: **Highland's Cafe** and **Merry-Go-Round** at Midway.

Freestyle Friday, a tradition at Aspen Highlands for 25 years, boasts some of the best freestyle bump and big air competitors in the state of Colorado every Friday from early January through mid-April. In this technical head-to-head competition, about 20 competitors bump their way down Scarlett's Run, and finish with a final jump that lands them within perfect view of lunchtime guests at the Merry-Go-Round Restaurant.

Highlands has 78 trails on 619 acres, served by nine lifts (two high speed quads, five double chairs, and two surface lifts).

Highlands is open from Thanksgiving through mid-April, daily from 9am to 4pm. See above for ticket prices and information sources.

BUTTERMILK MOUNTAIN   Buttermilk is a premier beginners' mountain. In fact, *Ski* magazine has rated it the best place in North America to learn how to ski. But there's plenty of intermediate and ample advanced terrain as well.

The smallest of Aspen's four mountains has three segments: Main Buttermilk, rising from the Inn at Aspen, with a variety of intermediate trails and the long, easy, winding Homestead Road; Buttermilk West, a mountaintop (9,900 ft.) novice area; and Tiehack, the intermediate-advanced section where Aspen town-league races are held. **The Cliffhouse** restaurant is atop Main Buttermilk, and there are cafes at the foot of the other two segments.

Seven lifts (one high-speed quad, five double chairs and a platter-pull) serve 45 trails on 410 acres, with a 2,030-foot vertical drop. Average annual snowfall at the summit is 200 inches (16 ft., 8 in.).

Special features include the Kevin Delaney Snowboard Camp, which offers an intensive adult learn-to-snowboard program; the Powder Pandas for 3- to 6-year-olds; and a snowboard park with a 23% grade.

Buttermilk is open from mid-December to early April, daily from 9am to 4pm.

SNOWMASS   A huge, intermediate mountain with something for everyone, Snowmass has 33% more skiable acreage than the other three Aspen areas combined! Actually four distinct self-contained areas, each with its own lift system and restaurant, its terrain varies from easy beginner runs to the pitches of the Cirque and the Hanging Valley Wall, the steepest in the Aspen area.

Big Burn, site of a forest fire set by 19th-century Utes to discourage settlers, boasts wide-open advanced and intermediate slopes and the expert drops of the Cirque. Atop the intermediate Alpine Springs trails is the advanced High Alpine Lift, from which experts can traverse to the formidable Hanging Valley Wall. Elk Camp is ideal for early intermediates who prefer long cruising runs. Sam's Knob has advanced upper trails diving through trees, and a variety of intermediate and novice runs around its northeast face and base. All areas meet in the scattered condominium developments that surround Snowmass Village Mall.

Hungry skiers head for **Ullrhof** restaurant at the foot of Big Burn, **High Alpine** atop Alpine Springs, **Café Suzanne** at the base of Elk Camp, and **Sam's Knob** at that peak's summit.

All told, there are 2,565 skiable acres at Snowmass, with a 4,208-foot vertical drop. The mountain has 78 trails served by 17 lifts (7 quad chairs, 2 triple chair, 6 double chairs, and 2 platter-pulls). Average annual snowfall at the 12,310-foot summit is 300 inches (25 ft.).

The renowned Snowmass ski school has hundreds of instructors, as well as Snow Cubs and Big Burn Bears programs for children 18 months and older. The area also caters to snowboarders with a half-pipe that is 545 feet long and 55 feet wide, with a 22% grade.

Snowmass is open from Thanksgiving through mid-April, daily from 8:30am to 3:30pm.

CROSS-COUNTRY SKIING   The Aspen/Snowmass Nordic Council operates a free Nordic trail system with nearly 50 miles of groomed double track extending throughout the Aspen-Snowmass area, and incorporating summer bicycle paths. Instruction and rentals are offered along the trail at the **Aspen Cross-Country Center,** Colo. 82 between Aspen and Buttermilk (☎ **970/925-2145**), and the **Snowmass Club Touring Center,** Snowmass Village (☎ **970/923-3148**), both of which provide daily condition reports and information regarding the entire trail system.

Ashcroft Ski Touring (☎ **970/925-1971**), has 30 kilometers (18 miles) of groomed trails around the old ghost town of Ashcroft in the Castle Creek Valley, 12 miles up Castle Creek Road off Colo. 82. Rentals, instruction, and guided backcountry day and overnight trips are available.

Independent backcountry skiers should consult **White River National Forest,** 806 W. Hallam St. (☎ **970/925-3445**), and the **avalanche conditions hot line** (☎ **970/920-1664**). Two hut systems provide shelter on multiday trips—the 14-hut **Tenth Mountain Trail Association** toward Vail, and the 6-hut **Alfred A. Braun Hut System** (☎ **970/925-5775** for both) toward Crested Butte. Call for hut reservations. Guided backcountry ski trips on the hut system routes are offered by **Aspen Alpine Guides, Inc.** (☎ **800/643-8621** or 970/925-6618).

DOGSLEDDING   For rides in winter or a kennel tour in summer, call **Krabloonik,** 4250 Divide Rd., Snowmass Village (☎ **970/923-3953**). Every day in winter, teams of 13 Alaskan sled dogs pull people and provisions into the Snowmass-Maroon Bells Wilderness Area. Half-day trips, departing at 8:30am and 12:30pm, include lunch at **Krabloonik's** restaurant (see "Where to Dine," below) and cost $185 per adult and $120 for children 3 to 8 years of age. Children under 3 are not permitted on the ride. One-hour kennel tours run from mid-June to Labor Day, Wednesday through Sunday. They depart at 11am and 2:30pm from the restaurant, at a cost of $3.50 for those over 12, $3 for 12 and under. Private and group tours can be arranged by calling, or writing to P.O. Box 5517, Snowmass Village, CO 81615.

ICE-SKATING   There's year-round ice-skating at the indoor **City of Aspen Ice Garden,** 233 W. Hyman Ave. (☎ 970/920-5141). Call for details. For outdoor skating, try the **Silver Circle** at the base of Aspen Mountain next to the Rubey Park Transit Center (☎ 970/925-6360). Rates are about $7 for adults, $5 for children, and rental skates are available.

SLEIGH RIDES   For a good old-fashioned horse-drawn sleigh ride, complete with bells, call **T Lazy 7 Ranch,** 3129 Maroon Creek Rd. (☎ 970/925-4614), which charges $20 for a 1-hour ride.

SNOWMOBILING   There's snowmobiling on 26 miles of groomed trails from the **T Lazy 7 Ranch,** 3129 Maroon Creek Road (☎ 970/925-4614), all the way to the base of the Maroon Bells. Guided 2-hour tours cost $100 for one person and $150 for two; and there's a 4-hour tour to the ghost town of Independence, with lunch that costs $160 for one person and $240 for two.

WARM-WEATHER & YEAR-ROUND ACTIVITIES

There's no lack of guides, outfitters, and sporting goods shops in Aspen. Among the best one-stop outfitters is **Blazing Adventures,** P.O. Box 2127, Aspen, CO 81612 (☎ 800/282-7238 or 970/925-5651), which operates under the names Blazing Paddles, Blazing Peddles, and Blazing Trails, and leads river rafting, canoeing, mountain biking, hiking, four-wheeling, ballooning, and rock climbing excursions. In addition, the company can help set up multiactivity vacation agendas. See below for specific activities.

Your best source of information on a wide variety of outdoor activities in the mountains around Aspen, including hiking, mountain biking, horseback riding, four-wheeling, fishing, and camping, is the **White River National Forest,** 806 W. Hallam St. (☎ 970/925-3445). Another good source of information and maps is **Ute Mountaineer,** 308 S. Mill St. (☎ 800/533-0883 or 970/925-2849), which sells hiking and mountaineering equipment, and rents tents, backpacks, sleeping bags, and stoves.

AIRBORNE SPORTS   **Unicorn Balloon Company** (☎ 800/468-2478 or 970/925-5752) floats high above Roaring Fork Valley and surrounding mountain slopes, offering spectacular bird's-eye views from their hot-air balloons. Prices are in the $170 to $200 range per person, and rides conclude with the traditional champagne toast.

Paragliding—popular among adventurous skiers—is taught by **Aspen Expeditions and Paragliding** (☎ 970/925-7625).

BICYCLING   There are two bike paths of note. One connects Aspen with Snowmass Village; it begins at Seventh Street south of Hopkins Avenue, cuts through the forest to Colo. 82, then follows Owl Creek Road and Brush Creek Road to the Snowmass Mall. Extensions link it with Aspen High School and the Aspen Business Park. The Rio Grande Trail follows the Roaring Fork River from near the Aspen Post Office, on Puppy Smith Street, through Henry Stein Park to the community of Woody Creek, off Colo. 82 near Snowmass.

CATTLE DRIVES   Those yearning for a taste of the real Old West can satisfy that urge by participating in a cattle drive. **Blazing Adventures** (see above) offers drives that start at $175 per person.

FISHING   Perhaps the best of a great deal of good trout-fishing in the Aspen area is to be found in the Roaring Fork and Frying Pan rivers, both considered gold medal streams. The Roaring Fork follows Colo. 82 through Aspen from Independence Pass; the Frying Pan starts near Tennessee Pass, northeast of Aspen, and joins the Roaring Fork at Basalt, 18 miles down valley.

The Taylor Creek Fly Shop, in the Frying Pan Shopping Center in Basalt (☎ 970/927-4374), is one of the nation's largest fly-fishing guide services and also operates a huge retail store with everything for the fly-fishing enthusiast, including rental equipment. Rates for half-day guided walk-and-wade trips are $150 for one person and $175 for two, and full-day trips cost $200 and $235, respectively. Rates for float fishing trips for one or two people is $210 for a half-day and $295 for a full day.

GOLF   There are two public 18-hole championship courses in the Aspen valley, both with pro shops, driving ranges, and PGA instruction. **Aspen Golf Course,** Colo. 82, 1 mile west of Aspen (☎ 970/925-2145), is one of the longer courses in Colorado at 7,165 yards, and also has a restaurant and a marvelous view of the scenic Maroon Bells. Fees are $35 for nine holes and $65 for 18 holes. **Snowmass Lodge & Golf Course,** Snowmass Club Circle, Snowmass (☎ 970/923-3148), is an 18-hole championship golf course with fees of $55 for nine holes and $95 for 18 holes, both including the required cart.

HEALTH CLUBS   Aspen's only public downtown health club is the **Aspen Athletic Club,** 720 E. Hyman Ave. (☎ 970/925-2531), with weights and exercise equipment, aerobics classes, racquetball courts, a lap pool, steam and suntan rooms, and a pro shop.

HIKING & MOUNTAINEERING   Among the best ways to see the spectacular scenery here is on foot. You can get maps and tips on where to go from White River National Forest offices (see above). One popular trail is the route past the Maroon Bells to Crested Butte; the trek would take 175 miles by mountain road, but it's only about 30 miles by foot—14 from the end of Aspen's Maroon Creek Road.

Guided half- and full-day wilderness hikes are offered by **Blazing Adventures** (see above), with rates of $52 for a half-day and $78 for a full-day; the cost for a 1-day rock-climbing excursion is $160. Hardy outdoors-lovers can also join **Aspen Expeditions,** 426 S. Spring St. (P.O. Box 2432, Aspen, CO 81612, ☎ 970/925-7625), for a variety of guided adventure-travel treks and peak ascents.

HORSEBACK RIDING   Several stables in the Aspen valley offer a variety of rides, and some outfitters even package gourmet meals and country-western serenades with their expeditions. Typical rates are $45 for a 3-hour breakfast ride and $90 for a 4-hour lunch ride. Inquire at **Brush Creek Ranch,** 1020 Brush Creek Rd., Snowmass Village, CO 81615 (☎ 970/923-4252); **Snowmass Stables,** 2735 Brush Creek Rd., Snowmass Village, CO 81615 (☎ 970/923-3075); or **T Lazy 7 Ranch,** Maroon Creek Road, Box 240, Aspen, CO 81612 (☎ 970/925-4614). The T Lazy 7 also offers lodging year round (☎ 970/925-7254), plus hayrides, fishing, and hiking in summer; and snowmobiling, cross-country skiing, stagecoach rides, and ice-skating in winter. The ranch has a large heated pool, sauna, and Jacuzzi.

LLAMA TREKKING   Get out into the wilderness, letting a llama carry all the gear. **The Pine Creek Cookhouse,** 11399 Castle Creek Rd. (☎ 970/925-1971), offers several trips into the mountains. The hike to the ghost town of Ashcroft is fairly easy terrain; the 3¹/₂-mile hikes to American, Cathedral, or Tabor Lakes are steeper and more strenuous. All start at 9,750 feet elevation. Treks operate from mid-June through September, cost $60 to $80 for adults, $25 to $35 for children under 12, and include a gourmet lunch.

MOUNTAIN BIKING   There are hundreds of miles of trails through the White River National Forest that are perfect for mountain bikers, offering splendid views of the mountains, meadows, and valleys. Check with the forest service (see above) and local bike shops for tips on the best trails. Among shops that provide information, and sell, rent, or service your bike, are **Ajax Bike & Sports,** 635 E. Hyman Ave. (☎ **970/925-7662**), and **Aspen Velo Bike Shop,** 465 N. Mill St. (☎ **970/ 925-1495**). Typically, a full-day rental is $20 to $25, but fancier bikes can cost a lot more. Among those leading guided mountain-biking tours is **Blazing Adventures** (see above), with rates starting at $50 for a half-day trip.

RIVER RAFTING, KAYAKING, & CANOEING   Colorado Riff Raft, 555 E. Durant (☎ **800/759-3939,** 970/925-5405, or 970/923-2220 in Snowmass), has been rafting the rapids since 1979. Trips are offered on the Roaring Fork, Arkansas, and Colorado rivers, with refreshments on half-day trips and lunch on full-day trips. Prices start at $63 for a half-day, $68 for a three-quarter day, and $85 for a full day. Also offering raft trips is **Blazing Adventures** (see above), charging $60 to $65 for half-day trips and $70 to $96 for full-day excursions.

Blazing Adventures also offers white-water canoeing trips for $65, and **Aspen Kayak School** (☎ **970/925-4433**) offers weekend and week-long kayaking classes, starting at $185.

SWIMMING   The James E. Moore City of Aspen Pool, 895 Maroon Creek Rd. (☎ **970/920-5145**), is open year-round for lap and recreational swimming.

TENNIS   The City of Aspen has 10 public outdoor courts. Call for reservations and locations (☎ 970/920-5146). In addition, there's a tennis complex at **Aspen Mead-ows, 845 Meadows Rd. (☎ **970/544-7111**) with two Har-Tru clay courts and four regular courts, all public; and **Snowmass Tennis Gardens,** in Snowmass Club at the intersection of Highline and Brush Creek roads (☎ **970/923-5600**), has 11 public courts.

THE FESTIVAL SCENE

The **Aspen Music Festival** (box office ☎ **970/925-8077**) has been held annually since 1949. Lasting 9 weeks from late June to late August, it offers more than 150 events, including classical music, opera, jazz, choral, and children's programs. Most concerts take place in the 1,700-seat Bayer-Benedict Music Tent and new 500-seat Joan and Irving Harris Concert Hall at Third and Gillespie streets. Free events in-clude the popular Saturday "Music on the Mountain" concerts atop Aspen Moun-tain. About 100,000 music lovers visit Aspen for the festival, so plan ahead. **Aspen Music Tours** (☎ **800/778-8576**), offers a variety of packages to the festival every summer. For instance, a $656 4-day package includes 4-nights lodging within walk-ing distance of the Music Tent, continental breakfast, a three-event Music Festival pass, and round-trip airfare from the West Coast. For more information, contact the festival office at 2 Music School Rd., Aspen, CO 81611 or call the number above. Most individual event tickets are $12 to $30, with some events as high as $40. Sea-son passes are also available.

The **DanceAspen Festival** (☎ **970/925-7718,** or 970/920-5770 after June 15) is considered one of the nation's leading summer dance festivals. Lasting 8 weeks from July through August, it features a broad spectrum of dance forms including classi-cal ballet, modern, and jazz. The festival takes place in the 550-seat Aspen School District Auditorium. For tickets, which cost $10 to $48, call the box office or write P.O. Box 8745, Aspen, CO 81612. Subscription series tickets are also available. Run-ning concurrently is the pre-professional DanceAspen summer school for 200 teen-agers, selected during a 28-city winter audition tour.

Jazz Aspen at Snowmass (110 E. Hallam St., Suite 204, Aspen, CO 81611, ☎ **970/920-4996,** or 970/920-5770 for tickets) is a 5-day festival at Snowmass

Town Park in late June. It kicks off with a French-Cajun meal and music program, and continues with legendary performers such as Lou Rawls, the Neville Brothers, and the Zion Harmonizers. Tickets start at $5, and the series includes two free outdoor concerts.

Aspen Theatre in the Park, P.O. Box 8677, Aspen, CO 81612 (☎ **970/ 925-9313**), which began in 1983, is the only professional theater company in the Roaring Fork Valley. In recent years it has presented *I Do! I Do!, Wait Until Dark,* and *Greater Tuna.* Performances are held during July and August, Wednesdays and Thursdays at 6:30pm, and Fridays and Saturdays at 8pm, in the company's tent in the Art Park near the Rio Grande parking garage. Plays run in repertoire, and tickets are $19 to $22 at the door, less when purchased in advance. Call for complete schedule.

MUSEUMS, ART CENTERS & HISTORIC SITES

The **Aspen Historical Society,** 621 W. Bleeker St. (☎ 970/925-3721), offers two walking tours of Aspen from mid-June to mid-September. One begins at the Visitor Center and covers the downtown area; the other is a 1-mile walk beginning on the grounds of the Wheeler/Stallard House Museum (see below) that explores the West End residential area. Both tours end in the lobby of the historic Hotel Jerome (see "Where to Stay," below). Cost is $10 per person. Guided tours of Ashcroft and Independence ghost towns are offered June through August, from Tuesday through Saturday. The Society has brochures with maps of the ghost towns for those who prefer to wander about on their own.

Anderson Ranch Arts Center. 5263 Owl Creek Rd., (P.O. Box 5598) Snowmass Village. ☎ **970/923-3181.** Free admission to the gallery. Workshop tuitions: $150–$995; $75–$175 for children's programs. Housing and meals are extra. Mon–Fri 9am–5pm, gallery.

What was once a sheep ranch in the Brush Creek Valley is now a highly respected arts center with an art gallery and two nationally acclaimed programs.

From June to September, about 90 workshops, catering to all levels, offer programs in ceramics, painting, drawing, sculpture, photography, computer imaging, woodworking, furniture, and interdisciplinary studies. Workshops last from 2 days to 3 weeks, and there's also a children's program. A free guided tour of the studios is offered at 4pm on Mondays, June through August.

The winter Studio Residency Program, October through April, offers artists an opportunity to create a body of work outside of professional or academic atmospheres, and receive critical feedback from their peers.

Aspen Art Museum. 590 N. Mill St., Aspen. ☎ **970/925-8050.** Admission $3 adults, $2 students and seniors, free for children under 12, free for everyone Thurs evening after 6pm. Tues–Sat 10am–6pm, Sun noon–6pm, plus Thurs evening until 8pm.

Though it has no permanent collection, the Aspen Art Museum presents rotating exhibits highlighting the work of local and nationally known contemporary artists. Lectures and art education programs for adults and children are offered year-round, and there's a free reception every Thursday evening from 6 to 8pm.

Wheeler/Stallard House Museum. 620 W. Bleeker St., Aspen. ☎ **970/925-3721.** Admission $3 adults, 50¢ children. Walking tours $10 per person. Mid-June–mid-Sept, Tues–Fri 1–4pm.

Silver baron Jerome B. Wheeler had this three-story Victorian brick home built in 1888. Its steeply pitched roofs, dormers, and gables have made it a landmark in Aspen's West End neighborhood ever since it was raised. A museum and archives of the Aspen Historical Society since 1969, the exterior of the house has been restored to its appearance in the heady days before the silver crash. Exhibits describe Aspen's history from Ute culture through the mining rush, and from railroads and ranching to the founding of the skiing industry. The Museum Annex presents changing exhibits, and the gift shop offers a variety of souvenirs. Guided walking tours of historic Aspen are offered during the summer (see above).

SHOPPING

To truly appreciate the Aspen experience (and possibly rub shoulders with Hollywood celebrities, royalty, and other gorgeous types), one must shop Aspen. Note that we say shop (meaning browse), rather than buy, because if you're not careful you just might blow next month's mortgage payment on some western fashion accessory that you probably won't wear much back home. No one ever brags about the great bargain they snagged last season in Aspen.

On the other hand, quality is usually tops, shop clerks are very friendly, and there's a good chance your neighbor doesn't already have one (maybe Princess Di does, though). Having said all that, we suggest you lock up your credit cards, put on some good walking shoes, and spend a few hours exploring the galleries and shops of Aspen. Following are a few of our favorites:

For **original art,** check out: **Pam Driscol Gallery** (magnificent bronze sculpture, and oils), 416 E. Cooper St. Mall (☎ **970/925-3881**); **Jill Vickers Gallery of Fine Art** (a unique collection of distinctive and internationally recognized American artists), 302 S. Galena St. (☎ **970/925-5797**); **Shaw Gallery** (antique North American Indian art), 525 E. Cooper Ave. (☎ **970/925-2873**); **Christy Lee Fine Arts** (fine 19th- and 20th-century prints and originals), 205 S. Mill St. (☎ **970/927-4399**); and **Patrick Collins Gallery** (wilderness photography), 520 E. Durant Ave. (☎ **970/920-4105**).

For **clothing,** the best places are: **Aspen Exotics** (leather goods), 205 S. Mill St. (☎ **970/925-2552**); **Bounty Hunter** (fine, handcrafted hats), 414 Hyman St. Mall (☎ **970/544-0570**); the **Freudian Slip** (lingerie), 416 S. Hunter St. (☎ **970/925-4427**); **Spurs** (western wear), 207 S. Galena St. (☎ **970/925-6029**); **Stefan Kaelin** (ski and casual wear), 447 E. Cooper St. (☎ **970/925-2989**); **Suzanne's** (locally knitted women's sweaters), 205 S. Mill St. (☎ **970/920-2535**); and for those who want a good-quality souvenir T-shirt or sweatshirt without breaking the bank, **Crazy Shirts,** 316 S. Galena St. (☎ **970/920-3145**).

When it's time to pick up a gift, we like **Aspen Mountain Christmas** (handcrafted and unique ornaments, nativities, and nutcrackers), 616 E. Hyman Ave. (☎ **970/925-8142**); **Chepita** (a toy store for adults), 525 E. Cooper Ave. (☎ **970/925-2871**), and at Snowmass Village Mall (☎ **970/923-6161**); **Curious George Collectibles** (western artifacts that used to belong to notorious cowboys), 410 E. Hyman Ave. (☎ **970/925-3315**); and **Solos Colorado** (original creations in clay, fibers, wood, metal, and stone), Mill Street Plaza, 205 S. Mill St. (☎ **970/925-9064**).

WHERE TO STAY

Occupancy rates run 90% or higher during peak winter and summer seasons, so it's essential to make reservations as early as possible. The easiest way to do so is to call **Aspen Central Reservations** (☎ **800/262-7736**). Additional lodging is available in Snowmass, 12 miles west of Aspen; call **Snowmass Central Reservations** (☎ **800/598-2004**). Those on especially tight budgets will find much lower room rates in Glenwood Springs, 42 miles away over a sometimes icy and snowpacked road (see chapter 12).

Many accommodations close during the spring and fall; if they're open, rates during those months are typically the lowest of any time during the year.

VERY EXPENSIVE

✪ **Hotel Jerome.** 330 E. Main St., Aspen, CO 81611. ☎ **800/331-7213** or 970/920-1000. Fax 970/925-2784. 77 rms, 16 suites. MINIBAR TV TEL. Mid-Apr–late May and Oct–late Nov, $160–$250 double; $395–$790 suite. Early Apr, late May–Sept, and late Nov–mid-Dec, $255–$355 double; $510–$1,020 suite. Christmas season, $585–$725 double; $895–$1,790 suite. Early Jan–Mar, $395–$495 double; $650–$1,300 suite. AE, CB, DC, MC, V. Underground valet parking.

Jerome B. Wheeler built the Jerome during the peak of the silver boom. It opened in 1889 as Colorado's first hotel with electricity and indoor plumbing, and the first west of the Mississippi with an elevator. The silver crash of 1893 ended Aspen's prosperity and the glory years of the Hotel Jerome. Happily, in the mid-1980s, a $5-million renovation of the Jerome began, restoring it to its original splendor. With its Eastlake Victorian architecture lovingly preserved, and furnished with period antiques, the Jerome is now on the National Register of Historic Places.

Each guest room is spacious and unique, containing period antiques and furnishings, with iron and brass double or king beds, down comforters, and crocheted bed dressings. Amenities include remote-control color TVs, VCRs, multiline telephones that are fax- and modem-ready, and minibars. Bathrooms, finished with white Carrera marble and reproduction 19th-century octagonal tiles, contain hair dryers, plush terry-cloth robes, showers, and oversize Jacuzzi tubs.

Dining/Entertainment: The Century Room offers savory American fare served in Victorian elegance. Main courses vary, but there's generally a choice of beef, seafood, poultry, wild game, and pasta, with prices in the $20 to $30 range. Mustard-crusted salmon is the chef's specialty and always on the menu. Jacob's Corner offers more casual surroundings for breakfast and lunch dining ($6–$13). Guests with lighter appetites can also visit the historical J-Bar where sandwiches and salads are available.

Services: 24-hour room service, concierge, 24-hour front desk, valet laundry, complimentary shuttle van, ski concierge, and business and secretarial services. Pets are permitted.

Facilities: Heated swimming pool with sun deck, two Jacuzzis, fitness center, retail ski shop, and meeting space for 400.

The Little Nell. 675 E. Durant Ave., Aspen, CO 81611. ☎ **800/525-6200** or 970/920-4600. Fax 970/920-4670. 78 rms, 14 suites. A/C MINIBAR TV TEL. Summer–early winter, and early spring $260–$400 double; $550–$1,650 suite. Spring, $195–$275 double; $400–$1,200 suite. Pre-Christmas and early Jan–early Apr, $425–$550 double; $775–$2,900 suite. Holiday period, call for rates. AE, CB, DC, DISC, MC, V. Valet parking $10 per day.

Located just 17 paces (yes, it's been measured) from the base terminal of the Silver Queen gondola, the Little Nell boasts the virtues of an intimate country inn with the personalized service and amenities of a grand hotel. All rooms have a view either of the town or the mountain.

No two guest rooms are alike, but all have gas fireplaces, Belgian-wool carpeting, down-filled lounge chairs and sofas, remote-control television, VCR, built-in bar/refrigerator unit, oversized beds with down comforters, three two-line telephones, and marble-finished bathrooms with two vanities, hair dryers, and Crabtree & Evelyn toiletries. Standard suites have separate Jacuzzi tubs and steam showers. Five executive apartments have all this and more, including their own fax machines.

Dining/Entertainment: The restaurant serves three meals daily in an arty atmosphere with large windows looking toward the hotel courtyard. The menu is constantly changing, offering fish and seafood, beef, chicken, and game with a regional flair. The Little Nell Bar is a plush living room with rich wood, a two-sided sandstone fireplace, historic photos of the Aspen ski scene, and outdoor terrace seating. The Ajax Tavern offers a more relaxed atmosphere.

Services: 24-hour room service, full-service concierge, winter ski concierge, ski technician on staff; same-day valet laundry; complimentary shuttle; in-room massage; baby-sitting; secretarial services; express check-out.

Facilities: Year-round outdoor heated swimming pool and Jacuzzi; fitness club with Nautilus equipment, steam room, and spa services, including massage; video rentals; arcade with eight shops; meeting space for 200.

The Ritz-Carlton. 315 E. Dean St., Aspen, CO 81611. ☎ **970/920-3300.** Fax 970/920-9555. 257 rms, 28 suites. A/C MINIBAR TV TEL. Mid-Apr–May and mid-Oct–mid-Nov, $98–$165 double; $195–$550 suite. June–mid-Oct and mid-Nov–mid-Dec, $165–$325 double; $375–$1,500 suite. Jan–mid-Apr, $295–$495 double; $595–$3,000 suite. Christmas holidays, $400–$700 double; $875–$4,000 suite. AE, CB, DC, DISC, JCB, MC, V. 24-hour valet parking.

Located at the base of Aspen Mountain, between the Gondola and Lift 1A, the Ritz-Carlton offers luxurious comfort amid casual elegance. You won't find any dress code here. There are many cozy seating areas in the lobby, some clustered about the large stone fireplace.

Rooms (except a few on the ground floor) have views of either the mountains or town. All have either two double beds or a king, fully stocked minibars, personal safes, plush terry bathrobes, remote control TVs, humidifiers, three telephones with dual phone lines, and AM/FM clock radios. Marble bathrooms feature double vanities, hair dryers, and scales. The Club Level offers keyed access to the floor for extra security, a private lobby, and food presentations five times daily. Pets are not allowed.

Dining/Entertainment: The full-service Terrace Restaurant serves continental cuisine with a regional flavor. The menu changes seasonally, but the Ritz-Carlton is known for its Colorado rack of lamb, and you'll usually find Colorado elk tenderloin plus other meat, seafood, and vegetarian dishes on the menu. The Mill Street Club & Grill offers more casual dining, with tableside preparations and evening entertainment.

Services: Twice daily housekeeping, turndown service, 24-hour room service, morning newspaper, free morning coffee in the lobby, 24-hour copy and fax services, secretarial service, baby-sitting, concierge, free ski shuttle.

Facilities: Fitness center with weight room, sauna and steam rooms, indoor and outdoor whirlpool spas, massage, and outdoor heated pool; gift shop; sports shop; hair and body salon; conference space for 900; nature trails, jogging track nearby, bicycle rental.

Expensive

The Sardy House. 128 E. Main St. (at Aspen St.), Aspen, CO 81611. ☎ **800/321-3457** or 970/920-2525. Fax 970/925-3840. 14 rms, 6 suites. TV TEL. Early/late ski season, $139–$219 double; $229–$349 suite. Pre-Christmas and Jan–Mar, $239–$329 double; $379–$549 suite. Holiday period, $339–$429 double; $499–$699 suite. Spring & Fall, $85–$135 double; $145–$195 suite. Summer, $160–$265 double; $285–$425 suite. Rates include breakfast. AE, DC, MC, V.

A red-brick Victorian mansion built in 1892, the handsome Sardy House stands among majestic spruce trees. Inside, lace curtains and period antiques lend a delicate elegance. An enclosed gallery bridges a private brick walkway, joining the Sardy House to its Carriage House wing. Rooms combine antique Victorian and modern furnishings: cherry-wood beds and armoires, wicker chairs and sofas. There are whirlpool tubs in all but two, which have antique claw-footed tubs. Other touches include down comforters, terry-cloth robes, and heated towel racks. Suites have entertainment centers with VCRs and stereos, kitchenettes, and hideaway sofas. Three have private entrances; one has a private balcony and sitting room; one has a fireplace. The Carriage House Suite features a winding, wrought-iron staircase to its second floor.

The Sardy House restaurant presents candlelit American dinners (6–9:30pm) with silver service in a plush fireplace room. Main courses include fish, pasta, free-range chicken, and game. It's also open for breakfast (7:30–10:30am, until noon Sun). Jack's Bar is open from 4pm daily. Room service morning and evening, a concierge, in-room massage, and valet laundry services are available. Facilities include a heated outdoor swimming pool, hot tub, sauna, private ski storage, and heated boot lockers.

MODERATE

Hearthstone House. 134 E. Hyman Ave. (at Aspen St.), Aspen, CO 81611. ☎ **970/ 925-7632.** Fax 970/920-4450. 17 rms. TV TEL. Summer, $118–$158 double; $168–$188 with whirlpool bath. Winter, $188–$228 double; $238–$268 with whirlpool bath. Rates include breakfast and afternoon tea. AE, MC, V.

Small and sophisticated in the tradition of European luxury inns, the Hearthstone House is located just two blocks west of the Wheeler Opera House. Guests share a large, elegant living room with teak-and-leather furnishings, a wood-burning fireplace, dining room with bright flowers, and an extensive library. Rooms are bright and homey, with queen-size or twin beds, and one room has a king-size bed. Three rooms feature whirlpool tubs. The inn also offers valet laundry and an Austrian herbal steam sauna. Smoking and pets are not permitted.

The Inn at Aspen. 38750 Colo. 82, Aspen, CO 81611. ☎ **800/952-1515** or 970/925-1500, **800/826-4998** in Colorado. Fax 970/925-9037. 120 rms, 4 suites. A/C TV TEL. Winter $150– $270 double; $250–$450 suite. Summer $80–$175 double; $140–$250 suite. Holiday period higher. AE, CB, DC, DISC, MC, V.

Nestled at the foot of Buttermilk Mountain, this ski-in/ski-out hotel offers views of either the slopes or the Roaring Fork valley. Studios are neat and cozy, with private balconies, queen-size Murphy beds, double sleeper sofas, easy chairs, dining tables, and vanities. Kitchenettes are stocked for four people and have microwave ovens, refrigerators, toasters, and coffeemakers. Executive studios are larger but furnished the same.

The restaurant serves three meals daily and has a full bar. The hotel also offers a heated outdoor swimming pool, hot tub, Jacuzzi, sauna, fitness center, masseuse; ski shop, ski lockers; meeting space for 220; room service, concierge, valet laundry, guest laundry, game room, and safe-deposit boxes.

Limelite Lodge. 228 E. Cooper Ave. (at Monarch St.), Aspen, CO 81611. ☎ **800/433-0832** or 970/925-3025. Fax 970/925-5120. 60 rms, 3 suites. TV TEL. Early/late ski season, $68–$98 double; $130 suite. Holiday period, $168–$208 double; $275 suite. Jan, $108–$138 double; $185 suite. Feb–Mar, $148–$168 double; $230 suite. May–June, $58–$98 double; $130 suite. July–Aug, $88–$118 double; $170 suite. Sept–Oct, $68–$98 double; $130 suite. Rates include continental breakfast. AE, CB, DC, DISC, MC, V.

Located within walking distance of practically everything in town, the lodge has two separate buildings facing each other across Cooper Avenue—one three stories, the other two—each with its own heated outdoor swimming pool and Jacuzzi. Rooms are well kept. Most have queen beds with comforters, a large dresser and other wood furnishings, floral wallpaper, and a small private bath on the other side of a walk-through closet/vanity. One Jacuzzi room is available, and pets are accepted.

The Columbine Room offers breakfast every morning and a warming fire at night. Hot beverages are available 24 hours a day. Services and facilities include a 24-hour desk, in-room massage, two heated outdoor swimming pools, Jacuzzi, sauna, sun deck, guest laundry, and ski lockers.

Snowflake Inn. 221 E. Hyman Ave., Aspen, CO 81611. ☎ **800/247-2069** or 970/925-3221. Fax 970/925-8740. 38 rms. TV TEL. Early/late ski season, $85–$195; holiday period, $206–$349; Jan–mid-Feb, $155–$229; mid-Feb–late Mar, $185–$259; spring and fall, $85–$120; summer, $109–$159. Call for 2–3 bedroom suite rates. Rates include continental breakfast in winter. AE, CB, DC, DISC, MC, V.

This is a comfortable ski-lodge–style inn with a variety of accommodations. Rooms have painted rough wood walls, overstuffed chairs and sofas, good lighting, and an in-room safe; some have gas fireplaces and some have skylights; all have kitchenettes. There's an outdoor heated pool, Jacuzzi, and sauna; a coin-operated laundry, 24-hour desk, and airport transportation for a fee. Centrally located just one block from downtown Aspen, it's within easy walking distance of the Aspen lifts. Pets are not allowed.

INEXPENSIVE

Innsbruck Inn. 233 W. Main St., Aspen CO 81611-1796. ☎ **970/925-2980.** Fax 970/925-6960. 29 rms, 2 suites. TV TEL. Jan–Mar, $129–$179 double; $200–$225 suite. Apr–Dec, $75–$105 double; $125–$153 suite; higher during holiday season. Rates include full breakfast in winter, continental in summer. AE, DC, DISC, MC, V.

This Tyrolean-style inn has a homey lobby, with a stone fireplace where you can relax and enjoy complimentary après-ski munchies. Each room is slightly different, though all have stucco walls, shower-tub combos, and ski racks. Upstairs rooms have hand-carved ceiling beams, and many have down comforters. Pets are not allowed. There's a year-round outdoor heated pool, sauna, and hot tub (robes are available).

The Mountain Chalet. 333 E. Durant Ave., Aspen, CO 81611. ☎ **800/321-7813** or 970/925-7797. Fax 970/925-7811. 47 rms, 4 apts. TV TEL. Winter, $150–$240 double, $340 apt, rates higher during holidays; spring-fall, $120–$210 double, $280 apt. Rates include full breakfast in winter, continental in summer. CB, DC, DISC, MC, V. Free parking, underground.

You'll find a friendly, ski-lodge atmosphere here, just $1^1/_2$ blocks from the lifts. There's a television and piano in the lobby. Rooms are light-colored, with wood furnishings, and twin, double, queen, or king beds, plus a few trundle beds. There are even some bunk rooms with four beds, rented by the bed at greatly reduced rates in ski season. There's a year-round heated outdoor pool, large indoor whirlpool, sauna and steam room, coin-operated laundry, exercise room, game room, aerobics classes, and ski lockers. Pets are not allowed.

St. Moritz Lodge. 334 W. Hyman Ave., Aspen, CO 81612. ☎ **800/817-2069** or 970/925-3220. Fax 970/920-4032. 12 dorm rms with 33 beds (shared bath), 13 standard rms. TV TEL. Peak summer season, $29 dorm bed; $69 standard room (double). Spring and fall, $19 dorm bed; $49 standard room. Winter (including continental breakfast), $25–$35 dorm bed; $69–$129 standard room. Holiday, $45 dorm bed; $169 standard room. AE, CB, DC, DISC, MC, V.

A friendly European-style lodge with a large fireplace in its lobby, the St. Moritz appeals to cost-conscious travelers with simple dorm rooms (small but sufficient), and recently renovated standard rooms with cable color television and private, tiled bathrooms. There's also a heated outdoor swimming pool, Jacuzzi, and sauna. Breakfast and après-ski refreshments are served daily in the lower lounge. One- and two-bedroom condos are also available; call for rates.

WHERE TO DINE

Most restaurants in the Aspen-Snowmass area are open during the winter (Thanksgiving–early Apr) and summer (mid-June–mid-Sept) seasons. Between seasons, however, some close their doors or limit hours. Call ahead if you're visiting at these times.

EXPENSIVE

The Chart House. 219 E. Durant Ave., at Monarch St. ☎ **970/925-3525.** Reservations recommended. Main courses $15.95–$29.95. AE, CB, DC, DISC, MC, V. Daily 5:30–10pm. STEAK/SEAFOOD.

The first Chart House in the United States was established here in Aspen in 1961. Rough-hewn wood walls with sports-action photos, planter boxes beside marble-top tables, and polished brass surround an extensive salad bar, included with all dinners. The menu emphasizes steaks, prime rib, and seafood.

The Golden Horn. 320 S. Mill St. ☎ **970/925-3373.** Reservations highly recommended. Main courses $15–$31. AE, MC, V. Daily 5:30–10pm. Closed mid-Apr–mid-June and mid-Sept–mid-Nov. SWISS.

An Aspen favorite since 1949, and the town's longest continually operating restaurant, the Golden Horn features the friendly alpine atmosphere of chef-owner Klaus Christ's native Switzerland. Named for the golden horn on the dark-paneled wall near the fireplace, it's famous for its hearty Swiss cuisine—Wiener schnitzel, lamb, filet mignon, venison, and fresh fish—and more recently for lighter fare including pasta and seafood. The Golden Horn's well-chosen 260-bottle wine list has earned it a place on the *Wine* Spectator's "top 100" list of U.S. restaurants.

Krabloonik. 4250 Divide Rd., off Brush Creek Rd., Snowmass Village. ☎ **970/923-3953.** Reservations recommended at lunch, essential at dinner. Main courses $9–$30 at lunch, $21–$50 at dinner. MC, V. Winter, daily 11am–2pm; year-round dinner seatings daily at 6 and 8:30pm. INTERNATIONAL/WILD GAME/SEAFOOD.

There's something very wild, something that hearkens to Jack London, perhaps, about sitting in a log cabin watching teams of sled dogs come and go as you bite into a caribou stew or wild-boar sandwich. That's part of the pleasure of Krabloonik. A venture of the largest dog kennel in America's lower 48 states, this rustic restaurant has huge picture windows with mountain views and seating around a sunken fireplace. Skiers drop into the restaurant from the Campground lift for winter lunch, or visitors can dine before or after an excursion on a dogsled (see "Dogsledding" above). You might try a buffalo burger or roasted elk sandwich for lunch, or a grilled boneless breast of quail. For dinner there's Krabloonik smoked trout for starters and a wide variety of game and fish for the main course. For those with hearty appetites there are two combination game entrees: caribou, elk and moose, or caribou, quail, and boar.

Piñons. 105 S. Mill St. ☎ **970/920-2021.** Reservations recommended. Main courses $22–$33. AE, MC, V. Daily 6–10pm. CREATIVE REGIONAL.

Tremendous attention to detail went into creating the contemporary western ranch setting of Piñons, with its aged stucco walls and braided whip leather around the stairwell. The innovative menu includes sautéed Colorado pheasant, roasted Colorado striped bass, fresh fish, wild game, and grilled meats. In summer lighter fare is also offered.

Renaissance. 304 E. Hopkins St. ☎ **970/925-2402.** Reservations recommended. Main courses $24–$36; complete five-course wine-tasting dinners, $95. AE, DC, MC, V. Daily 6–10:30pm. Closed late spring and fall. MODERN FRENCH.

Award-winning chef-owner Charles Dale has created a beautiful, intimate, and contemporary setting for his creative dishes, served as part of an elaborate wine-tasting dinner, or à la carte. The menu changes frequently, but nightly specials might include Chilean seabass with artichoke, exotically spiced grilled lamb loin, beef tenderloin, and honey-smoked duck breast. A choice from the award-winning wine list is a delightful addition.

The more casual attached bistro, **The R-Bar,** offers somewhat lighter fare such as chicken curry, Caesar salad, and a nightly pasta special, with prices from $14 to $20 or $25 for a three-course dinner. It's open for meals from 6 to 10pm, with entertainment continuing until 1:30am (☎ **970/925-2403**).

MODERATE

Takah Sushi. 420 E. Hyman Ave. ☎ **970/925-8588.** Reservations recommended. Main courses $15–$25. AE, DC, DISC, MC, V. Daily winter 5:30–11pm, summer 6–11pm. JAPANESE/PACIFIC RIM.

This lively sushi bar and Japanese restaurant has been praised by the *New York Times,* which called its sushi "some of the best between Malibu and Manhattan." A wide variety of sushi are sliced and rolled here, from halibut to octopus. For those not desiring sushi or sashimi, the menu also includes crisp Chinese duck, several vegetarian dishes, Chilean sea bass, and a teriyaki-tempura combination with beef, chicken, or salmon.

Wienerstube. 633 E. Hyman Ave., at Spring St. ☎ **970/925-3357.** Reservations not accepted. Breakfast $2.95–$9.95; lunch $5.95–$18.95. AE, CB, DC, MC, V. Tues–Sun 7am–2:30pm. AUSTRIAN.

Gerhard Mayritsch, a native of the Austrian city of Villach, has been serving genuine Austrian food in this beautiful garden restaurant since 1965, with the Aspen powers-that-be often gathered around the Stammitsch, a large community dining table. There are also private tables and booths where you can enjoy a changing menu that might include apple pancakes for breakfast and Austrian sausages, Wiener schnitzel, and other specialties at lunch. Viennese pastries are available any time.

INEXPENSIVE

China Fun. 132 W. Main St. ☎ **970/925-5433.** Main courses $8.95–$12.95, plus several more expensive house specialties. AE, DISC, MC, V. Daily 11:30am–11pm. CHINESE.

Lodged in an opulent century-old Victorian manor, this is Aspen's largest and, quite probably, finest Chinese restaurant. The decor is an interesting combination of Victorian and Oriental, with a mahogany bar from Liverpool, England. Chef Greg Qin trained in China and worked in New York City for 8 years before coming here. The menu includes an overwhelming array of Mandarin, Cantonese, Hunan, and Szechuan dishes.

Flying Dog Brew Pub. 424 E. Cooper Ave. ☎ **970/925-7464.** Lunch $5.25–$15.95; dinner $6.95–$17.95. AE, DISC, MC, V. Daily 11:30am–2am (may close 1 week in spring and fall). AMERICAN.

This is a cafe-style pub with red brick walls, tables, and booths and a view into the brewery on the side. As the name suggests, the decor celebrates all things canine. The food is good, and there's a wide variety, with starters such as vegetable quesadilla, chicken teriyaki, Cobb salad, and turkey chile. The lunch menu includes fish-and-chips, sandwiches, chicken pub pie, and brew pub bratwurst. The dinner menu is heavy on beef, with dishes such as Limousin beef, baby-back ribs, and French dip, but there are also plenty of pasta selections. There are about 20 different ales in the pub's inventory, with four to six available at any given time. A patio is open in summer, and there's a bluegrass band Sunday evenings.

La Piñata. Daly Lane, Snowmass Village. ☎ **970/923-2153.** Reservations not accepted. Main courses $12.95–$17.95. AE, MC, V. Winter, daily, après-ski 3–6pm; year-round dinner 5–10pm. SOUTHWESTERN.

Festive decor, a roaring fire, and a spacious deck make this a favorite Snowmass dining spot. Margaritas may be the house drink, while dinner specials can include ahi fajitas, seafood and vegetarian enchiladas, and honey chipotle chicken. Conventional steaks and chicken dishes are also served.

Little Annie's Eating House. 517 E. Hyman Ave. ☎ **970/925-1098.** Reservations not accepted. Lunch $4.95–$8.95; dinner $9.50–$20.95. MC, V. Daily 11:30am–11pm (bar open to 2am). AMERICAN.

A casual, western-style place, Little Annie's is locally famous for its barbecued ribs, chicken, and outrageous burgers. It's becoming equally popular for its newer, lighter offerings, including healthy summer salads, fresh pastas, vegetarian lasagna, and fresh fish specials.

✪ **Woody Creek Tavern.** Upper River Rd., Woody Creek. ☎ **970/923-4585.** Reservations not accepted. $3.50–$15.95. No credit cards. Daily 11:30am–10:30pm. AMERICAN/MEXICAN.

Woody Creek is a true local hangout. Locals say that celebrities like to visit too, but we didn't meet any on our last visit. Probably the only old-time, rustic tavern left in the Aspen area, its walls are covered with a variety of news clippings and other paraphernalia. The grilled buffalo beer sausage has just the right amount of spiciness, and their other dishes looked mighty tempting: barbecued pork ribs, thick steaks, and burgers. The Mexican food is pretty good, too, and goes well with the house specialty drink—fresh lime-juice margaritas.

To get there, drive three-quarters of a mile west of Brush Creek Road (the Snowmass Village turnoff) on Colo. 82, turn right into Woody Creek Canyon on Smith Road, take a left at the first fork, and continue 1¼ miles. This road can be icy in winter.

La Cocina. 308 E. Hopkins Ave. ☎ **970/925-9714.** Reservations not accepted. Main courses $6.50–$10.75. No credit cards. Daily 5–10pm. Closed mid-Apr–May and mid-Oct–Nov. MEXICAN.

Ski magazine calls La Cocina "one of the unmissables" in Aspen, and we fully agree. A basket of chips and spicy-hot salsa have greeted diners here for more than 2 decades. Start with the green-chile soup, then slide into a platter of blue-corn chicken enchiladas with a side of posole. There's no lard used for cooking here. Top it all off with a slice of chocolate velvet cake for dessert.

Moon Dogs. Village Shuttle Depot, Daly Lane, Snowmass Village. ☎ **970/923-6655.** $2–$6. No credit cards. Daily 8am–midnight. AMERICAN.

A 100-year-old cable car beside the Snowmass shuttle depot houses this self-proclaimed gourmet fast-food stand. Moon dogs—slow-grilled beef frankfurters—are the house favorite, but you can also get subs, breakfast burritos, gyros, Danish, and popcorn all day long.

The Red Onion. 420 E. Cooper St. ☎ **970/925-9043.** Reservations not accepted. Main courses $5–$11. MC, V. Daily 11:30am–10pm (bar open until 2am). Closed Apr 20–May 20 and Oct 20–Oct 28. AMERICAN/MEXICAN.

Aspen's oldest surviving bar started out as a saloon and casino during the silver boom. Now it has an indoor ski corral for folks just off the slopes. Burgers and Philadelphia steak sandwiches are big favorites at lunch; Mexican cuisine holds forth at night, with the likes of burritos, fajitas, and taco salads. Daily specials feature traditional American fare.

ASPEN AFTER DARK

The focus of the performing arts in Aspen is the 1889 **Wheeler Opera House,** 320 E. Hyman Ave. (☎ 970/920-5770 for the box office). Built at the peak of the mining boom by silver baron Jerome B. Wheeler, this stage—meticulously restored in 1984—hosts a year-round program of music, theater, dance, film, and lectures. The building itself is worth a visit, with brass wall sconces, crystal chandeliers, gold trim and stencils on the dark blue walls, rich wood, red carpeting, and red velvet seats. The box office is open Monday through Saturday from 10am to 5pm, with guided tours by appointment. The Music Associates of Aspen present operas in the theater from late June to late August. A monthly calendar of events is published; ticket prices generally range from $12 to $35.

For more information regarding performing arts events in Aspen, see "The Festival Scene," above.

To experience a more traditional western form of entertainment, head out to the lodge at **T Lazy 7 Ranch,** 3129 Maroon Creek Rd. (☎ 970/925-7254), on Wednesday and Thursday evenings during ski season. You'll get a sleigh ride, cook-your-own-steak-or-chicken dinner, and dance to a live country band. Cost, excluding alcoholic beverages, is $50 per person.

On the club scene, the **Club Soda,** 416 Hyman Ave. (☎ 970/925-8154), is a popular dance club where you'll find hipper-than-thou 20-somethings. **The Tippler,** 535 E. Dean St. (☎ 970/925-4977), near the gondola base, draws après-skiers, with enough energy remaining to get down on the dance floor, as well as major-league night owls. Its counterpart in the Snowmass Village Mall is the **Timber Mill** (☎ 970/923-4774). Country music lovers appreciate **Shooters Saloon,** 220 S. Galena St. (☎ 970/925-4567), and **Cowboys,** at the Silvertree Hotel in Snowmass (☎ 970/923-5249). The **Double Diamond,** 450 S. Galena St. (☎ 970/920-6905) opens periodically for shows by regional and sometimes national acts.

In Aspen, it seems the fashion to do one's drinking at a historic bar. The Hotel Jerome's **J-Bar** (our favorite), Main and Mill streets (☎ 970/920-1000), and the **R-Bar** in the Renaissance, 304 E. Hopkins St. (☎ 970/925-2402), have universal appeal, each with a live band 2 or 3 evenings most weeks. **Bentley's at the Wheeler,** 328 E. Hyman Ave. (☎ 970/920-2240), is an elegant English-style pub, good for the older crowd. The **Red Onion,** 420 E. Cooper Ave. (☎ 970/925-9043), is Aspen's oldest bar, and a noisy, popular hangout after a rough day on the slopes.

Aspen's requisite **Hard Rock Café,** 210 S. Galena St. (☎ 970/920-1666), opened in 1991. **Mezzaluna,** 600 E. Cooper Ave. (☎ 970/925-5882) has a $5 pizza during happy hour and draws scores of après-skiers, as does the **Lobby Lounge** at the Ritz-Carlton, at the base of Aspen Mountain (☎ 970/920-3300), where you can watch skiers come off the mountain at the end of the day. **Flying Dog Brew Pub,** at 424 E. Cooper Ave. (☎ 970/925-7464) has a bluegrass band Sunday evenings.

12 The Western Slope

Separated from Colorado's major cities by the mighty Rocky Mountains, the communities along the state's western edge are not only miles, but years away from the hustle-and-bustle of Denver and the California-style sophistication of Boulder. Even with the one million people it serves, Grand Junction remains a sprawling western town, and the rugged canyons and stark rocky terrain make you feel that you've stepped into a John Ford western. The lifeblood of this semi-desert land is its rivers—the Colorado, Gunnison, and Yampa—and not only have they brought life-giving water, but over tens of thousands of years their ceaseless energy has gouged out stunning canyons that have lured visitors from around the world. Here you'll see Colorado National Monument, west of Grand Junction, remarkable for its land forms and prehistoric petroglyphs; Dinosaur National Monument, in the state's northwestern corner, which preserves a wealth of fossil remains; and the Black Canyon of the Gunnison, east of Montrose, a dark, narrow, and almost impenetrable chasm that challenges adventurous rock climbers and rafters.

You'll also discover the Old West preserved at Pioneer Town in Cedaredge, and the even older West on display at Ute Indian Museum in Montrose. But it's not all rocks and six-guns here. In the tiny community of Palisade, outside Grand Junction, some of the West's best wine is produced; and downtown Grand Junction boasts a continually changing and evolving outdoor art exhibit with its delightful Art on the Corner sculpture display.

1 Grand Junction, Colorado National Monument & Dinosaur National Monument

Among our favorite Colorado cities, Grand Junction is an excellent base camp for those who want to drive or hike through the awe-inspiring red-rock canyons and sandstone monoliths of Colorado National Monument, as well as for families with budding paleontologists who want to see fossilized dinosaur bones at Dinosaur National Monument, about 2 hours north. Grand Junction is also the eastern entrance to one of the most scenic and challenging mountain-biking tracks in the world, Kokopelli's Trail, which ends

The Western Slope

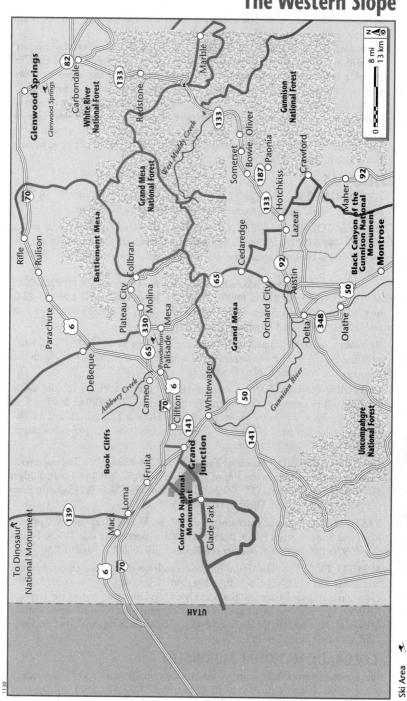

in Moab, Utah. And for the less athletically inclined, the Grand Junction area boasts half a dozen wineries that offer tours and tastings.

Located at the confluence of the Gunnison and Colorado rivers, the city was founded in 1882 where the spike was driven to connect Denver and Salt Lake City by rail. It quickly became the primary trade and distribution center between the two state capitals, and its mild climate, together with the fertile soil and irrigation potential of the river valleys, helped it grow into an important agricultural area. Soybeans, and later peaches and pears, were the most important crops. The city was also a center of the western Colorado uranium boom in the 1950s and the oil-shale boom in the late 1970s, and today is a fast-growing trade center serving practically all of western Colorado and eastern Utah.

ESSENTIALS

GETTING THERE　By Car　Grand Junction is located on I-70. U.S. 50 is the main artery from the south, connecting with Montrose and Durango.

By Plane　On the north side of Grand Junction, **Walker Field,** 2828 H Rd. (☎ **970/244-9100**), is less than a mile off I-70's Horizon Drive exit. Over 25 commercial flights connect Grand Junction with Denver, Phoenix, Salt Lake City, and other cities.

Airlines serving Walker Field include: **America West Express** (☎ 800/235-9292 or 970/728-4868), **Air 21** (☎ **800/FLY-AIR21**), **Mesa Airlines** (☎ **800/637-2247** or 970/243-3605), **SkyWest-The Delta Connection** (☎ **800/453-9417** or 970/ 242-5365), and **United Express** (☎ **800/241-6522**).

By Train　**Amtrak** has a passenger station at 337 S. First Street (☎ **800/USA-RAIL** or 970/241-2733). The *California Zephyr* stops daily on its main route from San Francisco and Salt Lake City to Denver and Chicago.

VISITOR INFORMATION　Contact the **Grand Junction Visitor & Convention Bureau,** 740 Horizon Dr., Grand Junction, CO 81506 (☎ **800/962-2547** or 970/ 244-1480). There's a Visitor Center on Horizon Drive at I-70 exit 31, and a Colorado Welcome Center at I-70 exit 19 (Fruita and Colorado National Monument), 12 miles west of Grand Junction.

GETTING AROUND　Sunshine Taxi (☎ **970/245-8294**) offers 24-hour service. Car rentals are available in the airport area from **Avis** (☎ 970/244-9170), **Budget** (☎ 970/244-9155), **Hertz** (☎ 970/243-0747), **National** (☎ 970/243-6626), **Sears** (☎ 970/244-9157), and **Thrifty** (☎ 970/243-7556).

FAST FACTS　In case of **emergency,** call **911. St. Mary's Hospital** is at Patterson Road and Seventh Street (☎ **970/244-2273**). The **post office** is at 241 N. Fourth St. (☎ **970/244-3400**). For **weather conditions,** call 970/242-2550 or 970/243-0914.

SPECIAL EVENTS　The Grand Junction area hosts the following annual events: Southwest Fest and Chile Cookoff, in late April; Cinco de Mayo, in early May; the Colorado Stampede Parade and Rodeo, in late June; Dinosaur Days, in late July; the Mesa County Fair, in early August; Junior College Baseball World Series, starting Memorial Day weekend; the Peach Festival, in Palisade in mid-August; and the Colorado Mountain Wine Fest in late September.

✪ COLORADO NATIONAL MONUMENT

Just minutes west of Grand Junction, this relatively undiscovered national monument is a delight, offering a colorful maze of steep-walled canyons filled with an array of naturally sculpted spires, pinnacles, arches, and other impressive sandstone rock formations. Easy to get to and easy to see, in many ways it's a miniature Grand Canyon, without the crowds. You can see much of the monument from your car on the 23-mile Rim Rock Drive, and there are also ample opportunities for hiking, horseback riding, and cross-country skiing. See "Sports & Outdoor Activities," below for details. Bighorn sheep, mountain lions, golden eagles, mule deer, and lizards are among the residents of the monument, which was established in 1911.

Carved by millions of years of erosion by water and wind, Colorado National Monument encompasses 32 square miles of red rock canyons and sandstone monoliths, some towering more than 1,000 feet above the Colorado River. A combination of upward lifts, erosion, and volcanic eruptions caused the chaos of formations here. Each layer visible in the striations of the canyon walls marks a time in the land's history. Fossils permit scientists to date these rocks back through the Mesozoic era of 225 million to 65 million years ago, and the Precambrian formation dates back 1.67 billion years.

The east entrance is only 5 miles west of Grand Junction, off Monument Road. But the best way to explore the monument is to begin at the west entrance, following the signs off I-70 from Fruita, 15 miles west of Grand Junction. It's here that **Rim Rock Drive,** created during the Great Depression as a Civilian Conservation Corps project, begins. Snaking up dramatic Fruita Canyon, it offers panoramic views across the Colorado River valley of fanciful and bizarre natural stone monuments to the cliffs and mesas beyond. At 4 miles it reaches the national monument headquarters and **Visitor Center.** Exhibits on geology and history, plus a slide show, introduce the park year-round, and rangers can help you plan your visit. Guided walks and campfire programs are offered during the summer.

Rim Rock Drive—open to bicycles as well as motor vehicles—offers access to hiking trails throughout the national monument, varying in length from 400 yards to 8^1/$_2$ miles. Many of the short, easy trails lead to spectacular canyon overlooks, while the longer backcountry trails head out across the mesas or down into the canyons. Strange formations such as Window Rock, the massive rounded Coke Ovens, the boulder-strewn Devils Kitchen, the barely touching Kissing Couple, and the free-standing Independence Monument—all of which can be viewed from the road—are easily reached by foot.

While the monument is worth visiting at any time of year, the best time is fall, when the air is crisp but not cold, the cottonwood trees turn a brilliant gold, and the summer crowds have departed. Like most vacation spots, summers—when kids are out of school—are the busiest. It's also often a bit hot. Winters are cold, although a frosting of white snow on the red rock is beautiful. Spring can be splendid—with warm, sunny days—or awful, with blustery winds, snow, and rain. Those visiting in May will want to carry insect repellent to combat the clouds of gnats that invade at this time.

The monument's Saddlehorn Campground, located in a piñon-juniper forest near the Visitor Center, has 80 sites, some shady, with rest rooms but no showers or R.V. hookups. At press time, the cost was $8 per night. Backcountry camping is free, and permitted throughout the monument, although campers must be at least 100 yards from trails and a quarter-mile from roads. Backcountry permits are not required. Also see "Camping," below.

Like most areas administered by the National Park Service, pets must be leashed and are not allowed on trails or in the backcountry, and removing anything—even rocks—is prohibited. Bicycles and all motor vehicles must stay on established roads, and are not permitted on trails.

At press time, admission was $4 per vehicle or $2 per person for cyclists, pedestrians, and bus passengers. The monument is open to visitors from Memorial Day to Labor Day, daily from 8am to 8pm; during the rest of the year, daily from 9am to 5pm. To obtain a brochure and other information, contact **Colorado National Monument,** Fruita, CO 81521-9530 (☎ **970/858-3617**). Those who want more in-depth information can order topographic maps, books, and other materials from the nonprofit Colorado National Monument Association at the monument's address and phone number above. Individual memberships in the association, which cost $10, entitle you to 15% discounts at this and many other national monument and national park bookstores.

DINOSAUR NATIONAL MONUMENT

This national monument, about 2 hours north of Grand Junction, is really two separate parks, divided by the Utah-Colorado border, that takes a close-up look at the world of dinosaurs on one side, and opens into a scenic wonderland of colorful rock, deep river canyons, and a forest of Douglas firs on the other.

About 145 million years ago this region was a suitable habitat for dinosaurs, including vegetarians such as diplodocus, brontosaurus, and stegosaurus, and sharp-toothed carnivores like allosaurus. Most of their skeletons decayed and disappeared, but in at least one spot floodwaters washed their carcasses onto a sandbar, where they were preserved in sand and covered with sediment.

This **Dinosaur Quarry,** accessible only from the Utah side of the park, is 7 miles north of Jensen, Utah, off U.S. 40 (Jensen is about 20 miles west of the town of Dinosaur, Co.). This is the only place in the monument to see dinosaur bones. The quarry contains the remains of many long-vanished species, including fossils of sea creatures two to three times older than any land dinosaurs, in one of the world's most concentrated and accessible deposits of the petrified remains of dinosaurs, crocodiles, turtles, and clams. The quarry—which looks like a long slab of frozen pudding with bones sticking out of it—is enclosed in the Visitor Center, along with exhibits that help make sense of this prehistoric zoo. There's one section of bones you can touch and models that show what paleontologists believe these dinosaurs looked like when they still had their skin. Sometimes visitors can see workers carefully chiseling away the hard rock to expose more bones, and park naturalists are on hand to explain the process.

But visitors who limit their Dinosaur National Monument trip to its namesake dinosaur quarry miss quite a bit. Encompassing 325 square miles of stark canyons at the confluence of the Yampa and Green rivers, there are hiking trails to explore, spectacular panoramic vistas, and the thrill of white-water rafting. From the Colorado side, your first stop will likely be the small Visitor Center located about 2 miles east of the town of Dinosaur, Colorado, at the intersection of U.S. 40 and Harpers Corner Drive. From here you can explore the Colorado section of the park before heading into Utah to see the dinosaur quarry. (You have to return to U.S. 40 to get to the Utah section of the park.)

To see some beautiful scenery from the comfort of your car, take the Harpers Corner Drive, allowing about 2 hours. This paved 62-mile round-trip drive has several overlooks offering panoramic views into the gorges carved by the Yampa and Green rivers, a look at the derby-shaped Plug Hat Butte, and close-ups of a variety of other colorful rock formations. The drive also offers access to the easy half-mile round-trip Plug Hat Nature trail, and the moderately difficult 2-mile round-trip Harpers Corner Trail, which is highly recommended for a magnificent view of the deep river canyons. In addition to several developed trails, experienced hikers with the appropriate maps can explore miles of unspoiled canyons and rock benches. Check with rangers on the numerous possibilities.

To many, the best way to see this rugged country is on the river, crashing through thrilling white water and gliding over the smooth, silent stretches. About a dozen outfitters are authorized to run the Yampa and Green rivers through the monument, offering trips ranging from 1 to 5 days, usually from mid-May through mid-September. Among companies providing river trips are **Hatch River Expeditions,** P.O. Box 1150, Vernal, UT 84078 (☎ **800/342-8243** or 801/789-4316), with prices starting at $60 to $70 for a 1-day trip. Reservations are recommended. A complete list of authorized river-running companies is available from monument headquarters.

Catfish are most often caught in the Green and Yampa rivers, although there are also some trout. Several endangered species of fish—including the Colorado squawfish and humpback chub—must be returned unharmed to the water if caught. You'll need either or both Utah and Colorado fishing licenses, depending on which side of the state line you're fishing.

The national monument entrance near Dinosaur, Colorado is about 110 miles north of Grand Junction. From Grand Junction, head west on I-70 about 12 miles to exit 15, turn right (north) onto Colo. 139 and go about 75 miles to Colo. 64, where you turn left, and follow it west, then north for 20 miles to the town of Dinosaur. Then turn right onto U.S. 40 and go east about 2 miles to the monument entrance. The monument is open around-the-clock, and the Visitor Centers are open daily year-round, except Thanksgiving, Christmas, and New Year's Day. Admission fee, charged only at the Utah entrance as of this writing, is $5 per vehicle, and $3 per person for those on foot, motorcycles, bicycles, or in buses.

Regulations here are similar to those at other national park service properties, which forbid damaging or taking anything, particularly fossils and other natural, historical, or archaeological items. Rangers warn that rivers are not safe for swimming or wading; water is cold, and the current is stronger than it may first appear. Backcountry camping requires free permits, available from park rangers. To get a copy of the national monument's color brochure and other information, contact **Dinosaur National Monument,** 4545 U.S. 40, Dinosaur, CO 81610 (☎ **970/ 374-3000**). In addition, the nonprofit **Dinosaur Nature Association,** 1291 E. U.S. 40, Vernal, UT 84078 (☎ **800/845-3466;** fax 801/781-1304), offers numerous publications, maps, posters, and videos on the park, its geology, wildlife, history, and especially its dinosaurs.

SPORTS & OUTDOOR ACTIVITIES

In addition to activities in Colorado and Dinosaur National Monuments, there are numerous opportunities for hiking, camping, mountain biking, off-roading, horseback riding, cross-country skiing, snowmobiling, and snowshoeing on other public lands administered by the federal government. Contact the **Bureau of Land Management,** 2815 H Rd., Grand Junction, CO 81506 (☎ **970/244-3000**) and the **Grand Junction Ranger District of Grand Mesa National Forest,** 764 Horizon Dr., Grand Junction, CO 81506 (☎ **970/242-8211**). You'll also find an excellent supply of outdoor recreation information at the Grand Junction Visitor & Convention Bureau (see "Visitor Information" above).

GOLF   The 18-hole **Tiara Rado Golf Course,** 2063 S. Broadway (☎ **970/245-8085**), is at the base of the Colorado National Monument canyons. The nine-hole **Lincoln Park Golf Course,** 12th Street and North Avenue (☎ **970/242-6394**), is in the center of town. Fees at both courses are $8.25 for nine holes and $14.50 for 18 holes Monday through Thursday, and $10 for nine holes and $17.50 for 18 holes Friday through Sunday.

HIKING   Hikers need look no further than Colorado National Monument for a wide choice of excellent day and overnight trips. A variety of descriptive brochures can be obtained at the monument's Visitor Center. If you're looking for an easy walk that leads to spectacular views of colorful rock formations, try the 1-mile (round-trip) Canyon Rim Trail, which follows the edge of a cliff to views of beautiful Wedding Canyon. Allow about an hour. An even shorter walk—the Window Rock Trail—also affords views of Wedding Canyon; and a free brochure available at the Visitor Center helps you identify the plants you'll see along the way. Allow a half hour for the quarter-mile loop.

Those who want to get down into the monument, rather than viewing it from above, will want to tackle one of the backcountry trails. The relatively difficult 12-mile round-trip Monument Canyon Trail drops 600 feet from the plateau into Monument Canyon, where you'll be surrounded by many of the monument's more dramatic rock formations, such as the aptly named Kissing Couple. This is home to rattlesnakes and scorpions, so you'll want to watch where you put your feet and hands. Also, it's hot and dry down there so be sure to carry plenty of water. If you'd like some panoramic views of the countryside, even to the canyon lands of Utah, try the Black Ridge Trail. The national monument's highest-elevation trail, it follows the rugged terrain of Black Ridge. Allow about 6 hours for the 11-mile round-trip hike, and again, carry plenty of water.

The Museum of Western Colorado manages four natural resource areas, each with self-guided trails and interpretive maps (available at museum shops). You can view ongoing excavations at Rabbit Valley, west of Grand Junction; and Little Park Desert Preserve is a 1,200-acre wilderness adjacent to the southern city limits—a great place for hiking and biking.

Hikers and walkers who want to stay closer to town can explore the trails in the Colorado Riverfront Project (see "Mountain Biking" below).

HORSEBACK RIDING   Trail rides near the west entrance of Colorado National Monument are available through **Rim Rock Adventures** (☎ 970/858-9555), with stables about a mile south of Fruita on Colo. 340. Rates for a 1-hour ride are $14 for adults and $12 for children, and a half-day ride into the wilderness of Devil's Canyon costs $36 for adults and $34 for children. Evening saddle horse and pack mule cookouts cost $30 per person or $50 per couple. Kids' pony rides, lasting about 15 minutes, cost $4. Those who thought to bring their own horses will enjoy the 14-mile (round-trip) Liberty Cap Trail through Colorado National Monument, which winds through a scrub forest and over a sagebrush mesa before dropping steeply into a valley.

MOUNTAIN BIKING   Grand Junction has become important to mountain bikers as the eastern terminus of Kokopelli's Trail to Moab, Utah. Winding for 142 miles through sandstone and shale canyons, it has an elevation differential of about 4,200 feet. There are primitive campsites at intervals along the trail. The Colorado gateway is at the Loma Boat Launch, 15 miles west of Grand Junction off I-70.

Another popular route is the Tabeguache Trail, running 142 miles from Shavano Valley, near Montrose, to No Thoroughfare Canyon, near the Colorado National Monument west of Grand Junction. For information on either trail, contact the **Colorado Plateau Mountain-Bike Trail Association,** P.O. Box 4602, Grand Junction, CO 81502 (☎ 970/241-9561). Send a self-addressed, stamped envelope for a free trail map.

Wine-Tasting and More Amid the Canyons

If you head east from Grand Junction, about 12 miles up the Grand Valley along U.S. 6 (or I-70 exit 42), you'll come to the farming community of **Palisade,** famous for its fruit orchards and vineyards. Most fruit is picked between late June and mid-September, when it's available at roadside fruit stands. For a fruit directory, harvest schedule, and map, contact the **Palisade Chamber of Commerce,** 309 S. Main (P.O. Box 729), Palisade, CO 81526 (☎ **970/464-7458**).

The half-dozen wineries in the area use the grapes and some of the fruits grown here. The state's oldest existing winery, **Colorado Cellars,** 3553 E Rd., Palisade (☎ **800/848-2812**), produces an excellent selection of award-winning wines, including a few chardonnays, a cabernet, rieslings, fruit wines, champagnes, and port. The winery grows its own grapes and produces some 15,000 cases of wine annually, plus more than 20 varieties of wine-based food products. Most Colorado Cellars' wines sell for $10 or less a bottle. Tours and tastings are given year-round, Monday through Saturday from noon to 4pm, and by appointment.

Carlson Vineyards, 461 35 Rd., Palisade (☎ **970/464-5554**), is a winery with a sense of humor, as well as a good product. Its wines, in the $7 to $8 range, have names such as Prairie Dog White and Tyrannosaurus Red, and are made with Colorado grapes. Visitors are welcome for free tours and tastings year-round, daily from 11am to 6pm.

Unique to Colorado is **Rocky Mountain Meadery,** 3701 G Rd., Palisade (☎ **970/464-0175**), which produces honey wine—also known as mead. Popular in medieval times, mead was known as "the drink of the gods," and is often served at Shakespearean festivals. It contains no grapes, but is made from orange blossom honey from citrus groves in Arizona, and ranges from very sweet to quite dry—appropriate as a table wine. Rocky Mountain Meadery also produces blends of honey wine and fruit, using fruit from local orchards. The tasting room, with large windows affording a view of the winery, is open daily from 10am to 5pm; and group tours are available by appointment.

Other local wineries include **Grande River Vineyards,** 787 Elberta Ave., Palisade (☎ **970/464-5867**) and **Plum Creek Cellars,** 3708 G Rd., Palisade (☎ **970/464-7586**). Call for hours and tour schedules.

There's also a bike route through and around Colorado National Monument (see above). Covering 33 miles, it follows Rim Rock Drive through the park and 10 additional miles on rural South Camp Road and South Broadway at the base of the canyons. Rim Rock Drive does not have a separate bike lane, nor shoulders, so be alert for motor traffic. The national monument publishes a free brochure.

The Colorado Riverfront Project includes several trails that meander along the Colorado River, offering the chance to see ducks, geese, blue heron, deer, and rabbits. Audubon Trail, $1^1/_2$ miles long, is accessed from Colo. 340 and Dike Road; Connected Lakes Trail, 1 mile long, is reached from the west end of Dike Road; Blue Heron Trail, 2 miles long, is accessible from Redlands Parkway; and Watson Island Trail, just under 1 mile, is entered at the intersection of South Seventh Street and Struthers Avenue. The Redlands Loop is an 8-mile trail that includes sections of the above trails. A free brochure with maps of the various river trails is available at the Grand Junction Visitor & Convention Bureau (see "Visitor Information" above).

RIVER RAFTING Colorado river-rafting trips through beautiful red sandstone canyons are provided by **Rim Rock Adventures,** Box 608, Fruita, CO 81521 (☎ 970/858-9555). Cost for a 1¹/₂-hour trip down the Colorado is $14 for adults and $12 for children; a full-day float trip costs about $35 per person, and multiday excursions from 2 to 7 days run $50 to $175 per person.

SKIING **Powderhorn,** Colo. 65, 7 miles west of Mesa (☎ 800/241-6997 or 970/ 268-5700; fax 970/248-2468), is located 35 miles east of Grand Junction on the north face of the Grand Mesa. A favorite of local powder skiers of all ability levels, it offers 400 acres of skiing, with an overnight lodge and condominiums, two restaurants, a lounge, shops, and full equipment rentals.

Colorado National Monument is also open to cross-country skiers. Among your best choice here is Liberty Cap Trail, which meanders across gently sloping Monument Mesa through a piñon-juniper forest and sagebrush flatlands. Total length of the trail is 14 miles (round-trip), but cross-country skiers may want to turn back before the last mile-and-a-half, which drops sharply into the Grand Valley.

SNOWMOBILING There's a trail connecting Powderhorn Resort to Ski Sunlight, running 120 miles from Grand Junction's local ski area to Glenwood Springs, the longest multiuse winter recreational trail in Colorado, traversing White River and Grand Mesa National forests. It is fully marked and continuously groomed. Other trails can be accessed from the parking areas along Colo. 65, between Mesa Lakes and Grand Mesa.

SWIMMING Centrally located **Lincoln Park,** at 12th Street and North Avenue (☎ 970/244-1548), has an outdoor heated swimming pool with a 351-foot water slide, open in summer, along with lighted tennis courts, playgrounds, picnic areas, and a nine-hole golf course. **The Orchard Mesa Community Center,** 2736 C Rd. (☎ 970/244-1485), has an indoor pool, open year-round, with a diving area and shallow-water section.

OTHER THINGS TO SEE & DO

Cross Orchards Historic Site, Dinosaur Valley, and the Museum of Western Colorado are all divisions of the Museum of Western Colorado, and combination passes to all three sites are available at substantial discounts.

Art on the Corner. Main St., from First to Seventh sts. ☎ 970/245-2926. Admission free. Daily 24 hours, with shops and restaurants open usual business hours.

This outdoor sculpture exhibit, with over 4 dozen works, helps make Grand Junction's Downtown Shopping Park one of the most attractive and successful in the country. Sculptures are loaned by the artists for 1 year, during which time they are for sale. The shopping park has art galleries, antique shops, restaurants, and a variety of retail stores, with wide, tree-lined pedestrian walkways.

Cross Orchards Historic Site. 3073 F Rd. ☎ 970/434-9814. Admission $4 adults, $3.50 seniors 60 and older and students with I.D., $2 children 3–12. May–Labor Day weekend, Tues–Thurs 10am–6pm, Fri 10am–8pm, Sat 10am–6pm, Sun 11am–5pm; reduced hours at other times.

Considered the finest remaining site from the early 20th-century Grand Valley agricultural boom era, Cross Orchards has re-created a lifestyle now usually found only in history books. On its 24.4 acres are a blacksmith shop, barn and packing shed, workers' bunkhouse, and former farm manager's residence, as well as an extensive collection of vintage farming and road-building equipment, a railway exhibit, a farm activity area, and a gift shop. Costumed guides lead personalized tours, explaining what life was really like "down on the farm," and living-history demonstrations are offered daily in summer. The original Cross Orchards Farm (1896–1923) covered 243 acres and contained 22,000 apple trees.

Devil's Canyon Science & Learning Center. 550 Crossroads Court, Fruita (just S. of I-70 exit 19). ☎ **800/DIG-DINO** or 970/858-7282. Admission $5 adults, $3.50 children 3–12 and seniors 55 and over, free for children under 3. Memorial Day–Labor Day, daily 8:30am–7pm; the rest of the year, Mon–Sat 9am–5pm, Sun 10am–5pm.

Enter a virtual time machine to journey back to the Jurassic period, where you'll encounter a mother stegosaurus defending her young from the fearsome allosaurus, and visit the last ice age alongside the mighty mammoth. Cleverly designed and constructed full-size models move, bellow, and occasionally spit. Hands-on, interactive exhibits allow kids of all ages to learn about and experience the forces that created the lands around us: feel the earth shake on an earthquake simulator; make a sandstorm; or touch the icy face of a glacier.

Dinosaur Valley. 362 Main St. ☎ **970/241-9210.** Admission $4 adults, $2 children 3–12, and $3.50 for students with I.D. and seniors 60 and older. May–Oct, Mon–Sat 9am–6pm, Sun 11am–5pm; the rest of the year, Tues–Sat 10am–5pm, Sun 11am–4pm.

Animated replicas of such dinosaurs as stegosaurus, triceratops, and apatosaurus bring the distant past alive at Dinosaur Valley, where visitors can try out the specialized tools paleontologists use to remove rock from bones, and stare through magnifying glasses to examine the intricate fossils of dinosaurs, fish, and even cockroaches. A simulated quarry lets children dig up actual dinosaur bones themselves, and there's a computer touch-screen display for those who want to learn more about dinosaurs. Exhibits also include a rare piece of fossilized dinosaur skin, and 1 day a week (usually Thursdays), a dinosaur dig workshop is offered (about $70 including lunch), in which participants join paleontologists at work in a quarry and the lab.

Doo Zoo Children's Museum. 635 Main St. ☎ **970/241-5225.** Admission $1 adults, $3 children, under age 2 free. Tues–Fri 10am–4pm, Sat 10am–5:30pm.

Children 1 to 12 get hands-on experience in a variety of activities, from playacting a grownup profession to performing scientific experiments and testing their creative artistic horizons. A toy store specializes in educational items. The Family Theater Company presents interactive, musical plays for and with children, plus "Diner Theatre" in a local diner. Theater tickets start at $5.

Museum of Western Colorado. 248 S. Fourth St., at Ute St. ☎ **970/242-0971.** Admission $2 adults, $1.50 students with I.D. and seniors 60 and up, $1 children 3–12. May–Oct, Mon–Sat 9am–6pm, Sun 11am–5pm; the rest of the year, Tues–Sat 10am–5pm, Sun 11am–4pm.

The history and culture of western Colorado are highlights of this worthwhile museum. Of special interest is the Western Colorado Timeline, with photos and exhibits from every decade since the 1880s, and an extensive collection of prehistoric Southwest pottery. The museum also has an extensive firearms collection, a pioneer section that includes an exhibit on one-room schools, natural history, and Old West–style paintings.

Rim Rock Adventures. On Colo. 340 about a half mile S. of I-70 exit 19, Fruita. ☎ **970/858-9555.** Admission to museum and Indian Village is free; admission to deer park $3.50 adults, $2.50 children 3–13, free for children under 3. May–Labor Day, daily 8am–5pm.

Exotic deer from around the world are the highlight of this park/zoo, where you can also see goats, sheep, and Roscoe the elk, who loves to be hand-fed by visiting children. There are Wild West rodeos on Tuesday evenings in July and August.

Western Colorado Center for the Arts. 1803 N. Seventh St. ☎ **970/243-7337.** Admission $2 adults, free for children under 12. Tues–Sat 9am–4pm.

This museum has hundreds of works of art, many with western themes, as well as traveling exhibits. The collection includes lithographs by Paul Pletka and more than 50 Navajo weavings dating from the turn of the century. There's also a gift shop featuring unique hand-crafted items, and community theater performances (call for schedule).

WHERE TO STAY

Major chains offering reasonably priced lodging in Grand Junction include **Holiday Inn,** 755 Horizon Dr. (☎ **800/HOLIDAY** or 970/243-6790), with 292 rooms and suites, and rates of $70 to $77 double, and $77 to $130 suite; and **Ramada Inn,** 2790 Crossroads Blvd. at Horizon Drive (☎ **800/2-RAMADA** or 970/241-8411), with 156 rooms and suites, charging $79 double and $85 and up for suites.

MODERATE

Grand Junction Hilton. 743 Horizon Dr., Grand Junction, CO 81506. ☎ **800/HILTONS** or 970/241-8888. Fax 970/242-7266. 248 rms, 16 suites. A/C TV TEL. $79–$129 double; $129–$225 suite. Children under 12 stay free in parents' room. AE, CB, DC, DISC, MC, V.

A modern eight-story hotel just off I-70 exit 31, the Hilton offers spacious guest rooms with southwestern decor, one king or two double beds, full-length curtains to separate the entry and bathroom from the sleeping area, and contemporary furnishings like clear-glass lamps and mirrored closet-doors. Rooms with refrigerators and coffeemakers are available. There are two restaurants and two lounges, one with entertainment. The Hilton also offers room service, valet laundry, an outdoor heated pool, a whirlpool, three lighted tennis courts, fitness center, volleyball court, horseshoe pits, a children's playground, game room, and meeting space for 600.

The Orchard House. 3573 E. ¹/₂ Rd., Palisade, CO 81526. ☎ **970/464-0529.** Fax 970/464-0681. 1 suite. A/C TV TEL. $79 double; $30 each additional person. Rate includes full breakfast. MC, V.

Situated in the midst of the scenic Grand Valley orchard and wine country, this pleasant country homestead is more than just a bed-and-breakfast. Hosts Bill and Stephanie Schmid have created a true home environment. The single suite, which can sleep from four to six, has a living room with sofa-sleeper that connects to an upstairs master bedroom (complete with king-size brass bed) and a second downstairs bedroom (with twin beds). Guests have two private entrances and their own kitchen, available for limited use, and can use the washer and dryer. Gourmet home-cooked candlelight dinners, complete with wine, are a nightly option at $60 per couple.

Stonehaven Bed & Breakfast. 798 N. Mesa St., Fruita, CO 81521. ☎ **800/303-0898** or 970/858-0898. 5 rms (4 with bath). A/C TEL. $55–$115 double, including full breakfast. AE, DISC, MC, V.

This elegant Victorian home, built in 1906, offers a relaxed country atmosphere within a few miles of both Grand Junction and Colorado National Monument. The inn is decorated with antiques and reproductions; mostly Victorian, but some earlier. The master suite, especially popular with honeymooners and those celebrating anniversaries, contains an 1840s brass bed, gas fireplace, two-person Jacuzzi tub plus separate shower, and large windows that provide spectacular views of Colorado National Monument. It also has a pew from a local church. Homemade breakfasts vary, but might include such items as baked potatoes stuffed with eggs or strawberry whole wheat crêpes. Dinners of smoked salmon or Alaskan salmon are available upon prior arrangement. Smoking and pets are not permitted.

INEXPENSIVE

Best Value Inn. 718 Horizon Dr., Grand Junction, CO 81506. ☎ **800/990-1143** or 970/243-5080. Fax 970/242-0600. 141 rms. A/C TV TEL. $34–$50 double. Children 12 and under stay free in parents' room. AE, CB, DC, DISC, MC, V. Free parking.

This Southwest-style motel, extensively remodeled in mid-1993, has spacious, quiet, comfortable rooms surrounding a courtyard with trees and a large grassy area. Most rooms have two sinks and queen beds, with some kings. All have individual thermostats, direct-dial phones with free local calls, and cable TV. There's a heated pool and kiddie pool, open in summer; a large lobby with spiral staircase and 24-hour free coffee and tea; and a laundromat. Pets are accepted.

Historic Hotel Melrose/International Hostel. 337 Colorado Ave., Grand Junction, CO 81501. ☎ **800/430-4555** or 970/242-9636. Fax 970/242-5613. 26 rms (12 with bath). $10 dorm bed; $18–$23 double with shared bath; $25–$35 double with private bath. DC, DISC, MC, V.

This centrally located historic brick building—dating from 1908—has been lovingly restored and now provides bargain-priced lodging to those seeking nostalgia and charm. Dorm rooms hold four to six, and private rooms vary considerably, but all are neat, clean, and comfortable. Hostel members have use of the kitchen, dining, and common rooms. Free pickup from the Grand Junction airport is available. Pets are not permitted.

CAMPING

In addition to campgrounds at Colorado National Monument (see above), there are several commercial campgrounds with complete R.V. hookups, hot showers, and all the usual niceties. We like **Junction West R.V. Park,** 793 22 Rd., Grand Junction (☎ **970/245-8531**), which not only has about the cleanest bathhouses we've seen anywhere, but is also quiet and conveniently located. There are 61 large, somewhat-shaded sites, a store, coin-operated laundry, and game room. Rates are in the $15 to $19 range. To get to Junction West, take U.S. 6 and 50 to 22 Road (or I-70 exit 26), and go north for half a mile.

WHERE TO DINE

MODERATE

G. B. Gladstone's. 2531 N. 12th St., at Patterson Rd. ☎ **970/241-6000.** Reservations recommended. Main courses $4.50–$8 at lunch, $7–$18 at dinner. AE, DC, DISC, MC, V. Daily 11am–10pm. STEAK/SEAFOOD.

Nostalgia dominates the mood of this popular restaurant. The Croquet Room, for instance, is decorated with early 20th-century sports regalia; and the Library would delight an old-book collector. The sunken central bar is most nostalgic and most packed on Friday nights, when blues records blast. Local business people enjoy the lunches: hot and cold sandwiches, flame-broiled burgers, soups, salads, quiche, and fish-and-chips. Dinners include exotic pastas, mesquite-smoked chicken, fresh-fish, prime rib (a house specialty), and Australian lobster tail.

INEXPENSIVE

Crystal Cafe and Bake Shop. 314 Main St. ☎ **970/242-8843.** Breakfast $2–$5.50; lunch $4.25–$9.50. No credit cards. Mon–Fri 7am–1:30pm; Sat 8:30am–1:30pm. AMERICAN.

You may have to wait for a table at this popular breakfast and lunch spot, but it's worth it. The simple, modern decor includes hardwood tables and bentwood cafe-style chairs, with woven place mats and napkins. Selections are mostly innovative variations on standard American dishes, highlighted by the cafe's own fresh-baked breads, rolls, pastries, and desserts. For breakfast there are a variety of pancakes, and egg dishes that include a Greek omelet—a two-egg omelet with fresh tomatoes, black olives, red onions, oregano, and feta cheese. Lunches include plenty of salads, hot and cold sandwiches, and a quiche of the day. Sandwiches, of course, are prepared on the bakery's own bread and rolls, and often include uniquely seasoned mayonnaise. We particularly enjoyed the smoked turkey with red onion and basil mayonnaise. Wine and beer are available.

Pantuso's Ristorante. 2782 Crossroads Blvd. ☎ **970/243-0000.** Main courses $3.50–$5.50 at lunch, $4.75–$9.75 at dinner; whole pizzas $6.75–$14.75. AE, DC, MC, V. Mon–Fri 11:30am–1:45pm; Mon–Thurs 5:30–9:30pm, Fri–Sat 5:30–10pm. ITALIAN.

Pantuso's has casual garden-style decor and an imaginative menu. There's pizza, pasta, and sandwiches for lunch; homemade ravioli and lasagna for dinner. House specialties include flounder primavera, stuffed manicotti, and cannolis. There's a full bar, draft beer, and Italian wine.

7th Street Café. 832 S. Seventh St. ☎ **970/242-7225.** Breakfast $1.75–$5.50; lunch $2.75–$5.75. DISC, MC, V. Daily 7am–3pm. AMERICAN.

The fifties are back at 7th Street Café, with an old-fashioned soda fountain (there's plenty of seating at tables also), photos of Marilyn and Elvis, and 45-r.p.m. records. Breakfasts include bacon and eggs, pancakes, and for the more adventurous, several spicy combinations. For lunch, there are numerous sandwiches and salads, good burgers, and hot-plate specials including Italian-style meat loaf, and hot turkey. Leave room for a banana split or a hot-fudge sundae.

2 Glenwood Springs

Scenic beauty and hot mineral water are the lures here. Members of the Ute tribe visited the Yampah mineral springs on the banks of the Colorado River for centuries. Calling it "big medicine," they came from miles around to heal their wounds or use nearby vapor caves as a natural sauna. But it wasn't until the 1880s that the springs were commercially developed. The three Devereux brothers, who had made a small fortune in silver at Aspen, built what was at the time the largest hot-springs pool in the world, then added a red sandstone bathhouse and built the Hotel Colorado. Soon everyone from European royalty to movie stars to President Theodore Roosevelt made their way to Glenwood Springs.

The springs supported the town until the Great Depression and World War II caused a business decline. But after the war, with the growth of the ski industry at nearby Aspen, Glenwood Springs began to reemerge as a resort town, but on a smaller scale. Today, this city of 6,000 is a popular recreational center. The hot springs complex underwent a total renovation in the 1970s, and additional improvements were made in 1993, as it celebrated its centennial.

Also completed that year was a 12-year $490-million project to build a four-lane interstate through the 18-mile Glenwood Canyon. One of the most expensive roadways ever built—as well as one of the most beautiful interstate highway drives in America—the road offers a number of trailheads and raft-launching areas as well as view points from which travelers can safely gaze at the Colorado River and its spectacular canyon.

ESSENTIALS

GETTING THERE   By Car   I-70 follows the Colorado River through Glenwood Springs. Colo. 82 (the Aspen Hwy.) links the city with Aspen, 42 miles southeast.

By Bus   Roaring Fork Transit Agency (RFTA) has daily service to and from Aspen (☎ 970/920-1905).

By Shuttle Van   There's daily commuter service to and from Aspen, and east on I-70 as far as Rifle, on 10-passenger vans with **Aspen Limousine,** 330 Seventh St. (☎ 800/222-2112 or 970/945-9400). A one-way ticket to Glenwood Springs costs $20 per person, and there are only two departures daily from Aspen: 8am and noon.

By Train   There's **Amtrak** (☎ 800/USA-RAIL) service to Glenwood Springs daily aboard the *California Zephyr,* direct from Denver and Salt Lake City. The depot is in the heart of the city at 7th Street and Cooper Avenue.

ORIENTATION   The northward-flowing Roaring Fork River joins the Colorado River at a T junction in the heart of Glenwood Springs, and streets follow the valleys carved by the two streams. Downtown Glenwood is south of the Colorado and east of the Roaring Fork, with north-south Grand Avenue (Colo. 82) its main thoroughfare. Old Glenwood, including the hot springs and Hotel Colorado, is on the north side of I-70 and the Colorado.

VISITOR INFORMATION   The Glenwood Springs Chamber Resort Association, 1102 Grand Ave., Glenwood Springs, CO 81601 (☎ 970/945-6589; fax 970/945-1531), maintains a Visitor Center on the south side of downtown, on the southeast corner of 11th and Grand. Brochures are available 24 hours a day.

GETTING AROUND   A **shuttle service** operates daily from Memorial Day through Labor Day, providing rides to and from hotels, motels, restaurants, shopping areas, and the Hot Springs Pool. Schedules and passes (about $1 per person) are available at the Chamber Resort Association office (see above).

FAST FACTS   In case of **emergency,** call **911. Valley View Hospital,** providing 24-hour emergency care, is at 1906 Blake Ave. (☎ 970/945-6535), a block east of Colo. 82 at 19th Street. The **post office** (☎ 970/945-5611) is at 113 Ninth Street.

SPECIAL EVENTS   Annual events in the Glenwood Springs area include the Ski Spree Winter Carnival, from late January to early February; Summer of Jazz, June through August; the Strawberry Days Festival, in the second full week of June; and the Fall Art Festival, in late September.

SPORTS & OUTDOOR ACTIVITIES

A busy local shop where you can get information on the best spots for hiking, mountain climbing, rock climbing, kayaking, camping, and cross-country skiing is **Summit Canyon Mountaineering,** 732 Grand Ave., Glenwood Springs (☎ 800/360-6994 or 970/945-6994). In addition to selling a wide variety of outdoor-sports equipment, it rents cross-country ski gear, tents, sleeping bags, and back packs.

BICYCLING   A paved bike trail runs from the Yampah Vapor Caves into Glenwood Canyon, and trails and four-wheel–drive roads in the adjacent White River National Forest are ideal for mountain bikers (see "Hiking," below). You'll find bike rentals ($5 per hour or $15 per day), plus repairs and accessories at **BSR Sports,** 210 Seventh St. (☎ 970/945-7317).

FISHING   Get licenses, equipment, and advice from **Roaring Fork Anglers,** 2022 Grand Ave. (☎ 970/945-0180), which also has been offering guided fly-fishing trips for some 25 years. Rates for one or two people on a full-day float trip are $275, including lunch and beverages; a full-day wading trip is $200 for one and $225 for two. Half-day trips are also available, and Roaring Fork also has 4 miles of private waters, with a charge of $40 per rod for a full day.

Taking the Waters: Visiting the Hot Springs of the Western Slope

There may be no better or more luxurious way to rejuvenate the dusty, tired traveler than a soak in a natural hot spring. In Glenwood Springs, there are two places to experience this ancient therapy.

Glenwood Hot Springs Pool

Named Yampah Springs—meaning "Big Medicine"—by the Utes, this pool, located at 401 N. River Rd., was created in 1888 when enterprising developers diverted the course of the Colorado River and built a stone bathhouse. The springs flow at a rate of 3.5 million gallons per day, and with a temperature of 122°F, it's one of the world's hottest springs. Its content is predominantly sodium chloride, but there are significant quantities of lime, potassium, and magnesium, and traces of other therapeutic minerals.

The two open-air pools together are nearly two city blocks in length. The larger pool, 405 feet long and 100 feet wide, holds more than a million gallons of water, and is maintained at 90°F. The smaller pool, 100 feet square, is kept at 104°F. There's also a children's pool with a water slide, plus a restaurant, sport shop, and miniature golf course.

The red-sandstone administration building overlooking the pools was the Hot Springs Lodge from 1890 until 1986, when a new hotel (see "Where to Stay" below) and bathhouse complex were built. An athletic club was also opened at that time.

Admission is $6.50 for adults, $4.25 for children 3 to 12; children 2 and under are admitted free. Reduced night rates are also available. The water slide costs $2.50 for four rides or $3.50 for eight rides. Suit and towel rentals and coin-operated lockers are available. Call 970/945-7428 for the athletic club non-member use charge. The facility is open during the summer months, daily from 7:30am to 10pm; during winter, daily from 9am to 10pm.

Yampah Spa and Vapor Caves

The hot Yampah Spring water flows through the floor of nearby caves, creating natural underground steam baths. Utes once used the chambers to take advantage of their curative powers. Today the cave, located at 709 E. Sixth St., has an adjacent spa where such treatments as massages, facials, herbal wraps, and body muds are offered. There's also a full-service beauty salon on the premises.

Admission to the caves is $7.75; spa treatments start at $32. They are open daily from 9am to 9pm. To reserve a treatment or obtain further information, call 970/945-0667.

GOLF   Glenwood Springs has two nine-hole courses: **Glenwood Springs Golf Club,** 193 Sunny Acres Rd. (☎ **970/945-7086**), and **Westbank Ranch Golf Club,** 1007 Westbank Rd. (☎ **970/945-7032**), with golfing from March through November. Fees are about $16 for nine holes at both courses; for 18 holes it's $24 at Glenwood Springs and $20 at Westbank. Some 27 miles west, near Rifle, is the championship 18-hole **Battlement Mesa Golf Course,** at I-70 exit 75 (☎ **800/275-5687** or 970/285-PAR-4), which charges $16 for nine holes and $28 for 18 holes of play ($14 and $24 respectively for those 55 and older).

HIKING   There are plenty of hiking opportunities in the area. Stop at the White River National Forest office, Ninth Street and Grand Avenue (☎ 970/945-2521), for a free copy of the "Hiking and Biking Trails" map plus free Recreational Opportunity Guide (ROG) sheets for most of the local trails. The forest service office also sells detailed forest maps and has other information.

Hikers will also find numerous trails in Glenwood Canyon, with some of the best scenery in the area. Hanging Lake Trail, 9 miles east of Glenwood Springs off I-70, is especially popular. The trailhead is accessible from eastbound I-70; westbound travelers must make a U-turn and backtrack a few miles to reach the parking area. The trail climbs 1,000 feet in 1 mile—allow several hours for the round-trip—and just beyond Hanging Lake is Spouting Rock, with an underground spring shooting out of a hole in the limestone cliff. The Grizzly Creek Trailhead is in the Grizzly Creek Rest Area, in Glenwood Canyon, where there is also a launching area for rafts and kayaks. The trail climbs along the creek, past wildflowers and dogwood trees.

One convenient walk is the Doc Holliday Trail, which climbs about half a mile from 13th Street and Bennett Street to an old cemetery that contains the grave of notorious gunslinger Doc Holliday (see "Places to Explore Glenwood Springs's Frontier Past," below). There's a panoramic view across the town from here.

HORSEBACK RIDING   Sometimes the best way to see this rugged country is the Old West way—on horseback. **A. J. Brink Outfitters,** at Sweetwater Lake Resort, 3406 Sweetwater Rd., Gypsum (☎ **970/524-9301**), about 35 miles northeast of Glenwood Springs, offers 1-hour rides for about $20; half-day rides for $50; and full-day trips starting at $75. Overnight pack trips, horseback fishing trips, and photography tours are also available. Sweetwater Lake Resort also has fully equipped cabins ($85–$130), several motel units ($50); camping ($9); boat rentals ($25 per day); and a restaurant that serves three meals daily.

RIVER RAFTING   Travel down the Colorado River through spectacular Glenwood Canyon in rafts or inflatable kayaks with **Rock Gardens,** 1308 County Rd. 129 (☎ **970/945-6737**), **Blue Sky Adventures,** 319 Sixth St. (☎ **970/945-6605**), or **Whitewater Rafting,** I-70 exit 114, West Glenwood Springs (☎ **970/945-8477**). Half-day trips cost about $32; full-day trips, which usually include lunch, cost about $55.

SKIING   **Ski Sunlight,** 10901 County Rd. 117 (☎ **800/445-7931** or 970/945-7491), is located 10 miles south of Glenwood Springs in the White River National Forest. Geared toward families, Sunlight is served by one triple and two double chair lifts and a ski-school surface lift. There is also a special area for snowboarders. For equipment rentals and repairs, see the **Ski Sunlight Ski Shop,** 1315 Grand Ave. (☎ **970/945-9425**).

Ski Sunlight's Cross-Country and Nordic Center has 29 kilometers (18 miles) of groomed and set track, available free, with rentals and lessons available. Information and equipment are also available at **Summit Canyon Mountaineering,** 732 Grand Ave., Glenwood Springs (☎ **800/360-6994** or 970/945-6994).

SNOWMOBILING   The Sunlight to Powderhorn Trail, running 120 miles from Glenwood's local ski area to Grand Junction's, on the Grand Mesa, is the longest multiuse winter recreational trail in Colorado, traversing White River and Grand Mesa National Forests. It is fully marked and continuously groomed. Other trails can be accessed from the end of County Road 11, 2 miles beyond Ski Sunlight and 12 miles south of Glenwood Springs. For information and rentals, contact **Rocky Mountain Sports,** 2177 300th Rd. (☎ **970/945-8885**).

PLACES TO EXPLORE GLENWOOD SPRINGS'S FRONTIER PAST

Doc Holliday's Grave. Linwood Cemetery.

After the famous shoot-out at the OK Corral, Doc Holliday began a final search for relief from his advanced tuberculosis. But even the mineral-rich waters of Glenwood Springs could not dissipate the ravages of hard drinking and disease, and Doc died in 1887 in bed at the Glenwood Hotel.

From the chamber office on Grand Avenue, walk or drive uphill on 11th to Bennett and turn right. On the left side of Bennett, you will shortly see the sign marking the trail to the cemetery. The trail is a half-mile hike, but you'll have a grand view of the city when you arrive. To find Doc's grave, just head for the flagpole.

Frontier Historical Museum. 1001 Colorado Ave. ☎ **970/945-4448.** Admission $3 adults, $2 seniors over 60, children under 12 free. May–Sept, Mon–Sat 11am–4pm; Oct–Apr, Mon, Thurs–Sat 1–4pm.

The highlight of this museum, which occupies a late Victorian home, is the original bedroom furniture of Colorado legends Horace and Baby Doe Tabor, brought here from Leadville. The collection also includes other pioneer home furnishings, antique dolls and toys, historic photos and maps, Native American artifacts, and minerals.

WHERE TO STAY

A **central reservation service** can help you book lodgings and obtain information on the area (☎ 800/221-0098). Among the chain lodgings in Glenwood Springs, your best bet is **Ramada Inn,** 124 W. Sixth St. (☎ 800/332-1472 or 970/945-2500), with 123 rooms and suites, and rates of $85 to $87 double, and $125 to $155 suites.

MODERATE

Hotel Colorado. 526 Pine St., Glenwood Springs, CO 81601. ☎ **800/544-3998** or 970/945-6511. Fax 970/945-7030. 101 rms, 25 suites. TV TEL. $70–$98 double; $110–$295 suite. Children under 18 stay free in parents' room. AE, CB, DC, DISC, MC, V.

The stately Hotel Colorado, constructed of sandstone and Roman brick in 1893, was modeled after Italy's Villa de Medici, and is a registered National Historic Landmark. Two American presidents—William Howard Taft and Theodore Roosevelt—spoke to crowds gathered beneath the orators' balcony in a lovely landscaped fountain piazza. In fact, this is reportedly the birthplace of the Teddy bear: One story has it that when a disappointed Roosevelt returned to the hotel in May 1905 after an unsuccessful bear hunt, hotel maids made him a small bear from scraps of cloth, causing a reporter to coin the phrase.

Guest rooms are individually decorated, most with double beds and the usual hotel furnishings; suites are more spacious, with upgraded decor and period antiques. Fifth-floor penthouse suites also have wet bars and refrigerators, as well as outstanding views. Two bell-tower suites, reached by stairs only, have double Jacuzzis and private dining balconies. They also have private staircases into the ancient bell towers, where 19th-century graffiti can still be deciphered.

Hotel restaurants serve three meals daily. There's a full bar and a large outdoor dining and cocktail area, with gardens and a fountain for summer use. Services and facilities include valet laundry; 24-hour concierge; a European-style health spa with sauna, Jacuzzi, massage, Nautilus and free weights; chiropractor; gift shop; and meeting space for 200.

Hot Springs Lodge & Pool. 415 Sixth St., Glenwood Springs, CO 81601. ☎ **800/537-SWIM** in Colorado, or 970/945-6571. Fax 970/945-6683. 107 rms. A/C TV TEL. $70–$95 double. AE, CB, DC, DISC, MC, V.

Heated by the springs that bubble through the hillside beneath it, this handsome modern motel overlooks the Glenwood Hot Springs Pool complex. Three quarters of the rooms have private balconies or patios. Rooms are spacious, with one king or two queen beds, cherry or light-wood furnishings, coffeemakers, and safes; some have hide-a-beds, refrigerators, and double vanities. The poolside restaurant serves coffee shop–style meals, and there's a small lounge. The hotel also offers guests discounts for the hot springs pools and athletic club (see "Taking the Waters: Visiting the Hot Springs of the Western Slope," above), plus a whirlpool, video arcade, guest laundry, and meeting space for 45.

INEXPENSIVE

Adducci's Inn Bed & Breakfast. 1023 Grand Ave., Glenwood Springs, CO 81601. ☎ **970/ 945-9341.** 5 rms. $48–$65 double. Rates include breakfast. MC, V.

A lovely turn-of-the-century Victorian home on Glenwood's main street houses this inn. Furnished with period antiques, it offers games in the parlor and complimentary transportation from train and bus depots. A restaurant serves lunch and dinner, and cross-country and downhill skiing is within 10 miles.

Glenwood Springs Hostel. 1021 Grand Ave., Glenwood Springs, CO 81601. ☎ **800/ 9-HOSTEL** or 970/945-8545. Fax 970/945-0984. 42 beds including dorm and 6 private rooms. $9.50 per night, $55 per week in dorm; $18 single, $24 double in private rooms. AE, MC, V.

Active travelers will find the bargain sports packages this hotel offers a real plus. Activities featured include downhill and cross-country skiing, rafting, kayaking, mountain biking, and spelunking. There's a large record library, free coffee or tea in the mornings, and two fully equipped kitchens for guests' use. Like most hostels, there are dormitory bunks, common toilets and showers, guest laundry, and other common areas. Linen is provided, and it's just a 5-minute walk from the train and bus. The individual rooms are great for couples and others who prefer more privacy.

CAMPING

Rock Gardens Camper Park. 1308 County Rd. 129 (I-70 exit 119), Glenwood Springs, CO 81601. ☎ **970/945-6737.** Fax 970/945-2413. 75 sites. $19 tent sites; $23 R.V. sites, with electric-and-water hookups. MC, V. Closed Nov–mid-Apr.

On the banks of the Colorado River in beautiful Glenwood Canyon, this campground is a great home base for those exploring this scenic wonderland. The Glenwood Canyon Bike Trail passes the campground on its way into Glenwood Springs, and hiking trails into the White River National Forest are nearby. Bathhouses are clean, showers are hot, and there's a dump station, although no sewer hookups. A store sells groceries, firewood, and ice, and can arrange bike rentals.

WHERE TO DINE

✪ **The Bayou.** 52103 U.S. 6, West Glenwood Springs. ☎ **970/945-1047.** Reservations suggested for large parties. Main courses $5.95–$15. AE, MC, V. Daily 4–10pm. CAJUN/CREOLE.

Western Colorado's classic New Orleans–style eatery can't be mistaken: Frog eyes bulge from the green awning over its deck, which looks toward I-70 near exit 114. Harlequin masks hang on the walls and zydeco music filters through this rustic and often entertaining restaurant. Come for down-home Cajun cuisine—including sautéed frogs' legs, deep-fried catfish, shrimp lagniappe, chicken étouffée, or swamp and moo (redfish and rib eye)—and stay for the staff-provided entertainment, including "dumb server tricks," birthday specials (ask if you dare), and the Frog Leg Revue. They have the largest selection of hot sauces in the valley, and on summer Sunday afternoons there's live music on the deck.

Delice. 1512 Grand Ave. ☎ **970/945-9424.** Reservations not accepted. $2.45–$5.95. No credit cards. Mon–Fri 10am–3pm. SANDWICH/PASTRY SHOP.

This family-run establishment serves excellent sandwiches, homemade soups, gourmet salads, Swiss sausage platters, and a variety of fresh-baked pastries in a friendly atmosphere in Glenwood's Executive Plaza.

✪ **Italian Underground.** 715 Grand Ave. ☎ **970/945-6422.** Reservations not accepted. Main courses $7.50–$9.50; pizzas $7.95–$13.95. AE, DISC, MC, V. Daily 5–10pm. ITALIAN.

Get here early and expect to wait. A favorite of locals, the Italian Underground offers good Italian food at excellent prices. Located in a basement below an antique shop, the restaurant has stone walls, brick floors, red-and-white checked tablecloths, candlelight, and exceedingly generous portions of fine food. Try the lasagna, linguine with pesto sauce, spaghetti with tomato and basil sauce or with *puttanesca* sauce. All entrees come with salad, bread, and ice cream. There's an excellent selection of Italian wines by the glass, as well as a full bar, and espresso and cappuccino are also served. The restaurant does not permit smoking.

19th Street Diner. 1908 Grand Ave. ☎ **970/945-9133.** Reservations not accepted. $2.50–$12.95. DISC, MC, V. Mon–Sat 7am–10pm, Sun 7:30am–3pm. AMERICAN.

This local hangout has stools at a counter facing the kitchen, a black-and-white tile floor, and all the usual diner selections. Breakfasts, served all day, include lots of omelets, French toast, and a breakfast banana split—banana, yogurt, blueberries, and granola. The lunch-and-dinner menu has hamburgers, sandwiches and salads, fajitas, southern-fried chicken, and blue-plate specials including an open-faced hot roast beef. There's also a children's menu, soda fountain, and full-service bar.

Restaurant Sopris. 7215 Colo. 82, 7 miles south of Glenwood Springs. ☎ **970/945-7771.** Reservations recommended. Main courses $8–$34. AE, DISC, MC, V. Daily 5–10pm. CONTINENTAL.

Luzern, Switzerland, native Kurt Wigger spent 17 years as chef at Aspen's Red Onion before opening the Sopris in 1974. Amid red-lit Victorian decor, accented by reproductions of classic oil paintings, Wigger serves up generous portions of veal-and-seafood dishes, as well as steaks and other meats. House specialties include Wiener schnitzel, rack of lamb, filet mignon chasseur, and lobster scampi in a garlic sauce. There's an extensive wine list and full bar.

3 Montrose & Black Canyon of the Gunnison National Monument

A ranching and farming center, this quiet city of just under 10,000 has an ideal location that is quickly being discovered by hikers, mountain bikers, anglers, and others who want to explore western Colorado. Surrounded by the Uncompahgre, Gunnison, and Grand Mesa national forests, and within a short drive of Black Canyon of the Gunnison National Monument and Curecanti National Recreation Area, it's becoming a major outdoor recreation center.

Ute Chief Ouray and his wife Chipeta ranched in the Uncompahgre Valley here until the government forced the tribe to migrate to Utah in 1881. Once the Utes were gone, settlers founded the town of Pomona, named for the Roman goddess of fruit. Later the town's name was changed to Montrose, for a character in a Sir Walter Scott novel. The railroad arrived in 1882, providing relatively reliable transportation and a means to ship out potatoes, beets, and other crops, and Montrose began in earnest its role as one of Colorado's major food producers, which continues today.

ESSENTIALS

GETTING THERE   By Car   Montrose is an hour's drive southeast of Grand Junction via U.S. 50, a 2^1/$_2$-hour drive north of Durango via U.S. 550, and a 5^1/$_2$-hour drive west of Colorado Springs via U.S. 50 through Salida and Gunnison.

By Plane   The Montrose Regional Airport, 2100 Airport Rd. (☎ **970/249-3203**), off U.S. 50 2 miles northwest of town, is served daily by **United Express** (☎ **800/241-6522** or 970/249-8455), with regular arrivals from and departures to Denver.

ORIENTATION   Montrose sits on the east bank of the Uncompahgre River. Its main street, Townsend Avenue (U.S. 50 and U.S. 550), parallels the stream in a northwest-southeast direction. Main Street (U.S. 50 and Colo. 90) crosses Townsend in the center of town. Numbered streets extend north and south from Main.

GETTING AROUND   Western Express Taxi (☎ 970/249-8880) provides local cab service. Car-rental agencies include **Budget** (☎ **970/249-6083**), **Dollar** (☎ **970/249-3770**), and **Hertz** (☎ **970/249-9447**).

VISITOR INFORMATION   Contact the **Montrose Visitors & Convention Bureau** (☎ **800/873-0244**) or the **Montrose Chamber of Commerce** (☎ **800/923-5515** or 970/249-5000), both at 1519 E. Main St., Montrose, CO 81401. At press time, plans were underway for expansion of the Ute Indian Museum (see "Other Things to See & Do," below), with inclusion of a town Visitor Center, scheduled to open early in 1997.

FAST FACTS   In case of **emergency,** call **911. Montrose Memorial Hospital** is at 800 S. Third St. (☎ **970/249-2211**). The **post office** is at 321 S. First St. (☎ **970/249-6654**). For **road conditions,** call 970/249-9363.

SPECIAL EVENTS   Each year Montrose hosts the Lighter Than Air Balloon Affaire in July, the Montrose County Fair in August, the Native American Lifeways in September, and the Chocolate Lovers' Affaire in December.

BLACK CANYON OF THE GUNNISON NATIONAL MONUMENT

"No other canyon in North America combines the depth, narrowness, sheerness, and somber countenance of the Black Canyon." So said geologist Wallace Hansen, who mapped the canyon in the 1950s and probably knew it better than anyone else. It was avoided by early Native Americans and later Utes and Anglo explorers, who believed that no human could survive a trip to its depths. Today, the deepest and most spectacular 12 miles of the 53-mile canyon comprise this national monument.

Located on Colo. 347, 6 miles north of U.S. 50, the Black Canyon ranges in depth from 1,730 to 2,700 feet. Its width at its narrowest point (cleverly called "The Narrows") is only 1,100 feet at the rim and 40 feet at the river. This deep slash in the earth was created by two million years of erosion, a process that's still going on—albeit slowed by the damming of the Gunnison River above the park.

Accessible only in summer, a road winds to the bottom of the canyon at the East Portal dam in the adjoining Curecanti National Recreation Area, but the only access to this part of the canyon floor is via hiking trails down steep side canyons. Few visitors make that trek. Most view the canyon from the South Rim Road, site of a **Visitor Center** (☎ 970/249-1915), or the lesser-used North Rim Road. Short paths branching off both roads lead to splendid viewpoints with signs explaining the canyon's unique geology. Brochures describe several hikes, and the sheer canyon walls are popular with rock climbers. Fishermen occasionally make their way to the bottom in a quest for brown and rainbow trout; only artificial lures are permitted. In winter, the monument is popular with cross-country skiers. See "Sports & Outdoor Activities," below.

The monument is home to a variety of wildlife, and you're likely to see chipmunks, ground squirrels, badgers, marmots, and mule deer. Although not frequently seen, there are also black bear, cougars, and bobcats; and you'll probably hear the lonesome high-pitched call of coyotes at night. The endangered peregrine falcon can sometimes be spotted along the cliffs, and you may also see red-tailed hawks, turkey vultures, golden eagles, and white-throated swifts.

There are **campgrounds** on both rims, usually open from May through October, with a limited water supply hauled in by truck. There are pit toilets, but no showers or R.V. hookups. Sites are available on a first-come, first-served basis, and cost in 1996 was $8 per site. The south rim campground has 102 sites, and the north rim campground has 13 sites. Campgrounds with hot showers and R.V. hookups are available in Montrose. See "Camping," below.

Pets must be leashed at all times and are not allowed in the inner canyon or in wilderness areas. Removing or damaging anything is prohibited, and bicycles are not permitted on hiking trails. Visitors are also warned to not throw anything from the rim into the canyon, since even a single small stone thrown or kicked from the rim could be fatal to people below; and to supervise children very carefully because many sections of the rim have no guard rails or fences.

To reach the south rim, travel east 6 miles from Montrose on U.S. 50 to the well-marked turnoff. To reach the north rim from Montrose, drive north 21 miles on U.S. 50 to Delta, east 31 miles on Colo. 92 to Crawford, then south on a 13-mile access road.

Admission in 1996 was $4 per vehicle. The Visitor Center is open daily from 8am to 7pm during the summer, has intermittent hours during spring and fall, and is closed in winter. The road to the south rim is open 24 hours a day year-round; the north rim road is open 24 hours except when closed by snow, usually between December and March. For a brochure and other information, contact Superintendent, **Black Canyon of the Gunnison National Monument,** 2233 E. Main St., Montrose, CO 81401 (☎ **970/249-7036**); or if you have specific questions, call the Visitor Center (☎ 970/249-1915).

OTHER THINGS TO SEE & DO

Montrose County Historical Museum. W. Main St. and Rio Grande Ave. ☎ **970/249-2085** or 970/249-6135. Admission $2 adults, 50¢ children 5–12, free for children under 5. Mid-May–Sept, Mon–Sat 9am–5pm.

Pioneer life is highlighted at this museum, housed in a historic Denver & Rio Grande Railroad Depot, which features an 1890s homesteader's cabin, railroad memorabilia, farm equipment, antique dolls and toys, a country store, and Native American artifacts.

✪ **Ute Indian Museum.** 17253 Chipeta Dr., S Montrose. ☎ **970/249-3098.** Admission $2.50 adults, $2 seniors over 65, $1.50 children 6–16, free for children under six. May 15–Sept, Mon–Sat 10am–5pm, Sun 1–5pm; Sept, modified hours. At this writing, plans were underway for an expansion of the museum, scheduled for early 1997, and a year-round operating schedule; for details, call the museum.

Located on the site of the final residence of southern Ute chief Ouray and his wife, Chipeta, the Ute Indian Museum—2 miles south of town off U.S. 550—offers the Colorado Historical Society's most complete exhibition of Ute traditional and ceremonial artifacts, including clothing. Several dioramas depict mid–19th-century lifestyles. Also on the grounds are Chipeta's grave and tiny, bubbling Ouray Springs.

SPORTS & OUTDOOR ACTIVITIES

In addition to boating and other outdoor recreational activities available in Black Canyon of the Gunnison National Monument and nearby Curecanti National Recreation Area (see "Gunnison & Curecanti National Recreation Area," in chapter 14), there are plenty of opportunities for hiking, mountain biking, horseback riding, off-roading, fishing, camping, cross-country skiing, and snowmobiling on other federal lands in the area.

FISHING For starters, you can drop a line into the Uncompahgre River from Riverbottom Park, reached via Apollo Road off Rio Grande Avenue. Most anglers seek rainbow trout here and at Chipeta Lake, behind the Ute Indian Museum, south of Montrose. About 20 miles east via U.S. 50 is the Gunnison River, which produces trophy-class brown and rainbow trout. Those fishing within Black Canyon of the Gunnison National Monument can use artificial lures only.

GOLF The 18-hole **Montrose Golf Course,** 1350 Birch St. (☎ **970/249-8551**), is open year-round, weather permitting. Greens fees are $14 for nine holes and $20 for 18 holes.

HIKING The best hiking is in the Black Canyon of the Gunnison National Monument (see above). Trails on the monument's rims range from short, easy nature walks to moderate-to-strenuous hikes of several miles. Permits are not needed, and leashed pets are permitted on some of the trails (check with rangers). On the south rim, the moderately difficult Rim Rock Nature Trail follows the rim along a relatively flat path to an overlook, providing good views of the Gunnison River and the canyon's sheer rock walls. A pamphlet available at the trailhead describes plant life along the half-mile (one-way) trail. Allow about a half-hour. A longer south rim hike is the 2-mile (round-trip) Oak Flat Loop Trail, rated moderate to strenuous, which drops slightly below the rim, offering excellent views into the canyon. Be aware that the trail is narrow in spots, and a bit close to steep drop-offs. Allow about an hour. On the monument's north rim, the North Vista Trail offers some of the best scenic views in the Black Canyon, and a good chance of seeing red-tailed hawks, white-throated swifts, Clark's nutcrackers, and ravens. You might also be lucky enough to see the rare peregrine falcon. The trail goes through a piñon-juniper forest along the canyon's rim about 1¹/₂ miles to Exclamation Point, which offers one of the best views into the canyon. Up to this point the trail is rated moderate, but it continues another 2 miles (rated strenuous) to Green Mountain, where you'll find broad, panoramic vistas.

Experienced hikers in excellent physical condition may want to hike down into the canyon. Although there are no maintained or marked trails, there are several routes that rangers can help you find. It usually takes from 4¹/₂ to 8 hours to get down to the river and back up, and free permits are required. There are also a limited number of campsites available for backpackers.

Other worthwhile hiking trails, outside the national monument, include the 4¹/₂-mile Ute Trail along the Gunnison River, 20 miles northeast of Montrose, and the 17-mile Alpine Trail from Silver Jack Reservoir in Uncompahgre National Forest, 35 miles southeast of Montrose via Cimarron on U.S. 50.

MOUNTAIN BIKING The Tabeguache Trail—142 miles from Shavano Valley, near Montrose, to No Thoroughfare Canyon, near the Colorado National Monument west of Grand Junction—is a popular and challenging route for mountain bikers. For information, contact the **Colorado Plateau Mountain-Bike Trail Association,** P.O. Box 4602, Grand Junction, CO 81502 (☎ **970/241-9561**). Send a self-addressed, stamped envelope for a free trail map. Bikers can also use the

Uncompahgre Riverway; it is eventually scheduled to connect Montrose with Delta (21 miles north) and Ouray (37 miles south).

A free map of city bike trails is available at the Visitor Center, chamber of commerce, and city hall. You can also obtain free maps, information, bike repairs, and accessories at **Cascade Bicycles,** 25 N. Cascade Ave. (☎ **970/249-7375**).

SWEETS FOR THE SWEET & A TOUCH OF THE GRAPE

Chocolate lovers can't leave Montrose without a stop at the **Russell Stover Candies Factory Outlet,** 2200 Stover Ave., just off Townsend Avenue on the south side of town (☎ **970/249-6681**), for bargain prices on holiday candy (after the holiday) and boxes of chocolates that may not look quite right but still taste great. **Rocky Hill Winery,** 1230 S. Townsend Ave. (☎ **970/249-3765**), is a fun place to stop and sample some of the winery's 11 locally produced wines. Grapes are Colorado grown, and free tours and tastings are offered; the wines sell for $6 to $9 per bottle.

WHERE TO STAY

Best Western Red Arrow Motor Inn. 1702 E. Main St. (P.O. Box 236), Montrose, CO 81402. ☎ **800/468-9323** or 970/249-9641. Fax 970/249-8380. 58 rms, 2 suites. A/C TV TEL. $99 double; $109 suite; $8 additional person; children under 12 stay free in parents' room. AE, CB, DC, DISC, MC, V.

The Red Arrow is a large two-story building near the east end of town, on the way to Black Canyon of the Gunnison National Monument. Spacious rooms, most with queen beds, have coffeemakers, bathrobes, hair dryers, and makeup mirrors. A handful of "spa rooms" have large Jacuzzi tubs and additional amenities. Facilities include a solarium with a hot tub and fitness center, an outdoor swimming pool, a children's playground and picnic area, guest laundry, and conference space for 360. The adjoining restaurant serves three meals daily.

Western Motel. 1200 E. Main St. (at Stough Ave.), Montrose, CO 81401. ☎ **800/445-7301** or 970/249-3481. 28 rms. A/C TV TEL. Memorial Day–Labor Day, $48–$58 double; Labor Day–mid-Nov, $40–$46 double; Mid-Nov–Memorial Day, $36–$45 double. Family units $52–$90. AE, DISC, MC, V.

A one-story red-brick building with a two-story annex, this pleasant motel offers cozy, clean, and comfortable rooms with good-size desks. A few family rooms and water-bed rooms are available, and most units have doorfront parking. VCRs are available to rent, and there's free coffee in the lobby. Facilities include a heated outdoor swimming pool.

CAMPING

In addition to the campgrounds in Black Canyon of the Gunnison National Monument mentioned above, we recommend:

The Hangin' Tree R.V. Park. 17250 U.S. 550 S., Montrose, CO 81401. ☎ **970/249-9966.** 25 sites. $13–$16.50. DISC, MC, V.

A conveniently located campground, open year-round, the Hangin' Tree has tent sites and large pull-through R.V. sites. Bathhouses are exceptionally clean but there are no private dressing areas. There's also a self-service laundry, convenience store, liquor store, antiques shop, and gas station. The campground is just a short walk from Chipeta Lakes, with excellent trout fishing.

WHERE TO DINE

Glenn Eyrie Restaurant. 2351 S. Townsend Ave. ☎ **970/249-9263.** Reservations recommended. Main courses $8.50–$23. AE, CB, DC, DISC, MC, V. Tues–Sat 5–9pm. CONTINENTAL/AMERICAN.

This small, chef-owned and -operated restaurant is lodged in a large colonial farmhouse on the south end of town. In summer, guests can dine outdoors in the wine garden; in winter, folks seek tables near the large central fireplace. Just about everything is made in-house, including rolls, jams, and sauces; and many items are grown on the grounds—fruits, herbs, and greens. Dinner choices include chateaubriand bouquetière, veal, duck, Colorado lamb, freshly made pastas, and fresh seafood including broiled lobster tail. There are also vegetarian dishes and a children's menu.

The Whole Enchilada. 44 S. Grand Ave., near W. Main St. ☎ **970/249-1881.** Main courses $3–$6 at lunch, $3–$12 at dinner. AE, MC, V. Mon–Sat 11am–10pm, Sun noon–9pm. Closes 1 hour earlier in winter. MEXICAN.

Come to this local favorite for well-prepared standard Mexican fare, such as burritos, tostadas, fajitas, tacos, and chimichangas; or more creative offerings, such as enchiladas Acapulco (filled with chicken, olives, and almonds), or the El Paso chimichanga (filled with beef and jalapenos). A variety of burgers are also available; and there's a full bar (known for its margaritas) and a children's menu. An outdoor patio is open in summer.

4 Side Trips to Delta (the City of Murals), Cedaredge, and the Grand Mesa Scenic Byway

Between Montrose and Grand Junction lies Delta County, bounded on the south by the Black Canyon of the Gunnison and on the north by the Grand Mesa. Its county seat is Delta, a town of about 4,000 people, 21 miles north of Montrose on U.S. 50. Delta is sometimes called "the city of murals" because many of its fine historical buildings display colorful murals on their outer walls, with themes ranging from Native American legends to wildlife to apple labels.

The highlight of a visit here is **Fort Uncompahgre,** in Confluence Park at the west end of Gunnison River Drive (☎ 970/874-8349), just north of Delta off U.S. 50. The original fort was built in 1826 at the confluence of the Gunnison and Uncompahgre rivers as a small fur-trading post, and abandoned in 1844 after an attack by Utes. Today it has been replicated as a living-history museum, with four hand-hewn log buildings facing a courtyard. Costumed traders, trappers, and laborers describe their lives, and zealous history buffs can arrange weekend stays to temporarily assume 19th-century lifestyles. Hours at the fort are 10am to 5pm. It's open Tuesday through Sunday from Memorial Day through Labor Day, closed January and February, and open Tuesday through Saturday at other times of the year. Admission costs $3.50 for adults, $2.50 for youths 6 to 16 and seniors 65 and older, and free for children under six.

Also in Delta is the **Delta County Museum,** 251 Meeker St. (☎ 970/874-8721). It's best known for its world-class butterfly collection; other exhibits include the historic Delta County Jail, built in 1886, early household appliances, Victorian memorabilia, a great collection of old photos and cameras, and dinosaur bones. The museum is open May to September, Tuesday through Saturday from 10am to 4pm. October to April it's open Wednesday and Saturday from 10am to 4pm. Admission costs $2 for adults, $1 seniors, and free for children under 12 accompanied by an adult.

WHERE TO STAY & DINE   If you're planning to stop in Delta, a good place to stay is the **Best Western Sundance,** 903 Main St. (☎ 800/626-1994 or 970/874-9781), with rates for two ranging from $40 to $54. Eat at **Daveto's,** 520 Main St. (☎ 970/874-8277), open for lunch and dinner Tuesday through Saturday, serving homemade pasta, cannoli, and pizza, plus sandwiches, salads, and burritos. Prices start at $2.30 for half-sandwiches, with dinners in the $6 to $8 range. Pizzas cost $7.10 to $16.55. For more **information,** contact the Delta County Tourism Council, P.O. Box 753, Delta, CO 81416 (☎ **800/436-3041** or 970/874-8616).

If you follow Colo. 92 4 miles east from Delta and turn north onto Colo. 65, you will come to Cedaredge (about 14 miles from Delta), where you can pick up the Grand Mesa Scenic Byway. This continues on Colo. 65 some 55 miles over the Grand Mesa before intersecting with I-70 to the north.

However, before heading off down the scenic byway, stop at **Pioneer Town** (☎ **970/856-7554**), just south of the main intersection in Cedaredge on Colo. 65. Visit the Byway Welcome Center, then take a tour of Pioneer Town, a re-creation of an early western town, complete with jail house, saloon, bank, country store, and other period buildings. It's open from Memorial Day to Labor Day, Monday through Saturday from 10am to 4pm, and Sunday from 1 to 4pm. Admission is $3 for adults, with reduced rates for senior citizens and children 8 to 17. Children under 8 are admitted free.

Lodging here includes the unique **Cedars' Edge Llamas Bed and Breakfast,** 2169 Colo. 65, Cedaredge (☎ **970/856-6836**), where guest rooms have private decks overlooking pastures of llamas. There's a cottage suite ($75) and three rooms, each with private bath ($50–$60 double; $10 per additional person). A full country breakfast is served privately in your room, on the deck, or in the cottage sun room. Farther on, atop the Grand Mesa at 10,200 feet, is the **Alexander Lake Lodge,** 2121 AA 50 Rd., Cedaredge (☎ **970/856-6700**), with two lodges and 17 cabins (13 with kitchenettes). Rates run $60–$70 double. The lodge has a full-service restaurant and lounge, R.V. park, gasoline and propane station, stables, mountain bikes, fishing boats and supplies, and winter snowmobiling tours.

Southwestern Colorado

A land apart from the rest of the state, Southwestern Colorado is set off by the spectacular mountain wall of the San Juan Range. The Anasazi who once lived here created cliff dwellings that more closely resemble structures found in New Mexico and Arizona than anything you might expect to see in Colorado. The ancient cliff dwellings of Mesa Verde National Park are a case in point, and there are many similar but less well-known sites throughout the area, primarily around Cortez.

Durango is the area's major city. Its vintage main street (circa 1880) and narrow-gauge railroad hearken back to the Old West days of the late 19th century, when it boomed as a transportation center for the region's rich silver and gold mines. Telluride, at the end of a box canyon surrounded by 14,000-foot peaks, has capitalized on its highly evident mining heritage in its evolution as a major ski and summer resort. And those who drive the Million Dollar Highway— down U.S. 550 from Ouray, over 11,008-foot Red Mountain Pass through Silverton, and on past the Purgatory resort to Durango— can't miss the remains of turn-of-the-century mines scattered over the mountainsides.

1 Durango

Born as a railroad town more than a century ago, Durango remains a railroad town to this day—at least in summer, when thousands of visitors take a journey back in time aboard the Durango & Silverton Narrow Gauge Railroad. Durango was founded in 1880 when the Denver & Rio Grande Railroad line was extended to Silverton to haul precious metals from high-country mines. Within a year, 2,000 new residents had turned the town into a smelting and transportation center. Although more than $300 million worth of silver, gold, and other minerals rode along the route over the years, the unstable nature of the mining business gave the town many ups and downs. One of the "ups" occurred in 1915, when southern Colorado boy Jack Dempsey, then 20, won $50 in a 10-round boxing match at the Central Hotel. Dempsey went on to become the world heavyweight champion.

Durango remained a small center for ranching and mining into the 1960s. In 1965 with the opening of the Purgatory ski resort, 25 miles north of Durango, a tourism boom began. When the railroad abandoned its tracks from Antonito, Colorado, to Durango in the late 1960s, leaving only the Durango-Silverton spur, the town panicked. But from that potential economic disaster blossomed a savior. The Durango & Silverton Narrow Gauge Railroad is now Durango's biggest attraction, hauling more than 200,000 passengers each summer. Durango also attracts mountain-biking enthusiasts from all over the country—in fact, opportunities abound for outdoor activities of all kinds, from river rafting to trout fishing.

ESSENTIALS

GETTING THERE   By Car   Durango is located at the crossroads of east-west U.S. 160 and north-south U.S. 550. From I-70, turn south at Grand Junction on U.S. 50, which joins U.S. 550 at Montrose. From I-25, turn west at Walsenburg on U.S. 160.

The most direct route from Denver, when snow conditions allow, is via U.S. 285 south to Del Norte, then west on U.S. 160 across Wolf Creek Pass to Durango. From Santa Fe, New Mexico, follow U.S. 84 north to Pagosa Springs, Colorado, and turn west on U.S. 160 to Durango. From Farmington, New Mexico, take U.S. 550 north. From the Grand Canyon area, follow U.S. 160 northeast through the "Four Corners" of Arizona, New Mexico, Utah, and Colorado.

By Plane   Durango/La Plata County Airport, 14 miles southeast of Durango off Colo. 172 (☎ 970/247-8143), has direct daily nonstop service from Denver; Phoenix, Arizona; and in winter, Dallas/Fort Worth, Texas; with connections to cities throughout North America. The airport is served by **America West Express** (☎ 800/247-5692) and **United Express** (☎ 800/241-6522 or 970/259-5178).

ORIENTATION   The city is situated on the banks of the Animas River, which flows south to join the San Juan River at Farmington, New Mexico. U.S. 160 brushes the south side of downtown Durango; U.S. 550 branches north at the river as Camino del Rio, turning northeast to intersect Main Avenue at 14th Street. Downtown Durango is built around Main Avenue (which takes the place of First Ave.), from Fifth Street north to 14th Street. Numbered streets run east-west, and numbered avenues run north-south, paralleling Main to the east and west. College Drive (Sixth St.), from Camino del Rio to East Eighth Avenue, is the principal downtown cross-street.

VISITOR INFORMATION   Contact the **Durango Area Chamber Resort Association,** 111 S. Camino del Rio (P.O. Box 2587), Durango, CO 81302 (☎ 800/GO-DURANGO or 970/247-0312). The chamber's **Visitor Center** is just south of downtown, on U.S. 160/550 opposite the intersection of East Eighth Avenue; it's open Monday through Friday from 8am to 7pm, Saturday from 10am to 7pm, and Sunday from noon to 7pm.

GETTING AROUND   The Durango Lift (☎ 970/259-LIFT) is the city bus, providing transportation throughout Durango from May to August, weekdays from 8am to 5:30pm; and September to April, weekdays from 7am to 6:30pm; closed major public holidays. The fare is 75¢ per ride. There are bus stops on Main Avenue at Sixth and Ninth, and at East Second Avenue and 15th Street; otherwise, you must "wave enthusiastically at the driver if you want him or her to stop," as the official route map urges.

A fun way to get around Durango in summer is the **Durango Trolley** (☎ 970/259-5438), which runs up and down Main Street weekdays, 7am to 7pm, from mid-June through mid-September. Although the trolley is intended for transportation rather than tours, drivers point out landmarks and talk about historic Durango as they

Southwestern Colorado

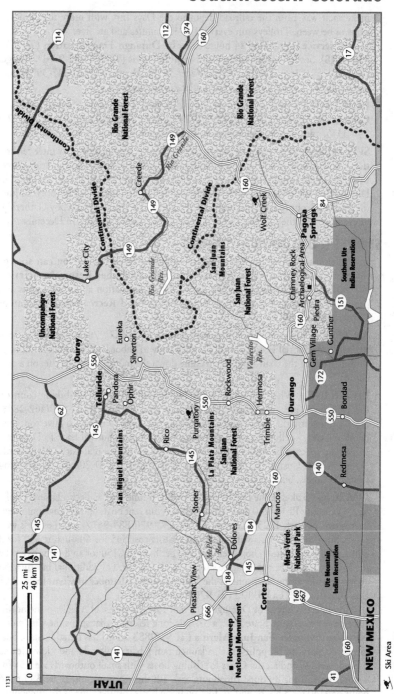

make their way from the railroad depot to the Days Inn, with more than a dozen stops in between. Trolleys run every 20 to 30 minutes and are free.

Taxi service is provided 24 hours a day by **Durango Transportation** (☎ 970/259-4818). Several car-rental agencies, including **Avis** (☎ 970/247-9761), **Budget** (☎ 970/259-1841), **Dollar** (☎ 970/259-3012), **Hertz** (☎ 970/247-3933), and **National** (☎ 970/259-0068), have outlets at the airport.

FAST FACTS In case of **emergency,** call **911.** The hospital, **Mercy Medical Center,** is at 375 E. Park Ave. (☎ **970/247-4311**). For **road conditions,** call 970/247-3355, and for a **weather forecast** and ski conditions, call 970/247-0930.

SPECIAL EVENTS Annual events in the Durango area include the winter celebration Snowdown!, in Durango and Purgatory, in early February; the Iron Horse Bicycle Classic in Durango, Memorial Day weekend; the Animas River Days, in Durango, on the last weekend of June; Music in the Mountains, in Purgatory, in July; the La Plata County Fair, in Durango, in August; the Durango Cowboy Gathering, in October; and the Durango Choral Society Christmas Program, in December.

SPORTS & OUTDOOR ACTIVITIES

In addition to contacting the various companies listed below, you can arrange for most activities through the **Durango Area Chamber Resort Association** (☎ 800/GO-DURANGO or 970/247-0312). Information about city parks and programs is available from the **Durango Parks and Recreation Department** (☎ 970/385-2950).

AN ALPINE SLIDE The **Purgatory Alpine Slide** (☎ 970/247-9000) is open weekends, Memorial Day to mid-June, then daily to Labor Day, weather permitting. Enthusiasts ride the chairlift up, then come down the mountain in a chute, on a self-controlled sled.

BICYCLING While Colorado is usually considered mountain-biking country, there are several great road trips in the Durango area. **Backroads** (☎ 800/462-2848) offers a 6-day trip that starts with a steam-train ride from Durango to Silverton, then bikes to Ouray, Telluride, and Mancos before riders are shuttled back to Durango. It includes spectacular scenery, a layover day in Telluride, and a visit to Mesa Verde National Park. Cost for campers is about $750, and about $1,200 for those opting to stay in hotels; bike rentals are available.

BOATING Lakes in the Durango area include 6-mile-long Vallecito Lake, 22 miles east via County Roads 240 and 501, where you can rent boats and fishing equipment at **Angler's Wharf,** 17250 County Rd. 501 (☎ 970/884-9477), on the lake's west shore. Small fishing boats with outboard motors cost $35 for 4 hours or $50 for 8 hours; and large pontoon boats rent for $35 per hour or $150 for an 8-hour day. The marina also has moorings, a tackle shop, and a snack bar. For additional information about activities at the lake, contact the **Vallecito Lake Chamber of Commerce,** P.O. Box 804, Bayfield, CO 81122 (☎ 970/884-9782).

Forty miles southeast of Durango on Colo. 151, the village of Arboles is the northern gateway to Navajo State Park, a 37-mile-long reservoir that spans the Colorado–New Mexico border. **San Juan Marina** (☎ 970/883-2343) has rental boats, a boat mechanic, parts and supplies, fuel, a launch ramp, bait, Colorado and New Mexico fishing licenses, and a cafe. Costs for fishing boats with small outboards are $35 for 4 hours or $60 for 8 hours; runabouts with 120-horsepower motors are $90 for 4 hours or $140 for 8 hours; and 24-foot pontoon boats cost the same as the runabouts. The marina also rents fully equipped houseboats from 36 to 50 feet, with prices from $460 to $760 for 3 days and 2 nights.

FISHING   Vallecito Lake (see "Boating," above) is a prime spot for rainbow trout, brown trout, kokanee salmon, and northern pike. Navajo State Park (see "Boating," above) also has good fishing, especially for huge northern pike and catfish, but although the park is in Colorado, much of the lake is in New Mexico and a New Mexico fishing license is required.

GLIDER RIDES   You can get a quiet, airborne look at Durango and the San Juan Mountains by taking a glider ride with **Durango Soaring Club (☎ 970/247-9037)**, located 2¹/₂ miles north of Durango on U.S. 550. Rides are given daily from May 15 through September; in 1996 rates were $70 for 25 minutes and $120 for a 50-minute flight.

GOLF   Two public 18-hole golf courses open in April, weather permitting. In Durango, there's **Hillcrest Golf Course,** 2300 Rim Dr. (☎ **970/247-1499**), adjacent to Fort Lewis College, with greens fees of $10 for nine holes and $16 for 18 holes; and **Dalton Ranch and Golf Club,** 589 County Rd. 252 (☎ **970/247-8774**), 6 miles north of Durango via U.S. 550, charging $18 for nine holes and $32 for 18 holes. Rates at both courses are lower on weekdays.

HIKING & BACKPACKING   Durango is at the western end of the 500-mile Colorado Trail to Denver. The trailhead is 3¹/₂ miles up Junction Creek Road, an extension of 25th Street west of Main Avenue. There are numerous other trails in the Durango area, including paths into the Weminuche Wilderness Area reached via the Durango & Silverton railroad. For information, contact the Animas Ranger District, San Juan National Forest, 701 Camino del Rio, Room 301 (☎ 970/247-4874), or the Bureau of Land Management, also at 701 Camino del Rio (☎ 970/247-4082).

Hikers and backpackers in this area should always carry rain gear and make an effort to reach their destination early in the day. Mountain thunderstorms are frequent on summer afternoons, causing temperatures to drop quickly and trails to become muddy.

HORSEBACK RIDING   To see this spectacular country as the pioneers did, arrange for a short horseback ride or a 2- to 6-day expedition into the San Juan National Forest or Weminuche Wilderness. Licensed outfitters include **Southfork Riding Stables and Outfitters, Inc.,** 5 miles south of Durango at 24481 U.S. 160 E. (☎ **970/259-4871**), which provides year-round horseback rides by the hour, half-day, day, overnight, and multiday wilderness pack trips. Prices start at $16 for a 1-hour ride, and a full day in the saddle costs about $85. You can also join in a cattle drive for about $150 per day, and breakfast rides and sunset supper rides are also offered.

HOT SPRINGS   **Trimble Hot Springs,** 6 miles north of Durango on U.S. 550 (☎ **970/247-0111**), at the junction of County Road 203 and Trimble Lane, is a national historic site. Facilities include an Olympic-size natural hot-springs pool, therapy pool, massage and therapy rooms, private tubs, a snack bar, park, and gardens. It's open daily from 8am to 11pm in summer and 9am to 10pm in winter. Day passes cost $7 for adults and $5 for children 12 and younger.

LLAMA TREKS   Llama hikes with gourmet lunches, or overnight expeditions accompanied by sturdy llamas, are the specialty of **Buckhorn Llama Co. (☎ 970/259-5965** or 970/667-7411), which charges $35 to $50 per person for a day hike with lunch. Pack trips cost about $150.

MOUNTAIN BIKING   The varied terrain and myriad trails of San Juan National Forest have made Durango a nationally known mountain-biking center. The Colorado Trail (see "Hiking & Backpacking," above), Hermosa Creek Trail (beginning

Southwestern Colorado on the Silver Screen

This area was John Wayne country, where the Duke slugged it out, shot it out, and sometimes yelled it out as he tamed the West on American movie screens from the late 1920s through the 1970s. It was also the location shoot for the multi-Oscar–winning 1969 hit, *Butch Cassidy and the Sundance Kid,* starring Robert Redford and Paul Newman. Most recently, it hosted *City Slickers,* the 1991 comedy starring Billy Crystal as a hapless city dweller on an Old West–style cattle drive.

Movie critics may argue this point but to many Americans, the king of them all was the Duke—none other than John Wayne. This bigger-than-life symbol of American manhood made numerous films in and around Gunnison, Ridgway, Delta, Durango, and Pagosa Springs, where you can still find the exact spots certain scenes were filmed.

The classic, if bleak 1956 John Ford film *The Searchers,* with Wayne, Jeffrey Hunter, Vera Miles, and Ward Bond, used a ranch near Gunnison as a military outpost. To reach the ranch, go north from Gunnison for 3 miles on Colo. 135, and then turn left onto Ohio Creek Road and drive for about 8 miles, where you'll see a barn and several other buildings off to the left. Ford's later western *How the West Was Won* (which, to the great disappointment of Wayne fans, didn't include the Duke) shows a wagon train crossing the Gunnison River west of Delta along 1800 road, as well as scenes of the Durango & Silverton Narrow Gauge Railroad.

As real John Wayne aficionados know, in 1969 he teamed with Glen Campbell and Kim Darby to make one of his most famous films, *True Grit.* The town of Ridgway becomes Fort Smith in the movie, and nearby is the ranch where Wayne jumps his horse over a river. (Contact the Montrose Chamber of Commerce for directions if you'd like to see it.) *The Cowboys,* filmed in 1972 outside Pagosa Springs,

---

11 miles north of Durango off U.S. 550), and La Plata Canyon Road (beginning 11 miles west of Durango off U.S. 160) are among favorite jaunts.

You can get information and rent mountain bikes at **Southwest Adventures,** 780 Main Ave. (☎ **800/642-5389** or 970/259-0370). Bike rentals are about $15 for a half day or $25 for a full day. Southwest also leads guided tours, both downhill and single track, starting at $30 for a half day.

The **Mountain Bike Specialists,** 949 Main Ave. (☎ **970/247-4066**), offers a 3-day Iron Horse Tour that includes a ride on the Durango & Silverton steam train, a soak in a hot spring, and goes around the ghost town of Animas Forks and along an old stagecoach road. Cost is about $395 per person with a three-person minimum, and includes several meals, lodging, guide, mountain bike, and gear.

For additional information on mountain-biking trails in the area contact the Animas Ranger District, San Juan National Forest, 701 Camino del Rio, Room 301 (☎ 970/247-4874) or the Bureau of Land Management, also at 701 Camino del Rio (☎ 970/247-4082).

MOUNTAINEERING   A variety of terrain offers mountaineering and rock and ice climbing opportunities for beginners as well as advanced climbers. Guided tours (which can range anywhere from 2 hours to several days) and instruction are offered by **Southwest Adventures,** 780 Main Ave. (☎ **800/642-5389** or 970/259-0370), with rates starting at $30 for a 2-hour climb.

finds Wayne as a cattleman who hires a group of schoolboys to drive his herd of 1,500 cattle after the gold rush lures away his crew. There are two location shoots from this film in the area. From the Pagosa Springs Chamber of Commerce, take U.S. 160 west about 3.5 miles to Upper Piedra Road. Turn right and travel about 10 miles to Jack Pasture Road; then turn left and go about 2 miles, where filming was done on both sides of the road. After returning to Upper Piedra Road, turn left and go about 5.5 miles; scenes were shot along the west side of the road.

But as we've said, Wayne wasn't the only one shooting up Colorado's southwest corner. Several movie companies have made use of the area, particularly the classic Durango & Silverton Narrow Gauge Railroad. But the best scene ever put on film has to be the one in *Butch Cassidy & the Sundance Kid,* where Butch, Sundance, and their gang attempt to blow open the train's safe and instead blow up the entire mail car, sending money flying in all directions. Reportedly the extent of this explosion was a surprise to everyone, even the special-effects technicians who apparently were a bit too liberal with their use of black powder. You can see the train at the depot at 479 Main Ave. in Durango, or in summer hop aboard for a ride to Silverton and back. There's a plaque commemorating the filming about 10 miles east of Durango; ask at the chamber of commerce for directions. The chamber can also give directions to two area ranches used in *City Slickers.*

Some of these locations are on private property, and some are difficult to find. For details, contact the chambers of commerce or visitor information centers in **Durango** (☎ 800/GO-DURANGO), **Gunnison** (☎ 800/274-7580), **Montrose** (☎ 800/873-0244), and **Pagosa Springs** (☎ 800/252-2204). And, if you're interested in being in a film yourself, the Colorado Film Commission in Denver operates a recorded bulletin board that lists film projects underway in the state that may be hiring crew members (☎ 303/620-4567).

RIVER RAFTING   The three stages of the Animas River provide excitement for rafters of all experience and ability levels. The churning Class IV and V rapids of the upper Animas mark its rapid descent from the San Juan Range. The 6 miles from Trimble Hot Springs into downtown Durango are an easy, gently rolling rush. Downstream from Durango, the river is mainly Classes II and III, promising a few thrills but mostly relaxation.

Most of the many outfitters in Durango offer a wide variety, from 2-hour raft trips that cost $20 to $30 to overnight guided excursions costing $300 to $400. Rafting companies include **Durango Rivertrippers** (☎ 970/259-0289); **Mountain Waters Rafting** (☎ 800/748-2507 or 970/259-4191); and **Southwest Adventures** (☎ 800/642-5389 or 970/259-0370), which also offers kayak trips and instruction.

RODEOS   From early June through the third week of August the **Durango Pro Rodeo** takes place every Tuesday and Wednesday night at the La Plata County Fairgrounds, Main Avenue and 25th Street (☎ 970/247-1666). The All-Women Rodeo takes place in early July, and the All-Indian Rodeo is planned in early September.

SKIING   Some 25 miles north of Durango on U.S. 550, **Purgatory,** operated by Durango Ski Corporation, #1 Skier Place, CO 81301 (☎ 800/525-0892 or 970/247-9000 for reservations), has a reputation of getting more sunshine than any other Colorado resort. Surprisingly, the sun doesn't come at the expense of snowfall: More than 250 inches a year (over 20 ft.) falls here. The 745 acres of skiable terrain are predominantly intermediate, but there are ample expert runs on the mountain's Backside, and plenty of easy runs for beginners. Seventy-five trails are served by nine chair lifts (one high-speed quad, four triples, and four doubles), with a vertical drop of 2,029 feet from a summit elevation of 10,822 feet.

Snowboarders are welcome on all lifts and trails, and a snowboard park offers jumps, slides, and a quarter pipe. The Purgatory Cross-Country Ski Center offers 16 kilometers (10 miles) of trails for Nordic skiers.

Three on-mountain restaurants complement the facilities of Purgatory Village, which include a hotel, condominiums, several restaurants and taverns, shops, equipment rentals, and activity centers. At press time, all-day tickets cost $39 for adults. All children 12 and younger ski free, except at the Christmas holidays and for a week in mid-March, and there is no parental ticket purchase required and no limit to the number of children in a family skiing free. Rates are subject to change. Purgatory is usually open from Thanksgiving to early April, daily from 9am to 4pm.

✪ THE DURANGO & SILVERTON NARROW GAUGE RAILROAD

Colorado's most famous train has been in continual operation since 1881. In all that time, its route has never varied: up the Rio de las Animas Perdidas (the River of Lost Souls), through 45 miles of mountain and San Juan National Forest wilderness to the tiny mining town of Silverton, and back. The coal-fired steam locomotives pull strings of Victorian coaches on the 3,000-foot climb, past relics of mining and railroad activity from the last century.

The trip takes 3¹/₄ hours each way, with a 2-hour stopover in the picturesque town of Silverton before the return trip. (You can also overnight in Silverton and return to Durango the following day.) Stops are made for water, and may also be made for hikers and fishermen at trailheads inaccessible by road. Refreshments and snacks are available on all trains; there's a bar in the first-class Alamosa Parlor Car. Several private cars are available for charter, including the 1878 *Nomad*—believed to be the oldest operating private car in the world, host of U.S. presidents from Taft to Ford.

Contact the railroad at 479 Main Ave. (☎ 970/247-2733). The round-trip fare is $42.70 adults, $21.45 for children 5–11; $73.45 for the parlor car (minimum age 21). Advance reservations are strongly advised. Railroad yard tours, which take about 45 minutes, are $5. Parking costs $6 per day per car. The train runs from mid-April through the last Sunday of October. At the peak of the summer season, July to mid-August, trains depart weekdays at 7:30, 8:30, 9:15, and 10:10am, weekends starting with the 8:30am run. The 8:30 and 9:15am trains have extended seasons. There's also a Winter Train to Cascade Canyon from Thanksgiving through late April, leaving at 10am (except on December 25). Call for fares.

YOUR STOP IN SILVERTON   Silverton calls itself "the mining town that never quit." Sitting at an altitude of 9,318 feet at the northern terminus of the railroad, the town has a year-round population of about 700. The entire town is a National Historic Landmark District, founded on silver production in 1871. Blair Street was such a notorious area of saloons and brothels a century ago that no less a character than Bat Masterson, fresh from taming Dodge City, Kansas, was imported to subdue the criminal elements. Today the original false-fronted buildings remain, but they now house restaurants and galleries, and are frequently used as Old West movie sets.

The **San Juan County Historical Society Museum,** in the turn-of-the-century jail on Greene Street at 15th Street (☎ 970/387-5838), displays memorabilia of Silverton's boom days daily from Memorial Day weekend to mid-October. Admission costs $2 adults and is free for children 12 and under. The adjacent San Juan

County Courthouse has a gold-domed clock tower, and a Colorado Historical Society grant has helped in the restoration of the Town Hall, at 14th and Greene streets.

Among the local art galleries are **Silverton Artworks,** 1028 Blair St. (☎ **970/ 387-5823**), featuring the work of weaver-ceramicist Ruth Ann Caitland; and the **Silver San Juan Gallery,** 116 W. 12th St. in the Grand Imperial Hotel building (☎ **970/387-0210**), showing watercolors, photographs, and prints by Michael Darr and other local artists.

You can get information and walking-tour maps of the historic commercial area from the **Silverton Chamber of Commerce,** Greene Street (Colo. 110) off U.S. 550 (P.O. Box 565), Silverton, CO 81433 (☎ **800/752-4494** or 970/387-5654).

Where to Stay & Dine Dating from 1883, the ♦ **Grand Imperial Hotel,** 1219 Greene St., Silverton (☎ **800/341-3340** or 970/387-5527), is an opulent showcase that houses the Hub Saloon, where the old song, "There'll Be a Hot Time in the Old Town Tonight," was penned. A stone facade, tin mansard roof, and pressed-tin ceilings usher guests into 40 Victorian-style rooms with private baths. Rates are $60 to $90 double, $125 to $150 suite. It's becoming a favorite getaway for people taking the Durango & Silverton train ride and spending the night in Silverton. The hotel is open year-round and has a saloon and dining room, where you can get burgers, steaks, shrimp, and various specialties, with dinner prices from $6 to $15.

OTHER DURANGO HIGHLIGHTS

Animas Museum. 31st St. and W. 2nd. Ave. ☎ **970/259-2402.** $2 adults, free for children under 12. May–Oct, Mon–Sat 10am–6pm.

An old stone schoolhouse in north Durango is the home of the La Plata County Historical Society museum, so it's appropriate that a turn-of-the-century classroom is one of its central displays. There is also a restored 1870s log home from the early days of Animas City (town that predated Durango), as well as exhibits depicting local history, Native Americans, and the West.

WHERE TO STAY

Durango has a definite lodging season. When the Durango & Silverton Narrow Gauge Railroad is running in summer, expect to pay top dollar for your room. But go in the off-season and you'll find much more reasonable rates. One exception is at the Purgatory Resort, where the holiday ski season—Christmas and Spring Break—is most expensive.

Among chain and franchise motels offering moderately priced rooms are the **Best Western Mountain Shadows,** 3255 N. Main Ave. (☎ **800/521-5218** or 970/ 247-5200), charging $75 to $94 double; and the **Comfort Inn,** 2930 N. Main Ave. (☎ **800/532-7112** or 970/259-5373), with rates from Memorial Day to Labor Day of $88 double, during the Christmas holidays of $86 double, and the rest of the year $49 double.

An easy way to book accommodations is to contact the **Durango Area Chamber Resort Association** (☎ **800/GO-DURANGO** or 970/247-0312).

VERY EXPENSIVE

The Wit's End Guest Ranch & Resort. 254 County Rd. 500, Bayfield, CO 81122. ☎ **970/ 884-4113.** Fax 970/884-3261. 16 cabins. TV TEL. From $2,940 per week for two guests. Additional adults $1,470. Rates include all meals and activities. These rates effective Memorial Day–Labor Day, Thanksgiving and Christmas holidays, with 7-day minimum stay. Off-season cabin-only rates available. AE, MC, V.

A delightful ranch encompassing 365 acres in a narrow valley at the head of Vallecito Lake, surrounded by the 12,000- to 14,000-foot peaks of the Weminuche Wilderness, the Wit's End offers guests a unique combination of rustic outdoors and sophisticated luxury. The activities and sports facilities are numerous. The main focus is a beautiful three-story log hunting lodge, dating from the 1870s, with a huge stone fireplace and walls mirrored with cut glass from London's 1853 Crystal Palace.

Log cabins, some of them 120 years old, have retained their rustic outer appearance but are totally renovated with knotty-pine interiors and modern luxuries. All have fully equipped kitchens, stone fireplaces, queen beds, full bathrooms, porches, and striking views.

Dining/Entertainment: Dinner and drinks are served in the Old Lodge at the Lake Restaurant and Colorado Tavern. The evening meal is included in all packages for resort guests, and is open to the public as well, by reservation, from 5 to 9:30pm nightly in summer; Thursday through Saturday only in winter. Filet mignon, roast duckling, chicken Culbertson, and other hearty American dishes are served. The Game Room, on the second floor, has an antique billiards table. Breakfast and lunch are served daily at the Cafe at "D" Creek, adjacent to the Wit's End General Store.

Services: Room service, masseur.

Facilities: Swimming pool (summer only), four spas, tennis courts, volleyball, horseshoes, mountain bikes, children's programs, trout fishing (five spring-fed ponds), winter sports equipment. Guided hiking, horseback riding, and motor-touring available, as well as fishing instruction. Additional charge for hunting and fishing packages, snowmobile rental, private horseback riding or fly-fishing lessons, private boat rentals, trap shooting, and airport transportation.

EXPENSIVE

Purgatory Village Hotel. Purgatory Resort, 5 Skier Place, Durango, CO 81301. ☎ **800/ 693-0175** or 970/383-2100. 155 units. TV TEL. Summer $60–$75 double; $85–$290 condo. Winter $85–$125 double; $95–$585 condo; higher for holidays. Weekly rates available Apr–Nov. AE, DISC, MC, V.

This ski-in/ski-out hotel at Purgatory Resort, 25 miles north of Durango, is located at the base of the mountain, surrounded by a village offering shops, bars, restaurants, and just about everything skiers want.

A variety of room types are available, both in the hotel building itself and in adjacent condominiums. Most rooms, regardless of size, have a kitchen, fireplace, and private deck, as well as a "snow room" with a ski locker in the entry. Standard one- and two-bedroom condominiums have whirlpool baths and/or steamer showers, classic furnishings, and full kitchens. Efficiency units make ultimate use of space with a Murphy bed that doubles as a dining table.

The hotel restaurant offers fine continental dining evenings during the winter and summer seasons. A cafeteria and lounge serves three meals daily. The pub adjacent to the hotel offers pizza and live music for dancing. There's a concierge, and babysitting can be arranged. You'll find a sports shop, rental shop, activities desk, indoor/ outdoor pool and hot tub, two rooftop hot tubs, and guest laundry.

✪ **Strater Hotel.** 699 Main Ave. (P.O. Drawer E), Durango, CO 81302. ☎ **800/247-4431** or 970/247-4431. Fax 970/259-2208. 93 rms. TV TEL. Mid-May–mid-Oct and Christmas holidays $115–$170 double; Jan–mid-May and mid-Oct–mid-Dec $78–$170 double. AE, CB, DC, DISC, MC, V.

Durango's most famous hotel, a four-story red-brick structure, is an exceptional example of American Victorian architecture. Built in 1887 by Henry H. Strater, a prominent druggist of the mining-boom era, the hotel boasts its original ornamental brickwork and white-stone cornices. Crystal chandeliers and a variety of ornate wood-working styles grace the public areas, along with intricately carved columns and ana-glyphic ceiling designs. The hotel has been in the family of current general manager Rod Barker for three generations (since 1926).

Spread throughout the guest rooms is one of the world's largest collections of American Victorian walnut antiques, and even the wallpaper is authentic to the 1880s. One of the most popular units is Room 222, at the corner of Seventh Street and Main Avenue and directly over the Diamond Belle Saloon, where prolific author Louis L'Amour gave life to his western heroes.

Henry's restaurant serves three meals daily in an elegant atmosphere, specializing in steak, seafood, fish, and pasta. Locals enjoy the Sunday brunch buffet. The Diamond Belle Saloon has live ragtime piano and summer melodrama (see "Durango After Dark," below). Room service and valet laundry are offered, plus a Victorian-style hot tub, by reservation only.

MODERATE

Iron Horse Inn. 5800 N. Main Ave. (U.S. 550 N.), Durango, CO 81301. ☎ **800/748-2990** or 970/259-1010. Fax 970/385-4791. 140 suites. A/C TV TEL. Mid-May–Sept and Christmas holidays $85–$110 double, $115–$120 deluxe room; Oct–mid-May (except Christmas holidays) $70–$80 double, $90 deluxe room. AE, CB, DC, DISC, MC, V.

All units at this modern motel are bi-level suites. Upstairs is the bedroom, usually with one queen bed, and downstairs there's a fireplace, television, dining table, bath-room, and either a couch and coffee table or a queen bed. Deluxe suites have two bathrooms and sleeping for up to five. Two suites have a refrigerator and microwave.

A restaurant serves American fare for breakfast and dinner, with an emphasis on beef; the adjoining lounge has a big-screen TV. The motel also has a large indoor pool, hot tub, sauna, a game room, guest laundry, and a car rental desk.

Silver Spur Motel. 3416 N. Main Ave., Durango, CO 81301. ☎ **800/748-1715** or 970/247-5552. 34 rms, 2 suites. A/C TV TEL. May–Oct $79–$89 double, $95 suite; Nov–Apr $36–$38 double, $65 suite. AE, CB, DC, DISC, MC, V.

Surrounded by junipers and pine trees, the Silver Spur is one of Durango's older hotels. It was a favorite of actor John Wayne, who stayed in room no. 4 when in town filming *True Grit* and several other movies. The recently renovated rooms are clean and comfortable, with refrigerators and microwaves. There's a family restaurant, lounge, room service, outdoor swimming pool, and sun deck.

INEXPENSIVE

Redwood Lodge. 763 Animas View Dr., Durango, CO 81301. ☎ **970/247-3895.** 16 rms. A/C TV TEL. Summer $44–$60 double; winter $31–$44 double. AE, DISC, MC, V.

This small, quiet mom-and-pop motel offers clean, comfortable rooms. Smaller rooms have one queen bed and a shower only; larger rooms come with two queen beds and a shower-tub combination, plus kitchenette with sink, two-burner stove, and small refrigerator. There's also a playground, large outdoor hot tub, and a sauna. The Redwood offers free local calls. Pets are not accepted.

WHERE TO DINE
MODERATE

Francisco's Restaurante y Cantina. 619 Main Ave. ☎ **970/247-4098.** Reservations not accepted. Breakfast $3.25–$6; lunch $5.50–$10; dinner $6–$18. AE, CB, DC, DISC, MC, V. Daily 11am–approximately 10pm; Sun breakfast 9am. MEXICAN/STEAK/SEAFOOD.

This large come-as-you-are family restaurant, with seating for 250, maintains a festive Mexican atmosphere in an adobe-style building with carved wood and a traditional *viga-and-latilla* ceiling. The menu ranges from south-of-the-border specialties such as enchiladas Durango (two blue-corn tortillas over a bed of beef and green chiles) and carne adovada burritos (marinated pork in a hot chile Caribe sauce) to aged Colorado beef, a good variety of fresh seafood, specialty salads, and a number of pasta and chicken dishes. There's a children's menu, and the bar mixes an excellent margarita.

The Palace Grill. 2 Depot Place. ☎ **970/247-2018.** Reservations not accepted. Main courses $12–$24. AE, CB, DC, DISC, MC, V. Mon–Fri 11:30am–2:30pm; daily 5:30–10pm. STEAK/SEAFOOD.

With its Victorian drawing-room atmosphere, adjacent to the Durango & Silverton Narrow Gauge Railroad terminal, this may be Durango's finest restaurant. Tiffany lamps hang over the tables, which are graciously positioned near a large fireplace; historical photos and classic oil paintings grace the walls. The menu is noted for its mesquite grills and daily fish specials. Also popular is the duck, roasted with a honey-and-almond sauce; and steak McMahon, a New York sirloin served on hash browns with a brown sauce and sautéed onions. Fish of the day may be salmon, swordfish, ahi tuna, or something entirely different. The Quiet Lady Tavern, named for the headless female sculpture at its entrance, is a beautiful lounge, complete with library.

INEXPENSIVE

Carvers Bakery/Cafe/Brewery. 1022 Main Ave. ☎ **970/259-2545.** Reservations not accepted. Main courses $3.25–$9.95. Mon–Sat 6:30am–10pm, Sun 6:30am–1pm. AMERICAN.

The Carver brothers have been baking since before they could see over the counter, and the morning bakers here start mixing dough and preparing fillings before the sun rises. The menu offers a wide selection of both meat and vegetarian dishes. Entrees include eggs Benedict on a fresh-baked sesame wheat English muffin, a variety of charbroiled sandwiches, and one of the house specialties: fresh-baked bread bowls filled with soups, stews, or salads. They have daily specials such as garlic basil lasagna, Navajo tacos, Thai pasta, chicken pot pie or cordon bleu, and deep dish enchiladas. There are rotating beer specials, plus wine.

Olde Tymer's Cafe. 10th St. and Main Ave. ☎ **970/259-2990.** Reservations not accepted. Most items $3.50–$7.50. MC, V. Daily 11am–10pm. AMERICAN.

This popular local hangout is located in a historic building with the original tin ceiling and antique bottles and tins from the early 20th-century Wall Drugstore once located here. We think its hamburgers—seven ounces of beef in an onion roll—are the best in Durango. The menu also features homemade chile, a variety of sandwiches, hearty salads such as chicken and cashews in pasta, and daily specials, including fried chicken on Tuesday and Mexican meals on weekends.

DURANGO AFTER DARK

During the summer season, the highly acclaimed **Diamond Circle Melodrama,** in the Strater Hotel, 699 Main Ave. (☎ **970/247-3400**), presents turn-of-the-century melodrama and professional vaudeville. Tickets are $14 per person.

2 A Spectacular Drive Along the San Juan Skyway

The San Juan Skyway, a 236-mile circuit that crosses five mountain passes, takes in the magnificent San Juan Mountains, as well as the cities and towns of the region. It can be accomplished in a single all-day drive from Durango or divided into several days, incorporating stops in Cortez, Telluride, and Ouray—all of which are discussed later in this chapter. Check for closed passes in winter and early spring.

The route can be driven either clockwise (heading west from Durango on U.S. 160) or counterclockwise (heading north from Durango on U.S. 550). We'll describe the clockwise route.

Leaving Durango, you'll pass first through the village of Hesperus, 11 miles west of Durango, from which a county road runs 10 miles north up the **La Plata Canyon,** with its mining ruins and ghost towns.

Farther west, U.S. 160 passes the entrance road to **Mesa Verde National Park** and on into the city of Cortez, 46 miles west of Durango.

Turn north here on Colo. 145, which passes through the historic town of Dolores, site of the **Anasazi Heritage Center and Museum** (see Section 4 of this chapter), then proceeds up the Dolores River Valley, a favorite of trout fishermen.

Sixty miles from Cortez, the route crosses 10,222-foot **Lizard Head Pass,** named for a startling rock spire that looms above the alpine meadows beside the road. It then descends 13 miles to the resort town of **Telluride,** set in a beautiful box canyon 4 miles off the main road.

Follow Colo. 145 west from Telluride down the San Miguel River valley to **Placerville,** then turn north on Colo. 62, across 8,970-foot Dallas Divide, to Ridgway, a historic railroad town and home of **Ridgway State Park** (☎ 970/ 626-5822), with a sparkling mountain reservoir, trout fishing, boating, swimming, hiking, mountain biking, horseback riding, and camping.

From Ridgway, turn south, and follow U.S. 550 to the scenic and historic town of **Ouray.** Here begins the remarkable Million Dollar Highway, so named for all the mineral wealth that passed over it.

The 23 miles from Ouray over 11,008-foot **Red Mountain Pass** to Silverton is an unforgettable drive. It shimmies up the sheer sides of the Uncompahgre Gorge, through tunnels and past cascading waterfalls, then follows a historic toll road built in the 19th century. Mining equipment and log cabins are in evidence on the slopes of the iron-colored mountains, many of them over 14,000 feet in elevation. Along this route you'll pass a monument to the snow plow operators who died trying to keep the road open during winter storms.

From Silverton, U.S. 550 climbs over the Molas Divide (elevation 10,910 ft.), then more or less parallels the track of the Durango & Silverton Narrow Gauge Railroad as it follows the Animas River south to Durango, passing en route the **Purgatory/ Durango** ski resort (see Section 1, above).

3 Mesa Verde National Park

Mesa Verde is the largest archaeological preserve in the United States, with some 4,000 known sites dating from A.D. 600 to 1300, including the most impressive cliff dwellings in the Southwest.

The area was unknown until ranchers Charles and Richard Wetherill chanced upon it in 1888. Looting of artifacts followed their discovery until a Denver newspaper reporter's stories aroused national interest in protecting the site. The 52,000-acre site was declared a national park in 1906—it's the only U.S. national park devoted entirely to the works of man.

The earliest known inhabitants of Mesa Verde (Spanish for "green plateau") built subterranean pit houses on the mesa tops. During the 13th century they moved into shallow caves and constructed complex cliff dwellings. These homes were obviously a massive construction project, yet they were only occupied for about a century; their residents left in about A.D. 1300 for reasons as yet undetermined.

The **Cliff Palace,** the park's largest and best-known site, is a four-story apartment complex with stepped-back roofs forming porches for the dwellings above. Accessible by guided tour only, it is reached by a quarter-mile downhill path. Its towers, walls, and *kivas* (large circular rooms used for spiritual ceremonies) are all set back beneath the rim of a cliff. Another ranger-led tour takes visitors up a 32-foot ladder to explore the interior of **Balcony House.**

Two more important sites—**Step House** and **Long House,** both on Wetherill Mesa—can be visited in summer only. Rangers lead tours to **Spruce Tree House,** another of the major cliff-dwelling complexes, only in winter, when other park facilities are closed. Three-hour ($10) and six-hour ($12) guided park tours are offered from Far View Lodge during the summer.

Although none of the trails to the Mesa Verde sites are strenuous, the 7,000-foot elevation can make the treks tiring for visitors who aren't used to the altitude. For those who want to avoid hiking and climbing, the 12-mile **Ruins Road** makes a number of pit houses and cliffside overlooks easily accessible by car.

In addition to the hidden cliffside villages, the park's **Chapin Mesa Museum,** open daily year-round, houses artifacts and specimens related to the history of the area, including other nearby sites.

Chapin Mesa, site of the park headquarters, museum, and a post office, is 21 miles from the park entrance on U.S. 160. **Morefield Village,** site of Mesa Verde's 477-site campground, is 4 miles in from U.S. 160. The **Far View Visitor Center** (open in summer only), site of the 150-unit Far View Lodge (see below), a restaurant, gift shop, and other facilities, is 15 miles off U.S. 160. In summer, rangers give nightly campfire programs. In winter, the Ruins Road and museum remain open, but many other facilities are closed.

Although this is not an outdoor recreation park per se—the reason to come here is to see the ancient cliff dwellings and other archaeological sites—you'll find yourself hiking and climbing to get to the sites. Several longer **hikes** into scenic Spruce Canyon let you stretch your legs and get away from the crowds. Hikers must register at the ranger's office before setting out.

Open from early May through mid-October, **Morefield Campground** (☎ 970/ 533-7731), 4 miles south of the park entrance, has almost 500 sites, including 15 with full R.V. hookups. There are modern rest rooms, showers, picnic tables, grills, and an R.V. dump station. Reservations are not accepted. Cost is about $10 for sites without hookups and about $17 for sites with hookups.

Admission to the park is $5 per vehicle; it's free for seniors (62 and over), children (12 and younger), and those with disabilities. There is also an additional fee of $1.25 per person for tours to Cliff Palace and several other sites. The park is open 24 hours a day, year-round. The cliff dwellings can be viewed daily from 9am to 5pm; the park museum is open daily from 8am to 6:30pm in summer, daily from 8am to 5pm the rest of the year. Food, gas, and lodging are available from May to October; full interpretive services are available from mid-June to Labor Day.

For a park brochure, contact Superintendent, P.O. Box 8, Mesa Verde National Park, CO 81330 (☎ 970/529-4461 or 970/529-4475). For information on camping, lodging, and dining, call park concessionaire ARA (☎ 970/533-7731).

WHERE TO STAY & DINE

You'll find a variety of lodging and dining possibilities in Cortez, a short drive west of the park entrance road, in addition to the one lodge in the park.

Far View Lodge. Mesa Verde National Park, Mesa Verde Co., P.O. Box 277, Mancos, CO 81328. ☎ **970/529-4421.** Fax 970/529-4411. 150 rms. Open late April–mid-Oct only. $89 double, with lower rates at beginning and end of season. AE, DISC, MC, V.

Fifteen miles from the park entrance, in the heart of Mesa Verde National Park, this facility lodges guests in 17 separate buildings spread across a hilltop. Rooms are cozy, with private balconies and southwestern decor, including original sand paintings. There's no TV or telephone, but the views are magnificent in all directions.

The lodge serves three meals daily, with two restaurants and a bar, has a 24-hour front desk, complimentary morning coffee and newspaper, and gift shop. Pets are accepted with a deposit. Half-day guided tours of the park leave the lodge daily at 9am and 1pm, and full-day tours leave at 9:30am.

4 Cortez: Gateway to the Anasazi Sites of the Four Corners Region

An important archaeological center, Cortez is surrounded by a vast complex of ancient villages that dominated the Four Corners region—where Colorado, New Mexico, Arizona, and Utah's borders meet—1,000 years ago. The inhabitants of those ancient villages, commonly called the Anasazi, are considered ancestral Pueblo people.

Mesa Verde National Park, 10 miles east, is certainly the most prominent nearby attraction, drawing hundreds of thousands of visitors annually. (See Section 3 of this chapter.) In addition, archaeological sites such as those at Hovenweep National Monument, Lowry Pueblo, the Dominguez and Escalante Ruins, and Ute Mountain Tribal Park are an easy drive from the city. San Juan National Forest, just to the north, offers many recreational opportunities.

ESSENTIALS

GETTING THERE   By Car   Cortez is located at the junction of U.S. 666 and U.S. 160. U.S. 666 runs north and west to Monticello, Utah (and on to Salt Lake City), and south to Gallup, New Mexico (on I-40); U.S. 160 runs east through Durango to Walsenburg, on I-25, and west through the Four Corners area to the Grand Canyon region of Arizona. Colo. 145, north to Telluride and Grand Junction, intersects U.S. 160 at the east end of town.

By Plane   Cortez—Montezuma County Airport, off U.S. 160 and 666, southwest of town (☎ **970/565-7458**), is served by **United Express Airlines** (☎ **800/ 241-6522** or 970/565-9510), with daily flights to Denver and Farmington, New Mexico. Providing car rentals at the airport is **U-Save** (☎ **800/272-USAV** or 970/565-9168).

ORIENTATION   U.S. 160 from Durango crosses north-south Colo. 145 (Dolores Rd.) as it enters Cortez from the east, then runs due west through town for about 2 miles as Main Street. The city's main thoroughfare, Main Street eventually intersects U.S. 666, which runs roughly southwest-northeast as Broadway at the west end of town.

VISITOR INFORMATION   Stop at the **Colorado Welcome Center at Cortez,** Cortez City Park, 928 E. Main St. (☎ **800/253-1616** or 970/565-3414); or contact the **Mesa Verde Country Visitor Information Bureau,** P.O. Box HH, Cortez, CO 81321 (also ☎ **800/253-1616**); or the **Cortez Area Chamber of Commerce,** P.O. Box 968, Cortez, CO 81321 (☎ **970/565-3414**).

SPECIAL EVENTS Major annual events in Cortez include the Indian Dances, held at the C.U. Center, 125 Market Street, Monday through Friday evenings at 7:30pm from Memorial Day through Labor Day, with free admission. Cortez events also include the Ute Mountain Roundup Rodeo, in mid-June; and the Montezuma County Fair, in early August. In nearby Dolores, the Moki Mush Dogsled Races take place in mid-January.

THE MAJOR ARCHAEOLOGICAL SITES
HOVENWEEP NATIONAL MONUMENT

This is located along the Colorado–Utah border, 41 miles west of Cortez. Take U.S. 160 south about 2 miles to County Rd. G, and follow signs into Utah and the monument. There are several other routes to the monument, but they include sections of graded dirt that become muddy during rainstorms.

This national monument contains some of the most striking and isolated archaeological sites in the Four Corners area. It's noted for mysterious, 20-foot-high sandstone towers, some of them square, others oval, circular, or D-shaped.

The towers have small windows up and down their masonry sides, and remain very solid today. Archaeologists have suggested their possible function as everything from guard or signal towers, celestial observatories, and ceremonial structures to water towers or granaries. *Hovenweep* is the Ute word for "deserted valley." The Anasazi apparently left the area around A.D. 1300, and even today it's often overlooked by tourists, who instead flock to the more famous Mesa Verde (see Section 3 of this chapter).

A ranger station, with exhibits, rest rooms, and bottled drinking water, is located at the **Square Tower Site,** in the Utah section of the monument, the most impressive and best preserved of the sites. The Tower Point Loop Trail here winds past the ruins and identifies desert plants used for food, clothing, medicine, and other purposes. The other five sites are difficult to find, and you'll need to obtain detailed driving directions and check on current road conditions before setting out.

The Hovenweep Campground, with 31 sites, is open year-round. It has rest rooms, drinking water, picnic tables, and fire pits, but no showers or R.V. hookups. Most sites will accommodate trailers. Cost is $6 per night, and reservations are not accepted, although the campground rarely fills up, even during the peak summer season.

Regulations are much the same here as at most National Park Service properties, with an emphasis on being careful to not damage archaeological sites. Summer temperatures can reach over 100° Fahrenheit, and water supplies here are limited; so take your own and carry a canteen even on short walks. During late spring and early fall, gnats can be a nuisance. Dogs must be leashed but are permitted on trails.

The ranger station is open daily from 8am to 5pm year-round, but may be closed for short periods while the ranger is on patrol. Admission is free. For advance information or questions about current road conditions, contact Hovenweep National Monument, P.O. Box 8, Mesa Verde National Park, CO 81330 (☎ 970/529-4461).

ANASAZI HERITAGE CENTER

When the Dolores River was dammed and McPhee Reservoir created in 1985, some 1,600 ancient archaeological sites were threatened. Four percent of the project costs were set aside for archaeological work, and some two million artifacts, samples, and other prehistoric records were rescued. The largest share are displayed in this museum, which opened in 1988. Located 10 miles north of Cortez, it is set into a hillside near the remains of 12th-century ruins.

Operated by the Bureau of Land Management, the center emphasizes visitor involvement. Children and adults are invited to examine corn-grinding implements, a loom and other weaving materials, and a re-created pit house. You can touch artifacts 1,000 to 2,000 years old, examine samples through microscopes, use interactive computer programs, and engage in video lessons in archaeological techniques.

A trail leads from the museum half a mile to the Dominguez and Escalante Ruins, atop a low hill, with a beautiful view across the Montezuma Valley.

The center is located at 27501 Colo. 184, Dolores (☎ **970/882-4811**). It's open daily from 9am to 5pm, except major holidays. Admission is free.

CORTEZ COLORADO UNIVERSITY CENTER AND MUSEUM

The center at 25 N. Market St., Cortez (☎ **970/565-1151**), is a clearinghouse for information on various Anasazi sites and related activities in southwestern Colorado, and the museum features interpretive exhibits from the sites as well as the Ute reservation. Evening programs, including Native American dances and cultural programs, are presented Monday through Saturday in summer, and about once a week the rest of the year. Admission is free, though donations are welcome. The center is open from June to August, Monday to Saturday from 10am to 9pm; in May, September, and October it's open Monday to Saturday from 10am to 6pm; from November to April, Monday to Saturday from 10am to 5pm.

LOWRY PUEBLO RUINS

An excavated 12th-century village, 26 miles from Cortez via U.S. 666 (on County Road CC, 9 miles west of Pleasant View; ☎ **970/247-4082**), Lowry Pueblo may have been a ritual center. Though believed to have been abandoned by A.D. 1200, during its heyday the 42-room pueblo was home to about 100 people. A short, self-guided interpretive trail leads past a *kiva*, or underground circular spiritual chamber, decorated with geometric designs. It then continues to the remains of a great kiva, which, at 54 feet in diameter, is among the largest ever found. The Bureau of Land Management, which maintains this designated National Historic Landmark, also maintains a picnic area and rest room facilities. Admission is free. The site is open daily from 8am to sunset, year-round (except when winter weather conditions close the gravel access road).

UTE MOUNTAIN TRIBAL PARK

If you liked Mesa Verde, but would have enjoyed the ruins more without the company of so many fellow tourists, you'll *love* the Ute Mountain Tribal Park, in Towaoc (☎ **800/847-5485** or 970/565-3751, ext. 282). Set aside by Ute Mountain Indian Reservation to preserve its heritage, the 125,000-acre park—which abuts Mesa Verde National Park—includes hundreds of surface ruins and cliff dwellings that compare in size and complexity with those in Mesa Verde, as well as wall paintings and ancient petroglyphs.

Accessibility to the park is strictly limited to guided tours. Full- and half-day tours begin at the Ute Mountain Museum and Visitor Center at the junction of U.S. 666 and U.S. 160, 19 miles south of Cortez. Mountain-biking and backpacking trips are also offered. No food, lodging, gasoline, or other services are available within the park. Be sure to take your own food and drinking water; and because most visitors use their own vehicles for transportation within the park, make sure your gas tank is full. Some climbing is necessary to get to several of the ruins. There's one primitive campground on the Mancos River for overnight stays ($10 per vehicle).

Charges for tours start at $15 for a half day, $25 for a full day; it's $5 extra to go in the tour guide's vehicle. Year-round tours begin daily at 8:30am, by confirmed reservation. Office hours are Monday to Friday 8am to 4:30pm..

OTHER NEARBY HIGHLIGHTS
FOUR CORNERS MONUMENT

Located one-half mile northwest of U.S. 160, about 38 miles southwest of Cortez, the monument is open year-round, daily 7am–8pm in summer, with shorter hours in winter. Admission costs $1.50 per person. Call the Navajo Parks and Recreation department in Window Rock, Arizona (☎ **520/871-4941, ext. 6647**).

This is the only place in the United States where you can stand, or sit if you prefer, in four states at once. Operated as a Navajo Tribal Park, there's a flat monument marking the spot where Utah, Colorado, New Mexico, and Arizona meet, and visitors perch for photos. Official seals of the four states are displayed, along with the motto, "Four states here meet in freedom under God." Surrounding the monument are the states' flags, flags of the Navajo Nation and Ute tribe, and the U.S. flag.

There are rows of booths where vendors sell traditional Navajo food, such as fry bread, along with plenty of traditional American junk food. There are often crafts demonstrations, and there's an abundance of jewelry, pottery, sand paintings, and other crafts, plus T-shirts, postcards, and souvenirs for sale.

Ute Mountain Casino. Towaoc (11 miles south of Cortez on U.S. 160/666). ☎ **800/ 258-8007** or 970/565-8800. Free admission. Daily 8am–4am.

Colorado's first tribal gaming facility has some 375 slot machines, plus ten blackjack tables, five poker tables, and high-stakes bingo. The electronic slots include video poker and keno, and bingo prizes up to $10,000 are offered Friday through Tuesday. Bingo is played evenings except Sunday, which is an afternoon session. As with all Colorado gambling, bets are limited to $5 and gamblers must be at least 21 years old, except for bingo where participants must be at least 18. The casino has a full-service restaurant offering southwestern cuisine. No alcoholic beverages are served or permitted in the building or on the grounds.

WHERE TO STAY

Among the major chains providing comfortable, reasonably priced lodging in Cortez are **Holiday Inn Express,** 2121 E. Main St. (☎ **800/626-5652** or 970/565-6000), with summer rates of $96 double, $125 suites, and rates the rest of the year of $70 to $85 double; and **Ramada Limited,** 2020 E. Main St., (☎ **800/2-RAMADA** or 970/565-3474), with rates of $75 to $90 double. Continental breakfast is included in both of the motels' rates.

✪ **Arrow Motel.** 440 S. Broadway, Cortez, CO 81321. ☎ **800/524-9999** or 970/565-7778. Fax 970/565-7214. 42 rms. A/C TV TEL. Memorial Day–Labor Day $48–$59 double; Labor Day– Memorial Day $28–$48 double. Children under 12 stay free in parents' room, $4 charge for children 12 and over. AE, DC, DISC, MC, V.

A small ma-and-pa–style motel affiliated with National 9 Inns, the Arrow is perfect for families on a budget. Flower boxes decorate the buildings, and facilities include an outdoor swimming pool, Jacuzzi, and guest laundry. Ten rooms have refrigerators and microwave ovens. Most of the attractive rooms have queen beds, although there are a few kings. Pets are not allowed.

WHERE TO DINE

Homesteaders Restaurant. 45 E. Main St. ☎ **970/565-6253.** Breakfast $2.50–$6; main courses $3–$6.50 at lunch, $4–$14 at dinner. AE, DISC, MC, V. Mon–Sat 7am–3pm and 5–9:30pm; Sun 5–9pm in summer. AMERICAN/MEXICAN.

A rustic barn provides the atmosphere for this popular family restaurant. A big waterwheel greets guests at the entrance, while throughout the dining room hang harnesses, skillets, and other pioneer artifacts. The menu ranges from tacos to chicken-fried steak, rainbow trout to barbecued spareribs. Their omelets start the day right.

Millwood Junction. U.S. 160 and Main St., Mancos. ☎ **970/533-7338.** Main courses $6.95–$18.50. MC, V. Daily 5:30–10:30pm. STEAK/SEAFOOD.

The atmosphere at this restaurant, 7 miles east (toward Durango) of the Mesa Verde National Park entrance, recalls a turn-of-the-century sawmilling industry that supported the Mancos-area economy. The food, though, is decidedly modern. House specials include steak Diane and blackened catfish; you can also get pastas, pork ribs, and a variety of other steaks and seafood. Especially popular are the homemade ice creams and desserts. On Friday night a seafood buffet draws folks from miles around.

✪ **Nero's.** 303 W. Main St. ☎ **970/565-7366.** Reservations recommended. Main courses $5.95–$15.95. AE, MC, V. Daily 5–10pm. ITALIAN/AMERICAN.

A small, homey restaurant with a southwestern art-gallery decor, Nero's doubles its capacity in summer with an outdoor patio. Main courses—which come with soup or salad and bread—include an excellent selection of beef, seafood, chicken, veal, and homemade pasta, prepared with an innovative flair by Culinary Institute of America–trained chef Richard Gurd. Southwestern specials, such as chorizo-stuffed chicken breast with red chile-garlic sauce, are offered frequently. There's a full bar and wine list, and a children's menu.

5 Telluride

This was one seriously rowdy town a century ago—in fact, this is where, in 1889, Butch Cassidy robbed his first bank. Incorporated with the boring name of Columbia in 1878, this mining town assumed its present name the following decade. Some say the name came from tellurium, a gold-bearing ore, while others insist the name really means "to hell you ride," referring to the town's boisterous nature.

Telluride became a National Historic District in 1964, and in 1968 entrepreneur Joe Zoline set to work on a "winter recreation area second to none." The Telluride Ski Company opened its first runs in 1972, and Telluride was a boom town again. Telluride's first summer festivals (bluegrass in June, film in September) were celebrated the following year. Today, the resort, at 8,745 feet elevation, is a year-round destination for mountain bikers, skiers, anglers, and hikers.

ESSENTIALS

GETTING THERE   By Car   Telluride is located on Colo. 145. From Cortez, follow Colo. 145 northeast for 73 miles. From the north (Montrose), turn west off U.S. 550 at Ridgway, onto Colo. 62. Proceed 25 miles to Placerville, and turn left (southeast) onto Colo. 145. Thirteen miles ahead is a junction—a right turn will take you to Cortez, but for Telluride, continue straight ahead 4 miles to the end of a box canyon. From Durango, in summer take U.S. 550 north to Colo. 62, and follow the directions above; in winter it's best to take the route through Cortez and avoid Red Mountain Pass above Silverton.

By Plane   Telluride Regional Airport, atop a 9,000-foot plateau 5 miles west of Telluride, is served by **United Express** (☎ **800/241-6522** or 970/728-4868) from Denver, and **America West Airlines** (☎ **800/235-9292** or 970/728-4868) from Phoenix.

ORIENTATION   The city is located on the San Miguel River where it flows out of a box canyon formed by the 14,000-foot peaks of the San Juan Mountains. Colo. 145, which enters town from the west, is known as Colorado Avenue and is Telluride's main street. The main part of historic downtown runs five blocks west from Aspen Street to Willow Street; beyond here is the Town Park, site of many summer festivals. Columbia Avenue parallels Colorado Avenue to the north, Pacific Avenue to the south.

Telluride Mountain Village, at 9,500 feet, can be reached by a gondola, scheduled for completion in late 1996. Motorists can take Mountain Village Boulevard off Colo. 145, a mile south of the Telluride junction.

VISITOR INFORMATION   Contact **Telluride Visitor Services/Telluride Central Reservations,** 666 W. Colorado Ave. (P.O. Box 653), Telluride, CO 81435 (☎ **800/525-3455**). The **Telluride Visitor Information Center** can be found with the visitor services and central reservations offices, located above Rose's Food Mart.

GETTING AROUND   With restaurants, shops, and attractions within easy walking distance of most lodging facilities, many visitors leave their cars parked and take to their feet. However, if you do want to ride, **Skip's Taxi and Shuttle Service** (☎ **970/728-6667**) and **Mountain Limo** (☎ **970/728-9606**) provide taxi service. And there's a free town shuttle in winter.

Budget (☎ **800/221-2419** or 970/728-4642), **Hertz** (☎ **800/654-3131** or 970/728-3163), and **Thrifty** (☎ **800/367-2277** or 970/728-3266) have car rentals, including vans and four-wheel–drive vehicles, at the airport.

FAST FACTS   In case of **emergency,** call **911**. The hospital, **Telluride Medical Center,** is at 500 W. Pacific Ave. (☎ **970/728-3848**). The **post office** (☎ **970/728-3900**) is at 101 E. Colorado Ave. For **road conditions,** call 970/249-9363.

SPECIAL EVENTS   Telluride has a number of annual cultural and athletic events, some of which are world-renowned and becoming more popular every year. In addition to the events mentioned under "The Festival Scene," below, there's the Melee in the Mines Mountain Bike Race, at the end of July; Imogene Pass Run, in early September; the Telluride Wine Festival, at the end of June; the World Aerobatic Hang Gliding Championships, in September; the Chamber Music Festival, in mid-August; and the Mushroom Festival, the fourth weekend of August.

SKIING

The elegant European-style Mountain Village Resort, built in 1987, offers a fascinating contrast to the laid-back community of artists, shopkeepers, and drop-outs in the 1870s mining town of stately Victorian homes below. The resort, midmountain at 9,450 feet elevation, offers ski-in, ski-out accommodations; three on-mountain restaurants including Gorrono Ranch, a historic homestead; spectacular scenery; and—of course—great skiing.

The mountain's **Front Face,** which drops sharply from the summit to the town of Telluride, is characterized by steep moguls, tree-and-glade skiing, and challenging groomed pitches for experts and advanced intermediates. **Gorrono Basin,** which rises from the Mountain Village Resort, caters to intermediate skiers. The broad, gentle slopes of the **Meadows** stretch beneath Gorrono Basin to the foot of Sunshine Peak. This part of the mountain, with trails over 2¹/₂ miles long devoted entirely to novice skiers, is served by a high-speed quad chair.

In all, Telluride offers 1,050 acres of skiable terrain. The vertical drop is an impressive 3,165 feet from the 11,890-foot summit. The mountain has 64 trails served by 10 lifts (two high-speed quads, two triples, five doubles, and a Poma). Twenty-one percent of the trails are rated for beginners, 47% for intermediates, and 32% for expert skiers. There are an additional 30 kilometers (18.6 miles) of Nordic trails, and helicopter skiing is available. Expansion is scheduled to begin in 1997. Average annual snowfall is 300 inches (25 ft.).

At press time, full-day lift tickets cost $45 adults; $20 children 6 to 12 and seniors 65 to 69; free for children under 6 and seniors over 69. Class lessons start at $35. Rates are subject to change. Call **800/525-3455** for snow reports. The resort is open daily from Thanksgiving to mid-April.

OTHER WINTER ACTIVITIES

In addition to downhill skiing at Telluride Ski Resort, virtually every cold-weather activity is available in the Telluride area. Much of it takes place at **Town Park,** at the east end of town (☎ **970/728-3071**), where there are groomed cross-country ski trails, daytime sledding and tubing at Firecracker Hill, and ice-skating (see below). The **River Corridor Trail** follows the San Miguel River from Town Park to the valley floor. Popular with bikers and hikers in warm weather, it's perfect for cross-country skiing and skate-skiing after the snow falls.

The major outfitter and arranger of outdoor activities here is the versatile and dependable **Telluride Outside,** 1982 W. Colo. 145 (☎ **800/831-6230** or 970/728-3895), which seems to be involved in every form of outdoor recreation except skiing.

HELISKIING   Those seeking untouched powder will find it with **Telluride Helitrax** (☎ **970/728-4904**), which uses a helicopter to reach those remote and beautiful mountain basins and bowls.

ICE-SKATING   There's free ice-skating in winter at Town Park (☎ 970/728-3071), and also at the outdoor rink in the Mountain Village (☎ 970/728-6727). Skate rentals are available at local sporting goods stores.

NORDIC SKIING & SNOWBOARDING   There are 30 kilometers (18.6 miles) of Nordic ski trails at Telluride Ski Resort (☎ 970/728-4424); rentals ($12/day), instruction, and tours are available. In addition, groomed trails at Town Park and River Corridor Trail add another 20 kilometers (12.4 miles), and all 50 kilometers (31 miles) are connected. Snowboarders are welcome anywhere on the mountain, and lessons are available.

For those who really want to put some miles behind them, there's the **San Juan Hut System** (☎ **970/728-6935**), providing backcountry huts with bunks, wood stoves and wood, and kitchens (see "Mountain Biking" below).

SLEIGH AND DOGSLED RIDES   Both dogsled ($125 half day and $190 full day) and old-fashioned horse-drawn sleigh rides, with dinner ($55 adults, $35 children 3–12), can be arranged with **Telluride Outside.**

SNOWMOBILING   Tours are offered by **Telluride Outside,** starting at $110 for one person on one snowmobile for a 2-hour ride, and $160 for two people on one machine for 2 hours. One- and two-hour dinner tours are also available.

WARM-WEATHER & YEAR-ROUND ACTIVITIES

Telluride isn't just a ski resort—there's a wide variety of year-round outdoor activities. **Town Park,** at the east end of town (☎ 970/728-3071), is home for the community's various festivals. It also has a public outdoor swimming pool, open in summer, plus tennis courts, sand volleyball courts, a small outdoor basketball court, skateboarding ramp, soccer and softball fields, picnic area, and a fishing pond (see "Fishing," below). A campground for tent and car campers, open in summer, with showers, costs $10 per night.

As with winter activities, the major outfitter and guide service here is **Telluride Outside,** 1982 W. Colo. 145 (☎ 800/831-6230 or 970/728-3895).

FISHING   There's excellent fishing in the San Miguel River through Telluride, but it's even better in nearby alpine lakes, including Silver Lake, reached by foot in Bridal Veil Basin, and Trout and Priest Lake, 12 miles south via Colo. 145. At **Town Park** there's Kids Fishin' Pond for children 12 and under, which is stocked from Memorial Day to Labor Day.

Equipment, licenses, and fly-fishing instruction are offered by **Telluride Outside,** with a walk-and-wade trip for two costing about $190 for a half day and $260 for a full day. A 1-day fishing float trip for two runs about $495, and a 3-day float trip for two into the Black Canyon of the Gunnison costs about $1,750.

FOUR-WHEELING   To see old ghost towns, mining camps, and spectacular mountain scenery from the relative comfort of a bouncing four-wheel–drive vehicle, join **Telluride Outside** for a full-day trip ($85) over the 14,114-foot Imogene Pass jeep road.

GOLF   The 18-hole par-71 **Telluride Golf Course** is located at Telluride Mountain Village (☎ 970/728-6800 or 970/728-6157). Greens fee with the required cart is $100 per person July through Labor Day, $80 at other times.

HIKING & MOUNTAINEERING   Sporting-goods stores and the Visitor Center have maps of trails in the Telluride area. Especially popular are the easy 4-mile Bear Creek Trail; the Jud Wiebe 4.8-mile loop trail that begins on Oak Street and ends a block away on Aspen Street; and the 1¹/₂-mile walk to the foot of Bridal Veil Falls, at the east end of Telluride Canyon.

A variety of guided mountain expeditions can be arranged through **Lizard Head Mountain Guides** (☎ 970/728-4904), or **Fantasy Ridge Alpinism,** 205 W. Colorado Ave. (☎ 970/728-3546), which also offers ice climbing and winter mountaineering instruction. Hiking, backpacking, and llama pack trips especially for women are offered by **Women in the Wilderness** (☎ 970/728-4538). **Herb Walker Tours** (☎ 970/728-4538) leads herb/nature hikes for those interested in learning about local plants, how to identify mushrooms, and the uses of plants. Call for rates and availability.

HORSEBACK RIDING   One of the best ways to see this spectacular country is by horse. **Telluride Horseback Adventures** (☎ 800/828-7547 through Telluride Sports, or 970/728-9611), offers "gentle horses for gentle people and fast horses for fast people," year-round, with 1-hour rides starting at $25 and all-day rides at $100. There are also breakfast ($50) and dinner ($60) rides; and ask about multiday pack trips in September and private rides for small groups of experienced riders.

MOUNTAIN BIKING   Telluride is a major mountain-biking center. **The San Juan Hut System** links Telluride with Moab, Utah, via a 206-mile-long network of backcountry dirt roads. Every 35 miles are primitive cabins, each with bunks, a wood stove, propane cooking stove, and cooking gear. The route is appropriate for intermediate level riders in good physical condition, and an advanced technical single track is found near the huts for more experienced cyclists. Cost for riders who plan to make the whole trip is about $450, which includes use of the six huts, three meals daily, sleeping bags at each hut, and maps and trail descriptions. Shorter trips, guide services, and vehicle shuttles are also available. Trail system offices are at 117 N. Willow St. (☎ **970/728-6935**). For a brochure write to P.O. Box 1663, Telluride, CO 81435.

Telluride Outside offers a 3-hour downhill tour, including a bike, for about $60.

RIVER RAFTING Those wanting to run the local rivers can hop in a raft with **Telluride Outside,** which charges about $70 for a half-day trip. The company also offers a spectacular full-day trip into the Black Canyon of the Gunnison that starts with a 1-mile hike to the river before rafting through 14 miles of pristine wilderness, where you'll quite possibly see bighorn sheep, river otters, and golden eagles. Cost is about $175, which includes lunch and dinner.

SEEING THE SIGHTS

The best way to see the Telluride National Historic District and get a feel for the West of the late 1800s, is to take to the streets, following the excellent **walking tour** described in the *Telluride Vacation Guide,* available at the Visitor Information Center. Among the buildings you'll see are the **San Miguel County Courthouse,** Colorado Avenue at Oak Street, built in 1887 and still in use today. A block north and west, at Columbia Avenue and Aspen Street, is the **L. L. Nunn House,** home of the late 19th-century mining engineer who created the first high-voltage alternating-current power plant in the world. Two blocks east of Fir Street, on Galena Avenue at Spruce Street, is **St. Patrick's Catholic Church,** built in 1895, whose wooden Stations of the Cross figures were carved in Austria's Tyrol region. Perhaps Telluride's most famous landmark is the **New Sheridan Hotel** and the **Sheridan Opera House,** opposite the County Courthouse at Colorado and Oak. The hotel, built in 1895, in its early days rivaled Denver's famed Brown Palace Hotel in service and cuisine. The exquisite Opera House, added in 1914, boasted a Venetian scene painted on its roll curtain.

Colorado's highest waterfall (365 ft.) can be seen from the east end of Colorado Avenue. **Bridal Veil Falls** freeze in winter, then slowly melt in early spring, creating a dramatic effect. Perched at the top edge of the falls is a National Historic Landmark, a hydroelectric power plant that served area mines at the turn of the century, and has been recently restored and is once again supplying power to the community. It is accessible by hiking or driving a switchback, four-wheel–drive road.

Telluride Historical Museum. 400 N. Fir St. ☎ **970/728-3344.** Admission $4 adults, $3 seniors, $1 children under 12. May–Oct Mon–Sat 10am–5pm, Sun noon–5pm; Nov–Apr Mon–Wed and Fri noon–5pm, Thurs noon–7pm. Possible closure of a week or two in late spring.

The museum was undergoing major renovation during 1996 and was expected to reopen in early 1997. Call to verify hours and admission charge. The museum has some 9,000 artifacts and 1,400 historic photos that show what Telluride was like in its Wild West days, when the likes of Butch Cassidy stalked the streets. Exhibits include a very rare prehistoric Anasazi blanket, mining memorabilia, a turn-of-the-century schoolroom display, and antique toys.

THE FESTIVAL SCENE

✪ **Telluride Film Festival.** An influential festival within the film industry that takes place over Labor Day weekend, the Telluride Film Festival has premiered some of the finest films produced in recent years (*The Crying Game, The Piano,* and *Ed Wood* are just a few examples). What truly sets it apart, however, is the casual interaction between stars and attendees. Open-air films and seminars are free to all. Contact the National Film Preserve (☎ **603/643-1255**) for further information.

Mountainfilm. Every Memorial Day weekend, filmmakers, writers, and outdoor enthusiasts gather to celebrate mountains, adventure, and the environment with 4 days of films, seminars, and presentations. Recent guests have included Sir Edmund Hillary and David Brower.

Telluride Bluegrass Festival. This is one of the most intense bluegrass, folk, and country jam sessions in the country. Held during the third full weekend of June in conjunction with the Bluegrass Academy, recent lineups have featured Mary Chapin Carpenter, Shawn Colvin, and James Taylor. Bluegrass Academy workshops for adults and children kick off the festival week. Call **800/624-2422** or 970/728-3041 for further information.

Telluride Jazz Celebration. Day concerts in Town Park and evening happenings in historic downtown saloons mark this 2-day event during the first week of August. Recent performers include Marleena Shaw, Paquito D'Rivera, Stanley Jordan, and Terence Blanchard.

WHERE TO STAY

Telluride's lodging rates probably have more different "seasons" than do those anywhere else in Colorado. Generally speaking you'll pay top dollar for a room over the Christmas holidays, during the film and bluegrass festivals, and at certain other peak times. Non-holiday skiing is a bit cheaper, summertime lodging (except for those festival times) is cheaper yet, and you may find some real bargains in spring and fall. The key to finding inexpensive lodging and at the same time avoiding crowds, is timing; unless you particularly want to attend the Bluegrass Festival, plan your trip to avoid visiting then. You're also much more likely to find attractive package deals on skiing and other activities if you can go during quieter times, and not on weekends.

Many of the lodging properties in Telluride (there are beds for approximately 3,900 visitors) are condominiums, managed by **Telluride Resort Accommodations** (☎ **800/538-7754** or 970/728-6621). Perhaps the best way to book lodging, however, is with **Telluride Visitor Services** (☎ **800/525-3455**), which not only represents Telluride Resort Accommodations properties, but practically all other accommodations in the area.

EXPENSIVE

✪ **The Peaks at Telluride.** 136 Country Club Dr. (P.O. Box 2702), Telluride, CO 81435. ☎ **800/789-2220** or 970/728-6800. Fax 970/728-6175. 181 rms and suites. TV TEL. $130–$435 double; $235–$585 suite. AE, DISC, MC, V. Free under cover parking; valet parking available.

Set on 6 acres in the Mountain Village above Telluride, this luxury resort is surrounded by 8,000- to 14,000-foot peaks. The lofty lobby, or Great Room, is elegantly decorated in southwestern style with beautiful leather couches, wooden tables and chairs, and handwoven rugs centered on a grand floor-to-ceiling fireplace.

Many rooms have a balcony or terrace to fully appreciate the breathtaking views of the magnificent mountains. The southwestern decor is luxurious and comfortable, all units have a stocked minibar, and there's ski-in and -out access to the ski area.

The Legends restaurant, open 6:30am to 10pm daily, offers meals costing $8 to $30. A concierge, room service, and tennis and ski valet services are available. Facilities include North America's highest championship 18-hole golf course; 42,000-square-foot spa with fitness center, heated pools, sauna, whirlpool, steam room, rock-climbing wall, KidSpa for ages 2½ to 11; day-care center; beauty salon; jeep tours; five tennis courts; mountain biking (rentals available); horseback riding; hiking; fly-fishing; cross-country skiing; snowmobiling; dogsledding.

MODERATE

Ice House Lodge and Condominiums. 310 S. Fir St. (P.O. Box 2909), Telluride, CO 81435. ☎ **800/544-3436** or 970/728-6300. Fax 970/728-6358. 42 rms. MINIBAR TV TEL. Summer $135–$260 double; Feb–Mar $185–$290 double; Christmas holidays $240–$385 double; rest of ski season $132–$270 double. Higher rates on some festival weekends. Rates include continental breakfast. AE, CB, DC, DISC, MC, V.

A full-service lodging just half a block from the Oak Street chairlift, the Ice House offers casual luxury in the European alpine style. Stairs or an elevator ascend from the ground-floor entrance to the lobby, with simple southwestern furniture. The decor carries to the guest rooms, each of which has a king bed and sleeper sofa or two full-size beds, European comforters, a 6-foot tub, and a gorgeous mountain view from a private deck. Room service from La Marmotte, the French restaurant next door, is available in season. There is a swimming pool, hot tub, and steam room on the premises.

New Sheridan Hotel. 231 W. Colorado Ave. (P.O. Box 980), Telluride, CO 81435. ☎ **800/200-1891** or 970/728-4351. Fax 970/728-5024. 32 rms (18 with bath), 6 suites. TV TEL. $75–$195 double; $155–$285 suite. Rates include breakfast. AE, CB, DC, JCB, MC, V.

The pride of Telluride when it was built in 1895, the New Sheridan reached the peak of its fame in 1902 when presidential candidate William Jennings Bryan delivered a speech from a platform outside. Decor is Victorian; roll-aways or day beds are available; and some units have whirlpool tubs. The suites, in a separate building, are condominium-style units, with full kitchen, bedrooms, and living room. The Sheridan lounge—with its Austrian-made cherrywood bar—is on the hotel's first floor. Neither pets nor smoking are permitted.

Pennington's Mountain Village Inn. 100 Pennington Court (P.O. Box 2428), Mountain Village Resort, Telluride, CO 81435. ☎ **800/543-1437** or 970/728-5337. Fax 970/728-5338. 12 rms. TV TEL. $275–$300. Rates include breakfast. AE, DISC, MC, V.

Located just off Colo. 145 at the entrance to Telluride Mountain Village, high above the San Miguel River valley, Pennington's is a luxurious getaway, the ultimate in bed-and-breakfasts, with French-country decor throughout. Every room has king or queen beds, private decks, and refrigerators stocked with beverages—included in the price of the room; and some have hot tubs. Breakfast can be served in your room (if you so choose) from 8 to 10am. There's a daily happy hour; a library lounge with books, games, and a large fireplace; billiards room; an indoor Jacuzzi and steam room; guest laundry facilities; and lockers for ski and golf equipment.

Riverside Condominiums. 450–460 S. Pine St. (P.O. Box 100), Telluride, CO 81435. ☎ **800/538-7754** or 970/728-6621. Fax 970/728-6160. 25 rms. $365–$555. Minimum stays may be required at busy times. AE, DISC, JCB, MC, V.

A luxury condo on the south bank of the San Miguel River, literally on the lower slopes of Telluride Mountain, rooms at the Riverside are among the best in town. Decor varies, but rooms typically have gas fireplaces, entertainment centers, private ski locker, private decks or balconies, steam showers, and washers and dryers. Upper-story units are especially spacious, with posh furnishings and fully stocked kitchens, complete with microwave ovens and dishwashers.

INEXPENSIVE

The Victorian Inn. 401 W. Pacific Ave. (P.O. Box 217), Telluride, CO 81435. ☎ **970/728-6601.** Fax 970/728-3233. 26 rms. TV TEL. $110–$140 double. Rates include continental breakfast. AE, CB, DISC, MC, V.

Built in 1976 in keeping with the turn-of-the-century flavor of the town of Telluride, the Victorian offers a sauna and hot tub. Rooms are fully carpeted, with individually controlled heating, queen beds, and refrigerators. There's no smoking and no pets allowed.

WHERE TO DINE

EXPENSIVE

Campagna. 435 W. Pacific Ave. ☎ **970/728-6190.** Reservations recommended. Main courses $16–$32. MC, V. Early June–early Oct and late Nov–early Apr, daily from 6pm. ITALIAN/TUSCAN.

Chef Vincent Esposito has converted an old miner's house into an open, friendly, country-style Italian restaurant. A third-generation chef, Esposito fell in love with Tuscan food while in the area studying art history. He changes the menu nightly, but it always includes wild game. Boar is a favorite, along with venison and quail.

La Marmotte. 150 W. San Juan Ave. ☎ **970/728-6232.** Reservations recommended. Main courses $17–$21. AE, DC, MC, V. Daily 6–10pm. FRENCH.

In a tiny house of exposed brick and weathered wood beside the Ice House Lodge—in fact, this building *was* Telluride's icehouse at the turn of the century—Bertrand and Nöelle Lepel-Cointet have fashioned a memorable dining experience of country-style French cuisine. You might begin with an hors d'oeuvre such as goat cheese ravioli or smoked salmon rolled with caviar. Entrees include innovative variations of grilled salmon or beef, sautéed sea bass or duck breast, roasted lamb loin, and braised veal sweetbreads.

MODERATE

Eddie's. 300 W. Colorado Ave. ☎ **970/728-5335.** Reservations not accepted. Most items $8–$20. AE, MC, V. Daily 10am–10pm. ITALIAN.

Eddie's specializes in New York–style pizza and gourmet pasta in a casually elegant atmosphere. The build-your-own pizza menu offers more than 2 dozen different toppings. Pasta includes spinach-and-chicken cannelloni, and a tortellini with smoked salmon. There are 12 microbrewery beers on tap, plus a full bar. Takeout and delivery are available.

INEXPENSIVE

Maggie's Bakery & Cafe. 217 E. Colorado Ave. ☎ **970/728-3334.** Reservations not accepted. Breakfast and lunch $2.95–$6.95. No credit cards. Daily 6:30am–4pm. VEGETARIAN/AMERICAN.

The atmosphere here is simple, with wooden tables in a rustic building, and the cuisine is geared toward natural-foods lovers. Breakfast dishes include raspberry granola and macadamia-nut oatmeal pancakes, or you can get the more traditional bacon and eggs with potatoes and fresh baked bread. Lunch possibilities include a variety of deli and vegetarian sandwiches, as well as handmade thick-crust pizza. Smoking is not permitted.

6 Ouray

Named for the greatest chief of the southern Ute tribe, whose homeland was in this area, Ouray, at 7,760 feet elevation, got its start in 1876 as a gold- and silver-mining camp, but within 10 years had 1,200 residents, a school, several churches, a hospital, and dozens of saloons and brothels. Today Ouray retains much of its 19th-century charm, with many of its original buildings still standing, and offers visitors a restful getaway while serving as home base for exploring the beautiful San Juan Mountains, with peaks rising to 14,000 feet.

ESSENTIALS

GETTING THERE   By Car   U.S. 550 runs through the heart of Ouray, connecting it with Durango to the south and—via U.S. 50, which it joins at Montrose—Grand Junction (and I-70) to the north.

ORIENTATION   As you enter from the north on U.S. 550, which parallels the Uncompahgre River, the highway passes the Ouray Hot Springs Pool and becomes known as Main Street. Most civic buildings are a block east of Main, on Sixth Avenue at Fourth Street; several motels are three blocks farther south on Third Avenue, and west on First Street. Above Third Avenue, U.S. 550 begins its climb up switchbacks to the Million Dollar Highway.

VISITOR INFORMATION   Stop in the Ouray Visitor Center beside the Hot Springs Pool, on U.S. 550 at the north end of town; or contact the **Ouray Chamber Resort Association,** P.O. Box 145, Ouray, CO 81427 (☎ **800/228-1876** or 970/325-4746). If you're planning a winter visit, be sure to ask about half-price skiing at Telluride when you stay in Ouray.

The Ouray Historical Museum (see "What to See & Do," below) has self-guided walking tour maps.

FAST FACTS   In case of **emergency,** call **911.** The **Ouray Medical Center** is on the south side of town at 302 Second Ave. (☎ **970/325-0600**). The **post office** (☎ **970/325-4302**) is at 620 Main St.

SPECIAL EVENTS   Annual events in Ouray include Cabin Fever Days, in mid-February; the Artists' Alpine Holiday, in August; and the Ouray County Fair, the first weekend of September.

WHAT TO SEE & DO

The main summertime outdoor activity here is exploring the mountains and forests, by foot, mountain bike, horse, four-wheel–drive vehicle, or even hot-air balloon. Local outfitters include **Switzerland of America,** 226 Seventh Ave. (☎ **800/432-5337** or 970/325-4484), which rents four-wheel–drive Jeeps, leads Jeep tours into the high country, and arranges horseback rides, fishing trips, raft rides, and balloon rides. Also offering four-wheel–drive tours are **San Juan Scenic Jeep Tours,** 480 Main St. (☎ **970/325-4444**).

At the southwest corner of Ouray, at Oak Street above Third Avenue, the ✪ **Box Canyon Falls** are among the most impressive in the Rockies. The Uncompahgre River tumbles 285 feet through—not over, *through*—a cliff: it's easy to get a feeling of vertigo as you study the spectacle. The trail to the bottom of the falls is easy; to the top it is strenuous. Admission to the area is $1.50 for adults, $1 for children and seniors, and it's open from mid-May to mid-October. Call **970/325-4464** or 970/325-4746 for information.

✪ **Bachelor-Syracuse Mine Tour.** 2 miles from Ouray via County Rd. 14. ☎ **970/325-0220.** $9.95 adults; $8.95 seniors 62 and older; $4.95 children under 12; free for children under 3. Mid-May–mid-Sept, 9am–5pm; shorter hours at the beginning and end of the season. Closed July 4. Reservations recommended, especially in July–Aug.

A mine train takes visitors 3,350 feet inside Gold Hill, to see where some $8-million in gold, $90 million in silver, and $5 million in other minerals have been mined since the first silver strike was made by three bachelor men in 1884. Guides, many of them former miners, explain the mining process and equipment, and recite the various legends of the mine. Also on the property is a blacksmith shop, where you can watch a blacksmith in action, and streams where you can learn the technique of gold-panning ($4.95 extra). There's also an outdoor cafe, serving an all-you-can-eat breakfast until noon and Texas-style barbecue all day. The mine temperature is a cool 50°, so jackets or sweaters are recommended even in summer.

Ouray County Museum. 420 Sixth Ave. ☎ **970/325-4576.** Admission $4 adults; $2 children 5–12. May–mid-June and early Sept–mid-Oct, Mon–Sat 10am–4pm, Sun 1–4pm; mid-June–early Sept, Mon–Fri 9am–6pm, Sat 9am–5pm, Sun 1–5pm; mid-Oct–Apr, Fri–Mon 1–4pm.

Lodged in the original Miners' Hospital, built in 1887 by the Sisters of Mercy, this three-story museum is packed to the rafters with fascinating exhibits from Ouray's past. Displays include pioneer and mining-era relics, memorabilia of Chief Ouray and the Utes, turn-of-the-century hospital equipment including some scary-looking medical devices, photographs, and other historic materials. Ask here for a walking-tour guide to the town's many historic buildings.

Ouray Hot Springs Pool. U.S. 550, at the north end of Ouray. ☎ **970/325-4638** or 970/325-4746. Admission $6 adults, $4.50 students 7–17, $3 children 3–6, and $5 seniors 65 and older. Summer Mon–Sat 10am–10pm, Sun 10am–8pm; winter Wed–Mon noon–9pm.

This pool, 250 feet long and 150 feet wide, holds nearly a million gallons of odorless mineral water. Spring water is cooled from 150°F; the pool is normally 80°F, but there's a hot soak of 104°F.

WHERE TO STAY

Ouray Victorian Inn. 50 Third Ave. (P.O. Box 1812), Ouray, CO 81427. ☎ **800/846-8729** or 970/325-7222. Fax 970/325-7225. 34 rms, 14 junior and one-bedroom suites. TV TEL. $49–$90 double; $75–$120 one-bedroom suites (up to four persons). AE, DC, DISC, MC, V.

Located in Ouray's National Historic District, this Victorian-style inn offers spacious rooms with outstanding views, in-room coffee, sun deck, and two outdoor hot tubs. Suites have either kitchenettes or full kitchens, and there are also four junior suites. A complimentary buffet breakfast is offered in winter.

St. Elmo Hotel. 426 Main St. (P.O. Box 667), Ouray, CO 81427. ☎ **970/325-4951.** Fax 970/325-0348. 9 rms. Summer and Christmas holidays, $88–$98 double; winter $62–$85 double. Rates include breakfast buffet. AE, DISC, MC, V.

An 1898 town landmark, restored to Victorian splendor, the St. Elmo has an old-fashioned lobby that's a meeting place for locals and guests alike. Its rooms contain many original furnishings. Throughout are stained glass, polished wood, and brass trim. There's a television in the parlor, and an outdoor hot tub and sauna for guests. All rooms are nonsmoking, and pets are not accepted. On the premises is the Bon Ton Restaurant (see "Where to Dine," below).

Wiesbaden Hot Springs Spa & Lodgings. Sixth Ave. and Fifth St. (P.O. Box 349), Ouray, CO 81427. ☎ **970/325-4347.** Fax 970/325-4358. 18 rms and suites, 5 cottages. TV TEL. $85–$100 double; $120–$150 suites and cottages; $12 per extra person. DISC, MC, V.

Built over a continually flowing hot-springs vapor cave, the Wiesbaden need never worry about artificial heating. The swimming pool, though outdoors, is open year-round and heated to between 95°F and 102°F; herbal wraps, Moor mud wraps, massages, facials, and other spa services are available. There's also a fitness center, float tank with sensory deprivation, and a "flow-through" Jacuzzi. The original structure was built in 1879, and today's rooms have an "old-country" ambiance with historic photographs on the walls. Some rooms with outside entrances have small refrigerators and coffeemakers.

WHERE TO DINE

Bon Ton Restaurant. In the St. Elmo Hotel, 426 Main St. ☎ **970/325-4951.** Reservations recommended. Main courses $9–$22.50. AE, DISC, MC, V. Daily 5–9pm; Sun 9:30am–1pm. ITALIAN.

A fixture in Ouray for more than a century—it had another location before moving into the St. Elmo Hotel basement in 1898—the Bon Ton is Ouray's finest. With stone outer walls, hardwood floors, and reproduction antique furnishings, it carries a Victorian rustic appeal. The menu, which varies nightly, includes a variety of pasta dishes, from tortellini carbonara to ravioli pesto; a "miner's medley" of sautéed veal, sausage, and chicken on fettucine; and various beef, veal, chicken, and fresh seafood dishes. There's a children's menu too.

Silver Nugget Cafe. 740 Main St. ☎ **970/325-4100.** Reservations recommended. Breakfast $2.50–$6; lunch $4.25–$6; dinner $5–$14. No credit cards. Daily 7am–10pm (closes 8pm in winter). AMERICAN.

A clean, contemporary eatery, the Silver Nugget occupies a historic building at the north end of Ouray. You can get a Denver omelet or huevos rancheros for breakfast, and a wide variety of deli-style sandwiches for lunch. The dinner menu runs the gamut from liver and onions to fish-and-chips, rib-eye steak to stuffed pork chops.

OURAY AFTER DARK

For summertime evening entertainment you've got two excellent choices. **Gary Davis's My Country—Chipeta Opry Show,** 630 Main St. (☎ **970/325-7354**), billed as an "all-American family musical revue," is a fast-paced 2 hours of music, comedy, an unbelievable Elvis revue, and a bang-up patriotic finale. A popular multimedia show, **San Juan Odyssey** (☎ **970/325-4020**) is presented in the historic Wright Opera House at Fifth and Main streets. The 35-minute program features spectacular five-screen panoramic photography of the area, using 15 computer-synchronized projectors and surround-sound stereo. Call for current schedules and prices.

7 Pagosa Springs

Pagosa (Ute for "boiling waters") took its name from the thermal springs that spurt from the ground at 146°. There was no major white settlement here until 1878, when Fort Lewis was constructed to help control the Utes. The town was incorporated in 1891, and although the spa never became a great commercial success, Pagosa Springs grew as an important lumbering area. Today it's a major recreational center, with hiking, camping, and fishing in summer, downhill and cross-country skiing, snowboarding, snowshoeing, and snowmobiling in winter. The hot mineral baths are fast becoming a great favorite of visitors.

ESSENTIALS

GETTING THERE   By Car   U.S. 160 connects Pagosa Springs with Durango and points west, and Alamosa and points east. It's also at the junction of U.S. 84, which runs south to Santa Fe, N. Mex.

ORIENTATION   The town is located on the banks of the San Juan River, which flows southwest from Wolf Creek Pass, eventually joining the Colorado River in Utah. Pagosa Street (U.S. 160) parallels the river through downtown until the river turns south. Hot Springs Boulevard, which crosses the river opposite Town Park, passes the Pagosa hot springs. U.S. 84 intersects U.S. 160 at the eastern edge of the town.

VISITOR INFORMATION   Consult the **Pagosa Springs Chamber of Commerce,** P.O. Box 787, Pagosa Springs, CO 81147 (☎ **800/252-2204** or 970/264-2360). The chamber has a Visitor Center on the south bank of the San Juan River at Hot Springs Boulevard, across from Town Park, which has picnic tables and a river walk.

FAST FACTS   In case of **emergency,** dial **911.** The **post office** (☎ **970/264-5440**) is on Hot Springs Boulevard three blocks south of U.S. 160. For road and weather conditions call 970/264-5555.

SPECIAL EVENTS   The Spanish Fiesta is held in mid-June; the Mountain Man Rendezvous takes place in late June; the Red Ryder Roundup and Rodeo is held on the Fourth of July weekend; the Archuleta County Fair is the first weekend in August; and Colorfest and the Hot Air Balloon Rally take place in late September.

SPORTS & OUTDOOR ACTIVITIES

Although it's not particularly well known outside the state, the **Wolf Creek** ski area is famous throughout Colorado as the area that consistently has the most snow in the state. In fact, it has an annual average of 465 inches (almost 39 ft.) of powder.

One of the state's oldest ski areas, Wolf Creek has terrain for skiers of all ability levels, but especially intermediates. The mountain has 50 trails served by five lifts (two triple chairs, two doubles, and a Poma). The Wolf Creek Lodge has restaurant and bar service, and ski sales and rentals.

For information, contact **Wolf Creek Ski Area,** U.S. 160, 25 miles east of Pagosa Springs (P.O. Box 2800), Pagosa Springs, CO 81147 (☎ **970/264-5629** for a ski report, or 970/264-5639 for the business office; fax 970/264-5732).

Surrounded by the two-million-acre San Juan National Forest, Pagosa Springs is an ideal base camp for hiking, horseback riding, mountain biking, rafting, fishing, hunting, and photography. Check with the **Pagosa Ranger District,** 180 Pagosa St. at Second St. (P.O. Box 310), Pagosa Springs, CO 81147 (☎ **970/264-2268**), for maps and other information. The chamber of commerce (see "Visitor Information," above) also has several free brochures describing hiking and mountain biking trails and other recreation possibilities.

Among local companies that provide **mountain-bike rentals, service, and guided tours** are **Pedal the Peaks** (☎ **800/743-3843**). Bike rentals cost about $15 for a half day, and a 3-hour tour costs $35. For those who prefer their travel by **horseback,** licensed outfitters that provide guided horseback rides in San Juan National Forest and Weminuche Wilderness Area include **Wolf Creek Outfitters** (☎ **970/264-5332**). Rides cost about $15 per hour or $70 per day. All ages and levels of riding ability are welcome, and the company also offers overnight pack trips, and fishing and hunting trips.

The San Juan and Piedra rivers are popular with **rafters.** One Pagosa Springs company that provides river trips is **Pagosa Rafting Outfitters & Wilderness Journeys** (☎ **970/731-4081**), with rates for raft trips from $27 to $100. The company also offers mountaineering and four-wheel–drive excursions.

Enthusiasts of **winter sports** will find plenty of snow and ample opportunities to play in it. In addition to the Wolf Creek ski area, **San Juan National Forest** (☎ 970/264-2268) has miles of trails and forest roads that lead **cross-country skiers, snowshoers, and snowmobilers** through tall firs and pines to spectacular vistas. Guided snowmobile tours ($45 for 1 hour, $70 for 2 hours) are available from Wolf Creek Outfitters (☎ 970/264-5332).

SEEING THE SIGHTS

A free brochure, available at the San Juan Historical Society Pioneer Museum (see below) or chamber of commerce, includes a map locating and describing 16 historic buildings or sites and the hot springs.

Chimney Rock Archaeological Area. About 20 miles southwest of Pagosa Springs via U.S. 160 and Colo. 151. ☎ 970/883-5359 or 970/264-2268. Admission $4 adults, $2 children 6–12, free for children under 6. Daily May 15–Sept 30. Call for tour times.

Home and sacred shrine to the Anasazi 1,000 years ago, this area, now managed by the U.S. Forest Service, is one of the most unique archaeological sites in the Four Corners region. Two developed trails lead to both excavated and undisturbed ruins of an ancient village, perched on a high mesa. One is an easy one-third-mile paved trail while the other is about a half mile, but more challenging, with loose rock. A Forest Service fire lookout tower offers an excellent view of the ruins. The site is open only to those who take 2-hour guided tours, offered four times daily during the summer.

Fred Harman Art Museum. 2560 W. U.S. 160, 2 miles west of downtown Pagosa Springs. ☎ 970/731-5785. Admission $1 adults, 50¢ children under 6. Summer, Mon–Sat 10:30am– 5pm, Sun 12:30–4pm; winter, Mon–Fri 10:30am–5pm, weekends by appointment.

Located in the artist's home, the museum features original works of Fred Harman and a collection of memorabilia from his life in the area. Harmon was one of five founders of the Cowboy Artists of America and creator of the "Red Ryder" and "Little Beaver" comic strips, which ran from 1938 to 1962 in over 750 newspapers on three continents.

Pagosa Hot Springs. Hot Springs Blvd., south of the San Juan River.

Here's the source of those great mineral baths and pools at several local motels (see below), which for years have lured those seeking cures for a large variety of ills. Designated a State Historic Site, the springs are privately owned and fenced, but several large signs give the mineral content of the 146° water and explain the geology of the area.

San Juan Historical Society Pioneer Museum. First and Pagosa Sts. ☎ 970/264-4424. Admission $1 adults, 50¢ children 6–18, free for children under 6 (suggested donations). Memorial Day–Labor Day Tues–Sat 10am–5pm.

Exhibits explain local history with a vast collection of antiques, memorabilia, and photos. There's also a replica of an old-time schoolroom and a blacksmith shop.

WHERE TO STAY

✪ **Echo Manor Inn.** 3366 U.S. 84, Pagosa Springs, CO 81147. ☎ 800/628-5004 or 970/ 264-5646. 10 rms (7 with bath), 1 suite. $55–$70 with shared bath, $65–$100 with private bath, $160–$280 suite. Rates include breakfast. AE, MC, V.

This four-story Dutch Tudor–style inn, with turrets, towers, and gables, is a delightful bed-and-breakfast, with its various rooms and suite all having very distinctive personalities. Rooms are comfortable, with country furnishings and little nooks and crannies everywhere—a good house for a game of hide-and-seek. The suite can accommodate up to 12, with its own kitchen, perfect for small family reunions. Owners Maureen and John Widmer serve quiche and a variety of other homemade breakfasts. There's a common family room and an outside deck with hot tub and Jacuzzi. The inn is not disabled accessible. Neither pets nor smoking are permitted inside.

Pagosa Lodge. U.S. 160 (P.O. Box 2050), Pagosa Springs, CO 81147. ☎ **800/523-7704** or 970/731-4141. Fax 970/731-4141. 100 rms and suites. A/C TV TEL. $75–$95 double; $130–$145 suite. AE, CB, DC, DISC, MC, V.

Located 3¹/₂ miles west of downtown Pagosa Springs, this lodge has a health spa, basketball and volleyball courts, and fishing. An 18-hole golf course is next door, and cross-country skiing is not far. Rooms have terrific views of the mountains to the north. There is a restaurant, lounge, heated indoor swimming pool, sauna, and whirlpool.

The Spring Inn. 165 Hot Springs Blvd. (P.O. Box 1799), Pagosa Springs, CO 81147. ☎ **800/225-0934** or 970/264-4168. Fax 970/264-4707. 21 rms, 3 suites, 1 cabin. A/C TV TEL. $54–$84 double; $74–$115 suites and cabin. CB, DC, DISC, MC, V.

Six outdoor hot tubs, open year-round and overlooking the San Juan River, provide therapeutic mineral baths with water from the nearby hot springs. Rooms have two entrances—to the parking area and to an inner hallway. There's a ski and sport shop and health club with massage. Small-to-medium–sized pets are accepted.

WHERE TO DINE

Branding Iron Bar-B-Q. 3 miles east of Pagosa Springs on Colo. Hwy. 160. ☎ **970/264-4268.** Reservations accepted for parties of six or more. Most items $2.25–$17.95. DISC, MC, V. Mon–Sat 11am–8pm. Closed Dec–Mar. BARBECUE.

You don't have to go to Texas for great barbecue. Here you'll find delicious barbecued ribs, along with barbecued chicken and brisket. This is an informal restaurant, where the toast gets branded and kids get to straddle little saddles instead of sitting in chairs. Save some room for dessert—owner Ed Campbell's chocolate-icebox pie took first place at the local county fair.

Greenhouse Restaurant & Bar. 505 Piedra Rd. ☎ **970/731-2021.** Reservations recommended. Main courses $10–$20. AE, CB, DISC, DC, MC, V. Sun–Thurs 5–9pm, Fri–Sat 5–10pm. NEW AMERICAN.

Creative variations on old favorites are what to expect at this upscale restaurant, with a menu that includes prime rib, fresh seafood, pasta, and vegetarian items. The emphasis is on fresh and natural, such as the use of organically produced beef and poultry and freshly grown herbs. The menu changes seasonally, with lighter selections in the summer, game during hunting season, and so forth. Outdoor dining was added for summer 1996, with dramatic views of the San Juan Mountains.

✪ **Rolling Pin Bakery & Cafe.** 214 Pagosa St. ☎ **970/264-2255.** Reservations not accepted. Breakfast $2–$5; lunch $4–$6. No credit cards. Mon–Sat 7am–5:30pm. AMERICAN.

The bakery is the king here, which you will quickly see as you sit at breakfast and watch just about everyone in Pagosa Springs stop in and walk away with a bag of buns, rolls, pastries, or whatever. Of course, it won't bother you, because you'll be eating the same, while sipping some of the restaurant's gourmet coffee. Lunches are good too, with quiches, burgers, salads, soups, and a variety of sandwiches and subs.

The Southern Rockies

14

If Colorado is the rooftop of America, then the southern Rockies are the peak of that roof. Some 30 of Colorado's fourteeners—14,000-foot-plus peaks—ring the area, and from Monarch Pass, at 11,312 feet, rivers flow in three directions.

Isolated from the rest of Colorado by its high mountains and rugged canyons, this region has historically bred proud, independent-minded people. In the 18th century, settlers came from what is now Taos, New Mexico, and built some of the region's striking Spanish architecture. To this day, the influence of these Spanish speakers remains strong, particularly in the San Luis Valley and Colorado's oldest town of San Luis, incorporated in 1851.

Today these mountain and river towns have earned a reputation as recreational capitals: Gunnison for fishing and hunting, Crested Butte for skiing and mountain biking, and Salida and Buena Vista for white-water rafting. Alamosa is within easy reach of numerous scenic attractions, including the remarkable Great Sand Dunes National Monument. In the foothills of the San Juan Range are the fascinating old mining towns of Creede and Lake City, and in the tiny community of Antonito you can hop a narrow-gauge steam train for a trip back to a simpler, but smokier time. This is a rugged and sparsely populated land, with numerous opportunities for seeing the wilds of mountain America at their best.

1 Gunnison & Curecanti National Recreation Area

A rough-and-ready western town, Gunnison is where you go to get a hot shower and a good meal after a week of camping, hiking, boating, or hunting in the rugged mountains and canyons that surround the town.

Utes began hunting here in the middle of the 17th century, and although Spanish explorers probably never penetrated this isolated region, mountain men, pursuing pelts, certainly had arrived by the 1830s. First mapped by U.S. Army captain John Gunnison in 1853, the town was established in 1874, soon growing into a ranching center and transportation hub for nearby silver and gold mines. Western State College was established in 1911; now with an enrollment of 2,500, it is the only college in the United States with a certified technical-evacuation mountain-rescue team.

ESSENTIALS

GETTING THERE **By Car** Gunnison is located on U.S. 50, midway between Montrose and Salida. From Denver, the most direct route is U.S. 285 southwest to Poncha Springs (near Salida), then west on U.S. 50. From Grand Junction, follow U.S. 50 through Montrose.

By Plane The **Gunnison County Airport,** 711 Rio Grande Ave. (☎ 970/641-2304), is just off U.S. 50, a few blocks south of downtown Gunnison. **United Express** (☎ 800/241-6522 or 970/641-0111) provides daily year-round service from Denver. During nearby Crested Butte's winter ski season, **Delta** (☎ 800/221-1212) flies direct from Atlanta, and **American Airlines** (☎ 800/433-7300) direct from Dallas/Fort Worth.

Alpine Express (☎ 800/822-4844 or 970/641-5074) provides shuttle service from Gunnison County Airport to Crested Butte and Telluride. It runs frequently during ski season, but call for availability at other times.

ORIENTATION The town is built on the southeast banks of the west-flowing Gunnison River. Tomichi Avenue (U.S. 50) runs east-west through town. Main Street (Colo. 135) intersects Tomichi Avenue in the center of town and proceeds north to Crested Butte. The campus of Western State College is three blocks north of Tomichi Avenue and four blocks east of Main Street.

VISITOR INFORMATION Contact the **Gunnison County Chamber of Commerce,** 500 E. Tomichi Ave. (P.O. Box 36), Gunnison, CO 81230 (☎ 800/274-7580 or 970/641-1501).

GETTING AROUND Car-rental agencies at Gunnison County Airport include **Avis** (☎ 970/641-0263), **Budget** (☎ 970/641-4403), and **Hertz** (☎ 970/641-2881).

FAST FACTS In case of **emergency,** call **911. Gunnison Valley Hospital** is at 214 E. Denver Ave. (☎ 970/641-1456), two blocks east of Main Street and six blocks north of U.S. 50. The **post office** (☎ 970/641-1884) is at Virginia Avenue and Wisconsin Street. For **road conditions,** call 970/641-8008. **Local sales tax** is about 7%.

SPECIAL EVENTS Annual events in Gunnison include the Gunnison County Airshow in mid-June; Cattlemen's Days and Rodeo, Colorado's oldest continually held rodeo, in the third week in July; and the Parade of Lights, in early December.

CURECANTI NATIONAL RECREATION AREA

Dams on the Gunnison River, just below Gunnison, have created a series of three very different reservoirs, extending 35 miles to the mouth of the Black Canyon of the Gunnison (see "Montrose & Black Canyon of the Gunnison National Monument," in chapter 12). **Blue Mesa Lake** (elevation 7,519 ft.), the easternmost (beginning 9 miles west of Gunnison), is the largest lake in Colorado when filled to capacity, and a water-sports paradise popular for fishing, motorboating, sailboating, board sailing, and other activities. Fjord-like **Morrow Point Lake** (elevation 7,160 ft.) and **Crystal Lake** (elevation 6,755 ft.) fill long, serpentine canyons accessible only by precipitous trails and thus are limited to use by hand-carried boats.

These lakes offer some of Colorado's best boating; rentals can be arranged at **Elk Creek Marina** on Blue Mesa Lake, 16 miles west of Gunnison off U.S. 50

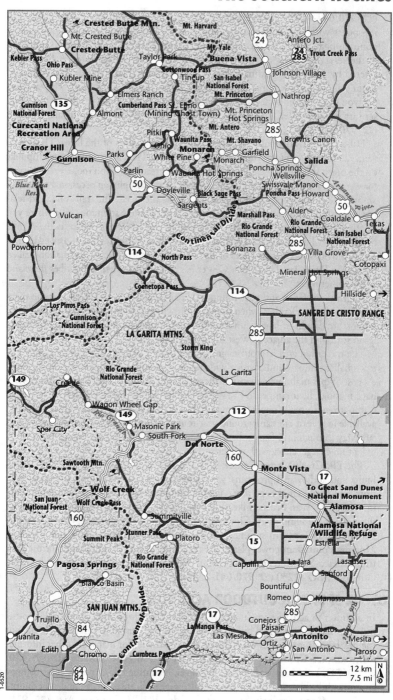

Crested Butte Mtn.
Mt. Harvard
Mt. Crested Butte
Antero Jct.
Crested Butte
24
24 285 Trout Creek Pass
Kebler Pass
Mt. Yale
Ohio Pass
Taylor Park
Buena Vista
Kubler Mine
Cottonwood Pass
Johnson Village
Tincup
San Isabel
National Forest
Elmers Ranch
Mt. Princeton
Nathrop
Gunnison 135
Cumberland Pass St. Elmo
National Forest
(Mining Ghost Town)
Almont
Mt. Princeton
Hot Springs
Curecanti National
Recreation Area
Pitkin
Mt. Antero
285
Cranor Hill
Waunita Pass
Mt. Shavano
Browns Canon
Ohio
Gunnison
Parks
White Pine
Garfield
Salida
Parlin
Monarch
Poncha Springs
Blue Mesa
Res.
Doyleville
Waunita Hot Springs
Wellsville
Swissvale Manor
50
Black Sage Pass
Poncha Pass Howard
Vulcan
Sargents
Marshall Pass
Alder
50
Continental Divide
Rio Grande
National Forest
Rio Grande
National Forest
Coaldale
Texas
Creek
San Isabel
National Forest
Powderhorn
114
North Pass
Bonanza
285
Villa Grove
Cotopaxi
Mineral Hot Springs
Cochetopa Pass
114
Hillside
Los Pinos Pass
SANGRE DE CRISTO RANGE
Gunnison
National Forest
285
LA GARITA MTNS.
Storm King
Rio Grande
National Forest
La Garita
149
Creede
Wagon Wheel Gap
112
149
Masonic Park
Spar City
South Fork
Sawtooth Mtn.
Del Norte
160
Wolf Creek
Monte Vista
17
Wolf Creek Pass
To Great Sand Dunes
National Monument
San Juan
National Forest
Summitville
Alamosa
160
Stunner Pass
Alamosa National
Wildlife Refuge
Summit Peak
Platoro
Estrella
Rio Grande
National Forest
15
Pagosa Springs
Capulin
La Jara
Lasauses
Blanco Basin
Sanford
Bountiful
SAN JUAN MTNS.
Romeo
Manassa
Trujillo
285
Conejos
84
17
Paisaje
Antonito
Juanita
La Manga Pass
Las Mesitas
Lobatos
Mesita
Edith
Chromo
Ortiz
San Antonio
Jaroso
64
84
Cumbres Pass
17

0   12 km
         7.5 mi

1-0520

(☎ 970/641-0707). Rates are about $10 per hour or $50 per day for small fishing boats with outboard motors, and about $25 per hour or $135 per day for pontoon boats. There's a second marina at Lake Fork, 25 miles west of Gunnison, at the reservoir's west end (☎ 970/641-3084), with similar rates. A **boat tour,** offered by Elk Creek Marina, leaves the Pine Creek Trail boat dock on Morrow Point Lake daily, Memorial Day through Labor Day, to explore the Upper Black Canyon of the Gunnison. Rates are $9.50 for adults, $8.50 for youths 13 to 17 and seniors 62 and older, and $6 for children under 13. Reservations are required (☎ **970/641-0402**).

Hikers find a variety of trails, often with splendid views of the lakes. Those who want to see birds can't go wrong with the Neversink Trail, a 1 1/2-mile round-trip hike on the north shore of the Gunnison River near a great blue heron rookery. Also watch for warblers, red-wing blackbirds, and great horned owls, plus an occasional mule deer among the cottonwoods and willows that shade the river. The trail is flat and relatively easy, and also provides fishing access. A moderately strenuous hike where you might see a golden eagle or two, and possibly some bighorn sheep, is the 4 mile round-trip Dillon Pinnacles Trail, which is open to horseback riders as well as hikers. It provides spectacular views of the strangely eroded volcanic formations called the Dillon Pinnacles. The Visitor Center has a free brochure that describes these and several other hikes.

Anglers visit Curecanti year-round—there's ice fishing in winter—but the main season is May to October, when rainbow, brown, and Mackinaw trout and kokanee salmon are caught in large numbers. Hunting, especially for elk and deer, is popular in season in the adjacent West Elk Mountains.

The recreation area has four major campgrounds, with almost 350 sites, plus several smaller campgrounds, with a wide range of facilities. Campgrounds with showers cost $9 per night, while most of those without showers cost $8 per night. Several have marinas, boat ramps, and R.V. dump stations, but there are no R.V. hookups. Campgrounds usually remain open until blocked by snow, and there are usually sites available in at least one campground year-round, although water is available only from late May through mid-September. Backcountry and boat-in camping is also permitted, at no charge; check with rangers.

The **Elk Creek Visitor Center,** 15 miles west of Gunnison off U.S. 50, has exhibits and audiovisual programs, as well as maps and publications. It's open daily from mid-May to mid-September, usually from 8am to 6pm, but only intermittently the rest of the year. Nature hikes and evening campground programs are presented throughout the summer. At **Cimarron,** 45 miles west of Gunnison, there's an information center (open in summer only) with a historic train exhibit and a road to **Morrow Point Dam** power plant. For a brochure and other information before your trip, contact: Superintendent, Curecanti National Recreation Area, 102 Elk Creek, Gunnison, CO 81230 (☎ **970/641-2337**).

OTHER SPORTS & OUTDOOR ACTIVITIES

In addition to activities in Curecanti National Recreation Area, there are opportunities for hiking, mountain biking, hunting, fishing, camping, and four-wheeling in the nearby national forest, which surrounds the town. For maps and other information, contact **Gunnison National Forest** at 216 N. Colorado St. (☎ 970/641-0471). Your best bet for sporting goods, including hiking boots, cross-country and downhill ski rentals, fishing and hunting gear, licenses, maps, and other information is **Gene Taylor's Sporting Goods,** 201 W. Tomichi Ave. (☎ 970/641-1845).

FISHING   The Gunnison River, both above and below town, and the tributary Taylor River, which joins the Gunnison at Almont, 11 miles north of town, are outstanding trout streams. In addition, the region's lakes are also rich in fish. **Willowfly Anglers,** at Three Rivers Resort, Almont (☎ **970/641-1303**), offers fly-fishing instruction, rentals, and guide service. Full-day float fishing trips cost $140 for one person and $180 for two, and walking trips are also available. **Elk Creek Marina** on Blue Mesa Lake (☎ **970/641-0707**), offers guided fishing trips in the Black Canyon of the Gunnison. Rates, which include guide, boat, lunch, and fishing poles and tackle, are about $150 for one person, $225 for two, and $300 for three. Ask at the chamber of commerce about other guide services, and for a free copy of the chamber's *Gunnison County Angling Guide.*

GOLF   The 18-hole **Dos Rios Country Club,** County Road 33, off U.S. 50 southwest of town (☎ **970/641-1482**), charges $20 for nine holes and $30 for 18 holes, and also has a driving range and practice facility.

HORSEBACK RIDING   **Tenderfoot Outfitter and Guide Services,** P.O. Box 246, Gunnison, CO 81230 (☎ **970/641-0504**), offers guided horseback rides into the West Elk Wilderness Area in the Gunnison National Forest, with rates of about $18 per hour or $90 for a full day, including lunch. Also offering horseback rides in the area is **Ferro's Trading Post,** P.O. Box 853, Gunnison, CO 81230 (☎ **970/641-4671**), with rates of about $13 per hour or $40 for a half-day. Pack trips are also available, starting at $100 per day. Ferro's is located on Soap Creek Road, about 26 miles west of Gunnison, overlooking Blue Mesa Reservoir.

RIVER RAFTING & KAYAKING   For trips on the Gunnison and other rivers, check with **Three Rivers Resort and Outfitting,** 11 miles north of Gunnison on Taylor Canyon Road, (P.O. Box 339, Almont, CO 81210 (☎ **970/641-1303**). Rates for 2-hour raft trips over relatively calm stretches are $14 for adults and $10 for children under 12; and for white-water trips run $45 to $60 per person, with a minimum age of 12. Three Rivers also offers guided white-water trips in inflatable kayaks called "duckies," with a minimum age of 16, and rates of $20 for 2 hours and $65 for a full day, which includes lunch.

SKIING   The two major winter-sports centers in the area are **Crested Butte** Mountain Resort, 32 miles north on Colo. 135 (see Section 2 of this chapter) and **Monarch** Ski Resort, 44 miles east on U.S. 50.

AN INTERESTING MUSEUM

Pioneer Museum. S. Adams St. and U.S. 50. ☎ **970/641-4530** or 970/641-0740. Admission $4 adults, $1 children 6–12, free for children under 6. Memorial Day–Labor Day, Mon–Sat 9am–5pm.

A Denver & Rio Grande narrow-gauge steam train, depot, and water tank are on display at this historical society museum. Other exhibits include a rural school house (circa 1905), 19th-century furnishings, minerals and arrowheads, antique cars and wagons, dolls, toys, and Gunnison's first post office (1876).

WHERE TO STAY

Major chain and franchise motels that provide reasonably priced lodging in Gunnison include the **Best Western Tomichi Village Inn,** on U.S. 50, 1 mile east of Gunnison (☎ **800/641-1131** or 970/641-1131), charging double rates of $70 to $90 in summer and $50 to $72 in winter; **Gunnison Super 8,** 411 E. Tomichi Ave., Gunnison (☎ **800/800-8000** or 970/641-3068), with rooms from $55 to $85 in summer and $45 to $72 in winter; and **Holiday Inn Express,** 400 E. Tomichi Ave., Gunnison

The Chief, the Miner, His Traveling Companions, and the Cooks Who Keep His Memory Alive: The Bizarre Tale of Alferd Packer

The winter of 1873 to 1874 was bad in southwest Colorado's San Juan Mountains—deep snow, staggeringly strong winds, and below-zero temperatures. But among the many miners who found themselves there, drawn by the hope of staking a claim among the region's newly discovered silver deposits, the temptation to change their fortunes in a day was just too powerful to resist. In February, six eager miners, led by Alferd Packer, set out from a Ute encampment near the present-day town of Delta, ignoring warnings from Ouray, chief of the Ute people. They took only 10 days' worth of food and weren't heard from for over 2 months, until Packer arrived alone at Los Piños Indian Agency, about 25 miles south of the present town of Gunnison.

Packer told Indian Agency officials that after he became ill, his companions abandoned him, and he survived on roots and bushes while making his way through the mountains. Curiously, he refused food upon his arrival. After resting, Packer traveled to the nearby community of Saguache, where he went on a drinking binge, paying with money from several wallets.

Since Packer had claimed to be penniless when the six men left the Ute encampment, and because Packer was the only one to return, Indian Agency officials became suspicious. Then, strips of what appeared to be human flesh were discovered along the path Packer had taken to the agency. Under questioning, Packer changed his story, claiming that others in the party had killed their companions, one by one, as they traveled, until only Packer and fellow miner Wilson Bell remained, and Packer was forced to kill Bell in self defense. Packer admitted eating the remains of his companions and was arrested and jailed.

That August, Packer escaped from jail, just about the time that five partially decomposed bodies were discovered along the northeast side of Lake San Cristobal, a few miles south of the present town of Lake City. Four of the men had apparently

---

(☎ **800/GUNNISON, 800/HOLIDAY,** or 970/641-1288), which charges $60 to $95 in summer and $50 to $88 in winter.

Mary Lawrence Inn. 601 N. Taylor St., Gunnison, CO 81230. ☎ **970/641-3343.** 3 rms, 2 suites. $69–$74 double; $89 and up suite. Rates include full breakfast. MC, V.

Built in 1885 and named for its longtime owner, the Mary Lawrence Inn is located in a quiet neighborhood near Western State College. Rooms are individually decorated with period furnishings, some four-poster beds, colorful quilts, and sponge-painted and stenciled walls. Creative breakfasts are served, with an assortment of juices, hot teas, and gourmet coffees. There's a large outdoor deck and yard, as well as a cozy sunroom. Children six and older are welcome, and smoking is not permitted inside.

Wildwood Motel. 1312 W. Tomichi Ave., Gunnison, CO 81230. ☎ **970/641-1663.** 18 units. TV TEL. $42–$49 double. Fishing and hunting packages available. DISC, MC, V.

Built in 1928 as a summer refuge for members of the Chicago underworld, the Wildwood today is a favorite hideaway for budget-conscious outdoor sports lovers. Rooms here aren't fancy, but they're very quiet, very clean and well maintained, and all include a kitchen nook with refrigerator. The grounds contain a play area, horseshoe

been murdered in their sleep, their heads split open with an ax, while a fifth had been shot. Chunks of flesh had been cut from at least two of the men's chests and thighs, and one was decapitated.

The search for Packer was now on in earnest, but he was nowhere to be found. Finally, about 9 years later, Packer was discovered living in Wyoming, using the name John Schwartz. Packer was arrested, and in April 1883, tried on a charge of premeditated murder, convicted, and sentenced to hang. That would have been the end of Packer, but the trial was declared unconstitutional on a technicality.

Packer was retried in 1886, convicted on five counts of manslaughter, and sentenced to 45 years in prison. However, due to poor health, Packer was pardoned by Governor Charles Thomas after only 5 years behind bars. He died of natural causes in the Denver area in 1907, at the age of 64, and was buried in the Littleton Cemetery. As an interesting aside, all through his life Packer's first name, Alferd, had been misspelled. Apparently, it was a problem that followed him into death, since today the name "Alfred" is prominently displayed on his tombstone.

Though many at the time considered it an open-and-shut case, some have questioned whether Packer was really guilty of murder, or if he was simply convicted because of the public's revulsion at his admission of cannibalism. In 1989, the bodies were exhumed, and it was determined that they had likely been victims of cannibalism; but no evidence has shown definitively that Packer killed them.

The site where the bodies were found is now known as Cannibal Plateau, and the surrounding community of Lake City (see "A Side Trip to Lake City," later in this chapter) commemorates the events with its annual Memorial Day weekend Alferd Packer Barbecue Cookoff, featuring coffin races, a dance, and a barbecue contest with four categories: chicken, pork, beef, and other.

pit, picnic tables, fish-cleaning station, and two duck ponds, where Tasmanian rainbow trout are raised for release into the Gunnison River. Pets may be accepted by prior arrangement.

CAMPING

There are campgrounds in Curecanti National Recreation Area (see above), as well as Gunnison.

Mesa Campground. 36128 W. U.S. 50, Gunnison, CO 81230. ☎ **800/482-8384** or 970/641-3186. 135 sites. $15 tent, $16.50 full R.V. hookup. DISC, MC, V. Closed Nov–Apr.

A good base camp for fishing, hunting, or sightseeing trips, this campground and R.V. park 3 miles west of Gunnison has grassy, shaded sites, and clean bathhouses with plenty of hot water. There's a self-service laundry; gas pumps; and a store with propane, groceries, and some R.V. supplies.

WHERE TO DINE

✪ **Cattlemen Inn.** 301 W. Tomichi Ave. ☎ **970/641-1061.** Reservations not accepted. Breakfast $1.50–$7; lunch $3–$7; dinner $6–$23. CB, DC, MC, V. Daily 6:30am–3pm and 5–9pm. AMERICAN.

Beef is the specialty here—only the best hand-cut steer beef—so you can bet you'll thoroughly enjoy your steak, prime rib, or even burger. There are two dining rooms; the downstairs one with attached bar has the look of a western steak house, with lots of rough wood, while the upstairs is more family-oriented. For breakfast, you can get all the standard selections, plus Southwest variations. Lunches include lots of sandwiches, fish-and-chips, burritos, pinto bean soup, and a salad bar. And at dinner, in addition to the great steaks, you can get many of the lunch items, plus trout, broiled chicken breast, and deep-fried breaded shrimp.

Josef's Restaurant. U.S. 50, 1¹/₂ miles east of Gunnison. ☎ **970/641-5032.** Reservations recommended at dinner. Main courses lunch $5–$9, dinner $6–$18. AE, CB, DC, DISC, MC, V. Mon–Fri 11am–2pm; daily 5–9pm. CONTINENTAL/GERMAN.

An Old World atmosphere pervades this fine restaurant adjacent to the Best Western Tomichi Village at the east end of town. The menu features a variety of charbroiled steaks, poultry, pasta, and fresh seafood, but the house specialties are true German, including traditional Wiener schnitzel and Bavarian sauerbraten. Lunch visitors enjoy Josef's burger, a variety of sandwiches, or a meal of Austrian pastries and coffee.

A SIDE TRIP TO LAKE CITY

The historic mining town of Lake City is 55 miles southwest via Colo. 149 (turn south off U.S. 50, 9 miles west of Gunnison). Founded in 1874, this former silver and gold town is set against a backdrop of 14,000-foot-plus peaks in three different national forests—the Gunnison, Uncompahgre, and Rio Grande.

One of Colorado's largest national historic districts, Lake City has more than 75 buildings that date from the 19th century. Visit the recently renovated **Hinsdale County Courthouse,** 317 N. Henson St., built in 1877 and still the home of county government. You'll see exhibits on the trial of the notorious Alferd Packer and the courtroom where the trial took place (see sidebar above). History buffs will also enjoy the **Hinsdale County Museum,** corner of Second and Silver streets (☎ **970/944-9515**) with exhibits about the Packer trial, of course, plus the area's silver mining heritage. Next door is the 1880s Smith-Grantham House, a small, furnished Victorian home where you can see how people here lived in the late 1800s. The museum is open Memorial Day through September; admission costs $2 for adults and 50¢ for children. The Hinsdale County Historical Society guides tours into some of the town's historic homes regularly throughout the summer. Check with the chamber of commerce (see below).

Surrounded by some 600,000 acres of public land, Lake City is also an important recreational center, offering hiking, mountain biking, horseback riding, jeeping, camping, and fishing in summer; and ice fishing, cross-country skiing, snowshoeing, and snowmobiling in winter. Lake San Cristobal, just south of town via County Road 30, is Colorado's second-largest natural lake and particularly popular with fishermen. Also nearby you'll find several ghost towns and historic sites, most of which will require a four-wheel–drive vehicle, horse, mountain bike, or a good pair of hiking boots.

For information, including lists of boat and jeep rentals, outfitters, stables, accommodations, and restaurants, contact the **Lake City/Hinsdale County Chamber of Commerce,** P.O. Box 430, Lake City, CO 81235 (☎ **800/569-1874** or 970/944-2527). The chamber operates a visitor information center on Silver Street, in the middle of town.

2 Crested Butte

The town of Crested Butte was born in 1880 as the Denver & Rio Grande line laid a narrow-gauge rail track from Gunnison to serve the gold and silver mines in the area. But coal, not the more precious minerals, sustained the town from the late 1880s until 1952, when the last of the mines closed. The economy then languished until Mount Crested Butte ski area was developed in 1961.

An influx of newcomers began renovating the old buildings in the 1970s, and in 1974 the entire town was designated a National Historic District. An architectural review board ensured that all construction was true to the town's heritage, with the result that Crested Butte is one of the most authentic Victorian towns in Colorado today. You won't find any rich miners' mansions here; this was and is a workingman's town, without the ostentation seen elsewhere in the state.

Today Crested Butte is known for skiing in winter, and hiking, bicycling, and other outdoor recreational activities in warmer weather. It has easily the best mountain biking in the state, and many Coloradans also consider it the best place in the state to see wildflowers.

ESSENTIALS

GETTING THERE   By Car   Crested Butte is 28 miles north of Gunnison on Colo. 135, the only year-round access. In summer, the gravel-surface Kebler Pass Road links Crested Butte with Colo. 133 at Paonia Reservoir, to the west; and four-wheel–drive vehicles can negotiate a difficult route south from Aspen, around the Maroon Bells.

By Plane   The **Gunnison County Airport** serves Crested Butte (see Section 1 of this chapter). **Alpine Express** (☎ 800/822-4844 or 970/641-5074) provides shuttle service from Gunnison County Airport to Crested Butte. It runs frequently during ski season, but call for availability at other times.

ORIENTATION   There are actually two separate communities here: the old mining town of Crested Butte and the modern resort village of Mount Crested Butte, 3¹/₂ miles away. Colo. 135 enters Crested Butte from the south and is intersected by Elk Avenue, which runs west-east as the town's main street. Numbered streets run north-south beginning with Fifth Street to the west of Colo. 135. Beyond Elk Avenue, Colo. 135 is called Gothic Road, which leads to the winding condominium-speckled roads surrounding the Mount Crested Butte village.

VISITOR INFORMATION   Consult the **Crested Butte–Mount Crested Butte Chamber of Commerce,** P.O. Box 1288, Crested Butte, CO 81224 (☎ 800/545-4505 or 970/349-6438). An **information center** is located downtown at the four-way stop at the corner of Elk Avenue and Sixth Street. Area lodging reservations can be made with **Central Reservations** (☎ 800/215-2226).

GETTING AROUND   Mountain Express (☎ 970/349-7318) provides free shuttle-bus service between Crested Butte, Mount Crested Butte, and area condominiums. Call for schedules. Local taxi service is available from **Town Taxi** (☎ 970/349-5543).

FAST FACTS   In case of **emergency,** call **911.** The **Crested Butte Medical Clinic,** Gothic Road at Emmons Road, Mount Crested Butte (☎ 970/349-6651), can handle most health needs. The **post office** (☎ 970/349-5568) is on the north side of Elk Avenue between Second and Third streets. **Local sales tax** is about 8%.

SPECIAL EVENTS   Crested Butte's annual events include the Fat Tire Bike Week, in late June; the Wildflower Festival, in early July; the Stepping Stones Children's Fun Festival, in late July; the Mountain Man Rendezvous, in early August; and the Vinotok Slavic Fall Festival, in mid-September.

SKIING & OTHER WINTER SPORTS

Crested Butte may be Colorado's best-kept secret. Situated at the intersection of two overlapping winter storm tracks, it's guaranteed outstanding snow. Offering abundant opportunities for beginners and intermediate skiers, Crested Butte has what many experts consider the most challenging runs—extreme-limits skiing—in the Rockies.

The resort has 1,160 acres of skiable terrain, including 550 acres of extreme limits, double black-diamond ungroomed terrain for experts only. Vertical drop is 3,062 feet from a summit of 12,162 feet. There are 85 trails served by 13 lifts (three triples, two quads, four doubles, and four surface lifts). Average annual snowfall is 229 inches, and there's snowmaking on trails served by all but two of the resort's lifts.

Crested Butte offers a ski program for the physically challenged, with specially trained and certified instructors; and a children's ski center providing lessons, rental equipment, day care, and nursery services. The resort also has a designated snowboarding area as well as snowboard rentals and lessons.

For more information, contact **Crested Butte Mountain Resort,** 500 Gothic Rd. (P.O. Box A), Mount Crested Butte, CO 81225 (☎ **800/544-8448** or 970/349-2222; 970/349-2323 for snow reports; fax 970/349-2250). At press time, lift tickets were $43 for an adult full day; children 12 and under pay their age; seniors 65 to 69 half price; seniors 70 and over free. Rates are subject to change, however. The resort operates from late November to mid-April, daily from 9am to 4pm.

CROSS-COUNTRY SKIING   The **Crested Butte Nordic Center,** based at Big Mine Park, Second Street and Whiterock Avenue in downtown Crested Butte (P.O. Box 1269), Crested Butte, CO 81224 (☎ **970/349-1707**), maintains 30 kilometers (18¹/₂ miles) of groomed trails and organizes backcountry tours over more than 100 miles of wilderness trail. It's open in winter daily from 9am to 4pm. The costs for track skiing are $7 per day for adults, $3 for children; rentals are $12 per day; all-day tours run $35 per person, with a two-person minimum. The center's Nordic Ski School offers instruction for all ages and levels of ability, with lessons starting at $22 per person. The center also maintains a lighted ice-skating rink and offers skate rentals, plus snowshoe tours and rentals.

SNOWMOBILING   Local companies that lead tours through Gunnison National Forest include **Action Adventures Snowmobiling** (☎ **800/383-1974** or 970/349-5909), **Alpine Outside** (☎ **800/833-8052** or 970/349-5011), **Burt Rentals** (☎ **970/349-2441**), and **Lost Lake Snowmobiling** (☎ **970/349-9709**). A wide variety of trips are available, at a wide range of prices. Typical prices are $35 for a 1-hour ride, and $120 for a half-day trip.

WARM-WEATHER SPORTS & OUTDOOR ACTIVITIES

BALLOONING   You can take a scenic hot-air balloon flight with **Big Horn Balloon** (☎ **970/596-1008** or 970/349-6335), with prices of about $90 per person for a 1-hour flight.

FOUR-WHEELING   There are plenty of opportunities here to use your four-wheel–drive rig on old mining and logging roads. Jeep Wranglers are rented by

Flatiron Sports, Treasury Center, 10 Crested Butte Way, Mount Crested Butte (☎ **970/349-6656**), for about $90 per day.

GOLF   Robert Trent Jones, Jr. designed the 7,200-yard, 18-hole course at **Skyland Country Club and Mountain Resort,** 385 Country Club Dr. (☎ **970/349-6131**), 2¹/₂ miles south of Crested Butte. Considered one of Colorado's best mountain courses, it has water hazards on the first nine holes; Scottish links and knolls on the back nine. The course is usually open from mid-May through October. Rates for 18 holes, including the mandatory cart, are $80 mornings and $50 afternoons in summer, and lower in the off-seasons.

HIKING   There are rich opportunities for hiking and backpacking in the Crested Butte area. Ask the chamber of commerce for trail suggestions, or contact the **Gunnison National Forest office,** 216 N. Colorado St., Gunnison (☎ **970/641-0471**).

HORSEBACK RIDING   Guided rides are offered from June through mid-October by **Fantasy Ranch** (☎ **970/349-5425**), ranging from 3-hour rides to week-long pack trips. Prices are about $80 for shorter rides, and range from $125 to about $800 for pack trips. **Teocalli Outfitters** (☎ **970/641-6656**) operates from June through November, offering day rides, pack trips, and hunting trips. A 1¹/₂-hour ride costs about $25, and pack trips average about $125 per day.

MOUNTAIN BIKING   Crested Butte has established a firm reputation as the place to mountain bike in Colorado. From jeep roads to hiking trails, there's something here to please every ability level. Popular rides include the challenging 25-mile ride over 10,707-foot Schofield Pass to the village of Marble, off Colo. 133; and the shorter Cement Creek Trail to the base of Italian Mountain.

   For trail information, maps, and mountain-bike rentals, stop at **Flatiron Sports,** Treasury Center, 10 Crested Butte Way, Mount Crested Butte (☎ **970/349-6656**). Mountain bikes rent for about $22 per day.

OTHER HIGHLIGHTS

The Crested Butte–Mount Crested Butte Chamber of Commerce can provide a free **self-guided walking tour** brochure describing more than 3 dozen historic buildings in Crested Butte, including the picturesque 1883 Town Hall, 1881 railroad depot, numerous saloons and homes, and a unique two-story outhouse.

Crested Butte Mountain Heritage Museum. 200 Sopris Ave., Crested Butte, CO 81224. ☎ **970/349-1880.** Call for hours.

This museum concentrates on the area's mining and ranching heritage, with a wide array of memorabilia from local settlers' cabins. Exhibits also include a 1920 fire truck, used by the Crested Butte Fire Department, and vintage mountain bikes. You can pick up a free copy of the Crested Butte walking tour map here.

WHERE TO STAY

The Claim Jumper. 704 Whiterock Ave. (P.O. Box 1181), Crested Butte, CO 81224. ☎ **970/ 349-6471.** 7 rms. TV. $89–$129 double. Rates include full breakfast. DISC, MC, V.

A huge log home packed with antiques and family heirlooms, this bed-and-breakfast easily qualifies as Crested Butte's most unique accommodation. Each guest room has a particular theme. The Rough and Ready Room is dedicated to cowboys; Prospector's Gulch, to miners; and Commodore Corrigan's Cabin, to seafarers. Fifties nostalgia buffs enjoy Ethyl's Room, complete with restored gas pump. Rooms have VCRs, and some 100 movies are available. The inn also features a redwood hot tub, sauna, and antique gaming parlor.

Elk Mountain Lodge. Second and Gothic streets. (P.O. Box 148), Crested Butte, CO 81224. ☎ **800/374-6521** or 970/349-7533. Fax 970/349-5114. 19 rms. TV TEL. Summer $69–$89 double; winter $88–$108 double. Rates include full breakfast. AE, DISC, MC, V.

Built in 1919 as a miners' hotel, this historic lodge has been beautifully renovated by owners John and Patty Vermillion. Located near the center of town, the lodge offers rooms with twin, queen, or king beds. Third-floor rooms have spectacular views of the town and surrounding mountains, and many have balconies. There's also an indoor hot tub, lobby bar, and free ski storage.

Grande Butte Hotel. 500 Gothic Rd. (P.O. Box A), Mount Crested Butte, CO 81225. ☎ **800/544-8448** or 970/349-4000. Fax 970/349-4466. 210 rms, 52 suites. TV TEL. $87–$200 double, $139–$589 suite. AE, CB, DC, DISC, MC, V. Check on spring and fall closures.

A luxurious property at the foot of the Silver Queen lift, this is the Crested Butte Mountain Resort's showcase hotel. Some 40,000 square feet of red cedar went into its construction, and an impressive collection of original oil paintings is on display. Every guest room has a private balcony, wet bar, refrigerator, and whirlpool tub. Standard rooms have a queen bed and sleeper sofa or two double beds. Pets are not permitted.

Fine continental dinners are served in the Grande Cafe, which boasts a wall of windows facing the ski slopes. A coffee shop serves three meals daily; its outdoor barbecue deck is especially popular. The hotel offers concierge, room service, and ski valet; indoor pool, indoor and outdoor hot tubs, sauna, fitness center, game room, guest laundry, ski shop, ice-skating rink (with rentals), business center, and meeting space for 500.

The Nordic Inn. 14 Treasury Rd. (P.O. Box 939, Crested Butte, CO 81224), Mt. Crested Butte, CO 81225. ☎ **970/349-5542.** Fax 970/349-6487. 24 rms, 2 suites, 2 chalets. TV TEL. Winter, $95–$175 room, $125–$315 suites and chalets; summer, $68–$114 room, $103–$140 suites and chalets. Rates include continental breakfast. AE, MC, V.

Among the first lodges built at the foot of the Crested Butte ski slopes, this well-kept, family-owned inn is still going strong. Its big fireplace is the focus of attention at breakfast, and there's a Jacuzzi on the sun deck, open year-round. Guest rooms have Scandinavian decor and two double beds. Some kitchen units are available, and families are especially welcome.

WHERE TO DINE
EXPENSIVE

Le Bosquet. Elk Ave. and Second St. ☎ **970/349-5808.** Reservations recommended. Main courses: lunch $4.95–$8.95, dinner $13.95–$33.95. AE, DISC, MC, V. Mon–Sat 11:30am–2pm, daily 5:30–10pm. Call about spring and fall closures. FRENCH.

Green plants are glimpsed through the lace curtains of this popular garden-style restaurant, operated by the same owners since 1978. The menu changes weekly, but usually includes fresh seafood, beef, lamb, and vegetarian entrees. Typical selections might include a Colorado lamb shank, grilled duck breast, or hazelnut chicken. There's also an excellent wine list. Smoking is not permitted.

INEXPENSIVE

The Bakery Cafe. 302 Elk Ave., at Third St. ☎ **970/349-7280.** Reservations not accepted. Meals $2.90–$5.95; pizzas $5.95–$13.95. DISC, MC, V. Mid-June–Sept and Thanksgiving–early Apr, daily 7am–9pm; off-season, daily 7am–6pm. DELI/BAKERY.

Large picture windows and a sun room give this cafe a bright, spacious atmosphere. All food is made fresh daily, including savory pastries, creative overstuffed deli-style sandwiches, soups, and desserts. There's a salad bar with greens plus homemade pre-pared salads such as seafood, cucumber and lentil, and potato salad. You can also fill up on pizza (served 4–9pm) or the complete bakery selection.

The Slogar Bar & Restaurant. Second St. at Whiterock Ave. ☎ **970/349-5765.** Reservations recommended. Fixed-price dinner $11–$16. AE, MC, V. Daily 5–9pm. AMERICAN.

If you do something right, why mess around with anything else? That's the way the Slogar feels about its skillet-fried chicken. The fixed-price menu offers chicken every night, accompanied by tangy coleslaw, mashed potatoes and gravy, biscuits with honey butter, creamed corn, and ice cream. Also offered is a family-style steak dinner. The atmosphere here, incidentally, is 1880s Victorian. The Slogar was the Slogar then, too, but nowhere near as elegant as it is today.

CRESTED BUTTE AFTER DARK

Call **Crested Butte Center for the Arts** (☎ 970/349-7487) for information on events in town, from Shakespeare to symphony performances.

3 Salida: White-Water Rafting Center of the Rockies

With a strategic location on the upper Arkansas River, near the headwaters of the Colorado River and Rio Grande tributaries, it was natural that Salida should become an important farming and transportation center in its early days, and a major river-rafting center today. Zebulon Pike opened the area for Americans in the 19th century, followed by trappers, and then miners after the discovery of gold in 1859. When Leadville boomed on silver in the late 1870s, the Denver & Rio Grande Railroad built a line up the Arkansas from Pueblo, and the town of Salida was founded at a key point on the line. The downtown core has kept its historic ambiance alive, and although the railway no longer carries passengers it still operates as a freight line.

ESSENTIALS

GETTING THERE   By Car   U.S. 50 connects Salida with Grand Junction, 193 miles west on I-70, and Pueblo, 96 miles east on I-25. U.S. 285 runs north to south 5 miles west of Salida (through Poncha Springs); it extends northeast 138 miles to Denver, and south 255 miles to Santa Fe, New Mexico. Colo. 291 provides a vital 9-mile link through Salida, completing a triangle that ties the two U.S. highways together. About 23 miles north of Salida, and 2 miles south of Buena Vista, U.S. 24 branches north off U.S. 285, connecting Salida with I-70 at Vail, via Leadville.

By Plane   The nearest airport with commercial service is at **Gunnison,** 65 miles west (see Section 1 of this chapter).

By Van   Chaffee Transit, 132 W. First St. (☎ 800/288-1375 or 719/539-3935), provides charter van service to and from Denver, Colorado Springs, Pueblo, and Albuquerque, New Mexico airports.

ORIENTATION   Salida sits on the southwestern bank of the Arkansas River, just above its confluence with the South Arkansas. U.S. 50 (Rainbow Blvd.), which follows the north bank of the South Arkansas, marks the southern edge of the town. At the eastern city limit, Colo. 291 (Oak St.) turns north off U.S. 50, and six blocks later, turns northwest as First Street through the historic downtown area. Though the southeastern quadrant of the city is platted north to south, most of Salida is oriented at a 45° angle: lettered streets (A through O) run southwest to northeast, and numbered streets (First through 17th) run northwest to southeast. The heart of town is around First through Third streets, where they are intersected by D and E streets.

VISITOR INFORMATION   Consult the **Heart of the Rockies Chamber of Commerce,** 406 W. U.S. 50, Salida, CO 81201 (☎ **719/539-2068**).

GETTING AROUND   **Chaffee Transit,** 132 W. First St. (☎ **800/288-1375** or 719/539-3935), provides charter van service throughout the Salida–Buena Vista–Monarch area.

FAST FACTS   In case of **emergency,** call **911.** Health care is provided by the **Heart of the Rockies Regional Medical Center,** 448 E. First St. (☎ **719/539-6661**), with a 24-hour emergency room. The **post office** is at 310 D St. (☎ **719/539-2548**). For **road conditions,** call ☎ 719/539-6688.

SPECIAL EVENTS   Annually, Salida sponsors the FIBArk Festival ("First in Boating on the Arkansas"), in mid-June; and the Chaffee County Fair, in early August.

RIVER RAFTING

Considered the white-water rafting center of the Rockies, Salida is the perfect base for enjoying the **Arkansas Headwaters Recreation Area,** a 148-mile stretch of river from Leadville to Pueblo Reservoir. With headquarters off Colo. 291, in downtown Salida at 307 W. Sackett St. (P.O. Box 126, Salida, CO 81201; ☎ **719/539-7289**), the recreation area includes more than a dozen developed sites along the river, offering raft and kayak access, fishing, hiking, camping, and picnicking. There are also undeveloped areas that offer access to the river, but be careful to avoid trespassing on private property.

The busiest stretch of the river is Browns Canyon, a granite wilderness between Buena Vista and Salida, with Class III and IV rapids (moderately difficult to difficult) along a 10-mile stretch of river from Nathrop to Stone Bridge. User fees are $1 per person per day, free for children under 10; $6 per night for camping.

Most people explore Colorado's rivers with experienced rafting companies, which provide trips on stretches of river that range from practically calm and suitable for everyone, to extremely difficult, with long, violent rapids that are recommended only for skilled white-water boaters. For a full listing of rafting companies, check with the Heart of the Rockies Chamber of Commerce. Leading outfitters include **Dvorak's Kayak & Rafting Expeditions,** 17921-B U.S. 285, Nathrop, CO 81236 (☎ **800/ 824-3795** or 719/539-6851), which offers half- and full-day trips, multiday excursions, plus one full-week trip each year with a flutist and string quartet, who give live concerts among the canyons and forests. Other major rafting companies include **Rocky Mountain Adventures,** 310 Charles St. (U.S. 24), **Buena Vista** (☎ **719/ 395-8594**); **River Runners, Ltd.,** 11150 U.S. 50, Salida, CO 81201 (☎ **800/ 525-2081** or 719/539-2144); and **Wilderness Aware,** P.O. Box 1550, Buena Vista, CO 81211 (☎ **800/462-7238** or 719/395-2112). Generally, half-day raft trips cost $30 to $35, full-day trips are in the $55 to $75 range, and multiday excursions start at about $200.

OTHER SPORTS & OUTDOOR ACTIVITIES

BICYCLING   **Otero Cyclery,** 108 F St. (☎ **719/539-6704**), sells and services mountain bikes, has rentals, and can provide information on biking throughout the region. Ask for a free copy of the *Mountain Bike Guide,* which gives details, including maps, for 15 area rides. Rentals of both dual and front suspension mountain bikes are available, priced from $20 to $30 per day.

FISHING   The Arkansas River is considered by many to be the finest fishing river in Colorado. There's also trout fishing in numerous alpine lakes, including Cottonwood Lake, Twin Lakes, Rainbow Lake, and O'Haver Lake.

GOLF   The Salida Golf Club, a regulation nine-hole municipal course, which opened in 1926, is at Crestone Avenue and Grant Street (☎ **719/539-1060**). Greens fees are $11 for nine holes and $19 for 18 holes.

HIKING   There are outstanding trails for all experience levels throughout the region, particularly in the San Isabel National Forest, along the eastern slope of the Continental Divide west of Salida. Of particular interest are hikes into the Collegiate Range (Mounts Harvard, Columbia, Yale, Princeton, and Oxford) off Cottonwood Creek Road west of Buena Vista, and trips from the ghost town of St. Elmo up Chalk Creek Road from Mount Princeton Hot Springs.

For maps and other information, stop at the **U.S. Forest Service,** 325 W. Rainbow Blvd., Salida (☎ **719/539-3591**).

HORSEBACK RIDING   Those who want to explore the backcountry on horseback can contact **Brown's Canyon Horse Leasing,** P.O. Box 123, Salida, CO 81201 (☎ **719/539-2095** or 719/395-6498), for scenic trail rides from 1 hour to multiday. Cost for a full-day ride with lunch is about $70.

LLAMA TREKS   Spruce Ridge Llama Treks, 4141 County Rd. 210, Salida, CO 81201 (☎ **719/539-4182**), offers full- and multiday hikes into the nearby national forests, with llamas carrying the gear. Trips are custom designed for couples, families, or groups, and all equipment is provided. Prices for a 1-day trip, including lunch, are $69 for adults, $29 for children 5 to 13, and $10 for children under 5.

ROCKHOUNDING   The richest mineral-and-gem beds in Colorado are found in the upper Arkansas River valley and the eastern slope of the Continental Divide, just west of Salida. For a free brochure on rockhounding locations, stop at the Chamber of Commerce office, or visit **D&J Rare Gems,** 112 F St. (☎ **719/539-7493**). Those wanting hammers, eye protection, and other prospecting equipment will find it at Homestead Sports, 444 U.S. 50, Poncha Springs (☎ 719/539-7507), 5 miles west of Salida.

SKIING   **Monarch** Ski Resort, 20 miles west of Salida at Monarch Pass on U.S. 50, is among the finest of Colorado's smaller ski and snowboarding areas, serving all levels of ability with 54 trails covering 670 acres. For information, contact the resort at 1 Powder Place, Monarch, CO 81227 (☎ **800/228-7943** or 719/539-3573).

SEEING THE SIGHTS

Salida Hot Springs. 410 W. Rainbow Blvd. ☎ **719/539-6738.** Admission $5 adults, $3 students 6–17, $2 children 5 and under, $3 seniors (60 and older). Memorial Day–Labor Day daily 1–9pm (adult lap swimming noon–1pm weekdays); Labor Day–Memorial Day Tues–Thurs 4–9pm, Fri–Sun 1–9pm.

Colorado's largest indoor hot springs have been in commercial operation since 1937, when the Works Progress Administration built the pools as a depression-era project. Ute tribes considered the mineral waters, rich in bicarbonate, sodium, and sulfate, to be sacred and medicinal. Today, the main 25-meter (27.3-yd.) pool, with two lap lanes available at all times, is kept at 90° to 92°, a shallow pool between 100° and 102°, and wading pool about 96°. European-style private hot baths, at 114° to 120°, are available for adults only ($5 per person per hour). Adjacent Centennial Park has tennis and volleyball courts and other recreational facilities.

Monarch Scenic Tram. Monarch Pass, U.S. 50, 22 miles west of Salida. ☎ **719/539-4789.** Admission $6 adults, $5 seniors, $3 children. Mid-May–late Sept, daily 9am–4pm.

Climbing from 11,312-foot Monarch Pass to the Continental Divide at an altitude of 12,012 feet, this tram offers views of five mountain ranges, up to 150 miles away when skies are clear. The tram includes six four-passenger gondolas.

Mt. Shavano Trout Rearing Unit. 7725 County Road 154. ☎ **719/539-6877.** Free admission. Daily 7:30am–4pm.

This state-run fish hatchery, about a half-mile northwest of town, produces some four million trout each year, which are then stocked in Colorado's numerous streams and lakes. Visitors can see how the hatchery operates, walk among the fish raceways and ponds, and feed the fish (food provided from coin-operated machines).

WHERE TO STAY

Aspen Leaf Lodge. 7350 W. U.S. 50, Salida, CO 81201. ☎ **800/759-0338** for reservations only, or 719/539-6733. 18 rms. A/C TV TEL. Mid-May–mid-Sept and holidays $45.50–$52.50 double; spring and fall $28.50–$48.50 double. Children under 16 stay free in parents' room. AE, DC, DISC, MC, V.

This small family-owned and -operated motel has a friendly feel, from the forest of small evergreens and aspens around a hot-tub pavilion, to the coffee pot that's on in the office each morning. There are single and double rooms. The more spacious doubles contain two queen beds, and rollaways and cribs are available at an extra charge. Pets are accepted.

Redwood Lodge. 7310 U.S. 50, Salida, CO 81201. ☎ **800/234-1077** or 719/539-2528. Fax 719/539-2528. 27 rms and suites. A/C TV TEL. May 15–Sept 15 and holidays $52–$65 double, $53–$86 suite. Other times $45–$52 double, $52–$72 suite. Rates include continental breakfast. DC, DISC, MC, V.

Red cedar is used throughout this attractive property, from construction to custom furnishings to the two outdoor hot tubs. Every room is unique, but each typically has king or queen beds, original artwork, and pedestal sinks; some have whirlpool tubs. Family suites have two full bedrooms and kitchenettes. There's a heated outdoor pool, open in summer.

River Run Inn. 8495 County Rd. 160, Salida, CO 81201. ☎ **800/385-6927** or 719/539-3818. Fax 719/539-3818. 7 rms (3 with bath), plus 13 dormitory beds (shared bath). $60 double without bath, $70 double with bath; $25 dorm bed. Rates include full breakfast. MC, V.

Built by Chaffee County in 1892 as a home for the indigent, this building—about 2 miles northwest of town—served that purpose for half a century. Since 1983, however, it has been a charming bed-and-breakfast, and is listed on the National Register of Historic Places. The grounds cover 11 acres, including a quarter-mile section of the Arkansas River. The wide front porch leads into a large sitting room and library, and the back porch looks out over a pond. The seven guest rooms have antique poster beds—two twins in one, one king in another, and queens in the rest—and most have mountain views. Pets and smoking are not allowed; children over 12 are welcome.

WHERE TO DINE

Country Bounty Restaurant & Gift Shoppe. 413 W. Rainbow Blvd. (U.S. 50). ☎ **719/539-3546.** Breakfast $2.50–$5.75; lunch $3.25–$8.25; dinner $7.25–$12.50. DISC, MC, V. Daily 6:30am–9pm. AMERICAN/MEXICAN.

This combination gift shop and restaurant gives diners plenty to look at while waiting for their mesquite-broiled tuna, hot beef sandwich, or country fried chicken. The gift shop seems to spill over into the restaurant with all manner of country-style crafts, southwestern jewelry, and other items. Breakfast selections include hotcakes, Denver omelets, and eggs Benedict; the lunch menu includes cheeseburgers, smoked turkey and avocado on rye, and homemade soup; and for dinner, selections include chicken-fried steak, pork chops, lemon herb chicken breast, and Rocky Mountain trout. There's also a Mexican menu and a variety of salads, plus locally famous pies and cobblers.

First St. Cafe. 137 E. First St. ☎ **719/539-4759.** Breakfast $3.25–$6; lunch $4–$7; dinner $7–$15. AE, DISC, MC, V. Apr–Sept, Mon–Sat 8am–10pm; call for Sun hours. Oct–Mar, Mon–Thurs 8am–8pm, Fri–Sat 8am–10pm. AMERICAN/MEXICAN.

In the heart of historic downtown Salida, First St. Cafe occupies a brick building dating from 1883, with hardwood floors and regional paintings and photographs that give the cafe a gallery feel. Among the city's most popular restaurants, it's a focal point for artists, musicians, and other creative types. The kitchen turns out gourmet home cooking; meals such as French toast stuffed with cream cheese and walnuts for breakfast; vegetarian casseroles and Monte Cristo sandwiches for lunch; steak, barbecued ribs, and halibut filets for dinner. You'll also find innovative Mexican selections, a salad bar, daily specials, and full liquor service.

4 Alamosa & Great Sand Dunes National Monument

If you're looking for Colorado's largest sandbox, here it is. Just 38 miles from town is a spectacular sight you wouldn't expect to find in Colorado: the tallest sand dunes in North America.

Founded in 1878 with the extension of the Denver & Rio Grande Railroad into the San Luis Valley, the town was named for the cottonwood (*alamosa*) trees that lined the banks of the Rio Grande. Soon rails spread out in all directions from the community, and it became a thriving transportation center for farmers and a supply depot for miners. Today this town of 9,500 remains a center for farming, especially vegetables. It is also an educational center with Adams State College, a 4-year institution founded in 1921, and a good home base for southern Colorado visitors.

ESSENTIALS

GETTING THERE   By Car   Alamosa is at the junction of U.S. 160, which runs east 73 miles to I-25 at Walsenburg and west to Durango and beyond; and U.S. 285, which extends south to Santa Fe, New Mexico, and north to Denver through Monte Vista and the upper Arkansas River valley. Because of a jog in U.S. 285, however, a more direct route into the city from the north is to take Colo. 17 the last 50 miles.

By Plane   The **Alamosa Municipal Airport** (☎ 719/589-6444), 3 miles off U.S. 285 South, has daily service to and from Denver with **United Express** (☎ **719/589-9446**).

ORIENTATION   Located on the southwestern bank of the Rio Grande, Alamosa is the center of the San Luis Valley—a vast basin bounded on the west by the San Juan Mountains and on the east by the sharp-ridged Sangre de Cristo Range. As you enter by car from the east, U.S. 160 crosses a bridge over the Rio Grande; immediately ahead, on Fourth Street at Chamber Drive, are the city hall, police station, and chamber of commerce. The arterial, however, runs south a block, then extends west as Main Street. Two blocks farther, Main is crossed by State Avenue, the principal north-south byway. Another six blocks ahead is the intersection of West Avenue, which runs south as U.S. 285. U.S. 160 continues in a northwesterly direction. First Street, four blocks north of Main, bisects the campus of Adams State College on the west side of town; numbered streets parallel First Street all the way south through 20th Street.

VISITOR INFORMATION   The **Alamosa County Chamber of Commerce,** Cole Park (Chamber Dr. at Third St.), Alamosa, CO 81101 (☎ **800/BLU-SKYS** or 719/589-3681), provides information on the entire six-county San Luis Valley region.

FAST FACTS   In case of **emergency,** call **911. San Luis Valley Regional Medical Center** is at 106 Blanca Ave. (☎ **719/589-2511**). The **post office** is at 505 Third St., off State Avenue (☎ **719/589-4908**). **Local sales tax** is 7%.

SPECIAL EVENTS   Annual area events include the Crane Festival, in mid-March, in Monte Vista; the Rendezvous of Cultures in Fort Garland on Memorial Day weekend; the Pro Rodeo, Dance, and Parade, in June, in Alamosa; and the Colorado State Mining Championships, on the Fourth of July weekend, in Creede.

✪ GREAT SAND DUNES NATIONAL MONUMENT

Just 38 miles northeast of Alamosa, on Colo. 150, you'll come to a startling sight— a 55-square-mile expanse of sand, piled nearly 700 feet high against the western edge of the Sangre de Cristo Mountains. The tallest sand dunes on the continent, they seem totally incongruous out here, far from any sea or major desert.

The dunes were created over thousands of years by winds blowing southwesterly across the valley. They began forming at the end of the last ice age, when streams of water from melting glaciers carried rocks, gravel, and silt from the mountains down into the valley. In addition, as the Rio Grande changed its course, it left behind sand, silt, and debris.

Even today the winds are changing the face of the dunes. So-called "reversing winds" from the mountains pile the dunes back upon themselves, building them higher and higher. Though it's physically impossible for sand to be piled steeper than 34°, the dunes often appear more sheer because of deceptive shadows and colors that change with the light: gold, pink, tan, sometimes even bluish. Climbing dunes is fun, but it can be tiring at this 8,200-foot altitude. The sand's surface can reach 140°F in summer.

Among the specialized animals that survive in this weird environment are the Ord kangaroo rat, a creature that never drinks water; and two insects found nowhere else on earth: the Great Sand Dunes tiger beetle and one type of darkling beetle. These animals and the flora of the adjacent mountain foothills are discussed in evening programs and guided walks during summer.

A quick way to see the monument is to walk the easy half-mile self-guided nature trail that begins in the parking area. If you've got some more time or want more of a challenge, hike the sandy 10-mile-long four-wheel–drive track that begins just beyond the monument's entrance. After about 5 miles, the terrain becomes rocky and somewhat challenging. If you make it all the way to the end, you'll be afforded spectacular views of the dunes and the surrounding mountains.

If you choose to camp in the monument, Pinyon Flats Campground, with 88 sites, is open year-round. It has flush toilets and drinking water, but no showers or R.V. hookups. Campsites are assigned on a first-come, first-served basis, and cost $10 per night. Admission to the monument is $4 per car. The **Visitor Center** (☎ **719/378-2312**) is open from 9am to 6pm daily in summer, with shorter hours at other times. For further information, contact: Great Sand Dunes National Monument, 11500 Colo. 150, Mosca, CO 81146.

From Alamosa, there are two main routes to Great Sand Dunes: east 14 miles on U.S. 160, then north on Colo. 150; or north 14 miles on Colo. 17 to Mosca, then east on Six Mile Lane to the junction of Colo. 150.

SPORTS & OUTDOOR ACTIVITIES

FISHING   The Rio Grande is an outstanding stream for trout, walleye, and catfish, and there are numerous reservoirs around the San Luis Valley. For licenses, tackle, and advice, visit **Spencer Sporting Goods,** 616 Main St. (☎ 719/589-4361), or **Alamosa Sporting Goods,** 1114 Main St. (☎ 719/589-3006). Many enjoy stays at **Mt. Blanca Game Bird & Trout, Inc.,** P.O. Box 236, Blanca, CO 81123 (☎ 719/379-DUCK; fax 719/379-3589). This lodge, 21 miles east of Alamosa on U.S. 160 and southwest about 5 miles on well-marked county roads, requires no license for guided bird hunting and fishing. Trout fishing is offered on two fully stocked lakes, catch and release. Rooms run $88, double occupancy, with three full meals an additional $30 per person.

GOLF   The Cattails Golf Club, 6615 N. River Rd. (☎ 719/589-9515), is an 18-hole, par-72 course along the Rio Grande on the north side of Alamosa. Generally open March through November, the club offers all the usual services. Cost is $18 for 18 holes. **The Zapata Ranch Golf Course,** 5303 Colo. 150 (☎ 719/378-2357), is a championship 18-hole course, 26 miles northeast of Alamosa. The course is usually open from mid-April through mid-November. Greens fees are $35 for 18 holes and $20 for nine holes, plus $10 cart rental. The nine-hole **Monte Vista Golf Club,** at 101 Country Club in the town of Monte Vista (☎ 719/852-4906), 17 miles west of Alamosa, is a particularly challenging course due to its small greens. Open April through October, the course is on the migratory path of sandhill and whooping cranes. Fees are $10 for nine holes and $15 for 18 holes.

HIKING   The best opportunities in the region are found in the surrounding **Rio Grande National Forest,** with nearly two million acres. The supervisor's office is at 1803 W. U.S. 160 in Monte Vista (☎ 719/852-5941), and district offices are located in Saguache, Del Norte, La Jara, and Creede.

One of the most popular hikes, with easy access, is **Zapata Falls,** reached off Colo. 150 about 20 miles northeast of Alamosa and south of Great Sand Dunes. This cavernous waterfall on the northwest flank of 14,345-foot Mount Blanca freezes in winter, turning its cave into a natural icebox that often remains frozen well into summer. More challenging hikes include trails into the **Wheeler Geologic Area,** set aside by President Theodore Roosevelt in 1911 because of its unique rock formations. Obtain directions at forest service offices.

IN-LINE SKATING   Kristi Mountain Sports, Villa Mall, on West U.S. 160 (☎ 719/589-9759) rents in-line skates, which you can use at Cole Park, on Chamber Drive at Third Street.

MOUNTAIN BIKING   There are plenty of opportunities for mountain biking on local federal lands. Stop at **Kristi Mountain Sports,** Villa Mall, on West U.S. 160 (☎ 719/589-9759) for information on the best places to go, rentals ($15 per day), repairs, and accessories.

SWIMMING   Splashland Hot Springs, Colo. 17 (☎ 719/589-6307 in summer, 719/589-5772 in winter), 1 mile north of Alamosa via U.S. 160, has a geothermally heated outdoor pool (94°F average temperature) measuring 150 feet by 60 feet, with both high dive and low dive. There's also an 18-inch-deep wading pool. Bathing suits, towels, flippers, goggles, and other pool paraphernalia can be rented. There's a snack

The Cumbres & Toltec Scenic Railroad

South from Alamosa, U.S. 285 cuts a nearly straight line through the heart of Conejos County. The best-known attraction in this part of the state is the Cumbres & Toltec Scenic Railroad, P.O. Box 668, Antonito, CO 81120 (☎ 719/376-5483). The depot is 28 miles south of Alamosa, just off the highway.

Born in 1880 to serve remote mining camps, this narrow-gauge steam railroad follows a spectacular 64-mile path through the San Juan Mountains from Antonito to Chama, New Mexico. The *Colorado Limited* weaves through groves of pine and aspen, and past strange rock formations, before ascending through the spectacular Toltec Gorge of the Los Piños River. At the rail-junction community of Osier, passengers picnic or have a catered lunch while the *Limited* stops to change engines with the *New Mexico Express*. Round-trip passengers return to their starting point in Antonito, while onward passengers continue a climb through tunnels and trestles to the summit of 10,015-foot Cumbres Pass, then drop down a precipitous 4% grade to Chama.

A through-trip from Antonito to Chama (or vice versa), traveling one-way by van, runs $52 for adults, $27 for children 11 and under. A regular round-trip, without transfers, is $34 adults, $17 children 11 and under, but this omits either the gorge or the pass. Either way, it's an all-day adventure, leaving between 8 and 10:30am, and returning between 4:30 and 6:30pm. Write or phone ahead for reservations: The train operates daily from Memorial Day weekend to mid-October. A joint venture by the states of Colorado and New Mexico, it's a registered National Historic Site.

bar, and the pool has public showers. It's open Memorial Day to Labor Day, Thursday through Tuesday. Hours weekdays are 10am to 6:30pm; noon to 6pm on Saturdays and Sundays. Admission is $3 for adults, $2 for children 3 to 12, $1 for babies, and $1.50 for senior citizens 60 and older.

OTHER HIGHLIGHTS

Adams State College—Luther Bean Museum. 208 Edgemont Blvd. ☎ **719/587-7121.** Free admission. Mon–Fri 1–4:30pm.

Located on the second floor of Richardson Hall, this museum has one of the Southwest's most complete collections of Hispanic *santos* (carved or painted images of saints), plus Anasazi artifacts, Rio Grande weavings, western art, and a priceless collection of European porcelains and furniture.

✪ **San Luis Valley Alligator Farm.** Two Mile Creek. ☎ **719/589-3032.** Admission $2 adults, $1.50 children 6–12, free for children under 6 and adults over 80. Daily June–Aug 7am–7pm, Sept–May 10am–3pm.

Geothermal wells keep the temperature at a cozy 87° at this alligator farm and wildlife habitat, located 18 miles north of Alamosa off Colo. 17.

NATURAL HIGHLIGHTS

The **Alamosa–Monte Vista National Wildlife Refuge Complex,** 6 miles southeast of Alamosa via U.S. 160 (9383 El Rancho Lane, Alamosa, CO 81101; ☎ 719/589-4021), has preserved nearly 25,000 acres of vital land for a variety of marsh birds and waterfowl, including many migrating and wintering species. Sandhill and whooping cranes visit in October and March; at other times of the year there may be egrets, herons, avocets, bitterns, and other avian species. A wide variety of ducks are year-round residents. Check at the refuge office about the best spots from which to see wildlife, hiking and biking trails, and a driving tour. Admission to the refuge is free. It's open daily from sunrise to sunset; the office is open Monday to Friday from 7:30am to 4pm.

In town, pleasant, grassy **Cole Park,** on Chamber Drive at Third Street, is home to the Alamosa County Chamber of Commerce, which is housed in a replica 1880s railroad depot, and displays a turn of the century steam engine. Also in the park, the **San Luis Valley History Center** has exhibits depicting the lives of the area's early inhabitants, the coming of the railroad, the military, and mining (the center is open daily June–September, 10am–4pm). There are picnic tables and benches in the park, as well as a quarter-mile walking track.

WHERE TO STAY
EXPENSIVE

Inn at Zapata Ranch. 5303 Colo. 150, Mosca, CO 81146. ☎ **800/284-9213** or 719/378-2356. Fax 719/378-2428. 14 rms, 1 suite. July–Oct $150–$180 double, $200–$250 suite; Nov–Dec $75–$90 double, $125–$140 suite; Apr–June $100–$120 double, $150–$170 suite. (Closed Jan–Mar.) Rates include breakfast. Golf packages available. AE, DC, DISC, MC, V. Take U.S. 160 14 miles east; turn north on Colo. 150 as if going to Great Sand Dunes National Monument. Then 4 miles before the monument gate, turn onto a gravel road (signposted ZAPATA RANCH) and proceed three-quarters of a mile to the inn.

Twenty-six miles northeast of Alamosa, beautiful cottonwood trees surround and shade this resort, on a former cattle ranch established by Spanish land grant in the early 19th century. The cattle aren't there anymore, but buffalo are raised on the ranch, and mule deer frequently browse the fairways of the 18-hole championship golf course (see "Golf" above). Guest rooms are intentionally rustic, with furnishings made by hand right on the ranch; but there are private baths, individually controlled heating, and quilted comforters. This is a getaway spot: no TVs or phones in the rooms, but plenty of great views. A gourmet restaurant (see "Where to Dine" below) specializes in contemporary American cuisine. Besides the golf course, facilities include a pool, sauna, hot tub, exercise and massage room, mountain-bike rentals, and horseback-riding stables. Children 10 and older are welcome.

INEXPENSIVE

Best Western Alamosa Inn. 1919 Main St., Alamosa, CO 81101. ☎ **800/528-1234** or 719/589-2567. Fax 719/589-0767. 119 rms, 2 suites. AC TV TEL. $72–$82 double; $125 suite. Slightly lower in winter. Children under 12 stay free in parents' room. AE, CB, DC, DISC, MC, V.

This comfortable, modern motel has clean, quiet rooms and an enclosed heated pool and whirlpool. Guests also have use of a full-service health club. The restaurant serves three meals daily. Pets are permitted.

✪ **The Cottonwood Inn & Gallery.** 123 San Juan Ave., Alamosa, CO 81101. ☎ **800/955-2623** or 719/589-3882. 7 rms and suites (5 with bath). $64–$85 double. Rates include breakfast. AE, CB, DISC, DC, MC, V.

This 1908 bungalow, three blocks north of Main Street, has a distinctly artsy orientation. Julie Mordecai has decorated the common areas and guest bedrooms as a gallery of regional art, much of which is for sale. Each room is unique: The Rosa Room, for instance, has queen and single beds to accommodate small families, along with children's books and stuffed animals. The Blanca Room weds southwestern decor with art-deco motifs, while the Verde Room features old prints and a hand-loomed coverlet. A television and video library are in the living room, and the full homemade breakfasts often feature regional specialties. Smoking is not permitted.

WHERE TO DINE

EXPENSIVE

Inn at Zapata Ranch. 5303 Colo. 150, Mosca, CO 81146. ☎ **800/284-9213** or 719/378-2356. Reservations required for dinner. Main courses lunch $4–$7, dinner $9–$25. AE, DISC, MC, V. Summer, daily 11:30am–3pm and 6–9pm. Call for winter hours. CONTEMPORARY AMERICAN.

While breakfast is served to guests only, the restaurant is open to the public daily for lunch and dinner, with outdoor seating in warm weather. The hearty cuisine includes entrees such as a grilled porterhouse, lemon sage grilled chicken breast, penne pasta, and five-bean cassoulet. There's a good selection of American wines and an excellent selection of microbrewed beers. Children 10 and older are welcome.

INEXPENSIVE

Oscar's Restaurant. 710 Main St. ☎ **719/589-9230.** Most items $3–$9. MC, V. Tues–Sun 11am–9pm. MEXICAN.

This is the place to come for spicy fajitas and carne adovada. The large dining room is distinctly Southwest, with beamed ceiling and chile ristras hanging on the rough plaster walls. In addition to more than 3-dozen Mexican dishes and numerous side orders, Oscar's offers several steaks, hamburgers, and sandwiches. Beer and margaritas are served.

St. Ives Pub & Eatery. 719 Main St. ☎ **719/589-0711.** $3.50–$5.50. DISC, MC, V. Mon–Sat 11am–midnight. BAR & GRILL.

You'll find the "eatery" in front, with plants and large sidewalk windows; and the "pub" in the rear, with a sports TV, pool table, pinball machine, and video games. The fare focuses on both hot and cold New York–style deli sandwiches. Soups, salads, and hamburgers satisfy most others.

True Grits Steak House. 100 Santa Fe Ave. at the junction of U.S. 160 and Colo. 17. ☎ **719/589-9954.** Main courses lunch $3.29–$6, dinner $6–$16. DC, MC, V. Daily 11am–10pm. STEAK/SEAFOOD.

The late actor John Wayne is, beyond question, the star of this popular local restaurant. A movie poster of his Oscar-winning *True Grit* greets visitors near the entrance, while various photos and paintings of the Duke are displayed elsewhere. Most folks come here for the mesquite-grilled steaks, but seafood and other selections are also offered. There's a children's menu and a large soup-and-salad bar, as well as a full lounge.

MANASSA & THE JACK DEMPSEY MUSEUM

Twenty-one miles south of Alamosa and 7 miles north of Antonito on U.S. 285, turn east on Colo. 142 for 3 miles to the town of Manassa (pop. 1,000), best known as the hometown of heavyweight boxing great Jack Dempsey. The former world champion (1919–26) was born here in 1895 and began his fighting career at the age of 14, earning $1 a bout in mining camps. He went on to international acclaim and was an elder statesman of the sport until his death in 1983. The **Jack Dempsey Museum,** on Main Street in a park across from Town Hall (☎ 719/843-5207), open from Memorial Day to Labor Day, Monday through Saturday from 9am to 5pm, has photographs and memorabilia of Dempsey and his family.

5 A Side Trip to Creede: A Slice of Colorado's Mining History

Another 17 miles beyond Del Norte (48 miles west of Alamosa), Colo. 149 forks north off U.S. 160 at South Fork and follows the Rio Grande nearly to its source in the San Juan Mountains. It's 23 miles from the junction to Creede (pop. 600, elevation 8,852 ft.), one of the best preserved of all 19th-century Colorado silver-mining towns. Founded in 1889, it had a population of 10,000 by 1892, when a balladeer wrote, "It's day all day in the daytime, and there is no night in Creede." Over $1 million in silver was mined every day, but the Silver Panic of 1893 eclipsed Creede's rising star. For most of the next century, area mines produced just enough silver and other minerals to sustain the community until the 1960s, when tourism and outdoor recreation became paramount.

WHAT TO SEE & DO   You can obtain information from the **Creede–Mineral County Chamber of Commerce,** north of the county courthouse at the north end of Main Street (P.O. Box 580), Creede, CO 81130 (☎ **800/327-2102** or 719/658-2374). The chamber will also provide directions to the **Wheeler Geologic Area,** a region of volcanic rock formations accessible only by Jeep, horseback, or 5-hour hike; and **North Creede Canyon,** where remnants of the old town of Creede still stand near the **Commodore Mine,** whose workings seem to keep a ghostly vigil over the canyon.

The former Denver & Rio Grande Railroad depot is now the **Creede Museum,** behind City Park, which tells the story of the town's wild-and-woolly heyday. There were dozens of saloons and gambling tables, and shoot-outs were not uncommon. Bob Ford, the killer of Jesse James, was murdered in his own saloon, and Bat Masterson and "Poker Alice" Tubbs were other notorious residents. Photographs and exhibits on gambling and other activities are among the museum's collection, and you can obtain a walking tour map of the town here. It's usually open Monday through Saturday from 10am to 4pm in summer.

Don't miss the **Creede Firehouse,** hewn out of solid rock; tours are offered Monday through Friday in summer. Next to the firehouse, the **Underground Mining Museum** takes visitors on a winding trip through a 250-foot tunnel inside a mountain, as they explore the history of mining. Call for hours and admission fees (☎ **719/658-0811**).

The **Creede Repertory Theatre,** P.O. Box 269, Creede, CO 81130 (☎ **719/658-2540**), was established in 1966 by a small troupe of young actors from the University of Kansas. Now nationally acclaimed, it has performances from June through mid-September in its theater on Creede Avenue at North First Street. Tickets for most performances run $12 to $14.

The 17-mile **Bachelor Historic Tour** is described in a booklet available from the Chamber of Commerce for $1. The route follows a U.S. Forest Service road through the mountains past abandoned mines, mining equipment, the original Creede cemetery, and 19th-century town sites. The road is fine for passenger cars in dry weather, but may be closed by winter snow.

Those who want to explore the surrounding mountains or fish or raft the waters of the upper Rio Grande can contact **Mountain Man Tours,** at Main Street and Colo. 149 in Creede (☎ **719/658-2663**) to arrange a guided raft trip, fishing float trip, or mountain-bike trip, or to rent a mountain bike. Half-day raft trips cost $30 for adults, $20 for children; and a full-day raft trip costs $60 for adults and $50 for children. Lunch is $6 extra. Guided half-day fishing trips for one or two cost $130, and full-day trips cost $195. Guided half-day mountain bike tours cost $38, with a minimum of two people. Those wanting to take off on their own on a mountain bike can rent one for $15 for a half-day or $25 for a full day.

WHERE TO STAY & DINE   Next door to the Rep Theatre is the **Creede Hotel & Restaurant,** 120 Main St. (☎ **719/658-2608**). Located in a restored 1892 hotel, this bed-and-breakfast inn is fully open May to October, with limited availability at other times. There are four rooms in the hotel, each with private bath, plus three additional rooms in an adjoining building. Rates run $69 to $79 double, $10 for each additional person, with full breakfast included, and discounts in the off-season. The restaurant also serves lunch and dinner, with dinner entrees such as lasagna, Rocky Mountain trout, charbroiled steak, and vegetarian dishes in the $10 to $19 range. Reservations are suggested at dinner.

Wason Ranch, a good choice for hunters, fishermen, and others seeking a secluded mountain getaway, is 2 miles southeast of Creede on Colo. 149 (☎ **719/658-2413**). The ranch has modern, two-bedroom log cabins for $54 per day, for up to four people; and three-bedroom cottages for $135 (2-day minimum). There is one large 100-year-old colonial home, starting at $160, which will accommodate four to eight. All units have fully equipped kitchenettes. The ranch can provide guided fishing and hunting trips, and guests also have opportunities to see eagles, elk, moose, mountain sheep, deer, and other wildlife.

6 La Garita: Rock Climber's Mecca

A quiet community about 43 miles northwest of Alamosa, and 8 miles west of U.S. 285, La Garita is widely known among rock climbers and mountain bikers. Rock climbers from around the world make their way to the gigantic boulders and sheer rock walls of **Penitente Canyon,** maintained by the Bureau of Land Management's San Luis Resource Area office, 1921 State Ave., Alamosa, CO 81101 (☎ **719/589-4975**). To reach the canyon, drive a little over a mile south of the La Garita Cash Store via County Road 38A (bear left when the road forks) to the well-marked turnoff. The rock climbing area is about 1¹/₂ miles west. Because of the area's growing popularity among rock climbers and the resulting number of bolts left in the rock walls, the Bureau of Land Management has implemented a bolting moratorium until a management plan can be completed.

About 3 miles south of the Penitente Canyon turnoff on County Road 38A is the turnoff for **Natural Arch,** administered by the Rio Grande National Forest, 13308 U.S. 160 (P.O. Box 40), Del Norte, CO 81132 (☎ **719/657-3321**). From the county road, go west on Road A32 through private land for just under 3 miles to the national forest boundary. After another mile bear right at a fork and travel about 1¹/₂ miles to the Natural Arch parking area, where you get a good view of the arch. It takes about 15 minutes on a short but steep trail to reach the arch itself, where you'll be rewarded with a beautiful view of surrounding mountain peaks and valleys.

Southeastern Colorado 15

Colorado's southeastern quadrant owes its life to the Arkansas River system. This mighty stream forges one of the world's most spectacular canyons—the deep, narrow Royal Gorge—as it wends its way down from the Rocky Mountain foothills. On its trek through Pueblo it supplies water for a major steel industry. Then it rolls across the Great Plains, providing life-giving water to an arid but soil-rich region that produces a wide variety of vegetables and fruits. Bent's Old Fort, a national historic site that has re-created one of the West's most important trading posts of the 1830s and 1840s, also rests beside the river. South of Pueblo down I-25, the towns of Trinidad and Walsenburg are the centers of a century-old coal-mining district.

1 Pueblo

Don't trust your first impressions. When you drive into Pueblo along the interstate, it's easy to think that this city's a dump, composed entirely of warehouses, rundown factories, and junked cars. But take the time to get off the interstate and discover the real Pueblo, and you'll find handsome historic homes, fine western art, a well-run zoo, and a surprising amount of outdoor recreation opportunities.

Although Zebulon Pike and his U.S. Army exploratory expedition camped at the future site of Pueblo in 1806, there was no white settlement here until 1842, when El Pueblo Fort was constructed as a fur-trading outpost. It was abandoned following a Ute massacre in late 1854, but when the Colorado gold rush began 5 years later, the town of Pueblo was born on the site of the former fort. Other towns were platted nearby, and eventually four of them grew together, each with its own street system, to become the Pueblo of today.

In the early 20th century the city grew as a major center for coal mining and steel production. Job opportunities drew large numbers of immigrants, especially from Mexico and eastern Europe. Modern Pueblo has diversified, with high-tech industries, as well as the University of Southern Colorado. As the largest city in southeastern Colorado, this city of 100,000 is the market center for a 15-county region extending to the borders of New Mexico, Oklahoma, and Kansas.

ESSENTIALS

GETTING THERE   By Car   I-25 links Pueblo directly with Colorado Springs, Denver, and points north; and Santa Fe, Albuquerque, and other New Mexico cities to the south. U.S. 50 runs east to La Junta and west to Cañon City, Gunnison, and Montrose.

By Plane   Pueblo Memorial Airport, Keeler Parkway off U.S. 50 East (☎ 719/948-3355), is served daily by **United Express** (☎ 800/241-6522 or 719/948-4423). In addition, air charter and air ambulance services are provided by **Travelaire Aviation** (☎ 719/948-3316).

ORIENTATION   The city of Pueblo is situated on the eastward-flowing Arkansas River at its confluence with Fountain Creek. The downtown core is located north of the Arkansas and west of the Fountain, immediately west of I-25. Santa Fe Avenue and Main Street, one block west, are the principal north-south thoroughfares; the cross streets are numbered (counting northward), with Fourth and Eighth streets the most important. Paralleling Main Street four blocks to its west is Elizabeth Street, another arterial that intersects U.S. 50 at I-25, opposite Pueblo Mall, at the north end of the city. U.S. 50 runs west from here toward Cañon City; U.S. 50 East exits I-25 about a mile farther south, and proceeds past the airport toward La Junta. Main and Fourth both cross the Arkansas River to the Mesa Junction residential district. Pueblo Boulevard circles the city on its south and west sides, with spurs leading to the Nature Center and Pueblo Reservoir.

VISITOR INFORMATION   Contact the **Pueblo Chamber of Commerce Convention and Visitors Council,** 302 N. Santa Fe Ave. (P.O. Box 697), Pueblo, CO 81002 (☎ 800/233-3446 or 719/542-1704), for most tourism needs. A **Visitor Information Center** is located in a modular unit adjacent to the caboose off I-25 exit 101, in the K-Mart parking lot on Elizabeth Street at U.S. 50 West (☎ 719/543-1742); it's open daily from 8am to 6pm in summer, 8am to 4pm in winter, and is accessible to handicapped travelers.

GETTING AROUND   Public transportation is provided by **City Bus** (☎ 719/542-4306). For taxi service, call **City Cab** (☎ 719/543-2525). Agencies providing rental cars at the airport include **Avis** (☎ 800/831-2847 or 719/948-9665), **Budget** (☎ 800/527-0700 or 719/948-3363), and **Hertz** (☎ 800/654-3131 or 719/948-3345).

FAST FACTS   In case of **emergency,** call **911.** Medical services are provided downtown by **Parkview Episcopal Medical Center,** 400 W. 16th St. (☎ 719/584-4000), or on the south side by **St. Mary-Corwin Regional Medical Center,** 1008 Minnequa Ave. (☎ 719/560-4000). The main **post office** is downtown at 420 N. Main St. (☎ 719/544-0132). For **road conditions,** call 719/545-8520. For **time, temperature, and weather,** call 719/542-4444. **State and local taxes** on rooms total 11.8%.

SPECIAL EVENTS   Major annual events include Bluegrass on the River, at the Greenway and Nature Center, in May; the Governor's Cup Regatta, at Pueblo Reservoir, in May; the Pueblo Chamber Golf Tournament, in June; the Rolling River Raft Race, in July; the Colorado State Fair, in late August; the Chile and Frijole Festival, in September; Oktoberfest, in September; the Parade of Lights, in November; the Christmas Posada, in December; and the Yule Log Festival, in Beulah, in December. The chamber of commerce has a recorded listing of weekly events (☎ 719/542-1776).

WHAT TO SEE & DO

Historic Pueblo runs along Union Avenue north from the Arkansas River to First Street, a distance of about five blocks. More than 40 buildings here are listed on the National Register of Historic Places, including the Vail Hotel, headquarters of the **Pueblo County Historical Society** museum and library (☎ **719/543-6772**), with railroad memorabilia, locally made saddles, and some 4,500 books, historical maps, and photographs depicting Pueblo's history. Union Depot, with its mosaic tile floors and beautiful stained-glass windows, still serves rail freight lines. **Walking-tour maps** can be obtained from the Chamber of Commerce, 302 N. Santa Fe Ave. (☎ **719/ 542-1704**), and Union Avenue businesses.

El Pueblo Museum. 324 W. First St. ☎ **719/583-0453.** Admission $2.50 adults, $2 ages 6–16 and over 65, children under 6 free. Mon–Sat 10am–4:30pm, Sun noon–3pm.

This downtown museum presents colorful exhibits of Native American, Mexican, and American cultures. Named for the site's original fur-trading post, the museum also has displays on frontier trapping, ranching, and agriculture, as well as the coming of industry to Colorado. In September the Chile & Frijole Festival features live music, traditional dances, and food.

Fred E. Weisbrod/International B-24 Memorial Museum. 1001 Magnuson Ave., Pueblo West. ☎ **719/948-9219.** Free Admission, but donations welcome. Mon–Fri 10am–4pm, Sat 10am–2pm, Sun 1–4pm.

About 2 dozen historic aircraft are on display here, as well as numerous exhibits on the B-24 bomber and its role in World War II.

✪ **The Greenway and Nature Center.** 5200 Nature Center Rd. ☎ **719/545-9114.** Free Admission, donations welcome. Grounds open daily dawn–10pm. Raptor Center: Tues–Fri 11am–4pm, Sat–Sun 10am–5pm. Interpretive Center and nature shop: Apr–Oct, Tues–Sat 9am–5pm, Sun 10am–5pm; Nov–Mar, Tues–Fri 9am–5pm, Sat–Sun 10am–4pm.

A major recreation and education center, this area provides access to more than 36 miles of biking and hiking trails along the Arkansas River. There's also a fishing dock, volleyball courts, horseshoe pits, an amphitheater, and interpretive nature trails. An interpretive center has exhibits on the flora and fauna of the area; and the **Cafe del Rio** (☎ 719/545-1009), serves American and southwestern dishes. At the **Raptor Center,** injured eagles, owls, hawks, and other birds of prey are nursed back to health and released to the wild. It also houses exhibits and several resident birds of prey.

Pueblo Zoo. City Park, 3455 Nuckolls Ave. ☎ **719/561-9664.** Admission $3 adult, $2 youths 13–18, $1 children 3–12, free children 2 and under. Summer daily 10am–5pm; winter daily 9am–4pm.

More than 300 animals are exhibited at this 30-acre zoo, which includes a tropical rain forest and the only underwater viewing of penguins in Colorado. You'll find all sorts of cold-blooded creatures in the herpetarium, including reptiles and insects; kangaroos and emus in the Australia Station; an excellent lion exhibit; endangered species such as cottontop tamarins, black and white ruffed lemurs and rusty spotted cats; plus numerous other animals. In the Pioneer Ranch-at-the-Zoo, visitors can feed a variety of rare domesticated animals, and the Discovery Room has hands-on exhibits for all ages.

✪ **Rosemount Museum.** 419 W. 14th St. ☎ **719/545-5290.** Admission $5 adults, $4 seniors 60 and over, $2 children 6–16, free for children under 6. June–Aug Tues–Sat 10am–4pm, Sun 2–4pm; Sept–Dec and Feb–May Tues–Sat 1–4pm, Sun 2–4pm. Last tour begins at 3:30pm.

Pueblo's most important historic attraction is this 37-room mansion, considered one of the finest surviving examples of turn-of-the-century architecture and decoration in North America. Built in 1891 for the pioneer Thatcher family, the three-story, 24,000-square-foot home is entirely of pink rhyolite stone. Inside you'll find handsome oak, maple, and mahogany woodwork; remarkable works of stained glass; hand-decorated ceilings; exquisite Tiffany lighting fixtures; and 10 fireplaces, each with a unique character. About 85% of the furnishings are original to the mansion. All visitors join a guided tour.

Sangre De Cristo Arts and Conference Center. 210 N. Santa Fe Ave. ☎ **719/543-0130.** Free Admission to galleries; Children's Museum $1 adults, 50¢ children. Children's Museum: Mon–Sat 11am–5pm; arts center: Mon–Sat 9am–5pm; galleries: Mon–Sat 11am–4pm; shop: Mon–Sat 11am–5pm.

Pueblo's cultural hub is a two-building complex that contains a 500-seat theater; two dance studios; four art galleries, including one that houses a fine collection of western art; a spacious conference room, gift shop, and a hands-on children's museum.

SPORTS & OUTDOOR ACTIVITIES

Lake Pueblo State Park, also called Pueblo Reservoir, is undoubtedly the water-sports capital of southern Colorado. The 17,000-acre park, with its 4,600 acres of water and 60 miles of shoreline, is open to boating of all kinds, swimming, hiking, biking, and horseback riding. From Pueblo, take U.S. 50 west for 4 miles, turn south onto Pueblo Boulevard and go another 4 miles to Thatcher Avenue, where you turn west and go 6 miles to the park.

AUTOMOBILE RACING   Top stock-car races are held from mid-April through September on the quarter-mile paved oval track at **Beacon Hill Speedway,** 400 Gobatti Place (☎ 719/545-6105). Nationally sanctioned drag racing, motocross, quarter scale, quarter-midget racing, and Sports Car Club of America competitions take place April through September at the **Pueblo Motor Sports Park,** U.S. 50 and Pueblo Boulevard in Pueblo West (☎ 719/547-9921).

BICYCLING   The Greenway and Nature Center includes more than 20 miles of bicycle paths along the Arkansas River. The Pueblo Chamber of Commerce can provide maps of the 35-mile River Trail System that stretches from Pueblo Reservoir to the University of Southern Colorado, where bicyclists and in-line skaters are welcome.

BOATING   The Pueblo Reservoir is one of Colorado's most popular water-sports areas. The park's **North Marina** (☎ 719/547-3880) has a gas dock, boating and fishing supplies, groceries, a restaurant, and boat rentals ($10–$15 per hour or $50–$75 per day for fishing boats). The marina is open year-round, but boats are available only from April through October. Boats and canoes can also be put into the Arkansas River at the **Greenway and Nature Center,** 5200 Nature Center Rd. (☎ 719/545-9114).

FISHING   The **Greenway and Nature Center,** 5200 Nature Center Rd. (☎ 719/545-9114), has a 150-foot fishing dock on the Arkansas River. Angling for rainbow trout, brown trout, crappie, black bass, and channel catfish is popular from shore or boat at Pueblo Reservoir, where you'll also find a fish cleaning station.

GOLF   Local courses open to the public include **Walking Stick,** 4301 Walking Stick Blvd. (☎ 719/584-3400), at the northwest corner of the University of Southern Colorado. Rated among Colorado's best courses and best values, this par-72, 18-hole course has a driving range and charges greens fees of $16 weekdays and $18 weekends for 18 holes. Other local courses include **City Park,** 3900 Thatcher Ave. (☎ **719/561-4946**), with an 18-hole regulation course plus an executive nine-hole course. Greens fees for 18 holes are $14 weekdays and $15 weekends, and for nine holes are $8.50 at any time. **Pueblo West,** 251 McCulloch Blvd. (☎ **719/ 547-2280**), is a par-72, 18-hole regulation course with practice facilities. Greens fees are $13 weekdays and $16 weekends for 18 holes, and $8 weekdays and $10 weekends for nine holes. **Hollydot Golf Course,** about 25 miles south of Pueblo, exit 74 off I-25, in Colorado City (☎ **719/676-3340**), is a 27-hole facility with an 18-hole regulation course. Greens fees are $13 weekdays and $15 weekends for 18 holes; $8 weekdays and $9 weekends for nine holes.

HIKING Pueblo is the headquarters of the Pike and San Isabel National Forests, and Comanche and Cimarron National Grasslands, 1920 Valley Dr. (☎ **719/ 545-8737**), with information on hiking and backpacking opportunities throughout central and southern Colorado and southwestern Kansas. Hikers also head to Pueblo Reservoir, which has 18 miles of trails.

SWIMMING The most popular local swimming hole is the **Rock Canyon Swim Beach** at the east end of Lake Pueblo State Park. The area has a beach (50¢ admission), a water slide ($7 for all day), and bumper boats ($1 for 5 minutes); lifeguards during summer.

There are also several public swimming pools in Pueblo, administered by the **City of Pueblo Parks and Recreation Department** (☎ 719/561-8502), including **Mineral Palace Pool,** 1600 N. Santa Fe Ave. (☎ **719/545-5319**); **City Park Pool,** City Park (☎ **719/564-2373**); and **Minnequa Park Pool,** 1708 E. Orman Ave. (☎ **719/ 564-2847**).

WINTER SPORTS Depending on weather conditions, you'll find ice fishing and cross-country skiing at Lake Pueblo State Park. Ice-skating is available year-round at **Pueblo Plaza Ice Arena,** 100 N. Grand Ave. (☎ **719/542-8784**). Admission costs $2 for adults, $1.50 for children 12 and under. Skate rentals and sharpening are also available.

WHERE TO STAY

Lodging possibilities in Pueblo include the **Ramada Inn,** 2001 N. Hudson (☎ **800/ 272-6232** or 719/542-3750), which charges $75 to $90 double in summer; and the **Hampton Inn,** 4703 N. Freeway, just west of I-25 exit 102 (☎ **800/972-0165, 800/HAMPTON,** or 719/544-4700), with rates, including continental breakfast, of $85 to $100 double. In Pueblo West, there's also the **Best Western Inn at Pueblo West,** 201 S. McCulloch Blvd. (☎ **800/448-1972** or 719/547-2111), charging $72 to $84 double in summer and $53 to $66 double in winter. Most area motels charge higher rates during the State Fair from mid-August to early September.

Abriendo Inn. 300 W. Abriendo Ave., Pueblo, CO 81004. ☎ **719/544-2703.** Fax 719/ 542-6544. 10 rms. A/C TV TEL. $58–$110 double. Rates include breakfast. AE, DC, MC, V.

Built in 1906 as the mansion of brewing magnate Martin Walter, his wife, and their eight children, this house—in traditional Foursquare architectural style—is one of Pueblo's finest bed-and-breakfasts. Located just three blocks north of historic Union Avenue, the inn offers guest rooms decorated with antique furniture and period reproductions, with brass or four-poster beds. All rooms have telephones with modem jacks. A full breakfast is served in the oak-wainscoted dining room or on an outside patio. Complimentary refreshments are available daily from 5:30 to 7pm. Smoking is permitted on the veranda only.

CAMPING

There are 401 campsites spread across Lake Pueblo State Park. There's a dump station and showers, and electric hookups at some sites. Sites cost $6 to $10 a night.

WHERE TO DINE

Ianne's Whiskey Ridge. 4333 Thatcher Ave. ☎ **719/564-8551.** Reservations recommended. Main courses $7–$21. AE, DISC, MC, V. Mon–Sat 4–10pm, Sun 11am–10pm. ITALIAN/STEAK/SEAFOOD.

Serving Pueblo for over 50 years, this family-owned and -operated restaurant prepares everything from scratch and warns evening diners that because each meal is cooked to order, they may have to wait. Pasta dishes are a specialty; our favorites are the lasagna and ravioli. There is also a large selection of fresh seafood, chicken, veal, and certified Angus steaks.

Irish Brew Pub & Grille. 108 W. Third St. ☎ **719/542-9974.** Main courses $5–$16. AE, CB, DC, DISC, MC, V. Mon–Sat 9am–11pm (bar open to 2am). ITALIAN/AMERICAN.

If you want to meet everybody who's anybody in Pueblo, squeeze into this brew pub any evening after work. Have a drink, hobnob with the locals, then head for a table for a great meal. The Calantino family, which opened the pub in 1944, is still there, serving everything from traditional bar food such as Philly cheese steak, buffalo burgers, and chicken club, to exotic pasta specialties, lamb, chicken, beef, and wild game.

La Renaissance. 217 E. Routt Ave., Mesa Junction. ☎ **719/543-6367.** Reservations recommended. Three-course lunch $4.95–$9.95; five-course dinner $9.75–$29. AE, CB, DC, DISC, MC, V. Mon–Fri 11am–2pm; Mon–Sat 5–9pm. STEAK/SEAFOOD.

Housed in a historic 1880s Presbyterian church, La Renaissance offers casual dining in a unique atmosphere, with stained-glass windows, high vaulted ceilings, and oak pews providing some of the seating. A three-course lunch and five-course dinner begin with a tureen of soup and finish with dessert, served at the table from a wooden cart. Broiled salmon filet and baked asparagus Virginia (wrapped in ham) are popular lunches, along with the pasta of the day; slow-roasted prime rib, New Zealand deep sea filet, and breast of chicken stuffed with broccoli and cheese are among dinner favorites. There's a wide variety of domestic and imported wine and beer. La Renaissance is located in Mesa Junction on the south side of Pueblo, two blocks southwest of Abriendo Avenue at the corner of Michigan Street.

2 Royal Gorge & Cañon City

The Royal Gorge, one of the most impressive natural attractions in the state, lies 8 miles west of Cañon City, at the head of the Arkansas River valley. This narrow canyon, 1,053 feet deep, was cut through solid granite by three million years of water and wind erosion. When Zebulon Pike encountered the gorge in 1806, he predicted that man would never conquer it. But by 1877 the Denver & Rio Grande Railroad had laid a route through the canyon, and it soon became a major tourist attraction.

The gorge is spanned by the world's highest suspension bridge and an aerial tramway, built for no other reason than to thrill tourists. The quarter-mile-long bridge was constructed in 1929, suspended from two 300-ton cables, and reinforced in 1983. A funicular railway, believed to be the world's steepest, was completed in 1931; it plunges from the rim of the gorge to the floor at a 45° angle. The tram opened in 1969.

Owned by the city of Cañon City, the park complex also includes a multimedia theater, miniature railway, children's attractions, restaurants, gift shops, an entertainment gazebo, and herds of tame mule deer. It's open every day, year-round, from dawn to dusk. Admission—$11 for adults, $8 for seniors and children 4 to 11—includes crossing the bridge and all other park attractions. For information, contact **Royal Gorge Bridge,** P.O. Box 549, Cañon City, CO 81215 (☎ **719/275-7507**).

To see this beautiful gorge from the river up and have some thrills at the same time, consider a raft trip. Rates for adults run $75 to $85 for full-day trips, including lunch; half-day trips are about $45. Most Royal Gorge raft trips include rough white-water stretches of the river, and those wanting trips over calmer sections should inquire with local rafting companies. Major outfitters include **Arkansas River Tours** (☎ **800/321-4352**); **Buffalo Joe River Trips** (☎ **800/356-7984**); **Echo Canyon River Expeditions,** (☎ **800/748-2953**); **Rocky Mountain Adventures** (☎ **800/858-6808**), and **Whitewater Adventure Outfitters** (☎ **800/530-8212**).

A popular location for filmmaking in the industry's early days, **Cañon City** was a particular favorite of silent screen actor Tom Mix, who reputedly was working as a cowboy in the area before he became a film star. The drowning death of a prominent actress sent film crews elsewhere, but the area's beautiful scenery and Old West heritage lured the industry back in the late 1950s with the creation of Buckskin Joe, a western theme park and movie set where dozens of films have been shot, including *How the West Was Won* and *Cat Ballou.* Located about 8 miles west of Cañon City on U.S. 50, **✪ Buckskin Joe Park & Railway** (☎ **719/275-5149**) is an authentic-looking Old West town, created from genuine 19th-century buildings relocated from around the state. Visitors can watch gunfights, pan for gold, see antique autos, ride horseback or in a horse-drawn trolley, wander around a western maze, and hop a train for a scenic 30-minute trip to the Royal Gorge rim. Open mid-May to late September, daily from 9am to 7:30pm. The railway runs from March through November, daily 8am to 8pm. Combination admission tickets are $12 adults, $10 children under 12; separate tickets are also available.

Other Cañon City attractions include the **✪ Colorado Territorial Prison Museum and Park,** 201 N. First St. (☎ **719/269-3015**). Housed in the state's former women's prison, just outside the walls of the original territorial prison that opened in 1871, the museum contains an actual gas chamber, historic photos of life behind bars, confiscated inmates' weapons, the last hangman's noose used legally in the state, and other artifacts and exhibits showing what prison life was like in the Old West. There's also a gift shop that sells arts and crafts made by inmates from the medium-security prison next door. The museum is open daily from 9am to 6pm from May through September, and Friday through Sunday from 10am to 5pm from October through April. Admission costs $3.50 for adults, $3 for senior citizens, $2 for children 6 to 12, and free for children under six. The **Cañon City Municipal Museum,** U.S. 50 (Royal Gorge Blvd.) at Sixth St. (☎ **719/269-9018**), contains Native American artifacts, guns, wild-game trophies, and pioneer memorabilia. Behind the main museum building you'll find the renovated 1860 log cabin built by Anson Rudd, local blacksmith and first warden of the Colorado Territorial Prison, as well as the Rudd family's three-story house built in 1881. The museum is open Tuesday through Sunday from early May through Labor Day, and Tuesday through Saturday the rest of the year. It is closed Christmas Eve plus all state and federal holidays. Hours are 10am to 4pm. Admission costs $1 for adults, 50¢ for children 6 to 12, and free for children under six.

For information on where to stay and eat, a walking tour of historic downtown Cañon City, and information on scenic drives and other attractions, contact the

Cañon City Chamber of Commerce, P.O. Bin 749, Cañon City, CO 81215 (☎ **800/876-7922** or 719/275-2331).

3 Trinidad

History and art are two reasons to stop in Trinidad when traveling along I-25 through southern Colorado. Bat Masterson was sheriff in the 1880s, Wyatt Earp drove the stage, Kit Carson helped open the trade routes, and even Billy the Kid passed through. Many historic buildings—handsome structures of brick and sandstone—survive from this era. Plains tribes roamed the area for centuries before the first 17th- and 18th-century forays by Spanish explorers and settlers. Later, traders and trappers made this an important stop on the northern branch of the Santa Fe Trail.

German, Irish, Italian, Jewish, Polish, and Slavic immigrants were drawn to the area around the turn of the century for jobs at area coal mines and cattle ranches, and agriculture and railroading were also important economic factors. Today there is some mining and ranching, along with a growing tourism trade.

ESSENTIALS

GETTING THERE   By Car   If you're traveling from north or south, take I-25: Trinidad straddles the interstate, halfway between Denver and Santa Fe, New Mexico. From the east, you can take U.S. 50 into La Junta, then turn southwest for 80 miles on U.S. 350. From Durango and points west, follow U.S. 160 to Walsenburg, then travel south 37 miles on I-25.

By Plane   Pueblo has the nearest commercial airport (see section 1, earlier in this chapter for flight information).

By Train   The **Amtrak** *Southwest Chief* passes through Trinidad twice daily—once eastbound, once westbound—on the main line between Chicago and Los Angeles. The depot is on Nevada Street north of College Street, beneath I-25 (☎ **800/ 872-7245**).

ORIENTATION   Trinidad is nestled in the foothills of the Rocky Mountains. To the west is the Sangre de Cristo Range; to the east, the Great Plains. El Rio de Las Animas en Purgatorio (the river of lost souls in Purgatory), better known as the Purgatoire River, flows from southwest to northeast through the center of town, par-alleling Main Street (U.S. 160/350). The historic downtown area is focused around Main and Commercial streets on the south side of the river. Main joins I-25 on the west side of downtown.

VISITOR INFORMATION   The **Colorado Welcome Center,** 309 N. Nevada Ave. (I-25 exit 14A), Trinidad, CO 81082 (☎ **719/846-9512**), open daily 8am to 5pm in winter and 8am to 6pm in summer, has information not only on Trinidad and southeastern Colorado, but on the entire state. The **Trinidad Chamber of Commerce** is in the same building (☎ **719/846-9285**).

GETTING AROUND   You can **rent a car** from Hadad Motor Sales (☎ **719/ 846-3318**) or Circle Chevrolet (☎ **719/846-9805**). Taxi service is provided by Freyta Garage (☎ **719/846-2237**).

The **Trinidad Trolley,** operating from Memorial Day to Labor Day, provides an excellent, and free, way to see this historic city. Running daily from 10am to 5pm, you can pick up the trolley at the Colorado Welcome Center (see "Visitor Information" above), and get on and off at the various museums and other attractions. Pick up a schedule at the Welcome Center.

FAST FACTS In case of **emergency,** call **911.** Medical services are provided at **Mt. San Rafael Hospital,** 410 Benedicta Avenue off Main Street (☎ **719/846-9213**). For **road conditions,** call 719/846-9262. The **post office** (☎ **719/846-6871**) is at 301 E. Main St. A tax of about 7% is added to lodging bills.

SPECIAL EVENTS Annual Trinidad events include the Santa Fe Trail Festival, the second weekend of June; Concerts in the Park many Fridays and Sundays from June through August; Cowboy Days, in early September; and Fallfest, in October.

WHAT TO SEE & DO

Main Street was once part of the Mountain Branch of the Santa Fe Trail, and many of the streets that cross it are paved with locally made red brick. The Trinidad Historical Society distributes a booklet titled *A Walk Through the History of Trinidad* ($2), available at local museums. Among the buildings it singles out for special attention are the Trinidad Opera House (1883), Columbian Hotel (1879), which are across from each other on Main Street, and the Trinidad Water Works (1879) on Cedar Street at the Purgatoire River.

✪ **A. R. Mitchell Memorial Museum of Western Art.** 150 E. Main St. ☎ **719/846-4224.** Free Admission. Apr–Sept Mon–Sat 10am–4pm; off-season by appointment.

More than 250 paintings and illustrations by western artist Arthur Roy Mitchell (1889–1977) are displayed here, along with works by other nationally recognized artists and a collection of early Hispanic religious folk art. The museum also contains the Aultman collection of photographs, taken by Oliver E. Aultman and his son Glenn from the late 1800s through much of the 20th century, a photographic time line from the early 1600s to the present, plus early cameras, darkroom equipment, and studio props. The huge building, originally a department store, is 1906 western-style with the original tin ceiling, wood floors, and a horseshoe-shaped mezzanine.

Louden-Henritze Archaeology Museum. Freudenthal Memorial Library, Trinidad State Junior College, near intersection of Park and Prospect streets. ☎ **719/846-5508.** Free Admission. May–Sept, Mon–Fri 10am–4pm; winter by appointment.

Millions of years of history are displayed here, including fossils, casts of dinosaur tracks, arrowheads, baskets, pottery, petroglyphs, and other artifacts from prehistoric man discovered during area excavations.

Old Firehouse No. 1 Children's Museum. 314 N. Commercial St. ☎ **719/846-8220** or 719/846-7721. Free Admission. June–Aug, Mon–Fri noon–4pm.

A historic fire truck, Trinidad's original 1930s-era alarm system, and a restored turn-of-the-century schoolroom are exhibited. There are also hands-on displays for children, including Grandma's trunk for dress-up.

✪ **Trinidad History Museum.** 300 E. Main St. ☎ **719/846-7217.** Call for admission fees. May–Sept daily 10am–4pm. Off-season by appointment.

Together, the Baca House, Bloom Mansion, and Santa Fe Trail Museum rank as Trinidad's principal attraction. The 1870 Baca House, along the mountain route of the Santa Fe Trail, is a two-story adobe in Greek Revival–style. Originally owned by sheep rancher Felipe Baca, the house contains some of the Baca family's original furnishings. Nearby stands the 1882 Bloom Mansion, a Second Empire–style Victorian manor embellished with fancy wood carving and ornate ironwork. The Colorado Historical Society operates both homes and the Santa Fe Trail Museum, located behind the homes in a building that was originally living quarters for ranch hands and sheepherders. Both the Baca House and Santa Fe Trail Museum are Certified Sites on the Santa Fe National Historic Trail; and the Denver Historical Society has named Felipe Baca one of the 100 most influential Coloradans.

SPORTS & OUTDOOR ACTIVITIES

Located 3 miles west of town on Colo. 12, **Trinidad Lake State Park** (☎ 719/846-6951) is the place to go for all sorts of outdoor recreation possibilities. Its 700-acre reservoir on the Purgatoire River is popular for powerboating, water-skiing, sailboating, and sailboarding. Swimming is prohibited, however. There's a boat ramp and dock, but no boat rentals or supplies. Fishermen go after largemouth bass, rainbow and brown trout, channel catfish, and walleye. There are 9 miles of hiking and mountain-biking trails, including the Levsa Canyon Trail, a 1-mile self-guided loop that also branches off for another 4 miles to the historic town of Cokedale. For those who thought to bring a horse, there are 4 miles of trails. An attractive 62-unit campground, with fees of $7 to $10, has electric hookups, a dump station, and showers. During the winter there's cross-country skiing, ice-skating, and ice fishing.

GOLF   The nine-hole, par-36 **Trinidad Municipal Golf Club,** off the Santa Fe Trail adjacent to I-25 at exit 13A (☎ 719/846-4015), is considered among the best nine-hole courses in the state. It has a driving range, putting green, pro shop, restaurant, and bar, with fees of $10 for nine holes, $15 for 18 holes, or $24 for all day.

SKIING   The **Cuchara Valley Ski Resort,** 946 Panadero Ave. #3, Cuchara, CO 81055 (☎ 800/227-4436 or 719/742-3163), is a family-oriented ski area with more than 20 runs covering some 230 acres, and it claims to never have a lift line. Located 60 miles west of Trinidad on Colo. 12, it has four lifts, including three double chairs and one triple chair, and trails are rated 40% beginner, 40% intermediate, and 20% advanced. There's a ski school, a day lodge with fast food, a restaurant, and equipment rentals. Snowboarders are welcome. Cross-country skiing trails are also located nearby.

WHERE TO STAY

Several national chains and franchises provide lodging in Trinidad. These include **Best Western Country Club Inn,** 900 W. Adams St. (I-25 exit 13A) (☎ 800/955-2211 or 719/846-2215), with summer rates of $79 to $95 double, and winter rates of $59 to $75 double; **Holiday Inn,** 9995 County Rd., just off I-25, exit 11 (☎ 800-HOLIDAY or 719/846-4491), with summer rates of $89 to $99 double, and winter rates of $74 to $79 double; and **Days Inn,** 702 W. Main St. (☎ 800/DAYS INN or 719/846-2271), charging $65 to $80 double in summer, and $43 to $60 double in winter.

WHERE TO DINE

El Capitan Restaurant & Lounge. 321 State St. ☎ **719/846-9903.** Sandwiches and à la carte Mexican items $2–$5.50; dinners $3–$10. AE, DISC, MC, V. Mon–Fri 11am–10pm, Sat 4:30–10pm. MEXICAN/ITALIAN/AMERICAN.

This attractive restaurant, with a relaxing, comfortable atmosphere, serves some of the best margaritas in southern Colorado. It's known for its Mexican and Italian dishes, although you can also get steaks, seafood, barbecued ribs, burgers, and sandwiches. Mexican items include green or red chile, bean or beef burritos, enchiladas, chimichangas, and a vegetable quesadilla. On the Italian side of the menu you'll find gnocchi, beef ravioli, and spaghetti with meatballs, meat sauce, or sausage. Desserts include fried ice cream. There's a children's menu and a full bar.

Nana & Nano's Pasta House. 415 University St. (I-25 exit 14A). ☎ **719/846-2696.** Main courses $5.50–$11.50; deli sandwiches $2.50–$3.50. AE, MC, V. Restaurant: Memorial

Day–Labor Day, Tues–Fri 4:30–8:30pm, Sat 4:30–9pm. Closes half an hour earlier in winter. Deli: Year-round Tues–Fri 10am–5pm, Sat 9am–1pm. ITALIAN.

The Monteleone family takes pride in the Italian specialties served here, each cooked to order (expect a 20-min. wait), and served with salad, bread, and butter. Daily specials include rigatoni, mostaccioli, and lasagna, and the regular menu includes a good selection of pasta, sandwiches, fish, or a rib-eye steak. Many pasta selections are available with a choice of meatballs or Italian sausage, and there is also a "Smaller Appetite" menu for all ages starting at $5.25. Monteleone's Deli, next to the restaurant, offers Italian and you-choose-it sandwiches, plus deli meats and cheeses, and take-out specialty items.

4 A Drive Along the Scenic Highway of Legends

Unquestionably the most fascinating day trip from Trinidad is the appropriately named Scenic Highway of Legends, which travels some 80 miles west, north, then northeast, mostly on Colo. 12, from Trinidad to Walsenburg.

Traveling west about 7 miles from Trinidad, past Trinidad Lake State Park, the first site of special note is **Cokedale,** just north of the highway. The best existing example of a coal camp in Colorado, Cokedale was founded in 1906 by the American Smelting and Refining Co. as a self-contained company town, and by 1909 was a thriving community of 1,500. When the mine closed in 1947, residents were offered the company-owned homes at $100 per room and $50 per lot. Some stayed, incorporating in 1948, and in 1984 Cokedale was placed on the National Register of Historic Places. Many of today's 120 or so residents are descendants of those miners, or retired miners themselves. As you drive in you'll see some of the 350 coke ovens, used to convert coal to hotter-burning coke, for which the town was named. Walking through the community you'll see the ice house, schoolhouse, mining office, Sacred Heart of Jesus and Mary Church, Gottlieb Mercantile Company, and other buildings, including the boardinghouse where bachelors could get room and board for $25 a month.

Proceeding west, you'll pass several old coal towns, including Segundo, Weston, and Vigil, and two coal mines, the Golden Eagle, where underground mining is still done, and New Elk Mine, now a processing plant, before entering **Stonewall Valley,** 33 miles west of Trinidad. Named for a striking rock formation, a vertical bed of lithified sandstone, Stonewall is both the site of a small timber industry and the location of many vacation homes. Lodging and camping are available.

From Stonewall, Colo. 12 turns north past **Monument Lake,** a resort and water supply for the city of Trinidad, named for a rock formation in the middle of the lake that some say resembles two Native American chiefs. Several miles past Monument Lake is **North Lake,** a state wildlife area and home to rainbow, cutthroat, kokanee, and brown trout.

The highway continues north across 9,941-foot **Cucharas Pass.** Overlooking the pass are the **Spanish Peaks,** eroded remnants of a 20-million-year-old volcano. The native Arapahoe believed them to be the home of the gods, and they served as guideposts to early travelers. Legends persist about the existence of a treasure of gold in this area, but none has been found. Several miles north of Cucharas Pass is **Cucharas River Recreation Area,** home of Blue Lake, named for its spectacular color.

Numerous geologic features become prominent as the road descends toward Walsenburg. Among them are the **Devil's Stairsteps,** one of a series of erosion-resistant igneous dikes that radiate out like spokes from the Spanish Peaks; **Dakota Wall,** a layer of pressed sandstone thrust vertically from the earth; and **Goemmer**

Butte, sometimes called "Sore Thumb Butte," a volcanic plug rising 500 feet from the valley floor.

At this point, about 65 miles from Trinidad, is the foothills village of **La Veta** (pop. 750), founded in 1862 by Colonel John M. Francisco, who reportedly said after seeing the pretty valley, "This is paradise enough for me." **Fort Francisco Museum,** on Francisco Street at Colo. 12 (P.O. Box 428, La Veta, CO 81055), occupies the original plaza buildings and incorporates a saloon, schoolhouse, blacksmith shop, Presbyterian church, and mining museum to depict frontier life. Operated by the Huerfano Historical Society, the museum celebrates Fort Francisco Days each August, usually on the third weekend. The museum is open from Memorial Day to Labor Day daily from 9am to 5pm; admission is $2 for adults, $1 for children aged 10 to 17, and free for those under 10. Among several attractive bed-and-breakfasts in La Veta is the **1899 Bed and Breakfast Inn,** 314 S. Main St., P.O. Box 372, La Veta, CO 81055 (☎ 719/742-3576). Listed in the National Register of Historic Places, the inn has five rooms ranging from $48 to $54 for two, including full breakfast, and there is a separate cottage that rents for about $70, also including breakfast for two.

Continuing east, Colo. 12 joins U.S. 160, which goes by **Lathrop State Park** (☎ 719/738-2376), the state's oldest state park, with two lakes for boating (no rentals), swimming, and fishing; camping ($6–$10); a 2-mile hiking and mountain biking trail; and cross-country skiing and ice-skating. There's also a nine-hole golf course (☎ 719/738-2739), with fees of $11 to $13 for nine holes, and an attractive Visitor Center.

From the park it's about 2 miles to Walsenburg on U.S. 160, and just under 40 miles south down I-25 to return to Trinidad.

5   La Junta

One of Colorado's pockets of fruit growing, this busy little town has several surprises for visitors, including some of the best Native American art in the country and nearby a handsome reconstruction of an historic fort.

Once the hunting and fishing grounds of the Arapahoe, Cheyenne, and Ute tribes, and visited briefly by Spanish soldiers in the 17th and 18th centuries, it was not until Zebulon Pike led his exploratory expedition into the Arkansas River valley in 1806 that the area became known to white Americans. Trappers and traders followed, creating the Santa Fe Trail; then brothers William and Charles Bent built Bent's Fort in 1833 as a trading post and the first American settlement in the region.

La Junta was founded in 1875 as a railroad camp. First called Manzaneras, then Otero, it was renamed La Junta—Spanish for "the junction"—on completion of rail links to Pueblo and Trinidad in 1877. The town flourished as a farming and ranching center. Today, with a population of about 8,500, its highly irrigated land produces a wide variety of fruits, vegetables, and wheat.

ESSENTIALS

GETTING THERE   By Car   La Junta is easily reached via U.S. 50, which comes into town from Kansas in the east, and continues west to I-25 at Pueblo. From New Mexico, exit I-25 at Trinidad and take U.S. 350; from Durango and southwestern Colorado, take U.S. 160 to Walsenburg, and continue on Colo. 10 to La Junta.

By Plane   Pueblo has the nearest commercial airport (see section 1 of this chapter).

By Train   Passenger service is available aboard **Amtrak,** with a depot on First Street at Colorado Avenue (☎ 800/872-7245). The *Southwest Chief* passes through daily on the main line between Chicago and Los Angeles.

ORIENTATION   La Junta is located on the Arkansas River at an elevation of 4,100 feet. U.S. 50, which runs through town as First Street, follows the river's south bank. Highways from Trinidad and Walsenburg join it just west of town. The downtown core focuses on First, Second, and Third streets, crossed by north-south Colorado and Santa Fe avenues. At the east edge of town, Colo. 109 (Adams Ave.) crosses the Arkansas into North La Junta (where it becomes Main St.); six blocks past the river, Colo. 194 (Trail Rd.) forks to the right and leads 5 miles to Bent's Old Fort.

VISITOR INFORMATION   Contact the **La Junta Chamber of Commerce,** 110 Santa Fe Ave., La Junta, CO 81050 (☎ **719/384-7411** and fax 719/384-2217).

FAST FACTS   In case of **emergency,** call **911.** Health services are rendered by the **Arkansas Valley Regional Medical Center,** 1100 Carson Ave. at 10th Street (☎ **719/384-5412**). The **post office** (☎ **719/384-5944**) is located at Fourth Street and Colorado Avenue. For **road conditions,** call 303/639-1111 (toll call).

SPECIAL EVENTS   Annual events include the Fur Trade Encampment, at Bent's Old Fort, in July; Kid's Rodeo, in August; Early Settlers Day, the Saturday after Labor Day; and 1846 Christmas, at Bent's Old Fort, in mid-December.

WHAT TO SEE & DO

A nice way to orient yourself to La Junta is to take the self-guided *Historic Homes of La Junta* walking/driving tour, described in a free brochure available from the La Junta Chamber of Commerce. On it, you'll pass by local homes built in the late 1800s and early 1900s that are listed on the National Register of Historic Sites.

✪ **Bent's Old Fort National Historic Site.** 35110 Colo. 194 E. ☎ **719/384-2596.** Admission $2 per person 17 and older. Summer daily 8am–5:30pm; winter daily 9am–4pm.

Once the most important settlement on the Santa Fe Trail between Missouri and New Mexico, Bent's Old Fort has been reconstructed as it was during its reign as a major trading post, from 1833 to 1849. Located 7 miles east of modern La Junta, this adobe fort on the Arkansas River was built by brothers Charles and William Bent and partner Ceran St. Vrain. It was the hub of trade between eastern U.S. merchants, Rocky Mountain fur trappers, and Plains tribes (mainly Cheyenne, but including Arapahoe, Ute, Apache, Kiowa, and Comanche).

As American settlement increased and drove off the buffalo that were the life blood of the tribes, the Bents were caught between two cultures. Serious hostilities began in 1847, and trade rapidly declined during a cholera epidemic in 1849. Part of the fort burned that year, and was not rebuilt until modern times, although it is as faithful as possible to the original design. Reproductions furnish the 33 rooms, which include a kitchen with an adjoining pantry, a cook's room, and a dining room; a trade room with robes, pelts, and blankets in stock; blacksmith-and-carpenter shops; William Bent's office and bedroom; quarters for Mexican laborers, trappers, and soldiers; a billiard room; and the quarters of a merchant's wife (who kept a meticulous diary).

It's a quarter-mile walk on a paved path from the historic site's entry station to the fort itself, where hosts in period costume greet visitors during the summer. You'll see demonstrations of frontier life, such as blacksmithing, adobe-making, trapping, cooking, and medical and survival skills. In summer, 45-minute guided tours begin on the hour daily.

✪ **Koshare Indian Museum and Kiva.** Otero Junior College, 115 W. 18th St. ☎ **800/ 693-5482** or 719/384-4411. Admission $2 adults, $1 students and senior citizens; dances $5 adults, $3 students and youth. Memorial Day–Labor Day daily 10am–5pm; rest of the year Tues–Sun 12:30–4:30pm. Dancers perform mid-June–mid-Aug, Fri and Sat at 8pm; call for additional times.

In Search of Dinosaur Tracks

Dinosaur tracks from the Jurassic period, about 150 million years ago, are a highlight of ✪ **Comanche National Grassland,** a 419,000-acre area south of La Junta that also draws bird-watchers, hunters, anglers, and hikers. Access to Picket Wire Canyonlands, where the dinosaur tracks are located, is limited to those hiking or on mountain bikes or horseback.

The tracks are believed to be from dinosaurs in the Sauropodmorpha "reptile-type feet" and Theropoda "beast feet" families, who lived here when the area was a savannah—a tropical grassland with a few scattered trees. There was plenty of food for the Sauropods, who were plant-eaters, and made them more tempting to their enemies, the meat-eating Theropods. The Sauropods, particularly the Brontosaurus, grew to about $14\frac{1}{2}$ feet tall, and weighed up to 33 tons. Theropods grew to about $16\frac{1}{2}$ feet tall, but were not as long, and weighed only about 4 tons. Still, with their sharp claws, they would attack the Sauropods whenever given the chance.

A high-clearance vehicle or four-wheel drive is needed to get to a parking area, and from there it's at least a 10.6-mile round-trip hike to the dinosaur tracks. Visitors should be prepared for temperature extremes (summer can exceed 100°F); carry lots of drinking water, and watch for flash floods, biting insects, and snakes. Maps to the area are available from the **Comanche National Grasslands office** at 1420 E. Third St., La Junta, CO 81050 (☎ **719/384-2181**). This office can also provide information on other attractions in the grasslands, including its wildlife, such as the lesser prairie chicken, a threatened species; and rock art that's hundreds of years old.

More than $10 million worth of Native American art—featuring tribal members both as artists and subjects—is the focus of this excellent museum. Authentic clothing, jewelry, and baskets, along with western paintings and sculptures are displayed. One of the finest collections of works by early Taos, New Mexico artists is presented as well. The museum itself, located one block west of Colorado Avenue, is an adobe-style building resembling a northern New Mexico pueblo and is on the Colorado Register of Historic Sites.

The Koshare Dancers, a nationally acclaimed troop of Boy Scout Explorers, perform an average of 60 times a year, primarily in their own great *kiva*, a circular chamber traditionally used for religious rites by southwestern tribes. Dances are held at least weekly in summer, and the Koshare Winter Ceremonials are a December tradition.

Otero Museum. Third and Anderson Sts. ☎ **719/384-7500** or 719/384-7406. Free Admission; donations welcome. June–Sept, daily 1–5pm; off-season tours by appointment.

This museum provides a look at what life was like in eastern Colorado between the 1870s and 1930s. There's a genuine 1876 stage coach, a complete grocery store, several early La Junta homes, a replica of the community's first school, a doctor's office, railroad equipment and memorabilia, and restored classic motorcars displayed in an early 20th-century gas station.

WHERE TO STAY

Among the national chain motels in La Junta is **Quality Inn,** 1325 E. Third St. (☎ **800/221-2222** or 719/384-2571, with rates of $44 to $57 double. The motel's restaurant is a good breakfast spot.

✪ **Mid-Town Motel.** 215 E. Third St., La Junta, CO 81050. ☎ **719/384-7741.** 26 rms. A/C TV TEL. $34 double. AE, CB, DC, DISC, MC, V.

A great little mom-and-pop motel off the main highway, the Mid-Town offers clean, quiet rooms with good-quality linens and cable television with HBO. Owners Jack and P. J. Culp are an invaluable source of information for area visitors. Pets are welcome, and there's free morning coffee.

WHERE TO DINE

Chiaramonte's Restaurant and Lounge. 208 Santa Fe Ave. ☎ **719/384-8909.** Lunch $4.75–$7.95; dinner $4.75–$27.50. DISC, MC, V. Sun–Fri 11am–2pm; Mon–Sat 5–9pm. STEAK/SEAFOOD.

This casually elegant basement restaurant, with polished wood walls, looks fancy but welcomes everyone. A local favorite for its pepper steak, green chile burger, and daily luncheon specials, it's also the place to come for a wide variety of charbroiled steaks, chicken alfredo, halibut, salmon, or shrimp, and the Friday and Saturday night prime-rib specials. There's full bar service.

Appendix

LODGINGS

Best Western International, Inc.
800/528-1234 North America
800/528-2222 TDD

Budget Host
800/BUD-HOST Continental USA

Clarion Hotels
800/CLARION Continental USA and Canada
800/228-3323 TDD
http://www.hotelchoice.com/cgi-bin/res/webres?clarion.html

Comfort Inns
800/228-5150 Continental USA and Canada
800/228-3323 TDD
http://www.hotelchoice.com/cgi-bin/res/webres?comfort.html

Courtyard by Marriott
800/321-2211 Continental USA and Canada
800/228-7014 TDD
http://www.marriott.com/lodging/courtyar.htm

Days Inn
800/325-2525 Continental USA and Canada
800/325-3297 TDD
http://www.daysinn.com/daysinn.html

Doubletree Hotels
800/222-TREE Continental USA and Canada
800/528-9898 TDD

Drury Inn
800/325-8300 Continental USA and Canada
800/325-0583 TDD

Econo Lodges
800/55-ECONO Continental USA and Canada
800/228-3323 TDD
http://www.hotelchoice.com/cgi-bin/res/webres?econo.html

Embassy Suites
800/362-2779 Continental USA and Canada
800/458-4708 TDD
http://www.embassy-suites.com/

Fairfield Inn by Marriott
800/228-2800 Continental USA and Canada
800/228-7014 TDD
http://www.marriott.com/lodging/fairf.htm

Guest Quarters Suites
800/424-2900 Continental USA

Hampton Inn
800/HAMPTON Continental USA and Canada
800/451-HTDD TDD
http://www.hampton-inn.com/

Hilton Hotels Corporation
800/HILTONS Continental USA and Canada
800/368-1133 TDD
http://www.hilton.com

Holiday Inn
800/HOLIDAY Continental USA and Canada
800/238-5544 TDD
http://www.holiday-inn.com/

Howard Johnson
800/654-2000 Continental USA and Canada
800/654-8442 TDD
http://www.hojo.com/hojo.html

Hyatt Hotels and Resorts
800/228-9000 Continental USA and Canada
800/228-9548 TDD
http://www.hyatt.com

Intercontinental Hotels
800/327-0200 Continental USA and Canada

ITT Sheraton
800/325-3535 Continental USA and Canada
800/325-1717 TDD

La Quinta Motor Inns, Inc.
800/531-5900 Continental USA and Canada
800/426-3101 TDD

Loews Hotels
800/223-0888 Continental USA and Canada
http://www.loewshotels.com

Marriott Hotels
800/228-9290 Continental USA and Canada
800/228-7014 TDD
http://www.marriott.com MainPage.html

Park Inns International
800/437-PARK Continental USA and Canada
http://www.p-inns.com/parkinn.html

Quality Inns
800/228-5151 Continental USA and Canada
800/228-3323 TDD
http://www.hotelchoice.com/cgi-bin/res/webres?quality.html

Radisson Hotels International
800/333-3333 Continental USA and Canada

Ramada
800/2-RAMADA Continental USA and Canada
http://www.ramada.com/ramada.html

Red Lion Hotels and Inns
800/547-8010 Continental USA and Canada

Red Roof Inns
800/843-7663 Continental USA and Canada
800/843-9999 TDD
http://www.redroof.com

Renaissance Hotels International
800/HOTELS-1 Continental USA and Canada
800/833-4747 TDD

Residence Inn by Marriott
800/331-3131 Continental USA and Canada
800/228-7014 TDD
http://www.marriott.com/lodging/resinn.htm

Ritz-Carlton
800/241-3333 Continental USA and Canada

Rodeway Inns
800/228-2000 Continental USA and Canada
800/228-3323 TDD
http://www.hotelchoice.com/cgi-bin/res/webres?rodeway.html

Super 8 Motels
800/800-8000 Continental USA and Canada
800/533-6634 TDD
http://www.super8motels.com/super8.html

Travelodge
800/255-3050 Continental USA and Canada

Westin Hotels and Resorts
800/228-3000 Continental USA and Canada
800/254-5440 TDD
http://www.westin.com/

Wyndham Hotels and Resorts
800/822-4200 Continental USA and Canada

CAR-RENTAL AGENCIES

Advantage Rent-A-Car
800/777-5500 Continental USA and Canada

Airways Rent A Car
800/952-9200 Continental USA

Alamo Rent A Car
800/327-9633 Continental USA and Canada
http://www.goalamo.com/

Avis
800/331-1212 Continental USA
800/TRY-AVIS Canada
800/331-2323 TDD
http://www.avis/com/

Budget Rent A Car
800/527-0700 Continental USA and Canada
800/826-5510 TDD

Dollar Rent A Car
800/800-4000 Continental USA and Canada

Enterprise Rent-A-Car
800/325-8007 Continental USA and Canada

Hertz
800/654-3131 Continental USA and Canada
800/654-2280 TDD

National Car Rental
800/CAR-RENT Continental USA and Canada
800/328-6323 TDD
http://www.nationalcar.com/index.html

Payless Car Rental
800/PAYLESS Continental USA and Canada

Rent-A-Wreck
800/535-1391 Continental USA

Sears Rent A Car
800/527-0770 Continental USA and Canada

Thrifty Car Rental
800/367-2277 Continental USA and Canada
800/358-5856 TDD

U-Save Auto Rental of America
800/272-USAV Continental USA and Canada

Value Rent-A Car
800/327-2501 Continental USA and Canada
http://www.go-value.com/

AIRLINES

American Airlines
800/433-7300 Continental USA and Western Canada
800/543-1586 TDD
http://www.americanair.com/aa_home/aa_home.htm

America West Airlines
800/235-9292
800/526-8077
http://www.americawest.com

Canadian Airlines International
800/426-7000 Continental USA and Canada
http://www.cdair.ca/

Continental Airlines
800/525-0280 Continental USA
800/343-9195 TDD
http://www.flycontinental.com:80/index.html

Delta Air Lines
800/221-1212 Continental USA
800/831-4488 TDD
http://www.delta-air.com/index.html

GP Express
800/525-0280

Mark Air
800/627-5247

Martinair Holland
800/366-4655

Mesa Airlines
800/637-2247

Mexicana
800/531-7921

Northwest Airlines
800/225-2525 Continental USA and Canada
http://www.nwa.com/

Southwest Airlines
800/435-9792 Continental USA and Canada
http://iflyswa.com

Sun Country
800/359-5786

Trans World Airlines
800/221-2000 Continental USA
http://www2.twa.com/TWA/Airlines/home/home.htm

United Airlines
800/241-6522 Continental USA and Canada
http://www.ual.com/

USAir
800/428-4322 Continental USA and Canada
http://www.usair.com/

Index

FROMMER'S COMPLETE TRAVEL GUIDES

(Comprehensive guides to destinations around the world, with selections in all price ranges—from deluxe to budget)

Acapulco/Ixtapa/Taxco
Alaska
Amsterdam
Arizona
Atlanta
Australia
Austria
Bahamas
Bangkok
Barcelona, Madrid & Seville
Belgium, Holland & Luxembourg
Berlin
Bermuda
Boston
Budapest & the Best of Hungary
California
Canada
Cancún, Cozumel & the Yucatán
Caribbean
Caribbean Cruises & Ports of Call
Caribbean Ports of Call
Carolinas & Georgia
Chicago
Colorado
Costa Rica
Denver, Boulder & Colorado Springs
Dublin
England
Florida
France
Germany
Greece
Hawaii
Hong Kong
Honolulu/Waikiki/Oahu
Ireland
Italy
Jamaica/Barbados
Japan
Las Vegas
London
Los Angeles
Maryland & Delaware
Maui

Mexico
Mexico City
Miami & the Keys
Montana & Wyoming
Montréal & Québec City
Munich & the Bavarian Alps
Nashville & Memphis
Nepal
New England
New Mexico
New Orleans
New York City
Northern New England
Nova Scotia, New Brunswick & Prince
    Edward Island
Paris
Philadelphia & the Amish Country
Portugal
Prague & the Best of the Czech Republic
Puerto Rico
Puerto Vallarta, Manzanillo & Guadalajara
Rome
San Antonio & Austin
San Diego
San Francisco
Santa Fe, Taos & Albuquerque
Scandinavia
Scotland
Seattle & Portland
South Pacific
Spain
Switzerland
Thailand
Tokyo
Toronto
U.S.A.
Utah
Vancouver & Victoria
Vienna
Virgin Islands
Virginia
Walt Disney World & Orlando
Washington, D.C.
Washington & Oregon

FROMMER'S FRUGAL TRAVELER'S GUIDES
(The grown-up guides to budget travel, offering dream vacations at down-to-earth prices)

Australia from $45 a Day

Berlin from $50 a Day

California from $60 a Day

Caribbean from $60 a Day

Costa Rica & Belize from $35 a Day

Eastern Europe from $30 a Day

England from $50 a Day

Europe from $50 a Day

Florida from $50 a Day

Greece from $45 a Day

Hawaii from $60 a Day

India from $40 a Day

Ireland from $45 a Day

Italy from $50 a Day

Israel from $45 a Day

London from $60 a Day

Mexico from $35 a Day

New York from $70 a Day

New Zealand from $45 a Day

Paris from $65 a Day

Washington, D.C. from $50 a Day

FROMMER'S PORTABLE GUIDES
(Pocket-size guides for travelers who want everything in a nutshell)

Charleston & Savannah

Las Vegas

New Orleans

San Francisco

FROMMER'S IRREVERENT GUIDES
(Wickedly honest guides for sophisticated travelers)

Amsterdam

Chicago

London

Manhattan

Miami

New Orleans

Paris

San Francisco

Santa Fe

U.S. Virgin Islands

Walt Disney World

Washington, D.C.

FROMMER'S AMERICA ON WHEELS
(Everything you need for a successful road trip, including full-color road maps and ratings for every hotel)

California & Nevada

Florida

Mid-Atlantic

Midwest & the Great Lakes

New England & New York

Northwest & Great Plains

South Central &Texas

Southeast

Southwest

FROMMER'S BY NIGHT GUIDES
(The series for those who know that life begins after dark)

Amsterdam

Chicago

Las Vegas

London

Los Angeles

Miami

New Orleans

New York

Paris

San Francisco

WHEREVER YOU TRAVEL, *H*ELP IS NEVER FAR AWAY.

From planning your trip to providing travel assistance along the way, American Express® Travel Service Offices are always there to help.

Colorado

American Express Travel Service
Anaconda Towers
555 17th Street
Denver
303/298-7100

American Express Travel Service
250 Steele Street
Denver
303/388-7600

Travel

http://www.americanexpress.com/travel

American Express Travel Service Offices are found in central locations throughout Colorado.
For the location nearest you please call 1-800-AXP-3429.